A Hubert

A Hubert Harrison Reader

Edited with Introduction and Notes by

Jeffrey B. Perry

Wesleyan University Press | Middletown, Connecticut

Published by Wesleyan University Press, Middletown, CT 06459

© 2001 by the Estate of Hubert Henry Harrison

Introduction, commentary, and notes © 2001 Jeffrey B. Perry

Printed in the United States of America

Design and composition by Julie Allred, B. Williams & Associates

Library of Congress Cataloging-in-Publication Data

Harrison, Hubert H.

A Hubert Harrison reader / edited with introductions and notes by Jeffrey B. Perry.

    p. cm.

Includes index.

ISBN 0-8195-6469-9 (cloth) — ISBN 0-8195-6470-2 (pbk.)

1. Afro-Americans — Intellectual life — 20th century. 2. Afro-Americans —
Politics and government — 20th century. 3. Afro-Americans — Book reviews.
4. Harrison, Hubert H. — Political and social views. 5. Harlem Renaissance.
6. United States — Race relations. 7. United States — Social conditions —
20th century. I. Perry, Jeffrey Babcock. II. Title.

E185.6.H28 2001

973'.0496073 — dc21   00-051322

5   4   3   2   1

To Aida Harrison Richardson

Becky Hom

Perri Lin Hom

Theodore William Allen

and the memory of

William Harrison

For the Cause that lacks assistance;

For the Wrongs that need resistance;

For the Future in the distance

And the good that we can do.

The Voice, front-page banner box; adapted
from the poem "What I Live For" by Mrs.
George Linnaeus [Isabella] Banks (1821–1897)

Contents

5. Politics

6. Leaders and Leadership

7. Anti-imperialism and Internationalism

8. Meditations

9. Lynching, the Klan, "Race Relations," and "Democracy" in America

10. Literary Criticism, Book Reviews, and Book Reviewing

11. Theater Reviews

12. Poets and Poetry

13. The International Colored Unity League and the Way Forward

Acknowledgments

During the 1960s, I, like many others, was deeply affected by the civil rights movement and other struggles for social change in the United States. As a student I was afforded some opportunity to study, research, and interact with scholars. My ancestral roots, as far back as they are identifiable, are entirely among working people. These factors and many related experiences have led me to a life in which I have tried to mix worker-based organizing with historical research and writing. My major preoccupation has been the successes and failures of efforts at social change in the United States, and my major focuses have been on the role of white supremacy in undermining efforts at social change and the importance of struggle against white supremacy to social change.

These assorted influences and interests have provided me with a certain openness to the contributions of working class and anti–white-supremacist intellectuals. It was in this context that I encountered the work of Hubert Harrison in the early 1980s. When I first read microfilm copies of Harrison's two published books I was arrested by the clarity of his writing and the perceptiveness of his analysis. I immediately sensed that I was encountering a writer of importance. I searched for what information I could find on him and was several hundred pages into a dissertation and projected biography when, through the help of two Virgin Islanders — G. James Fleming, Professor Emeritus of Morgan State University in Baltimore, and June A. V. Linqvist (a relative of Harrison), librarian at the Enid M. Baa Library and Archives in Charlotte Amalie, St. Thomas — I was put in contact with Harrison's daughter, Aida Harrison Richardson, and his son, William Harrison.

I met Aida and William for the first time in 1983. Aida was a former schoolteacher and principal, and William a former attorney; both were socially aware, race-conscious individuals who knew the value of their father's work. They, along with their mother, the late Irene Louise Horton Harrison, had preserved the remains of Hubert Harrison's once-vast collection of papers and books in a series of Harlem apartments. After several meetings and discussions of their father's work they very generously granted me access to their father's materials. To Aida and William and to Aida's son, Charles Richardson, and William's daughter, Ilva, who have similarly extended support and encouragement, I am forever grateful. Their generous spirit, human kindness, and willingness to support my efforts as biographer and chronicler of Hubert Harrison's life have left a lasting impression on me and inspired my work.

I was influenced toward serious study of matters of race and class in America by the work of an independent scholar and close personal friend, Theodore William Allen, whose insightful and seminal writings on the role of white supremacy in United States history and on "race" in America have attracted increased attention. Familiarity with Allen's work disposed me to be receptive to the work of Harrison, another independent, anti–white-supremacist, working class intellectual.

When I was a doctoral student at Columbia University in the 1980s, my principal advisors, Hollis R. Lynch and the late Nathan I. Huggins, offered the encouragement, support, and constructive critical comments that strengthened my research in its early stages and emphasized Harrison's importance. Their assistance included helping me to put together an exceptional team of dissertation readers, which included Professors Eric Foner, Charles V. Hamilton, and Elliot Skinner. These scholars read my manuscript critically and offered constructive suggestions and encouragement that pushed me to improve my work.

Subsequent drafts of writings on Harrison were read, commented on, and encouraged by Ernest Allen Jr., Theodore William Allen, Gene Bruskin, Robert Fitch, Bill Fletcher Jr., Henry Louis Gates Jr., Geoffrey Jacques, Portia James, and Jack O'Dell. Winston James, when called on, offered helpful discussion, and Manning Marable encouraged further work on Harrison by helping to publish a shortened form of the introduction to this work in *Souls*, the critical journal of Black studies that he edits.

Readers of either my dissertation or the *Souls* piece who offered comments and encouragement applied toward this work include Sean Ahearn, Norman Allen, Tomie Arai, Rosalyn Baxandall, Peter Bohmer, Alexis Buss, Kwame Copeland, James P. Danky, Ossie Davis, Ruby Dee, Ralph Dumain, Steve Early, Dan Georgakas, Ted Glick, Don Hazen, Donna Katzin, Yuri Kochiyama, Kazu Iijima, Jane Latour, David Lawyer, Mike Merrill, Carole Mihalko, Jim Murray, Reverend Kay Osborn, Angelica Santamauro, David Slavin, Ann Sparanese, Michael Spiegel, Clarence Taylor, Andres Torres, Timothy B. Tyson, Joyce Turner, Michael Votichenko, Joel Washington, and Komozi Woodard. Important encouragement, feedback, and constructive criticism has also been offered by brothers and sisters in Local 300 of the National Postal Mail Handlers Union and by other trade union activists.

Throughout my research I have found librarians and library workers to be consistently helpful and generous with their time and expertise. (I note, however, that a great gap often exists between the value of the services they provide and the compensation in wages and benefits they receive.) I am particularly thankful to the staffs at the Schomburg Center for

Research in Black Culture (SCRBC), New York, New York; the New York Public Library (NYPL); the Columbia University libraries; the Tamiment Institute in the Elmer Holmes Bobst Library at New York University; the Moorland-Spingarn Research Center at Howard University (MSRC); the Library of Congress (LOC); the National Archives (NA) in Washington, D.C., New York, New York, and formerly in Bayonne, New Jersey; the Florence Williams Public Library, Christiansted, St. Croix; the Frederiksted, St. Croix, Public Library; the Landarskivet, Archives of Sealand, Lolland-Falster and Bornholm, Copenhagen, Denmark; the Marx Memorial Library, London; the British Library, London; the Hoover Institution of War, Revolution, and Peace, Stanford University; the Municipal Archives and Records Center, New York, New York; the United States Postal Record Center, St. Louis, Missouri; the Brooklyn, New York, Public Library; the Paterson, New Jersey, Public Library; the Free Library of Philadelphia; the Westwood, New Jersey, Public Library; the Rutgers University libraries; the Firestone Library at Princeton University; the Lenin State Library, Moscow; the Amistad Research Center, Tulane University, New Orleans, Louisiana; the Minnesota Historical Society, St. Paul, Minnesota; and the University of Minnesota libraries, Minneapolis, Minnesota.

This research developed over many years, and virtually everyone I asked for help responded positively. Among the librarians, curators, and records administrators I would like to thank are Eleanor Alexander, Morgan State University, Baltimore, Maryland; Otis D. Alexander, Frederiksted Public Library; Jorgen H. Anderson, Landarskivet; Joellen El Bashir, MSRC; David A. Benjamin, Government of the Virgin Islands of the United States; J. Scott Blackman, Immigration and Naturalization Service, New York, New York; J. Donald Blevins, U. S. Department of State, Washington, D.C.; Thomas Bourke, NYPL; Jacqueline Brown, Wilberforce College, Wilberforce, Ohio; Margaret J. Brink, Swarthmore College, Swarthmore, Pennsylvania; Joel Buchwald, NA, Bayonne and New York; James G. Cassedy, NA, Washington, D.C.; Mary Ellen Chijoke, Swarthmore College; Kenneth R. Cobb, Municipal Archives, City of New York; Anna L. Cook, Lane College, Jackson, Tennessee; Betty M. Culpepper, MSRC; Charles Cummings, Newark, New Jersey, Public Library; Susan E. Davis, NYPL; Eppie D. Edwards; National Library of Jamaica, Kingston, Jamaica; Denise English, Carter G. Woodson Regional Library, Chicago; Peter J. Filardo, Tamiment Institution; Martha Foley, NYPL; Charlie Hall, Marx Memorial Library; James K. Hall, U.S. Department of Justice, Washington, D.C.; Linda K. Harvey, Tuskegee University, Tuskegee, Alabama; Reverend A. Ivan Heyliger, St. John's Episcopal Church, Christiansted, St. Croix; Jean Blackwell Hutson, SCRBC; Diane M. Johnston, NYPL; Ernest D. Kaiser, SCRBC; Karl Kabelac, University of Rochester; G. Kürti, Hungarian Academy of Sciences, Budapest, Hungary; Diana Lachatanare, SCRBC; Ethel Lobomon, Tamiment Institution; Marilyn N. Loesch, Hampton University, Hampton, Virginia; William R. Massa, Yale University, New Haven, Connecticut; Linda M. Matthews, Emory University, Atlanta, Georgia; Gene McAfee, Harvard Divinity School, Cambridge, Massachusetts; Douglas

McDonald, Boston University; Susan McElrath, Mary McLeod Bethune National Historic Site, Washington, D.C.; Mary R. McGee, Christian Science Monitor, Boston, Massachusetts; Genna Rae McNeil, NYPL; R. Michael McReynolds, NA, Washington, D.C.; Alan Moss, University of the West Indies, Cave Hill, Barbados; Ardie S. Myers, LOC; Charles G. Palm, Hoover Institution; Warner W. Pflug, Wayne State University, Detroit; Mary Jo Pugh, University of Michigan; Ralph A. Pugh, Chicago Historical Society; Linda Seidman, University of Massachusetts, Amherst, Massachusetts; Alan Saltman, LOC; Susan Sampietro, Westwood, New Jersey, Public Library; Oswald Schjang, recorder of deeds, Christiansted, St. Croix; Burtin R. Scholl, Board of Education of the City of New York; John H. Sengstacke, *Chicago Daily Defender*; Ann Allen Shockley, Fisk University Library, Nashville, Tennessee; Janet L. Sims-Wood, MSRC; Charles A. Shaughnessy, NA, Washington, D.C.; Robert Sink, NYPL; David Stivers, Nabisco Company, Parsippany, New Jersey; Sister Marguerita Smith, Archdiocese of New York, Yonkers, New York; Ronald E. Swerczak, NA, Washington, D.C.; Anastacio Teodoro, NYPL; Wendy Thomas, Radcliffe College, Cambridge, Massachusetts; Robert H. Terte, New York City Board of Education; Ernest C. Wagner, College of the Virgin Islands, St. Thomas, United States Virgin Islands; William J. Walsh, NA, Washington, D.C.; Michael R. Winston, MSRC; Daoud-David Williams, Jersey City, New Jersey Public Library; Deborah Willis-Thomas, SCRBC; Lucinda Wong, Pacifica Foundation Radio Archives, Universal City, California; and Mary Yearwood, SCRBC.

Others who either responded to requests or assisted in the search for material and information include Neil Arlin, Sol Auerbach, Henry Black, Lloyd Brown, Mercer Cook, Carl Cowl, Sam and Emma Darcy, Raya Dunayevskaya, William French, David J. Garrow, Walter Goldwater, Gilbert Green, June Gunn, Jack Handler, Louis R. Harlan, John Haynes, Janis M. Jaynes, Gloria Joseph, Harvey Klehr, Bernard K. Johnpoll, Ivan Lorand, Joseph McDonald, Jim Murray, Helen K. Nearing, Guishard Parris, Louise Thompson Patterson, Evelyn Richardson, Helga Rogers, Franklin Rosemont, Lenny and Sara Smollet, Mark D. Solomon, Ted Vincent, Hope McKay Virtue, Ella G. Wolfe, Peter Wong, and Lionel Yard. Gregory Grazevich of the Modern Language Association helped at various times with questions on usage.

Early in my research I received much-needed assistance from the Marian Davis Scholarship Fund, now the Davis-Putter Scholarship Fund, which is to be commended for its continuing work in support of academic efforts of social activists.

I wish to extend special appreciation to Margaret Fisher Dalrymple, formerly of Louisiana State University Press and currently of the University of Nevada Press. She understood the importance of Harrison's work many years ago, and over the years she has consistently supported efforts to bring his work to a wider audience.

Tom Radko, the director of Wesleyan University Press, was thoughtful, kind, helpful, and responsive as I looked to place this work. His willingness to take a chance on Harrison is to be commended; this work would not have been possible without him.

Suzanna Tamminen, the editor-in-chief at Wesleyan, has been a joy to work with — every writer should be so fortunate. She offered guidance and encouragement, listened to my thoughts, and repeatedly extended efforts to develop this work. To Suzanna and Tom and to the entire Wesleyan staff I extend special thanks.

This book's managing editor, Maura High; its copyeditor, Elizabeth Gardner; and its designer and compositor, Julie Allred, have been exceptional, and it has been my pleasure to work with them. Their expertise has helped to bring this work to the high standards that Wesleyan maintains, and they have responded to my every query promptly, knowledgeably, and with understanding.

On a more personal level, I thank my late mother and father for their struggles to enable me to be the first in our family's line to attend college, for their love, and for encouraging me to take a responsible approach to the work I undertake. To my sisters, Pam and Deb; to my in-laws Paul, Billy, Eddie, and Blanche; to the Giblin, Buco, and Fong families; and to long-time family friends Ted, Sande, and Albo, I extend special thanks with much love for their patience and support.

To my wife, Becky Hom, and to my daughter, Perri Lin Hom, go my deepest thanks and my love. They have been enormously supportive, and their freely and frequently offered "suggestions" have sustained this project and always made it fun while recognizing that the work was important. Without Becky's love, support, and assistance and Perri's love and many questions this project would never have been completed as the joyous labor that it was.

Brief Chronology of the Life of Hubert Harrison

St. Croix

1883   Born April 27 in Concordia, St. Croix, Danish West Indies.

1896–1900   Completes elementary education and works as underteacher.

Self-Education and Early Intellectual Growth in New York

1900   Arrives New York City during nadir for African Americans.

1901–7   Completes high school education, breaks from organized Christianity, and is attracted to freethought.

1905–9   Active with St. Benedict's and St. Mark's Lyceums, White Rose Home for Working Girls, YMCA, and postal worker press club.

1907   Publishes in the *New York Times*, hired as a postal clerk, starts diary, moves to Harlem.

1908–11   Attracted to freethought, the single tax movement, and socialism; starts scrapbooks.

1909   Marries Irene Louise Horton.

1910   Criticizes Booker T. Washington in the *Sun*; first daughter, Frances Marion, born.

1911   Fired from post office through efforts of Washington's "Tuskegee Machine."

Socialist Party Years

1911   Leading Black in Socialist Party of New York; writes series on "The Negro and Socialism" in the *Call*; assistant editor of *The Masses*; founds Colored Socialist Club; second daughter, Alice Genevieve, born.

1912   Organizes for the Colored Socialist Club; writes on "The Black Man's Burden" and "Socialism and the Negro" in the *International Socialist Review*; third daughter, Aida Mae, born; speaks throughout New York and New Jersey.

1913   Featured speaker at Paterson, N.J., silk strike; prominent Socialist speaker in New York and Connecticut.

1914   Teaches at Socialist Party school; criticizes Socialists in letter to the *New Review*; suspended from Socialist Party.

Interregnum

1914   Teaches at the Ferrer Modern School; publishes "The Negro A Conservative" in
        the *Truth Seeker*; starts Radical Forum; fourth daughter, Ilva Henrietta, born.

1915   Lectures throughout New York City; begins writing "Negro Society and the
        Negro Stage"; writes for the *New York News* and the *Colored American Review*.

Founding and Nurturing the New Negro Manhood Movement

1916   Develops plans for "a Negro newspaper" based on the principle of "Africa First!";
        "race first" lectures at Lafayette Hall mark the beginning of the "New Negro
        Manhood Movement."

1917   Founds the Liberty League and *The Voice*; introduces Marcus Garvey to New
        York crowds; publishes *The Negro and the Nation*.

1918   Serves as American Federation of Labor organizer among hotel and restaurant
        workers; co-chairs (with William Monroe Trotter) National Liberty Congress;
        resurrects *The Voice* and publishes "The Descent of Dr. Du Bois"; rejoins and
        then resigns from Socialist Party.

1919   Lectures in Washington, D.C., and Virginia; ill health causes him to cease publi-
        cation of *The Voice*; edits *New Negro* magazine and writes "Two Negro
        Radicalisms."

Editor of the Negro World

1920   Becomes managing editor of the *Negro World* and reshapes the newspaper;
        speaks on "Lincoln vs. Liberty"; is selected by Garvey to head UNIA delegation
        to Liberia; writes "Race First versus Class First" and "Crab-Barrel" series; writes
        critical appraisal of "Garvey's Character" and "The Garvey Movement" in his
        diary; shapes resolutions for the First International Convention of the Negro
        Peoples of the World; publishes *When Africa Awakes*; breaks from Garvey; organ-
        izes all-Black Liberty Party; fifth child, son William born; ceases work as manag-
        ing editor of the *Negro World* and writes columns as associate editor; travels to
        Virginia and Philadelphia on speaking tours.

1921   Contributing editor and book reviewer for the *Negro World*; writes "Wanted —
        A Colored International" and review of "Emperor Jones."

1922   Serves as contributing editor and then ceases work for the *Negro World*.

Freelance Educator

1922   Begins five-year employment as staff lecturer for New York Board of Education;
        talks on "The Brother in Black" at the Great Hall of Cooper Institute; writes for
        the *New York World*, the *Daily Negro Times*, the *New York Age*, the *New York
        Tribune*, and the *New York Times*.

1923   Challenges Ku Klux Klan in Paterson, N.J.; delivers radio talks on "The Brother
        in Black" and "The Negro and the Nation"; writes for *The Nation*, the *New York
        Tribune*, the *Amsterdam News*, the *New York World*, the *New Republic*, and the
        National Star.

The International Colored Unity League Period

1924   Writes columns in the *New York Inter-State Tattler* and the *Boston Chronicle* and reviews for the Indianapolis *Freeman*; founds the International Colored Unity League; travels to Massachusetts and the Midwest on speaking tours.

1925–26 Helps found New York Public Library Department of Negro Literature and History; joins American Negro Labor Congress; writes for *Modern Quarterly*, the *Negro Champion, Opportunity*, and the *Amsterdam News*; teaches "World Problems of Race" course; suffers ill health.

1927   Writes for the *West Indian Statesman*, the *Pittsburgh Courier*, and the *Chicago Defender*; edits and publishes *Embryo of The Voice of the Negro* and *The Voice of the Negro*; resurrects the International Colored Unity League; dies suddenly (December 17) at Bellevue Hospital and thousands attend his Harlem funeral.

Abbreviations Used

Manuscript Collections

HHHDI   Hubert Henry Harrison, Diary, HHHP

HHHP   Hubert Henry Harrison Papers, private collection

     Bo   Books

     Co   Correspondence

     Mi   Miscellany

     Scr   Scrapbooks

         Scr A   *Early Writings of Hubert H. Harrison*: Mainly in the *Truth Seeker*, the *New York Call*, the *International Socialist Review*, *The Voice*, and *The New Negro*. Also *Zukunfdt*, The *Colonies Magazine*, and the *Medical Review of Reviews*.

         Scr B   *"Writings of Hubert Harrison Contributed to the Negro World Jan 1920 to Feb 1922"*: Major Pieces — Book Reviews, Editorial Contributions, Minor Pieces, Book Reviews, Editorial, Contributions, Verses, etc., Duplicates (unpasted).

         Scr C   *Mainly About Me: The Radical and Racial Phase.* Newspaper Clippings & Other Items Relating to Hubert H. Harrison, 8/11/12 [November 8, 1912].

         Scr D   *"M.O.M" [Mainly About Me] vol. 2: Hubert H. Harrison, Public Notices, Records and References, vol. 2; The Upward Climb.*

         Scr 3   *The Negro American vol. 6: Economic.* Facts, Thought.

         Scr 8   *The Negro-American vol. 14: The Negro and the War.* A. In the U.S.; B. Elsewhere.

         Scr 28   *The Negro American. vol. 3: Lynching.*

     Wr   Writings

Published Works

AN   *Amsterdam News* [1909–1919]; New York *Amsterdam News* [1919–]

ANB   John A. Garraty and Mark C. Carnes, eds. *American National Biography*. 24 vols. New York: Oxford University Press, 1999.

BC   *Boston Chronicle*

BTWP   Louis R. Harlan and Raymond W. Smock, eds. *The Booker T. Washington Papers*. 13 vols. Urbana: University of Illinois Press, 1972–1984.

BWA   Darlene Clark Hine, Elsa Barkley Brown, and Rosalyn Terborg-Penn, eds. *Black Women in America: An Historical Perspective*. 2 vols. Bloomington: Indiana University Press, 1993.

CBS   *Contributions in Black Studies*

CD   *Chicago Defender*

CSM   *Christian Science Monitor*

DANB   Rayford W. Logan and Michael R. Winston, eds. *Dictionary of American Negro Biography*. New York: W. W. Norton, 1982.

FSAA   Theodore Kornweibel Jr. *Federal Surveillance of Afro-Americans (1917–1925): The First World War, the Red Scare, and the Garvey Movement*. 25 microfilm reels. Lanham, Md.: University Publications of America: 1986.

HATB   Winston James. *Holding Aloft the Banner of Ethiopia: Caribbean Radicalism in Early Twentieth-Century America*. New York: Verso, 1998.

HHN   *Harlem Home News*

HR   Bruce Kellner, ed. *The Harlem Renaissance: A Historical Dictionary for the Era*. New York: Methuen, 1987.

ISR   *International Socialist Review*

JAH   *Journal of American History*

JCH   *Journal of Caribbean History*

KI   *The Kaiser Index to Black Resources 1948–1986*. From the Schomburg Center for Research in Black Culture of the New York Public Library. 5 vols. Brooklyn: Carlson Publishing, 1992.

LH   *Labor History*

L&L   Robert A. Hill, ed., and Barbara Bair, associate ed. *Marcus Garvey: Life and Lessons, A Centennial Companion to the Marcus Garvey and Universal Negro Improvement Papers*. Berkeley: University of California Press, 1987.

MGP   Robert A. Hill, ed. *The Marcus Garvey and Universal Negro Improvement Association Papers*. 12 vols. projected. Berkeley: University of California Press, vols. 1–7 and vol. 9, 1983–1995.

NAAAL   Henry Louis Gates Jr. and Nellie Y. McKay, eds. *Norton Anthology of African American Literature*. New York: W. W. Norton, 1997.

N&N   Hubert Henry Harrison. *The Negro and the Nation*. New York: Cosmo-Advocate Publishing, 1917.

NN   *New Negro*

NR   *New Review*

NW   *Negro World*

NYA *New York Age*

NYB Monroe N. Work. *Negro Year Book: An Annual Encyclopedia of the Negro.* Tuskegee Institute, Ala., nine editions beginning in 1912.

NYC *New York Call*

NYEM *New York Evening Mail*

NYEP *New York Evening Post*

NYES *New York Evening Sun*

NYN *New York News*

NYS *New York Sun*

NYT *New York Times*

NYTSRB *New York Times Saturday Review of Books*

NYW *New York World*

OCAAL William L. Andrews, Frances Smith Foster, and Trudier Harris, eds. *The Oxford Companion to African American Literatrue.* New York: Oxford University Press, 1997.

OP   *Opportunity*

PC   *Pittsburgh Courier*

RCAH Eric Foner and John Garraty, eds. *The Reader's Companion to American History.* Boston: Houghton Mifflin, 1991.

RF   Tony Martin. *Race First: The Ideological and Organizational Struggle of Marcus Garvey and the Universal Negro Improvement Association.* Westport, Conn.: Greenwood Press, 1976.

TS   *Truth Seeker*

WAA Hubert Henry Harrison. *When Africa Awakes: The "Inside Story" of the Stirrings and Strivings of the New Negro in the Western World.* New York: Porro Press, 1920.

WGMC J[oel] A. Rogers. *World's Great Men of Color.* Edited with an introduction, commentary, and new bibliographical notes by John Henrik Clarke. New York: Collier Books, 1972.

WNBD *Webster's New Biographical Dictionary.* Springfield, Mass.: Merriam-Webster, 1988.

Other Symbols and Abbreviations

ACL African Communities League

AFL American Federation of Labor

BI   Bureau of Investigation

BSL Black Star Line

CC   Central Committee

CP   Communist Party

CSC Colored Socialist Club

DNA National Archives, Washington, D.C.

EC   Executive Committee

HH   Hubert Harrison
HHH   Hubert Henry Harrison
ICUL   International Colored Unity League
IWW   Industrial Workers of the World
LNY   Local New York
MG   Marcus Garvey
MID   Military Intelligence Division
NAACP   National Association for the Advancement of Colored People
NFC   Negro Factories Corporation
NYPL   New York Public Library
RG   Record Group
SP   Socialist Party of America
SCRBC   Schomburg Center for Research in Black Culture
UNIA   Universal Negro Improvement Association

A Note on Usage

Hubert Harrison used the word *Negro* with a capital *N* (as opposed to such words as *colored* and *negro*), and he struggled to have others do the same. He founded the New Negro Manhood Movement, presided over the Liberty League of Negro-Americans, and edited the *New Negro* monthly, the *Negro World,* the *Embryo of The Voice of the Negro,* and *The Voice of the Negro.* Results of the capitalization struggles included the change to the capital *N* by the *International Socialist Review* in 1912 and by the *New York Times* in 1930 (after Harrison's death).

In the 1960s, however, there was a shift from that usage and today *Negro* has generally been replaced in the United States by *Black, African American, African-American,* or *Afro-American.*

In this text, *Negro* is retained in titles, names, and quoted passages. When the term is contextually appropriate, it is enclosed in quotation marks. In general discussions *African American* or *Black* are used.

Because Harrison and others struggled to capitalize the *N* in *Negro* as both a statement of pride *and* as a challenge to white supremacy, when the word *Black* is used as its equivalent it is used with a capital *B*. There is no similarly compelling basis for capitalizing the *w* in *white.*

Hubert Harrison, undated, from the Hubert Harrison Papers.

Introduction

A brilliant writer, orator, educator, critic, and political activist, Hubert Harrison (1883–1927) is one of the truly important, yet neglected, figures of early twentieth-century America. Harrison was described by the historian Joel A. Rogers, in *World's Great Men of Color*, as "the foremost Afro-American intellect of his time" and "one of America's greatest minds." Rogers adds (after insightful chapters on Booker T. Washington, William Monroe Trotter, W. E. B. Du Bois, and Marcus Garvey), "No one worked more seriously and indefatigably to enlighten his fellow-men" and "none of the Afro-American leaders of his time had a saner and more effective program."[1]

Variants of Rogers's lavish praise were offered by other contemporaries. The novelist Henry Miller, a socialist in his youth, remembered Harrison on a soapbox as his "quondam idol" and as an unrivalled, electrifying speaker who "had the ability to demolish any opponent."[2] William Pickens, field secretary of the National Association for the Advancement of Colored People (NAACP), a former college dean and an oratory prize winner at Yale, described him as "a plain black man who can speak more easily, effectively, and interestingly on a greater variety of subjects than any other man I have ever met in the great universities."[3] W. A. Domingo, the first editor of Marcus Garvey's *Negro World*, underscored the fact that Garvey, A. Philip Randolph, and the leading Black activists of their generation "all followed Hubert Harrison."[4]

During his relatively short life, Harrison made his mark by struggling against class and racial oppression, by participating in and helping to create a remarkably rich and vibrant intellectual life, and by working for the enlightened development of the lives of "the common people." His political and educational work emphasized the need for working-class people to develop class consciousness; for Black people to develop race consciousness, self-reliance, and self-respect; and for all those he reached to develop modern, scientific, critical, and independent thought as a means toward liberation.

More than any other political leader of his era, Harrison combined class consciousness and (anti–white-supremacist) race consciousness in a coherent political radicalism. He opposed capitalism and maintained that white supremacy was central to capitalist rule in the United States, that racism was not in white workers' class interests, that Blacks must not wait for whites while struggling to shape their own future, and that Americans should oppose U.S. imperialist intervention abroad. He served as the foremost Black organizer, agitator, and theoretician in the Socialist Party (SP) of New York during its 1912 heyday; as the founder and leading figure of the militant, World War I–era "New Negro" movement; as the editor of the *Negro World*; and as a principal radical influence on the Garvey movement during its radical high point in 1920.[5]

Among African American leaders of his era Harrison was the most class conscious of the race radicals, and the most race conscious of the class radicals.[6] His views profoundly influenced a generation of "New Negro" militants that included the class-radical socialists A. Philip Randolph and Chandler Owen, the future communists Cyril V. Briggs and Richard B. Moore, and the race radical Marcus Garvey. Considered more race conscious than Randolph and Owen and more class conscious than Garvey, Harrison is a key link in the ideological unity of the two great trends of the Black Liberation Movement—the labor and civil rights trend of Martin Luther King Jr. and the race and nationalist trend of Malcolm X. Randolph and Garvey were, respectively, the direct links to King marching on Washington (with Randolph at his side) and to Malcolm (whose father was a Garveyite preacher and whose mother was a writer for the *Negro World*) speaking militantly and proudly on Lenox Avenue.[7]

In the era of World War I, as the center of national Black leadership shifted from Booker T. Washington's Tuskegee, Alabama, headquarters to New York City, Harlem increasingly became an "international Negro Mecca" and "the center of radical Black thought."[8] In this period Harrison earned the title "The Father of Harlem Radicalism."[9] During the 1910s and 1920s, he either created or was among the founders of "almost every important development originating in Negro Harlem—from the Negro Manhood Movement to political representation in public office, from collecting Negro books to speaking on the streets, from demanding Federal control over lynching to agitation for Negroes on the police force."[10]

Harrison was not only a political radical, however. Rogers describes him as an "Intellectual Giant and Free-Lance Educator" whose contributions were wide-ranging, innovative, and influential. Rogers's appraisal is accurate. Harrison was an immensely popular orator and freelance educator; a highly praised journalist, critic, editor, and book reviewer who initiated the first "regular book-review section known to Negro newspaperdom"; a promoter of Black writers and artists (including Rogers, Andy Razaf, Claude McKay, Charles Gilpin, and Augusta Savage); a pioneer Black activist in the freethought and birth control movements; and a bibliophile and library popularizer who helped develop the 135th Street

Public Library into an international center for research in Black culture. In his later years he was the leading Black lecturer for the New York City Board of Education and one of its foremost orators. He was also a trailblazing literary critic during the period known as the Harlem Renaissance.[11]

Biographical Background

Hubert Henry Harrison was born at Estate Concordia, St. Croix, Danish West Indies, on April 27, 1883. Little is known with certainty about his parents. Rogers writes that they were of "unmixed African ancestry" and church records indicate that Harrison's mother was a poor, laboring-class woman, who was not formally married at the time of Hubert's birth, had several other children, and died in 1899. Other available information suggests that Hubert spent his early years pursuing his educational interests and that as a teenager he worked as an underteacher in an island school. These opportunities were possible, in part, because in St. Croix (unlike in the United States) there were no formal segregation, no lynchings, and no system of severe racial proscriptions against class advancement for those of African descent. Shortly after his mother died, Hubert emigrated to the United States, arriving in 1900 as a seventeen-year-old orphan.[12]

Harrison's move from the rural, agricultural island of St. Croix to the teeming urban industrial metropolis of New York was truly a move from the nineteenth into the twentieth century. His arrival coincided with U.S. capitalism's ascent to new imperialist heights, with the period of intense racial oppression of African Americans known as the "nadir," and with the era of critical writing and muckraking journalism that, according to the social commentator Daniel Bell, produced "the most concentrated flowering of criticism in the history of American ideas." These factors would shape the remainder of his life.[13]

Harrison's life in the United States was never easy. Soon after his arrival in New York he began working menial jobs and attending high school at night. He finished school and read constantly and, after several years, obtained postal employment, married Irene Louise Horton (whose family probably came from Antigua and Demerara, a region in present-day Guyana), and started to raise a family that eventually included five children. His insatiable thirst for knowledge and his critical mind led him to break from "orthodox and institutional Christianity" and to develop an agnostic philosophy of life, which stressed rationalism, modern science, and evolution and placed humanity at the center of its worldview. It also led to involvement in Black intellectual circles, workers' groups, community organizations, and the freethought movement.[14]

In this stimulating intellectual environment and with a developing self-confidence, Harrison began lecturing, teaching, and writing letters to newspapers. His boldness soon affected him economically. In late 1910, he wrote two letters that criticized Booker T. Washington, the most powerful Black leader in America, and in 1911 he lost his postal employment through the efforts of Washington's powerful "Tuskegee Machine." It was a devastating blow, and the resultant loss of income and security seriously affected his remaining years with his family and, at times, influenced his political and educational efforts.[15]

Shortly after his postal firing, Harrison turned to full-time work with the Socialist Party. From 1911 to 1914 he was America's leading Black Socialist — a prominent party speaker and campaigner (especially in the 1912 presidential campaign of Eugene V. Debs), an editor of *The Masses*, an articulate and popular critic of capitalism, the leading Black Socialist organizer in New York, and the initiator of the Colored Socialist Club (CSC), an unprecedented effort by U.S. socialists to organize African Americans. In his writings he made major theoretical contributions on the subject of "The Negro and Socialism" by advocating in the *New York Call* and the *International Socialist Review* that socialists champion the cause of African Americans as a revolutionary doctrine, that they develop a special appeal to and for African Americans, and that they affirm the duty of all socialists to oppose race prejudice. His proposal that "the crucial test of Socialism's sincerity" was its duty to champion the cause of the African American anticipated by more than a year Du Bois's dictum that the "Negro Problem . . . [is] the great test of the American Socialists."[16]

Such efforts were to little avail. Socialist Party theory and practice, including segregated locals in the South, the failure to route the campaign of the 1912 presidential candidate Eugene V. Debs through the South, racist positions on Asian immigration at the 1912 national convention, and the failure to support the CSC politically and economically soon led Harrison to conclude that Socialist Party leaders, like organized labor, put the white "race first and class after."[17]

As Harrison started to move away from the Socialist Party he turned his efforts toward the more egalitarian, militant, and action-oriented Industrial Workers of the World (IWW). He was a featured speaker (along with the IWW leaders "Big Bill" Haywood, Elizabeth Gurley Flynn, Carlo Tresca, and Patrick Quinlan), and the only Black speaker, at the historic 1913 Paterson silk strike. He publicly defended Haywood against attack by the right wing of the Socialist Party on the issue of sabotage. SP leaders soon moved to restrict his speaking, however, and as their attacks on both his political views and his principal means of livelihood intensified, his disenchantment grew, he was suspended, and finally he left the party.

After leaving the Socialists, Harrison took what he revealingly described as the first truly self-initiated step of his life — the founding of the Radical Forum in the summer of 1914. The forum was an effort to draw together radicals from various movements who were "sick of the insincerities of cults and creeds" and sought "the awakening breath of the larger liberalism, from which all alike may draw inspiration."[18] In this period he also began teaching at the Ferrer Modern School (with some of America's foremost artists and intellectuals) and lecturing indoors and out on birth control, the racial aspects of World War I, religion, science, literature, education, evolution, and a wide variety of other subjects.

Harrison's outdoor lectures pioneered the tradition of militant street-corner oratory in Harlem. As a soapbox orator he was brilliant and unrivalled. He had a charismatic presence, a wide-ranging intellect, a remarkable memory, impeccable diction, and exceptional mastery of language. Factual and interactive, he utilized humor, irony, and a biting sarcasm. With his popular indoor and outdoor style he paved the way for those who followed — including A. Philip Randolph, Marcus Garvey, and, much later, Malcolm X.[19]

By 1915–16 his experiences with the racial oppression, glaring racial inequality, and white supremacy of U.S. society as well as with the "white first" attitude of the organized labor movement and the Socialists led Harrison, the former leading Black Socialist, to respond with a "race first" political perspective.[20] Important steps in this direction were made through the frontier of art: Harrison wrote several theater reviews in which he described how the "Negro Theatre" revealed the "social mind . . . of the Negro."[21] With his new "race first" approach, Harrison served over the next few years as the founder and intellectual guiding light of the "New Negro Manhood Movement,"[22] better known as the "New Negro" movement[23] — the race-conscious, internationalist, mass-based, autonomous, radical, and militantly assertive movement for "political equality, social justice, civic opportunity, and economic power." This "New Negro" movement[24] laid the basis for the Garvey movement[25] and, by fostering a mass interest in literature and the arts, contributed significantly to the climate leading to the 1925 publication of Alain Locke's well-known *The New Negro*. Harrison's mass-based political movement was qualitatively different, however, from the more middle-class, arts-based, and apolitical movement associated with Locke.[26]

In 1917, as the Great War raged abroad along with race riots, lynchings, segregation, discrimination, and white-supremacist ideology at home, Harrison founded the Liberty League and *The Voice*. They were, respectively, the first organization and the first newspaper of the "New Negro" movement. The Liberty League was called into being, he explained, by "the need for a more radical policy" than that of existing civil rights organizations such as the National Association for the Advancement of Colored People. He felt that the NAACP limited itself to paper protests, was dominated by white people's conceptions of how African Americans should act, concentrated too much on the "Talented Tenth" of the "Negro race," and repeatedly stumbled over the problem of what to do "if these [white] minds at which you are aiming remain unaffected" and refused "to grant guarantees of life and liberty."[27]

In contrast to the NAACP, the Liberty League was not dependent on whites and aimed beyond the "Talented Tenth" at the common people. Its program emphasized internationalism, political independence, and class and race consciousness. In response to white supremacy, the *Voice* called for a "race first" approach, full equality, federal antilynching legislation (which the NAACP did not support at the time), enforcement of the Fourteenth and Fifteenth Amendments, labor organizing, support of socialist and anti-imperialist causes, and armed self-defense in the face of racist attacks. It stressed that new Black leadership would emerge from the masses.[28]

From the Liberty League and *The Voice* (whose weekly circulation reached eleven thousand and estimated readership reached fifty-five thousand) came the core progressive ideas and leaders later utilized by Marcus Garvey in both the Universal Negro Improvement Association (UNIA) and the *Negro World*. Harrison himself claimed, with considerable basis, that from the Liberty League "Garvey appropriated every feature that was worthwhile in his movement" and that the secret of Garvey's success was that he "[held] up to the Negro masses those things which bloom in their hearts — racialism, race-consciousness, racial solidarity — things taught first in 1917 by the *Voice* and The Liberty League."[29]

Contemporaries readily acknowledged that Harrison's work laid the groundwork for the Garvey movement. Anselmo Jackson, a writer for both Harrison's *Voice* and Garvey's *Negro World*, claimed that "Garvey publicly eulogized Harrison, joined the Liberty League and took a keen interest in its affairs" and that "the success of Garvey" was built on Harrison's work. The *Negro World* assistant editor and assistant president general of the UNIA, William H. Ferris, maintained that Garvey "rapidly crystallized" Harrison's ideas. W. A. Domingo, the first editor of the *Negro World*, said that "Garvey came at the psychological moment. There had been the East St. Louis riot, he visited the scene and then came back here. However, before him there was Hubert Harrison. He was a brilliant man, a great intellectual, a Socialist and highly respected. Garvey like the rest of us followed Hubert Harrison." J. A. Rogers, a frequent contributor to the *Negro World*, wrote that "one of the men who was very much influenced by Harrison was Marcus Garvey." Rogers added that "Garvey's emphasis on racialism was due in no small measure to Harrison's lectures on Negro history and his utterances on racial pride, which animated and fortified Garvey's views." He concluded that the Garvey movement was "fructified by the spirit and teaching of Harrison."[30]

After *The Voice* ceased publication in early 1918, Harrison briefly served as an organizer for the American Federation of Labor (AFL) and then chaired the Liberty Congress. The June 1918 Liberty Congress (co-headed by the longtime activist William Monroe Trotter) was the major wartime protest effort of African Americans and an important precursor to subsequent protests during World War II and the Vietnam War. The Congress issued demands against discrimination and segregation and petitioned the U.S. Congress for federal antilynching legislation.[31] This autonomous and militant effort was undermined by the U.S. Army's antiradical Military Intelligence Bureau (MIB) in a campaign that was spearheaded by the NAACP board chairman Joel E. Spingarn and involved Du Bois.[32]

Following the Liberty Congress, Harrison initiated "New Negro" criticism of Du Bois for urging African Americans to forget justifiable grievances, for "closing ranks" behind President Woodrow Wilson's war effort, and for following Spingarn's lead and seeking a captaincy in Military Intelligence, that branch of government that monitored radicals and the African American community. Harrison's exposé, "The Descent of Dr. Du Bois," was a principal reason that Du Bois was denied the captaincy he sought in Military Intelligence, and more than any other document it marked the significant break between the "New Negroes" and the older leadership.[33]

To articulate this new direction, Harrison restarted *The Voice* in July 1918 and worked on a daring, though unsuccessful, plan to bring it into the Deep South. After the resurrected *Voice* failed in March 1919 Harrison edited the monthly *New Negro* magazine from August through October 1919. The *New Negro* was "intended as an organ of the international consciousness of the darker races — especially of the Negro race" and it aimed to be for African Americans what *The Nation* was for white Americans.[34]

In January 1920 Harrison became the principal editor of the *Negro World*, the organ of Marcus Garvey's UNIA. He reshaped and developed the newspaper — changing its style, format, content, and editorial page — and was primarily responsible for developing it into the preeminent radical, race-conscious political and literary publication of the day. Many of his most important editorials and reviews from this period (as well as from the earlier Liberty League period) were reprinted in his book *When Africa Awakes* (1920). During the first eight months of 1920 he was the *Negro World's* chief radical propagandist and in August, at the UNIA's 1920 convention, he was the one who gave "radical tone" to the UNIA's "Declaration of the Negro Peoples of the World."[35]

By the 1920 convention, however, a campaign was under way to have Harrison dismissed from the editorship of the paper. Harrison, in turn, was highly critical of Garvey and worked against him. His criticisms concerned the extravagance of Garvey's claims, his ego, the conduct of his stock-selling schemes, and his politics and practices. Though Harrison continued to write columns and book reviews for the *Negro World* into 1922, their political differences grew and he sought to develop political alternatives to Garvey.[36] In particular, Harrison urged political action in terms of electoral politics; attempted to build an all-Black Liberty Party to run African American candidates for political offices, including the presidency; consistently maintained the position that African Americans' principal struggle was in the United States and that they should therefore not seek to develop a state in Africa; opposed imperialism and did not seek an African empire; argued that Africans, not African Americans, would lead struggles in Africa; vociferously opposed the Ku Klux Klan; and favored reason, science, and fact-based knowledge over emotional appeals and exaggerated claims to the masses.

In the 1920s after breaking with Garvey, Harrison continued his full schedule of activities. He lectured on a wide range of topics for the New York City Board of Education and for its elite "Trends of the Times" series, which included prominent professors from the city's foremost universities. His book and theater reviews and other writings appeared in many of the leading periodicals of the day — including the *New York Times*, the *New York Tribune*, the *New York World*, the *Nation*, the *New Republic*, *Modern Quarterly*, the *Pittsburgh Courier*, the *Chicago Defender*, the *Amsterdam News*, the *Boston Chronicle*, and

Opportunity magazine. He also spoke out against the revived Ku Klux Klan and the horrific pogrom and air attacks on the Tulsa, Oklahoma, Black community, and he worked with numerous groups, including the Virgin Islands Congressional Council, the Democratic Party, the Farmer-Labor Party, the single tax movement, anticensorship activists, the American Friends Service Committee, the Urban League, the American Negro Labor Congress, and the Workers (Communist) Party.[37]

One of his most important activities in this period was the founding of the International Colored Unity League (ICUL) and its organ, *The Voice of the Negro*. The ICUL was Harrison's most broadly unitary race-organizing effort (particularly in terms of work with other Black organizations and with the Black church) and it attempted "to do for the Negro the things which the Negro needs to have done without depending upon or waiting for the co-operative action of white people." It urged Blacks to develop "race consciousness" as a defensive measure — to be aware of their racial oppression and to use that awareness to unite, organize, and respond as a group. The 1924 ICUL platform had political, economic, and social planks urging protests, self-reliance, self-sufficiency, and cooperatives and included as its central idea the founding of "a Negro state, not in Africa, as Marcus Garvey would have done, but in the United States," as an outlet for "racial egoism." It was a plan for the harnessing of "Negro energies" and for "economic, political and spiritual self-help and advancement," and it preceded a somewhat similar plan by the Communist International by four years.[38]

Overall, in his writing and oratory, Harrison's appeal was to both the masses and the individual. He focused on the man and woman in the street and emphasized the importance of each individual's development of an independent, critical attitude. The period during and after World War I was one of intense racial oppression and great Black migration from the South and the Caribbean into urban centers, particularly in the North. Harrison's race-conscious mass appeal utilized newspapers, popular lectures, and street-corner talks and marked a major shift from the leadership approaches of Booker T. Washington and W. E. B. Du Bois, the paramount Black leaders of his youth. He rejected Washington's reliance on white patrons and a Black political machine and Du Bois's reliance on a "Talented Tenth of the Negro Race." Harrison's effective appeal (later identified with that of Garvey) was aimed directly at the urban masses and, as the Harlem activist Richard B. Moore explained, "More than any other man of his time, he [Harrison] inspired and educated the masses of Afro-Americans then flocking into Harlem."[39]

Though he was extremely popular among the masses who flocked to hear him, Harrison, as Rogers points out, was often overlooked by "the more established conservative Negro leaders, especially those who derived support from wealthy whites." Others, "inferior . . . in ability and altruism, received acclaim, wealth, and distinction" that was his due. When he died from appendectomy complications on December 17, 1927, the Harlem community, in a major show of affection, turned out by the thousands for his funeral. A church (ironically) was soon named in his honor, and his portrait was to be placed prominently on the main floor of the 135th Street Public Library, where he, along with bibliophile Arthur Schomburg and others, had helped to found and develop the world-famous Department of Negro Literature and History (which grew into the Schomburg Center for Research in Black Culture).[40]

Despite these manifestations of love and respect from his contemporaries, Harrison has been greatly neglected in death. He lies buried in an unmarked, shared plot in Woodlawn Cemetery in the Bronx; the church named in his honor was abandoned; the portrait donated to the library cannot be found; and his life story and contributions have largely been ignored. The historian Winston James observes that "seldom has a person been so influential, esteemed, even revered in one period of history and so thoroughly unremembered in the space of a generation." James correctly emphasizes that Harrison "deserves better than that."[41]

Given Harrison's enormous contributions, why has he been all but forgotten? Some reasons are readily apparent. Harrison was poor, Black, foreign-born, and from the Caribbean. Each of these groups has suffered discrimination and neglect in the United States. He opposed capitalism, racism, and the Christian church—dominant forces of the most powerful society in the world. He supported socialism, race consciousness, racial equality, women's equality, freethought, and birth control. The forces arrayed against the expression of such ideas were, and continue to be, formidable. Others, most notably the similarly poor, Black, Caribbean-born Garvey, who challenged the forces of white supremacy only began to emerge from similar historical neglect with the increase in Black studies and popular history that were byproducts of the civil rights and Black power struggles of the 1960s. Even then, however, Harrison was largely overlooked. In part this was undoubtedly due to his radicalism on issues other than race—particularly on matters of class and religion.[42]

There are, however, additional reasons for this neglect of Harrison. First, although he was personally amiable, he was an inveterate critic whose style was candid and at times bitingly sarcastic. Though his comments were usually perceptive and well researched, they often challenged the established order and existing leaders. As Rogers explains, "Most of the enmity against Harrison was incurred by his devastating candor."[43]

In particular, Harrison's willingness to directly challenge prominent leaders in leftist and African American circles stung many of the people most likely to keep his memory alive. Though he pointed out that "those who live by the people must needs be careful of the people's gods,"[44] it was advice he did not always heed himself. He was often more candidly critical than calculatingly cautious, and organizations that might have publicly preserved his memory made little effort to do so; some actually led in the great neglect that followed.[45]

Also important is that Harrison was more of a freelance educator and activist then an "organization man." He was not "somebody's man, whether that somebody was a Vesey

Street Liberal, or Northern millionaire or a powerful politician." He would not, as he said, "bow the knee to Baal, because Baal is in power." He did not suffer fools gladly and he neither wheedled nor cajoled supporters. He felt quite uncomfortable with praise, and though he worked with many organizations and played important roles in several key ones, Harrison had no long-term relationship with any organization or institution.[46]

While these reasons help to explain why Harrison has been largely overlooked, the omission of his life and work from historical accounts is a significant loss. He is far too important and influential, and his writings are far too seminal, to be neglected.[47]

The Development of Harrison's Thought and the Selected Writings

This *Reader* presents a selection of Harrison's writings and contans one hundred thirty-eight individually introduced items out of approximately seven hundred substantial Harrison pieces that have been located. The selections are divided into thirteen broad themes which present Harrison's views on a wide range of issues, social movements, and individuals. To further assist the reader, the following brief overview of the development of Harrison's thought (with parenthetical references to the selections) is offered.

Harrison's early years were spent on St. Croix, where his intellectual bent was nurtured and shaped. He utilized the library at St. John's Anglican Church in Christiansted, befriended schoolmate D. Hamilton Jackson (who became the island's foremost labor leader), studied under one of the island's best teachers (Jackson's father, Wilford Jackson), and excelled enough as a student that he was chosen as an underteacher for younger children.[48] Hubert learned the islanders' African traditions and their history of mass struggle, which included the 1848 slave-led emancipation struggle directed by "Buddhoe" [Gotlieb Bordeaux] and the 1878 week-long, island-wide labor protest known as "The Great Fireburn" (led by rebel leaders "Queen Mary" Thomas, "Queen Agnes," and "Queen Matilda" and inspired by the watchword "Our Side"). He also knew poverty, and that experience, he said, helped to keep his "heart open to the call of those who are down" and kept him from developing "such airs as might make a chasm between myself and my people." St. Croix did not have the lynching, formal segregation, severe racial proscriptions, or virulent white supremacy of the United States, and Harrison maintained (selection 81) that as a youth he knew nothing of the "doctrine of chromatic inferiors and superiors" which was thrust on islanders by the occupying U.S. Navy after his departure. In the absence of the suffocating racial oppression of the United States, Hubert was able to pursue his educational interests on St. Croix and dream the "long, long thoughts" of youth.[49]

After arriving in New York in 1900, Harrison was quickly forced to confront a bitter racial oppression unlike anything he had known at home. It was the period known as the nadir for African Americans, and New York City had recently had a race riot, lynchings marred the land, and racial discrimination marked every area of life. Most immediately, he had to confront racial discrimination in housing and employment.

Harrison was determined to learn, however, and after his arrival he immediately sought to enter school. Despite working a full-time day job and several nights each week, he attended high school at night, excelled in oratory and Latin, and was described as a "genius" by one of New York's daily newspapers. His interests included literature, the classics, history, politics, religion, evolutionary science, and current affairs, and these subjects were only part of his life-long pursuit of self-education.[50]

Harrison was an omnivorous reader of newspapers and books. The journalist Oscar Benson described him as "bookish, but not of the sort classed as a bookworm." He read assiduously and "when he grabbed a book he knew just what parts to digest, what passages to mark, what dogma to criticize and whether any book was worth a second reading." Hodge Kirnon explained that Harrison "took pains with whatever he planned to do in his educational efforts to an extraordinary degree; yet he would often times say that he memorized, assimilated, and transposed his wide range of reading upon technical subjects into their simplest and most understandable forms with but little or no effort." Kirnon added that Harrison always "found time to do his own thinking" and that he carried many social and philosophical problems in his mind for years, during which he would examine and probe them for hours, shelve them for a short period, then "take them out again and again to be subjected to his rigid tests of critical inquiry."[51]

Around 1907 Harrison started to maintain scrapbooks and keep a diary, and these materials reveal much about his thought processes. Approximately forty scrapbooks remain on subjects such as "The Negro-American," "The Negro in Africa," "History," "Biography," "Politics," "Literature," "Religion," "The State of Society," and "Mainly about Me." The scrapbooks (and an accompanying clippings section) include thousands of articles clipped primarily from six of New York's daily papers, from the *Literary Digest*, from New York City's Black papers (particularly the *New York Age*, the *Amsterdam News*, and the *New York News*), and from other Black publications. They also contain Harrison's writings, memorabilia, and marginal comments. The clippings and writings were classified and as Harrison began work on a subject he would pull his file or scrapbook and begin to subclassify according to need. His mind was not so much concerned with trivia as with understanding logical relations, and he constantly worked at building internal systems and testing hypotheses. The numbered scrapbooks served as a factual resource during the remainder of his life.[52]

The 1907 diary was actually Harrison's second. He first started one shortly after arriving in the United States, but it was not continued, and that copy has not been located. After securing work as a postal clerk, he began the new diary on September 18, 1907, and maintained it until days before his death. Harrison would often make entries in it in the early morning hours after working a late-night shift at the post office and returning to his apartment to read and write. When he restarted his diary at age twenty-four, he wrote down his thoughts on why he made that decision:

> It must surely be instructive to look back after long years on one's past thoughts and deeds and form new estimates of ourselves and others. Seen from another perspective large things grow small, small ones large and the lives of relative importance are bound to change position. At any rate it must be instructive to compare the impression of the moment, laden as it may be with the bias of feeling and clouded by partisan or personal prejudice, with the more broad and impartial review which distance in time or space makes possible.
>
> This may serve me in some sort as a history of myself twisted of two threads — what I do, and what I think. I hope I shall not make any conscious effort to impress upon it a character of any sort. So far as life is concerned as it comes so must it be set down. And if I omit any one phase of my life's experience I do so for judicial reasons and not for the sake of seeming better in my own eyes when memory has ceased to testify.[53]

While Hubert wrote his diary for himself, its content and occasional marginal comments leave no doubt that it was also written for those who would come after him to read it — an indication that even as a young man he had a strong sense of self-worth and was aware of the importance of the work he undertook.[54]

During his first decade in New York, in addition to his self-study, Harrison began to participate in the vibrant intellectual life that was created by working class Black New Yorkers. He was active in church lyceums, the YMCA and YWCA, the White Rose Home social-work center, a postal worker study circle, and a press club. He befriended working class scholars and activists such as bibliophiles Arthur Schomburg and George Young, journalist John E. Bruce, actor Charles Burroughs, and the social worker, educator, and activist Frances Reynolds Keyser. Harrison's approach, especially his efforts at getting "in full-touch with the *life* of my people" as an aid "to understanding them better," (selection 3) makes clear that he was what Antonio Gramsci would later describe as an "organic intellectual."[55]

Influenced by the atmosphere of muckraking criticism in early twentieth-century New York, Harrison developed critical skills which would remain an important part of his intellectual framework. His study of history, religion, and evolutionary science led him in the direction of freethought — thought based on adherence to scientific methodology and not "fettered by the dogmas and principles of religion." He grappled with his own religious faith (he had been reared an Episcopalian), broke from Christianity, and became an agnostic of the ilk of Thomas Huxley. Like Huxley, he refused "to put faith in that which does not rest on sufficient evidence." He chose, instead, to "look the universe in the face," to believe in "the sanctity of human nature," and to develop "a deep sense of . . . responsibility" for his actions. As he explained in his diary (selection 4), he would never "be anything but an honest Agnostic" because he preferred "to go to the grave with [his] eyes open." Harrison's new worldview placed humanity, not God, at the center, and his approach to life was based on the scientific method of investigation, not on a system of religious belief.[56]

Hubert went through much of this intellectual struggle in "inner loneliness." In his diary (selection 2) he commented that since his boyhood he had turned to "Sorrow" as his heritage, though he knew not why. In one of his more personally revealing passages he wrote that "The infinite sorrow in the face of the Christ-man, deeper than unfathomable seas, the face of [Thomas] Carlyle, ridged with the furrows of travail and turmoil; the fire-chastened face of Dante [Alighieri] that bearer of an immortal grief to the regions of underlying woe—these have always had a strange attraction for me. The things that sadden are more to me than the things that gladden." He concluded that God was "Unknown and Unknowable" and humanity was "more than life." With this understanding he placed the burden of human actions squarely on human shoulders—"For every man who *does* is God and in his work he lives, as God, forever." To those, "who think," he added, there was assured "an immortality more precious than that of their own individual existence."[57]

Harrison's developing worldview and beginning social activism, particularly against racism, are evident in his early writings. One letter to the editor (selection 1) and three articles (selections 7–9) criticize the racist press. Entries from his diary reveal an early pledge to help "the Mother race" (selection 2) and a desire to write a history of African Americans to counter existing white-supremacist historical interpretations (selection 3). A subsection on freethought details Harrison's break from religion (selection 4), his interest in reason and democratic dissent as advocated by Thomas Paine (selection 5), and his conviction that Christianity and organized religion were major causes of conservatism among African Americans (selection 6). This last theme appears again in later writings (selections 85, 86, 95, 110, and 111), and a letter from this period (selection 96) presents his early views on literary criticism.

Harrison was increasingly attracted to the protest philosophy of activists such as W. E. B. Du Bois, and, like Du Bois, he began to criticize the words and actions of Booker T. Washington. Washington, the president of Tuskegee Institute in Alabama and the most powerful Black man in the America, had achieved his position of influence by building an extensive patronage machine made possible through ties to powerful whites including former president Theodore Roosevelt and financial giants John Wanamaker and Andrew Carnegie. His loyalty to his white backers and the Republican Party was at times extreme, as in 1906 when, in reference to Roosevelt, he said that "I will oppose nothing that he wants done and will help forward all that he desires to have done." Overall, Washington's policy was one of Black subordination in political and economic spheres and his core philosophy emphasized industrial over higher education for African Americans, Christian character-building, constructing an economic base before demanding equal civic and political rights, and cooperation with wealthy and powerful Southern "white friends." He warned that "the agitation of questions of social equality is the extremist folly," advised that African Americans must begin "at the bottom of life" and "not at the top," and emphasized that "the Negro" was "not given to strikes and lockouts." He also firmly opposed those African Americans who dared to criticize him.[58]

Harrison's criticisms of Washington (selections 6–8, 12–13, and 52), whom he described as "subservient," were all-encompassing. He said that Washington's philosophy was "one of submission and acquiescence in political servitude." In contrast to Washington, Harrison was staunchly opposed to the Republican Party, and he favored protests and struggles for equality, "modern education," thought unfettered by religion, and support of trade unions. He also urged that Black leaders should be chosen by, and responsible to, Black people (selections 42–51, 55, 59). Only in the area of economic base-building would Harrison articulate views remotely similar to Washington (selection 135), and these views would never be at the expense of equal rights.[59]

In the first decades of the twentieth century Harrison began to encourage a break from the Republican Party to which African Americans had been wedded since the Civil War era (selections 14, 40–41 and 48–49). He arrived at this position through critical readings on Lincoln, the Civil War, and the Compromise of 1876; in response to political developments including the increase in lynchings, disfranchisement, and segregation while Republicans controlled the federal government; as a counter to the Brownsville, Texas, affair (and President Theodore Roosevelt's racist response to it); and as an answer to President William Howard Taft's pushing out of Black officeholders.[60] In addition, as his readings extended further into history, sociology, economics, evolution, and single taxism, he became familiar with authors such as Karl Marx, Friedrich Engels, Karl Kautsky, Paul Lafargue, Herbert Spencer, Lester F. Ward, Charles Darwin, Thomas Huxley, Mary Maclean, and Francisco Ferrer, and he moved in the direction of socialism. The rejection of the Republican Party and the sympathy for the socialist message accelerated his move toward third-party politics and toward the Socialist Party. In 1911–12 he began lecturing on "Lincoln and Liberty" and developed these talks into a series of articles (selections 40–41), which, particularly after their publication in the *Negro World*, played an important role in stimulating African American political independence and in fueling the Black community's break from the Republican Party in the 1920s (selection 42).[61]

Harrison became a full-time activist with the Socialist Party in late 1911 and quickly rose to prominence with his writings and talks in support of Socialist candidates and on socialism and a wide variety of other subjects including economics, religion, and philosophy. His most important theoretical contributions were two series of articles on the subject of "The Negro and Socialism" which appeared in the Socialist Party's *New York Call* (selections 8–11) and in the *International Socialist Review* (selections 12–14). The articles provided a comprehensive political, economic, social, and educational analysis and broke new ground by calling on Socialists to champion the cause of African Americans, to oppose white supremacy, and to develop a special appeal to reach "the Negro."

Despite his efforts, the theory and practice of the Socialist Party led Harrison to conclude that it, like the organized labor movement (selections 12 and 16), put the white "race first and class after" (selections 15, 31, 33, and 34). He then moved increasingly to the left, toward the militant socialist Industrial Workers of the World (selections 16–18). From 1912–14, while still a Socialist, he consistently supported direct action and sabotage, spoke of the revolution "working its way up from the depths . . . not coming from above," agitated on behalf of the Paterson silk strikers, and defended IWW founder and SP leader "Big Bill" Haywood, who was under attack by the Socialists for his pro-sabotage views.[62]

In 1914–15 Harrison withdrew from the Socialist Party and began to work with freethinkers; with the freethought-influenced Modern School Movement, founded by the martyred Spanish anarchist and educator Francisco Ferrer; and with his own Radical Forum. The freethought influence is reflected in his *Truth Seeker* article, "The Negro A Conservative" (selection 6), which calls for a new race leadership, abreast of modern and scientific thought, in order to "shake off the trammels of such time-serving leaders as Mr. [Booker T.] Washington." It also appears in his revealing letter to Frances Reynolds Keyser (selection 4), in a *Truth Seeker* piece on Thomas Paine (selection 5), and in two later articles on education (selections 35 and 36).

Dissatisfied with the established political parties, with the Socialists, and with conservative Black leadership (selections 24 and 30), Harrison, in the 1915–16 period, decided to concentrate his work in Harlem (selection 32). The final, decisive step in this direction was made through the frontier of art. His reviews on the "Negro Theater" (selections 126 and 127) analyzed what he considered to be truly distinctive in "Negro society" and in the psychology of the "Negro." His vehicle was the stage and through it he gained a perspective on the psychology of race relations in the United States. In his effort to glimpse "the Negro's soul" he focused on the central role of the playgoer in determining "the form and substance of the Negro drama" and concluded that there was a distinct "Negro culture" (marked by color prejudice by light-skinned African Americans toward those of darker color) and that "the craze for color runs all through Negro society in the United States." (He elaborates further on within-race color discrimination in selections 58 and 94.)[63]

In this 1915–16 period Harrison developed his race-conscious, "race first" message in response to systematic racial oppression and the "white first" attitude of the organized labor movement and the Socialists. It was also an alternative to the leadership message offered by contemporary Black leaders. The core race-conscious message, which would became more pronounced during the sacrifices and social upheaval of World War I, would be his political staple for the remaining thirteen years of his life. Harrison's call to race consciousness would become the center of his strategic perspective; it was basically a call to African Americans to recognize the racial oppression they faced and to use that awareness to unite, organize, and respond as a group (selections 26, 27, and 34).

Harrison had grown dissatisfied with strategies such as those advocated by the NAACP that sought "to secure certain results by affecting the minds of white people" when, in fact,

African Americans had no control over those minds and had "absolutely no answer to the question, 'What steps do you propose to take if those minds at which you are aiming remain unaffected?'" As an alternate strategy he began to advocate "the mobilizing of the Negro's political power, pocket book power and intellectual power," which were "within the Negro's control," in order "to do for the Negro the things which the Negro needs to have done." This would be accomplished "without depending upon or waiting for the co-operative action of white people." Though interracial cooperation, whenever it came, would be "a boon" which "no Negro, intelligent or unintelligent" would despise, he emphasized that they could not "afford to predicate the progress of the Negro upon such co-operative action" — because such action "may not come" (selections 18, 45, 57).

At first, in the early stages from perhaps 1915 through around 1920, Harrison advocated the propagandistic doctrine of "race first" (the phrase subsequently was treated as the essence of the Garvey movement in Tony Martin's *Race First*). He considered it "propaganda" and described it as "a response to the Class First of the Socialists" and to the "America First" put forth by Woodrow Wilson in an April 1915 speech on American neutrality in relation to the European conflict. Harrison emphasized to the Socialists that "We say Race First, because you have all along insisted on [white] Race First and class after when you didn't need our help" (selection 30).

When first developed, Harrison's call for "race first" seemed to be a reflexive response to both the "white race first" theory and practice of the Socialists and to the inadequacy of the Socialists's "class first" propaganda in the face of class *and* racial oppression. "Race first" urged placement of the racial struggle at the fore, before the class struggle. It tended to de-emphasize struggle against class oppression, and in its fervor it at times suggested an almost fatalistic biological permanency to racism among European Americans. There was little indication of anything temporal in the use of the slogan, which seemed to be a response to a white supremacy that appeared both ubiquitous and permanent. The slogan suggested minimal hope concerning work with whites and it suggested a minimizing of within-race class differences in the face of an oppressor white race.

The historian Ernest Allen points out particular difficulty with Harrison's decision to respond to the Socialists' "rigidly determinist" "class first" with the "equally dogmatic 'race first'" slogan. He concludes that "Whereas 'class first' ignored the *special* oppression which blacks *qua* blacks suffered above and beyond that borne by white laborers, 'race first' obliterated the class aspects of the African American struggle." Though Harrison did not himself obliterate class struggle with his propagandist use of the slogan, Allen's comment is insightful.[64]

Over time, Harrison seemed to replace his call for "race first" with a call to develop race consciousness (selection 34). Though the phrases were at times interchangeable, the call to race consciousness suggested a broader and deeper appeal, more compatible with class consciousness, not "rigidly determinist," and more temporal. It seemed to emphasize "race" as a sociohistorical rather than a biological concept.[65] It is this message that his children remembered Harrison delivering. There was, however, overlap in his use of the slogans, and nowhere did he clearly compare and differentiate the concepts.[66]

In his writings (selections 26 and 34) Harrison explained that race consciousness was needed as a self-defense measure under existing societal conditions and that it was a necessary corrective to white supremacy. It was also a strategic component in the struggle for a racially just and socialist society. Thus, where "the feeling of racial superiority" among the white population was pronounced, there was necessarily produced "in the mind of the masses of the black, brown and yellow peoples" what is termed in psychology "a protective reaction." This protective reaction was "race consciousness" and like loyalty it was "neither an evil nor a good." The "good or evil of it" depended "upon the uses to which it [was] put." As long as the outer situation remained the same, reasoned Harrison, "We must evoke race-consciousness to furnish a background for our aspirations, readers for our writers, a clientele for our artists and professional people, and ideals for our future." So long as a Black child could "not aspire to be Governor of Massachusetts or President of the United States, like the son of an immigrant, German or Russian, so long will we need race-consciousness."

Race consciousness took various forms. Harrison cited opposition to "Jim Crow" and to mimicking whites, objection to "educational starvation," striving for "racial independence in business," rejection of "our conservative leaders," and "reaching out into new fields of endeavor" as manifestations of it. The slogan did not mean that Blacks "hate white people," he noted, but it did mean "that in sheer self-defense, we too must put race very high on our list of necessities." If such effort had not been made all along, there would have been no "'Negro progress' to boast about" as proof of equal human potential. Black churches, newspapers, life insurance companies, banks, fraternities, colleges, and political appointees all indicated Black race consciousness.[67]

Organizing efforts among working people offer a clear example of what Harrison's race-conscious message entailed. Essentially, it was a proactive policy that did not wait for white laborers to act in their class interest by struggling against white supremacy. Harrison pointed out that "the black worker was opposed by the general run of white working men, who kept him out of their unions for the most part and yet called him 'scab' for getting their jobs at the only time when those jobs were available to him." Though he called on Black workers to support "the program of the advanced labor movement in this country," he also advocated that African American workers should—when confronted by racist, exclusionary unions—"Form [their] own unions." By 1921, in the face of racist, exclusionary unions, he would urge the use of "every effort to line up all Colored workers in unions composed of Colored workers only." These unions could then "co-operate in every possible way with the white unions," when "allowed that right." He considered this policy not "the best," but "the most helpful."[68]

The strategic importance of this race conscious message in terms of labor was strikingly revealed in 1920, in a review (selection 17) of the labor leader William Z. Foster's *The Great Steel Strike and Its Lessons*. Harrison emphasized that it was a principal duty of whites to oppose racism and he explained that until that was done there would be little prospect for real joint effort:

> It is up to the white unions and the American Federation of Labor and the great railroad brotherhoods themselves and not up to the Negro leaders to change this deep seated aversion which American Negroes have for white American labor. It is conceded on all sides that the white organized labor movement has been and still is pronouncedly anti-Negro. And as long as that remains true, just so long will self-respecting Negro leaders abstain from urging the laboring masses of their race to join forces with the stupid and short-sighted labor oligarchy which refuses to join forces with them.

In 1921, in the pages of the *Negro World*, Harrison offered more on the importance to his strategic perspective of both race consciousness by African Americans and white worker opposition to racism (selection 75). After clarifying that the principal enemy of the darker peoples of the world was "capitalist imperialism" and its "economic motive," he explained that "structures of racial self-protection" were "defensive structures" that arose in response to white "racial solidarity." He emphasized that it was particularly the task of white revolutionists to "show their sincerity by first breaking down the exclusion walls of white workingmen before they ask us to demolish our own defensive structures of racial self-protection." The reason was that Black race consciousness "arose as a consequence of the former [white racial solidarity], and the cause should be removed before the consequence can fairly be expected to disappear." He emphasized that those "who will meet us on our common ground will find that we recognize a common enemy [capitalist imperialism] in the present world order and are willing to advance to attack it in our joint behalf."[69]

Thus, for Harrison, the key to the class question and to class unity was the breaking down of white racial solidarity and the system of racial oppression. Harrison, a former leading Black Socialist and a consistent class radical, concluded that in the United States progressives would have to go through race to get to class. Most particularly, as long as white supremacy and racial oppression remained, proponents of working-class struggle would have to fight against them to succeed. For this reason he saw the Liberty League's demand for genuine democracy for African Americans to be a "startling program" with most radical implications.

The particular significance of Harrison's call for race consciousness should not be overlooked. The historian Nathan Huggins has argued that race consciousness "most likely leads to provincialism," that it can be tied to an identity crisis and to race guilt, and that it is often reflected in a hatred of whites. In Harrison's case we see something quite different.

Rather than a provincial, he was a genuinely well-educated and critically independent intellectual. He had traveled some, he was abreast of domestic and international events, and he was well versed in modern and scientific thought. He was not undergoing an identity crisis or expressing race guilt; rather, he quite rationally and in a well-thought-out fashion was attempting to point a way forward. His analysis was based on his study of society.[70]

Rather than moving from a "hate white" analysis, Harrison, an internationalist and a true educator, was approaching the Black masses with a call for self–awareness and group awareness. Quite simply, he had concluded, after considerable practical experience and intellectual analysis, that as long as the United States remained a white supremacist society, a needed and necessary corrective in the interest of all was for African Americans to develop race consciousness. In the United States (where a system of racial oppression was central to capitalist rule), to heighten the class struggle people would have to struggle against racial oppression and the supremacy of "the white race." In that way, the leading class-conscious African American leader led in the advocacy of race consciousness. It was a profound transformation with profound implications for the future of United States radicalism.[71]

Harrison's "race first" program was first put forth with the Liberty League and *The Voice* in 1917. The organization called for enforcement of the Fourteenth and Fifteenth Amendments, federal antilynching legislation, militant armed resistance in response to racist attacks (such as those in the East St. Louis pogrom), and a political voice (selections 16, 18–23, 67, and 100). Harrison understood the new political reality of the changing consciousness and changing demographics of northern urban centers (including Black majority concentrations in certain areas). He agitated for elective representation; for campaigns to support independent Black candidates responsive to Black voters; and for an end to barnacle-like Black leaders who were tied to the Republican Party and subservient to "white friends" (selections 42–46 and 48–50).

The Liberty League and *The Voice* stimulated a generation of activists and, as Harrison explained (selection 64), laid the basis for the Garvey movement. Marcus Garvey's experiences in the United States — with virulently organized white supremacy, with the race consciousness of African Americans, and with activists like Harrison — began to reshape his views. Garvey had at first eschewed politics and possessed what historian Robert A. Hill has described as a "static view of political abstinence." Harrison, the Liberty League, *The Voice,* and activists around them played particularly important roles in Garvey's decision to stay in the United States and in his developing ideas and the organization he would create. Domingo, a Liberty League officer who had known Garvey in Jamaica, introduced him to Harrison. After observing Harrison's work, Garvey decided to remain in New York. Domingo also aided Garvey in parliamentary procedures during 1917 and 1918. Liberty League member Charles C. Seifert developed the idea for the Black Star Line steamship company (BSL). (Harrison unequivocally stated that the BSL was "an idea which Garvey took bodily from Seifert, one of the original members of the Liberty League" [selection

64].) Many of the people who were key progressive leaders of the Garvey movement over the next few years came from Harrison's Liberty League and *The Voice*, including the first three editors of the *Negro World*; two presidents and one general secretary of the UNIA; the president, director, and officers of the Black Star Line; and the president of the Ladies Division of the UNIA.[72]

The founding of the Liberty League and *The Voice* not only laid the basis for the Garvey movement, it also propelled Harrison to national prominence as a Black leader. Less than one year later, the June 1918 Liberty Congress brought him to the pinnacle of protest leadership (selection 53). The Harrison-led Congress was the major autonomous protest effort of African Americans during World War I and, in an ominous foreshadowing of later practices, government officials moved to undermine it (with a series of actions that involved prominent civil rights leaders).

Leading in the effort was the NAACP's Joel E. Spingarn, who enlisted the support of Emmett Scott (special adjutant to the secretary of war and the former chief assistant to Booker T. Washington) and Du Bois in speedily calling a preemptive June Editors' Conference of more moderate leaders to undermine the Liberty Congress and support President Wilson's war effort. During this period Du Bois attempted to secure a commission in Military Intelligence, the agency of the U.S. General Staff that monitored and intimidated both Blacks and radicals. He also wrote what was probably the most controversial editorial of his life, "Close Ranks," which appeared in the July 1918 issue of the *Crisis*. The piece was only two paragraphs long; its last two sentences were aimed at the African American community and read, "Let us, while this war lasts, forget our special grievances and close ranks shoulder to shoulder with our own white fellow citizens and allied nations that are fighting for democracy. We make no ordinary sacrifice, but we make it gladly and willingly with our eyes lifted to the hills."[73]

Though Du Bois denied that there was any relation between the editorial and the commission, Harrison took him to task over this in an editorial published in the July 25, 1918, issue of *The Voice* (selection 54). Harrison opened by citing a War Department bulletin that declared that "'justifiable grievances' were producing and had produced 'not disloyalty, but an amount of unrest and bitterness which even the best efforts of their leaders may not be able always to guide.'" He emphasized that this was "the simple truth." He then characterized the "essence of the present situation" as one of reevaluation of leadership in which both "those whom our white masters have 'recognized' as our leaders (without taking the trouble to consult us) and those who, by our own selection, had actually attained to leadership among us are being reevaluated and, in most cases, rejected." The "most striking instance from the latter class" was Du Bois, and, wrote Harrison, his case was "the more significant because his former services to his race" were "undoubtedly of a high and courageous sort."[74]

This was Harrison's most forceful criticism of Du Bois, but over the years he had developed others (selections 55–59). He was particularly critical of Du Bois's notion of the "Talented Tenth"—the "educated and gifted" group whose members, according to Du Bois, "must be made leaders of thought and missionaries of culture among their people" in order to lead African Americans forward. Harrison, in contrast, emphasized education and self-development of the masses, the so-called "common people." He also increasingly equated the "Talented Tenth" concept with the concept of "colored" or "mulatto" as opposed to "Negro" leadership of the "Negro race." He did not believe that such a "Talented Tenth" was in any way preordained to lead the "Negro race," and he did not think that it had provided the leadership needed by African Americans. Harrison rejected the white domination that unchallenged acceptance of such leadership implied. As he explained (selection 58) in harsh and pointed language, for two centuries African Americans had been "told by white Americans that we cannot and will not amount to anything except in so far as we first accept the bar sinister of their mixing with us." Thus, "always when white people had to select a leader for Negroes they would select some one who had in his veins the blood of the selector." Under slavery, according to Harrison, "it was those whom Denmark Vesey of Charleston described as 'house niggers' who got the master's cut-off clothes, the better scraps of food and culture which fell from the white man's table, who were looked upon as the Talented Tenth of the Negro race" (selection 93). Historically, "the opportunities of self-improvement, in so far as they lay within the hand of the white race, were accorded exclusively to this class of people who were the left-handed progeny of the white masters."[75]

Harrison was also critical of the NAACP leadership that Du Bois supported. He favored more militant protest and thought that the NAACP was limited by white people's conceptions of how Black people should act. He observed (selection 72) that "some white people seem to think a certain public attitude toward white people to be fit and proper, and a certain other attitude—an attitude which white people would maintain if they were in the same situation—as unbecoming to black people." For the NAACP the race problem was "to be settled by the words, the mandates, the principles, the judgments and opinions coming from one side only—the white side."[76]

Though Harrison had started out as a Du Bois supporter in his first decade in New York, his differences with Du Bois extended beyond the "Talented Tenth," relations with "white friends," and the NAACP program. Other differences over the years included those on the question of lynchers and lynching—Harrison called for armed self-defense and federal antilynching legislation (selections 89–91) when Du Bois and the NAACP did not; on the Socialist Party's approach to African Americans—Harrison had called for a special effort, the Colored Socialist Club, which Du Bois opposed; on the 1912 presidential election —Harrison had supported the Socialist candidate Debs while Du Bois left the Socialists in order to support the Democratic candidate Wilson; on segregated military camps during World War I—Harrison had opposed them, while Du Bois supported them; and, finally, on domestic protests for equality and redress of grievances during World War I — Harrison favored them while Du Bois rejected that approach. Clearly, Harrison's dissatisfactions with Du Bois's leadership had been building and the whole series of events around Du Bois's "Close Ranks" editorial and the captaincy was the last straw — it represented, wrote Harrison, "the moral downfall of another great leader."[77]

By the end of the war Harrison's differences with Du Bois seemed to center on the strategic question, "'What steps do you propose to take if those [white] minds at which you are aiming remain unaffected?'" (selection 57). To Harrison, Du Bois's answer revolved around "the Talented Tenth," paper protests, and hoped-for interracial cooperation; Harrison increasingly advocated the alternate strategy of "mobilizing of the Negro's political power, pocket book power and intellectual power" and not "depending upon or waiting for the co-operative action of white people."

What was particularly new in Harrison's strategy was his conception of and approach to race unity. As he later explained (selections 136 and 137), many who sought race unity were unclear of what they actually meant — was it to be "unity of thought and ideas," "unity of organization," "unity of purpose," or "unity of action"? For Harrison unity of thought was neither desirable nor possible except in the graveyard, and unity of organization was exceedingly difficult and therefore not likely. Unity of purpose was a real possibility, however. The fault with previous efforts was that the uniters, such as Washington and Du Bois, had "generally gone at the problem from the wrong end." As he explained, "they have begun at the top when they should have begun at the bottom." "To attempt to unite the 'intellectuals' at the top" was "not the same thing as uniting the Negro masses" who were the key to racial solidarity."[78]

During World War I Harrison's concerns extended beyond domestic struggles for democracy, equality, voting rights, an end to lynching and segregation, and a new approach to leadership. He was also deeply concerned with international matters and the racial implications of the conflict (selections 66 and 67). In particular, he opposed the imperialist and white-supremacist aims of the major war powers, the imperialist oppression of nations, the imperial powers' designs on Africa, and the use of working people as cannon fodder. He also emphasized, however, that the conflict was destroying many resources of the "white world" and facilitating contact among oppressed peoples and thus was providing the oppressed an opportunity to press their demands and improve their conditions. After the armistice on November 11, 1918, he offered instructive comments on the forthcoming Peace Conference in Paris (selections 68 and 69).

Harrison's concentration on international matters continued, and over the next several years he wrote many powerful pieces critical of imperialism ("the most dangerous phase of developed capitalism") and supportive of internationalism. His writings reveal a solid grasp of current international events and included in this *Reader* are pieces on India, Africa, Asia, the Islamic world, and the Caribbean (selections 70–84, 103, 105–106, 111, and

125). Harrison repeatedly began his analysis of contemporary situations from an international perspective and emphasized that it was important for African Americans to overcome ignorance of international events and "to get in international touch" with "the downtrodden section of the human population of the globe" in order to "establish business, industrial and commercial relations with them" (selection 72). Quite interesting in this regard also is the fact that Harrison, a supporter of armed self-defense, recognized the pacifist mass leader Mohandas K. Gandhi "as the greatest, most unselfish and powerful leader of the modern world" (selection 105).

Consistent with his race-conscious, international approach, Harrison in 1919 assumed the editorship of the *New Negro* magazine. The monthly sought to become "an organ of the international consciousness of the darker races — especially of the Negro race." In addition to editorials on international duty (selections 24 and 25) and the need for a race-conscious publication (selections 26 and 27), other *New Negro* pieces in this *Reader* include an article on "The Women of Our Race" (selection 28) and two selections — "Negro Culture and the Negro College" (selection 35) and "Two Negro Radicalisms" (selection 27) — that laid the basis for Harrison's forthcoming work with Garvey.

In December of 1919 when Marcus Garvey first asked Harrison to work with him, it was to head a college that Garvey planned to develop. Harrison spent much time and effort on educational work, especially in the Black community, and he considered such modern educational work a revolutionary endeavor (selections 35, 36, and 55). He called attention to this revolutionary importance in "Education and the Race" (selection 36), and explained how, in "the dark days of Russia, when the iron heel of czarist despotism was heaviest on the necks of the people, . . . Leo Tolstoi and the other intelligentsia began to carry knowledge to the masses." Then, as "knowledge spread, enthusiasm was backed by brains, and the developing Russian revolution 'began to be sure of itself,' thus confirming the age-old wisdom that 'Knowledge *is* power.'" Harrison elsewhere emphasized that knowledge offered the power to open "political, social and economic" doors and "only by brains and by the product of brains" could Black people "pull [them]selves up."[80]

Emphasis on education was a central concern for Harrison. He had long opposed the "educational starvation" of the Black masses (see selections 11, 13, 32, 52, 56, 93, and 121), and he stressed that "it behooves my race as well as the other subject races to learn the wisdom of the weak and to develop to the fullest that organ whereby weakness has been able to overcome strength; namely, the intellect." He urged that "Negroes must take to reading, study and the development of intelligence as we have never done before." As an example he cited the Japanese who had gone to school in Europe but "never used Europe's education to make them the apes of Europe's culture." They had "absorbed, adopted, transformed and utilized," and, he reasoned, "we Negroes must do the same."[81]

Harrison was a superb educator, and his views on education (selections 35–39) differed notably from those of Washington and Du Bois. Though he had in part supported Du

Bois's challenge to Washington (a call for higher education as opposed to industrial education), Harrison emphasized education of the masses, as opposed to Du Bois's emphasis on "the higher education of a Talented Tenth." The intellectual leaders, explained Harrison (selection 36), would have to "come down from the Sinais" and teach "the common people." They would have to "simplify and make clear, to light the lamps of knowledge that the eyes of the race may see; that the feet of their people may not stumble."[82]

Harrison's conception of the education needed by the Black masses was significantly influenced by the rationalist, freethought, anarchist, and socialist theories to which he had been exposed. In particular, he favored integral education, emphasis on the process of learning over emphasis on instruction, teaching by example and experience over teaching by rote and memorization, and education as life over education as preparation for life. Thus, for Harrison, the real "essence" of the within-race debate over education was not "the easy distinction between 'lower' and 'higher' education" discussed by Washington and Du Bois, but rather that of "'the knowledge of things' versus 'the knowledge of words'" — a debate that had been waged in England since Thomas Huxley's youth. The questions to be answered, said Harrison, were: "Shall education consist of Latin and Greek, literature and metaphysics, or of modern science, modern languages and modern thought?" and should children be trained "to grapple effectively with the problems of life that lie before them, or to look longingly back upon the past standards of life and thought?" Harrison's answer was that Black people needed "above all a knowledge of the wider world and of the long past" as provided in "modern science and modern thought." Science, he emphasized, was "organized observation, experiment, and common sense," and it was used both politically and economically. Those who had the most of it were "able to impose their will" on those who had "less or none at all."[83]

To the African American masses he urged "Read! Read! Read!" In a *Voice* editorial of that title (selection 39) he observed that "as a people our bent for books is not encouraging," and "we mostly read trash." This was true of both the rank and file and the leaders. He used Kelly Miller, Dean of the College of Arts and Sciences of Howard University, as an example of a leader who exhibited "ignorance of modern science and modern thought," whose biology seemed that of "eighteen hundred years ago," and who knew little of astronomy and geology. To Harrison, such ignorance was typical of most Black leaders, and he reasoned that little could be expected from them. Therefore, he called on the Black masses to take the issue of education into their own hands and read and study in order to obtain the "New Knowledge" that was needed.[84]

Though Garvey approached Harrison in December 1919 to head a UNIA college, he actually had something more immediate in mind: he wanted Harrison to edit the *Negro World*. By the first week of January 1920 Harrison assumed the principal editorship of the *Negro World* and proceeded to reshape it into the most powerful organ of Black race consciousness in the world. How this magnificent and historic journalistic effort was accomplished is detailed in his diary (selection 60).

One of the first issues that involved Harrison as editor of the *Negro World* was an intense debate with the Black Socialists (selections 30–33), particularly the "class first" Black Socialists led by A. Philip Randolph and Chandler Owen. Harrison charged that the Socialist Party had "secretly subsidized both a magazine and a newspaper to attempt to cut into the splendid solidarity which Negroes are achieving." He also argued against the Socialist position that "there is no race problem, only an economic problem." In the course of the debate he defended the "New Negro" movement, the "race first" approach, and his opposition to white domination of the African American movement, and he made clear that his objection was not to socialism, but to Socialist Party practice.

While serving as editor of the *Negro World*, Harrison called on the Black community to move in new political directions (selections 46–51). One such effort was an attempt to establish an all-Black Liberty Party and run a Black candidate for President (selection 46). He also tried to break the hold that the Republican Party held on Black voters (selections 40, 41, and 47–51) and emphasized the need to use the powers and privileges of the vote to independently support candidates and causes (selection 49). In "The Black Tide Turns in Politics" (selection 51) Harrison discussed Republican betrayals, the new mood of Black voters, Democrats vying for Black votes, and how "the two largest mass-meetings [with political candidates] ever held among Negroes in America" were "cases of political thimble-rigging."

As he sought to move African Americans in these new political directions, Harrison focused considerable attention on the question of leadership. He had previously written on Booker T. Washington (selections 6 and 52) and W. E. B. Du Bois (selections 53–55), and he now offered some general comments on leadership (selections 56–59). His talks on political leadership centered on his understanding that "New Negro" leadership would be "based not upon the ignorance of the masses, but their intelligence." The old leadership had maintained itself "partly because the masses were ignorant," but as African Americans became more educated and literate, and gained more access to educational facilities, Harrison saw the possibility of successfully challenging the old leadership.[85]

In discussing characteristics needed by "New Negro" leaders, Harrison focused on training, irreverence, and courage (selection 56). In a direct reference to Du Bois during the war, he emphasized that "New Negro" leaders could not take a moral vacation, but must "stand four-square to *all* the winds that blow" (selection 55). He also urged that new leaders must concentrate on Black "political power, pocketbook power and intellectual power" without "waiting for the co-operative action of white people" which might not come (selection 57), and that they must stand clear of outside interference, which was one "of the knottiest problems Negroes faced."[86] Harrison felt that the "outside interference" issue emerged in both white-dominated organizations and in "the claim advanced, explicitly and implicitly, by Negroids of mixed blood to be considered the natural leaders of Negro activities on the ground of some alleged 'superiority' inherent in their white blood" (selection 58).

Related to the leadership question are Harrison's profound comments on Marcus Garvey (selections 60–65). They are some of the most important selections in this collection, and they help to establish that Harrison, the Liberty League, and *The Voice* laid the basis for the Garvey movement.[87] They also establish Harrison's major role in developing the *Negro World*. These writings indicate many of Harrison's differences from Garvey, including his desire to move in a more political, more radical, more anti-imperialist direction; his opposition to the KKK; his different approach to ending lynching; his desire for more rational and factual appeals rather than more emotional ones; and his more personal and political differences concerning attitudes toward co-workers, followers, and truth.

The material in this *Reader* should lead to new interpretations of Garvey and the Garvey movement. The diary entries from March 17 and 18, 1920 (selection 60), detail how Harrison reshaped the *Negro World* and turned it into the preeminent radical, race-conscious Black publication in the world. The materials offer important insights into the Black Star Line (Garvey's biggest fund-raiser) and the Liberian Commission (the delegation that Garvey planned to send to Africa to facilitate the opening of economic ties on the continent). Harrison's diary entry (selection 61) of May 24, 1920, provides a revealing analysis of Garvey's character. It discusses what Harrison considers to be the "defect" in "the size of Garvey's soul" and Garvey's ignorance in matters pertaining to ships and the Black Star Line. It also comments on how Garvey "lies to the people magniloquently, bragging about impossible things while not owning the ships outright." The diary entries of August 28th and 30th (selections 62 and 63) describe how, as part of the publicity for the 1920 UNIA convention, Garvey "plastered the air with lies," how he ran the convention undemocratically, and how he was the "chief mountebank" of "Negrodom."

In "Marcus Garvey at the Bar of United States Justice" (selection 64), written in 1923 upon Garvey's conviction for mail fraud, Harrison maintains that Garvey's trial was fair. He says that Garvey had collected hundreds of thousands of dollars by "false and misleading advertisements"; that the Black Star Line "was designed as a money-getter for Garvey"; and that Garvey never accounted for much of the money he collected. The article also discusses how dedicated Garvey followers refused to recognize such things as "the receipts of the poor people for passage money," false "advertisements in the *Negro World* of sailings of the *Phyllis Wheatley*," "printed lies" and "faked pictures," and "telling of 20,000 delegates to a convention in which anyone who could count would find only a hundred." In recounting his personal history with Garvey, Harrison explains that the UNIA program "was based on the belief that Negroes should finance the foundations of their future and not go begging to the white race either for help, leadership or a program," and that this was "the program of the Liberty League of which Garvey was a member in 1917." He emphasizes that "From that league Garvey appropriated every feature that was worth while in his movement."

Another major difference between Harrison and Garvey is treated in a 1923 Harrison radio talk (selection 96) and a 1924 *Boston Chronicle* editorial (selection 65). By 1924 Garvey's program centered on the notion of "African Redemption." In contrast, Harrison argued that "The American Negro is — after all — an American; and generally a deeper, truer American than nine-tenths of the whites." The "Negro Problem," he asserted, is "an American problem," and will be settled "here in America upon American lines." He had made a similar point earlier, at the time of the 1919 Paris Peace Conference (selections 68 and 69), when he criticized those, including Garvey, who were "seeking to get money from the unsuspecting masses of our people 'for the purpose of sending delegates.'" Harrison considered such efforts "sublimely silly" and "a useless waste of the money of poor people who can ill afford it." He stressed that instead of elaborating plans on how to liberate Africa, African Americans should "LEARN WHAT THEY [Africans] HAVE TO TEACH US," and he emphasized that "Lynching, disfranchisement and segregation are evils HERE; and the place in which we must fight them is HERE."[88]

While Harrison commented regularly on the pressing political issues of the day, he also on many occasions became more reflective and offered "meditations" in his diary and in whatever publication he was editing. These often very insightful meditations reveal a more pensive Harrison. In "Goodwill Toward Men" (selection 85) he suggested that Jesus, "despised and rejected of men," was nearer "to the despised and down-trodden Negro than to his haughty Anglo-Saxon oppressor." In "Heroes and Hero-Worship, and the Heroic in Human History" (selection 86) he discussed the stern responsibilities and duties of leadership and suggested that one reason true heroes are so rare is that "it is the virtue of the crowd to be crowd-minded, and the hounds of slander and the curs of foul abuse often follow yelping at the heels of him who dares to venture on the better way." In "A Soul in Search of Itself" (selection 87) Harrison came as close as he ever did to offering a personal creed, and in "On Praise" (selection 88) he discussed his disdain for most flattery — and in so doing suggested why his intellectual bent and personality characteristics may have placed limits on his becoming a mass leader.

During the 1920s Harrison extended earlier comments (selections 89–91) on lynching and the Klan, and he also developed insightful thoughts on race relations and democracy in America (selections 92–96). His editorial on the 1920 census (selection 92) treated it as "a lying document" and called attention to how the social sciences can be used to deceive. His Board of Education lecture "Bridging the Gulf of Color" (selection 93) stressed the importance of increased social contact as a "first desideratum" for improved race relations. In "At the Back of the Black Man's Mind" (selection 94) Harrison attempted to unveil the secret thoughts of African Americans on racial matters, and in "'Democracy' in America" (selection 95) he expressed his opposition to "white [capitalist] civilization," "capitalist imperialism," and its "color line" (selections selections 46, 102, and 106).

In "The Negro and the Nation" (selection 96), a June 21, 1923, radio talk, Harrison developed the theme that the "destiny of the American Negro lies in the future of America," and in a direct challenge to Garvey, he added that the "strands of his soul are woven into the fabric of our national existence and no mere demagogue can untwist them." Harrison also posited that "An American character, physically and spiritually one, is emerging from this complex of cultural forces" and that America's "great experiment in democracy" would "make these United States the herald of the Dawn that is to be."

Harrison never limited himself to sociopolitical matters, and some of his finest writings are those pertaining to literature — particularly his book and theater reviews and comments on criticism. His first published comments on book reviewing and theories of literary criticism appeared in 1907, when he was twenty-three, in the *New York Times Saturday Review of Books* (selection 97). He wrote occasional reviews over the next decade, and then, in 1917, he began "plying the trade" professionally in *The Voice*. Over the last decade of his life, reviews and poems were important parts of every publication that he edited. Approximately seventy reviews by Harrison have been located.

On March 4, 1922, Harrison described (selection 98) how in the 1920 *Negro World* he "inaugurated" the "first (and up to now the only) regular book-review section known to Negro newspaperdom" and, in a February 1923 letter to Clifford Smyth, editor of the *International Book Review*, he claimed that he was "the only professional Negro book-reviewer in captivity." He discussed his broad subject range and mentioned that he was reviewing books on "the Negro here and in Africa" for the *New York World*, *New York Tribune*, and *New York Evening Post*, and that he had recently reviewed books on Persia, the Balkan Peninsula, and the history of Christianity for the *Nation*. Throughout the twenties Harrison used the skills he had developed over two decades to provide reviews with the "twofold aim" of "bring[ing] to the knowledge of the Negro reading public those books which were necessary" to "know what the white world was thinking and planning and doing in regard to the colored world" and of bringing the wares of the white publisher "to a market which needed those wares."[89]

In selections in this work Harrison offers comments on book reviewing in general (selections 97 and 106) and on the particular difficulties of Black reviewers (selections 98, 99, and 107). His reviews (selections 97–125 and 128–134) are wide-ranging and include as subjects works by the historians J. A. Rogers (selections 101 and 102), Carter G. Woodson (selections 115 and 116), and Hendrik Van Loon (122); by the sociologist and economist Thorstein Veblen (selection 109); of the social commentators W. E. B. Du Bois (selection 107 and 119) and T. Lothrop Stoddard (selections 103–106); by the humorist Octavus Roy Cohen (selections 113 and 114); and by the novelist Carl Van Vechten (selections 117 and 118). Harrison also provides reviews on the Harlem Renaissance (selections 119–121), Africa (selections 110–112), Haiti (selection 125), the *Satyricon* of Petronious (selection 123), and Herodotus (selection 29).

Harrison's theater reviews (selections 126–130) are especially important for their coverage of Black stage efforts. They include important theoretical essays on the Black theater (selections 126 and 127), an early review of the Lafayette Players (126), and comments on the comedian "String Beans" and on the performance duos of Bert Williams and George Walker and Bob Cole and J. Rosamond Johnson (selection 127). His theater reviews from the 1920s — on *Canary Cottage* (selection 128), Eugene O'Neill's "The Emperor Jones" (selection 129), The Ethiopian Art Theater's *The Chip Woman's Fortune*, and Oscar Wilde's *Salome* (selection 130) offer Harrison's insights on efforts at the development of a Black theater.

Poetry was another of Harrison's interests — he considered it a major art form and component of culture. Beginning with *The Voice* in 1917, he included a "Poetry for the People" section in all his publishing efforts, and he continually encouraged poets such as Andy Razaf, Lucian B. Watkins, Walter Everette Hawkins, and Claude McKay to submit their works. The "Poetry for the People" section of the *Negro World* was a major contribution to that paper, and the historian Tony Martin points out in *Literary Garveyism* that by 1920 "the *Negro World* was already well on its way to becoming the focal point of a mass preoccupation with the arts, especially poetry, unequalled by any of the better known publications of the Harlem Renaissance."[90]

The selections in the poetry section of this work include Harrison's race-conscious response to Rudyard Kipling's internationally famous "The White Man's Burden" (selection 131), a piece that discusses the passing of poet Lucian B. Watkins (selection 132), and two pieces on Claude McKay, whom Harrison refers to as "the greatest living poet of Negro blood in America today" (selections 132 and 133). In his review of James Weldon Johnson's *The Book of American Negro Poetry*, Harrison offers some very strong criticism of the selections and the presentation of materials in Johnson's often-reprinted work (selection 134).

The final section of this work, *The International Colored Unity League and The Way Forward*, offers Harrison's most mature political thoughts from the last four years of his life. It presents his most broadly unitary effort and program for progress. "The Program and Principles of the International Colored Unity League" (selection 135) discusses cooperatives; political, economic, and educational action; youth work; a new (for Harrison) desire to emulate "the elements of racial strength and co-operation already existing in the Negro Church, which has done more for the education and spiritual uplift of the masses than any other agency in the race"; and a separate state for the "racial egoism" of African Americans.[91]

The program's primary focus was on the common people and on how to achieve unity of purpose. Harrison stressed that the "way to unity" was "through the hearts of the multitude" (selection 136). His advice was to "light the fire at the bottom" and "set those hearts on fire with a common zeal for a common object, equally desired and equally attained by all in common." The fire of that common feeling would then "flame in every lodge, every church, every city and state in the nation," and "unselfishness, humility, courage and usefulness" would be "the fuel to kindle it." He added that "by and large the Common People are the real race," and what they have to give—"loyalty, respect, friendliness and help in the hour of need"—they give "without stint." If you do right by them "they always do the right thing by you." They are "the dependable back-bone of every good cause." Such emphasis on the masses was Harrison's unwavering message.[92]

It is hoped that this *Reader* will help to introduce Harrison and his writings to new generations of "common people."

1

A Developing Worldview and Beginning Social Activism

Hubert Harrison's earliest writings during his first decade in New York suggest some of the influences on his intellectual development as a humanist and social activist. He was forced to confront the class exploitation and racial oppression of U.S. society as he pursued his wide-ranging reading interests in history, the sciences, and literature. Items in this section include his first response to the racist press and diary entries on his committment to African peoples, on the need to counter white supremacist history writing, and on his break from religion. Also included are two articles influenced by freethought and a longer piece on the role of the press in perpetuating white supremacy.

A Product of Black Working-Class Intellectual Circles in New York

1. "A Negro on Chicken Stealing: Assails the Statement That His Race Is Addicted to Vice," letter to the editor, *New York Times*, December 11, 1904, 6.

In 1904 Black residents of the Hell's Kitchen area of New York City (which included the San Juan Hill area where Harrison lived) suffered a particularly brutal race riot. Harrison believed that the press was largely responsible for inflaming racial tensions and that the *New York Times*, in particular, reflected Southern sentiment on the race question. On November 28, in the wake of the riot and after one particularly offensive *Times* editorial that stereotyped Blacks as "chicken-stealers," he wrote a letter to the editor. ("Stealing," according to historian Rayford Logan, "was the [derogatory] characteristic most frequently attributed to Negroes." The chicken-stealer stereotype, which had been popularized by the racist author Thomas Nelson Page in his 1887 collection *In Ole Virginia*, was a staple of many racist white minstrel shows.)[1]

The twenty-one-year-old Harrison's response exhibits the reasoned and forceful historical knowledge and race pride that mark his efforts for the remainder of his life. The letter also exhibits a familiarity with evolutionary thought and a critical attitude toward the use of religion and religious myth to justify specious, pseudo-scientific arguments. Historical criticism and evolutionary thought were among the leading intellectual trends of the day and Harrison utilizes each.

Harrison used *Negro* as a term of racial pride. In the text the word *Negro* is capitalized as Harrison would have written it. It appeared with a small *n* in the *New York Times*, consistent with that paper's editorial policy until March 7, 1930, when it made the change to capital *N* as an "act in recognition of racial self-respect."[2]

To the Editor of the *New York Times*:

I have been a constant reader of your paper. I have had occasion to differ from you on many questions; but through all those differences I have constantly maintained that your editorial manners were above reproach. Against a news item, as such, a mere reader can have no just cause for complaint. But with an editorial the case is different. An editorial expresses the opinion of the newspaper in which it appears.

Therefore a mere reader may justly take offense at an editorial which heaps insults and indignities on his race. Such an editorial was the one in to-day's *Times* on gamecocks in New Jersey. I, Sir, am a Negro, and, strange as it may appear, I am proud of it. In the name of my race I resent the indignity which your editorial has put upon us.

The editorial expressly stated that Africans (Negroes) "of any age, sex, (sic!) or previous condition of servitude" had been wont to steal chickens since the days of Ham and Noah's ark. I may remark that the Noah's ark story, far from being a fact, is an impossible myth, and I refer the writer to Prof. [Thomas] Huxley's *Lay Sermons, Critiques, and Addresses.* I would also submit that any man of ordinary intelligence can prove from the Christian Bible itself that Ham (if there ever was a Noah) was not a Negro at all. This narrows the chicken-stealing period considerably, and when I point out that under the tribal governments of Africa chicken culture was a thing unknown it is narrowed still more closely.

I would also point out that in the West Indies, where fowls are plenteous, chicken stealing is much less common than suicide is here. Therefore it cannot be true that all Negroes are prone to steal fowls, nor that some Negroes have been wont to do so since the days of the wine-bibbing Noah.

I, as a Negro, can have no objection to a bit of news that reports a Jersey Negro, or many Jersey Negroes, as being dexterous stealers of chicken; but I strongly object to the sweeping opinion of any newspaper that we are a race of thieves — either of fowls or of anything else.

2. Pledge to the Mother Race from an Untamed African, November 11, 1907, 10:30 P.M., HHHDI.

In this addendum at the end of one of his earliest diary entries, the twenty-four-year-old Harrison, "an untamed, untamable African," dedicates himself to a life of service for the "Mother Race." "Africa," he later explains, should "be taken in its racial rather than its geographical sense."[3]

Poor heart-sore and soul-starved Mother Race, who shall minister to thy deep desires, who shall bind up thy wounds and raise thee up again if these and such as these are to be thy prophets and thy priests? Oh Africa! when shall be the term of thy long degradation? Behold here, even now, I pledge thee, O my Mother, that I shall devote my years to thee, shall work for thy redemption even in the land of thine exile and set before mine eyes an ideal of service to thee inextricably blent with service for myself; shall love thee and be proud of thee and glory in thy power now lying dormant and shall strive to bring it to the light. Take my youth, my labors, my love, my life, my all and do thou when I shall have died for thee, take me to thy bosom, an untamed, untamable African.

 3. Plan to Write a "History of the Negro in America," November 25, 1907, 10:30 P.M., HHHDI.

In this diary entry Harrison mentions one of the often hidden injuries of class, the effects of harmful workplace lighting, as an introduction to comments on how important reading is to his future work. The twenty-year project that he sets for himself is to write "A History of the Negro in America," in order to counter the great role that prejudices play in history, to show the capabilities of Black scholars and Black scholarship, and to "do something for [his] race." His approach includes getting "in full-touch with the *life* of [his] people" in order "to understand them better" and is clearly that of an organic intellectual produced from the ranks of the working class.

Harrison proposes two important steps for the course of writing his history. First, he seeks to apply a philosopher's insight in his efforts to articulate laws of history. This scientific approach probably reflects in part the influence of the nineteenth-century English historian Henry Thomas Buckle whose scientific approach to history Harrison admired. Second, in his approach to Reconstruction, Harrison seeks to break from previous white-supremacist historiography, and plans to depict and interpret events "from the Negro's side." This approach takes on added significance because on November 15, 1908, Harrison gave his personal notebooks on Reconstruction to his friend Charles Burroughs, a former student of W. E. B. Du Bois, who was to deliver them to Du Bois. In 1909 Du Bois received a letter from James R. L. Diggs, President of Virginia Seminary and College, suggesting he write "a set of histories of reconstruction from the Negro point of view," and in December 1909 Du Bois read a paper on "Reconstruction and Its Benefits" at a meeting of the American Historical Association in New York. Du Bois's thesis was critical of previous historical interpretations and, like the view articulated by Harrison, it maintained that Reconstruction should be treated "from the Negro's side." Twenty-five years later Du Bois would elaborate further on these themes in *Black Reconstruction in America*, his most influential historical work.[4]

Today I laid aside my books for a week. My eyes pain very much and have been troubling me for some time past—in fact since last February in New Rochelle. As soon as I draw my salary on Saturday I shall go to the eye and ear hospital to have my eyes examined and get a pair of glasses. What with excessive reading by lamplight and the glare of the electric lights down at the Post Office I think I have hurt my eyes seriously. I hope it is not irremediable. For I have much to do with my eyes—especially reading. I have work to do in the next twenty years that will require hard reading, and much of it, on my part. So far, I have not confided to anyone what is the work whose production demands twenty years of labor. It is a history of the Negro in America. I was led to embrace this partly by the surprisingly great ignorance on the part of American whites of what the Negro was and is in this country, and partly by the deplorable ignorance of themselves evinced by the great majority of Negroes here. Then again, American historians have treated us not too well. Prejudice plays as great a part in history as in life. Therefore to produce a work which will make it impossible for a white historian not to know—and dangerous to mis-represent—the Negro historically made a strong appeal to me. Moreover I am not free from the desire to measure arms with the white man and to force him to see that he is not *facile princeps* in everything—even at present. We can do some other things besides writing poetry and being otherwise emotional—as Du Bois is showing them. The Negro Scholar is a fact of today. I also have the ambition to do something for myself as a black man and to do something for my Race as one of her children. She needs it. For all these reasons I have projected this work. Years of patient research, of examination of authorities and of the sources back of them will be necessary. Then when I shall have traversed the field and examined and exhausted all the sources of information I shall sit down to *make* my book.

The great lack of Negro scholarship today is, in the field of history, a competent authority such as [Henry C.] Lea is on the Inquisition, [James Ford] Rhodes on Reconstruction (its white aspect), or [Walter L.] Fleming on the same subject & on Reconstruction in Alabama. And that reminds me that in doing my research work much knowledge will come to me which I cannot incorporate in the final work. This I expect to throw off from time to time in incidental volumes and I think that the first of these will be "The Negro and Reconstruction". Reconstruction has been treated both statically and dynamically, as a social process and a political one, as a process of adjustment and a phase of national development. But no one, to my knowledge, has yet condescended to regard it from the Negro's side as a process of racial development, one phase of the progressive adjustment of a people to the life of another people. This I purpose to do and the outlines which I drew up six months ago to serve as the basis from my class-work at the Y.M.C.A. are the first preliminary.

I have heard Capt. [probably George] Young speak of [George Washington] Williams' "History of the Negro Race" (by a Negro), but I don't think much of it. I have not yet seen the work and thought at first he referred to a stupid little green book, [Edward A.] Johnson's "School History of the Negro Race in America", of which St. Benedict's Lyceum's Library had a few copies. But I am bound to get it if it is now obtainable (it was 2 vols published in '83) and from the reference in [William A.] Dunning I judge that it is valuable. But I expect to go far beyond this. I do not intend to confine myself to proving that the race has progressed and is rising. That needs no such deep study. But a history of the American Negro that will bring a knowledge of psychology and sociology to the exposition of Negro history, that will be a storehouse of information yet no mere cyclopedia, that will attempt to bring to the history of the race something of a philosopher's insight [and] the perception of laws running thru the mesh of deeds — all this my history must be. And this my haunting of the YWCA, YMCA, the White Rose Home, disreputable clubs, streets of evil and sordid associations; my social work with the rest among the children of 62nd St., my attendance at revival meetings and prayer meetings which but for the psychologic interest would disgust me — all this by putting me in full-touch with the *life* of my people will aid me in understanding them better than many another and fit me to write their *history*.

Freethought

In his first decade in the United States, Harrison was attracted to the freethought movement. Freethinkers sought to approach social issues with scientific methodology and thought that was freed from the dogmas and principles of religion. As explained in the freethought journal the *Truth Seeker*, they prided themselves on fearless examination of both sides of issues and stood in support of free inquiry, free publicity of ideas, and free discussion of convictions. Though the movement was several hundred years old, it experienced its most rapid growth in the nineteenth century in the wake of Charles Darwin's work on evolution. Freethought attracted many prominent followers including suffragists Susan B. Anthony and Elizabeth Cady Stanton; birth control advocate Margaret Sanger; orator Robert G. Ingersoll; antislavery editor Horace Greeley; Union Army colonel and writer Thomas Wentworth Higginson; attorney Clarence Darrow; socialist Eugene V. Debs; authors Samuel L. Clemens (Mark Twain), Moncure D. Conway, and Herbert Spencer; and the popular European scientist Ernst Haeckel.[5] Many Black leaders and writers of the early twentieth century in addition to Harrison were influenced by freethought or atheism. These included labor activists and socialists A. Philip Randolph and Chandler Owen; writers J. A. Rogers and George S. Schuyler; poets Claude McKay and Walter Everette Hawkins; and activists Cyril V. Briggs, Richard B. Moore, and Rothschild Francis. W. E. B. Du Bois, according to his biographer David Levering Lewis, was "agnostic and anticlerical."[6]

In the following three entries Harrison details his break from religion, his new world view, and how freethought influenced his analysis of issues.

4. Letter To Miss Frances Reynolds Keyser, May 20, 1908, HHHDI.

The activist and educator Frances Reynolds Keyser, like Harrison, is an important, but neglected, figure of early twentieth-century America. After graduating with honors from Hunter College and heading a small parochial school in Florida, the widowed Keyser returned to New York and served as superintendent of the White Rose Home, a principal social work agency for young Black women started by Victoria Earle Matthews, one of the leading female Black activists of the nineteenth century. She also served as a board member of the Young Women's Christian Association, as the first president of the National Association of Colored Women's Clubs Empire State Federation, as a founding member of the NAACP (serving on both its executive committee and its first board of directors), and later as the principal assistant to Mary McCleod Bethune, at the Daytona Educational and Industrial School for Negro Girls in Florida. Keyser became a very close personal friend and confidant to Harrison and a person from whom he said he drew immense "spiritual values." She had similarly befriended poet Paul Laurence Dunbar, who confided in her so much that he submitted his *Lyrics of a Lowly Life* to her for criticism, and she would similarly befriend Bethune.[7]

In these excerpts from a letter to Mrs. Keyser, which Harrison transcribed into his diary, he details his break from Christianity and his turn to agnosticism as an intellectual approach similar to that of Thomas Huxley. To Huxley, agnosticism was "not a creed but a method," the essence of which was to "follow . . . reason as far as it can carry you" and to "not pretend the conclusions are certain that are not demonstrated or demonstrable." Drawing from Huxley, Harrison explains his desire to be "an honest Agnostic" — because, he says, "I prefer to go to the grave with my eyes open."[8]

In this letter Harrison also makes reference to the Lamarckian theory of inherited adaptations that would at times influence and cloud his theories on race and racial oppression.[9] Lamarckians believed in the transmission of acquired characteristics. The implications of Lamarckian theory were that if race characteristics and race consciousness were biologically transmitted, then direct social action might have little bearing on racial oppression or racism (at least in any current generation), and strategies for change should not focus on changing white supremacist attitudes. If, on the other hand, race was a social category and race consciousness socially derived (as Harrison most frequently maintained), than racial oppression and racism could be eliminated by social action. In that case, strategies for change could be directed at challenging white supremacy. These implications would become more important as Harrison's interest in broader social problems related to class and race increased.[10]

You may not have known that seven years ago I divorced myself from orthodox and institutional Christianity. You are well enough acquainted with both literature and life to know that this is neither a proof of depravity nor of indifference. Not in minds like mine at any rate. *Au contraire.* The complete severance was not effected at once. In the course of my reading I came across [Thomas] Paine's *Age of Reason.* The religion of Deism as advocated by [Jean-Jacques] Rousseau, Voltaire [François-Marie Arouet], and Volney [Constantin-François Chasseboeuf], when considered intellectually is a barren, sterile hybrid. If my untried faith had first encountered the purely intellectual *non possumus* which deism presented it would have survived. But Paine, the least learned of the 18th century deistic writers, presented certain rationalistic results which bore their own proof on their face. Certain forms of the *reductio ad absurdum* . . . were to me then irresistible. Conviction quick as a flash did its dynamite work. Did it hurt? I said already that I was not one of those who did not care: I suffered. Oh, how my poor wounded soul cried out in agony! I saw the whole fabric of thought and feeling crumbling at its very foundations, and in those first fearful weeks of stern reaction I could not console myself as so many have done with the husks of a superior braggadocio. I began with feverish anxiety to pick from the ruins those pieces that would serve for the building of another fabric. What *had* gone was the authenticity of the Bible, that which I had been taught was the word of God. For my God was the Bible God, the Jahveh of Hebrew tradition plus the tribune God fused from four centuries of Persian, Babylonian and Hindu teaching and the Alexandrine cobwebs of Porphyry, Plotinus, and the Neo-Platonists. So when my Bible went my God went also. But I had to get one to worship, and I proceeded to build me a God of what was left. Do you remember [Alexander] Pope's *Universal Prayer*?

"Father of all, in every age
In every clime adored,
By saint, by savage & by sage
Jehovah, Jove, or Lord."

It was what I came to. But in the meanwhile, Time, the great healer, closed the wound and I began again to live — internally. But I now had a new belief — Agnosticism. I said belief: what I did mean was philosophy-of-life, point-of-observation, attitude-toward-things. You *must* have one you know, or you will cease to live.

Well, at first the great stumbling block was the personality of Jesus. Volney's pious fraud explanation couldn't do for me — for I lived in the 20th century when comparative mythology had more rational explanations to offer. The power of his personality haunted me for a long time, but in the end that also went.

Now I am an Agnostic; not a dogmatic *dis*believer nor a bumptious and narrow infidel. I am not at all of Col. [Robert G.] Ingersoll's school and it gives me the keenest pleasure to engage in dialectic with the vulgarian infidels who assume the name of

Agnostic without knowing what it means. If I am to explain myself by another I would say that I am (in my mental attitude) such an Agnostic as [Thomas] Huxley was and my principles are the same.

But I have been so genuinely interested in the bases of religion that I have tried to keep in touch with it all along the line: Christian apologetics, ecclesiastics, history, higher criticism — I have been into them all and I would need but little more reading, I fancy, to qualify for clerical honors.

I wish to admit here something that most Agnostics are unwilling to admit. I would pay a tribute to the power of that religion which was mine. It is only fair to confess that Reason alone has failed to satisfy all my needs. For there are needs, not merely ethical, but spiritual, inspirational — what I would call personal dynamics; and these also must be filled. So I have often felt a hungering after the fleshpots of Egypt. I do not necessarily commit myself to [belief in] immortality or any allied doctrine when I say that the *soul* yearns for the support of something. Scientifically, of course, I translate this as the power of inherited adaptabilities manifesting themselves in the sphere of psychology, even as it does in the sphere of biology [zoology]. And, rationally, I believe the scientific explanation to be the correct one. And yet — Shall we stunt the soul by refusing to develop it in any one direction while conceding the necessity for development in all other directions? Precisely because I am an Agnostic I object to this limitation. Now, if it can be shown that any given belief or set of beliefs can develop the spiritual side of man, why should we refuse the aid of the belief because its correspondence with fact can not be demonstrated?

So much for Christianity in general. Now for Catholicism in particular. Not long after the historical impulse came to me I busied myself to find out what were the actual objective conditions under which Christianity originated. I had already reached a point in my bias and, in addition to the literary, I had now a scientific or, if you like, an evolutionary interest. I began, as usual, to work back — from the Reformation helped by the Translations & Reprints from Original Sources of European History which Mr. [James Harvey] Robinson of Columbia has edited for the University of Pennsylvania. Altho my researches were comparatively superficial I managed to strike the right road. Many beliefs and types of thought and feeling inexplicably bound up with the orderly development of Christianity but repudiated by the Protestants were made clear to me. But it was when I had got as far back as the fourth and third centuries that I really *saw*. Using the Council of Nicaea as a suspension point, I swang alternately backward (as far as Irenaeus) and forward (to the Council of Antioch). And when I had dug into that mine of religious history I came back to our day gathering the different strands as I came.

One of the main conclusions at which I had arrived was this: that Catholicism was the representative type of Christianity; whatever was absurd in it (the three great doctrines of transubstantiation, papal infallibility and Mariolatry for example) was due to an absurdity inherent in the very texture of Christianity. So far as the Reformation went intellectually, its main results were self-destructive. For the right of private judgment gave to all conclusions logically drawn from the Bible an equal validity in Reason; and as I found Protestantism more satisfactory as reason I found it less satisfactory as Faith. But all this was as an outsider. Yet it was enough to convince me that if I ever went back to orthodox Christianity it would be by way of Catholicism and I never hesitated to say so. I cannot here enter into the emotional bases of my preference for it; but one cause was the beauty and solemnity of its ritual, another the dignity, antiquity and power of that vulnerable institution itself. Besides as I got to know more I found that Reason was not everything and I admired the sublime courage of the Church which boldly demands the subjection of Reason to faith. Then again Protestantism mainly tries to hide from itself that the fundamental basis of theism is an assumption and constructs an elaborate chain of religious syllogisms to aid it. Catholicism hardly avows the Assumption; it says "Believe!" while Protestantism says "Believe because — " Hence the difference. You couldn't mistake [Joseph] Butler's "[The] Analogy [of Religion 1736)]" for a product of Catholicism. And St. Paul in the 15th chapter of the 1st Corinthians is the great prototype of your Protestant divine — appealing to *logic,* yet failing to see that logic gives the quietus to his case.

As to utilitarian considerations that incline me to Catholicism, they are two-fold — subjective and objective. I am one of those natures that are the better for being curbed. Intellectually I range wherever I please — and that has its dangers. I sometimes think that to acknowledge some restraint would do me good.

Again, I think that I have a contribution to make to the world and, naturally, I could would have that as perfect as possible. For this, I should like to master the Latin language — to read it and write it as well as I do English. If I were a Catholic I could obtain the great-advantage of a Jesuit's training in Latin. And here, you will say, appears the cloven hoof, Eh bien! Suppose I sell myself for knowledge, suppress a few negative convictions? Whose is the very small loss? Whose is the very great gain? But enough my friend. This is the painful part which I would rather discuss face to face than on paper. Suppose we defer it until we meet again.

But all this is only intended to explain why I have thought seriously of becoming a Catholic. Entre nous, I doubt whether I will ever be anything but an honest Agnostic because I prefer, as I once told you, to go to the grave with my eyes open.

Yet — who knows? Is it not true now, as ever that

> "There is a divinity that shapes our ends,
> Rough-hew them how we will!"

So take what I have written as you please. I know it will seem remarkable as a chapter in the autobiography of opinion at least. Take it at any rate as a compliment in the highest and truest sense of that word.

5. "Paine's Place in the Deistical Movement," *Truth Seeker* 38, no. 6 (February 11, 1911): 87–88.

Thomas Paine (1737–1809), the most famous pamphleteer of the American Revolution, was born in England and attended grammar school there before apprenticing to his father's corset making trade and working as a tax collector. In 1774 he immigrated to Philadelphia where he served as editor of the *Pennsylvania Magazine* and contributor to the rival *Pennsylvania Journal.* His 1776 pamphlet *Commom Sense* advocated American independence, articulated ideas of equal rights for all citizens and Republican government over monarchy, and stressed the international significance of the American Revolution. The influential pamphlet was intended for a mass audience and sold some 150,000 copies in its first year. Paine returned to Europe in 1787, and four years later, in *The Rights of Man*, advocated political reforms such as progressive taxation and public employment. After being charged with seditious libel for advocating an end of British monarchy he fled to France where he took part in the French Revolution, was elected to the National Convention, and wrote *The Age of Reason* (part 1, 1794; and part 2, 1796). This last work attacked Christianity, put forth his views on deism, and sought to apply rationalism to religion as it had been applied to the two revolutions.[11]

In February 1911 Harrison spoke on "Tom Paine's Place in the Deistical Movement" at a Thomas Paine Commemoration Dinner sponsored by the freethought movement. His lecture explored Paine's "dual aspect of . . . militant unbelief and democratic dissent" and noted that these characteristics were "truly representative" of contemporary thought. Since Harrison often encouraged smilar ideas, it is clear that he saw his own developing views as being at one with the leading thought of his era. Drawing from Paine, Harrison repeatedly argued for a democratization of scientific knowledge and the development of critical skills.

If you should ask a man in the street who Thomas Paine was, he would say he was an Atheist; and he might probably qualify his statement with an adjective more forceful than polite. If you had asked a cultured liberal like Leslie Stephen the same question fifty years ago, he would has said that Paine was one of the cruder kinds of Infidels, fit perhaps for the unlettered minds of the mob, but not worthy of any serious attention from the illuminati. Both these estimates, false as they are in themselves, express a truth concerning Paine which we may not safely ignore. For it is this dual aspect of Paine — militant unbelief and democratic dissent — that is most truly representative of him in the thought of our time.

In other words, the theological aspect of Paine is the most typical. To me, at least, a consideration of him from this viewpoint seems more fruitful than from any other. Paine popularized the arguments against Christianity and brought them down to the level of the democracy, and this broadened and quickened the advance of Freethought as it could not be done by the learned tomes of Hume, Spinoza or any other thinker whose words were restricted to the aristocracy of intellect.

If we would fully appreciate this fact it is necessary to sketch that broad movement of the human mind which, beginning in the seventeenth century, grew and developed until it shattered the very foundations of superstition in the latter half of the nineteenth century. The sources of this movement are to be found in the intellectual impulses of the Renaissance. Galileo and Copernicus had destroyed the traditional conception of the universe and of man's relation to it, while Descartes in physics and Bacon in philosophy, with the foundations of empirical science, paved the way for [Isaac] Newton and [Baruch] Spinoza's *Ethica* and *Tractatus Theologico-Politicus* had begun that metaphysical and theological criticism which was to broaden out, in Germany at least, into the destructive energies of the Higher Criticism of the nineteenth century.

This movement I call the Deistical movement, and I define Deism as a current of theological thought which appeared as such in the latter part of the seventeenth century and spread over the greater portion of the eighteenth. The protagonists of this movement were known as Deists and were often referred to as Rationalists. While they did not believe in the traditional god of Christian revelation, they did, at first, believe in a personal god not only distinct from the universe but apart from its affairs. It is a curious fact that the thinking minority of Christians today, like the bishop of London and Dr. [Samuel Rolles] Driver, hold to a view of God hardly distinguishable from that of the Deists of the eighteenth century.

The efficient momentum was given to Deism by the French thinkers — the encylopedists like [Denis] Diderot, [Jean Le Rond] d'Alembert, Rousseau, Voltaire, Condorcet [Marie-Jean-Antoine-Nicolas de Caritat], and [Paul-Henri-Dietrich] D'Holbach. These French Deists, however, made certain false premises which we smile at today. They believed in the physical and moral perfection of the prehistoric savage and former universal monotheism — which was absurd; in the worship of nature — which was foolish; and in the origin of religion as conscious fraud — which was demonstrably unsound. The proponents of this last thesis were Rousseau, Volney, in his *Ruins of Empires*, and [Jean] Meslier, in his *History of Superstition*.

In England the movement began as textual criticism; then came the Natural Religion of Lord [Edward] Herbert [1583–1648] and [Henry St. John, 1st Viscount] Bolingbroke, which [Joseph] Butler demolished in his famous *Analogy* [*The Analogy of Religion*]. Afterwards came the slow growth of historical criticism contributed to by [Edward] Gibbon's celebrated two chapters and (despite his own intentions) by [Nathaniel] Lardner's *Credibility of the Gospel Narratives* [*Credibility of Gospel History* (1727)]. The scientific criticism which on its literary side was to be known as Higher Criticism; on its philosophical side as Agnosticism; and in its rigidly scientific aspect as Atheism, was left for the nineteenth century.

The broad result of this concerted attack upon the foundations of theological thinking was the pulverization of the case for orthodoxy, and it had its curious result, viz.: that Lardner, [Conyers] Middleton, [John] Toland, [Matthew] Tindal, and [Henry]

Dodwell — all the orthodox defenders save that small minority which could neither learn nor forget — were practically all heterodox.

Paine's personal deism came to him as the legacy of this conflict. Its elements were (1) the belief in a personal god — which he held firmly at first; (2) the belief in the immortality of the soul; (3) a tenuous religious sentiment, and (4) a strong ethical sense which he expressed in the phrase, "The world is my country; to do good is my religion."

Its positive aspects were presented as (1) common sense criticism as exemplified in his treatment of certain numerical blunders in Chronicles and his comparison of genealogy of Jesus as given in Matthew with that given in Luke; (2) historical criticism, as shown by his presentation of the simple fact that the Pentateuch [the first five books of the Old Testament] could not have been written by Moses since it related events that occurred after Moses' day — including the death and burial of Moses himself, and his analysis of the time-elements in Job; (3) comparative and literary criticism, scattered over the second part of the "Age of Reason." He also made certain critical anticipations such as the hint of the existence of different strata in the gospel narratives; the suspicion of two different elements in Isaiah, and the precedence of certain Pauline epistles over the other books of the New Testament. All these things modern biblical criticism has established even in orthodox circles, and they are known to every theological tyro — except, perhaps, in America.

Paine's contributions closed the deistical controversy. Thereafter the theological conflict was to center around himself and the war was to be waged with vilification, calumny, and lies. The twilight of reason in religion had come and the *Age of Reason* was to initiate a different method of dissent. The battle could no longer be fought above the clouds, for Paine had brought it down to the level of all men. Thus, his place in the deistical movement was established. He was "the Apostle to the Gentiles" of the Freethought movement. He brought the results of that great conflict down to the level of the democracy and was therefore the forerunner of the English and American Rationalists of today.

6. "The Negro a Conservative: Christianity Still Enslaves the Minds of Those Whose Bodies It Has Long Held Bound," *Truth Seeker* 41 (September 12, 1914): 583; reprinted with deletions as "On a Certain Conservatism in Negroes," in *The Negro and the Nation*, 41–47.

In late 1914 Harrison tried to analyze what he called the "conservatism in Negroes." In his analysis he paid particular attention to the role of Christianity. The Black church was extraordinarily influential in the realm of ideas in the African American community, and as Harrison's rationalist analysis developed and became more public it tended to distance him from the church. In this article Harrison challenges the role of Christianity and he also calls for "Negroes . . . [to] shake off the trammels of such time-serving leaders as Mr. [Booker T.] Washington." Washington was, at the time, the most powerful Black leader in the country. At age thirty-one Harrison was challenging the most powerful institution and the most powerful individual in the African American community. (In the original article the journal did not capitalize the *N* in *Negro*. When Harrison reprinted it, he did.)

It would be a difficult task to name one line of intellectual endeavor among white men in America, in which the American Negro has not taken his part. Yet it is a striking fact that the racial attitude has been dominantly conservative. Radicalism does not yet register to any noticeable extent the contributions of our race in this country. In theological criticism, religious dissent, social and political heresies such as Single Tax, Socialism, Anarchism — in most of the movements arising from the reconstruction made necessary by the great body of that new knowledge which the last two centuries gave us — the Negro in America has taken no part. And today our sociologists and economists still restrict themselves to the compilation of tables of statistics in proof of Negro progress. Our scholars are still expressing the intellectual viewpoints of the eighteenth century. The glimmer of change is perceptible only in some of the younger men like [Alain Leroy] Locke of Howard University and James C. Waters, Jr.

It is easy to account for this. Christian America created the color line; and all the great currents of critical opinion, from the eighteenth century to our time, have found the great barrier impassible and well-nigh impervious. Behind the color line one has to think perpetually of the color line, and most of those who grow up behind it can think of nothing else. Even when one essays to think of other things, that thinking is tinged with the shades of the surrounding atmosphere.

Besides, when we consider what Negro education is to-day, when we remember that in certain southern counties the munificent sum of 58 cents is spent for the annual education of a Negro child; that the "great leader" of his race decries "higher" education for them; that Negro boys who get as far as "college" must first surmount tremendous special obstacles — we will cease to wonder at the dearth of thinkers who are radical on other than racial matters.

Yet, it should seem that Negroes, of all Americans, would be found in the Freethought fold, since they have suffered more than any other class of Americans from the dubious blessings of Christianity. It has been well said that the two great instruments for the propagation of race prejudice in America are the Associated Press and the Christian Church. This is quite true. Historically, it has nearly always been true of the Church. It was the name of religion that cloaked the beginnings of slavery on the soil of America, and buttressed its continuance. The church saw to it that the religion taught to slaves should stress the servile virtues of subservience and content, and these things have bitten deeply into the souls of black folk. True, the treasured music of these darker millions preserves, here and there, the note of stifled rebellion; but this was in spite of religion — not because of it. Besides, such of their "sorrow-songs" as have this note in them were brutally banned by their masters, and driven to the purlieus of the plantation, there to be sung in secret. And all through the dark days of slavery, it was the Bible that constituted the divine sanction of this "peculiar institution." "Cursed be Canaan," "Servants obey your masters" and similar texts were the best that the slaveholders' Bible could give of consolation to the brothers in black, while, for the rest, teaching them to read was made a crime so that whatever of social dynamite there might be in certain parts of the book, might not come near their minds.

[James Russell] Lowell in his *Biglow Papers* has given a caustic but correct summary of the Christian slaveholders' theology in regard to the slavery of black working-people:

> "All things wuz gin to man for's use, his sarvice an' delight;
> An' don't the Greek an' Hebrew words that mean a man mean white?
> Ain't it belittlin the good book in all its proudes' features
> To think 't wuz wrote for black an' brown an' 'lasses-colored creatures,
> Thet couldn't read it ef they would — nor aint by lor allowed to,
> But ought to take wut we think suits their naturs, an' be proud to?
> * * * * * * * * *
> Where'd their soles go ter, I'd like to know, ef we should let 'em ketch
> Freeknowledgism an' Fouerism an' Speritoolism an' sech?"

When the fight for the abolition of slavery was on, the Christian church, not content with quoting scripture, gagged the mouths of such of their adherents as dared to protest against the accursed thing, penalized their open advocacy of abolition, and opposed all the men like [William Lloyd] Garrison, [Elijah Parish] Lovejoy, [Wendell] Phillips and John Brown, who fought on behalf of the Negro slave. The detailed instances and proofs are given in the last chapter of [Eugene Montague Macdonald's] *A Short History of the Inquisition*, wherein the work shows the relation of the church and slavery.

Yet the church among the Negroes today exerts a more powerful influence than anything else in the sphere of ideas. Nietzsche's contention that the ethics of Christianity are the slave's ethics would seem to be justified in this instance. Show me a population that is deeply religious, and I will show you a servile population, content with whips and chains, contumely and the gibbet, content to eat the bread of sorrow and drink the waters of affliction.

The present condition of the Negroes of America is a touching bit of testimony to the truth of this assertion. Here in America the spirit of the Negro has been transformed by three centuries of subjection, physical and mental, so that they have even glorified the fact of subjection and subservience. How many Negro speakers have I not heard vaunting the fact that when in the dark days of the South the Northern armies had the Southern aristocracy by the throat, there was no Negro uprising to make their masters pay for the systematic raping of Negro women and the inhuman cruelties perpetrated on Negro men. And yet the sole reason for this "forbearance" is to be found in the fact that their spirits had been completely crushed by the system of slavery. And to accomplish this, Christianity—the Christianity of their masters—was the most effective instrument.

A recent writer, Mr. E. B. Putnam-Weale [B. L. Putnam Weale was the psuedonym of Bertram Lenox Simpson], in his book, *The Conflict of Color*, has quite naively disclosed the fact that white people are well aware of this aspect of Christianity and use it for their own ends. Mr. Putnam-Weale makes no pretense of believing in the Christian myth himself, but he wants it taught to the Negroes; and comparing it with Islam, he finds it a more efficient instrument of racial subjugation. The Mohammedan, he finds, preaches the equality of all true believers—and lives up to it. The white Christian preaches the brotherhood of man, but wants "niggers" to sit in the rear pews, to ride in "Jim Crow" cars, and generally to "keep in their place." He presents this aspect of the case under the caption of "The Black Sampson and the White Delilah," and, with less fear than an angel, frankly advises the white Lords of Empire not so much to civilize as to Christianize Africa, so that Delilah's work may be well done.

Here in America her work has been well done; and I fear that many years must pass before the leaders of thought among my people in this country contribute many representatives to the cause of Freethought. Just now, there are a few Negro Agnostics in New York and Boston, but these are generally found to be West Indians from the French, Spanish, and English islands. The Cuban and Porto Rican cigar-makers are notorious Infidels, due largely, as Mr. Arthur Schomburg informs me, to their acquaintance with the bigotry, ignorance and immorality of the Catholic priesthood in their native islands. Here and there one finds a [Negro] American who is reputed to have Agnostic tendencies; but these are seldom, if ever, openly avowed. I can hardly find it in my heart to blame them, for I know the tremendous weight of the social proscription which it is possible to bring to bear upon those who dare defy the idols of our tribe. For those who live by the people must needs be careful of the people's gods; and

> "An up-to-date statesman has to be on his guard,
> If he must have beliefs not to b'lieve 'em too hard."

Myself, I am inclined to believe that freedom of thought must come from freedom of circumstance; and so long as our "leaders" are dependent on the favor of our masses for their livelihood, just so long will they express the thought of the masses, which of itself may be a good thing or a bad according to the circumstances of the particular case. Still, there is a terrible truth in Kipling's modern version of Job's sarcastic bit of criticism:

> "No doubt but ye are the people — your throne is above the King's
> Whoso speaks in your presence must say acceptable things;
> Bowing the head in worship, bending the knee in fear —
> Bringing the word well-smoothen — such as a King should hear."

And until this rising generation of Negroes can shake off the trammels of such time-serving leaders as Mr. Washington, and attain the level of that "higher education" against which he solidly sets his face; until they, too, shall have entered into the intellectual heritage of the last two hundred years, there can be little hope of a change in this respect.

The Press

7. "The Negro and the Newspapers," c. early 1911, reprinted in *The Negro and the Nation*, 59–64.

By early 1911 Harrison had developed a general critique of the racist press in the United States. He was especially concerned with "how the Negro is being 'done' by headlines and other newspaper devices" and he advocated more struggle against such treatment. A decade later, he still maintained this position and explained that the "need of some formal protest [over newspaper coverage] has been growing in the minds of those thinking Negroes who are not compelled to 'crook the pregnant hinges of the knee'; and it has grown largely because the practices complained of have grown to alarming proportions."[12]

In this circa 1911 article Harrison describes how "The newspapers of this country have many crimes to answer for" with their constant appeals "to the putrid passion of race hatred." He expresses some confidence, however, in the ability of truth and reason to counter newspaper bias. Such an attitude was similarly expressed by W. E. B. Du Bois, who, in the same period, described his "long-term remedy" as "Truth." Within a few years both Harrison and Du Bois would become far less sanguine about truth and reason and far more aware of economic and sociopolitical factors and of the power of irrational thought and action.[13]

> It is not an easy task to plead in the courts of the oppressor against oppression and wrong. It is not easy to get the judgment of the white men of the world against the white man's injustice to the black. But, nevertheless the attempt must be made and made again until the seared conscience of the civilized world's hall throbs with righteous indignation at such outrage. "To sin by silence when we should protest makes cowards out of men. The human race has climbed on protest. Had no voice been raised against injustice, ignorance and lust, the Inquisition yet would serve the law and guillotines decide our least disputes. The few who dare must speak and speak to right the wrongs of many."

The urgent need of speaking out is shown by the following communication from Mr. J. Ellis Barker of London in an interview given to a correspondent of *The New York Age* and published in that paper on December 29th 1910.

"We people in Europe," says Mr. Barker, "do not understand the race problem, and we do not know the colored people, for the simple reason that there are not any colored people in Europe. In London, where I live, there are only a few hundred colored students whom one does not meet. Before I came to the United States my prejudice against the colored people was as great as that of any southern planter. My prejudice against your race, as I believe the prejudice of most white people, was due rather to ignorance than to ill-will. I had been told in the books and papers published in Europe that the colored were a race of barbarians and savages. I had been told that the colored people were a worthless set of people, dressed in rags, working a day or two during the week, and loafing during the rest of the time. I was told that the colored people were idle, diseased and vicious. So I imagined that all of them lived in slums and alleys and that the aristocracy of the race consisted of the waiters and railway porters.

I had been told that the colored people only played at science; that their doctors and lawyers were charlatems [charlatans]. I had been told that the people of a mixed race were even worse than pure Negroes; that the mulattoes had lost the primitive virtues of the Negroes and acquired all of the vices of the whites. A chance encounter with a cultured man of color induced me to look into the race problem and I was perfectly amazed when I discovered how greatly the colored people have been libeled and traduced. I have spent a considerable amount of time with colored people and have met many who are highly cultivated. I have found that among your race you have excellent lawyers, and some of the foremost physicians and surgeons. I have been over a large number of your elementary and higher grade schools and colleges and over Howard University, and I have admired the earnest and resolute determination with which your children try to improve their minds and to raise themselves. In your night schools I have found old men and women, former slaves, who are anxious to learn writing and reading. I have been to the homes of many colored people and I have found them cosy, comfortable, elegant, and peopled by happy and harmonious families. I have come to the conclusion that the race is oppressed and persecuted and very largely because it is not known."

But it is not in Europe alone that these baneful effects of calumny appear. Here in America, and even in the south where the bulk of the Negroes live in the midst of a people who resentfully declare that they should be left to deal with the Negro because they alone know him — even there the notion of the Negro, fostered by the press and other agencies of public opinion is as wide of the truth as it can be. To illustrate:

In the March number of *Van Norden's Magazine* in 1907 there appeared a symposium on The Negro Question. It was composed of expressions of opinion from twelve intelligent southerners, and was followed by an article by Mr. Booker T. Washington. The humor of the think lay in this, that these men were Southern college presidents and heads of banks, had lived all their lives among Negroes, and were, by their own words, proved to be either woefully or willfully ignorant of what the Negro had done and was doing. The mordant irony of fate decreed that Mr. Washington should be the one to present the facts that changed their seeming sapience to Falstaffian farce. The president of Randolph-Macon Woman's College, Va. set forth that the Negro will not work regularly, that he needs but three dollars a week, and, therefore, works but three days to get it and "quits work to spend it." The president of Howard College, Alabama declared that, "My deliberate opinion is that the days of the Negro as a fair, honest laborer are numbered, and are few at that. He is becoming daily more shiftless, more unreliable, more restless, less inclined to work steadily." The president of the University of South Carolina and the president of the North Carolina College of Agriculture and Mechanic Arts re-echoed the same doleful dictum while the president of the First National Bank of Birmingham, Ala. and the president of the Bank of Lexington, N.C. declared that it was a mistake to grant the rights of citizenship to the Negro and that education was a curse to him. The president of Guilford College repeated the "lazy, shiftless" argument while the president of Randolph-Macon College, Va. said, "Reduce their wages so that they shall have to work all the time to make a living and they will become better workmen or disappear in the struggle for existence," repeating in substance, the argument of his brother-president of the Woman's college.

Mr. Washington's article did not show any sign that it had been written as a reply of any sort. But it did show among other things, that the census of 1900 proved that the Negro people *owned* in the very states of these college presidents, "23,383 square miles of territory, an area nearly as large as that of Holland and Belgium combined"; that this represented only a quarter of the farms *worked* by them; that, "after a searching investigation, I have not been able to find that a single graduate of Tuskegee, Hampton or any of the Negro colleges can now be found in the prisons of the South"; that in a single county of Virginia — Gloucester Co. — Negroes were paying taxes on land valued at 88 million dollars and on buildings assessed at 80 millions, and all this on the soil where they had been slaves forty years before.

Is not this eloquent of the value of American opinion on the American Negro as given in the American press? And the question suggested is, whether such statements are published in ignorance or ill-will? In either case it is equally damnatory.

In December 1907 Professor R. R. Wright, Jr., an eminent Negro sociologist, published in *McGirt's Magazine* an article on "The Newspapers and the Negro," showing how the Negro is being "done" by headlines and other newspaper devices. *The Horizon* [edited by Du Bois], at that time the most brilliant Negro periodical, dealt with the subject in its issue from April 1908. Under the caption, "The Color Line in the Press Dispatches," it quoted approvingly these words of a Socialist paper — the *Appeal to Reason* — "The hand that fakes the Associated Press is the hand that rules the world." European readers who are acquainted with the occasional diversions of Reuter's Hong Kong and Shanghai correspondents will appreciate the point.

The Horizon was constrained to refer to the matter again in its August issue. In both instances specific cases were cited and proof given. Since that time the need of some formal protest has been growing in the minds of all those thinking Negroes who are not compelled to "crook the pregnant hinges of the Knee"; and it has grown largely because the practices complained of have grown to alarming proportions.

The newspapers of this country have many crimes to answer for. They feature our criminals in bold head-lines: our substantial men when noticed at all are relegated to the agate type division. Their methods, whether they obtain through set purpose or through carelessness, constantly appeal to the putrid passion of race hatred. They cause rapine to break loose by nurturing rancor. They help create untold sorrow. They are weak-kneed and apologizing when the hour is bloody.

But how can such a protest be effectively put? Though Truth come hot on the heels of Falsehood it could not quite undo its devil's work. And the detractors of the weak and helpless are well aware of this.

But Truth in the Negro's case is not even unleashed. Truth, in fact, is chained up and well guarded, and it is this terrible task of setting Truth free that the Negro must essay in the very teeth of the American press. It is not an easy task to voice an adequate protest, for it needs the widest publicity. And since prejudice will oppose, it needs prestige also. Any such effort must feel itself feeble, and yet it must be made.

Hubert Harrison, Elizabeth Gurley Flynn, and William D. "Big Bill" Haywood, c. 1913. (Courtesy of the Elizabeth Gurley Flynn Collection, Tamiment Institute, Bobst Library, New York University.) This photo was probably taken when Harrison spoke to striking silk workers in Paterson and Haledon, New Jersey (April 17 and May 19, 1913) or when he spoke in New York City at a mass protest meeting of the Paterson Defense Committee (February 4, 1913). In early 1913 Harrison was the leading Black Socialist in America and the Industrial Workers of the World leaders Flynn and Haywood were two of America's most prominent labor agitators and class radicals.

Class Radicalism

Socialism

The Socialist Party of America was founded in 1901 out of various socialist organizations including the Social Democratic Party of Eugene V. Debs and Victor L. Berger and a split-off faction from Daniel DeLeon's Socialist Labor Party headed by Morris Hillquit. In general, socialists believed that capitalism was an outmoded system and the principal cause of both the rapidly intensifying economic inequality and the erosion of democracy in the United States; and that an inevitable cooperative commonwealth was near and obtainable through political and parliamentary means. By the 1908 presidential election, the party had more than 40,000 members and polled more than 400,000 votes (3 percent of all votes cast). It was the largest class-radical movement in U.S. history.[1]

The Socialist Party proclaimed itself "the party of the working class"; explained that political parties were "the expression of economic class interests"; attacked monopolies and trusts, the high courts, and Congress; and called for nationalization of industries, the eight-hour work day, a graduated income tax, women's suffrage, and public works programs for the unemployed. The party's rational appeal was symbolized by *Appeal to Reason*, the national newspaper with a half million subscribers, considered by historian Paul M. Buhle "the clearest expression of indigenous American socialism." Author Daniel Bell has described this appeal simply, though in male-oriented terms — "society was heading in a rational direction because men in the nature of their social evolution were becoming more rational, were mastering nature and harnessing it to men's purposes; they would also, in the course of events, harness society and turn it to the common good rather than the profit of a few."[2]

The SP's major internal debate was whether socialism would come by evolution (through gradual political gains) or by ever-more militant strikes and revolution. Related to this evolution versus revolution issue was a second, pivotal question — the trade union question. The debate centered on whether or not the party should concentrate work within the generally conservative (and racist) trade union movement headed by the 1.7-million-member American Federation of Labor (AFL).[3]

In 1911 when Harrison became active with the Socialists, the party had few Black members, offered no special program on the "Negro Question," and it opposed reforms which were badly needed in the African American community. It also had no significant political power and was relatively powerless to implement change. In addition, as historian Philip S. Foner has described in the only book-length treatment of the subject, "racism was well entrenched in the Socialist party."[4]

Harrison was hired by the Socialist Party to do work among African Americans in November 1911, and the following month he founded the Colored Socialist Club, a pioneering effort at developing such special work. In those first two months he wrote a five-part theoretical series on "The Negro and Socialism" for the *New York Call*. The lead article took the position that the "Negro Problem" had a history in past social relationships and was at root a question of "social adjustment," of social control of relationships. Harrison argued against a biological analysis of the race problem and maintained that race relationships have a history "much as the class struggle and the system of production have theirs."

Harrison clearly saw the revolutionary implications of simple democracy for African Americans, describing it as a "revolution . . . startling even to think of." In addition, by identifying the locus of the problem in the white race, he directly challenged the opinion, expressed by influential SP writers, that Black people were a hindrance to social change. In treating African Americans as "the touchstone of the modern democratic idea" he pointed out that "the broad denial of justice to colored men as exemplified in lynchings, segregation, public proscription and disfranchisement" resulted "in the vitiation of democratic faith" and provided "the supplying power" for other deceitful practices such as the lack of concern about the unsafe conditions which led to the Triangle Shirtwaist Factory fire on March 25, 1911, in which 146 workers (mostly women) died.[5]

8. "The Negro and Socialism: I — The Negro Problem Stated," *New York Call* (November 28, 1911) 6, HHHP Scr A.

In the opening article of his *Call* series Harrison sets the tone for his social, as opposed to biological, approach to "the Negro problem." He emphasizes that the "problem" has "roots in the past relationships of both races in America" and has a history that must be comprehended before it can be overcome. He then sets out to review important sociohistorical aspects of the problem. Such a scientific approach was a keystone of Harrison's analysis of social problems. (The *New York Call* did not capitalize the *N* in *Negro*.)

The Negro problem of today has its roots in the past relationships of both races in America. It has its history, therefore, much as the class struggle and the system of production have theirs. And in neither case is it possible to get a clear comprehension of the present without some knowledge of the past. But before we go further, it might be well to state just what we mean by "The Negro Problem." Setting aside the special definitions of partisans, such as the "Negro baiter," the "friend of the Negro," the professional "leader," or the politician — and regarding the question in its broad, general aspects, the Negro problem is a problem of social adjustment. How can the white American and the black American adjust themselves satisfactorily to the presence of each other? When the question is stated in this form, it is clear that both sides must be heard from. But so far it has been assured that the proper adjustment must be wholly in the hands of one party to that adjustment. This is not equitable, and all the resultant friction has sprung from this one-sided view of the matter, so that, in the white man's mind, the Negro problem presents itself in this form: How shall I fit the status of the black man to my satisfaction?

In the *Atlantic Monthly* for March, 1909, the Rev. Quincy Ewing, himself a Southerner, writing on "The Heat of the Race Problem," expresses the crux of the matter in these words: "The foundation of it, true or false, is the white man's conviction that the Negro, as a race and as an individual, is his inferior; not human in the sense that he is human; not entitled to the exercise of human rights in the sense that he is entitled to the exercise of them. The problem itself, the essence of it, the heart of it, is the white man's determination to make good this conviction, coupled with constant anxiety lest by some means he should fail to make it good. The race problem, in other words, is not that the Negro is what he is in relation to the white man — the white man's inferior — but this, rather: How to keep him what he is in relation to the white man; how to prevent his ever achieving or becoming that which would justify the belief on his part or on the part of other people that he and the white stand on common ground."

Historically, the roots of the problem are to be found in slavery. After [Bartolomé de] Las Casas, the great missionary of Columbus' time, and the adventurous servants of His most Catholic and Christian Majesty, the King of Spain, had starved and flogged and murdered all the available natives of Santo Domingo and the adjacent islands, they felt the necessity of a fresh supply of people who could be made to work and produce wealth for them. Out of this was born the African slave trade, with which the Spaniards supplied their need for cheap labor power in their colonies in the West Indies and South America. Brazil, in the seventeenth century, was the great slave mart of the New World and the Dutch of New Netherland bought their slaves direct from Brazil or "captured" them from the Spanish slave ships. In fact, the first cargo of Negro slaves brought to Jamestown in 1619 had been so "captured." Not that they were the first slaves in North America. Under Spanish rule, the Indians of Florida and California had been enslaved, and under English rule white men, women and children from Ireland had been sold into American slavery as a result of [Oliver] Cromwell's Irish campaigns. And many of the English working class condemned to penal servitude shared the same fate.

Since the Negroes were brought here as chattels, their social status was fixed by that fact. To the credit of our common human nature, it was found necessary to reconcile the public mind to the system of slavery. This was effected by building up the belief that the slaves were not really human: that they belonged to a different order of beings. Of course, this belief could not be rigidly adhered to, inasmuch as the slave would often reveal qualities almost human, such as fidelity, courage, intelligence and the power to procreate. This latter quality was very serviceable to the slave owner. He could gratify his carnal desires with the slave woman while he sold for cash the children which were his and hers. And wherever the system was most profitable, the belief that the slave was not human was strongest. This belief dies hard, and, before it finally vanished, assumed many curious forms. In the early part of the nineteenth century, defenders of American slavery argued that the Negro was a beast. Later they conceded that he was a man of an inferior sort, consigned to slavery by God as the only human condition that was good for him. Then, when the freed black began to produce men of mark and lift themselves far above the slave level, it was argued that certain craniological peculiarities would prevent them from assimilating the learning and culture of Europe. Finally, when they gave such evidence of that assimilation as even their friends could not deny, it was suddenly discovered that this is a white man's country.

One broad, general implication of this belief seems to be the denial of social, political, and economic justice to all people not white. Since this is a white man's country all other occupants of it must be pariahs subsisting on sufferance, and the future of civilization imperatively demands that their status as "inferiors" shall be fixed and determined for them by the "superior" caste. Which, as I said before, involves injustice. But this is at the bottom of race problems everywhere.

The factors of the Negro problem are many. Of these the social factor is easily first in the public knowledge. The man of sense will recognize it as the age-long, world-wide problem of caste. Here today it is mostly concerned with keeping "niggers" in their place. But it pales in insignificance and unimportance beside the economic factor. And this contains the real root of all race difficulties. As long as white men can be taught to believe that the presence of black men threatens their means of existence, so long will their general attitude be one of enmity. So long as the fallacy of economic fear survives, so long will economic competition create race prejudice. Politically, the Negro is the touchstone of the modern democratic idea. The presence of the Negro puts our democracy to the proof and reveals the falsity of it. Take the Declaration of Independence, for instance. That seemed a splendid truth. But the black man merely touched it and it became a splendid lie. And in this matter of the suffrage in the Southern States it is expedient to keep the Negro a serf politically because he is still largely an economic serf. If he should attain to political freedom he would free himself from industrial exploitation and contempt. Of course, such a revolution is startling even to think of, and, therefore, we find that the prevailing social philosophy among Negroes — that which white capitalism will pay to have them taught — is one of submission and acquiescence in political servitude.

Now, there are certain broad general implications of these facts which it might be well to emphasize. And the chief of these is that, so far, democracy in America has not yet been kept beneath the level of other Americans. When any portion of the people of a commonwealth are denied the rights accorded to the rest, that commonwealth ceases to be a republic in fact, whatever it may be in name. Then, again, the broad denial of justice to colored men as exemplified in lynchings, segregation, public proscription and disfranchisement results in the vitiation of democratic faith. Herein is seen the supplying power of a false practice. The public mind accustoms itself to seeing these things until it can look with complacency upon the jailing of innocent labor leaders and the murder of working girls in a fire trap factory.

In the face of these facts the sending of American missionaries to Asia and to Africa is so horribly humorous that it might well make the devil laugh.

9. "Race Prejudice—II," *New York Call* (December 4, 1911): 6, HHHP Scr A.

In his second article in the *Call* series Harrison maintained that racism has economic causes and that capitalists benefit from racial discrimination and consciously foster race prejudice. This materialist analysis contrasted sharply with the more idealist view that the "Negro Problem" was simply a mental attitude which could be solved in the realm of ideas. To Harrison, the "mental attitude" argument contained the real core of all racist theory— the notion "that race prejudice is innate" (and therefore nothing significant could be done about it). By maintaining that race prejudice arose from socioeconomic causes Harrison suggested that it could be subjected to eliminative social action. He also maintained that racism was not in workers' class interests and that by pitting workers "white against black," the capitalists kept the wage level low and fostered disunity in the working class. Thus, he emphasized, race prejudice was a "very useful tool" for dividing the workers. (The *New York Call* did not capitalize the *N* in *Negro.*)

There was a time when it was not even necessary to defend race prejudice. That time is past. Today it is becoming increasingly necessary to defend the odious thing. And there are ever so many arguments put forward in its behalf. They range all the way from the plea-for-posterity arguments of Mr. [William Benjamin] Smith, of Tulane, and Dr. [Robert Wilson] Shufeldt to the dirty drivel of ex-Governor [James K.] Vardaman and Tom Dixon. Eventually these arguments thin down to the point where it is necessary to declare that race prejudice is innate. The method is fairly familiar. Every stupid dislike makes the same plea for itself. But the idea has so many adherents that it may merit a formal challenge.

The Southern aristocrat has lived longest among Negroes. He is also the ablest defender of innate race prejudice in America. Let us interrogate him, since he may be supposed to know. How is it then, that the greatest of them preferred to have colored women to give their children suck? How is it that they still prefer to have black people around them as servants? If there is such innate repulsion between white men and black men, how is it that there is none between white men and black women? Did the bad colored women assault the dear, good white Southerner? Or how must we account for our millions of mulattoes? Let us confess the naked truth that there is nothing innate in race prejudice.

Had it been innate it would not be necessary to teach it to children by separate schools or to adults by separate cars. And every single fabric in the great wall of segregation which America is so laboriously building is an eloquent argument against the belief that race prejudice is innate. If it were innate it would never be necessary to bolster it up by legislative enactments or otherwise.

No, race prejudice is not innate. But it is diligently fostered by those who have something to gain by it. Let me explain. If white working people in the South can be made to hate black working people the result will be that the economic interests of the white workers will be advanced at the cost of the black man's economic interests. If there exist side by side one body of workers protected to a certain extent by the courts, public opinion and the ballot and another not protected at all, whenever they are thrown into economic competition the protected workers will take away the jobs of the other body of workers. That is what is happening in the South and elsewhere today. But the inevitable result of this is that there is created a body of workers whose standard of living has been permanently lowered. They are forced to live on a lower level, while as wage slaves they are as industrially efficient as the other group.

Then, now, the protected group demands for itself a larger share of its product in the form of higher wages or better conditions of labor and of life. Its demands are met with the cold fact that other wage slaves are doing as hard work or harder and doing it for less. And if they strike, the strike can always be broken by making use of that same body of workers whom the others have thus been breeding artificially as strikebreakers. It is therefore to the interests of the capitalists of America to preserve the inferior economic status of the colored race, because they can always use it as a club for the other workers. Besides, the lower the lowest wage level, the lower the average wage. They are interested in keeping the average wage as low as possible so they pit the workers, white against black, to keep the lowest wage level as low as possible. To this end they must divide the workers, and they find race prejudice a very useful tool to do this with. So the newspapers, owned by the capitalist class of the South, with their brother barons in the North, have entered upon a campaign of deprecation, vilification, calumny and lies in an endeavor to use the ignorance and superstition of the workers against the workers. So far, they have had a tremendous success, especially those larger Northern papers, like the *New York Times*, that are controlled by Southern capitalists.

They do this work in many ways. First by playing up Negro crime in their columns while they remain as close as clams as to Negro achievement. Then in addition, these same papers will twist an Associated Press dispatch so as to give it a meaning more damning than the original. Cases of assault by black men are written as if they were cases of sexual assault and that overworked word derives a dubious meaning their columns. But they will go even farther and tell deliberate lies as in the case of Dr. Du Bois and the Lyceum Club of London, or the Asbury Park murder of this year.

What is the object of the newspapers in doing things of this sort? They evidently wish to make their readers think along one certain line and to make them think that everyone else thinks and feels in the same way. Thus public opinion is built up in favor of race prejudice. And since a man's individual opinions are mostly derived from the social atmosphere, it is easy to see how people who grow up reading such newspapers, surrounded by others who are subjected to the same influence, get to believe that this carefully built up antipathy is innate.

Race prejudice when acquired takes care of itself. And that seems quite human, quite American. The word "inferior" sounds so nice in a republic that, really the temptation to think, if not to say it, is irresistible — except to the truly civilized.

For let it be noted that men rise out of their superstitions as they advance in civilization. A nation whose murder rate can climb from twenty-one per million in 1900 to fifty-nine per million in 1910 — leading the murder rate record of the civilized world — such a nation can fittingly lead in such savage and primitive superstitions as race prejudice and lynching bees.

Let us be assured that there is no justification of American race prejudice on scientific, social, or ethical grounds. The only grounds on which it can be maintained are those of caste. It is, perhaps, well that we should understand this so that we may not delude ourselves. And now, I shall conclude this section with a few words from an article which Comrade H. G. Wells wrote for the *Independent* in February, 1907.

> I am convinced myself that there is no more evil thing in this present world than race prejudice; none at all. I write deliberately — it is the worst single thing in life now. It justifies and holds together more baseness, cruelty and abomination than any other sort of error in the world. Through its body runs the black blood of coarse lust, suspicion, jealousy and persecution and all the darkest poison of the human soul . . . . It is a monster begotten of natural instincts and intellectual confusion, to be fought against by all men of good intent, each in our dispersed modern manner doing his fragmentary, inestimable share.

 10. "The Duty of the Socialist Party," *New York Call* (December 13, 1911): 6, HHHP Scr A.

Harrison's third article in the *Call* series addressed the Socialist Party's duty to combat race prejudice and extend its socialist message to African Americans. He argued that it was necessary for the party to make clear that it stood for "Socialism" over "Southernism." In making his argument he explained that socialism, as put forth by Karl Marx, Friedrich Engels, and Karl Kautsky, aimed "to put an end to the exploitation of one group by another, whether that group be social, economic or racial." This was the message the party must deliver, and Harrison praised the fact that in December 1911 it was beginning to do this by developing plans for organizing Socialist propaganda work among African Americans in New York. This work soon grew into the Colored Socialist Club. (The *New York Call* did not capitalize the *N* in *Negro*.)

If the Socialist movement is to draw all men to itself, it is but natural to expect that within its limits there will be found various and divergent opinions. These differences of opinion may even extend to the fundamental postulates of Socialism, for, of course, there will be in the beginning some calling themselves Socialists who do not quite understand what Socialism means. Of such is the dainty gentleman (or was it a lady?) who wrote the curious letter in *The Call* during the latter part of January, signing himself (or herself) "A Southern Socialist." The shrinking anonymity of the professional Southerner when writing to a Northern newspaper on the race problem is really praiseworthy. At least, they have the decency to be ashamed of the views which they champion. That letter in *The Call* and others in the *Weekly People* suggest that south of the 40th parallel are some people who think that the Socialist movement can be made into a vehicle for the venom of their caste consciousness. I am wondering what the Socialist philosophy would be if Marx had been a Mississippian.

The recent experience of Mrs. [Theresa] Malkiel in the South has made it necessary to note the views of the professional Southerner — and to condemn them. Of course, we do not believe that white women should be forced to marry black men or black women to marry white men. We do not believe that black men should be forced to invite white people to their homes, and vice versa. Neither do we believe in talking foolishness. But the particular attitude expressed in such forms as I have referred to constitute the challenge of caste. The Socialist party is not in a position to evade the issue. How will it meet it? By reaffirming its position in no uncertain tones. If it is to be Southernism versus Socialism, we take our stand on Socialism.

Here we are and here we stand, with no intention of receding. We are not a white man's party or a black man's party, but the party of the working class. And the historic mission of the Socialist movement is to unite the workers of the world. The party can never hope to advance to the conquest of capitalism with the taint of trimming about it.

Undoubtedly, votes will be necessary. But for what? For the enthronement of a narrowed, emasculated movement, or for the success of Socialism? In this we succeed if we succeed as Socialists; if we succeed as Southernists, we fail.

There are certain Southern people with parochial minds — and Northern ones, too —

who, when they are asked in the name of democracy and decency to treat the black man as a man, will rise up in wrath and demand, Shall I let him marry my daughter? Such petty people are always haunted with the specter of "social equality," which, like Banquo's ghost, will not down. Now, there never can be any such thing as "social equality," in this world. But there is such a thing as social justice, which requires that society shall not dictate to a man what friends he shall choose. The Southern idea would dictate to the other white people that they shall not choose black friends — and that is the whole sum and substance of this "social equality" scare. I would advise the Southern friends to invest in a large chunk of common sense. It cools the head and quiets the restless imagination.

I do not expect that the advent of Socialism will at once remove race prejudice — unless it remove ignorance at the same time. But I do expect that it will remove racial injustice and lighten the black man's burden. I do expect that it will take the white man from off the black man's back and leave him free for the first time to make of himself as much or as little as he chooses. And these expectations I share with the overwhelming majority of Socialists North and South.

And the Socialist party will do this because it cannot do otherwise and live as the Socialist party. If there are any people who think otherwise, now is the time to set them right.

Socialism is here to put an end to the exploitation of one group by another, whether that group be social, economic or racial. This is the position of Marx, Engels, Kautsky and every great leader of the Socialist movement. It is imbedded in the very fabric of the Socialist philosophy. And the affirmation of this is the present duty of the Socialist party as I see it.

But a more practical duty lies close at hand. It is the duty of extending the message of Socialism to the Negroes of America, of teaching its tenets to them; of organizing them; of stimulating them with the splendid hope of that new republic which will emerge out of the sordid selfishness of the present, under the benignant auspices of an inspiring social ideal — the Brotherhood of Man. In this battle for bread and economic justice, the services of these auxiliaries may prove to be of the highest value. And if they are to help us win victory for the exploited workers of the world, they must first be enlisted, then organized.

Some time ago, the Executive Committee of Local New York took under advisement certain plans for the organization of the Socialist propaganda work among the Negroes of New York. These plans were approved and a subcommittee was subsequently appointed to work out the details of this plan. This is the first step in that direction which the party has taken in the East and it is a timely one.

It means that the party is beginning to recognize its duty in this respect.

11. "How to Do It — And How Not," *New York Call* (December 16, 1911): 6, HHHP Scr A.

In the fourth article in the *Call* series Harrison offers advice on how to attract African Americans to the Socialist Party. He counsels white party members, "If your heart be in the right place, and this is assumed at the start, it will appear in your actions." Harrison cites campaign work in the 1911 New York City municipal election and reviews the work of his Black socialist predecessors, the Reverends George Woodbey and George W. Slater, as he makes a plea for a special appeal and a special group of organizers to reach Black people. Harrison, with his scientific and secular approach, made a significant break from the Christian Socialist tradition of activists like Woodbey and Slater. (The *New York Call* did not capitalize the *N* in *Negro*.)

One who comes into contact with strange people is often forced to ask himself, How shall I treat them? The answer to this varies as the culture and courtesy of the one who asks the question. The barbarian, white or black, answers, Treat them as "inferior" folk to whom one may be kind, but only as a special favor to be set off, perhaps with a suave and careful condescension. But the truly civilized, of any color, will answer, "Treat them frankly as human beings, for only by so doing can we make good our own claim to that title." This brings to mind Hamlet's advise to Polonious, in which the difference between the two types of culture is strikingly illustrated, for those were also "inferior" folk. Hamlet had instructed the old chamberlain to see the players well bestowed, to which he replied: "My lord, I will use them according to their desert." But the prince, with short patience laid down the true ethics of social contact. " 'Od's bodikins, man, much better! Use every man after his desert and who shall 'scape whipping? Use them after your own honor and dignity, the less they deserve, the more merit is in your bounty. Take them in."

It seems necessary at this time to tender a word of advice to many members of the party under this head. From so many of them one may hear such declarations as "I have always been friendly with colored people." "I have never felt any prejudice against Negroes," and so forth. All of which may be well meant, but is wholly unnecessary. If your heart be in the right place, and this is assumed at the start, it will appear in your actions. No special kindness and no condescension is either needed or expected. Treat them simply as human beings, as if you had never looked at the color of their faces. It is wonderful but true that what people will be to you depends very largely upon what you are to them. So much for personal contact.

But, the real object of this article is to explain just how the work of Socialism may be carried on among Negroes. I have shown in a previous article how the bonds of allegiance in parties are breaking and how the Negro public's mind has been prepared to listen to new doctrine. It may be well to add that the Negro vote is the balance of power in the elections in six Northern States, including Ohio, Indiana, Pennsylvania and New

York. This establishes two things — that the Negro vote can be got and that it is worth getting. How, then, are they to be reached?

First, we would do well to remember the special nature of the work. Some comrades believe that "Socialism is the same for all people — women, Finns, Negroes and all." Quite true. But the minds of all these are not the same and are not to be approached in the same way. Even an ordinary commercial dreamer will tell you this. I have already explained that the Negro has lived behind the color line, where none of these social movements have come to him. Those that did broke down as soon as they had to cross the color line. So that his mind is somewhat more difficult of approach, and consequently the work of taking the message of Socialism to him is really a special work. In the first place, the literature with which we cover a Negro district must be of a special nature. In the last [municipal election] campaign, Local New York got out a pamphlet entitled *The Colored Man's Case as Socialism Sees It*, written by Comrade [George W.] Slater, of Chicago, a colored minister, to which I added a special argument for that campaign. We would take one of these pamphlets and hold it so that the title showed plainly and walk up to a colored man with it. As soon as his eyes fell on the words "Colored Man's Case," his attention was arrested. Hide bound Republican healers and Democratic politicians would take it, where they would put aside any less special literature with a wave of impatience. And having taken it, they would read it, and stop to listen to our street speaker. The Debs pamphlet with the two pictures illustrating wage slavery and chattel slavery was *just* as welcome. So we demonstrated in the territory of Branch 5 that the special literature had a special effectiveness. Then there was the special form of address. Our arguments were the ABC arguments. But we crammed them full of facts — facts for the most part drawn from the Negro's own history and experience and hitting the bull's eye of his own affairs every time. That did not deprive our speeches of any general effectiveness, for very often from a third to a half of our audience would be made up of white people, whose attention and interest were held just the same. On the Tuesday before election, when we stampeded the crowd from the opposite corner, where they had women speakers as well as men, a large wagon and music, and held all of them for two hours in a driving rain — about two-fifths of the crowd were white people. So we demonstrated again the tremendous power of special addresses. And in that district they are talking about it yet — all of them — doctors, lawyers, longshoremen, clerks and waiters.

Now for such work a special equipment is necessary. One must know the people, their history, their manner of life, and modes of thinking and feeling. You have to know the psychology of the Negro, for if you don't you will fail to attract or impress him. You will fail to make him think — and feel. For many of your arguments must be addressed to his heart as well as to his head. This is more true of him than of most other American groups.

It stands to reason that this work can be better done by men who are themselves Negroes to whom these considerations come by second nature. If they are intelligent and well versed in the principles of Socialism they can drive home an argument with such effectiveness that white Socialists must despair of achieving.

And this brings me to the question of colored organizers. Comrade [Eugene V.] Debs has said that there are already three or four such national organizers. I know only one, Comrade [George W.] Woodbey, of California. He has been very effective. There should be more. But there is no need to wait until we can get colored national organizers. It ought to be taken up by the various Local and State organizations. Something of this sort is needed right here in New York where we have a Negro population of 100,000 in the city alone. The work must be done if the party would not be derelict in its duty and it should be done in no half-hearted way. For it is not a question of charity. Does the Socialist party feel that it needs the Negroes as much as the Negro needs Socialism? That is the question. What is the answer? If we feel that we can advance to the conquest of capitalism with one part of the proletariat against us, let us say so. But I haven't the slightest doubt that our program requires all the proletariat and we are all agreed on that. Let us act, then, in the light of this knowledge and add to the strength of the organized, all inclusive class conscious working class movement.

12. "The Black Man's Burden [I]" *International Socialist Review* 12 (April 1912): 660–63; reprinted with slight changes in *The Negro and the Nation*, 2–11; reworked as "The Real Negro Problem," *Modern Quarterly* 3, no. 4 (September–December 1926): 314–21. Also typescript in HHHP Wr.

The *International Socialist Review* (ISR) was a monthly magazine privately owned by Charles H. Kerr with a nationwide circulation in 1912 of between forty and fifty thousand, a markedly leftist political orientation, and a willingness to open its pages to debate on the "Negro Problem." Harrison prepared three articles in late 1911 that were published in the *ISR* in 1912 and posed a pointed challenge to Socialists preparing for the party convention in Indianapolis in May of that year. "The Black Man's Burden" appeared in two parts, in April and May, while "Socialism and the Negro" did not appear until July, after the convention had ended.

"The Black Man's Burden" directly challenged the thrust of Rudyard Kipling's internationally famous poem, the "The White Man's Burden" (first published in *McClure's Magazine* in February 1899). Kipling's argument in defense of British imperialism was the racist idea that whites should take up the task of trying to regulate the affairs of backward and undeveloped peoples of color. The *Times* of London called it "an address to the United States." Harrison's "Black Man's Burden" stood Kipling on his head and simultaneously posed a challenge to the position expressed by Socialist Party leader Eugene V. Debs, who in 1903 made reference to "the white burden bearer" in his article on "The Negro in the Class Struggle." Harrison pointed out that, rather than the white man being faced with the "tremendous burden of regulating the affairs of men of all other colors, who . . . are backward and undeveloped," it was quite possible that "the shoe may be on the other foot" so far as the colored three-fourths of humanity is concerned. In contrast to Kipling's white man's view, Harrison put forth a comprehensive rebuttal, based on facts, from the "other side." He felt that those political, economic, educational, and social facts would "furnish such a damning indictment of the Negro's American over-lord as must open the eyes of the world." [Though it is capitalized here, the *N* in *Negro* was not capitalized in the first two articles in this *ISR* series.[6] In selection 131 Harrison also offers a poetic response to Kipling.]

Providence, according to Mr. Kipling, has been pleased to place upon the white man's shoulders the tremendous burden of regulating the affairs of men of all other colors, who, for the purpose of his argument, are backward and undeveloped — "half devil and half child." When one considers that of the sixteen hundred million people living upon this earth, more than twelve hundred million are colored, this seems a truly staggering burden.

But it does not seem to have occurred to the proponents of this pleasant doctrine that the shoe may be on the other foot so far as the other twelve hundred million are concerned. It is easy to maintain an *ex parte* argument, and as long as we do not ask the other side to state their case our own arguments will appear not only convincing but conclusive. But in the court of common sense this method is not generally allowed and a case is not considered closed until *both* parties have been heard from.

I have no doubt but that the colored peoples of the world will have a word or two to say in their own defense. In this article I propose to put the case of the black man in America, not by any elaborate arguments, but by the presentation of certain facts which will probably speak for themselves.

I am not speaking here of the evidences of Negro advancement, not even making a plea for justice. I wish merely to draw attention to certain pitiful facts. This is all that is necessary — at present. For I believe that those facts will furnish such a damning indictment of the Negro's American over-lord as must open the eyes of the world. The sum total of these facts and of what they suggest constitute a portion of the black man's burden in America. Not all of it, to be sure, but quite enough to make one understand what the Negro problem is. For the sake of clarity I shall arrange them in four groups: political, economic, educational and social. And first as to the political.

Political I

In a republic all the adult male natives at least are citizens. If in a given community some are citizens and others subjects, then your community is not a republic. It may call itself so. But that is another matter. Now, the essence of citizenship is the exercise of political rights; the right to a voice in government, to say what shall be done with your taxes, and the right to express your own needs. If you are denied these rights you are not a citizen. Well, in sixteen southern states there are over eight million Negroes in this anomalous position. Of course, many good people contend that they may be unfit to exercise the right of suffrage. If that is so, then who is fit to exercise it for them? This argument covers a fundamental fallacy in our prevailing conception of the function of the ballot. We think that it is a privilege to be conferred for "fitness." But it isn't. It is an instrument by which the people of a community express their will, their wants and their needs. And all those are entitled to use it who have wants, needs and desires that are worth consideration by society. If they are not worth considering, then be brutally frank about it; say so, and establish a protectorate over them. But have done with the silly cant of "fitness." People vote to express their wants. Of course, they will make mistakes. They are not gods. But they have a right to make their own mistakes — the Negroes. All other Americans have. That is why we had ["Boss" Abraham] Ruef in San Francisco, and still have ["Boss" Charles F.] Murphy in New York.

But the American republic says, in effect, that eight million Americans shall be political serfs. Now, this might be effected with decency by putting it into the national constitution. But it isn't there. The national constitution has two provisions expressly penalizing this very thing. Yet the government — the President, Congress, the Supreme Court — wink at it. This is not what we call political decency. But, just the same, it is done. How is it done? By fraud and force. [Benjamin] Tillman of South Carolina has told in the United States Senate how the ballot was taken from Negroes by shooting them — that is, by murder. But murder is not necessary now. In certain southern states in order to vote a man must have had a grandfather who voted before Negroes were freed. In others, he must be able to interpret and understand any clause in the Constitution — and a white registration official decides whether he does understand. And the colored men of states like Virginia, North Carolina, Georgia, Alabama, Mississippi and Louisiana who meet such tests as these states provide are disfranchised by the "white primary" system. According to this system only those who vote at the primaries can vote at the general elections. But the South Carolina law provides that: "At this election only white voters . . . and such Negroes as voted the Democratic ticket in 1876 and have voted the Democratic ticket continuously since . . . may vote." Of course, they know that none of them voted that ticket in 1876 or have done so continuously since. In Georgia the law says that: "All white electors who have been duly registered . . . irrespective of past political affiliations . . . are hereby declared qualified and are invited to participate in said primary election."

Under the new suffrage law of Mr. Booker T. Washington's state of Alabama, Montgomery County, which has 53,000 Negroes, disfranchises all but one hundred of them. In 1908 the Democrats of West Virginia declared in their platform that the United States Constitution should be so amended as to disfranchise all the Negroes of the country. In

December, 1910, the lower house of the Texas legislature, by a vote of 51 to 34, instructed its federal senators and Congressmen to work for the repeal of the two amendments to the national constitution which [by implication] confer the right of suffrage upon Negroes. But the funniest proposal in that direction came from Georgia, where J. J. Slade proposed an amendment to the state constitution to the effect that colored men should be allowed to vote only if two *chaste* white women would swear that they would trust them in the dark! But, however it has been effected, whether by force or fraud, by methods wise or otherwise, the great bulk of the Negroes of America are political pariahs today. When it is remembered that they once had the right of suffrage, that it was given them, not upon any principle of abstract right, but as a means of protection from the organized ill-will of their white neighbors, that ill-will is now more effectively organized and in possession of all the powers of the state, — it can be seen at a glance that this spells subjection certain and complete.

Economic II

Political rights are the only sure protection and guarantee of economic rights. Every fool knows this. And yet, here in America to-day, we have people who tell Negroes that they ought not to agitate for the ballot so long as they still have a chance to get work in the south. And Negro leaders, hired by white capitalists who want cheap labor-power, still continue to mislead both their own and other people. The following facts should demonstrate the economic insecurity of the Negro in the South.

Up to a few years ago systematic peonage was wide-spread in the South. Now, peonage is slavery unsanctioned by law. In its essence it is more degrading than mere chattel slavery. Any one who disputes this may look to modern Mexico for proofs. This peonage in the South had reduced many black men to slavery. And it isn't stamped out yet. It was on January 3, 1911, that the Supreme Court, in the case of Alonzo Bailey, declared unconstitutional the Alabama peonage law, which had been upheld by the state Supreme Bench. About the same time W. S. Harlan, a nephew of the late Justice Harlan of the United States Supreme Court, and manager of a great lumber and turpentine trust doing business in Florida and Alabama, was sentenced to eighteen months' imprisonment and fined $5,000 for peonage. He was pardoned soon after and had his fine remitted by President [William Howard] Taft.

One of the forms of this second slavery is the proprietary system, according to which the Negro laborer or tenant farmer must get his supply at the proprietor's store — and he gets it on credit. The accounts are "cooked" so that the Negro is always in debt to the modern slave-holder. Some of them spend a life-time working out an original debt of five or ten dollars.

But peonage isn't all. The professional southerner is always declaring that whatever else the south may not do for the Negro it supplies him with work. It does — when he works for some one else. When he works for himself it is often very different. For instance, there was the Georgia Railroad strike of May, 1909. The Negro firemen were getting some fifty cents to a dollar a day less than the white firemen, they had to do menial work, and could not be promoted to be engineers. They could be promoted, however, to the best runs by the rule of seniority. But the white firemen, who had fixed the economic status of the black firemen, objected to even this. They went on strike and published a ukase to the people of the state in which they said: "The white people of this state refuse to accept social equality."

On the eighth of March, last year [1911], the firemen of the Cincinnati, New Orleans & Texas Pacific Railroad did the same thing. In the attacks made on the trains by them [the white firemen] and their sympathizers many Negro firemen were killed. Occurrences of this sort are increasing in frequency and they have a certain tragic significance. It means that the Negro, stripped of the protection of the ballot, holds the right to earn his bread at the mere sufferance of the whites. It means that no black man shall hold a job that any white man wants. And that, not in the South alone. There was the case of the Pavers' Union of New York City. The colored pavers, during the panic of 1907, got behind in their dues. The usual period granted expired on Friday. On Monday they sent in their dues in full to the national organization. The treasurer refused to receive the dues and at once got out an injunction against them. This injunction estopped them from appealing to the National Executive Committee [of the union] or to the National convention. They are still fighting the case. Last January [1911] the several walking delegates of the Painters', Plumbers', Masons', Carpenters', Steam Fitters', Plasterers' and Tinsmiths' Unions compelled the Thompson & Starrett Construction Co., the second largest firm of contractors in New York, to get rid of the colored cold painters who were engaged on the annex to Stearns' department store. They would not admit them to membership in the union; they merely declared that colored men would not be allowed to do this work. And these are the same men who denounce Negro strike-breakers. They want them out of the unions and also want them to fight for the unions. Presumably they would have them eating air-balls in the meantime.

Last February [1911] the New York Cab Company was dropping its Negro cab drivers because it said its patrons demanded it. In November of that year the white chauffeurs of New York were trying to terrorize the colored chauffeurs by a system of sabotage in the garages, because they, too, believed that these jobs were white men's jobs.

It is but a short step from the denial of the right to work to the denial of the right to own. In fact, the two are often linked together, as in the next case. In the latter part of 1910, land speculators in Hominy, Oklahoma sold some land for cotton farms to Negroes. The Negroes paid for this land, took possession, and were getting along splendidly when — "the local whites protested." "Night-riders (i.e. Ku Klux) around Hominy, several days before, served notice that all Negroes must leave the town at once, and to emphasize the warning they exploded dynamite in the neighborhood of Negro houses." So the Negroes fled, fearing for their lives. At Baxterville, Miss., the same thing happened in March [1911]. In November 1910, a colored man named Matthew Anderson in Kansas City was having a fine $5,000 house built. But the jealousy of the white neighbors prevented its completion. It was blown up by a dynamite when it had been almost finished. In Warrentown, Ga., notice was sent to three colored men and one widow, who had prospered greatly in business, to the effect that they must leave immediately because the white people of Warrentown "were not a-goin' to stand for rich niggers." One of them has been forced to sell out his business at a loss. Another never answers a knock and never leaves his house by the front door. And all through these things Mr. [Booker T.] Washington told his race that if it would work hard, get property and be useful to a community it would not need to strive for a share in the government, and they call this man a "leader"!

(to be continued)

 13. "The Black Man's Burden [II]," *International Socialist Review* 12, no. 11 (May 1912): 762–64; reprinted with slight changes in *The Negro and the Nation,* 11–20. (*The International Socialist Review* did not capitalize the *N* in *Negro* in this article.)

Educational III

EDUCATION is the name which we give to that process of equipment and training which, in our day, society gives the individual to prepare him for fighting the battle of life. We do not confer it as a privilege, but it is given on behalf of society for society's own protection from the perils of ignorance and incompetence. It is a privilege to which every member of society is entitled. For without some equipment of this sort the individual is but half a man, handicapped in the endeavor to make a living. Here in America, we subscribe to the dangerous doctrine that ten [reprint gives *twelve*] million of the people should receive the minimum of education. And in order to reconcile ourselves to this doctrine, we deck it in the garments of wisdom. Because of the serf idea in American life, we say that the Negro shall have a serf's equipment and nothing more. It is the same idea that the aristocracy of Europe evolved when the workers demanded that their children should be trained better than they themselves had been. "Why," said the masters, "if we give your children schooling will they be educated out of their station in life. What should the son of a carpenter need to know of Euclid or Virgil? He should learn his father's vocation that he may be well equipped to serve in that station of life into which it has pleased God to call him. We need more plowmen than frocks [priests], more servants than savants."

In our own land, when Negroes demand education, we say, "Why, surely, give them industrial education. Your race has a great opportunity — to make itself useful. It needs trained craftsmen and workers and, perhaps, a few parsons. Teach your sons and daughters to work. That is enough." And we dexterously select leaders for them who will administer the soothing syrup of this old idea with deftness and dispatch. The General Education Board which disburses millions of dollars annually in the South for education has, so far, given to forty-one Negro schools the sum of $464,015. Only in two instances has any money been given to a real college. Practically all of it went to the labor-caste schools [HH removed the word *caste* in the reprint]. Why? Because the dark degradation of the Negro must be lightened by no ray of learning. That would never do. We need them as "hewers of wood and drawers of water." And in the meanwhile, this is what the richest country on earth offers to ruthlessly exploited people as a training for life.

Before the Twelfth Annual Conference for Education in the South (1910), Mr. Charles L. Coon, superintendent of schools in North Carolina, read a paper on Negro education in the South ["Public Taxation and New Schools"]. His investigations extended over eleven states: Virginia, North Carolina, South Carolina, Georgia, Florida, Alabama, Mississippi, Louisiana, Texas, Arkansas and Tennessee. In these states the Negroes made up 40.1 per cent of the population, but received only 14.8 per cent of the school fund. He showed that even if the school funds disbursed were apportioned to each race according to taxes paid the colored people of Virginia should receive $507,305 instead of the $482,228 which they now receive; in North Carolina they should get $429,127 instead of $402,658, and in Georgia $647,852 instead of $506,170. So that these three states expended for Negro education $93,278 less than what the Negroes themselves pay for — and that sum is contributed by Negroes to the white children of the state.

But, as a matter of fact, in no modern country is education made to depend upon the tax-paying power of the parents. If that were so, the children of 80,000,000 [the reprint gives *40,000,000*] American proletarians would live and die without schooling. So that the case is really much worse than it seems.

South Carolina spent in 1910 $10.34 for the education of each white child and $1.70 for the *education* of each colored child. In Lawrence County the state gave to each colored child 97 cents worth of education that year; in Lexington county, 90 cents; in Bamberg, 89 cents; in Saluda, 68 cents, and in Calhoun, 58 cents worth. The smallest sum spent on a white child for education that year was $4.03. In Georgia it was quite as bad. One county of this state owned 19 of the 27 school houses for Negroes. The valuation of the entire 19 was $2,500; that is $131.58 for each school house for Negroes! *The annual cost of the education of a Negro child in six counties of this civilized state was 39 cents.* Meanwhile the whites were protesting against the building of a new Negro school! In Louisiana the report of the Department of Education showed that the average monthly salary of white male teachers is $75.29, while that of colored male teachers is $34.25. The average monthly salary of white female teachers is $50.80 and that of colored female teachers is $28.67. The average length of the annual school term for white children is eight months and a quarter; for colored children, four months and a half.

In Wilcox County, Alabama, where there are 2,000 white children and 10,758 colored children, $32,660.48 is devoted to education. Of this amount the 10,758 colored children received one-fifth — $6,532.09, or sixty cents each per annum — while the 2,000 white children receive the remaining four-fifths — $26,128.13, or about $13 each per annum. Mr. Booker Washington, who lives in this state, sends his own children to the best colleges and to Europe while advising the rest of his people to "make your condition known to the white people of the state."

Now, if education — of any sort — is training for life, is it not evident here that black children are being robbed of their chance in life? Why? Is it to be supposed that their fathers are so stupid as to allow this if they could vote their own needs? Yet Mr. Washington decries the agitation for the ballot as unwise and never loses an opportunity of sneering at those who see something of value in it. But to continue. The number of white children of school age in Alabama is 364,266; the number of colored children of school age is 311,552. But the teachers of the white children receive in salaries $2,404,062.54, while the teachers of the colored children receive $202,251.13. The value of all schoolhouses, sites and furniture for white children is $6,503,019.57; for colored children, $273,147.50.

In South Carolina there are 316,007 Negro children of school age and 201,868 white children; but the state spends on its Negro children $368,802, and on its white children $1,684,976. Thus does America keep knowledge from her Negroes. She is afraid of the educated black man. Of such are the people who taunt Negroes with ignorance.

Social IV

When a group has been reduced to serfdom, political and economic, its social status becomes fixed by that fact. And so we find that in "the home of the free and the land of the brave" Negroes must not ride in the same cars in a train as white people. On street-cars, certain sections are set apart for them. They may not eat in public places where white people eat nor drink at the same bar. They may not go to the same church (although they are foolish enough to worship the same God) as white people; they may not die in the same hospital nor be buried in the same grave-yard.

So far as we know, the segregation ends here. But why is segregation necessary? Because [*some* is added in the reprint] white Americans are afraid that their "inherent" superiority may not, after all, be so very evident either to the Negro or to other people. They, therefore, find it necessary to enact it into law. So we had the first Ghetto legislation in an American nation last year [1911] in Baltimore. Hard on the heels of this followed legislative proposals along the same line in Richmond, Va., Kansas City, Mo.,

St. Louis, Mo., and Birmingham, Ala. In Memphis, Tenn. Negroes pay taxes for public parks in which they are not allowed to enter. A year ago they petitioned for a Negro park and were about to get it when "500 white citizens protested." That settled it with the park.

But discrimination goes even farther and declares that Negroes shall not possess even their lives if any white persons should want them. And so we have the institution called the lynching-bee. The professional southerner continues to assert that Negroes are lynched for rape committed upon white women. Why not? It is perfectly American. If you want to kill a dog call it mad; if you want to silence a man call him an Anarchist [the 1926 revision gives *Bolshevist*], and if you want to kill a black man call him a rapist. But let us see what the facts actually are.

In the two decades from 1884 to 1904 there were 2,875 lynchings in the United States. Of these 87 per cent, or 2,499 occurred in the South. The national total was grouped as follows:

1. For alleged and attempted criminal assault (i.e., rape) 564
2. For assault and murder and for complicity 138
3. For murder 1277
4. For theft, burglary and robbery 326
5. For arson 106
6. For race-prejudice (?) 94
7. For unknown reasons 134
8. For simple assault 18
9. For insulting whites 18
10. For making threats 16

The causes for the remainder were: slander, miscegenation, informing, drunkenness, fraud, voodooism, violation of contract, resisting arrest, elopement, train-wrecking, poisoning stock, refusing to give evidence, testifying against whites, political animosity, disobedience of quarantine regulations, passing counterfeit money, introducing small-pox, concealing criminals, cutting levees, kidnapping, gambling, riots, seduction, incest and forcing a child to steal.

Yes, there are courts in the South; but not for the black people — not when the mob chooses to relieve civilization of the onus of law and order. At Honeapath, S.C., a Negro was lynched in November last, charged, of course, with "the usual crime." The charge had not been proven, or even investigated; but the man was lynched. The howling mob which did him to death was composed of "prominent citizens" who made up automobile parties to ride to the affair. Among those prominently present was the *dis*honorable Joshua Ashley, a member of the state legislature. He and his friends cut off the man's fingers as souvenirs and were proud of their work. Why shouldn't they? You see, it helps to keep "niggers" in their place. And then, besides, isn't this a white man's country? Governor [Cole] Blease of South Carolina was also proud of the event and said that instead of stopping the horrible work of the mob he would have resigned his office to lead it. In Okemeah, Oklahoma, last June [1911] a band of white gentlemen raped a Negro woman and then lynched her and her fourteen-year-old son. Nothing has been done to them. And it is not that the facts are unknown. At Durant, Okla., and elsewhere, the savages [*white christians* in the reprint] have posed around their victims to have their pictures taken. One man, from Alabama, sent to the Rev. John Haynes Holmes, of Brooklyn, New York, a post-card (*by mail*) bearing a photograph of such a group. "This is the way we treat them down here," he writes, and, after promising to put Mr. Holmes' name on his mailing list, declares that they will have one, at least, each month.

In Washington, Ga., Charles S. Holinshead, a wealthy white planter, raped the wife of T. B. Walker, a decent, respectable Negro. As his wife returned to him disheveled and bleeding from the outrage perpetrated on her, Walker went to Holinshead's store and shot him dead. For this he was tried and condemned, and, while the judge was yet pronouncing sentence, Holinshead's brother shot Walker in the court-room. They held his head up while the judge finished the sentence. Then he was taken out and lynched — not executed. Nothing was done to the other Holinshead.

The New York *Evening Post*, on October 23rd [1911], said in an editorial that "there has hardly been a single authenticated case in a decade of the Negroes rising against the whites, despite the growing feeling, among them that there should be some retaliation since no tribunal will punish lynchers or enforce the law." I am glad that the *Post* noticed this. I had begun to notice it myself. When President Roosevelt discussed lynching some years ago, he severely reprobated *the colored people* for their tendency to shield their "criminals" and ordered them to go out and help hunt them down. So was insult added to injury.

But, putting my own opinion aside, here are the facts as I have seen them. In the face of these facts, the phrase, "the white man's burden," sounds to me like a horrid mockery.

14. "Socialism and the Negro," *International Socialist Review* 13 (July 1912): 65–68, reprinted with minor changes in *The Negro and the Nation*, 21–29.

Harrison concluded his nationwide theoretical series with his seminal piece on "Socialism and the Negro," which delineated his ideas on the "Negro Question" and was based on a pro-IWW speech he delivered on December 31, 1911. The printed version is noteworthy because it marked the first time that the pro-IWW *International Socialist Review* printed the word *Negro* with a capital *N*. This was probably due in part to Harrison's insistence. It also showed some progress in racial understanding; Harrison's two earlier articles in the *ISR* did not capitalize the word, and the more right-wing socialist paper the *New York Call* had also refused to capitalize it.[7]

In this article Harrison reasoned that since the Socialist Party mission was avowedly "to free the working class from exploitation," and since the African American was the "most ruthlessly exploited working class group in America," then "the duty of the party to champion his cause" was "as clear as day." He added, anticipating W. E. B. Du Bois by a year, that this duty was "the crucial test of Socialism's sincerity."[8]

The implications of Harrison's analysis were profound. For the majority in the party, the key political debates concerned positions on the political (evolutionary) and the industrial (revolutionary) approaches to socialism. Harrison, in 1911–12, addressed the two large factions in the party on their own terms. In each case, using the logic of their theoretical positions, he called for special emphasis on African Americans in the interests of the working class. He stressed to the political socialists that in their work for "the abolition of capitalism, by legislation," the "Negro, who feels most fiercely the deep damnation of the capitalist system, can help." To the revolutionary socialists he stressed that Black workers possessed "labor power — which they can be taught to withhold," and that they could organize themselves "at the point of production"; "work to shorten the hours of labor, to raise wages, [and] to enforce laws for the protection of labor"; and work toward "a progressive control of the tools of production and a progressive expropriation of the capitalist class." In putting forth these arguments, Harrison, "on grounds of common sense and enlightened self-interest," effectively proposed a new test for U.S. Socialists — "to champion" the cause of the "Negro." He thought this was the key to revolutionary change.[9]

Economic Status of the Negro

The ten million Negroes of America form a group that is more essentially proletarian than any other American group. In the first place the ancestors of this group were brought here with the very definite understanding that they were to be ruthlessly exploited. And they were not allowed any choice in the matter. Since they were brought here as chattels their social status was fixed by that fact. In every case that we know of where a group has lived by exploiting another group, it has despised that group which it has put under subjection. And the degree of contempt has always been in direct proportion to the degree of exploitation.

Inasmuch then, as the Negro was at one period the most thoroughly exploited of the American proletariat, he was the most thoroughly despised. That group which exploited and despised him, being the most powerful section of the ruling class, was able to diffuse its own necessary contempt of the Negro first among the other sections of the ruling class, and afterwards among all other classes of Americans. For the ruling class has always determined what the social ideals and moral ideas of society should be; and this explains how race prejudice was disseminated until all Americans are supposed to be saturated with it. Race prejudice, then, is the fruit of economic subjection and a fixed inferior economic status. It is the reflex of a social caste system. That caste system in America today is what we roughly refer to as the Race Problem, and it is thus seen that the Negro problem is essentially an economic problem with its roots in slavery past and present.

Notwithstanding the fact that it is usually kept out of public discussion, the bread-and-butter side of this problem is easily the most important. The Negro worker gets less for his work—thanks to exclusion from the craft unions—than any other worker; he works longer hours as a rule and under worse conditions than any other worker, and his rent in any large city is much higher than that which the white worker pays for the same tenement. In short, the exploitation of the Negro worker is keener than that of any group of white workers in America. Now, the mission of the Socialist Party is to free the working class from exploitation, and since the Negro is the most ruthlessly exploited working class group in America, the duty of the party to champion his cause is as clear as day. This is the crucial test of Socialism's sincerity and therein lies the value of this point of view—Socialism and the Negro.

The Need of Socialist Propaganda

So far, no particular effort has been made to carry the message of Socialism to these people. All the rest of the poor have had the gospel preached to them, for the party has carried on special propaganda work among the Poles, Slovaks, Finns, Hungarians and Lithuanians. Here are ten million Americans, all proletarians, hanging on the ragged edge of the impending class conflict. Left to themselves they may become as great a menace to our advancing army as is the army of the unemployed, and for precisely the same reason: they can be used against us, as the craft unions have begun to find out. Surely we should make some effort to enlist them under our banner that they may swell our ranks and help to make us invincible. And we must do this for the same reason that is impelling organized labor to adopt an all-inclusive policy; because the other policy results in the artificial breeding of scabs. On grounds of common sense and enlightened self-interest it would be well for the Socialist party to begin to organize the Negroes of America in reference to the class struggle. You may depend on it, comrades, the capitalists of America are not waiting. Already they have subsidized Negro leaders, Negro editors, preachers and politicians to build up in the breasts of black people those sentiments which will make them subservient to their will. For they recognize the value (to them) of cheap labor power and they know that if they can succeed in keeping one section of the working class down they can use that section to keep the other sections down too.

The Negro's Attitude toward Socialism

If the Socialist propaganda among Negroes is to be effectively carried on, the members and leaders of the party must first understand the Negro's attitude toward Socialism. That attitude finds its first expression in ignorance. The mass of the Negro people in America are ignorant of what Socialism means. For this they are not much to blame. Behind the veil of the color line none of the great world-movements for social betterment have been able to penetrate. Since it is not yet the easiest task to get the white

American worker — with all his superior intellect — to see Socialism, it is but natural to expect that these darker workers to whom America denies knowledge should still be in ignorance as to its aims and objects.

Besides, the Negroes of America — those of them who think — are suspicious of Socialism as of everything that comes from the white people of America. They have seen that every movement for the extension of democracy here has broken down as soon as it reached the color line. Political democracy declared that "all men are created equal," meant only all white men; the Christian church found that the brotherhood of man did not include God's bastard children; the public school system proclaimed that the school house was the backbone of democracy — "for white people only," and the civil service says that Negroes must keep their place — at the bottom. So that they can hardly be blamed for looking askance at any new gospel of freedom. Freedom to them has been like one of

> "those juggling fiends
> That palter with us in double sense;
> That keep the word of promise to our ear,
> And break it to our hope."

In this connection, some explanation of the former political solidarity of those Negroes who were voters may be of service. Up to six years ago the one great obstacle to the political progress of the colored people was their sheep-like allegiance to the Republican party. They were taught to believe that God had raised up a peculiar race of men called Republicans who had loved the slaves so tenderly that they had taken guns in their hands and rushed on the ranks of the southern slaveholders to free the slaves; that this race of men was still in existence, marching under the banner of the Republican party and showing their great love for Negroes by appointing from six to sixteen near-Negroes to soft political snaps. Today that great political superstition is falling to pieces before the advance of intelligence among Negroes. They begin to realize that they were sold out by the Republican party in 1876; that in the last twenty-five years lynchings have increased, disfranchisement has spread all over the south and "jim-crow" cars run even into the national capital — with the continuing consent of a Republican congress, a Republican Supreme Court and Republican presidents.

Ever since the Brownsville affair, but more clearly since [William Howard] Taft declared and put in force the policy of pushing out the few near-Negro officeholders, the rank and file have come to see that the Republican party is a great big sham. Many went over to the Democratic party because, as the *Amsterdam News* puts it, "they had nowhere else to go." Twenty years ago the colored men who joined that party were ostracized as scalawags and crooks — which they probably were. But today, the defection to the democrats of such men as Bishop [Alexander] Walters, [Robert N.] Wood, [James

D.] Carr and [Ralph E.] Langston — whose uncle was a colored Republican congress-man from Virginia — has made the colored democracy respectable and given quite a tone to political heterodoxy.

All this loosens the bonds of their allegiance and breaks the bigotry of the last forty years. But of this change in their political view-point the white world knows nothing. The two leading Negro newspapers are subsidized by the same political pirates who hold the title-deeds to the handful of hirelings holding office in the name of the Negro race. One of these papers [the *New York Age*] is an organ of Mr. Washington, the other [the *Amsterdam News*] pretends to be independent — that is, it must be "bought" on the installment plan, and both of them are in New York. Despite this "conspiracy of silence" the Negroes are waking up; are beginning to think for themselves; to look with more favor on "new doctrines." And herein lies the open opportunity of the Socialist party. If the work of spreading Socialist propaganda is taken to them now, their ignorance of it can be enlightened and their suspicions removed.

The Duty of the Socialist Party

I think that we might embrace the opportunity of taking the matter up at the com-ing national convention. The time is ripe for taking a stand against the extensive dis-franchisement of the Negro in violation of the plain provisions of the national consti-tution. In view of the fact that the last three amendments to the constitution contain the clause, "Congress shall have the power to enforce this article by appropriate legisla-tion," the party will not be guilty of proposing anything worse than asking the govern-ment to enforce its own "law and order." If the Negroes, or any other section of the working class in America, is to be deprived of the ballot, how can they participate with us in the class struggle? How can we pretend to be a political party if we fail to see the significance of this fact?

Besides, the recent dirty diatribes against the Negro in a Texas paper [the *Rebel*], which is still on our national list of Socialist papers; the experiences of Mrs. Theresa Malkiel in Tennessee, where she was prevented by certain people from addressing a meeting of Negroes on the subject of Socialism, and certain other exhibitions of the thing called southernism, constitute the challenge of caste. Can we ignore this chal-lenge? I think not. We could hardly afford to have the taint of "trimming" on the gar-ments of the Socialist party. It is dangerous — doubly dangerous now, when the temper of the times is against such "trimming." Besides it would be futile. If it is not met now it must be met later when it shall have grown stronger. Now, when we can cope with it, we have the issue squarely presented: Southernism or Socialism — which? Is it to be the white half of the working class against the black half, or all the working class? Can we hope to triumph over capitalism with one-half of the working class against us? Let us settle these questions now — for settled they must be.

The Negro and Political Socialism

The power of the voting proletariat can be made to express itself through the ballot. To do this they must have a political organization of their own to give form to their will. The direct object of such an organization is to help them to secure control of the powers of government by electing members of the working class to office and so secure legislation in the interests of the working class until such time as the workers may, by being in overwhelming control of the government, be able "to alter or abolish it, and to institute a new government, laying its foundation on such principles, and organizing its power in such form, as to them shall seem most likely to effect their safety and happiness" — in short, to work for the abolition of capitalism, by legislation — if that be permitted. And in all this, the Negro, who feels most fiercely the deep damnation of the capitalist system, can help.

The Negro and Industrial Socialism

But even the voteless proletarian can in a measure help toward the final abolition of the capitalist system. For they too have labor power — which they can be taught to withhold. They can do this by organizing themselves at the point of production. By means of such organization they can work to shorten the hours of labor, to raise wages, to secure an ever-increasing share of the product of their toil. They can enact and enforce laws for the protection of labor and they can do this at the point of production, as was done by the Western Federation of Miners in the matter of the eight-hour law, which they established without the aid of the legislatures or the courts. All of this involves a progressive control of the tools of production and a progressive expropriation of the capitalist class. And in all this the Negro can help. So far, they are unorganized on the industrial field, but industrial unionism beckons to them as to others, and the consequent program of the Socialist party for the Negro in the south can be based upon this fact.

15. "Southern Socialists and the Ku Klux Klan," letter to the editor, *New Review*, written c. 1914 but not published by the paper; reprinted in the *Negro World*, January 8, 1921; HHHP Scr B, where Harrison handwrote above it "An Unpublished letter of 1914 or 1915."

The *New Review* first appeared on January 4, 1913, and its stated purpose was to "enable the Socialists of America to attain a better knowledge and clearer understanding of the theories and principles, history and methods of the International Socialist Movement." It paid particular attention to the race question, and in its inaugural issue W. E. B. Du Bois wrote "A Field for Socialists," in which he maintained, echoing Harrison in the *International Socialist Review*, that "there is a group of ten million persons in the United States toward whom Socialists would better turn serious attention." In the February 1 issue

Du Bois declared, again echoing Harrison's July 1912 *ISR* article, that "the Negro problem is the great test of the American Socialist." In September 1913 NAACP founder Mary White Ovington wrote an article for the *New Review* on "The Status of the Negro in the United States." Ovington's piece reviewed instances of disfranchisement and loss of property rights and evaluated the work of the NAACP, the IWW, and the SP on "the Negro Question." She commented that "in some Southern states [the Socialists] . . . have, at times, shown a race prejudice unexcelled by the most virulent Democrats."[10]

Ovington's article elicited a controversial response from Ida M. Raymond, state secretary of the Socialist Party of Mississippi, which was published as "A Southern Socialist on the Negro Question." Raymond responded to the Ovington article with what the *New Review* termed "a frank and sincere statement of the views of certain Southern Socialists." She opposed Blacks and whites meeting together, and she opposed integrated locals of the Socialist Party, stating that such integration would "do more to retard" efforts at educating both races "than any other thing that can be done." She maintained that the "Negroes" of the South were without education and "worse than the 'Uncle Tom' of slavery days," adding that if "Negroes" were given rights currently denied them by state constitutions they would resurrect those "awful days" of "Negro domination" that were seen after the Civil War. According to Raymond, this "Negro domination" had necessitated the rise of the Ku Klux Klan in order "to take matters in their own hands and save their women, their homes, and their country."[11]

Shortly after Raymond's letter was published Harrison wrote the following response to the editors of the *New Review*. It put forth serious criticisms of the Socialist Party and the editors chose not to publish it. The article was only published years later by the *Negro World* when Harrison was a contributing editor.

To the Editor of the *New Review*:

Sir — Perhaps a Negro may fittingly consider the subject brought up in the December number of the *New Review* by the letter of Mrs. Ida Raymond, State Secretary, Socialist Party of Mississippi. Mrs. Raymond opposes Miss Ovington's advocacy of having the white and black people meet on equal terms "at this present time." I should like to know whether she would be in favor of it at any future time. Apart from this, it seems to me that Mrs. Raymond misreads the meaning of Miss Ovington's demand, which is quite natural — in the South. She had already named "the creation of a segregated class in our democracy," the "jim crow" legislation, lynching, caste education and the suppression of those rights considered to all other citizens under the fourteenth and fifteenth amendments of the Federal Constitution. On these matters even Southerners like E. G. Murphy and Rev. Quincy Ewing are agreed upon "equal terms." These two men, are not Socialists. And the question arises whether any Socialists — in the South or elsewhere — can afford to take a position to the rearward of this. To my mind, Mrs. Raymond is thinking of "social equality," the fetish of all Southerners. And Miss Ovington wasn't. As for me, I can't conceive what the two words mean. Mrs. Raymond, however, has imbibed the Southern attitude from her Southern environment, and it vitiates even her notions of history.

For example, she asserts that "the South had a taste of what the Negroes would do if they were to be allowed [the] full political rights accorded them by the Constitution," and that "the Ku Klux Klan had to take matters in their own hands and save their women, their homes, and their country from the terrible outrages that were perpetrated by the Negroes." It might interest her to know that the constitutional right to vote was given to Negroes in 1868, while the Ku Klux Klan began its terrorism in the winter of 1865, long before the vote was given to Negroes in the South. Congress was induced to give the vote to the Negro to enable him to protect himself from his friends, of the Ku Klux Klan, the Society of the Pale Faces, and the Knights of the White Camelias. The great authoritative work on the period is *A Documentary History of Reconstruction*. Its author is Prof. Walter L. Fleming, a Southerner. His work can easily be had, and I should recommend Mrs. Raymond to go there for her facts rather than to the traditions current in her neighborhood.

What most interests me, however, is not the misstatements of well-known facts in her letter, but the attitude of Southern Socialists which it so naively reveals. The experience of Mrs. Malkiel in Tennessee and the letter of a "Southern Socialist" to the *Call* some time ago have shown us that Southern Socialists are "Southerners" first and "Socialists" after. And the Socialist party, in the laudable ambition of increasing its membership and vote among all classes of the population is apt to keep in the rear whatever implications of its doctrine may offend and scare off the desired elements. This may be sound tactics, but may it not mask a definite danger? I think so. Wherefore, so long as the tattered remains of the Granger and Populist movements rally to your standards in the South, we shall have to keep from saying that Socialism stands for the full civic and political equality of all workers at least.

The I. W. W., of course, has no scruples about affirming the full import of its revolutionary doctrine at all times and all places — even in the South. It actually opposes race prejudice, with success, as in Louisiana, where it organized 14,000 black timber workers, together with 18,000 white timber workers, with "mixed" locals, too, in spite of Southern sentiment.

I wonder, now, whether any Socialist, Southern or other, could blame me for throwing in my lot with the I. W. W.

The Labor Movement

Harrison was a strong proponent of working-class struggle and a firm critic of the class-collaborationist policies of the American Federation of Labor, which was presided over by Samuel Gompers (1850–1924). The AFL under Gompers (from 1886 to 1894 and 1896 to

1924) was generally recognized as one of the most conservative labor federations in the world. The organization had a strong base in lily-white construction trade unions and railroad brotherhoods and it, in general, opposed the more all-encompassing industrial unionism advocated by the Industrial Workers of the World. Both the AFL bureaucracy and Gompers, in an effort to prevent job competition with their members, countenanced segregated and racist unions, denied Black unionists charters in federated locals, and facilitated American empire building. As Gompers explained in 1905, "We are not going to let the [white] standard of living be destroyed by Negroes, Chinamen, Japs or any others."[12]

Harrison was critical of the AFL's class collaboration and its racist and exclusionary practices. His criticisms of white supremacy grew in the wake of labor's (and Gompers's) role in the East St. Louis riot of 1917. He later explained that "my long previous acquaintance with the American Federation of Labor did not predispose me to be friendly to its unions. Their policy seemed so constructed that, whereas the white worker could consider his fight for bread to be directed solely against the capitalist, the black worker was opposed by the general run of white working men, who kept him out of their unions for the most part and yet called him 'scab' for getting their jobs at the only time when those jobs were available to him. My attitude on this has been maintained consistently since 1917, when Samuel Gompers assumed at Carnegie Hall, in the face of Colonel [Theodore] Roosevelt, responsibility for the East St. Louis riots on the ground of an alleged necessity for the white unionists to defend their jobs by murder against the Negro workers whom they had shut out of their unions — as Negroes."[13]

In the following 1917 editorial Harrison emphasizes that he had been a member of a party which "stood for the rights of labor and the principle of Industrial Unionism" and that he desired to see the working class victorious, but as editor of *The Voice*, his first duty, was "to the Negro race." In the second piece, written several years later as a book review in the *Negro World*, Harrison elaborates on the duty of white labor to open its ranks and make serious efforts at organizing Black workers.

16. "The Negro and the Labor Unions," *The Voice*, (c. August 1917); reprinted in *When Africa Awakes*, 20–22.

From July 1 to July 3, 1917, East St. Louis, Illinois, suffered the most severe race riots since the Springfield, Illinois, riot (almost a decade earlier) that had led to the formation of the National Association for the Advancement of Colored People. East St. Louis was one of the major industrial sites on the Mississippi River, and its African American population had doubled to almost 13,000 between 1910 and 1917. Due to oppressive conditions in the South (hardships that were intensified by drought, heavy rains, and boll weevils) and war-related production needs, East St. Louis became a destination site of the "Great Migration" north. The city's African American population increased by some 2,400 in 1916 and 1917. Local Democrats attributed the increase to Republicans, whom, they said, were importing Black workers to be used as voters and potential strikebreakers.[14]

In this racially inflamed situation there occurred two series of race riots. In the first, from May 27 to May 30, one African American was killed and hundreds were forced to flee.

The second riots, from July 1 to July 3, were bloody, and the Illinois National Guard was called in. The number of African Americans killed was reported to be from thirty-nine to 250, property damage was at least $373,000, and 244 buildings were totally or partially destroyed. Historian Edward Robb Ellis reports that in the heinous assault Black women were actually scalped and four Black children were slaughtered.[15]

These riots were widely attributed to white labor's opposition to Black workers coming into the labor market, and they were directly precipitated by a car of white joyriders who fired guns into the Black section of the city. Officials of organized labor served as prominent apologists for white labor's role in the rioting. AFL President Gompers placed principal blame for the riots on "the excessive and abnormal number of negroes" in East St. Louis. W. S. Carter, president of the Brotherhood of Locomotive Firemen and Enginemen, added that "evidently the purpose of the railroads in importing Negro labor is to destroy the influence of white men's labor organizations." The House of Representatives established a committee to investigate the riots, and the committee subsequently charged the local police and Illinois National Guard with inadequate riot training, ineptness, indifference, and, in specific instances, supporting the white mobs.[16]

The white-supremacist attitude of AFL President Gompers regarding East St. Louis prompted Harrison to take to task the white AFL labor leadership and elaborate his views on trade unions in the following *Voice* editorial on "The Negro and Labor Unions." Harrison favored the inclusive unionism of the IWW rather than the white supremacy of the AFL and Gompers. As he explained several years later, the Liberty League supported "the program of the advanced labor movement in this country." But, due in large part to government repression, the IWW declined over the next few years, and the League was confronted more frequently by Gompers and the AFL, whom Harrison believed blocked class solidarity. By 1921 the Liberty League would urge the formation of all-Black unions, which would co-operate with white unions when allowed that right.[17]

There are two kinds of labor unionism; the A. F. of L. kind and the other kind. So far, the Negro has been taught to think that all unionism was like the unionism of the American Federation of Labor, and because of this ignorance, his attitude toward organized labor has been that of the scab. For this no member of the A. F. of L. can blame the Negro. The policy of that organization toward the Negro has been damnable. It has kept him out of work and out of the unions as long as it could; and when it could no longer do this it has taken him in, tricked him, and discriminated against him.

On the other hand, the big capitalists who pay low wages (from the son of Abraham Lincoln [Robert Todd Lincoln] in the Pullman Co. to Julius Rosenwald of the Sears Roebuck Co.) have been rather friendly to the Negro. They have given their money to help him build Y. M. C. A.s and schools of a certain type. They have given him community help in Northern cities and have expended charity on him—and on the newspapers and parsons who taught him. Small wonder, then, that the Negro people are anti-union.

Labor unions were created by white working men that they might bring the pressure of many to bear upon the greedy employer and make him give higher wages and better living conditions to the laborer. When they, in turn, become so greedy that they keep out the majority of working people, by high dues and initiation fees, they no longer represent the interests of the laboring class. They stand in the way of this class's advancement — *and they must go*. They must leave the way clear for the 20th century type of unionism which says: "To leave a single worker out is to leave something for the boss to use against us. Therefore we must organize in One Big Union of *all* the working-class." This is the type of unionism which organized, in 1911, 18,000 white and 14,000 black timber workers in Louisiana. This is the I. W. W. type of unionism, and the employers use their newspapers to make the public believe that it stands for anarchy, violence, law-breaking and atheism, because they know that if it succeeds it will break them.

This type of unionism wants Negroes — not because its promoters love Negroes — but because they realize that they cannot win if any of the working class is left out; and after winning they cannot go back on them because they could be used as scabs to break the unions.

The A. F. of L., which claims a part of the responsibility for the East St. Louis outrage, is playing with fire. The American Negro may join hands with the American capitalist and scab them out of existence. And the editor of *The Voice* calls upon Negroes to do this. We have stood the American Federation of Labor just about long enough. Join hands with the capitalists and scab them out of existence — not in the name of scabbery, but in the name of a real organization of labor. From your own unions (the A.C.E. is already in the field) and make a truce with your capitalist enemy until you get rid of this traitor to the cause of labor. Offer your labor to capitalism if it will agree to protect you in your right to labor — and see that it does. Then get rid of the A. F. of L.

The writer has been a member of a party which stood for the rights of labor and the principle of Industrial Unionism (the 20th century kind). He understands the labor conditions of the country and desires to see the working man win out. But his first duty, here as everywhere, is to the Negro race. And he refuses to put ahead of his race's rights a collection of diddering jackasses which can publicly palliate such atrocities as that of East St. Louis and publicly assume, as Gompers did, responsibility for it. Therefore, he issues the advice to the workers of his race to "can the A. F. of L." Since the A. F. of L. chooses to put Race before Class, let us return the compliment.

17. "The Negro in Industry," review of *The Great Steel Strike and Its Lessons* by William Z. Foster, *Negro World* 9 (August 21, 1920): 2, HHHP Scr B.

In August 1920 Harrison published a review of William Z. Foster's *The Great Steel Strike and Its Lessons*. Foster (1881–1961), a former socialist and syndicalist, was one of the outstanding radical labor organizers in the country and would become a leading member of the Communist Party, which he joined around 1921. The steel strike of 1919 was one of the great labor battles of the decade and an important component of Foster's efforts to establish a significant left wing in the American Federation of Labor. The review, with its comments on the role of white workers and their duty to oppose racism, was one of Harrison's more important pieces on the white organized labor movement and African Americans.[18]

The Great Steel Strike and Its Lessons, by William Z. Foster, published by B. W. Huebsch, has already received so many well merited encomiums from periodicals and newspapers of national scope that I don't find it necessary to dwell upon its general excellence. As a first-hand study of the actual machinery of industrial control in one great department of the nation's economical [HH changed this to *economic*] life, it stands almost unrivalled. Any one who has gone through the book will realize that the great trusts which are empowered to organize, arm and equip a military and police of their own, control in addition the political machinery of government, national and state, and utilize this machinery to beat down the opposition of the workers, organized and unorganized. But this has been known in a general way for a long time by all those who cared to take their heads out of the sand of conservatism long enough to look at the actual facts by which they are surrounded.

What we are mainly concerned with is the relation of the Negro worker to the white workers and to this militant machinery of brutal repression. The facts presented by Mr. Foster in the 11th chapter of this serviceable little volume produce the impression that the Negro worker at present is largely hostile to organized labor.

"The indifference, verging often into open hostility with which Negroes largely regard organized labor activities, manifested itself strongly in the steel campaign. Those employed in the industry were extremely resistant to the trade-union program: those on the outside allowed themselves to be used freely as strikebreakers."

He goes on to say that in the Homestead steel works out of 14,000 employees, 1,700 were Negroes. "During the organized campaign, of all these men, only eight joined the union. And of these, but one struck. . . . The degree of this abstention may be gauged when it is recalled that of the white unskilled workers in the same plants, at least 75 per cent. joined the union and 90 per cent. struck. In Duquense, of 344 Negroes employed, not one struck; in Clairton, of 300, six joined the unions and struck for two weeks. Of the several hundred working in the Braddock plants, not one joined the union or went on strike, and a dozen would cover those from the large number employed in the mills in Pittsburgh proper who walked out with the 25,000 white on September 22. Similar tendencies were shown in Chicago, Youngstown, Buffalo, Pueblo, Sparrows' Point, and other districts. In the entire steel industry, the Negroes beyond compare, gave the movement less co-operation than any other element, skilled or unskilled, foreign or native. . . . Those on the outside of the industry seemed equally unsympathetic. National committee secretaries reports indicate that the Steel Trust recruited and shipped from 30,000 to 40,000 Negroes into the mills as strike-breakers. Many of these were picked up in the northern cities, but the most of them came from the South. They were used in all the large districts and were a big factor in breaking the strike. . . . Most of them seemed to take keen delight in stealing the white men's jobs and crushing their strike."

Here is a terrible indictment of the Negroes' failure to respond to the call of labor. But, for this, labor itself is to blame, as Mr. Foster very cheerfully admits further on. He insists that "the unions will have to meet the issue honestly and broad-mindedly. They must open their ranks to Negroes, make an earnest effort to organize them and then give them a square deal when they do join. Nothing short of this will accomplish the desired result." Negroes, therefore, will be at a loss to understand why Mr. Foster should expect that "the best Negro leaders must join heartily in destroying the pernicious anti-union attitude so deeply rooted among their people." It is up to the white unions of the American Federation of Labor and the great railroad brotherhoods themselves and not up to the Negro leaders to change this deep seated aversion which American Negroes have for white American labor. It is conceded on all sides that the white organized labor movement has been and still is pronouncedly anti-Negro. And as long as that remains true, just so long will self-respecting Negro leaders abstain from urging the laboring masses of their race to join forces with the stupid and short-sighted labor oligarchy which refuses to join forces with them.

But, apart from this matter, *The Great Steel Strike and its Lessons* is a book for intelligent, work-a-day Negroes to read. They need to see the photographs of the Pennsylvania Cossacks in brutal action on the streets of Homestead, Gary and other cities They need to look at the pictures of Mrs. Fannie Sellins, trade union organizer, disfigured and shot to death by steel trust gunmen in West Natrona, Pa.; they need to see the forces of respectability marshalled in favor of disorder and violence against white workers whose only crime is the demand that enough of the profits of their labor be deflected into their pockets to enable them to live with the ordinary decency of a common horse or cow. For when the Negro sees this he will know how to estimate properly the lying statements made in newspapers and on pulpits concerning the criminality of the laboring man.

Race Radicalism

I n the period from 1914 to 1916, Harrison developed a "race first" message in response
to the racial oppression of U.S. society and the "white first" attitude of the organized
labor and socialist movements. It was his primary political message when he founded
the Liberty League and *The Voice* in 1917. As Harrison explained to the Socialists: "We
say Race First, because you have all along insisted on [white] Race First and class after
when you didn't need our help."[1]

Over time, Harrison tended to replace his call for "race first" with a call to develop race
consciousness. He considered race consciousness "a protective reaction" under existing
societal conditions and a necessary corrective to white supremacy. It was also a strategic
component in the struggle for a racially just and socialist society. He stressed that as long
as the outer situation remained the same, "we must evoke race-consciousness."[2]

Though the phrases "race first" and "race consciousness" were at times interchangeable,
the call to race consciousness suggested a broader and deeper appeal that was more compatible with class consciousness, was not rigidly determinist, and was more temporal than
"race first."

The Liberty League and *The Voice*

In the "Introductory" to his 1920 book *When Africa Awakes*, Harrison, explained from
an international perspective how the Great War of 1914–1918 helped "to liberate many
ideas undreamt of by those who rushed humanity into that bath of blood." Most important among these ideas was "democracy," which was widely advertised, particularly
in the English-speaking world. It was used, however, as "a convenient camouflage behind
which competing imperialists masked their sordid aims" and those who proclaimed it
loudly didn't intend to extend it; this was demonstrated in the cases of Ireland, India,
Egypt and Russia. The "flamboyant advertising of 'democracy'" returned to plague its
inventors, however, and the subject millions demanded what was advertised. To Harrison,

this desire for democracy, not "'sedition' and Bolshevism," was "the main root" of the "great unrest" that developed.[3]

The most serious aspect of this new unrest, explained Harrison, was the racial one. The white world played with the catchwords of democracy "while ruthlessly ruling an overwhelming majority of black, brown and yellow peoples to whom these catchwords were never intended to apply." But these oppressed millions, having participated in the war "to make the world safe for democracy," now insisted "that democracy shall be made safe for them." Their demands challenged the "international control" of the imperialist white nations and led to a crisis of "white civilization."[4]

In the United States, wrote Harrison, this new situation was reflected "in the mental attitude of the Negro people" who developed a new sense of their own place in the world and "new conceptions of their powers and destiny," which quickened the development of their "race-consciousness." Black people made new demands on themselves and on the world around them, which applied "to politics, domestic and international, to education and culture, [and] to commerce and industry." Interpretations that focused on "the spread of 'Bolshevism' among Negroes" couldn't explain the change in the minds of the people.[5]

In 1916 Harrison began to hammer out some of the ideas of what came to be known as the "New Negro Movement." Then, in the summer of 1917, he launched the movement's first organization, the Liberty League, at a historic June 12 meeting at Harlem's Bethel African Methodist Episcopal Church on West 132nd Street off Lenox Avenue. At the Bethel meeting lynching was the main subject, and particular attention was paid to the recent horrific burning at the stake of Ell Persons amid a public lynching orgy in Memphis, Tennessee. Announcement was also made about the organization's forthcoming newspaper, *The Voice*, to be edited by Harrison. Among the speakers at Bethel was Marcus Garvey, a relatively unknown former printer from Jamaica, who had spent time in Costa Rica and England, and had toured the United States. Within three years of his introduction by Harrison, Garvey would build on Harrison's work and lead what became the largest mass movement of Black people in history up to that time.[6]

In the article that follows Harrison details the early history of the Liberty League.

 18. "The Liberty League of Negro-Americans: How It Came to Be," *The Voice* (July 4, 1917); reprinted in *The Voice* (September 19, 1917), HHHP Wr; and reprinted as "Launching the Liberty League," in *When Africa Awakes*, 9–11.

The Liberty League of Negro-Americans, which was recently organized by the Negroes of New York, presents the most startling program of any organization of Negroes in the country today. This is nothing less than the demand that the Negroes of the United States be given a chance to enthuse over democracy for themselves in America before they are expected to enthuse over democracy in Europe. The League is composed of "Negro-Americans, loyal to their country in every respect, and obedient to her laws."

The League has an interesting history. It grew out of the labors of Mr. Hubert H. Harrison, who has been on the lecture platform for years and is well and favorably known to thousands of New Yorkers from Wall Street to Washington Heights. Two years ago Mr. Harrison withdrew from an international political organization, and, a little more than a year ago, gave up lecturing to white people, to devote himself to lecturing exclusively among his own people. He acquired so much influence among them that when he issued the first call for a mass-meeting "to protest against lynching in the land of liberty and disfranchisement in the home of democracy," although the call was not advertised in any newspaper, the church in which the meeting was held was packed from top to bottom. At this mass meeting, which was held at Bethel Church on June 12, the organization was effected and funds were raised to sustain it and to extend its work all over the country.

Harrison was subsequently elected its president, with Edgar Grey and James Harris as secretary and treasurer, respectively. At the close of this mass-meeting he hurriedly took the mid-night train for Boston, where a call for a similar meeting had been issued by W. Monroe Trotter, editor of *The Boston Guardian*. While there he delivered an address in Faneuil Hall, the cradle of American liberty, and told the Negroes of Boston what their brothers in New York had done and were doing. The result was the linking up of the New York and the Boston organizations, and Harrison was elected chairman of a national committee of arrangements to issue a call to every Negro organization in the country to send delegates to a great race-congress which is to meet in Washington in September or October and put their grievances before the country and Congress.

At the New York mass-meeting money was subscribed for the establishment of a newspaper to be known as *The Voice* and to serve as the medium of expression for the new demands and aspirations of the new Negro. It was made clear that this "New Negro Movement" represented a breaking away of the Negro masses from the grip of old-time leaders — none of whom was represented at the meeting. The audience rose to their feet with cheers when Harrison was introduced by the chairman. The most striking passages of his speech were those in which he demanded that Congress make lynching a Federal crime and take the Negro's life under national protection, and declared that since lynching was murder and a violation of Federal and State laws, it was incumbent upon the Negroes themselves to maintain the majesty of the law and put down the law-breakers by organizing all over the South to defend their own lives whenever their right to live was invaded by mobs which the local authorities were too weak or unwilling to suppress.

The meeting was also addressed by Mr. J[ames]. C. Thomas, Jr., a young Negro lawyer, who pointed out the weakness and subserviency of the old-time political leaders and insisted that Negroes stop begging for charity in the matter of their legal rights and demand justice instead.

[The next two sentences were not in the original — they were inserted in the 1920 version.] Mr. Marcus Garvey, president of the Jamaica Improvement Association, was next introduced by Mr. Harrison. He spoke in enthusiastic approval of the new movement and pledged it his hearty support.

After the Rev. Dr. [A. R.] Cooper, the pastor of Bethel, had addressed the meeting, the following resolutions were adopted and a petition to Congress was prepared and circulated. In addition the meeting sent a telegram to the Jews of Russia, congratulating them upon the acquisition of full political and civil rights and expressing the hope that the United States might soon follow the democratic example of Russia.

19. "Resolutions [Passed at the Liberty League Meeting]," (c. June 12, 1917); reprinted as "Resolutions" in *The Voice* (September 19, 1917); and reprinted as "Resolutions Passed at the Liberty League Meeting," in *The Negro and Nation*, 11–12.

The resolutions, adopted by the Liberty League at the Bethel Church meeting and forwarded to Congress, focused on democratic demands, both international and domestic. The league planned to fight the evils of lynching, disfranchisement, segregation, Jim Crowism and peonage by seeking enforcement of the Thirteenth, Fourteenth, and Fifteenth Amendments and aimed "to protest and to agitate by every legal means," to "create adequate instruments for securing these ends," and to "make our voice heard."

Two thousand Negro-Americans assembled in mass-meeting at Bethel A.M.E. Church to protest against lynching in the land of liberty and disfranchisement in the home of democracy have, after due deliberation, adopted the following resolutions and make them known to the world at large in the earnest hope that whenever the world shall be made safe for democracy our corner of that world will not be forgotten.

We believe that this world war will and must result in a larger measure of democracy for the peoples engaged therein—whatever may be the secret ambitions of their several rulers.

We therefore ask, that when the war shall be ended and the council of peace shall meet to secure to every people the right to rule their own ancestral lands free from the domination of tyrants, domestic and foreign, the similar rights of the 250,000,000 Negroes of Africa be conceded. Not to concede them this is to lay the foundation for more wars in the future and to saddle the new democracies with the burden of a militarism greater than that under which the world now groans. [The emphasis is added in the 1917 reprint.]

Secondly, we, as Negro-Americans who have poured out our blood freely in every war of the Republic, and upheld her flag with undivided loyalty, demand that since we have shared to the full measure of manhood in bearing the burdens of democracy we should also share in the rights and privileges of that democracy.

And we believe that the present time, when the hearts of ninety millions of our white fellow-citizens are aflame with the passionate ardor of democracy which has carried them into the greatest war of the age with the sole purpose of suppressing autocracy in

Europe, is the best time to appeal to them to give to twelve millions of us the elementary rights of democracy at home.

For democracy, like charity, begins at home, and we find it hard to endure without murmur and with the acquiescence of our government the awful evils of lynching, which is a denial of the right to life; of segregation, Jim Crowism and peonage, which are a denial of the right to liberty; and disfranchisement, which is a denial of justice and democracy.

And since Imperial Russia, formerly the most tyrannous government in Europe, has been transformed into Republican Russia, whereby millions of political serfs have been lifted to the level of citizenship rights; since England is offering the meed of political manhood to the hitherto oppressed Irish and the down-trodden Hindu; and since these things have helped to make good the democratic assertions of these countries of the old world now engaged in war;

> Therefore, be it resolved:
>
> That we, the Negro people of the first republic of the New World, ask all true friends of democracy in this country to help us to win these same precious rights for ourselves and our children;
>
> That we invite the government's attention to the great danger which threatens democracy through the continued violation of the 13th, 14th and 15th amendments, which is a denial of justice and the existence of mob-law for Negroes from Florida to New York;
>
> That we intend to protest and to agitate by every legal means until we win these rights from the hands of our government and induce it to protect democracy from these dangers, and square the deeds of our nations with its declarations;
>
> That we create adequate instruments for securing these ends and make our voice heard and heeded in the councils of our country, and
>
> That copies of these resolutions be forwarded to the Congress of the United States and to such other public bodies as shall seem proper to us.

20. "Declaration of Principles [of the Liberty League]," *Clarion* (September 1, 1917); reprinted as "What It Stands For: Declaration of Principles," in *The Voice* (September 19, 1917), HHHP Wr.

Harrison wrote the powerful "Declaration of Principles" of the Liberty League which pledged support "to the program of the manhood movement for Negroes" and "to the elevation of our race as to at least equal standing with any other race." To achieve those goals the declaration put forth its international perspective; focused domestically on lynching, segregation, equal rights, and developing a "political voice"; and proclaimed a special duty to Africa and Africans worldwide. It began, as did so much of Harrison's political analysis, from an international perspective and paid particular attention to the era of "revolutionary ferment all over the world." It also praised and cited the Irish Home Rule struggle as it called on its own members to "be loyal to our race first in everything."

The directness of the challenge posed by the declaration's Prohibition analogy is striking. The South, which was the home of lynching and of "states' rights," was also home to strong Prohibition sentiment against the sale and use of alcohol. The logic of the Prohibition argument (federal intervention) directly challenged the logic of the southern argument (states' rights) that was used to oppose federal antilynching legislation.[7]

The Liberty League Declaration also called for direct action and armed self-defense. Harrison, a longtime proponent of direct action, recognized that Southern Blacks decreased lynching by the direct action of migrating North. Black migration "struck a body blow at the most powerful interests in the South" and "compelled them to exert their influence against lynching," he later wrote. The ultimate form of direct action, however, was armed self-defense, and Harrison argued that with Black life no longer cheap, "the cure follows from the nature of the cause."[8]

Two of the declaration's comments on democracy are of special interest. First, it describes the "essence of democracy" by quoting President Woodrow Wilson's war message to Congress on "the right of those who submit to authority to have a voice in their own government." Second, the declaration indicates the Liberty League's support for women's suffrage (prior to passage of the Nineteenth Amendment) by stating its aim to organize "to secure the ballot for every adult Negro man or woman who owe[s] allegiance to our flag and who obey[s] our country's laws."

The Liberty League, in June 1917, also adopted a black, brown, and yellow tricolor flag because of the "Negroes'" "dual relationship to our own and other peoples" and because the colors were "symbolic of the three colors of the Negro race in America." It was from this tricolor that Marcus Garvey would later, according to Harrison, draw the idea for the red, black, and green tricolor racial flag, which the UNIA popularized, and which later became identified as Black liberation colors.[9]

DECLARATION OF PRINCIPLES
(Drawn up by Hubert H. Harrison, President of the League)

The Liberty League of Negro-Americans was born of the great World War into which Europe entered in 1914 and the United States in 1917.

Whatever the compelling causes of this conflict may have been, the participants on that side which our country has embraced are all declaring at the present time that they are fighting "to make the world safe for democracy" [and] out of this welter of war will come democracy — the right of every people to rule their own ancestral lands, free from the domination of tyrants, domestic and foreign. And this result will be attained no matter what the will of the rulers and spokesmen on either side may be. Already the Russian people, the Irish and the Hindu have seized the moment to strike for the realizing of those ideals which their respective governments professed.

The Negro people of America feel that this is the right time to make a bold bid for some of that democracy for which their government has gone to war. They insist that the constant recurrence of horrible lynchings, where perpetrators go unpunished, and the status of disfranchisement for ten millions of Negroes living in the Southern Section of this land, can not be reconciled with any idea of liberty or democracy. And the Liberty League came into existence to voice not merely their protest, but the demand that this nation of which they are a part shall first abolish the twin evils of lynching and disfranchisement at home before it can expect the world to take seriously its professions of democracy.

This is the era of revolutionary ferment all over the world, and we realize that we, too, are living in the world. Not to voice our demands for equal justice, protection and opportunity at this time, would be to brand ourselves as the only people in the world who are quite fit for serfdom.

The first right of all men is their right to their lives. This elementary right is denied us by mobs of our white fellow-citizens all over this land, with the continuing consent of the national government which has never taken a single step to discourage and put down lynching; and with the active connivance of state and county authorities in the south where the greater portion of our people live.

The Liberty League, in the face of such conditions, demands, and will continue to work for, the enactment by the U.S. Congress of such legislation as will make lynching a Federal Crime, and thus take the Negroes of America under national protection, pending the granting to them of universal adult suffrage. This can be done if the nation has the will to do it.

The nation invades the domain of state to put down the illicit distilling of whiskey. It wants the enforcement of the revenue laws and therefore will not trust such cases to the local prejudices of a local court and jury. It makes illicit whiskey distilling a federal offense. The lives of its Negro subjects are worth more to the government than the revenues saved by the putting down of moonshiners; if the national government can override the state government for the raising of revenues, it can and should override them for the protection of life. We therefore demand that the Congress pass laws making lynching a federal crime punishable by the Federal Courts which shall have exclusive jurisdiction, thus taking the Negro subjects of the country under the direct protection of the same flag which is powerful to protect foreign born white citizens even when residing in China or Armenia.

But if the national government should refuse to take any steps to protect its Negro people from murderous mob-violence, then we should call upon our people to defend themselves against murder with the weapons of murder.

The essence of democracy today is, as president Wilson says, "the right of those who submit to authority to have a voice in their own government." It is only those who intend to tyrannize who deny this right to those over whom they rule. The Liberty League is organized to secure the ballot for every adult Negro man or woman who owe allegiance to our flag and who obey our country's laws.

The continued violation of the 14th and 15th amendment to the U.S. Constitution with the consent of the national government constituted the gravest menace to stability of that government. For it accustoms some of the people to despise that portion of the organic law which they are encouraged to override. And if they despise any portion of it to-day, what guarantee has the government that they will respect any portion of it to-morrow? We therefore, call upon the Negro people of America to join hands in an effort to have all parts of the constitution equally enforced, as the first step toward the securing of absolutely equal political rights.

And we go even further than this. We ask the Negroes of the North, who have the ballot, to disclaim allegiance to any and all political parties; to organize their votes independently, and by swinging them in their own interest, to play the same part which the Irish Home Rule party played in British politics. We must be loyal to our race first in everything.

But the Liberty League has an international as well as a national duty to the seventeen hundred millions [who] are colored—black and brown and yellow. We cannot look without concern upon the struggle of this great majority, of which we are a part, to live their lives free from the domination of a minority, howsoever good or wise. The Liberty League therefore stands ready to affiliate itself with similar organizations of the darker races in other lands; to sympathize with their just aims and afford them such aid as may be within its power. With the 250 millions of our brethren in Africa we feel a special sympathy, and we will work for the ultimate realization of democracy in Africa —for the right of these darker millions to rule their own ancestral lands—even as the people of Europe—free from the domination of foreign tyrants.

Because of the dual relationship to our own and other peoples, we have adopted as our emblem the three colors, black brown and yellow, in perpendicular stripes.

We pledge ourselves to the program of the manhood movement for Negroes; to the elevation of our race as to at least equal standing with any other race.

21. "The Liberty League's Petition to the House of Representatives of the United States, July 4, 1917," reprinted in *When Africa Awakes*, 12–13.

The Liberty League's Petition to the House of Representatives focused on the need for federal antilynching legislation and federal action to ensure suffrage rights in the South. The significance of the antilynching demand should not be underestimated. It was a notable departure from the position taken by the nation's leading civil rights organization, the National Association for the Advancement of Colored People. from 1918 to 1922, the NAACP refused to call for such legislation while it sought southern support. Its president and principal legal adviser, Moorfield Storey, repeatedly raised constitutionality issues to federal legislation and in so doing conceded considerable ground to the states' rights arguments of the South. The historian Robert L. Zangrando explains that after Congressman Leonidas Dyer (D., Mo.) asked the NAACP to sponsor a bill making lynching a federal crime in March 1918, its Board of Directors explored various options in May and "[t]he NAACP actually declined to make an open push for such legislation" on the grounds that it was "not constitutional as written and could not, even if revised, be made so." This position relied heavily on the advice of Storey, "who at the time took a very conservative, traditional position." The NAACP followed Storey's advice and muted its lobbying role for an antilynching bill.[10]

We, the Negro people of the United States, loyal to our country in every respect, and obedient to her laws, respectfully petition your honorable body for a redress of the specific grievances and flagrant violations of your own laws as set forth in this statement.

We beg to call your attention to the discrepancy which exists between the public profession of government that we are lavishing our resources of men and money in this war in order to make the world safe for democracy, and the just as public performances of lynching-bees, Jim Crowism and disfranchisement in which our common country abounds.

We should like to believe in our government's profession of democracy, but find it hard to do so in the presence of the facts; and we judge that millions of other people outside of the country will find it just as hard.

Desirous, therefore, of squaring our country's profession with her performance, that she may not appear morally contemptible in the eyes of friends and foes alike, we, the Negro people of the United States, who have never been guilty of any disloyalty or treason to our government, demand that the nation shall justify to the world her assertions of democracy by setting free the millions of Negroes in the South from political and civil slavery through the enactment of laws which will either take the Negroes under the direct protection of the U.S. Congress by making lynching a Federal crime, or (by legislative mandate) compelling of several States which now deprive the Negroes of their right to self-government, to give them the suffrage as Russia has done for her Jews. We ask this in the name of the American declaration that the world shall be made safe for democracy and fervently pray that your honorable body will not go back upon democracy.

East St. Louis, Houston, and Armed Self-Defense

National attention was drawn to the Liberty League's July 4, 1917, rally at the Metropolitan Baptist Church by Harrison's bold call for armed self-defense and the appearance of the first edition of *The Voice: A Newspaper for the New Negro*. The rally to celebrate "Liberty's Birthday" (July 4th) and to protest lynching and disfranchisement came on the heels of the racist pogrom in East St. Louis, Illinois on July 1–3, 1917 (see selection 16), and following a racist flare-up in the San Juan Hill section of New York on July 3. The *New York Times* reported that a thousand Black men and women were present at the rally and enthusiastically cheered the speakers who were "all Negroes." Each speaker reportedly denounced the East St. Louis rioters as ruthless murderers and each condemned the authorities for not protecting citizens and preventing the atrocities.[11]

The call for armed self-defense made in the following *Voice* editorial was characteristic of much of Harrison's work in 1917. He had already, on several occasions, made clear his belief in the need to fight back in defense of lives and community. This attitude has been decribed by the historian Robert A. Hill as "the touchstone of the new black militancy." On June 12 at the Bethel Church meeting Harrison had called for retaliatory violence, and he did so again on June 13 in Boston. To Hill this was "especially noteworthy" because it "was *uttered* before the outrages committed against blacks in the East St. Louis riot."[12]

 22. "The East St. Louis Horror," *The Voice* (July 4, 1917); reprinted in *New Negro* 4, no.1 (September 1919): 8; and reprinted in *When Africa Awakes*, 14–16.

In the East St. Louis editorial Harrison praised the African American community for fighting back and called for an economic boycott and armed self-defense. He also ominously warned that "Unbeknown to the white people of this land a temper is being developed among Negroes with which the American people will have to reckon." The original article has numerous typographical errors, so the *When Africa Awakes* version is used here.

This nation is now at war to make the world "safe for democracy," but the Negro's contention in the court of public opinion is that until this nation itself is made safe for twelve million of its subjects the Negro, at least, will refuse to believe in the democratic assertions of the country. The East St. Louis pogrom gives point to this contention. Here, on the eve of the celebration of the Nation's birthday of freedom and equality, the white people, who are denouncing the Germans as Huns and barbarians, break loose in an orgy of unprovoked and villainous barbarism which neither Germans nor any other civilized people have ever equalled.

How can America hold up its hands in hypocritical horror at foreign barbarism while the red blood of the Negro is clinging to those hands? So long as the President and Congress of the United States remain dumb in the presence of barbarities in their own land which would tip their tongues with righteous indignation if they had been done in Belgium, Ireland, or Galicia?

And what are the Negroes to do? Are they expected to re-echo with enthusiasm the patriotic protestations of the boot-licking leaders whose pockets and positions testify to the power of the white man's gold? Let there be no mistake. Whatever the Negroes may be compelled by law to do and say, the resentment in their hearts will not down. Unbeknown to the white people of this land a temper is being developed among Negroes with which the American people will have to reckon.

At the present moment it takes this form: If white men are to kill unoffending Negroes, Negroes must kill white men in defense of their lives and property. This is the lesson of the East St. Louis massacre.

The press reports declare that "the troops who were on duty during the most serious disturbances were ordered not to shoot." The civil and military authorities are evidently winking at the work of the mobs — horrible as that was — and the Negroes of the city need not look to them for protection. They must protect themselves. And even the United States Supreme Court concedes them this right.

There is, in addition, a method of retaliation which we urge upon them. It is one which will hit those white men who have the power to prevent lawlessness just where they will feel it most, in the place where they keep their consciences — the pocket-book. Let every Negro in East St. Louis and the other cities where race rioting occurs draw his money from the savings-bank and either bank it in the other cities or in the postal savings bank. The only part of the news reports with which we are well pleased is that which states that the property loss is already estimated at a million and a half dollars.

Another reassuring feature is the one suppressed in most of the news despatches. We refer to the evidences that the East St. Louis Negroes organized themselves during the riots and fought back under some kind of leadership. We Negroes will never know, perhaps, how many whites were killed by our enraged brothers in East St. Louis. It isn't the news-policy of the white newspapers (whether friendly or unfriendly) to spread such news broadcast. It might teach Negroes too much. But we will hope for the best.

The occurrence should serve to enlarge rapidly the membership of the Liberty League of Negro-Americans which was organized to take practical steps to help our people all over the land in the protection of their lives and liberties.

 23. "Houston vs. Waco," *The Voice* (August 28, 1917), HHHP Wr.

Less than two months after the East St. Louis riots, Harrison wrote another fiery editorial after an August 23 incident in Houston, Texas. Seasoned regular troops of the United States Army's Twenty-fourth Infantry, Third Battalion, were stationed in Houston while they built nearby Camp Logan. The soldiers, Black men from North and South, faced Jim Crow regulations so strict that they resisted: they refused to be segregated in theaters and streetcars, to drink from separate water barrels in camp, and to be denied the dignity their service and their military status should have commanded. The city of Houston responded through its police force and the soldiers were repeatedly insulted, beaten, and arrested.[13]

On August 23 a Black soldier intervened as a white policeman beat a Black woman. The soldier was then beaten and arrested, and when Corporal Charles Baltimore of the Third

Battalion went to inquire, he, too, was beaten and arrested, and the rumor quickly spread that he was killed. Pitched battles ensued between Black soldiers and white police and armed white civilians. Two Black soldiers and seventeen whites, including five policemen, were killed.

Soldiers of the Twenty-fourth Regiment were disarmed and immediately arrested; sixty-four were subjected to "the largest court-martial in American military history." The trial lasted twenty-two days, included 169 prosecution and twenty-seven defense witnesses, and filled 2,100 typed transcript pages. The results were thirteen death sentences, forty-two life sentences, four long prison terms, and five acquittals.[14]

At 7:17 A.M. on the morning of December 11, before their sentences were publicly announced, thirteen of the men (who sang a hymn on the way to the gallows) were summarily and secretly hanged. The army then tried an additional fifty-five soldiers in two more courts-martial; sixteen more were sentenced to hang (six did), and twelve to life in prison. The African American community was incensed — especially since the December 11 hangings were in private, before the public knew of the verdicts, and before the president or the secretary of war had reviewed and given approval to the decision. Community pressure eventually saved ten of those sentenced to death; their sentences commuted to life in prison. Immediately after this event, racist white Southern sentiment against the stationing of Black troops in the South reached new highs.[15]

In this editorial, written shortly after the killings but before the courts-martial, Harrison compared the Houston incident to one in Waco, Texas, in the year before. On May 8, 1916, fifteen hundred white people had expressed enjoyment as a mentally handicapped Black adolescent, Jesse Washington, was castrated and had his eyes gouged out and his ears and fingers cut off in a public square before being burned to death in an iron cage that was repeatedly lowered into flames in the presence of "thousands of white women and children" and the mayor and other city officials.[16]

> Houston and Waco are both in Texas, and both have had killings. At the Waco killing 15,000 people enjoyed themselves while a helpless Negro was put in an iron cage and roasted to death. His eyes were gouged out, and nameless horrible mutilation was practiced on him before thousands of white women and children.
>
> Just about a year later comes the Houston killing. In this one, whites were the sufferers and Negroes the perpetrators. While the first killing was being staged, Negro soldiers were dying at Carizal, Mexico, in defence of Texas. Today those Negro soldiers are in Texas, and they have staged a killing on their own account.
>
> Both killings were illegal. But every fool knows that the spirit of lawlessness, mob-violence and race hatred which found expression in the first was the thing which called forth the second. Negro soldiers (disguise it how we will) must always be a menace to any state which lynches Negro civilians.
>
> How true are Lincoln's words:
>
> "The Almighty has his own purposes. . . . Fondly do we hope, fervently do we pray, that the terrible scourge of war may speedily pass away. Yet if God wills that it continue

until all the wealth piled by the bondman's two hundred and fifty years of unrequited toil shall be sunk, and until every drop of blood drawn with the lash shall be paid by another drawn with the sword, as was said three thousand years ago, so, still it must be said, that the judgments of the Lord are true and righteous altogether."

The *New Negro*

From August through October 1919, Harrison edited the short-lived monthly magazine, the *New Negro*, which was "intended as an organ of the international consciousness of the darker races — especially of the Negro race" and aimed to "be for Negro-America what *The Nation* is for white America." The magazine's major editorials and articles were written by Harrison and foreshadowed those he would write for Garvey's *Negro World* when he became the de facto managing editor of that paper in January 1920.

 24. "As the Currents Flow," *New Negro* 3, no. 7 (August 1919): 3–4.

In the August 1919 *New Negro* Harrison's "As the Currents Flow" column offered paragraphs of commentary on domestic events. Writing in the wake of the resistance shown by the Black community during the Chicago and Washington, D.C. race riots of July and August 1919, he offered a description of the New Negro, stated that the New Negro was "identifying . . . with every progressive and radical movement," and posited that "the New Negro spirit" was "a *fait accompli*." Though he considered the riots "tragical," he noted that the Black community armed and fought back in self-defense in both cities and he deemed these actions "brilliant events in the history of the Negro race in America." In the Washington riot (July 19–22) the African American community armed on July 21, and that night fifteen people were killed: six white policemen, one white marine, and three white and five Black civilians. In the week-long Chicago riot, which began on July 27 and was provoked in large part by the hostility of white workers, at least fifteen white and twenty-three Black people were killed, and 537 people were injured. In both cities, the postwar spirit of militancy, particularly among returning Black soldiers, was unmistakable.[17]

During the past fortnight great events have taken place. The race battles in Washington and Chicago, although tragical, are nevertheless to be recorded as brilliant events in the history of the Negro race in America. It is most gratifying for us to note that the New Negro spirit is a *fait accompli*. It has found an abode in the hearts of all the truly liberty-loving and progressive Negroes. It has been too long the practice of the Southern Negro victim to beg and plead for mercy at the hands of a sordid mob. We have often wondered why these men, at the first sign of trouble, do not arm themselves preparatory for self-defence. If they are to die at the hands of a "legalized" mob, then it is up to them to sell their lives as dearly as possible. The white man must be made to take his own medicine so that he may learn to appreciate its disagreeable and disgusting flavor. . . .

The white press of this country has noted that the Negro American has entered a new epoch in the history of his country. The baneful effects of the lessons forced upon him during his period as a chattel slave is wearing off. The New Negro — unlike the Negro of the "old conservative crowd" who is ever willing to compromise everything that is held dear to his race in order to obtain for himself a miserable pittance and some sympathy from his former master — is identifying himself with every progressive and radical movement; he is uncompromising and non-partisan, as the *New York World* stated in an editorial a part of which we reproduce here:

> There are enough points of friction between the races without introducing party. The Negro owes nothing to any party. He has been abandoned by all of them, most notably by the Republicans, who in 1877 TRADED HIS RIGHTS AT THE SOUTH TO PERFECT THE TITLE OF A STOLEN PRESIDENCY. Colored men assuming to lead their people should know this by this time that the political and incidentally the legal privileges conferred upon them can never be enjoyed so long as they are the mere chattels of a party. . . .

The New Negro is Negro first, Negro last, and Negro always. He needs not the white man's sympathy; all he is asking for is equal justice before the law and equal opportunity in the battle of life. He needs and asks for no special privileges that are not granted to the other races; he is not a weakling. He has proven his physical strength as well as his intellectual equality which enables him to live both as a savage among savages and as the most cultured and civilized being among those who profess to have reached that stage of life. . . .

That stuff about "he who humbleth himself shall be exalted" is being left untouched by him in the book in which it is written, so that the Anglo-Saxon and other allied mixtures, may use it to their hearts' content and gratification. Then there is the other stuff about turning the left cheek to the assailant after the right cheek has been smitten. There can be no stronger proof of the positive rejection of this unmanly teaching than the expositions of the New Negro spirit during the recent royal racial battles in Washington — the most cultured and civilized city in the world — and Chicago. . . .

"An eye for an eye, a tooth for a tooth," and sometimes two eyes or a half dozen teeth for one is the aim of the New Negro. Since life is sweet, our first object is to preserve life. If any one is to be killed let it be the other fellow as self-preservation is the first law of nature. Render good for evil? Bah! it is not practical among christianized hypocrites, and furthermore, that is the kind of argument the fellow who does the evil puts forward. Why? Because he fears retaliation. That is what the conservative and reactionary white press has discovered, and much space is now dedicated to its discussion. But while editorials are written, many of which we have produced in this issue, singing the praises of the Negro, the news and reports concerning him occupy the front page, are, in the majority of cases, biased, discreditable, and heartrending.

Who is foolish enough to assume that with 239,000 colored men in uniform from the Southern states alone, as against 370,000 white men, the blacks whose manhood and patriotism were thus recognized and tested are forever to be flogged, lynched, burned at the stake, and chased into concealment whenever Caucasian desperadoes are moved to engage in these infamous pastimes?

It is a dreadful thing to see a man of ideals and principles desert them and reveal his traitorous soul to public scorn and contempt, in order that he may serve a master.

25. "Our Larger Duty," *New Negro* 3 (August 1919): 5, reprinted in *When Africa Awakes*, 100–104.

In the first issue of the *New Negro* that he edited, Harrison indicated the importance that internationalism played in his worldview. In "Our Larger Duty," he emphasized that "before the Negroes of the Western world can play any effective part they must first acquaint themselves with what is taking place in the larger world whose millions are in motion." He explained that the "superior[ity]" of the white race was due to "its control of the physical force of the world — ships, guns, soldiers, money and other resources," not to anything innate. Harrison also put forth the view that the "cant of 'democracy'" was "intended as dust in the eyes of white voters" and that "as long as the Color Line exists, all the perfumed protestations of Democracy on the part of the white race" were "simply downright lying." Harrison saw the lack of democracy and the "similarity of suffering on the part of colored folk" throughout the world as giving rise to an international revolutionary ferment.[18]

The problem of the twentieth century is the problem of the Color Line. But what is the Color Line? It is the practice of the theory that the colored and "weaker" races of the earth shall not be free to follow "their own way of life and of allegiance," but shall live, work and be governed after such fashion as the dominant white race may decide. Consider for a moment the full meaning of this fact. Of the seventeen hundred million people that dwell on our earth today more than twelve hundred million are colored — black and brown and yellow. The so-called white race is, of course, the superior race. That is to say, it is on top by virtue of its control of the physical force of the world — ships, guns, soldiers, money and other resources. By virtue of this control England rules and robs India, Egypt, Africa and the West Indies; by virtue of this control we of the United States can tell Haytians, Hawaiians, Filipinos, and Virgin Islanders how much they shall get for their labor and what shall be done in their lands; by virtue of this control Belgium can still say to the Congolese whether they shall have their hands hacked off or their eyes gouged out — and all without any reference to what Africans, Asiatics or other inferior members of the world's majority may want.

It is thus clear that, as long as the Color Line exists, all the perfumed protestations of Democracy on the part of the white race must be simply downright lying. The cant of "Democracy" is intended as dust in the eyes of white voters, incense on the alter of their own self-love. It furnishes bait for the clever statesmen who hold the destinies of their people in their hands when they go fishing for suckers in the waters of public discussion. But it becomes more and more apparent that Hindus, Egyptians, Africans, Chinese and Haytians have taken the measure of this cant and hypocrisy. And, whatever the white world may think, it will have these peoples to deal with during the twentieth century.

In dealing with them in the past it has been considered sufficient that the white man should listen to his own voice alone in determining what colored peoples should have; and he has, therefore, been trying perpetually to "solve" the problems arising from his own assumptions of the role of God. The first and still the simplest method was to kill them off, either by slaughter pure and simple, as in the case of the American Indians and the Congo natives, or by forcibly changing their mode of life, as was done by the pious prudes who killed off the Tasmanians; or by importing among them rum, guns, whiskey and consumption, as has been attempted in the case of the Negroes of Africa and North America. But unlike the red Indians and Tasmanians, most of these subject peoples have refused to be killed off. Their vitality is too strong.

The later method derives itself into internal and external treatment. The internal treatment consists of making them work, to develop the resources of their ancestral lands, not for themselves, but for their white over-lords, so that the national and imperial coffers may be filled to overflowing, while the Hindu ryot, on six cents a day, lives down to the level of the imperialist formula:

> "The poor benighted Hindoo,
> He does the best he kin do;
> He never aches
> For chops and steaks
> And for clothes he makes his skin do."

The external treatment consists of girdling them with forts and battleships and holding armies in readiness to fly at their throats upon the least sign of "uppishness" or "impudence."

Now this similarity of suffering on the part of colored folk has given, and is giving, rise to a certain similarity of sentiment. Egypt has produced the Young Egypt movement; India, the Swadesha, the All-India Congress, and the present revolutionary movement which has lit the fuse of the powder-keg on which Britain sits in India today; Africa has her Ethiopian Movement which ranges from the Zulus and Hottentots of the Cape to the Ekoi of Nigeria; in short, the darker races, chafing under the domination of the alien whites, are everywhere showing a disposition to take Democracy at its word and to win some measure of it — for themselves.

What part in this great drama of the future are the Negroes of the Western world to play? The answer is on the knees of the gods, who often make hash of the predictions of men. But it is safe to say that, before the Negroes of the Western World can play any effective part they must first acquaint themselves with what is taking place in the larger world whose millions are in motion. They must keep well informed of the trend of that motion and of its range and possibilities. If our problem here is really a part of a great world-wide problem, we must make our attempts to solve our part [and] link up with the attempts being made elsewhere to solve the other parts. So will we profit by a wider experience and perhaps be able to lend some assistance to that ancient Mother Land of ours to whom we may fittingly apply the words of Milton:

> "Methinks I see in my mind a mighty and puissant nation, rousing herself like a strong man after sleep and shaking her invincible locks; methinks I see her like an eagle mewing her mighty youth and kindling her undazzled eyes at the full noonday beam; methinks I see her scaling and improving her sight at the fountain itself of heavenly radiance, while the whole noise of timorous and flocking birds—with them also that love the twilight—hover around, amazed at what she means, and in their useless gabble would prognosticate a year of sects and schisms."

26. "The Need for It [and The Nature of It]," *New Negro* 4, no. 1 (September 1919): 1.

The September 1919 issue of the *New Negro* provided a fuller editorial statement of the magazine's purpose and scope. This lead editorial by Harrison discussed why "Negro-Americans" needed to develop "racial consciousness," understand world events, and have a publication which served their interests.

The meeting and mingling of the darker peoples on the plains of France under stress of war has served to bring more clearly before the minds of Negro-Americans these three things:

(1) The need and value of extending racial consciousness beyond the bounds of the white countries in which we find ourselves.

(2) That the basis of such extension must be found in a common current knowledge of the facts and happenings of the international world, especially in so far as they affect the status and welfare of the darker races and of subject peoples everywhere.

(3) That, as a people, we Negro Americans need to know and understand events and their trend; we need a publication which will not only chronicle events of world-importance, but will also interpret them for us in the light of our own race's intents and aims, and keeps us at the same time in touch with the interpretation put on these world events by the controlling culture of the white world.

The Nature of It

As things stand now, such a service can not be rendered by a weekly newspaper. What we need is a monthly which will be in touch with colored writers in Asia, South Africa, West Africa, Egypt, Europe, America and the West Indies. Only so can it render effective aid in molding international consciousness of the darker races.

Such a journal will contain, first and foremost N E W S —not a mere reprint of newspaper articles and items, but well-digested summaries of the world's news of the month in so far as it has special significance for the darker races. These summaries will be at the same time presentation and interpretation—after the manner of *The Nation*. In short, *The New Negro* must be for Negro-America what *The Nation* is for white America.

It will carry every month special articles written mainly by colored men—articles giving information, and articles furnishing interpretation, simple, clear and enlightening. By this means its readers will receive all the different currents of ideas that flow into the sea of racial consciousness.

 27. "Two Negro Radicalisms," *New Negro* n.s. 4 (October 1919): 4–5, reprinted with revisions and minus second and third last paragraphs as "The Negro's Own Radicalism" in *When Africa Awakes*, 76–79.

One of Harrison's most important *New Negro* editorials was his "Two Negro Radicalisms" in the October 1919 issue. It identified the cause of the New Negro radicalism not in socialism or Bolshevism, but in the theory and practice of the color line. In response, it put forth a plea for developing race-conscious radicalism. In addition, for the first time, Harrison publicly discussed Marcus Garvey and stated that the key to Garvey's success was that he effectively publicized that which had been advocated by *The Voice* and the Liberty League. This editorial, along with one on "Negro Culture and the Negro College" (selection 35), set the stage for the joint work that would take place between Garvey and Harrison beginning in January 1920.

Harrison's three most important paragraphs were the last three—the first two of which did not appear in later reprints of the editorial. In these last paragraphs he explained the dual nature of race consciousness, that Garvey's mass appeal was due to his Liberty League-like call to "racialism, race-consciousness, racial solidarity," and that the new awakening was due to race consciousness, not to the less appealing, more purely class radicalism of the Black socialists (such as A. Philip Randolph and Chandler Owen).

Twenty years ago all Negroes known to the white publicists of America could be classed as conservatives on all the great questions on which thinkers differ. In matters of industry, commerce, politics, religion, they could be trusted to take the backward view. Only on the question of the Negro's "rights" could a small handful be found bold enough to be tagged as "radicals"—and they were howled down by both the white and colored adherents of the conservative point of view. Today Negroes differ on all those great questions on which white thinkers differ, and there are Negro radicals of every imaginable stripe — agnostics, atheists, I. W. W.'s, Socialists, Single Taxers, and even Bolshevists.

In the good old days white people derived their knowledge of what Negroes were doing from those Negroes who were nearest to them, generally their own selected exponents of Negro activity or of their white point of view. A classic illustration of this kind of knowledge was afforded by the Republican Party; but the Episcopal Church, the Urban League, or the U.S. Government would serve as well. To-day the white world is vaguely, but disquietingly, aware that Negroes are awake, different and perplexingly uncertain. Yet the white world by which they are surrounded retains its traditional method of interpreting the mass by the Negro nearest to themselves in affiliation or contact. The Socialist party thinks that the "unrest" now apparent in the Negro masses is due to the propaganda which its adherents support, and believes that it will function largely along the lines of socialist political thought. The great dailies, concerned mainly with their chosen task of being the mental bellwethers of the mob, scream "Bolshevist propaganda" and flatter themselves that they have found the true cause; while the government's unreliable agents envisage it as "disloyalty." The truth, as usual, is to be found in the depths: but they are all prevented from going by mental laziness and that traditional off-handed, easy contempt with which white men in America, from scholars like Lester Ward to scavengers like [Archibald E.] Stevenson, deign to consider the colored population of 12 millions.

In the first place the cause of the "radicalism" among American Negroes is international. But it is necessary to cause clear distinctions at the outset. The function of the Christian church is international. So is art, war, the family, rum and exploitation of labor. But none of these is entitled to extend the mantle of its own peculiar "internationalism" to cover the present case of the Negro discontent — although this has been attempted. The international Fact to which Negroes in America are now reacting is not the exploitation of laborers by capitalists; but the social, political and economic subjection of colored peoples by white. It is not the Class Line, but the Color Line, which is the incorrect but accepted expression for the Dead Line of racial inferiority. This fact is a fact of Negro consciousness as well as a fact of externals. The international Color Line is the practice and theory of that doctrine which holds that the best stocks of Africa, China, Egypt and the West Indies are inferior to the worst stocks of Belgium, England, and Italy, and must hold their lives, lands and liberties upon such terms and conditions as the white races may choose to grant them.

On the part of the whites, the motive was originally economic; but it is no longer purely so. All the available facts go to prove that, whether in the United States or in Africa or China, the economic subjection is without exception keener and more brutal when the exploited are black, brown and yellow, than when they are white. And the fact that black, brown, and yellow also exploit each other brutally whenever Capitalism has created the economic classes of plutocrat and proletarian should suffice to put purely economic subjection out of court as the prime cause of racial unrest. For the similarity of suffering has produced in all lands where whites rule colored races a certain similarity of sentiment, viz.: a racial revulsion of racial feeling. The peoples of those lands begin to feel and realize that they are so subjected because they are members of races condemned as "inferior" by their Caucasian overlords. The fact presented to their minds is one of race, and in terms of race do they react to it. Put the case to any Negro by way of test and the answer will make this clear.

The great World War, by virtue of its great advertising campaign for democracy and the promises which were held out to subject peoples, fertilized the Race Consciousness of the Negro people into the stage of conflict with the dominant white idea of the Color Line. They took democracy at its face value — which is — Equality. So did the Hindus, Egyptians, and West Indians. This is what the hypocritical advertisers of democracy had not bargained for. The American Negroes, like the other darker peoples, are presenting their checques and trying to "cash in," and delays in that process, however unavoidable to the paying tellers, are bound to beget a plentiful lack of belief in either their intention or in their ability to pay. Hence the run on Democracy's bank — "the Negro unrest" of the newspaper paragraphers.

This Race Consciousness takes many forms, some negative, others positive. On the one hand we balk at Jim Crow, object to educational starvation, refuse to accept goodwill for good deeds, and scornfully reject our conservative leaders. On the other hand, we are seeking racial independence in business and reaching out into new fields of endeavor. One of the most taking enterprises at present is the Black Star Line, a steamship enterprise being floated by Mr. Marcus Garvey of New York. Garvey's project (whatever may be its ultimate fate) has attracted tens of thousands of Negroes. Where Negro "radicals" of the type known to white radicals can scarce get a handful of people, Garvey fills the largest halls and the Negro people rain money on him. This is not to be explained by the argument of "superior brains," for this man's education and intelligence are markedly inferior to those of the brilliant "radicals" whose "internationalism" is drawn from other than racial sources. But this man holds up to the Negro masses those things which bloom in their hearts — racialism, race-consciousness, racial solidarity — things taught first in 1917 by *THE VOICE* and The Liberty League. That is the secret of his success so far.

All over this land and in the West Indies Negroes are responding to the call of battle against the white man's Color Line. And, so long as this remains, the international dogma of the white race, so long will the new Negro war against it. This is the very Ethiopianism which England has been combatting from Cairo to the Cape.

Undoubtedly some of these newly-awakened Negroes will take to Socialism and Bolshevism. But here again the reason is racial. Since they suffer racially from the world as at present organized by the white race, some of their ablest hold that it is "good play" to encourage and give aid to every subversive movement within that white world which makes for its destruction "as it is." For by its subversion they have much to gain and nothing to lose. But they build on their own foundations. Parallel with the dogma of Class-Consciousness they run the dogma of Race-Consciousness. And they dig deeper. For the roots of Class-consciousness inhere in a temporary economic order; whereas the roots of Race-consciousness must of necessity survive any and all changes in the economic order. Accepting biology as a fact, their view is the more fundamental. At any rate, it is that view with which the white world will have to deal.

28. "The Women of Our Race," *New Negro* 4 (October 1919): 6–7; reprinted in *When Africa Awakes*, 89–91.

In the October 1919 *New Negro*, Harrison wrote about Black women, and praised their "native grace," "greater beauty," "fire and passion," and "charm." Though the tone is one of laudatory "esthetic appreciation," the article appears to be addressed primarily to men. At times Harrison accepted a double standard — viewing, studying, thinking, and writing being viewed as men's work and home responsibilities and beauty as women's concerns.[19]

America owes much to the foreigner and the Negro in America owes even more. For it was the white foreigner who first proclaimed that the only music which America had produced that was worthy of the name was Negro music. It naturally took some time for this truth to sink in, and, in the meantime, the younger element of Negroes, in their weird worship of everything that was white, neglected and despised their own race-music. More than one college class has walked out, highly insulted, when their white teachers had asked them to sing "Swing Low Sweet Chariot" and "My Lord, What a Morning." It is to be hoped that they now know better.

But the real subject of this editorial is not Negro music, but Negro women. If any foreigner should come here from Europe, Asia or Africa and be privileged to pass in review the various kinds of women who live in our America he would pick out as the superior of them all — the Negro woman. It seems a great pity that it should be left to the foreigner to "discover" the Negro-American woman. For her own mankind has been seeing her for centuries. And yet, outside of the vague rhetoric of the brethren in church and lodge when they want her to turn their functions into financial successes, and outside of Paul Dunbar and perhaps two other poets, no proper amount of esthetic appreciation of her has been forthcoming from their side.

Consider the facts of the case. The white women of America are charming to look at — in the upper social classes. But even the Negro laundress, cook or elevator girl far surpasses her mistress in the matter of feminine charms. No white woman has a color as beautiful as the dark browns, light-browns, peach browns, or gold and bronze of the Negro girl. These are some of the things which make a walk through any Negro section of New York or Washington such a feast of delight.

Then, there is the matter of form. The bodies and limbs of our Negro women are, on the whole, better built and better shaped than those of any other women on earth — except perhaps, the Egyptian women's. And their gait and movement would require an artist to properly describe. The grace of their carriage is inimitable.

But their most striking characteristic is a feature which even the crude mind of mere man can appreciate. It is [*to quote "Gunga Din,"* added in reprint] "the way in which they carry their clothes." They dress well — not merely in the sense that their clothing is costly and good to look at; but in that higher sense in which the Parisian woman is the best dressed woman in Europe. From shoes and stockings to shirtwaists and hats, they choose their clothes with fine taste and show them off to the best advantage when they put them on. That is why a man may walk down the avenue with a Negro cook or factory girl without anyone's being able to guess that she has to work for a living.

And, finally, in the matter of that indefinable something which, for want of a better word, we call simply "charm" — the Negro women are far ahead of all others in America. They have more native grace, more winsomeness, greater beauty and more fire and passion. These facts have already begun to attract attention, here and elsewhere, and, eventually, the Negro woman will come into her own.

What say you, brothers? Shall we not love her while she is among us? Shall we not bend the knee in worship and thank high heaven for the great good fortune which has given us such sisters and sweethearts, mothers and wives?

29. "In the Melting Pot (re Herodotus)," *New Negro* 4 (October 1919): 14–15.

In his October 1919 *New Negro* column "In the Melting Pot," written under the pseudonym "The Taster," Harrison offered some thoughts after rereading Herodotus (c. 484–c. 425 B.C.), the wide-traveling Greek scholar known as "The Father of History." Harrison argues that an accurate knowledge of Egypt's contributions to civilization would benefit Black youth and, as a step in this direction, he advocates a reprint of Herodotus's works at popular prices.

A recent re-reading of Herodotus, the "Father of History," has brought to the mind of The Taster a favorite ambition of his earlier years. It was the issuing of a series of reprints dealing with the history of Negro lands and lands in which Negroes are interested, from the works of those great writers of the past whose works are no longer "protected by copyright." This could be done at a price to suit the pocket of the average man, women or child — say at 25 and 50 cents. A good beginning could be made with the second book of Herodotus which gives invaluable and interesting facts about Egyptian history, as known to the Greeks. He points out, among other things, that many of the Egyptians were black and all of them were dark; that the Greeks derived their art and science and religion from them; that the black Ethiopians gave civilization to Egypt and often reigned and ruled over them. In face of the lies of Anglo-Saxon scholars, and the cheap assumption of our near-scholars that Herodotus (in English) is hard to read, such a reprint would be a blessing to our Negro youth.

The *Negro World*

30. "Race First versus Class First," *Negro World* (March 27, 1920), reprinted in *When Africa Awakes*, 79–82.

The short-lived *Emancipator* appeared as a weekly from March 13 to April 24, 1920. It was published by the New Negro Publishing Co., Inc., whose president was Thomas A. E. Potter, a seventeen-year Socialist Party member, and its secretary and treasurer were the Socialists W. A. Domingo and Frank R. Crosswaith. The *Emancipator*'s articles came from Black radicals in or near the SP, including its editor, former Liberty Leaguer Domingo; its secretary, Crosswaith; and radical community activists Chandler Owen, A. Philip Randolph, Cyril Briggs, Richard B. Moore, and Anselmo Jackson. Of that group only Owen and Randolph were U.S.-born; the others were from the Caribbean — Domingo was from Jamaica, Moore was from Barbados, Briggs was born in Nevis and educated in St. Kitts, and Jackson and Crosswaith were from the Virgin Islands. In an editorial entitled "Our Reason for Being," the editors explained that the paper was the outgrowth of a merger of two monthlies, Briggs's *Crusader* and Randolph and Owen's *Messenger*, and sought to be a weekly that would work for industrial unionism, cooperation, social democracy, and a more complete emancipation than that achieved fifty years earlier.[20]

The *Emancipator*'s editors were not of one mind, particularly on the subject of "class first" vs. "race first." Owens and Randolph were "class first" socialists. Briggs, on the other hand, had strong sympathies for the "race first" position. In the March 1920 *Crusader*, he published an editorial entitled "Race First!" which cited examples of how whites put race first and expressed the hope that those examples were "sufficient to convince the asses who would have the Negro give loyalty first to any country, while white men who derive the greatest benefits and protection from those countries give their first loyalty, not to the country, but to their race." Briggs's *Crusader* offered another "race first" appeal in June.[21]

On March 27 Harrison's "Race First versus Class First" appeared in the *Negro World*. Harrison indicated that he still considered himself a socialist, though he refused to put either socialism or the Socialist Party "above the call of his race." He did this because the Socialist Party has "insisted on Race First and class after." To substantiate his charges he quoted from the Majority Report on Immigration from the Party's 1912 Convention that "race consciousness is inborn and cannot be wholly unlearned" and that there is a "white man's domain" that is being invaded "by other races."[22]

"In the old days white people derived their knowledge of what Negroes were doing from those Negroes who were nearest to them, largely their own selected exponents of Negro activity or of their white point of view. * * * Today the white world is vaguely, but disquietingly, aware that Negroes are awake; different, but perplexingly uncertain. Yet the white world by which they are surrounded retains its traditional method of interpreting the mass by the Negro nearest to themselves in affiliation or contact. The Socialist party still persists in thinking that the unrest now apparent in the Negro masses is due to their propaganda which its paid adherents support, and believes that the unrest will function largely along the lines of Socialist political thought."

It is necessary to insist on this point today when the Socialist party of America has secretly subsidized both a magazine and a newspaper to attempt to cut into the splendid solidarity which Negroes are achieving in response to the call of racial necessity. It is necessary to point out that "radical" young Negroes may betray the interests of the race into alien hands just as surely as "the old crowd." For, after all, the essence of both betrayals consists in making the racial requirements play second fiddle to the requirements dictated as best for it by other groups with other interests to serve. The fact that one group of alien interests is described as "radical" and the other as "reactionary" is of very slight value to us.

In the days when the Socialist Party of America was respectable, although it never drew lines of racial separation in the North, it permitted those lines to be drawn in the South. It had no word of official condemnation for the Socialists of Tennessee who prevented Theresa Malkiel in 1912 from lecturing to Negroes on Socialism either in the same hall with them or in meetings of their own. It was the national office of the party which in that same presidential year refused to route Eugene V. Debs in the South because the Grand Old Man let it be known that he would not remain silent on the race question while in the South. They wanted the votes of the white South then, and were willing to betray by silence the principles of inter-racial solidarity which they espoused on paper.

Now, when their party has shrunk considerably in popular support and sentiment, they are willing to take up our cause. Well, we thank honest white people everywhere who take up our cause, but we wish them to know that we have already taken it up ourselves. While they were refusing to diagnose our case we diagnosed it ourselves, and, now that we have prescribed the remedy — Race Solidarity — they came to us with their prescription — Class Solidarity. It is too late, gentlemen! This racial alignment is all our own product, and we have no desire to turn it over to you at this late day, when we are beginning to reap its benefits. And if you are simple enough to believe that those among us who serve your interests ahead of ours have any monopoly of intellect or information along the lines of modern learning, then you are the greater gulls indeed.

We can respect the Socialists of Scandinavia, France, Germany or England on their record. But your record so far does not entitle you to the respect of those who can see all around a subject. We say Race First, because you have all along insisted on Race First and class after when you didn't need our help. We reproduce below a brief portion of your record in those piping times of peace, and ask you to explain it. If you are unable to do so, set your lackeys to work; they may be able to do it in terms of their own "radical scientific" surface slush. The following is taken from the majority report of one of your national committees during one of your recent national conventions. It was signed by Ernest Untermann and J. Stitt Wilson, representing the West, and Joshua Wanhope, editor of the *Call*, and Robert Hunter, representing the East, and it was adopted as a portion of the party program. We learn from it that —

> Race feeling is not so much a result of social as of biological evolution. It does not change essentially with changes of economic systems. It is deeper than any class feeling and will outlast the capitalist system. It persists even after race prejudice has been outgrown. It exists not because the capitalists nurse it for economic reasons, but the capitalists rather have an opportunity to nurse it for economic reasons because it exists a product of biology. It is bound to play a role in the economics of the future society. If it should not assert itself in open warfare under a Socialist form of society, it will nevertheless lead to a rivalry of races for expansion over the globe as a result of the play of natural and sexual selection. We may temper this race feeling by education, but we can never hope to extinguish it altogether. Class-consciousness must be learned, but race consciousness is inborn and cannot be wholly unlearned. A few individuals may indulge in the luxury of ignoring race and posing as utterly raceless humanitarians, but whole races never.
>
> Where races struggle for the means of life, racial animosities cannot be avoided. When working people struggle for jobs, self-preservation enforces its decrees. Economic and political considerations lead to racial fights and to legislation restricting the invasion of the white man's domain by other races.

It is well that the New Negro should know this, since it justifies him in giving you a taste of your own medicine. The writer of these lines is also a Socialist; but he refuses in this crisis of the world's history to put either Socialism or your party above the call of his race. And he does this on the very grounds which you yourself have given in the document quoted above. Also because he is not a fool.

31. "Just Crabs," *Negro World* (c. April 1920), reprinted in *When Africa Awakes*, 73–75.

In his diary, Harrison discussed the new methods and changes he brought to the *Negro World* after becoming its principal editor. In this context he mentioned "writing 'The

Crab-Barrel' series," which was part of his larger, intense debate with the socialist-leaning editors of the *Emancipator*.[23]

"Just Crabs" appeared in the *Negro World* around March 27, 1920. Harrison described it as "a delightful inspiration in the course of defending, not Mr. Garvey personally, but the principles of the New Negro Manhood Movement, a portion of which had been incorporated by him and his followers of the U.N.I.A. and A.C.L." The piece, said Harrison, was "the opening gun of the defense, of which some other salvos were given in the serial satire of 'The Crab Barrel' and which gave rise to related editorials." "Just Crabs" was clearly a barb directed at the *Emancipator* crowd of Black socialists, to whom it referred as "The Subsidized Sixth" in an obvious allusion to Du Bois's "Talented Tenth" and to their Socialist Party financial backing. Harrison described the series of prose and poetry as the "Crab and Just So" stories in another allusion—to Booker T. Washington's homespun "Crab" stories and Rudyard Kipling's *Just So Stories for Little Children* (1902).[24]

The debate with the *Emancipator* became extremely personal and revealed little-known sides of Randolph, Owen, Domingo, and Harrison. It seemed, at least temporarily, to silence criticism from Garvey's opponents. It also may have had an important, though long-ignored, role in the rightward political transformation of Chandler Owen, who, over the next few years, would abandon socialism and move toward the Republicans (from whence, according to Harrison, he came).[25]

Once upon a time a Greedy Person went rummaging along the lagoon with a basket and a stick in quest of Crabs, which he needed for the Home Market. (Now, this was in the Beginning of Things, Best Beloved.) These were Land Crabs—which, you know, are more luscious than Sea Crabs, being more primitive and more full of meat. He dug into their holes with his stick, rousted them out, packed them on their backs in his basket and took them home. Several trips he made with his basket and his stick, and all the Crabs which he caught were dumped into a huge barrel. (But this time he didn't pack them on their backs.) And all the creatures stood around and watched. For this Greedy Person had put no cover on the barrel. (But this was in the Beginning of Things.)

He knew Crab Nature, and was not at all worried about his Crabs. For as soon as any one Crab began to climb up on the side of the barrel to work his way toward the top the other Crabs would reach up, grab him by the legs, and down he would come, kerplunk! "If we can't get up," they would say—"if we can't get up you shan't get up, either. We'll pull you down. Besides, you should wait until the barrel bursts. There are Kind Friends on the Outside who will burst the barrel if we only wait, and then, when the Great Day dawns, we will all be Emancipated and there'll be no need for Climbing. Come down, you fool!" (Because this was in the Beginning of Things, Best Beloved.) So the Greedy Person could always get as many Crabs as he needed for the Home market, because they all depended on him for their food.

And all the creatures stood around and laughed. For this was very funny in the Beginning of Things. And all the creatures said that the Reason for this kink in Crab nature was that when the Creator was giving out heads he didn't have enough to go around, so the poor Crabs didn't get any. And the Greedy Person thanked his lucky stars that Crabs had been made in that Peculiar way, since it made it unnecessary to put a cover on his barrel or to waste his precious time a-watching of them. (Now, all this happened long ago, Best Beloved, in the very Beginning of Things.)

The above is the first of our Just-So Stories—with no apologies to Rudyard Kipling or any one else. We print it here because, just at this time the Crabs are at work in Harlem, and there is a tremendous clashing of claws as the Pull 'Em Down program goes forward. It's a great game to be sure, but it doesn't seem to get them or us anywhere. The new day that has dawned for the Negroes of Harlem is a day of business accomplishment. People are going into business, saving their money and collectively putting it into enterprises which will mean roofs over their heads and an economic future for themselves and their little ones.

But the Subsidized Sixth are sure that this is all wrong and that we have no right to move an inch until the Socialist millennium dawns, when we will all get 'out of the barrel' together. It does not seem to have occurred to them that making an imperfect heaven now does not unfit any one for enjoying the perfect paradise which they promise us—if it ever comes. Truly, it is said of them that "the power over a man's subsistence is the power over his will"—and over his "scientific radicalism," too. But we remember having translated this long ago into the less showy English of "Show me whose bread you eat, and I'll tell you whose songs you'll sing." Surely this applies to radicals overnight as well as to ordinary folk. And if not, why not?

But when the reek of the poison gas propaganda has cleared away and the smoke of the barrage has lifted it will be found that "White Men's Niggers" is a phrase that need not be restricted to old-line politicians and editors. Criticism pungent and insistent is due to every man in public life and to every movement which bids for public support. But the cowardly insinuator who from the safe shelter of nameless charges launches his poisoned arrows at other people's reputation is a contemptible character to have on any side of any movement. He is generally a liar who fears that he will be called to account for his lies if he should venture to name his foe. No man with the truth to tell indulges in this pastime of the skulker and skunk. Let us, by all means, have clear, hard-hitting criticism, but none of this foul filth which lowers the thing that throws it. In the name of common sense and common decency, quit being Just Crabs.

32. "Patronize Your Own," *Negro World* (May 1, 1920): 2, reprinted in *When Africa Awakes*, 87–89.

In 1915, Gertrude Cohen, the librarian at New York's 135th Street Public Library, and James Weldon Johnson, editorial writer for the *New York Age*, both urged Harrison to concentrate his efforts on work among the African American masses in Harlem. At about the same time, John T. Clark, housing and industrial secretary of the Urban League, was "working out the details of such an idea." Clark broached "the proposition of speaking on the streets in the Negro neighborhood on behalf of the Negro business men in a propaganda designed to induce Negro purchasers to patronize Negro businessmen." Clark was supposed to help "bring the business men together to organize and launch the propaganda," but obstruction from both United Colored Democracy leaders and Booker T. Washington's followers undermined the effort.[26]

Several years later Harrison described how such "Patronize Your Own" campaigns were put into effect in Harlem in the period from 1915 to 1920.

The doctrine of "Race First," although utilized largely by the Negro businessmen of Harlem, has never received any large general support from them. If we remember rightly, it was the direct product of the out-door and in-door lecturers who flourished in Harlem between 1914 and 1916. Not all who were radical shared this sentiment. For instance, we remember the debate between Mr. Hubert Harrison, then president of the Liberty League, and Mr. Chandler Owen, at Palace Casino in December, 1918, in which the "radical" Owen fiercely maintained "that the doctrine of race first was an indefensible doctrine"; Mr. Harrison maintaining that it was the source of salvation for the race. Both these gentlemen have run true to form ever since.

But to return to our thesis. The secondary principle of "patronize your own," flowing as it does from the main doctrine of "race first," is subject to the risk of being exploited dishonestly—particularly by business men. And business men in Harlem have shown themselves capable of doing this all the time. They seem to forget that "do unto others as you would have them do unto you" is a part of the honest application of this doctrine. Many of these men seem to want other black people to pay them for being black. They seem to think that a dirty place and imperfect service and 3 cents more a pound should be rewarded with racial patronage regardless of these demerits.

On the other hand, there have grown up in Harlem Negro businesses, groceries, ice cream parlors, etc., in which the application of prices, courtesy and selling efficiency are maintained. This is the New Negro business man, and we say "more power to him." If this method of applying the principle should continue to increase in popularity we are sure to have in Harlem and elsewhere a full and flowing tide of Negro business enterprises gladly and loyally supported by the mass of Negro purchasers to their mutual benefit.

The Negro business man who is unintelligently selfish, makes a hash of racial welfare in the attempt to achieve individual success. A case in point is that of the brown-skinned dolls. Twenty years ago the Negro child's only choice was between a white Caucasian doll and the "nigger doll." On the lower levels the one was as cheap as the other. Then, a step at the time came the picturesque poupee, variously described as the "Negro doll," the "colored doll" and the "brown-skinned doll." This was sold by white stores at an almost prohibitive price. It was made three times as easy for the Negro child to idolize a white doll as to idolize one with the features of its own race. When the principle of "Race First" began to be proclaimed from scores of platforms and pulpits, certain Negro business men saw a chance to benefit the race and, incidently to reap a wonderful harvest of profits, by appealing to a principle for whose support and maintenance, here and elsewhere, they had never paid a cent. "Factories" for the production of brown-skinned dolls began to spring up — most of the factoring consisting of receiving these dolls from white factories and either stuffing them with saw dust, excelsior or other filling, or merely changing them from one wrapper to another. Bear in mind that the proclaimed object was to make it easier for the Negro mother to teach race patriotism to her Negro child. Yet it was soon notorious that these leeches were charging $3, $4, and $5 for Negro dolls which could sell at prices ranging from 75 cents to $1.25, and yet leave a handsome margin of profit.

The result is that even today in Negro Harlem nine out of ten Negro children are forced to play with white dolls, because rapacious scoundrels have been capitalizing the principle of "patronize your own" in a one-sided way. By lowering the prices to a reasonable level, they could extend their business tremendously. Failing to do this, they are playing into the hands of the vendors of white dolls and making it much easier for the Negro to select a white doll for her child; limiting at once their own market and restricting the development of a larger racial ideal.

33. "An Open Letter to the Socialist Party of New York City," *Negro World* 8 (May 8, 1920): 2, reprinted with deletions in *When Africa Awakes*, 82–86.

Harrison's "An Open Letter to The Socialist Party of New York City" in the *Negro World* of May 8, 1920, sought to make clear that the rise in Black radicalism was not due to the propaganda of Black Socialists (those whom the SP "had selected to interpret Negro sentiment for them"), despite what they were telling white party leaders. The new radicalism was due, he explained, to the "new Negro" "race first" sentiment, which emerged during the war in response to white supremacy. He also pointed out that Blacks would be receptive to socialism's appeal if it was freed from "rancor and hatred of the Negro's . . . defensive racial propaganda."

Gentlemen: During 1917 the white leaders of the Republican party were warned that the Negroes of this city were in a mood unfavorable to the success of their party at the polls and that this mood was likely to last until they changed their party's attitude toward the Negro masses. They scouted this warning because the Negroes whom they had selected to interpret Negro sentiment for them still confidently assured them that there had been no change of sentiment on the part of the Negro people, and white politicians did not think it necessary to come and find out for themselves. Consequently they were lied to by those whose bread and butter depended on such lying. Then came the mayoralty campaign, and, when it was too late they discovered their mistake. At a memorable meeting at Palace Casino John Purroy Mitchel, the candidate of the Republican party, and Theodore Roosevelt, its idol, were almost hissed off the stage, while the Mitchel outdoor speakers found it impossible to speak on the street corners of Harlem. The party went down to defeat and Judge John F. Hylan was elected.

All this is recent history, and it is called to your attention at this time only because you are in danger of making a similar costly mistake. You, too, have selected Negro spokesman on whose word you choose to rely for information as to the tone and temper of Negro political sentiment. You have chosen to adopt the same faulty method of the white Republican politicians, and you do not care to go behind the word of your selected exponents of Negro thought and feeling. Yet the pitiful vote which you polled in the last election might have warned you that something had gone wrong in your arrangements. What that something is we shall now proceed to show you — if you are still able to see.

During the recent world war the Negro in America was taught that while white people spoke of patriotism, religion, democracy and other sounding themes, they remained loyal to one concept above all others, and that was the concept of race. Even in the throes of war, and on the battlefields of France it was "race first" with them. Out of this relation was born the new Negro ideal of "race first" for us. And today, whether Negroes be Catholics or Protestants, capitalists or wage workers, Republicans or Democrats, native or foreign-born, they begin life anew on this basis. Alike in their business alignments, their demands on the government and political parties, and in their courageous response to race rioters, they are responding to this sentiment which has been bred by the attitude of white men here and everywhere else where white rules black. To be sure, neither [Postmaster General Albert S.] Burleson nor [Attorney General A. Mitchell] Palmer have told you or the rest of the white world this. The Anglo-Saxon white man is a notorious hypocrite; and they have preferred to prate of Bolshevism — your "radicalism" — rather than tell the truth of racialism, our "radicalism," because this was an easier explanation, more in keeping with official stupidity. But we had supposed that you were intelligent enough to find this out. Evidently, you were not.

Your official Negro exponents, on behalf of their bread and butter, have seized on this widely-published official explanation to make you believe that the changed attitude of the Negro masses was due to the propaganda which you were paying them (at their published request) to preach. But this is a lie. Don't take our word for it. Do some reading on your own account. Get a hundred different Negro newspapers and magazines, outside of those which you have subsidized, and study their editorial and other pronouncements, and you will see that this is so.

But let us come nearer home. The propaganda of Socialism has been preached in times past in Harlem by different people without awakening hostility of any sort. Today it elicits a hostility which is outspoken. Send up and see; then ask yourselves the reason. You will find a Negro Harlem reborn, with business enterprises and cultural arrangements. And these things have been established without any help from you or those who eat your bread. Even the work of Socialist propaganda was neglected by you between 1912 and 1917. Consult your own memories and columns of the *Call*.

All these things are the recent products of the principle of "race first." And among them the biggest is the Universal Negro Improvement Association, with its associate bodies, the Black Star Line and the Negro Factories Corporation [NFC]. No movement among American Negroes since slavery was abolished has ever attained the gigantic proportions of this. The love and loyalty of millions go out to it as well as the cold cash of tens of thousands. Yet your Negro hirelings have seen fit to use the organs which you give them to spread Socialist propaganda for the purpose of attacking all these things, and the Black Star Line in particular. Do you wonder now that they meet with such outspoken opposition that they have been driven to seek an underhanded alliance with the police (as your Negro Socialist organ avows in its latest issue)? Isn't that a glorious alliance for purposes of Negro propaganda? When such things can happen you may depend upon it that someone has been fooling you.

On their own avowal your chief militant representatives among us are Messrs. Chandler Owen, A.P. Randolph, W. A. Domingo and Cyril V. Briggs [this sentence was omitted from the reprint]. And, just as the white Republicans did, you have assumed that those whom chance or change brought your way have somehow, achieved a monopoly of the intellect and virtue of the Negro race. Do you think that this is sound sense on your part? Of course, it was natural that they should tell you so. But was it natural for you to be so simple as to believe it? On March 27 this newspaper in an editorial quoted a passage from one of your official documents [The 1912 convention position on immigration; see selection 30] showing that the white men of your party officially put "race first" rather than "class first," which latter phrase is your henchmen's sole contribution to "sociology" — for us. The quoted passage cuts the very heart out of their case. And yet, those whom you have selected to represent you are so green and sappy in their Socialism that, although six weeks have elapsed since this was hurled at their thick heads, not one of them has yet been able to trace its source, this quotation from one of your own official documents. Think of it! And in the meantime you yourselves are such "easy marks" that you believe them, on their own assertion, to be the ablest among the Negroes of America. It is not easy to decide which of the two groups is the bigger joke — you or they.

You have constantly insisted that "there is no race problem, only an economic problem," but you will soon be in a fair way to find out otherwise. Some day you will, perhaps, have learned enough to cease being "suckers" for perpetual candidates who dickered with the Democrats up to within a month of "flopping" to your party only because they "couldn't make it" elsewhere; some day, perhaps you will know enough to put Socialism's cause in the hands of those who will refrain from using your party's organ for purposes of personal pique, spite and venom. When that day dawns Socialism will have a chance to be heard by Negroes on its merits. And even now, if you should send anyone up here (black or white) to put the cause of Karl Marx, freed from admixture of rancor and hatred of the Negro's own defensive racial propaganda, you may find that it will have as good a chance of gaining adherents as any other political creed. But until you change your tactics or make your exponents change theirs your case among us will be hopeless indeed.

The *Boston Chronicle* and *The Voice of the Negro*

34. "Race Consciousness," *Boston Chronicle* (March 15, 1924), HHHP Wr, reprinted in *The Voice of the Negro* 1, no. 1 (April 1927): 3–4.

Harrison's very important editorial on race consciousness appeared in the March 15, 1924, *Boston Chronicle*. It offered his mature, well-thought-out views on the subject and, by treating race consciousness as a "protective reaction," suggested a more temporal and conditional tone than was indicated by the more reflexive and absolutist "race first" of seven years earlier.

The general facts of the outside world reflect themselves not only in ideas but in our feelings. The facts that make up a general social condition are reflected in social states of mind. Thus the feeling of racial superiority which the white races so generally exhibit is produced by the external fact of their domination in most parts of the world. That same fact, by the way, produces in the minds of the masses of black, brown and yellow peoples in Africa, Asia and elsewhere what is called in psychology a protective reaction; and that is their race-consciousness. So that race-consciousness is like loyalty, neither an evil nor a good. The good or evil of it depends upon the uses to which it is put.

The recent World War has chiseled the channels of race-consciousness deeper among American Negroes than any previous external circumstances. For weal or woe that is a fact to be reckoned with. During the war we learnt that the Other People held race to be higher than patriotism when American army officers treated their Negro fellow soldiers worse than they did the German enemy. In times of peace we are taught that race is stronger than religion—as the existence of Negro churches prove. All of which need not mean that we have to hate white people. But it does mean that in sheer self-defense, we too must put race very high on our list of necessities. In fact if we hadn't been doing this all along there would have been no "Negro progress" to boast about as proof of our equal human possibilities. Negro churches, Negro newspapers, Negro life-insurance-companies, banks, fraternities, colleges and political appointees — all mean Negro race-consciousness.

So even if self-seekers have vilely exploited the thing that is no reason why we should condemn it as an evil. What is an evil is the ignorance and gullibility of those who let themselves be exploited. So long as the outer situation remains what it is we must evoke race-consciousness to furnish a background for our aspirations, readers for our writers, a clientele for our artists and professional people, and ideals for our future. For so long as a black boy may not aspire to be Governor of Massachusetts or President of the United States, like the son of an immigrant German or Russian, so long will we need race-consciousness.

Education

Harrison viewed education of the masses as essential to any movement which aimed to overthrow oppression. But, as he explained in 1914, he saw "little hope of change" for the African American community under Black intellectual leaders whose "scholastic development" consisted of "superficial acquaintance with 'letters' and a flair for the cryptic phrase." What was needed, he said, was a "new leadership . . . based not upon the ignorance of the masses, but upon their intelligence."[1]

Between 1914 and 1920 Harrison began to articulate the type of educational work he thought was needed. He challenged both the concern with industrial education associated with Booker T. Washington and the emphasis on training of the "Talented Tenth" emphasized by W. E. B. Du Bois. His new approach was marked by its concern with the masses, its encouragement of reading and self-education, its emphasis on modernism, and its internationalism. Harrison admonished the "Talented Tenth" to "come down from their Sinais" to teach and viewed such educational work as crucial because an enlightened mass was a potential source of real power.[2]

Central to this concern for the masses was his emphasis on self-study and self-education. In every publication that he edited Harrison offered lists of recommended books. He urged his audiences to "Get the reading habit," and he suggested books which he believed provided "the essentials of modern science and modern thought."[3]

Harrison was particularly influenced by the work of the Spanish anarchist and educator Francisco Ferrer y Guardia (1859–1909), who established an *Escuela Moderna* in Barcelona in 1901 and saw that secular educational movement grow rapidly throughout Spain before he was murdered in a joint effort of church and state for his role in mass demonstrations against sending reservists to fight in Morocco. The Modern School Movement aimed to create schools that served as instruments of development and self-development and as vehicles for social change. Modern Schools (including one founded in New York in 1910, at which Harrison taught in 1914 and 1915) encouraged self-expression, individual freedom, and practical knowledge, and reinforced brotherhood, cooperation, support for the poor and oppressed, anticapitalism, antimilitarism, and antistatism. The Modern School Movement was openly internationalist and drew from the writings of the French philosopher Jean-Jacques Rousseau, the Swiss educational reformer Johann Heinrich Pestalozzi, the German educator Friedrich Froebel, the Russian anarchist Pyotr Alekseyevich Kropotkin, and the Russian writer and social critic Leo Tolstoy.[4]

Additional international influences came from many sources, including the Russian, Jewish, and Japanese peoples, who used education as a means to fight oppression and seek power. Harrison repeatedly emphasized the important role of education to each of these peoples. In one typical example from 1920, he described how he had consistently stressed the need for "subject races" to be like the Japanese and develop intellectual power:

> With most of the present sources of power controlled by the white race it behooves my race as well as the other subject races to learn the wisdom of the weak and to develop to the fullest that organ whereby weakness has been able to overcome strength; namely, the intellect. It is not with our teeth that we will tear the white man out of our ancestral land. It isn't with our jaws that we can wring from his hard hands consideration and respect. It must be done by the upper and not the lower parts of our heads. Therefore, I have insisted ever since my entry into the arena of racial discussion that we Negroes must take to reading, study and the development of intelligence as we have never done before. In this respect we must pattern ourselves after the Japanese who have gone to school in Europe but have never used Europe's education to make them the apes of Europe's culture. They have absorbed, adopted, transformed and utilized, and we Negroes must do the same.[5]

35. "Negro Culture and the Negro College," *New Negro* 4, no. 1 (September 1919): 4–5; reprinted with deletions as "The Racial Roots of Culture," *Negro World* (July 31, 1920): 2, and as "The Racial Roots of Culture," in *When Africa Awakes*, 129–31. [The first sentence, the last sentence of the second paragraph, and the last paragraph appear in the original, but not in the reprints.]

Harrison's major editorial in the September 1919 issue of the *New Negro* was on "Negro Culture and the Negro College," and it called for "Negro colleges" to develop "courses in Negro history and the culture of West African peoples" and to become general "institution[s] of Negro learning." Shortly after this editorial appeared, Marcus Garvey approached Harrison and asked him to head a college that he wanted to establish, presumably "in line with the modern thought of Negroes."[6]

> The modern line of discussion in education runs more to aim, intent and object than to forms and frills. Education is the name of the game which we give to that process by which the ripened generation brings to bear upon the rising generation the stored-up knowledge and experience of the past and present generations to fit it for the business of life. If we are not to waste money and energy, our educational systems should shape our youth for what we intend them to become. Where (as in the case of white America) we are muddled as to what the young are to be made into, there also we are muddled in

our methods, since it is the character of the aim that finally fixes the character of the methods.

We Negroes, in a world in which we are the under dog, must shape our youth for living in such a world. Shall we shape them mentally to accept the status of under-dog as their predestined lot? Or shall we shape them into men and women fit for a free world? To do the former needs nothing more than continuing as we are. To do the latter is to shape their souls for continued conflict with a theory and practice in which most of the white world that surrounds them are at one. This is the pivotal fact which we can not safely ignore.

The educational system in the United States and the West Indies was shaped by white people for white youth, and from their point of view, it fits their purpose well. Into this system came the children of Negro parents when chattel slavery was ended — and their relation to the problems of life was obviously different. The white boy and girl draw exclusively from the stored-up knowledge and experience of the past and present generations of white people to fit them for the business of being dominant whites in a world full of colored folk. The examples of valor and virtue on which their minds are fed are exclusively white examples. What wonder, then, that each generation comes to maturity with the idea imbedded in its mind that only white men are valorous and fit to rule and only white women are virtuous and entitled to chivalry, respect and protection? What wonder that they think, almost instinctively, that the Negro's proper place, nationally and internationally, is that of an inferior? It is only what we should naturally expect.

But what seems to escape attention is the fact that the Negro boy and girl, getting the same (though worse) instruction, also get from it the same notion of the Negro's place and part in life which the white children get. Is it any wonder, then, that they so readily accept the status of inferiors; that they tend to disparage themselves, and think themselves worth while only to the extent to which they look and act and think like the whites? They know nothing of the stored-up knowledge and experience of the past and present generations of Negroes in their ancestral lands, and conclude there is no such store of knowledge and experience. They readily accept the assumption that Negroes have never been anything but slaves and that they have never had a glorious past as other fallen peoples like the Greeks and Persians have. And this despite the mass of collected testimony in the works of [Heinrich] Barth, [Georg August] Schweinfurth, Mary Kingsley, Lady [Flora Luisa (Shaw)] Lugard, [Edmund D.] Morel, [Job] Ludolphus, [Edward Wilmot] Blyden, [George Washington] Ellis, [Friedrich] Ratzel, [Dudley] Kidd, [Abd al-Rahman al] Es-Saadi, [Joseph Ephraim] Casely Hayford and a host of others, Negro and white.

A large part of the blame for this deplorable condition must be put upon the Negro colleges like Howard, Fisk, Livingstone and Lincoln in the United States, and Codrington, Harrison and Mico in the West Indies. These are the institutions in which our cultural ideals and educational systems are fashioned for the shaping of the minds of the future generations of Negroes. It cannot be expected that it shall begin with the common schools; for, in spite of logic, educational ideas and ideals spread from above downwards. If we are ever to enter into the confraternity of colored peoples it should seem the duty of our Negro colleges to drop their silly smatterings of "little Latin and less Greek" and establish modern courses in Hausa and Arabic, for these are the living languages of millions of our brethren in modern Africa. Courses in Negro history and the culture of West African peoples, at least, should be given in every college that claims to be an institution of learning for Negroes. Surely an institution of learning for Negroes should not fail to be also an institution of Negro learning.

Up to the present, the only Negro college which has even planned such courses is the Baptist Seminary and College at Lynchburg, Virginia, which, quite fittingly, is "owned and controlled" entirely by Negroes and has a Negro president [Dr. R. C. Woods] responsible to a Negro board of trustees. *The New Negro* would be glad to hear of others and would willingly extend its aid to any college desirous of getting in line with the modern thought of Negroes. Until such steps are taken the Negro college must bear the burden of this open shame.

 36. "Education and the Race," in *When Africa Awakes*, 126–28.

In "Education and the Race," written in August 1920 for his book *When Africa Awakes*, Harrison considers the example of Russia, with its mass education campaigns prior to its revolution as instructive for African Americans desirous of "freedom and power." He also discusses the examples of the Japanese and Jewish peoples, the need for the "Talented Tenth" to "come down from their Sinais," and the need for his readers to "Get the reading habit" and "Go to school whenever [they] can."

In the dark days of Russia, when the iron heel of Czarist despotism was heaviest on the necks of the people, those who wished to rule decreed that the people should remain ignorant. Loyalty to interests that were opposed to theirs was the prevailing public sentiment of the masses. In vain did the pioneers of freedom for the masses perish under the knout and rigors of Siberia. They sacrificed to move the masses, but the masses, strong in their love of liberty, lacked the head to guide the moving feet to any issue. It was then that Leo Tolstoi and the other intelligentsia began to carry knowledge to the masses. Not only in the province of Tula, but in every large city, young men of university experience would assemble in secret classes of instruction, teaching them to read, to write, to know, to think and to love knowledge. Most of this work was underground at first. But it took. Thousands of educated persons gave themselves to this work — without pay: their only hope of reward lay in the future effectiveness of an instructed mass movement.

What were the results? As knowledge spread, enthusiasm was backed by brains. The

Russian revolution began to be sure of itself. The workingmen of the cities studied the thing that they were "up against," gauged their own weakness and strength as well as their opponents'. The despotism of the Czar could not provoke them to a mass movement before they were ready and had the means; and when at last they moved, they swept not only the Czar's regime but the whole exploiting system upon which it stood into utter oblivion.

What does this mean to the Negro of the Western world? It may mean much, or little: that depends on him. If other men's experiences have value for the New Negro Manhood Movement it will seek now to profit by them and to bottom the new fervor of faith in itself with the solid support of knowledge. The chains snap from the limb of the young giant as he rises, stretches himself, and sits up to take notice. But let him, for his future's sake, insist on taking notice. To drop the figure of speech, we Negroes who have shown our *manhood* must back it by our *mind*. This world, at present, is a white man's world — even in Africa. We, being what we are, want to shake loose the chains of his control from our corner of it. We must either accept his domination and our inferiority, or we must contend against it. But we go up to win; and whether we carry on that contest with ballots, bullets or business, we can not win from the white man unless we know at least as much as the white man knows. For, after all, knowledge *is* power.

But that isn't all. What kind of knowledge is it that enables white men to rule black men's lands? Is it the knowledge of Hebrew and Greek, philosophy or literature? It isn't. It is the knowledge of explosives and deadly compounds: that is chemistry. It is the knowledge which can build ships, bridges, railroads and factories: that is engineering. It is the knowledge which harnesses the visible and invisible forces of the earth and air and water: that is science, modern science. And that is what the New Negro must enlist upon his side. Let us, like the Japanese, become a race of knowledge-getters, preserving our racial soul, but digesting into it all that we can glean or grasp, so that when Israel goes up out of bondage he will be "skilled in all the learning of the Egyptians" and competent to control his destiny.

Those who have knowledge must come down from their Sinais and give it to the common people. Theirs is the great duty to simplify and make clear, to light the lamps of knowledge that the eyes of their race may see; that the feet of their people may not stumble. This is the task of the Talented Tenth.

To the masses of our people we say: Read! Get the reading habit; spend your spare time not so much in training the feet to dance, as in training the head to think. And, at the very outset, draw the line between books of opinion and books of information. Saturate your minds with the latter and you will be forming your own opinions, which will be worth ten times more to you than the opinions of the greatest minds on earth. Go to school whenever you can. If you can't go in the day, go at night. But remember always that the best college is that on your bookshelf: the best education is that on the inside of your own head. For in this work-a-day world people ask first, not "Where were you educated?" but "What do you know?" and next, "What can you do with it?" And if we of the Negro race can master modern knowledge — the kind that counts — we will be able to win for ourselves the priceless gifts of freedom and power, and we will be able to hold them against the world.

37. "English as She Is Spoke," *Boston Chronicle* (January 26, 1924), HHHP Wr.

In the first half of 1924, Harrison wrote a regular weekly column, "The Trend of the Times," for the *Boston Chronicle*. In this January piece he offered advice on speaking and writing well. He maintained that "Our manner of speaking is an absolute indication of the manner of our thinking" and if "you master your language you will be mastering your ideas." He also urged his readers to eagerly use dictionaries and spelling books, and to take time to read a few good books.

Just last week I overheard a man reading to his friend a paragraph from a newspaper. As soon as he had finished his friend enquired in a casual way, "That's from a colored paper, isn't it?" And the answer was simply, "Of course." It made me take notice and think. Isn't it true that we Negroes who speak English achieve in the mass something less than mastery of the language? Our ordinary speech, as well as our ordinary writing, is a thing set apart, bearing the badge of an inferior product, as if we were in a mental class by ourselves. I have seen editorials written by Negro graduates of Harvard (the writers so described themselves) in which pronouns and their antecedents, nouns and verbs, were as hopelessly at odds as if the writers were trying to master a foreign language. What is the basic reason of all this?

The Polish Jew can use five different languages: Hebrew and Yiddish, Polish, German and Russian. If he speaks any one of them imperfectly he has some excuse for doing so. The American Negro has but the one language to learn. From birth to death he sees, hears, and is surrounded by, only that language. No language is difficult for one who is born to it; yet most of us speak and write ours as if it were, for us, the hardest thing in the world. We read the newspapers every day, the magazines every month, as well as books and pamphlets; yet we put a dot over a capital "I" and confound "its" (in "its own fashion") with "it's" (in "it's a boy"). We say "Ah'm go'n burn 'tup too" for "I shall burn it up too," "Un'nkyeah" for "I don't care," and "Neh mine" for "Never mind." No one deserves any special credit for speaking his own language correctly and distinctly. That is the least that he can do. But he should do at least that. Our manner of speaking is an absolute indication of the manner of our thinking. The man who slurs his words always slurs his thoughts and he who runs his words together does the same thing with his ideas. People whose mental incompetence is evident in their failure to master the A.B.C's of their mother-tongue should not be surprised at the fact that no one cares what their ideas may be on literature, business, religion or the race problem.

After all, the question of our speech is closely connected with the larger question of our mental capacity. Whether you are in Africa, Germany or New York, the white man whose speech you can tell by the way in which you use it whether he shall consider you as Sambo or Mr. Jones; and he naturally concludes that when you speak like "inferior cattle" you are "inferior cattle." Nor will the use of grand words which you don't understand help in any way. When you say, "What do you mean to infer?" for "What do you mean to imply?" or "The proposition is extremely hypothetical" for "The idea isn't practicable" you are tagged and ticketed as one who is incompetent to put his thoughts into language that is clear, precise and distinct.

You may know only three thousand words; but if you can use them properly, then you must go back to the little grammar, the spelling book and the dictionary. Never be ashamed to do this; it will stand you in good stead in the days to come. You will find that as you master your language you will be mastering your ideas. And, until you master them your mental life will be a muddle.

Reading a few good books will be a great help: the Bible, [John Bunyan's] *The Pilgrim's Progress*, [Charles] Dickens' *Christmas Carol*, [Thomas Babington] Macaulay's *Essays*—these can be bought for a few cents each, and they will repay reading and study. Commit a few paragraphs of each to memory, and they will serve as standards by which to test your own everyday speech. And if you don't need to do this, then this article was not meant for you.

38. "Education out of School," *Boston Chronicle* (February 23, 1924),
HHHP Wr.

In a later *Chronicle* column the autodidactic Harrison wrote on "Education out of School"—a subject about which he had a particular competence. He emphasized the golden opportunity provided by "free schools and colleges, free public libraries and the second-hand bookshops," and offered examples of self-educated people who had made major contributions to society.

To the Negro America offers Jim Crow, segregation, disfranchisement and the lynching-bee. But at the same time she also offers him free schools and colleges, free public libraries and the second-hand bookshops where he can "sit with Shakespeare," walk with [George Bernard] Shaw, commune with poets, philosophers, scientists, historians, novelists, and draw "sweetness and light" from the noblest souls of the past and present. What a blessing it would be if, while we fight against the evil in America's left hand, we should utilize the powers which she holds in her right to make our fight more effective!

For, after all, it is the wisdom of the weak that enables them to overthrow the strength of the strong. When the European Jews found themselves proscribed and trampled on, without rights or protection in the Middle Ages they began to specialize in two things: mind-power and money-power—and the first was parent of the second.

They became the most intelligent people in all Europe, and although they number less than the Negroes in America and are hated more cordially both there and here, they have become by their intelligence more powerful than any people in Europe in proportion to their numbers.

With education open to us, in the North, as freely as to others, we fail to avail ourselves of the golden opportunity. True, some of our boys go to college; but going to college is not necessarily education. The last day in college is called Commencement Day because it is only after college that the youth *commences* to learn. His college course (if well conducted) gives him the key to the door of the Temple of Learning. But too often he stands in the porch of wisdom twirling the key in his hand for others to admire, and never opens the door; while many a man who forges a key for himself goes in and enjoys all her treasures. Herbert Spencer knew more than any other European of the 19th century, yet he had never been in college. [Henry Thomas] Buckle, Lincoln, Toussaint Louverture and Frederick Douglass were all educated men, but none of them had ever been to college or high school.

How did they achieve education? These ways are still open to every American, black as well as white. After all, the most that they can teach you in college is how to gather knowledge, and if you can't go to college as long as you can read you may still master that art. How to use knowledge — that no one can teach you, either in college or out of it.

"Knowledge is power." We have heard that so often that we fail to grasp its significance. But until we do, we will always be asking for crumbs of pity, chips of charity and scraps of assistance. While we chatter about "segregation" we segregate ourselves from that community of culture and knowledge that is as wide open to us as the winds of heaven and limitless as the eternal sea. In this respect the West Africans are far ahead of us. Let us pray for the will to follow in the footsteps of John Mensah Sarbah, Casely Hayford, S. Beoku Betts, Kobyna Sekyi and our other black brothers whom we ignorantly aspire to lead.

39. "Read! Read! Read!" *The Voice* (July 18, 1918), HHHP Wr.

In this July 1918 article in *The Voice*, Harrison encourages people to read and offers a list of books suggested for the "New Negro." Two months later he would write that since the list's publication, "thousands of people" expressed an eagerness "to get in touch with the stored-up knowledge the books contain[ed]." Because of such a response, Harrison would frequently make similar exhortations and periodically offer similar lists of recommended books. In September 1919 he offered another list in the *New Negro*, and that list is appended to this article.[7]

As a people our bent for books is not encouraging. We mostly read trash. And this is true not only of our rank and file but even of our leaders. When we heard Kelly Miller address the Sunrise Club of New York at a Broadway hotel two or three years ago, we were shocked at the ignorance of modern science and modern thought which his remarks displayed. His biology was of the brand of Pliny who lived about eighteen hundred years ago. For him Darwin and Spencer and Jacques Loeb had never existed nor written. His ignorance of the A. B. C.'s of astronomy and geology was pitiful.

If this is true of the leaders to whom our reading masses look, what can we expect from those reading masses? The masses must be taught to love good books. But to love them they must first know them. The handicaps placed on us in America are too great to allow us to ignore the help which we can get from that education which we get out of school for ourselves — the only one that is really worth while.

Without the New Knowledge the New Negro is no better than the old. And this new knowledge will be found in the books. Therefore, it would be well if every Negro of the new model were to make up his (or her) mind to get the essentials of modern science and modern thought as they are set down in the books which may be easily had. Don't talk about Darwin and Spencer: read them!

To help the good work along we append the following list of books that are essential. When you *master* these you will have a better "education" than is found in nine-tenths of the graduates of the average American college.

Modern Science and Modern Thought, by Samuel Laing; *The Origin of the Species* and *The Descent of Man*, by Charles Darwin; *The Principles of Sociology* and *First Principles*, by Herbert Spencer; *The Childhood of The World* and *The Childhood of Religion*, by Edward Clodd; *Anthropology*, by E[dward] B. Tylor (very easy to read and a work of standard information on Races, Culture and the origins of Religion, Art and Science); [Henry Thomas] Buckle's *History of Civilization*; [Edward] Gibbon's *Decline and Fall of the Roman Empire*; *The Martyrdom of Man*, by [W.] Winwood Reade; the books on Africa by Livingstone and Mungo Park, and *The Mind of Primitive Man*, by Franz Boas.

To stimulate an interest in good books we are about to start a book shop at the offices of *THE VOICE* where we will supply second-hand books cheap and save our readers the expense and bother of seeking them in down-town stores. We will also have new books in stock or will get them for you cheaper than any bookstore in Harlem is furnishing them now.

So we end with the slogan with which we began: Read! Read! Read!

[In the September 1919 *New Negro*, Harrison's "Our Little Library" column listed books "for general education" and "for the study of Negro History and Culture." This followed a "Books of the Month" section which included Arthur Ransome's *Russia in 1919*, George Creel's *Ireland's Fight for Freedom*, William Hard's *Theodore Roosevelt a Tribute*, Charles W. Wood's *Hurrah for Sin!*, Frank A. Vanderlip's *What Happened to Europe*, [Lala] Lajpat Rai's *The Call to Young India*, J. A. Rogers's *From Superman to Man*, and *The Complete History of Colored Soldiers in the World War* by Sergt. J. A. Jamieson and others. Harrison also suggested "the formation of Study Clubs which may meet every week to take up, one by one, the study of the works." "For General Education" he recommended:

> *Man's Place in Nature* by Thomas Henry Huxley,
> *The Childhood of the World* by Edward Clodd,
> *Modern Science and Modern Thought* by Samuel Laing,
> *A History of Modern Science* by Arabella Buckley,
> *Education* by Herbert Spencer,
> *Anthropology* by Edward B. Tylor,
> *Mutual Aid* by Prince Peter [Pyotr] Kropotkin,
> *Elementary Principles of Economics* by Richard T. Ely and George Ray Wicker,
> *Readings in European History,* by James Harvey Robinson,
> *A Short History of the English People* by John R. Green,
> *Civilization in England* by Henry T. Buckle,
> *Modern Europe* by Christopher Fyffe,
> *The Conflict Between Religion and Science* by John William Draper,
> *Workers in American History* by James Oneal.[8]

For "Negro History and Culture" he suggested:

> *African Life and Customs* by Edward Wilmot Blyden,
> *White Capital and Coloured Labor* by Sir Sidney Olivier,
> *Negro Culture in West Africa* by George W. Ellis,
> *Europe in Africa in the Nineteenth Century* by Elizabeth Wormeley Latimer,
> *Ethiopia Unbound: Studies in Race Emancipation* by Joseph Ephraim Casely
>   Hayford (Acca Agrimun),
> *From Superman to Man* by J. A. Rogers,
> *The Aftermath of Slavery,* by Dr. William A. Sinclair,
> *The Haytian Revolution* by T. G. Stewart,
> *West African Studies* by Mary H. Kingsley,
> *A Tropical Dependency* by Lady Florence Lugard
> *The Negro and the Nation* by Hubert H. Harrison

Harrison also promised that "a review and summary" of one of these books would appear each month "for the benefit of our readers." This piece appeared again in the October *New Negro*, the last one that Harrison edited.][9]

Politics

5

Throughout his adult life Harrison advocated the importance of developing a political voice and organizing politically. In this he both differed from and influenced Marcus Garvey. Garvey, according to historian Robert A. Hill, had eschewed political involvement before learning from Harrison the need of a political voice.[1]

After the 1906 incident in Brownsville, Texas, Harrison emphatically urged African American voters to break from the Republican Party (the party to which Booker T. Washington and the "Tuskegee Machine" were so fully aligned). He first turned to the Socialists, W. E. B. Du Bois also did, but unlike Du Bois, he stayed with the Socialists in 1912 and did not back the Democratic Party's Woodrow Wilson.[2]

Beginning around 1916, Harrison repeatedly called for African Americans to maintain their political independence, put "race interests" first in evaluating candidates, organize politically, seek a political voice, and run Black candidates for office. Overall, this quest for a new Black political voice distinguished Harrison from the leadership of Washington, Du Bois, and Garvey and was, according to Robert A. Hill, the cornerstone of the "New Negro Movement" which he founded.[3]

Lincoln and Liberty

During his first decade in the United States, Harrison studied American history carefully and developed a critical reinterpretation of Reconstruction history that broke from the white-supremacist mold and focused on the actions and leading role of African Americans. In the course of his research he obtained a book that deeply affected his political thinking, *Letters and Addresses of Abraham Lincoln*, edited by Mary Maclean, a socialist and a writer for the *New York Times*. Maclean became a leading activist with the NAACP, managing editor of that organization's *Crisis* magazine, and one of the few close white friends of W. E. B. Du Bois (until her untimely death in 1912). In her book, Lincoln, the "Father of Emancipation" and standard bearer of the Republican Party to which Blacks had been wedded since the Civil War, had his racial, and at times racist, views exposed.[4]

Harrison, particularly since the Brownsville incident, had increasingly become disillusioned with the Republicans. (On the day after election day in 1906, the Republican President Theodore Roosevelt, on insufficient evidence, dishonorably discharged from the army and debarred from future government employment all 167 men of three companies of Black troops of the Twenty-fifth Regiment stationed near Brownsville.)[5] In developing his overall criticism of the Republican Party, Harrison routinely cited the historical record (including Congress's apparent willingness to make slavery perpetual under a proposed thirteenth amendment), and he quoted Lincoln. Beginning in 1911, he developed a series of lectures on "Lincoln and Liberty — Fact versus Fiction," which were finally published in four parts in the *Negro World* in 1921. At that time they were used as principle examples of the need for political independence for African Americans and they helped to facilitate the African American community's break from the Republican Party.

Over the years, Harrison applied an analogy from the Civil War to his efforts with workers. He was a strong proponent of the need for workers to form unions for self-defense and to strengthen their collective power in struggle against capitalists. However, his position changed markedly after American Federation of Labor President Samuel Gompers visited Carnegie Hall in New York in 1917 and placed responsibility for the East St. Louis pogrom on the alleged necessity of "white" unionists to defend their jobs by murder against the Black workers whom they had shut out of their unions. Harrison thenceforth made it clear that, unlike Abraham Lincoln, his primary objective was not "to save the union" (be it a union of states or an AFL union), but "to free the slaves." It was a position that he first highlighted in "Lincoln and Liberty."

The following articles are numbers 2 and 3 in the "Lincoln and Liberty" series. Though published in 1921, they were based in large part on a talk Harrison developed in late 1911. Of particular interest, in addition to his "free the slaves" proclamation, are Harrison's discussions of the proposed thirteenth amendment of 1861, which, with Republican support, sought to make slavery perpetual.

 40. "Lincoln and Liberty: Fact versus Fiction; Chapter Two. Lincoln Not an Abolitionist, Republicans Opposed Abolitionist Doctrine," *Negro World* (March 12, 1921), 8, HHHP Scr B.

What was Lincoln's relation to all this? I shall endeavor to show that Lincoln was not an Abolitionist; that he had no special love for Negroes; that he opposed the abolition of the Domestic Slave Trade and favored the Fugitive Slave Law; that he opposed citizenship for Negroes; that he favored making slavery perpetual in 1861; that he denied officially that the war was fought to free the slaves; that he refused to pay Negro soldiers the same wage that he paid the white soldiers; that without these Negro soldiers the North could not have won the war; that the Emancipation Proclamation was issued, not for the slave's sake, but solely as an act to cripple the army of the South; and finally, that it did not abolish slavery and was not intended to.

These are the things that I shall prove in regard to Abraham Lincoln and in regard to the men of his party.

I shall also prove that the war was fought for economic and not for moral reasons. Indeed, I think I have done that already.

Next, I shall prove that: the Republican party opposed the Abolitionist doctrine; that they offered to sell out the Negro in 1861, and the only reason why the sale was not consummated was that the buyer picked up his basket and went home. And I shall prove that as late as 1864 the Republican party, in control of the Government, refused to pass an amendment to the Constitution abolishing slavery.

Now for the proof.

I shall turn first to page 118 of *The Letters and Addresses of Abraham Lincoln.* I am quoting from Lincoln's opening speech in the second joint debate with Stephen Douglas, August 27, 1858, at Freeport, Illinois. In regard to the Fugitive Slave Law, Lincoln said:

> I have never hesitated to say, that I think, under the Constitution of the United States, the people of the Southern States are entitled to a congressional fugitive-slave law. . . . I should not with my present views be in favor of endeavoring to abolish slavery in the District of Columbia unless it would be upon these conditions: First, that the abolition should be gradual; second, that it should be on a vote of the majority of qualified voters in the District; and third, that compensation should be made to unwilling owners. . . . In regard to the fifth interrogatory, I must say here that as to the question of the abolition of the slave trade between the different states I can truly answer, as I have, that I am pledged to nothing about it. . . . I must say, however, that if I should be of opinion that Congress does possess the Constitutional power to abolish the slave trade among the different states, I should still not be in favor of that power. . . .

These facts seem to make against the story that you get from little Mary's Fairy Tales about the young man sailing down the Mississippi and seeing slaves in a slave gathering, and coming back and saying: "If I ever get a chance to hit slavery I will hit it and hit it hard." It sounds beautiful but it isn't true.

In his first inaugural address in Washington, Abraham Lincoln said:

> Apprehension seems to exist among the people of the Southern States that by the accession of a Republican administration their property and their peace and personal security are to be endangered. There has never been any reasonable cause for such apprehension. Indeed, the most ample evidence to the contrary has all the while existed and been open to their inspection. It is found in nearly all the published speeches of him who now addresses you. I do but quote from one of those speeches when I declare that "I have no purpose, directly or indirectly, to interfere with this institution of slavery in the states where it exists. . . ."

And in his first inaugural, to support his contention, he quoted from the Republican party's platform:

> Resolved, That the maintenance inviolate of the rights of the states, and especially the right of each state to order and control its own domestic institutions according to its own judgment exclusively, is essential to that balance of power on which the perfection and endurance of our political fabric depend, and we denounce the lawless invasion by armed force of the soil of any state or territory, no matter under what pretext, as among the gravest of crimes.

First, you have Lincoln and then you have Lincoln's party. I do not mean to insinuate when I present these truths that Abraham Lincoln was a hypocrite. When I think that Abraham Lincoln was a hypocrite at a particular point, I shall take occasion to say so plainly and manfully. My own information is simply that Abraham Lincoln was a politician, or if you like, a statesman. You see, a statesman, is a politician with a circumbendibus.

In his opening speech in his fourth joint debate at Charleston, Illinois, September 18, 1858, he said:

> I will say then that I am not, nor ever have been, in favor of the bringing about in any way the social and political equality of the white and black races — that I am not, nor have ever been, in favor of making voters or jurors of Negroes, nor of qualifying them to hold office. . . .

In his rejoinder to Douglas at the same place, September 1858, he said:

> Judge Douglas has said to you that he has not been able to get from me an answer to the question whether I am in favor of Negro citizenship. So far as I know, the judge never asked me the question before. He shall have no occasion to ever ask it again, for I tell him very frankly that I am not in favor of Negro citizenship. . . .

Further on he says:

> Now my opinion is that the different states have the power to make a Negro a citizen under the Constitution of the United States, if they choose. The Dred Scott decision decides that they have not the power. If the state of Illinois had that power, I should be opposed to the exercise of it. That is all I have to say about it.

So much for the proof of that.

I said that I should prove that he favored making slavery perpetual in 1861. Take [James G.] Blaine's *Twenty Years in Congress* — a rather hefty book, both physical and otherwise. Blaine was one of the biggest politicians or statesmen that this country has produced. He was in Congress for something like twenty years on and off, and this book was written, partly as a summary of the activities of his Congressional era, and partly as a history of the United States by a politician who had to do with the making of history.

I shall show that the first thirteenth Amendment was proposed to entrench slavery so securely that it should be safe from attack by the Supreme Court of the United States itself; and the Republican party and Abraham Lincoln himself, specifically, by explicit statement, supported that move.

Early in 1861, the Southern representatives in Congress began to drop out as their states seceded and issued cartels, some of defiance and some of simple explanation, telling why they were leaving. When the North and the northern politicians saw that, did they use the great arm of the government as our friend Postmaster [Albert S.] Burleson is trying to do as regards Negro papers? No! They compromised. They got together and offered to sell out the cause of the Negro. White men of the North did not, on the whole, care much about Negroes then. Those who did were called Abolitionists, and the Abolitionists had no party. You may remember that there was a break between Frederick Douglass and William Lloyd Garrison, between the Radical and Abolitionist groups, as to whether they should support the Free Soil or any other party, by which they could get a percentage of their demands realized and enacted into law.

41. "Lincoln and Liberty: Fact versus Fiction; Chapter Three. Lincoln and Republican Party Favor Perpetual Slavery," *Negro World* (March 19, 1921), HHHP Scr.B.

Early in 1861, while the Northern legislators were kow-towing to Southern sentiment, a committee composed of thirteen members of the Senate and thirty-one members of the House was created to bring in resolutions on the basis of the Crittenden compromise, which had been previously offered to Congress. "The record of that committee," says Mr. Blaine, "is one which cannot be reviewed with pride or satisfaction by any citizen of a State that was loyal to the Union. [. . .] Mr. Charles Francis Adams proposed that the Constitution of the United States be so amended that no subsequent amendment thereto having for its object any interference with slavery shall originate with any State that does not recognize that relation, within its own limits, or shall be valid without the assent of every one of the States composing the Union."

Says Mr. Blaine in comment: "No Southern man, during the long agitation of the slavery question extending from 1820 to 1860, had ever submitted so extreme a proposition as that of Mr. Adams. The most precious muniments of personal liberty never had such deep embedment in the organic law of the Republic as Mr. Adams now proposed for the protection of slavery." Yet, the proposition was opposed by only three members of the committee of thirty-three, and they were Mason W. Tappan of New Hampshire, Cadwallader C. Washburn of Wisconsin and William Kellogg of Illinois.

"The first amendment proposed that in 'all [the territory] of the United States south of the old Missouri line, either now held or to be hereafter acquired, the slavery of the African race is recognized as existing, not to be interfered with by Congress, but to be protected as property by all the departments of the Territorial Government during its continuance.'

"The second amendment declared that 'Congress shall have no power to interfere with slavery even in those places under its exclusive jurisdiction in the slave States.'

"The third amendment took away from Congress the exclusive jurisdiction over the District of Columbia as guaranteed in the Constitution, declared that Congress should "never interfere with slavery in the District except with the consent of Virginia and Maryland so long as it exists in the States of Virginia and Maryland."

"The fourth amendment prohibited Congress from interfering with the transportation of slaves from one State to another, or from one State to any Territory south of the Missouri line."

That meant that slaveholders could by migration to the Northern States re-establish slavery which had been abolished by the Legislature as a domestic institution in those Northern States.

"The sixth amendment," says Mr. Blaine, "provided for a perpetual existence of the five amendments just quoted by placing them beyond the power of the people to change or revise — declaring that no future amendment to the Constitution shall ever be passed that shall affect any provision of the five amendments just recited; that the provision in the original Constitution which guarantees the court of three-fifths of the slaves in the basis of representation, shall never be changed by any amendment, that no amendment shall ever be made which alters or impairs the original provision for the recovery of fugitives from service; that no amendment shall be made that shall ever permit Congress to interfere in any way with slavery in the States where it may be permitted.

"When the report of the committee came before the House for action the series of resolutions were first tested by motion to lay upon the table, which was defeated by a vote of nearly two to one: and after an angry debate running through several days the resolutions [. . .] were adopted by a large majority" on February 27, 1861. "When the constitutional amendment was reached, Mr. [Thomas] Corwin substituted for that which was originally drafted by Adams, an amendment declaring that 'no amendment shall be made to the Constitution which will authorize or give to Congress the power to abolish, or interfere, within any State with the domestic institutions thereof, including that of persons held to labor or service by the law of said State.' This was adopted by a vote of 133 to 65. It was numbered as the Thirteenth Amendment to the Federal Constitution and would have made slavery perpetual in the United States, so far as any influence or power of the national government could affect it.

"It entrenched slavery securely in the organic law of the land and elevated the privilege of the slaveholder beyond that of the owner of any other species of property. It received the votes of a large number of Republicans who were then and afterwards prominent in the councils of the party. Among the most distinguished were Mr. [John] Sherman of Ohio, Mr. [Schuyler] Colfax, Mr. C[harles]. F. Adams, Mr. [Jacob] Howard of Michigan, Mr. [William] Windom of Minnesota and Messrs. [James K.] Moorhead and [Edward] McPherson of Pennsylvania."

Now how did Abraham Lincoln stand connected with this? For the answer you have to turn to Abraham Lincoln's first inaugural address. So many of us read this State paper just as we read the emancipation proclamation and we do not seem to understand what it is that they really tell us. In the first inaugural, Abraham Lincoln, said in reference to this proposal, which was then before the Congress: "I understand that a proposed amendment to the Constitution — which amendment, however, I have not seen — has passed Congress to the effect that the Federal Government shall never interfere with the domestic institutions, including that of persons held to labor or service. To avoid misconstruction of what I have said, I depart from my purpose not to speak of particular amendments, so far as to say that, holding such a provision now to be implied constitutional law, I have no objection to its being made express and irrevocable."

"To Save the Union — Not To Free The Slaves"

During the first year and a half of the war the white working men of England and Europe made repeated requests to Lincoln to declare that the freedom of the Negro slaves was one of the objects of the war. Karl Marx and the working men of Great Britain particularly urged him to do this pointing out that the Tories of England were making capital of the fact that they could get England into the war on the side of the Confederacy. Said the working men of England: "If you would now declare that this is a war to free the slaves, we will smoke them out and in the name of human altruism we will compel the Government of Britain to keep its hands off." And even so — even though their requests were backed up by such big men in America as Moncure D. Conway, Augustus Stalla, Judge Lorenzo Taft and Horace Greeley — even though the support of the Liberal parties of Europe hung in the balance, Abraham Lincoln was so wedded to his view (which is not the view currently ascribed to him) that he would not say that the war was a war to free the slaves, but insisted instead in saying again and again that the war was not a war to free slaves.

Greeley was impatient at this attitude of the President. He held that it was ignoble Morality — the morality of the slick politician — and he had the courage to write an open letter to the President in which he stated that point of view. In this letter replying to Greeley's, Lincoln said, among other things:

I would save the Union. I would save it the shortest way under the Constitution. The sooner the national authority can be restored, the nearer the Union will be "the

Union as it was." If there be those who would not save the Union unless they could at the same time save slavery, I do not agree with them. If there be those who would not save the Union unless they could at the same time destroy slavery, I do not agree with them. *My paramount object in this struggle is to save the union and is not either to save or destroy slavery. If I can save the union without freeing any slave, I would do it. If I can save it by freeing all the slaves, I would do it, and if I could save it by freeing some and leaving others alone—, I would also do that.*

— and I might add parenthetically that that is exactly what he did, as I shall prove to you later. "What I do about slavery," he goes on, "and the colored race, I do because I believe it helps to save the union, and what I forbear I forbear because I do not think it helps to save the union. I shall do less whenever I shall believe what I am doing hurts the cause; I shall do more whenever I shall believe doing more will help the cause."

I wish to say that it is a very sensible reason which Mr. Lincoln gives. It is statesman-like and it merits approval for statesmanship. But since "you cannot eat your cake and have it, too" it effectively disposes of any claim to the Negroes' gratitude on the grounds of high moral altruism and benevolence.

"New Negro Politics"

In mid-1917, less than two years after the death of Booker T. Washington, the old Tuskegee political machinery was breaking up, and new avenues for political action were opening. The Washington option (of a client–patron relationship to white politicians) and the Du Bois option (of "uniting the intellectuals at the top" and moving in favor of whoever made the most symbolic gesture toward "fair treatment" — as in the 1912 and 1916 presidential elections) — were no longer the only alternatives. The Black vote in certain northern aldermanic and assembly election districts held the balance of power and there was the possibility for Black pressure groups and Black self-assertion to influence and shape elections. As the objective conditions changed with the formation of concentrated communities of Black voters the tasks of awakening racial consciousness and of developing organizational means to voice political demands became pressing. In this setting, Harrison came forward advocating a new strategy: the uniting, not of those at the top, but those at the bottom — the "Negro masses."[6]

In New York City there were no Black elected officials. The Republican Party maintained a segregated political club system and the Democratic Party had a segregated city-wide organization (the United Colored Democracy) and under these systems, Black political leaders were directly accountable, not to the African American community, but to white party leaders. There was opportunity, however, in both the Nineteenth Aldermanic District and the Twenty-sixth Assembly District where independent Black leaders could mobilize the masses and influence the outcome of the elections. In the summer of 1917, Harrison emerged as a leader in the "campaign for Black district leadership" as Harlem's "New Negroes" sought an independent political voice.[7]

ᛚᛚᛚᛚ 42. "The Drift in Politics," *The Voice* (c. July 25, 1917), reprinted with minor
ᛚᛚᛚᛚ changes in *When Africa Awakes*, 41–43.

As Harlem's Black population grew and sentiment for elective leadership intensified, a meeting was scheduled for the Palace Casino on Sunday, July 29, 1917. A citizen's committee was to report to Harlem's Black voters on how it had been turned down by the local Republican Party when it sought to have Black candidates run on the party slate. Immediately prior to that meeting, as part of the build-up campaign, Harrison published "The Drift in Politics." Its first four paragraphs were drawn almost verbatim from his July 1912 "Socialism and the Negro" article. However, where in 1912 Harrison saw an "open opportunity of the Socialist party," in 1917 he explained that Black voters were "not Republicans, Democrats or Socialists any longer." They were now "Negroes first" and they were "no longer begging for sops" but demanding representation.[8]

The Negroes of America — those of them who think — are suspicious of everything that comes from the white people [the 1912 version gives *Socialist Party*]of America. They have seen that every movement for the extension of democracy here has broken down as soon as it reached the color line. Political democracy declared that "all men are created equal," [but] meant only all white men. The Christian church found that the brotherhood of man did not include God's bastard children; the public school system proclaimed that the school house was the backbone of democracy — "for white people only," and the civil service says that Negroes must keep their place — at the bottom. So that they can hardly be blamed for looking askance at any new gospel of freedom. Freedom to them has been like one of

> "those juggling fiends
> That palter with us in double sense;
> That keep the word of promise to our ear,
> And break it to our hope."

In this connection, some explanation of the former political solidarity of those Negroes who were voters may be of service. Up to six years ago the one great obstacle to the political progress of the colored people was their sheep-like allegiance to the Republican party. They were taught to believe that God had raised up a peculiar race of men called Republicans who had loved the slaves so tenderly that they had taken guns in their hands and rushed on the ranks of the southern slaveholders to free the slaves; that this race of men was still in existence, marching under the banner of the Republican party and showing their great love for Negroes by appointing from six to sixteen near-Negroes to soft political snaps. Today that great political superstition is falling to pieces before the advance of intelligence among Negroes. They begin to realize that they were sold out by the Republican party in 1876; that in the last twenty-five years lynchings have increased, disfranchisement has spread all over the south and "Jim-crow" cars run even into the national capital — with the continuing consent of a Republican Congress, a Republican Supreme Court and Republican President.

Ever since the Brownsville affair, but more clearly since [President William Howard] Taft declared and put in force the policy of pushing out the few near-Negro officeholders, the rank and file have come to see that the Republican party is a great big sham. Many went over to the Democratic party because, as the *Amsterdam News* puts it, "they had nowhere else to go." Twenty years ago the colored men who joined that party were ostracized as scalawags and crooks — which they probably were. But today, the defection to the democrats of such men as Bishop [Alexander] Walters, [Robert N.] Wood, [James D.] Carr and [Ralph E.] Langston — whose uncle was a colored Republican congressman from Virginia — has made the colored democracy respectable and given quite a tone to political heterodoxy.

All this loosens the bonds of their allegiance and breaks the bigotry of the last forty years. But of this change in their political view-point the white world knows nothing. The two leading Negro newspapers are subsidized by the same political pirates who hold the title-deeds to the handful of hirelings holding office in the name of the Negro race. One of these papers is an organ of Mr. [Booker T.] Washington, the other pretends to be independent — that is, it must be "bought" on the installment plan, and both of them are in New York. Despite this "conspiracy of silence" the Negroes are waking up; are beginning to think for themselves; to look with more favor on "new doctrines." [HH removed two lines in the reprint: And herein lies the open opportunity of the Socialist party. If the work of spreading Socialist propaganda is taken to them now, their ignorance of it can be enlightened and their suspicions removed.]

Today the politician who wants the support of the Negro voter will have to give something more than piecrust promises. The old professional "friend to the colored people" must have something more solid than the name of Lincoln and party appointments.

We demand what the Irish and the Jewish voter get: nominations on the party's ticket in our own districts. And if we don't get this we will smash the party that refuses to give it.

For we are not Republicans, Democrats or Socialists any longer. We are Negroes first. And we are no longer begging for sops. We demand, not "recognition," but representation, and we are out to throw our votes to *any* party which gives us this, and withhold them from any party which refuses to give it. No longer will we follow any leader whose job the party controls. For we know that no leader so controlled can oppose such party in our interests beyond a given point.

That is why so much interest attaches to the mass-meeting to be held at Palace Casino on the 29th where the Citizens' Committee will make its report to the Negro voters of Harlem and tell them how it was "turned down" by the local representatives of

the Republican party when it begged the boon of elective representation. All such re-
buffs will make for manhood — if we are men — and will drive us to play in American
politics the same role which the Irish party played in British politics. That is the new
trend in Negro politics, and we must not let any party forget it.

43. "The New Policies for the New Negro," *The Voice* (September 4, 1917),
HHHP Wr, reprinted with minor changes as "The New Politics for the
New Negro," in *When Africa Awakes*, 39–41.

Harrison's editorial "The New Policies for the New Negro" continued the 1917 campaign
for elective representation. He explained that the "new Negro" was "no longer begging or
asking" but "demanding representation," and that "New Negro" political leaders would
have to be chosen by those they were to represent. Drawing on international examples, he
expressed the view that anyone who aspired "to lead the Negro race" had to "follow the
path of the Swadesha movement of India and the Sinn Fein movement of Ireland" and
seek to build a politically independent party for the benefit of "ourselves first."

The world of the future will look upon the world of today as an essentially new turning
point in the path of human progress. All over the world the spirit of democratic striving
is making itself felt. The new issues have brought forth new ideas of freedom, politics,
industry and society at large. The new Negro living in this new world is just as responsive to these new impulses as other people are.

In the "good old days" it was quite easy to tell the Negro to follow in the footsteps of
those who had gone before. The mere mention of the name Lincoln or the Republican
party was sufficient to secure his allegiance to that party which had seen him stripped
of all political power and of civil rights without protest — effective or otherwise.

Things are different now. The new Negro is demanding elective representation in
Baltimore, Chicago and other places. He is demanding it in New York. The pith of the
present occasion is, that he is no longer begging or asking. He is demanding as a right
that which he is in position to enforce.

In the presence of this new demand the old political leaders are bewildered, and
afraid; for the old idea of Negro leadership by virtue of the white man's selection has
collapsed. The new Negro leader must be chosen by his fellows — by those whose strivings he is supposed to represent.

Any man today who aspires to lead the Negro race must set squarely before his face
the idea of "Africa first" ["*Race First*" in the reprint]. Just as the white men of these and
other lands are white men before they are Christians, Anglo-Saxons or Republicans; so
the Negroes of this and other lands are intent upon being Negroes before they are
Christians, Englishmen or Republicans.

Sauce for the goose is sauce for the gander. Charity begins at home, and our first duty is to ourselves. It is not what we wish but what we must, that we are connected with. The world, as it ought to be, is still for us, as for others, the world that does not exist. The world as it is, is the real world, and it is to that real world that we address ourselves. Striving to be men, and finding no effective aid in government or in politics, the Negro of the Western world must follow the path of the Swadesha movement of India and the Sinn Fein movement of Ireland. The meaning of both these terms is "ourselves first." This is the mental background of the new politics of the New Negro, and we commend it to the consideration of all the political parties. For it is upon this background that we will predicate such policies as shall seem to us necessary and desirable.

In the British Parliament the Irish Home Rule party clubbed its full strength and devoted itself so exclusively to the cause of Free Ireland that it virtually dictated for a time the policies of Liberals and Conservatives alike.

The new Negro race in America will not achieve political self-respect until it is in a position to organize itself as a politically independent party and follow the example of the Irish Home Rulers. This is what will happen in American politics. [This last paragraph is italicized in the reprint.][9]

44. "The Coming Election," *The Voice* (October 18, 1917), HHHP Wr.

The 1917 New York municipal elections featured a four-way mayoral contest that was among the most hotly contested in city history. William Bennett was the Republican nominee. John Purroy Mitchel, the incumbent, lost the Republican primary and ran as a Fusion candidate (the Fusion Party was an alliance of defecting Republicans and anti-Tammany Democrats) with the backing of Republican former presidents Theodore Roosevelt and William Howard Taft and former New York Governor and 1916 Republican presidential candidate Charles Evans Hughes. Brooklyn Judge John Hylan, the Democrat, was a low-profile Tammany candidate, while Morris Hillquit was the Socialist contender. In addition to a host of Socialists contesting other offices, there were also two Black candidates who had fought their way to nominations in the primaries — attorney Edward A. Johnson, for assemblyman in the Nineteenth Assembly District, and attorney James C. Thomas Jr. for alderman in the Twenty-sixth Aldermanic District. The Nineteenth Assembly District was from one-third to one-half Black and the gerrymandered Twenty-sixth Aldermanic District included parts of the Nineteenth, Twentieth, Twenty-first, and Twenty-second Assembly Districts and was about one-third Black. The 1917 ballot was also to decide on the question of women's suffrage.[10]

Harrison accurately predicted that "the Negro vote will be worth more than it ever was worth before." Due in large part to migration from the South and arrivals from the Caribbean, Harlem in 1917 had approximately 60,000 Blacks, about one-fifth of whom were West Indians. In this "New Negro Mecca," where Black males had the vote, African Americans were moving to a position where they could clearly influence (and soon determine) election results. This significant change was helping to reshape Black political strategy and leadership. Though Black voters did not decide the final election, the situation in which Black votes didn't matter (a situation which historian Nathan Huggins has suggested was a reason for the relative impotency of Black leadership) was changing.[11]

Harrison addresses this new reality in "The Coming Election."

In the coming election the Negro vote will be worth more than it ever was worth before. The different parties are willing to pay a higher price for it than they have ever paid. It will be a remarkably close contest, and whoever wins will win by a neck. For the first time in the city's history the Negro's vote can be the pivotal, the deciding, element. Will the Negro voter see this? He ought to ask, of course, all that he can get. That is the way in which sensible men get profit out of politics. Of course, if we are in politics for the gratitude, altruism or goodness, then there is nothing to be said. But if we are in politics to benefit our race, then it must be that we are in it to get something out of it.

What is this something? And how much of it are the various parties offering? Let us examine and see.

First, let us take the Republican Party. What is it fighting for? It isn't quite easy to say. Bennett won the verdict of the party's voters at the primaries. But Mitchel, backed by Roosevelt, Taft and Hughes, and the organized plunderbund of Wall Street, refuses to abide by that verdict. That splits the Republican vote squarely in two and makes their need for the Negro vote all the greater. Therefore, it is up to the Negro voters to demand a higher price from them. So far, our "colored" Republican leaders have not seen fit to formulate this demand. They are still sunk in the sloth of stupid "allegiance."

The present Negro candidates do not owe their candidacy to the white leaders of the Republican Party; because they had to fight them tooth and nail—and beat them—to get it. And there is no absolute certainty that these leaders who deliberately gerrymandered the Negro district to make the election of a Negro highly improbable, will be quite straight behind the screen. Some few of them, like Frank McCabe, are quite fair, honest and above-board. But we have reason to fear that most of them, like Mayor Mitchel, are not.

It seems to us that the proper play for the Negro leaders was to demand—and get—things before election. They should have gone down to City Hall—not like Fred Moore [editor and publisher of the strongly pro-Republican *New York Age*], a lick-spittle leader of nothing but himself—to promise to fight like h—— for Mitchel; but to have the city administration pass at once the bill for a big bathhouse in Harlem. They should have got before election twenty Negro policeman appointed in Harlem and the condign punishment of those white policemen and detectives who have "beaten up" Negro citizens. They should have got a few Negroes appointed on the Fire Department and stationed here. But they didn't. This failure shows their fatuousness; and fatuousness is, in plain English, just plain damfoolishness. Because of this, we are not likely to get from the Mitchel wing of the party of plutocracy any more than we got before. What that has been, the raidings, clubbings, shootings, insults, and neglect will abundantly testify.

From the Bennett wing, of course, nothing is to be had before election, except a little cash; because it has nothing to give. After election it is open speculation. But Bennett is not likely to be elected. His only value will consist in splitting the Republican vote and helping to insure Mitchel's well-deserved defeat.

Then, there is the party of Judge Hylan. Tammany Hall has dealt more decently by the Negroes than Negroes have by Tammany Hall. But, we are told that Tammany Hall is corrupt, and the good old game of "Swat the tiger!" goes merrily on. This is a game in which the Negro is not concerned. Too many fakers, like [District Attorney, William Travers] Jerome, have made their political fortunes by fooling the people into believing that when they swat Tammany Hall their troubles will be over. And Tammany Hall thrives and is always there to be swatted. Why? Because Tammany Hall is no more vicious than the voters of New York are. That's why.

But the Negro voters of New York have not had horse-sense enough to make an honest deal with Tammany Hall. Therefore, they have no right to expect much from it. If Judge Hylan is elected we may get a better deal from the Democratic Party in this city, than we ever got from the Republican. But that is only a hope.

Finally, there is the Socialist Party — clean and straight and standing out of the muck of mere politics, with the sunlight on its face, fronting the dawn of a better day. Its candidate is Morris Hillquit. Here are a man and a party from whom no oppressive act toward the Negro has ever come. Three years ago a Negro was on its City Central Committee, helping to manage the affairs of tens of thousands of white Socialists — without any Negro voters behind him as the price of this high office. What has this party to offer the Negro in this election? Nothing special. Nothing but what it offers to all downtrodden workers: Justice, liberty, and absolute equality — not only in words, but in deeds. That is why Mitchel fears it and, when challenged to debate the high price of bread and milk, meat and rents, skulks behind the meaningless platitudes about patriotism. That is why Hylan fears it, that is why Bennett fears it.

The Socialist Party in power would mean the absolute cessation of police brutality and the conscienceless evictions by conscienceless landlords; would mean bathhouses and playgrounds; municipal markets to cut down the high cost of living, municipal ownership of ice and milk, They have not put forward these issues for this coming election. They have had the same issues at every campaign. These are the things that a Socialist Party means — here and everywhere else.

Now, for the first time in years, they have a chance to win. Tammany Hall concedes this. The editors of the *World* and other big newspapers concede it. If the Negroes of this great city want and need the things for which they stand, let them vote for the Socialist candidates (and for Thomas and Johnson) in this election. This time, at any rate, the talk of "throwing away your vote" is sheer humbug. For, even if it came to the worst, it is better to vote for what you want, and not get it, than to vote for what you don't want — and get it.

45. "Our Professional 'Friends,'" *The Voice* (November 7, 1917), reprinted with deletions in *When Africa Awakes*, 55–60.

As election results were tabulated in New York City's 1917 municipal elections, *The Voice* carried a scorching editorial by Harrison entitled "Our Professional 'Friends.'" The country was at war, and Harrison was a critic of the country's war policy, of the federal government's opening of segregated officers training camps, and of the role played by NAACP leader Joel E. Spingarn in supporting the war effort and developing the camps. Spingarn had arranged with General Leonard Wood, the commander of the Easter Division, to establish a camp for Black officers if two hundred suitable applicants were found. Three hundred and fifty applicants, mostly from Howard University and the Hampton Institute, quickly applied, and at Spingarn's urging, the War Department approved the plan on May 19. In June, qualified candidates reported to Fort Des Moines, Iowa, and by October the camp had produced 629 officers of the total of 1,200 that would ultimately be commissioned.[12]

The segregated officers' training camps issue prompted W. E. B. Du Bois to utter his famous "condition, not a theory" position. Du Bois at first opposed the segregated camps as an "insult" to all African Americans, but, he claimed, "strong, sober second thought" (influenced by Spingarn) led him to change his position, arguing that "We face a condition, not a theory." There was to Du Bois "not the slightest chance" of African Americans being admitted to white camps and he viewed the choice as simply one between either segregated camps or "no colored officers."[13]

The camps issue proved to be a major point of difference between the "New Negroes" and the "old" leadership. Harrison maintained that "the government was just getting ready to open the camps to Negroes" when certain leaders (such as the NAACP's Joel E. Spingarn) "piped up" for a Jim Crow training camp.[14] Charles Flint Kellogg, historian of the NAACP, supports Harrison's contention. Kellogg points out that the "Negro press as a whole bitterly condemned" Spingarn's proposal and cites leading papers, including the *New York Age*, the *Chicago Defender*, the *Boston Guardian*, the *St. Paul Appeal*, and the *Baltimore Afro-American*, that opposed segregated camps. Because of actions by the NAACP like those regarding the camps, Harrison began to refer to it as the "National Association for the Acceptance of Color Proscription." Because of the leading role of whites like Spingarn in obtaining the camps, Harrison would charge that "the brighter minds among Negroes of today hate them [such white friends] with a hatred [the original gives *savagery*] comparable only to the way in which a similar class of Negroes hated the white supporters of the American Colonization Society [the original gives *Booker Washington*]."[15]

Harrison and the Liberty League challenged the NAACP's policies and leadership because of the camps issue, just as Du Bois and the Niagara Movement had when they opposed the leadership of Booker T. Washington. Harrison recognized that the NAACP had "done much good work for Negroes — splendid work — in fighting lynching and segregation" and that as Negroes "we owe it more gratitude and good will than we owe the entire Republican party for the last sixty years of its existence." But he felt strongly that gratitude should not mean that African Americans should "abdicate our right to shape more radical policies for ourselves." It was, as he explained, "the realization of the need for a more radical policy than that of the N.A.A.C.P. that called into being the Liberty League of Negro Americans." Challenging the role of "Professional Friends" was an important part of developing that policy. In the article that follows, Harrison criticizes the actions of leading white members of the NAACP, including Oswald Garrison Villard, Mary White Ovingon, and Joel E. Spingarn.

This country of ours has produced many curious lines of endeavor, not the least curious of which is the business known as "being the Negro's friend." It was first invented by politicians, but was taken up later by "good" men, six-per-cent philanthropists, millionaire believers in "industrial education," benevolent newspapers like the *Evening Post*, and a host of smaller fry of the "superior race." Just at this time the business is being worked to death, and we wish to contribute our mite toward the killing — by showing what it means.

The first great "friend" of the Negro was the Southern politician, Henry Clay, who in the first half of the nineteenth century organized the American Colonization Society. This society befriended the "free men of color" by raising funds to ship them to Liberia, which was accepted by many free Negroes as high proof of the white man's "friendship." But Frederick Douglass, William Still, James McCune Smith, Martin R. Delaney, and other wide-awake Negroes were able to show (by transcripts of its proceedings) that its real purpose was to get rid of free Negroes because, so long as they continued to live here, their freedom was an inducement to the slaves to run away from slavery, and their accomplishments demonstrated to all white people that the Negro (contrary to the claims of the slave-holders) was capable of a higher human destiny than that of being chattels — and this was helping to make American slavery odious in the eyes of the civilized world.

Since that time the dismal farce of "friendship" has been played many times, by politicians, millionaires and their editorial adherents, who have been profuse in giving good advice to the Negro people. They have advised them to "go slow," that "Rome was not built in a day," and that "half a loaf is better than no bread," that "respect could not be demanded," and, in a thousand different ways have advised them that if they would only follow the counsels of "the good white people" who really had their interests at heart, instead of following their own counsels (as the Irish and the Jews do), all would yet be well. Many Negroes who have a wish-bone where their back-bone ought to be have been doing this. It was as a representative of this class that [Mayor John Purroy]

Mitchel's man, Mr. Fred R. Moore, the editor of *The Age*, spoke, when in July he gave utterance to the owlish reflection that,

> The Negro race is afflicted with many individuals whose wagging tongues are apt to lead them into indiscreet utterances that reflect upon the whole race . . . The unruly tongues should not be allowed to alienate public sympathy from the cause of the oppressed.

To which *The Voice* replied:

> Good God! Isn't it high time to ask, "Of what value is that kind of sympathy which is ready to be alienated as soon as Negroes cease to be 'niggers' and start to be men?" Is that the sort of sympathy on which *The Age* has thrived? Then we will have none of it.

It was as a fairly good representative of the class of "good white friends of the colored people" that Miss Mary White Ovington, the chairman of the New York Branch of the National Association for the Advancement of Colored People, sent to *The Voice* the following bossy and dictatorial note:

My dear Mr. Harrison,

I don't see any reason for another organization, or another paper. If you printed straight socialism it might be different. I hope you were in the parade.

Yours truly,

MARY. W. OVINGTON.

Aug. 3, 1917

My dear Miss Ovington,

I wish I could help you to see. But does it matter so very much? *The Voice* goes ten thousand strong each week just the same.

As I am not [at present] a member of the Socialist [Party] organization, printing "Straight Socialism" — whatever that is — would seem to be out of my line.

I hope you will attend the carnival, in person or by proxy. I am sure you would be startled by what you should see.

HUBERT H. HARRISON

Editor of THE VOICE

P. S. — Just to let you see the difference between my spirit and yours, I am sending my membership fee to the secretary of your organization. H. H.

Comment is hardly necessary. These "good white people" must really forgive us for insisting that we are not children, and that, while we want all the friends we can get, we need no benevolent dictators. It is we, and not they, who must shape Negro policies. If they want to help in carrying them out we will appreciate their help.

Just now the white people — even in the South — have felt the pressure of the new Negro's Manhood Demands, in spite of the fact that backward-looking Negroes like *The Age's* editor condemn the inflexible spirit of these demands. All over the south, the white papers, scared by the exodus of Negro laborers who are tired of begging for justice overdue, are saying that we are right, and friendlier legislation has begun to appear on Southern statute books. Mr. [H. L.] Mencken and other Southern writers are saying that the Negro is demanding, and that the south had better accede to his just demands, as it is only a matter of time when he will be in a position to enforce them. One should think, then, that those who have been parading as our professional friends would be in the van of this manhood movement. But the movement seems to have left them in the rear. Now, that we are demanding the whole loaf, they are begging for half, and are angry at us for going further than they think "nice."

It was the N. A. A. C. P. which was urging us to compromise our manhood by begging eagerly for "Jim Crow" training camps. And the same group is asking, in the November *Crisis*, that we put a collective power-of-attorney into their hands and leave it to them to shape our national destiny. The N. A. A. C. P. has done much good work for Negroes — splendid work — in fighting lynching and segregation. For that we owe it more gratitude and good will than we owe the entire Republican party for the last sixty years of its existence. But we cannot, even in this case, abdicate our right to shape more radical policies for ourselves. It was the realization of the need for a more radical policy than that of the N. A. A. C. P. that called into being the Liberty League of Negro Americans. And the N. A. A. C. P., as mother, must forgive its offspring for forging further ahead.

Then, there is the case of the New York *Evening Post*, of which Mr. [Oswald Garrison] Villard is owner. This paper was known far and wide as "a friend to Negroes." But its friendship has given way to indifference and worse. In the good old days every lynching received editorial condemnation. But the three great lynchings this year which preceded East St. Louis found no editorial of condemnation in the *Post*. It was more than luke-warm then. But alack and alas! As soon as Negro soldiers in Houston, goaded to retaliation by gross indignities, did some shooting on their own account, the *Evening Post*, which had "no condemnation of the conduct of the lynchers," joined the chorus of those who were screaming for "punishment" and death. Here is its brief editorial on August 25th:

> As no provocation could justify the crimes committed by mutinous Negro soldiers at Houston, Texas, so no condemnation of their conduct can be too severe. It may be that the local authorities were not wholly blameless, and that the commanding officers were at fault in not foreseeing the trouble and taking steps to guard against it. But nothing can really palliate the offence of the soldiers. They were false to their uniform; they were false to their race. In one sense, this is the most deplorable aspect

of the whole riotous outbreak. It will play straight into the hands of the men like Senator [James K.] Vardaman who have been saying that it was dangerous to draft colored men into the army. And the feeling against having colored troops encamped in the South will be intensified. The grievous harm which they might do to their own people should have been all along in the minds of the colored soldiers, and make them doubly circumspect. They were under special obligation, in addition to their military oath, to conduct themselves so as not to bring reproach upon the Negroes as a whole, of whom they were in a sort representative. Their criminal outrage will tend to make people forget the good work done by other Negro soldiers. After the rigid investigation which the War Department has ordered, the men found guilty should receive the severest punishment. As for the general army policy affecting colored troops, we are glad to see that Secretary [of War Newton] Baker appears to intend no change in his recent orders.

The attitude of one who is just, rather than expedient for political reasons, is different and is well expressed in the citation, from OUR DUMB ANIMALS which will be found on page 6 of our [*The Voice*'s] last issue under News and Views. We ourselves cannot forget that while the question of whether the *Post's* editor would get a diplomatic appointment (like some other editors) [this is a probable reference to the NAACP's James Weldon Johnson, former editor of the *New York Age* and consul to Venezuela and Nicaragua] was under consideration during the first year of Woodrow Wilson's first administration, the *Post* pretended to believe that the President didn't know of the segregation practiced in the government departments. The N. A. A. C. P., whose letter sent out at the time is now before us, pretended to the same effect.

After viewing these expressions of frightful friendliness in our own times, we have reached the conclusion that the time has come when we should insist on being our own best friends. We make many mistakes, of course, but we ought to be allowed to make our own mistakes — as other people are allowed to do. If friendship is to mean compulsory compromise foisted on us by kindly white people, or by cultured Negroes whose ideal is the imitation of the urbane acquiescence of these white friends, then we had better learn to look a gift horse in the mouth whenever we get the chance.

Politics in the 1920s

46. "A Negro for President," *Negro World* 8 (June 19, 1920): 2, reprinted in *When Africa Awakes*, 44–46.

In 1920 Harrison, who had continually tried to inject politics into the Garvey movement, and William Bridges, another critic of Garvey, organized a new, all-Black political party —

the Liberty Party. The new organization had a short life: it lasted from about June to November 1920, but in that time it sought to put into practice the militant political independence that Harrison had been advocating. It aimed to break from the established political parties, sought to run its own candidates for political office, and argued for militant self-defense in the face of racist attacks. The Liberty Party was a major departure from Garvey's relatively apolitical approach, and Harrison hoped to draw followers from the Garvey movement and the broader "New Negro" movement into political action. The following editorial, "A Negro for President," assesses the principal theme of the campaign and emphasizes the need for "a Negro party."[16]

For many years the Negro has been the football of American politics. Kicked from pillar to post, he goes begging, hat in hand, from a Republican convention, to a Democratic one. Always is he asking someone else to do something for him. Always is he begging, pleading, demanding or threatening. In all these cases his dependence is on the good will, sense of justice or gratitude of the other fellow. And in none of these cases is the political reaction of the other fellow within the control of the Negro.

But a change for the better is approaching. Four years ago, the present writer was propounding in lectures, indoors and outdoors, the thesis that the Negro people of America would never amount to anything much politically until they should see fit to imitate the Irish of Britain and to organize themselves into a Political Party of their own whose leaders, on the basis of this large collective vote, could "hold up" Republican, Democrats, Socialists or any other political group of American whites. As in many other cases, we have lived to see time ripen the fruits of our own thought for some one else to pluck. Here is the editor of the *Challenge* [William Bridges] making a campaign along these very lines. His version of the idea takes the form of advocating the nomination of a Negro for the presidency of the United States. In this form we haven't the slightest doubt that this idea will meet with a great deal of ridicule and contempt. Nevertheless, we venture to prophesy that, whether in the hands of Mr. Bridges or another, it will come to be ultimately accepted as one of the finest contributions to Negro statesmanship.

No one pretends, of course, that the votes of Negroes can elect a Negro to the high office of president of the United States. Nor would anyone expect that the votes of white people will be forthcoming to assist them in such a project. The only way in which a Negro could be elected President of the United States would be by virtue of the voters not knowing that the particular candidate was of Negro ancestry. This, we believe, has already happened within the memory of living men. But, the essential intent of this new plan is to furnish a focusing-point around which the ballots of the Negro voters may be concentrated for the realization of racial demands for justice and equality of opportunity and treatment. It would be carrying "Race First" with a vengeance into the arena of politics. It would take the Negro voter out of the ranks of the Republican,

Democratic and Socialist parties and would enable their leaders to trade the votes of their followers, openly and above-board, for those things for which masses of men largely exchange their votes.

Mr. Bridges will find that the idea of a Negro candidate for president presupposes the creation of a purely Negro party and upon the prerequisite he will find himself compelled to concentrate. Doubtless, most of the political wise-acres of the Negro race will argue that the idea is impossible because it antagonizes the white politicians of the various parties. They will close their eyes to the fact that politics implies antagonism and a conflict of interest. They will fail to see that the only things which count with politicians are votes, and that, just as one white man will cheerfully cut another white man's throat to get the dollars which a black man has, so will one white politician or party cut another one's throat politically to get the votes which black men may cast at the polls. But these considerations will finally carry the day. Let there be no mistake. The Negro will never be accepted by the white American democracy except in so far as he can by the use of force, financial, political or other, win, seize or maintain in the teeth of the opposition that position which he finds necessary to his own security and salvation. And we Negroes may as well make up our own minds now that we can't depend upon the good-will of white men in anything or at any point where our interests and theirs conflict. Disguise it as we may, in business, politics, education or other departments of life, we as Negroes are compelled to fight for what we want to win from the white world.

It is easy enough for those colored men whose psychology is shaped by their white inheritance to argue the ethics of compromise and inter-racial co-operation. But we whose brains are still unbastardized must face the frank realities of this situation of racial conflict and competition. Wherefore, it is well that we marshal our forces to withstand and make head against the constant racial pressure. Action and reaction are equal and opposite. Where there is but slight pressure a slight resistance will suffice. But where, as in our case, that pressure is grinding and pitiless, the resistance that would re-establish equal conditions of freedom must of necessity be intense and radical. And it is this philosophy which must furnish the motive for such a new and radical departure as is implied in the joint idea of a Negro party in American politics and a Negro candidate for the Presidency of these United States.

47. "U-Need-A Biscuit," *Negro World* 8 (July 17, 1920): 2, reprinted as "U-Need-a Biscuit" in *When Africa Awakes*, 98–100.

In a July 1920 editorial Harrison used as a take-off the National Biscuit Company's masterful soda cracker advertising campaign, which had driven home the message "Uneeda Biscuit" since 1902. The editorial drew special praise from *Negro World* reader Leonard Brathwaite of New York, who wrote that it accurately described "the correct cause of the new spirit that has overshadowed the Negro peoples of the western world as well as the people of all the world." Brathwaite added that he had "been reading the *Negro World* for some time," and, while the editorials were often "masterfully written," special attention was due this one for revealing both "the character of the writer — a close observer of humanity" and "the ills that affect us."[17]

There is one advertisement which appears in the magazines, on the streets and bill boards which has always seemed to us a masterly illustration of the principle of repetition. When going to work in the morning we look up from our daily newspaper and see the flaring sign which states that U-need-a Biscuit, we may ignore its appeal the first time, but as the days go by the constant insistence reaches our inner consciousness and we decide that perhaps after all we do need a biscuit. At any rate, whenever we have biscuits to buy it is natural that the biscuit which has been most persistently advertised should recur at once to our minds and that we should buy that particular biscuit.

We beg to call the above apologue to the attention of the white people of this country who guide the ship of state either in the halls of Congress or through the columns of the white newspapers. They are seemingly at a loss to account for the new spirit which has come over the Negro people in the Western world. Some pretend to believe that it is Bolshevism — whatever that may be. Others tell us that it is the product of alien agitators, and yet others are coming to the front with the novel explanation that it springs from a desire to mingle our blood with that of white people.

Perhaps we are wasting our time in offering an explanation to the white men of this country. It has been proven again and again that the Anglo-Saxon is such a professional liar that with the plain truth before his eyes he will still profess to be seeing something else. Nevertheless we make the attempt because we believe that a double benefit may accrue to us thereby. Does any reader who lived through the years from 1914 to 1919 and is still living remember what "Democracy" was? It was the U-need-a Biscuit advertised by Messrs. Woodrow Wilson, [David] Lloyd George, Georges Clemenceau and thousands of perspiring publicists, preachers and thinkers, who were on one side of a conflict then raging in Europe.

Now, you cannot get men to go out and get killed by telling them plainly that you who are sending them want to get the other fellow's land, trade and wealth, and you are too cowardly or too intelligent to go yourself and risk getting shot over the acquisition. That would never do. So you whoop it up with any catch word which will serve as sufficient bait for the silly fools whom you keep silly in order that you may always use them in this way. "Democracy" was such a catch-word, and the honorable gentlemen to whom we referred above advertised it for all it was worth — to them. But, just as we prophesied in 1915, there was an unavoidable flare-back. When you advertise U-need-a Biscuit incessantly people will want it; and when you advertise Democracy incessantly the people to whom you trumpet forth its deliciousness are likely to believe you, take you at your word, and, later on, demand that you make good and furnish them with the article for which you yourself have created the appetite.

Now, we Negroes, Egyptians and Hindoos, under the pressure of democracy's commercial drummers, have developed a democratic complex which in its turbulent insistence is apt to trouble the firms for whom these drummers drummed. Because they haven't any of the goods which they advertised in the first place, and, in the second place, they haven't the slightest intention of passing any of it on — even if they had.

So, gentlemen, when you read of the Mullah, of Said Zagloul [Zaghlul] Pasha and Marcus Garvey or Casely Hayford; when you hear of Egyptian and Indian nationalist uprisings, of Black Star Lines and West Indian "seditions" — kindly remember (because *we* know) that these fruits spring from the seeds of your own sowing. You have said to us "U need a biscuit," and, after long listening to you, we have replied, "We do!" Perhaps next time — if there is a next time — you will think twice before you furnish to "inferior" peoples such a stick as "Democracy" has proved for the bludgeoning of your heads. In any case your work has been too well done for even you to obliterate it. The Negro of the Western world can truthfully say to the white man and the Anglo-Saxon in particular, "You made me what I am today, I hope you're satisfied." And if the white man isn't satisfied — well, we should worry. That's all.

48. "The Grand Old Party," *Negro World* (c. July 1920), reprinted in *When Africa Awakes*, 49–53.

In July 1920 Harrison, in "The Grand Old Party," called attention to the fact that there were "'intellectual' Negroes" who were attempting to "perpetuate the bonds of serfdom" which tied Blacks to the Republican party. He appealed to the historical record to oppose this and to show that if Blacks owed any debt to the Republicans, it was "a debt of execration and of punishment rather than one of gratitude." This was so, he explained, because the Republican Party was "the most corrupt influence among Negro Americans." The article gave additional impetus to the movement of African Americans out of the Republican Party.

In the early days of 1861, when the Southern Senators and Representatives were relinquishing their seats in the United States Congress and hurling cartels of defiant explanation broadcast, the Republican party in Congress, under the leadership of Charles Francis Adams of Massachusetts, organized a joint committee made up of thirteen members of the Senate and thirty-three members of the House to make overture to the seceding Southerners. The result of this friendly gesture was a proposed thirteenth amendment, which, if the Southerners had not been so obstinate, would have bridged the chasm. For this amendment proposed to make the slavery of the black man in America eternal and inescapable. It provided that no amendment to the Constitution, or any other proposition affecting slavery in any way, could ever be legally presented upon the floor of Congress unless its mover had secured the previous consent of *every Senator and Representative from the slave-holding States*. It put teeth into the Fugitive Slave Law and absolutely gave the Negro over into the keeping of his oppressors.

Most Negro Americans (and white ones, too) think it fashionable to maintain the most fervid faith and deepest ignorance about points in their national history of which they should be informed. We therefore submit that these facts are open and notorious to those who know American history. The record will be found slimy and shamefacedly given in [Edward] McPherson's *[Political] History of the Rebellion*; at indignant length in [James G.] Blaine's *Twenty Years of Congress* and Horace Greeley's *The Great American Conflict*. The document can be examined in Professor William Macdonald's *Select Documents of United States History [Select Documents Illustrative of the History of the United States]*. These works are to be found in every public library, and we refer to them here because there are "intellectual" Negroes today who are striving secretly, when they dare not do so openly, to perpetuate the bonds of serfdom which bind the Negro Americans to the Republican party. This bond of serfdom, this debt of gratitude, is supposed to hinge on the love which Abraham Lincoln and his party are supposed to have borne towards the Negro; and the object of this appeal to the historical record is to show that the record demonstrates that if the Negro owes any debt to the Republican party it is a debt of execration and of punishment rather than one of gratitude.

It is an astounding fact that in his First Inaugural Address Abraham Lincoln gave his explicit approval to the substance of the Crittenden resolutions which the joint committee referred to above had collectively taken over. This demonstrates that the Republican party at the very beginning of its contact with the Negro was willing to sell the Negro, bound hand and foot, for the substance of its own political control. This Thirteenth Amendment was adopted by six or eight Northern States, including Pennsylvania and Illinois; and if Fort Sumter had not been fired upon it would have become by State action the law of the land.

The Republican party did not fight for the freedom of the Negro, but for the maintenance of its own grip on the government which the election of Abraham Lincoln had secured. If anyone wants to know for what the Republican party fought he will find it in such facts as this: That thousands of square miles of the people's property was given away to Wall Street magnates who had corrupted the Legislature in their efforts to build railroads on the government's money. The sordid story is given in *Fifty Years in Wall Street*, by the banker, Henry Clews, and others who took part in this raid upon the resources of a great but stupid people.

But the Civil War phase of the Republican party's treason to the Negro is not the only outstanding one, as was shown by the late General [Henry Edmund] Tremaine in his *Sectionalism Unmasked*. Not only was General [Ulysses S.] Grant elected in 1868 by the newly created Negro vote, as the official records prove, but his re-election in 1872 was effected by the same means. So was the election of Rutherford B. Hayes in 1876. Yet when the election of Hayes had been taken before the overwhelmingly Republican Congress this shameless party made a deal whereby, in order to pacify the white "crackers" of the South, the Negro was given over into the hands of the triumphant Ku-Klux; the soldiers who protected their access to the ballot box in the worst southern states were withdrawn, while the "crackers" agreed as the price of this favor to withdraw their opposition to the election of Hayes. For this there exists ample proof which will be presented upon the challenge of any politician or editor. As a Republican Senator from New England shamelessly said, it was a matter of "Root, hog, or die" for the helpless Negro whose ballots had buttressed the Republican party's temple of graft and corruption. So was reconstruction settled against the Negro by the aid and abetting of the Republican party.

And since that time lynching, disfranchisement and segregation have grown with the Republican party in continuous control of the government from 1861 to 1920 — with the exception of eight years of Woodrow Wilson and eight years of Grover Cleveland. With their continuing consent the South has been made solid, so that at every Republican convention delegates who do not represent a voting constituency but a grafting collection of white postmasters and their Negro lackeys can turn the scales of nomination in favor of any person whom the central clique of the party, controlled as it always has been by Wall Street financiers, may foist upon a disgusted people, as they have done in the case of Harding. So long as the South remains solid, so long will the Republican delegates from the South consist only of this handful of hirelings; so long will they be amenable to the "discipline" which means the pressure of the jobs by which they get their bread. Therefore the Republican leaders will know that the solidarity of the South is their most valuable asset; and they are least likely to do anything that will break that solidarity. The Republican party's only interest in the Negro is to get his vote for nothing; and so long as Negro Republican leaders remain the contemptible grafters and political procurers that they are at present, so long will it get Negro votes for nothing.

Through it all the Republican party remains the most corrupt influence among Negro Americans. It buys up by jobs, appointments and gifts those Negroes who in politics should be the free and independent spokesmen of Negro Americans. But worse than this is its private work in which it secretly subsidizes men who pose before the public as independent radicals. These intellectual pimps draw private supplementary incomes from the Republican party to sell out the influence of any movement, church or newspaper with which they are connected. Of the enormity of this mode of procedure and the existent to which it saps the very springs of Negro integrity the average Negro knows nothing. Its blighting, baleful influence is known only to those who have trained ears to hear and trained eyes to see.

And now in this election the standards will advance and the cohorts go forward under the simple impulse of the same corrupting influence. But whether the movement for a Negro party comes to a head or not, the new Negro in America in will never amount to anything politically until he enfranchises himself from the Grand Old Party which has made a political joke of him.

49. "When the Tail Wags the Dog," *Negro World* (c. July 1920), reprinted in *When Africa Awakes*, 46–48.

In the July 1920 editorial "When the Tail Wags the Dog," Harrison described how "ignorant, stupid and vicious" forces in both the Democratic and Republican Parties affected Black interests. Under the nation's Democratic Party leadership, racist southern whites, particularly those elected in white-only primaries, ran roughshod over African Americans. At the Republican Party convention, vulnerable and corruptible Southern Black delegates (appointed by whites, not elected), led their Northern Black peers. In both cases, argued Harrison, the tail wagged the dog, and African Americans paid the price for not opposing more strongly the social and political reduction of disfranchised Southern Blacks.

The degree of Southern Black disfranchisement by intimidation, poll taxes, registrations tests, grandfather clauses, understanding clauses, and other techniques was truly staggering. In 1920 the South was home to more than 80 percent of the voting-age African American population and, though exact figures by race were not kept, the historian Paul Lewinson had found that "the Negro vote in the South was so small as to be negligible." In Mississippi, Alabama, and Georgia, for instance, the percentage of Blacks of voting age who were registered Black voters was less than one percent, two percent, and three percent, respectively. In Mississippi, no more than 850 Blacks were registered out of an African American population of more than 290,000 who were literate and at least twenty-one years old.[18]

Politically, these United States may be roughly divided into two sections, so far as the Negroes are concerned. In the North the Negro population has the vote. In the South it hasn't. This was not always so. There was a time when the Negro voters of the South sent in to Congress a thin but steady stream of black men who represented their political interests directly. Due to the misadventures of the reconstruction period, this stream was shut off until at the beginning of this century George White, of North Carolina, was the sole and last representative of the black man with a ballot in the South.

This result was due largely to the characteristic stupidity of the Negro voter. He was a Republican, he was. He would do anything with his ballot for Abraham Lincoln — who was dead — but not a thing for himself and his family, who were all alive and kicking. For this the Republican party loved him so much that it permitted the Democrats to disfranchise him while it controlled Congress and the courts, the army and the navy, and all the machinery of law-enforcement in the United States. With its continuing consent, Jim-crowism, disfranchisement, segregation, and lynching spread abroad over the land. The end of it all was the reduction of the Negro in the South to the position of a political serf, an industrial peon and a social outcast.

Recently there has been developed in the souls of black folk a new manhood dedicated to the proposition that, if all Americans are equal in the matter of baring their breasts to foreign bayonet, then all Americans must, by their own efforts, be made equal in balloting for President and other officers of the government. This principle is compelling the Republican party in certain localities to consider the necessity of nominating Negroes on its local electoral tickets. Yet the old attitude of that party on the political rights of Negroes remains substantially the same.

Here, for instance, is the Chicago convention, at which the Negro delegates were lined up to do their duty by the party. Of course, these delegates had to deal collectively with the white leaders. This was to their mutual advantage. But the odd feature of the entire affair was this, that, *Whereas the Negro people in the South are not free to cast their votes, it was precisely from these voteless areas that the national Republican leaders selected the political spokesman for the voting Negroes of the North.* Men who will not vote at the coming election and men who, like Roscoe Simmons, never cast a vote in their lives were the accredited representatives in whose hands lay the destiny of a million Negro voters.

But there need to be no fear that this insult will annoy the black brother in the Republican ranks. A Negro Republican generally runs the rhinoceros and the elephant a close third. In plain English, the average Negro Republican is too stupid to see and too meek to mind. Then, too, here is Fate's retribution for the black man in the North who has never cared enough to fight (the Republican party) for the political freedom of his brother in the South, but left him to rot under poll-tax laws and grandfather clauses. The Northern white Democrats, for letting their Southern brethren run riot through the Constitution, must pay the penalty of being led into the ditch by the most ignorant, stupid and vicious portion of the party. Even so, the Northern Negro Republican, for letting his Southern brother remain a political ragamuffin, must now stomach the insult of this same ragamuffin dictating the destiny of the freer Negroes of the North. In both cases the tail doth wag the dog because of "the solid South." Surely, "the judgments of the Lord are true and righteous altogether!"

 50. "Our Political Power," *Negro World* 9 (August 21, 1920): 2.

Harrison's editorial "Our Political Power" was written during the month-long UNIA Convention. It explained that there were "opportunities, rights and privileges" related to political action in the United States that were not available in the Caribbean and elsewhere. Most important among these was the right to vote, and Harrison urged African Americans in northern states to exercise this and other political rights to help themselves as well as to help Black people in the South and in the Caribbean. This repeated emphasis on political struggle was one of Harrison's major contributions to the Garvey movement.

It is a matter of general knowledge that the Negro in America is lynched, disfranchised, jim-crowed and discriminated against. But it is also true that the Negro in America has a few opportunities, rights and privileges which he does not enjoy in the West Indies, for instance. In the Northern States the Negro has only himself to blame when he fails to utilize these powers and privileges in his own behalf. Here in New York any Negro can send his child to the public schools and the high schools for an education identically the same in every respect with that which is given to the most favored Anglo-Saxon. The College of the City of New York and Hunter College furnish collegiate instruction, with the B. A. and the M. A. degrees, absolutely free. Yet how many of us avail ourselves of these educational rights and privileges? Right in our very midst, in West 138th street, there is a trade school from which may be seen issuing any afternoon hundreds upon hundreds of white boys from the Bronx and downtown, who have come to this school built in the Negro neighborhood to get such instruction as will enable them to begin life above the level of a railroad porter or waiter. It is seldom that one sees a black boy among them. Yet in the days to come black men who are now black boys will be insisting that all the fault for their low economic condition is due to the white people. No one who knows us will accuse us of any excessive friendliness for white people, but we must point out that it is the Negro's duty to avail himself of every means to power which is now furnished in New York and America at large, if he would eventually and successfully maintain a position of independence in the world uncontrolled by the whims and prejudices of the whites.

But it is in politics particularly that we Negroes fail in this respect. Agitation and propaganda which have been outlawed in Hayti, the Virgin Islands and the British West Indies can still be carried on in the Northern states of the union. If the condition of our brothers in those territories can be affected for better or for worse by the action of the American Government, it becomes our duty here in the North to exercise some effective influence on the machinery of that government. If Negroes in the North had intelligently organized their votes they would be able to now call the hand of the Secretary of the Navy, who has been waging brutal war against the liberties and property of our brothers in black in Hayti and Santo Domingo and has given to the Virgin Islands the awful anomaly of Danish laws in American territory, and sexual and physical outrages perpetrated by the marines.

Propaganda is pertinent to the point, but politics and propaganda are more powerful than propaganda alone. As it is now, we stand in this respect naked to the scorn of the world. What have we done? What can we do to make our privileged position here in the North tell on behalf of our brothers not so far away? We have done nothing, although we could do much. And because we have virtually made ourselves impotent, we can expect nothing. It behooves every Negro in the North who hasn't the vote to acquire it and it behooves all those who vote to use it. If they use it wisely they will be able to secure the ballot for their voteless brethren in the South by withholding their votes from the Republican party or any other party and by using their votes in the city, State and nation to compel the enforcement of the 13th, 14th and 15th amendments to the American Constitution. But, if they could do this by their votes, they could also secure the appointment of Negro governors for the Virgin Islands. They could, at any rate, bring effective pressure to bear against the horrifying brutalities which black people are now compelled to endure from the "cracker" in the Caribbean.

The machinery of government has already been provided. On this machinery we are privileged to lay our hands to guide, direct and control some of its application. And if we fail to do this, the blame will be laid squarely by future generations, not upon the criminality of the white but upon the stupidity and cowardice of the black. Let us see to it, therefore, that we make in this regard a record which our posterity will respect.

 51. Frances Dearborn (pseudonym), "The Black Tide Turns in Politics," (c. December 1921?), HHHP Wr. [Frances was the name of Harrison's firstborn child.]

Around December 1921 Harrison wrote "The Black Tide Turns in Politics" under the pseudonym "Frances Dearborn." Harrison sought to challenge the Republican party's record in relation to African Americans, the general practice by whites of using one Black person as their "selected index" of Black sentiment, and the "superstition" that Blacks were born Republicans. To illustrate his point, he introduced the subject with an aphorism.

At the April 1872 Black workers' convention in New Orleans, Frederick Douglass had told his audience that "The Republican party is the deck, all else is the sea." That aphorism had captured the essence of African American political allegiance for most of the next half-century, but by late 1921 that reality was changing. African Americans were breaking from the Republican party and white political leaders, who, according to Harrison, relied on appraisals and assurances from their selected Black exponents, were largely ignorant of these developments. The selected exponents told white political leaders what they wanted to hear rather than what was true.[19]

In New York City only one of nine Black newspapers was aggressively pro-Republican in the 1921 municipal elections, and some 65 percent of the Black vote went Democratic. White leaders were still ignorant of these developments, and Harrison used the example of "the two largest [political] mass-meetings ever held among Negroes in America," in early November 1921, as examples of "political thimble-rigging" which demonstrated that the white party leaders were out of touch.

It is a singular fact that the white people of America know more about the white people of England and Ireland than they do about the twelve million black people in their midst. And nowhere is this shown more strikingly than in the domain of politics. It is here where superstitions are rife that the great superstition persists that the Negro is a born Republican. His political philosophy is presumed to be summed up in the aphorism that "The Republican Party is the ship and all else is the open sea." Undoubtedly, there was a period when the superficial observer might feel justified in holding by the myth of the Negro's simon-pure Republicanism; but that period is now at an end. Yet those white people who shape the ideas of the nation on this and other matters have remained strangely ignorant of that fact. Editors, lecturers, authors and politicians seem equally unaware of this transformation of the Negro's political sentiments. The reason for this is not far to seek.

Here in America the white world and the black world move side by side; but they seldom intermingle. Those white people, like the politicians, who have business in the black world generally do their business in the following fashion. They select one Negro as their exponent of Negro activities who is also the exponent of their own white point of view. They then multiply him indefinitely to serve as a working concept of "The Negro," taking his word religiously and excluding from their consideration any other whose word is not in tune with that of their selected bell-wether. This has been the traditional method of getting at the Negro's mind employed by politicians and patriots, professional Southerners and Vesey Street Liberals. It is small wonder, then, that their easy complacence comes a cropper in the face of revolutionary facts.

Such catastrophes have not been lacking in the domain of politics. Most white people will be surprised to learn that in the New York Municipal campaign of 1917 Colonel Theodore Roosevelt and Mayor [John Purroy] Mitchel were hissed off the platform at the Palace Casino by an audience of more than three thousand Negroes. In this case the editor of the *New York Age*, was the selected index. Most of the Negro ministers had received for their support sums ranging from two to six hundred dollars, and the high-priests of pure government from whom the money came were assured that the votes were safely stowed away in some one's vest pocket ready for delivery. The real truth was that the Negro masses were seething with hostility. But the Republican leaders only learned this when it was too late. And during the rest of the campaign their speakers were hardly able to show their faces at street-meetings in Harlem, the Negro section. Yet they learned nothing from the lesson; but lapsed again into their traditional dependence on a selected exponent.

During the last week of the recent campaign the two largest mass-meetings ever held among Negroes in America were held in Liberty Hall the home of Marcus Garvey's adherents. In both cases the hall had been hired by politicians; The Democrats held their meeting on Thursday night, the Republicans held theirs on Friday night. Both were cases of political thimble-rigging. The hall holds six thousand people and is filled nearly every night in the week by Garvey's crowd — who have no votes, being for the most part aliens. It was this same crowd, plus about 400 voters, who filled the house on both nights.

But this, although known to the canny colored local leaders, was not even suspected by the white politicians who naturally gave great credit to the local party-riggers for turning out such a multitude of "voters" to listen to them. But although the Garvey people hadn't votes they had plenty of the local feeling in regard to politics. So they applauded the Democrats with enthusiasm Thursday night and Garvey himself spoke in their behalf. But when [mayoral candidate] Major [Henry H.] Curran and his Republican team-mates attempted to speak for their ticket the next night they were heckled, hissed, jeered and booed. The reserves were called out and the meeting broke up in disorder. The audience was expressing the deep detestation in which the Republican Party is held in Negro Harlem. But of this detestation which was enough to reach even the remote non-voters the official Republican Party hadn't an inkling.

On the afternoon before that meeting at the headquarters of one of the Republican candidates a colored campaign worker had asked "how could they expect to carry Harlem without spending money for Republican workers to canvass the district?" "Oh," said one of the chiefs, airily, "they always vote the Republican ticket!" The day after the meeting this same chief, with the tears streaming down his face, was asking the same colored worker appealingly, "what can we do? Tell us, what can we do?"

Only one out of nine local Negro newspapers [the *New York Age*] thumped for the Republicans during the campaign: The editor of that one [Fred R. Moore] has been "the selected index" and the bursar of party funds for years. The others were either quiescent like the *Amsterdam News*, insurgent like the *Despatch*, or Democratic like the *Pictorial News*. And for the first time in all the long history of American politics more than 65 per cent of the Negro vote was cast for the Democratic Party. Yet the American white continues to know less of the Negro in his midst than of any other people except the Russian. For, it was *The Nation* which in its post-election issue blandly informed us that "the colored vote is now more than ever attached to the Republican Party." Now, if *The Nation* is unreliable in a matter of this sort and size, what white interpreter can be depended on? It certainly suggests that if white people want to get accurate interpretations of what's what in the colored world they must go to properly equipped Negroes who are not in leading-strings to them. And in the present disturbed state of race-relations in America the thinking portion of the white public needs the truth about the Negro situation as it never did before.

But the facts which challenge the correctness of *The Nation's* assertion are very much wider than has been indicated above. In many states like Maryland and Virginia the Negroes, with the hope of defeating the Republicans, put independent tickets in the field.

This had been done once before in the last Presidential campaign. In Virginia last year they put up a complete state ticket and voted exclusively for men and women of their race with the result that the "Lily-White" Republicans who were squeezing the Negroes out of the party went down in ignominious defeat. As one Negro newspaper expressed it: "The Republican Party can not close its eyes to the fact that a measure of resentment entered into the results."

For such a tremendous change in the political sentiment of the Negroes there must exist adequate and ascertainable causes. What are these causes? In the first place, Negroes are beginning to read American history, and in so doing they have begun to find out things that are not consistent with the claims on the strength of which they have been held in political tutelage. If the fairminded white reader will go through Lincoln's reply to Horace Greeley and also consult, [James G.] Blaine's *Twenty Years of Congress* for his account of how the joint committee of Congress secured the passage of an amendment to the U.S. Constitution making slavery perpetual, as a sop to the seceding Southerners; if he will then read Lincoln's explicit concurrence in that move as stated in his First Inaugural — he will get a shock which may destroy his easy-going belief that Lincoln and the Republican Party had any original intention of freeing the Negroes. They themselves have been discovering these facts and, naturally, disillusionment has been doing its work. They have also noted that it was while the Republican Party was in control of both Houses of Congress, the Army, Navy and Supreme Court that "Jim-Crow," lynching and disfranchisement have increased — the latter especially with the continuing consent of the party; since, if the 14th and 15th amendments to the Constitution were found to be legally incompetent, both of them carry the proviso that "Congress shall have power to enforce this article by appropriate legislation."

The Negroes have recalled also that in the disputed count of the [Rutherford B.] Hayes–[Samuel J.] Tilden electoral contest in 1877, a deal was put through by which the Republicans sold them out and left them politically naked to the tender mercies of the Southern whites. They recall that in every sectional party-crisis they have been sacrificed as an offering on the altar of friendship. Roosevelt paid the South for the Booker Washington lunch with the discharge of the Brownsville Battalion — in the late afternoon of Election Day, after the votes were in. [William H.] Taft offered them up as a wedding present when he laid down the famous dictum that no Negro should ever be appointed to office anywhere if white men anywhere objected. And these few appointments were the only return which the Republican Party made for the Negro vote in the "doubtful" states. Negroes have seen "Lily-White-ism" increase in that party from [William] McKinley to Will Hayes — that theory of party practice which insists that the Southern Negro is a liability rather than an asset, and that he should be politely thrown overboard. They have heard President [Warren G.] Harding re-expounding the principle laid down by Taft; and in his Birmingham address asking them please to leave the party. What wonder that they are taking him at his word and leaving it?

But the President's invitation comes just a trifle late. Negroes have been leaving the party for some time back. Twenty years ago those Negroes who joined the Democratic Party were regarded by their fellows much as white Americans regarded pacifists and pro-German in War time — and they were treated accordingly. [At this point Harrison deleted the following two sentences: I can recall how even as late as 1916 I had to mediate between an angry Harlem street crowd and a group of colored Democrats including Ferdinand Q. Morton, the present head of the United Colored Democracy. I was not a member of the Democratic Party, but I appealed successfully for fair play and a hearing on a platform from which they had been driven the night before.]

Now the pendulum has swung to the other side. How far will it go? And what does it all mean? It means first that the Negro voter is developing political common-sense. He is seeking to work out for himself his own political emancipation and is striving to win political consideration for his vote. Formerly, while both parties in an overwhelmingly Jewish district would put Jews on the local ticket to insure the Jewish vote they would put in a Negro neighborhood no Negro at all. Now the Negroes are demanding this right of "Elective representation." In New York City the one party which fought against this was "The Grand Old Party." But the change has gone so far that in the 21st Aldermanic District [Harrison's own] the Aldermanic candidates of all three parties were Negroes. Thus Negroes are forcing the politicians to give them something for something.

If one may speculate as to the ultimate aims of this new spirit, it seems that it will not rest satisfied until Negroes return to Congress as national legislators. And it seems likely that this will first be done in the North. They will continue to capitalize on the neighborhood segregation which has been forced on them, as they are now doing in Chicago and New York, and thus reap some of "the advantages of their disadvantages." They certainly intend to make a real use of their balance of power in the doubtful States to trade with the enemy, as did the Irish Parliamentary *bloc* under [Charles Stewart] Parnell and [Justin] McCarthy. And we may confidently look for a *rapprochement* between Negro voters and the Democrats of Virginia and the other Southern States in which they still have the ballot, since by so doing they will be able to block the "Lily-White" Republicans. It is not to be expected that they will choose to condemn themselves to perpetual political sterility in such States. Since they can defeat the Republicans (as they did in Virginia last fall) they might as well do it for something as do it for nothing. And those who want to defeat the Republicans in States like Virginia will be willing to concede some solid gains, however slight, to those who can insure that defeat. At any rate, from now on, the two major parties will have to compete for the Negro vote — and that is a sign of healthy political life.

6 Leaders and Leadership

One matter that Harrison considered of prime importance to African Americans was the question of leadership, which he defined broadly as "the direction of a group's activities, whether by precept, example or compulsion." He was convinced that amid "all the tangles of . . . awakening race consciousness" there were no problems "more knotty" than those relating to leadership and he paid special attention to this in several 1919 and 1920 editorials.[1]

In the writings that follow Harrison offers insightful comments on the paramount Black leaders of his day — Booker T. Washington, W. E. B. Du Bois, and Marcus Garvey; on Black leadership during World War I; and on Black leadership in general. The material on Washington caused Harrison to lose his job at the post office; the material on Du Bois (the accuracy of which has been confirmed by subsequent scholarship) led to Du Bois's being denied a captaincy in Military Intelligence and to his downfall in the eyes of militant "New Negroes";[2] the material on Garvey is a profound critique of his efforts by one who knew him well and offers cause for considerable reevaluation of Garvey. In the final pieces Harrison discusses what he refers to as a new element in the leadership question — the problem of "outside interference," or, as he termed it, the issue of whether "the leading of our group in any sense be the product of our group's consciousness or of a consciousness originating from outside that group." Related to that issue, he also discusses a part of the leadership problem "seldom touched upon by Negro Americans," namely, "the claim advanced, explicitly and implicitly, by Negroids of mixed blood to be considered the natural leaders of Negro activities on the ground of some alleged 'superiority' inherent in their white blood."

On Booker T. Washington

Booker Taliaferro Washington (1856–1915) was the most powerful Black leader in the United States from the time of his 1895 address at the Cotton States Exposition in Atlanta until his death in late 1915. In 1881 Washington became principal of Tuskegee Institute in

Alabama and, while concentrating on industrial education, developed it into the leading Black college in America. His Atlanta address, before a racially mixed audience, suggested that the best way to ensure peaceful progress in the South was for whites to respect African Americans' desires for improved economic opportunities and gradual improvement and for Blacks to accept the political status quo, to cast down their buckets where they were, and to respect whites' desires for racial separation. With this philosophy and with ties to powerful whites, Washington built a potent political patronage machine to reward friends with federal and state positions and to punish opponents. Harrison was strongly critical of Washington for his inadequate protest of racial oppression and class exploitation, his subservience to powerful whites, his opposition to trade unions, his views on education, his unbreakable ties to the Republican Party, his efforts to control sentiment in the Black community, and his unwillingness to directly and forthrightly discuss the problems faced by African Americans.[3]

52. "Insistence upon Its Real Grievances the Only Course for the Race," letter to the editor, *New York Sun* (December 8, 1910): 8.

In September 1910 Washington, who was traveling in Europe, was quoted in the London *Morning Post* as saying that the situation in the South was becoming "more and more reassuring" and "offer[ed] to the Negro a better chance than almost any other country in the world." This statement was uttered despite the fact that lynching, segregation, disfranchisement, and peonage marked the period as a "nadir" of post-Emancipation race relations in the United States. An "Appeal" signed by thirty-two notable "Negro Americans" of "The National Negro Committee on Mr. [Booker T.] Washington," including W. E. B. Du Bois and William Monroe Trotter, charged that Washington skirted instances of wrongdoings and was unduly optimistic about race relations. The *Sun*, a major New York daily, published the "Appeal" on December 1 and this was followed by an editorial and a series of letters. The editorial implied that the signatories were envious "exes" (former holders of prominent positions) who were jealous of Washington's position and advised these "uninvited spokesmen" that they were "not helping their cause" and that what was needed was "patience and perseverance" not "impotent lamentations." Responses included a rabidly racist one on December 5 signed by "D" who argued that "the white man will not, cannot, accord social equality, because he will not in a day or in a generation, in public or private, accept him [the African American] as an equal."[4]

It was in this setting that Harrison wrote a letter to the *Sun* that was titled "Insistence upon Its Real Grievances the Only Course for the Race." It criticized the *Sun* editorial and was a pointed attack on the leadership of Washington. Harrison publicly criticized America's most powerful Black leader, and he soon paid the price when Washington's powerful "Tuskegee Machine" engineered his dismissal from the post office. [Note: the *Sun* did not capitalize the *N* in *Negro*.][5]

To the editor of *The Sun*:

Sir: I wish to put to *The Sun* this question in regard to its editorial comment on the letter recently addressed to England and Europe by certain American colored men:

whether it is assumed that the human nature of black men differs from that of white men. There was evinced in the article I refer to that patronizing attitude of the American mind toward the Negro intellect which is so unpleasant to self-respecting black people. In other words, while it is assumed that progressive Jews are more competent than outsiders to appraise the leaders of any Jewish propaganda, such as Zionism, it is everywhere assumed that outsiders are better able to do this for Negroes than progressive Negroes are to do it for themselves. May I ask why?

I wish to present a part of the case of the Negro protestants, and I shall put it without any "hysterical peevishness," not merely because I am averse to that kind of thing, but more because I wish to show that their case is grounded upon reason. Of course if Negroes have no right to think, the case ends there. Mr. Booker Washington declares to the world that all is well with the Negro. His special mouthpiece *The New York Age*, said in its Thanksgiving number that the Negro had more to be thankful for than any other group of Americans; and this right on the heels of the Baltimore legislation [imposing residential segregation], the Oklahoma elections [in which a grandfather clause disfranchising two-thirds of the state's African Americans was passed], and the instructions of Texas to its Congressional representatives to work for the repeal of the last two amendments [the Fourteenth and the Fifteenth, which granted citizenship to African Americans and the right to vote to African American males] to the Constitution. These protestants, on the other hand, declare that there are, as you say, "real and great grievances" crying for redress. If these are not to be righted by "peevish and fruitless wailing," are they any more likely to be righted by saying that they do not exist? How have human wrongs been righted all through the ages? First, by insisting that they were wrongs: and secondly, by fighting against them with tongue and pen and sword. But if that is so, then these protesting Negroes are adopting the policy which has in its favor the experience of all kinds and conditions of men and six thousand years of trial.

Mr. Washington says that if black people will cease insisting on these "real and great grievances" and acquire property and manual skill, the grievances, which are the crux of the Negro problem, will decrease and finally disappear. I will make no appeal to the philosophy of history or to anything that may even faintly savor of erudition, because Mr. Washington and his satellites say that that is bad. But I will appeal to the hard facts.

Superintendent [Charles L.] Coon of North Carolina has shown that in Virginia, North Carolina and South Carolina the Negroes being 40 per cent of the population receive only 14 per cent of the school fund. Not only this but they pay school taxes amounting to $93,278 more than they get in school funds. South Carolina spends annually for the education of each white child $10.36 and for each black child $1.70. In some counties the average has run down to 58 cents. If education of any sort is a training for life, is it not evident that black children are being deprived of their chance in life? Why? Is it to be supposed that their fathers are so stupid as to allow this if they could vote their own needs? But Mr. Washington decries the agitation for the ballot as unwise.

In Baltimore the colored people have shown industry and thrift, have acquired wealth, and are now, as a result of that wealth, reaching out and buying better homes. But the white people, through their city council, say the right of Negroes to buy what they can pay for must be restricted in the interests of white people. In Kansas City a colored man was putting up a $5,000 building and it was dynamited by his white neighbors. Yet Mr. Washington says that if the Negro will become a house owner he will get the good will and respect of his white neighbors. Presumably he gets also their envy and ill will.

The Georgia railroad strike of 1909 served to show that any training which makes black men more efficient will bring them into keener competition with white men. When the white workers are armed with the ballot, the courts and the Legislatures, what do you suppose will happen to their colored competitors? Precisely what happened in Georgia and is happening unsolicited elsewhere. Their jobs will be taken away.

When, now in the light of facts which could easily be multiplied and extended, you look at the Negro's position do you think it advisable to say that he is "very well, thank you, and doing nicely"?

Mr. Washington is a great leader, by the grace of the white people who elect colored people's leaders for them, as he himself says in the November *World's Work*. But he has his great limitations. By the very nature of these he can adequately represent only one side of the Negro's life to-day. But when he essays to represent other sides he is likely to make mistakes as any other son of man. Why then do you presume to say that any criticism of his views coming from black men must needs be based on envy? As to the absurdity of an appeal addressed to England, it might be said that there is no race prejudice against Negroes in England. India and Egypt are not England, and Anglo-Indians are slightly different from England and Englishmen.

The Liberty Congress and W. E. B. Du Bois

The Liberty Congress of June 24–29, 1918, was the major wartime national meeting of militant Black leaders. It had been planned for over a year and grew, in particular, out of the work of William Monroe Trotter in Massachusetts and of Harrison in New York. It was attended by 115 delegates (including five women) from 33 states and the District of Columbia. Harrison served as president of the board and then as both chairman and president of the Congress, and Trotter served as chairman of the board.[6]

The Liberty Congress's importance, according to Harrison, was that it called attention "to the danger into which democracy is put by disfranchisement, discrimination, and lynching." It gained national notice when it petitioned Congress for federal legislation against lynching. The "Petition to the House of Representatives" was submitted to Representative Frederick Huntington Gillett of Massachusetts and entered in the *Congressional Record* on June 28.[7]

Hubert Harrison and delegates at the Liberty Congress, Washington, D.C., June 23–29, 1918, from the Hubert Harrison Papers. Harrison (second from right, front row) was at the pinnacle of militant race leadership when he and William Monroe Trotter (third from right, front row) co-chaired the major national protest meeting of African Americans during World War I. The Liberty Congress opposed segregation and discrimination, sought enforcement of the Thirteenth, Fourteenth, and Fifteenth Amendments, and petitioned Congress for federal anti-lynching legislation. In the same period, in contrast, W. E. B. Du Bois advocated that African Americans forget their special grievances and close ranks behind Woodrow Wilson's war effort and the National Association for the Advancement of Colored People refused to advocate permanent federal anti-lynching legislation.

While plans for this militant, autonomous, all-Black effort were underway, steps were taken to undermine it, consistent with a general three-pronged government effort. The offensive included direct dissemination of propaganda to the Black press, threats against Black dissidents and protesters, and flattery and co-optation of "select" Black editors and leaders, including those who were hastily called together in Washington for a June 19–21 Editors Conference immediately prior to the opening of the Liberty Congress. At the Editors Conference there were no women in attendance, labor was not represented, and the South was underrepresented. This principal effort to undermine the Liberty Congress was engineered by Joel E. Spingarn—the white chairman of the NAACP's executive board and one of those "friends of the Negro" that Harrison often warned against. Spingarn, a major in the anti-radical Military Intelligence Branch of the War Department, enlisted his close personal friend, Du Bois, in his efforts.[8]

53. [The Liberty Congress], July 1, 1918 HHHDI.

Harrison's diary entry offers a unique inside look at aspects of the Liberty Congress as well as his more intimate reflections on his personal involvement and the leadership offered. Overall, he considered it "the most notable gathering of Negro-Americans in a generation."

Monday July 1st 1918 Washington, D.C.

Well the 1st Convention of the Colored National Liberty Congress has passed into history. And I like to cuddle the hope that its influence will pass into the spirit of these days, with good results.

I came here on Saturday about six o'clock to undertake the duties of Organizer of the "International Federation of the Workers in the Hotel and Restaurant Industry"—a white organization which wishes to get the Negro workers in their ranks. Sometime ago I did some fruitless work for them in Philadelphia.

But, although they are paying me $35.00 a week and my expenses, I threw myself into the maelstrom of the Congress' activities. I went into the Church in which the sessions were being held (the John Wesley A.M.E. Church, corner of 14 St. and Corcoran) on Monday morning and was at once reminded that I had been elected Chairman of the Board of Managers in Boston [in] May 1917. (This had been done in my absence and by ministers, of all people!) I was, therefore, escorted to the chair, as this was a meeting of that preliminary body. My conduct of the business in hand seems to have been such a clear improvement upon what went before that, when it was moved that we go into permanent organization (for the period of the Congress) I was unanimously elected Chairman, or president, of the body.

I had been presiding hardly an hour before enthusiastic commendations were expressed from the floor and later, to the chagrin of Monroe Trotter, I was elected President of the Congress. If I were given much to megalomania my head would have grown as big as the church.

We had three sessions each day from Monday to Saturday, and I was present from Monday to Friday. The morning and afternoon sessions were for delegates only and they came from 33 states: some from as far as Oklahoma 1500 miles away and paying their own fares.

There were many men of prominence and achievement, doctors, lawyers, ministers, editors and teachers. One of these last, Professor [J. W.] Bell from Kentucky, was elected Secretary — and a most efficient secretary he was. Unfortunately, many of the delegates were bent upon interminable wrangling and disputation of a childish sort, and it was only by the most skillful combination of tact and repression that they were constrained to do practical work.

And yet, on the whole, this was the most notable gathering of Negro-Americans in a generation — and most of the delegates felt this. We waited upon the President of the Senate (whom we didn't see) and upon the Speaker of the House of Representatives, [James B.] Champ Clark [Dem., MO], who accorded us a kindly and genial reception. This was on Tuesday (I think). We had gone upon instructions of the Congress, appointing a Committee of three (Harrison of New York, Trotter of Massachusetts, and Sandiford of Washington, D.C. [probably J. A. Lankford of Indiana] to ask for a joint session of the two houses of Congress to consider the grievances of the 12 million people of our race and their demand for democracy at home from the nation which was at war "to make the world safe for democracy." Some of us thought the request for a joint session silly, in as much as this is done only when the President addresses Congress and when war is declared. But we went as we were bid. The speaker, for all his genial kindliness, couldn't see his way to a joint session, and I reported this to the afternoon session of *our* Congress.

In three days more we finished up most of our work: the Committees on Resolutions, on Suffrage, on the Petition to the U.S. Congress and the other Committees made their reports, and we wound up in fine fettle.

The Negro people of Washington turned out in large numbers night after night and gave us a fine reception. I spoke on Monday night and again on Wednesday night. On the former occasion Judge [Robert H.] Terrell was among the prominent people who came up to shake hands and make their felicitations. I seemed to have taken Washington by storm. But that was nothing to the occurrence of Wednesday night. The first speaker was representative [Leonidas] Dyer of Illinois [a Democrat from Missouri] who had presented to Congress an anti-lynching bill. He was followed by [Allen W.] Whaley of Boston, Trotter's assistant and alter ego, who delivered the best speech that I had ever heard from his lips. Then Dr. M. A. N. Shaw, of Boston, a West Indian by birth, spoke and, for the happy welding of critical thought and forceful presentation, I have never heard that speech surpassed. I could have listened all night.

When he ended it was 5 minutes of midnight and Washington folk go to bed at 10:30. The Chairman, Mr. Morris Spencer, then introduced me and I begged the audience to agree to hear me on the next night instead. At this there were cries from all over the church for "Harrison! Harrison!" So, the chairman asked those who insisted on hearing me that night to stand — and about 4/5 of them rose to their feet. Thereupon, I spoke and held them until 12:35 A.M.

On the preceding night we had heard two brilliant and eloquent speakers: Mr. Charles Morris, Jr., "The Boy Orator" — just 19 years old, but thoughtful and capable beyond his years, a young man who is destined to go far; and the Secretary of the Congress, Professor Bell of Kentucky, a man of engaging eloquence.

There can be no doubt that the administration's "white men's niggers" and their masters are worried about the size and quality of the protest we are making.

54. "The Descent of Dr. Du Bois," *The Voice* (July 25, 1918), reprinted in *When Africa Awakes*, 66–70.

William Edward Burghardt Du Bois (1868–1963) was the most prominent Black protest leader in the United States from the early 1900s until World War I. He was a scholar and writer of outstanding talent and leader of the Pan-African movement. In 1905 Dr. Du Bois helped to found the Niagara Movement in opposition to Booker T. Washington's more conservative policies and "Tuskegee Machine," and in 1909–1910 he was instrumental in founding the National Association for the Advancement of Colored People. From 1910 until 1934 he served as the influential editor of the NAACP's *Crisis* magazine. In later years Du Bois chaired the Department of Sociology at Atlanta University, directed the NAACP's research department (1944–1948), cochaired the Council of African Affairs (1948–1956), was prosecuted and persecuted for his support of the Soviet Union, and when finally freed to travel went to the Soviet Union and Africa. In 1961 he became a member of the Communist Party; in 1963 he became a citizen of Ghana.

Harrison's devastating "The Descent of Dr. Du Bois" was written on July 17, 1918, at the request of Major Walter Howard Loving of military intelligence, while Du Bois "was being preened for a desk captaincy [in military intelligence] at Washington." Du Bois had written a very controversial "Close Ranks" editorial in June for the July *Crisis* magazine. It urged African Americans, "while this war lasts, [to] forget our special grievances and close ranks shoulder to shoulder with our own white fellow citizens and allied nations that are fighting for democracy." Loving, who probably wanted to block Du Bois's rise in military intelligence, had solicited a summary of the situation from Harrison who was viewed "as one of those 'radicals' qualified to furnish such a summary." Harrison, who desired the federal government to intervene against lynching, segregation, and disfranchisement, published his summary a week later as an editorial in *The Voice* on July 25, 1918, without changing a single word. Loving subsequently informed him that the editorial "was one of the main causes of the government's change of intention as regards the Du Bois captaincy." Harrison and the New Negro militants viewed the overall process as the "collapse of his [Du Bois's] leadership." The exposé of Du Bois's role in the matter led to Du Bois's descent from the pinnacle of leadership in the mind of many of the militant "New Negroes."[10]

Though Du Bois denied that there was any relation between his "Close Ranks" editorial and the commission, Harrison took him to task over this. Du Bois's motives quickly became a subject of intense debate in the Black community, and, as Harrison correctly predicted, the controversy severely tarnished Du Bois's position as an "influential person among Negroes" and as an uncompromising opponent of race discrimination. Partly because of this editorial, Du Bois, over the next forty years, would refer to his activity around the period of the Great War with what historian Mark Ellis describes as, "a mixture of shame and bitterness."[11]

Harrison's editorial did more than cast grave doubt on Du Bois as a leader and lead to the denial of his captaincy commission. It also marked Harrison as a spearhead of the opposition to "Close Ranks" and as a spokesman for the militant New Negro Movement. Trotter soon issued a similar critique, and in a short time so did the *Negro World*.[12]

In a recent bulletin of the War Department it was declared that "justifiable grievances" were producing and had produced "not disloyalty, but an amount of unrest and bitterness which even the best efforts of their leaders may not be able always to guide." This is the simple truth. The essence of the present situation lies in the fact that the people whom our white masters have "recognized" as our leaders (without taking the trouble to consult us) and those who, by our own selection, had actually attained to leadership among us are being revaluated and, in most cases, rejected.

The most striking instance from the latter class is Dr. W. E. B. Du Bois, the editor of the *Crisis*. Du Bois's case is the more significant because his former services to his race have been undoubtedly of a high and courageous sort. Moreover, the act by which he has brought upon himself the stormy outburst of disapproval from his race is one which of itself, would seem to merit no such stern condemnation. To properly gauge the value and merit of this disapproval one must view it in the light of its attendant circumstances and of the situation in which it arose.

Dr. Du Bois first palpably sinned in his editorial "Close Ranks" in the July number of the *Crisis*. But this offense (apart from the trend and general tenor of the brief editorial) lies in a single sentence: "Let us, while this war lasts, *forget our special grievances* and close our ranks, shoulder to shoulder with our white fellow-citizens and the allied nations that are fighting for democracy." From the latter part of the sentence there is no dissent, so far as we know. The offense lies in that part of the sentence which ends with the italicized words. It is felt by all his critics, that Du Bois, of all Negroes, knows best that our "special grievances" which the War Department Bulletin describes as "justifiable" consist of lynching, segregation and disfranchisement, and that Negroes of America can not perceive either their lives, their manhood or their vote (which is their political life and liberties) with these things in existence. The doctor's critics feel that America can not use the Negro people to any good effect unless they have life, liberty and manhood assured and guaranteed to them. Therefore, instead of the war for democracy making these things less necessary, it makes them more so.

"But," it may be asked, "why should not these few words be taken merely as a slip of the pen or a venial error in logic? Why all this hubbub?" It is because the so-called leaders of the first-mentioned class have already established an unsavory reputation by advocating this same surrender of life, liberty and manhood, masking their cowardice behind the pillars of war-time sacrifice? Du Bois's statement, then, is believed to mark his entrance into that class, and is accepted as a "surrender" of the principles which brought him into prominence — and which alone kept him there.

Later, when it was learned that Du Bois was being preened for a berth in the War Department as a captain-assistant (adjutant) to Major [Joel E.] Spingarn, the words used by him in the editorial acquired a darker and more sinister significance. The two things fitted too well together as motive and self-interest.

For these reasons Du Bois is regarded much in the same way as a knight in the middle ages who had had his armor stripped from him, his arms reversed and his spurs hacked off. This ruins him as an influential person among Negroes at this time, alike whether he becomes a captain or remains an editor.

But the case has roots much further back than the editorial in July's *Crisis*. Some time ago when it was learned that the *Crisis* was being investigated by the government for an alleged seditious utterance a great clamor went up, although the expression of it was not open. Negroes who dared to express their thoughts seemed to think the action tantamount to a declaration that protests against lynching, segregation and disfranchisement were outlawed by the government. But nothing was clearly understood until the conference of editors was called under the assumed auspices of Emmett Scott and Major Spingarn. Then it began to appear that these editors had not been called without a purpose. The desperate ambiguity of the language which they used in their report (in the War Department Bulletin), coupled with the fact that not one of them, upon his return would tell the people anything of the proceedings of the conference — all this made the Negroes feel less and less confidence in them and their leadership; made them (as leaders) less effective instruments for the influential control of the race's state of mind.

Now Du Bois was one of the most prominent of those editors "who were called." The responsibility, therefore, for a course of counsel which stresses the servile virtues of acquiescence and subservience falls squarely on his shoulders. The offer of a captaincy and Du Bois's flirtation with that offer following on the heels of these things seemed, even in the eyes of his associate members of the N. A. A. C. P. to afford clear proof of that which was only a suspicion before, viz.: that the racial resolution of the leaders had been tampered with, and that Du Bois had been privy to something of the sort. The connection between the successive acts of the drama (May, June, July) was too clear to admit of any interpretation other than that of deliberate, cold-blooded, purposive planning. And the connection with Spingarn seemed to suggest that personal friendships and public faith were not good working team-mates.

For the sake of the larger usefulness of Dr. Du Bois we hope he will be able to show that he can remain as editor of the *Crisis*; but we fear that it will require a good deal of explaining. For our leaders, like Caesar's wife, must be above suspicion.

55. "When the Blind Lead," *Negro World* (c. February 1920), reprinted in *When Africa Awakes*, 70–73.

In "When the Blind Lead" Harrison offered a stinging critique of Du Bois for his cessation of struggle in wartime and for blindly believing the empty words of Woodrow Wilson. He recounted Du Bois's actions and emphasized that future leaders would have "to stand by us in war as well as in peace" — "to stand four-square to *all* the winds that blow."

In the February [1920] issue of the *Crisis* its editor begins a brief editorial on "Leadership," with the touching reminder that "Many a good cause has been killed by suspected leadership." How strikingly do these words bring back to us Negroes those dark days of 1918! At that time the editor of the *Crisis* was offering certain unique formulas of leadership that somehow didn't "take." His "Close Ranks" editorial and the subsequent slump in the stock of his leadership have again illustrated the truth since expressed in Latin: "*descensus Averni facilis; sed revocare gradus — hoc opus est*," which, being translated, might mean that, while it's as easy as eggs for a leader to fall off the fence, it is devilishly difficult to boost him up again. In September, 1918, one could boldly say, "*The Crisis says, first* your Country, *then* your Rights!" Today, when the Negro people everywhere are responding to Mr. Michael Coulsen's sentiment that "it's Race, not Country, first," we find the "leader" of 1918 in the position described by [James Russell] Lowell in these words:

> "A moultin' fallen cherubim, ef he should see ye'd snicker,
> Thinkin' he warn's a suckemstance."

How fast time flies!

But the gist of Dr. Du Bois's editorial is the moral downfall of another great leader. "Woodrow Wilson, in following a great ideal of world unity, forgot all his pledges to the German people, forgot all his large words to Russia, did not hesitate to betray Gompers and his unions, *and never at any single moment meant to include in his democracy twelve millions of his fellow Americans, whom he categorically promised 'more than mere grudging justice,' and then allowed 350 of them to be lynched during his Presidency.* Under such leadership what cause could succeed?" He notes that out of the World War, with the Allies triumphant, have come Britain's brutal domination of the seas, her conquest of Persia, Arabia and Egypt, and her tremendous tyranny imposed on two-thirds of Africa.

But we saw these things, as early as 1917, to be the necessary consequences of the Allies' success, when the editor of the *Crisis* was telling his race: "You are not fighting simply for Europe; you are fighting for the world." Was Dr. Du Bois so blind that he couldn't see them? And if he was, is he any less blind today? In 1918 the lynchings were still going on while Dr. Du Bois was solemnly advising us to "forget our grievances." Any one who insisted then on putting such grievances as lynchings, disfranchisement and segregation in the foreground was described by the *Crisis'* editor as seeking "to turn his country's tragic predicament to his own personal gain." At that time he either believed or pretended to believe every one of the empty words that flowed from Woodrow Wilson's lips, and on the basis of this belief he was willing to act as a brilliant bellwether to the rest of the flock. Unfortunately, the flock refused to follow the lost leader.

"If the blind lead the blind they will both fall into the ditch." But in this case those being led were not quite so blind as those who wanted to lead them by way of captaincies in the army. Which was why some captaincies were not forthcoming. The test of vision in a leader is the ability to foresee the immediate future, the necessary consequences of a course of conduct and the dependable sentiments of those whom he assumes to lead. In all these things Dr. Du Bois has failed; and neither his ungrateful attack on Emmett Scott [former special assistant to the secretary of war for Negro affairs"] nor his belated discovery of Wilsonian hypocrisy will, we fear, enable him to climb back into the saddle of race leadership. This is a pity, because he has rendered good service in his day. But that day is past. The magazine which he edits still remains as a splendid example of Negro journalism. But the personal primacy of its editor has departed, never to return. Other times, other men; other men, other manners.

Even the Negro people are now insisting that their leaders shall in thought and moral stamina keep ahead of, and not behind, them.

> "It takes a mind like Willun's [fact!] ez big as all out-doors
> To find out thet it looks like rain after it fairly pours."

The people's spiritual appetite has changed and they are no longer enamoured of "brilliant" leaders, whose chorus is:

> "A marciful Providence fashioned us holler
> O' purpose that we might our principles swaller;
> It can hold any quantity on 'em — the belly can —
> An' bring 'em up ready fer use like the pelican"

And this is a change which we commend to the kindly consideration of all those good white friends who are out selecting Negro "leaders." It is a fact which, when carefully considered, will save them thousands of dollars in "overhead expense." The Negro leaders of the future will be expected not only to begin straight, take a moral vacation, and then go straight again. They will be expected to go straight all the time; to stand by us in war as well as in peace; not to blow hot and cold with the same mouth, but "to stand four-square to *all* the winds that blow."

Problems of Leadership

▧▧▧▧ 56. "To the Young Men of My Race," *The Voice* (January 1919), reprinted in *When*
▧▧▧▧ *Africa Awakes*, 91–95.

In January 1919 Harrison wrote an inspiring editorial which aimed to point the way forward for the African American masses. Entitled "To the Young Men of My Race," it offered (in a male supremacist context) a scorching critique of the old "Negro leadership" and suggested some of the characteristics that "New Negro" leadership should possess, including training, irreverence, and courage. It also quoted from Paul Laurence Dunbar's poem "Right's Security" to emphasize the important role of "minorities."[13]

The Negro is already at work on the problems of reconstruction. He finds himself in the midst of a world which is changing to its very foundations. Yet millions of Negroes haven't now — and have never had — the slightest knowledge or idea of what those foundations are. How can they render effective aid to the world without understanding something of how the world, or society, is arranged, how it runs, and how it is run?

No one, friendly or unfriendly, can deny that the Negroes of America do wish to help in constructing this world of men and things which will emerge from the Great War. They want to help, because they realize that their standing and welfare and happiness in that world will very largely depend upon what kind of world it is. They have not been happy, so far, in America — nor, so far as the white man's rule is concerned, — anywhere else under it. And they want to be happy, if that be possible. For which reason they want to help in the re-shaping of the world-to-be.

They feel the burdens put on them by the White Lords of subjection and repression, of 39 cents worth of education a year in Alabama, of the deep race hatred of the Christian Church, the Y. M. C. A. and the Associated Press; of lynching in the land of "liberty," disfranchisement in "democratic" America and segregation on the Federal trains and in the Federal departments. They feel that the world should be set free from this machinery of mischief — for their sakes as well as that of the world.

Such is the state of mind of the Negro masses here. And now what does this attitude of the Negro masses require? GUIDANCE! Guidance, shaping and direction. Here is strength, here is power, here is a task to call forth the sublimest heroism on the part of those who should lead them. And what do we find? No guidance, no shaping of the course of these millions. The blind may not safely lead the blind in these critical times — and blind men are practically all that we have as leaders.

The old men whose minds are always retrospecting and reminiscing to the past, who are "trained" to read a few dry and dead books which they still fondly believe are hard to get — these do not know anything of the modern world, its power of change and travel, and the mighty range of its ideas. Its labor problems and their relation to wars and alliances and diplomacy are not even suspected by these quaint fossils. They think that they are "leading" Negro thought, but they could serve us better if they were cradled in cotton-wool, wrapped in faded roses, and laid aside in lavender as mementos of the dead past.

The young men must gird up their loins for the task of leadership — and leadership has its stern and necessary duties. The first of these is TRAINING. Not in a night did the call come to Christ, not in a day was HE made fit to make the great sacrifice. It took thirty years of preparation to fit him for the work of three. Even so, on you, young men of Negro America, descends the duty of the great preparation. Get education. Get it not only in school and college, but in books and newspapers, in market-places, institutions, and movements. Prepare by knowing; and never think you know until you have listened to ten others who know differently — and have survived the shock.

The young man's second duty is IRREVERENCE. Reverence is in one sense, respect for what is antiquated because it is antiquated. The race has lived in a rut too long to reverence the rut. Oldsters love ruts because they help them to "rub along," they are easy to understand; they require the minimum of exertion and brains, they give the maximum of ease. Young man! If you wish to be spiritually alert and alive; to get the very best out of yourself — shun a rut as you would shun the plague! Never bow the knee to Baal because Baal is in power; never respect wrong and injustice because they are enshrined in "the sacred institutions of our glorious land"; never have patience with either Cowardice or Stupidity because they happen to wear venerable whiskers. Read, reason, and think on all sides of all subjects. Don't compare yourself with the runner behind you on the road; always compare yourself with the one ahead; so only will you go faster and farther. And set it before you, as a sacred duty always to surpass the teachers that taught you — and this is the essence of irreverence.

The last duty is COURAGE. Dear man of my people, if all else should fail you, never let *that* fail. Much as you need preparation and prevision you are more in need of Courage. This has been, and is yet, A DOWNTRODDEN RACE. Do you know what a downtrodden race needs most? If you are not sure, take down your Bible and read the story of Gideon and his band. You will then understand that, as Dunbar says:

> "Minorities since time began
> Have shown the better side of man;
> And often, in the lists of time,
> One man has made a cause sublime."

You will learn the full force of what another American meant when he told young men of his age:

> "They are slaves who dare not choose
> Hatred, scoffing and abuse
> Rather than in silence shrink
> From the truth they needs must think,
> They are slaves who dare not be
> In the right with two or three."

A people under the heel of oppression has more need of heroic souls than one for whom the world is bright. It was in Egypt and in the wilderness that Israel had need of Moses, Aaron and Joshua. No race situated like ours, has any place of leadership for those who lack courage, fortitude, heroism. You may have to turn your eyes away from the fleshpots of Egypt; you may be called on to fight the wild beasts at Ephesus; you may have to face starvation in the wilderness or crucifixion on Calvary. Have the courage to do that which the occasion demands when it comes. And I make you no promise that "in the end you will win a glorious crown." You may fail, fall and be forgotten. What of it? When you think of our heroic dead on Messines Ridge, along the Aisne and at Chateau Thierry—how does your heart act? It thrills! It thrills because

> "Manhood hath a larger span
> And wider privilege of life than Man."

And you, young Negro men of America, you are striving to give the gift of manhood to this race of ours. The future belongs to the young men.

57. "Shillady Resigns," *Negro World* 8 (June 19, 1920): 2, reprinted in *When Africa Awakes*, 60–61.

John R. Shillady, the white executive secretary of the NAACP in 1918 and 1919, resigned his position after being beaten into unconsciousness in August 1919 by a group of white men (led by a county judge) as he unsuccessfully attempted to meet with the governor and attorney general of Texas in Austin. Shillady never fully recovered from the assault and was succeeded by James Weldon Johnson. Harrison used Shillady's comments on the incident of the beating as a lead for a June 19, 1920, *Negro World* editorial on "the great weakness" of the NAACP.[14]

Mr. John R. Shillady, ex-secretary of the N. A. A. C. P., states in his letter of resignation that "I am less confident than heretofore of the speedy success of the association's full program and of the probability of overcoming within a reasonable period the forces opposed to Negro equality by the means and methods which are within the association's power to employ." In this one sentence Mr. Shillady, the worker on the inside, puts in suave and serenely diplomatic phrase the truth which people on the outside have long perceived, namely, that the N. A. A. C. P. makes a joke of itself when it affects to think that lynching and the other evils which beset the Negro in the South can be abolished by simple publicity. The great weakness of the National Association for the Advancement of Colored People has been and is that, whereas it aims to secure certain results by affecting the minds of white people and making them friendly to it, it has no control over these minds and has absolutely no answers to the question, "What steps do you propose to take if these minds at which you are aiming remain unaffected? What do you propose to do to secure life and liberty for the Negro if the white Southerner persists, as he has persisted for sixty years, in refusing to grant guarantees of life and liberty?" The N. A. A. C. P. has done some good and worth-while work as an organization of protest. But the times call for something more effective than protests addressed to the other fellow's consciousness. What is needed at present is more of the mobilizing of the Negro's political power, pocketbook power and intellectual power (which are absolutely within the Negro's own control) to do for the Negro the things which the Negro needs to have done without depending upon or waiting for the co-operative action of white people. This co-operative action, whenever it does come, is a boon that no Negro, intelligent or unintelligent, affects to despise. But no Negro of clear vision, whether he be a leader or not, can afford to predicate the progress of the Negro upon such co-operative action, because it may not come.

Mr. Shillady may have seen these things. It is high time that all Negroes see these things whether their white professional friends see them or not.

58. "A Tender Point," *Negro World* 8 (July 3, 1920): 2, reprinted with deletions in *When Africa Awakes*, 63–66.

In "A Tender Point" Harrison addressed the leadership problem related to "the claim advanced, explicitly and implicitly, by Negroids of mixed blood to be considered the natural leaders of Negro activities on the ground of some alleged 'superiority' inherent in their white blood." That light-skinned African Americans were prominent in Black leadership there is little doubt. The historian Florette Henri has found that some ninety percent of prominent African American leaders of the era — the kind mentioned in "Who's Who" type lists of race leaders — were light skinned. The historian Willard B. Gatewood found that "for at least a half century, the aristocracy of color that emerged in the post–Civil War era continued to exercise influence in Black America" and "dominated and often monopolized the choicest positions open to blacks in education, politics, government, and business."[15]

When the convention of turtles assembled on the Grand Banks of Newfoundland it was found absolutely impossible to get a tortoise elected as leader. All turtles, conservative and radical, agreed that a land and water creature, who was half one thing and half another, was not an ideal choice for leader of a group which lived exclusively in the water. Whenever a leader of the Irish has to be selected by the Irish it is an Irishman who is selected. No Irishman would be inclined to dispute the fact that other men, even Englishmen like John Stuart Mill and the late Keir Hardie, could feel the woes of Ireland as profoundly as any Irishman. But they prefer to live up to the principle of "Safety First."

These two illustrations are to be taken as a prelude to an important point which is not often discussed in the Negro press because all of us — black, brown and particolored — fear to offend each other. That point concerns the biological breed of persons who should be selected by Negroes as leaders of their race. We risk the offense this time because efficiency in matters of racial leadership, as in other matters, should not be too tender to these points of prejudice when they stand in the way of desirable results. For two centuries in America we, the descendants of the black Negroes of Africa, have been told by white men that we cannot and will not amount to anything except in so far as we first accept the bar sinister of their mixing with us. Always when white people had to select a leader for Negroes they would select some one who had in his veins the blood of the selectors. In the good old days when slavery was in flower, it was those whom Denmark Vesey of Charleston described as "house niggers" who got the master's cast-off clothes, the better scraps of food and culture which fell from the white man's table, who were looked upon as the Talented Tenth of the Negro race. The opportunities of self-improvement, in so far as they lay within the hand of the white race, were accorded exclusively to this class of people who were the left-handed progeny of the white masters.

Out of this grew a certain attitude on their part towards the rest of the Negro people which, unfortunately, has not yet been outgrown. In Washington, Boston, Charleston, New York and Chicago these proponents of the lily-white idea are prone to erect around their sacred personalities a high wall of caste, based on the grounds of color. And the black Negroes have heretofore worshipped at the alters erected on these walls. One sees this in the Baptist, Methodist and Episcopal churches, at the various conventions and in fraternal organizations. Black people themselves seem to hold the degrading view that a man who is but half a Negro is twice as worthy of their respect and support as one who is entirely black. We have seen in the social life of some of the places mentioned how women, undeniably black and undeniably beautiful, have been shunned and ostracized at public functions by men who should be presumed to know better. We have read the fervid jeremiads of "colored" men who, when addressing the whites on behalf of some privilege which they wished to share with them, would be, in words, as black as the ace of spades, but, when it came to mixing with "their kind," they were professional lily-whites, and we have often had to point out to them that there is no color prejudice in America — except among "colored" people. Those who may be inclined to be angry at the broaching of this subject are respectfully requested to ponder that pungent fact.

In this matter white people, even in America, are inclined to be more liberal than colored people. If a white man has no race prejudice, it will be found that he doesn't care how black is the Negro friend that he takes to his home and his bosom. Even these white people who pick leaders for Negroes have begun in these latter years to give formal and official expression to this principle. Thus it was that when the trustees of Tuskegee had to elect a head of Tuskegee and a putative leader of the Negroes of America to succeed the late Dr. Washington, they argued that it was now necessary to select as leader for the Negro people a man who could not be mistaken by any one for anything other than a Negro. Therefore, Mr. Emmett Scott was passed over and Dr. Robert R. Moton was selected. We are not approving here the results of this selection, but merely holding up to Negroes the principle by which it was governed.

So long as we ourselves acquiesce in the selection of leaders on the ground of their unlikeness to our racial type, just so long will we be met by the invincible argument that white blood is necessary to make a Negro worth while. Every Negro who has respect for himself and for his race will feel, when contemplating such examples as Toussaint Louverture, Phillis Wheatley, Paul Laurence Dunbar, Samuel Ringgold Ward and Marcus Garvey [Garvey is deleted in the reprint] the thrill of pride that differs in quality and intensity from the feeling which he experiences when contemplating other examples of great Negroes who are not entirely black. For it is impossible in such cases for the white men to argue that they owed their greatness or their prominence to the blood of the white race which was mingled in their veins. It is a legitimate thrill of pride, for it gives us a hope nobler than the hope of amalgamation whereby, in order to become men, we must lose our racial identity. It is a subject for sober and serious reflection, and it is hoped that sober and serious reflection will be given to it.

59. "Our White Friends," *Negro World* 8 (July 3, 1920): 2, reprinted in *When Africa Awakes*, 61–63.

On June 20, 1920, members of the Star Order of Ethiopia held a procession in front of a South Chicago café and burned an American flag. A Black police officer who attempted to stop the destruction of a second flag was shot and wounded, a white sailor who intervened was killed, and a restaurant employee was also killed. The police arrested the Black procession leader, Grover Cleveland Redding, and charged him with murder, accessory to murder, and rioting. R. D. Jonas, the white head of the "Back to Abyssinia Movement," was released with no evidence found of his direct connection with the shooting. Jonas, a former secretary of the League of Darker Peoples (whose founders included hair products millionaire Madame C. J. Walker and *Messenger* editors Chandler Owen and A. Philip Randolph), was reportedly "able to show he had no part in the riot." Jonas had worked for U.S. military intelligence as an informant on "Negro subversion" and was working for British intelligence (who had supplied his reports to U.S. military intelligence). While Jonas was released, Redding, who denied participation in the activity, was convicted of murder and hanged on June 24, 1921.[6]

Harrison's scathing editorial, "Our White Friends," followed a *Negro World* article that described the incident. The editorial discusses the new "New Negro" attitude toward "white friends," calls attention to the blindness of "Anglo-Saxon civilization," and urges Blacks to choose and support their own leaders.

In the good old days when the black man's highest value in the white man's eye was that of an object of benevolence especially provided by the Divine mind for calling out those tender out-pourings of charity which were so dear to the self-satisfied Caucasian — in those days the white men who fraternized with black people could do so as their guides, philosophers and friends without incurring any hostility on the part of black folk. Today, however, the white man who mixes with the black brother is having a hard time of it. Somehow Ham's offspring no longer feels proud of being "taken up" by the progeny of Japhet. And when the white man insists on mixing in with him the colored brother will persist in attributing ulterior motives.

What is the cause of this difference? The answer will be found only by one who refuses to wear the parochial blinkers of Anglo-Saxon civilization and sees that the relations of the white and the black race have changed and are changing all over the world. Such an observer would note that the most significant fact of the growing race consciousness is to be found in the inevitable second half of the world. It isn't because these darker people are motivated by race that their present state of mind constitutes a danger to Caucasian over-lordship. It is because they have developed consciousness, intelligence, understanding. They have learned that the white brother is perfectly willing to love them — "in their place." They have learned that that place is one in which they are not to develop brains and initiative, but must furnish the brawn and muscle whereby the white man's brain and initiative can take eternally the products of their brawn and muscle. There are today many white men who will befriend the Negro, who will give their dollars to his comfort and welfare, so long as the idea of what constitutes the comfort and welfare comes entirely from the white man's mind. Examples like those of Dr. [Joel E.] Spingarn and Mr. E. D. Morel are numerous.

And not for nothing does the black man balk at the white man's "mixing in." For there are spies everywhere and the *agent provocateur* is abroad in the land. From Chicago comes the news by way of the Associated Press (white) that Dr. [R. D.] Jonas, who has always insisted in sticking his nose into the Negro people's affairs as their guide, philosopher and friend, has been forced to confess that he is a government agent, presumably paid for things which the government would later suppress. Dr. Jonas is reported to have said that he is connected with the British secret service; but since the second year of the European war it has been rather difficult for us poor devils to tell where the American government ended and the British government began, especially in these matters. In any case, we have Dr. Jonas' confession, and all the silly Negroes who listened approvingly to the senseless allegations made by Messrs. Jonas, Gabriel, and others of a standing army of 4,000,000 in Abyssinia and of Japanese-Abyssinian diplomatic relations and intentions, must feel now very foolish about the final result.

How natural it was that Jonas, the white leader, should have gone scot free, while Redding and his other Negro dupes are held! How natural that Jonas should be the one to positively identify Redding as the slayer of the Negro policeman! And so, once again, that section of the Negro race that will not follow except where a white man leads will have to pay that stern penalty whereby Dame Experience teaches her dunces. Under the present circumstances we, the Negroes of the Western world, do pledge our allegiance to leaders of our own race, selected by our own group and supported financially and otherwise exclusively by us. Their leadership may be wise or otherwise; they may make mistakes here and there; nevertheless, such sins as they may commit will be our sins, and all the glory that they may achieve will be our glory. We prefer it so. It may be worth the while of the white men who desire to be "Our Professional Friends" to take note of this preference.

Time as Editor of the *Negro World* and Comments on Marcus Garvey

Marcus Mosiah Garvey (1887–1940) was born in St. Ann's Bay, Jamaica, apprenticed as a printer, and traveled to Costa Rica, Panama, and England before returning home in 1914 to start the Universal Negro Improvement and Conservation Association and African Communities League. He traveled to the United States in 1916 and, while on the verge of returning to Jamaica, was deeply influenced by Harrison. Garvey then started a UNIA in New York in 1917, began the *Negro World* in 1918, and in 1919–20 saw his organization, his newspaper, and his Black Star Line take off in meteoric fashion. The UNIA became the largest mass movement of Black people in the United States and in the world, and the newspaper swept the globe. In 1923 Garvey was convicted of mail fraud related to the sale of stock for the Black Star Line, and his sentence was commuted by President Calvin Coolidge. On his release Garvey was deported to Jamaica where he lived until moving to London in 1935.[17]

The following items on Garvey and the *Negro World* provide what is arguably the most intimate, profound, and insightful critique of Garvey from one of his contemporaries.

 60. Connections with the Garvey Movement, March 17 and 18, 1920, HHHDI.

Harrison began work with the *Negro World* on January 2, 1920, while Garvey was honeymooning in Canada with his first wife, Amy Ashwood. He served as principal editor (without the formal title) until around November 1920 and then served as associate editor until December 25, 1920, and as contributing editor from around January 1, 1921 to March 25, 1922. Under Harrison's expert editorship, with news for the race, pithy identifiable editorials, and a host of new features, the *Negro World* came to be viewed as a publication of the masses. Before Harrison's editorship it had a circulation of about ten thousand. On May 1, 1920, it went from six to ten pages per issue, and in June it reached a circulation of fifty thousand as it swept the globe with its race-conscious message. The growth was in large part due to Harrison's skillful editing.[18]

On St. Patrick's Day, Wednesday, March 17, 1920, Harrison began to write in his diary the early history of his connection with the Garvey movement and *The Negro World*. In his comments he offers an overview of the major reworking of the *Negro World* that he undertook and it stands as an important page in the history of African American journalism. Harrison reshaped and developed the paper — changing its style, format, content, and editorial page — and was primarily responsible for developing it into the preeminent radical, race-conscious political and literary publication of that time. (Historian Tony Martin writes that it was "the most highly political of newspapers" and "simultaneously the most literary of newspapers.")[19]

In this diary entry Harrison also discusses problems surrounding the first voyage of the Black Star Line's thirty-two-year-old freighter, the *Yarmouth*, as well as Garvey's early plans to have him head a commission to Liberia, where Garvey proposed to establish a center for future colonization and trade efforts.

Wednesday
March 17th 1920.

I must attempt to set down here the early history of my connection with the Garvey movement (The Universal Negro Improvement Association and African Communities League, and its products: The Black Star Line Corporation, The Negro Factories' Corporation and *The Negro World*). If I should delay it longer the fine edge of certain impressions might be worn down and certain minor details might vanish from my memory. The account of my own labors in the field of New Negro sentiment can be left for later shaping. The materials for that narrative may be found partly in the pages of *The Voice*, the weekly newspaper which I issued between July 4th 1917 and March 1919 — especially in the first number. I shall here confine myself to my connection with the later and larger movement.

It was in the first week in December of last year (1919) that Mr. Marcus Garvey met me on West 136th Street between Lenox and Fifth avenues and, after a hearty handshake, told me that he had been looking for me for several weeks and had concluded that I had gone out of town. I explained to him that, although Dr. [R. C.] Woods, president of the Baptist Seminary and College of Lynchburg, Va., had engaged me to come down there and organize and set going a Department of Negro History, I had finally decided to remain in New York and was at that time acting as Director of Publicity and head of the Speakers' Bureau for Sam Duncan's project of a Negro Bank (The Pioneer Development Corporation). He thereupon made me the offer of the presidency or principalship of the new college which he had projected as one of the main institutions of the U.N.I.A. I told him that I would consider it seriously and give him my reply later. I think it was a week later that I went to his office to give him my reply. This office was at the time a curious shambles. The work of the U.N.I.A., of the Black Star Line and of the newspaper, were all jumbled together in one room—although much of the financial work of the B.S.L. and also that of the U.N.I.A. was done on the floor above. There was, consequently, no privacy for the discussion of business in the office. We, therefore, went out on the landing. There it turned out he wanted to associate me with Ferris ("Professor" and "Rev." Wm. H. Ferris, "author of *The African Abroad*") in the editing of the paper at that time and later to assume the headship of the school or college when it was organized.

I accepted provisionally, and asked for more time to make my acceptance binding and to formulate the conditions under which I would work. I think it was on the 24th of December, the day before his wedding, that I made my acceptance final. I was to work for $30 a week as Associate Editor (not *Assistant* Editor), and I stipulated that I was not to be expected to lecture at Liberty Hall as any part of my duties, although I was willing to help out in an emergency.

My connection with the paper began on January 2nd (1920) although I had no hand in the issue dated Jan. 3rd which was already out on Dec. 30th. When it became known that I was to be connected with the *Negro World* many of the rank and file and of the officials of the movement were enthusiastic in their congratulations. Chief among these was the bright young secretary E[dward]. D[avid]. Smith-Green, who was just then convalescent from a pistol shot wound in his leg inflicted by a murderous footpad who, for the purpose of robbery, had waylaid him in the dark hallway of his home. The shock had killed his wife who was at the time enceinte.

My first business was to improve the appearance and general makeup of the paper. A reference to the files will show how much has been achieved in two months and a half. The "heads" of news articles and special articles often ran to six and eight lines, with "banks" of eight and ten lines that sprawlingly attempted to tell all about what was contained in the articles. Letters went galloping all over its ten pages and opinion-items, which should have been sparingly used and confined to the supplementary sections, appeared on the front page all in the wasteful glory of "heads," "subheads" and "banks" eight lines long. It seemed that every ass in the universe who was of the Negro race was writing "poetry," and everyone spewed his hog-wash in the pages of the *Negro World*. The general idea seemed to be that if each line began with a capital letter, if grammar's neck was wrung and rhymes like "boat" and "joke" were occasionally interspersed, "poetry" was achieved.

I had to stop all this. I began by herding the poetry on one page under the standing feature-head, "Poetry For the People." I made that page the Magazine Page and tethered there the literary effusions in which Mr. Ferris and his friends were prolific. Then I set to work cutting down the "heads" and "banks" and guiding a large portion of the letters into the harmless harbor of the waste-basket.

Two other defects must not be forgotten. The editorials were almost endless. Many of them consumed nearly four columns (set as two double-columns). They might have been all right as literary essays; but, then, a newspaper (especially one designated for the masses black or white) cannot afford to let its editorials run to literary essays. They should have terseness, point, pungency and force. But I did not criticize: I turned out samples instead, and, by dint of putting my initials at the end of my editorials during the first few weeks, I soon forced on my associate a change of form; for readers began to note the difference. Then there was the matter of clippings. Most of our news came from that source — mainly from the white newspapers. Mr. Ferris, although a Harvard and Yale M.A. hasn't the slightest idea of newspaper work. He seemed to read certain papers by chance and if he found in them something which pleased him he would snip it out and put it in even if it were six months or a year old, never changing a word or a heading. His desk was as untidy as his person, strewn with the accumulated rubbish of months. This he could never arrange into any semblance of order and in it he could consequently find nothing when it was wanted. He is a brilliant "scholar" within a certain narrow rut or range; but his mind is innocent of order, plan, or arrangement. Anyone who has read his two volumes, *The African Abroad*, that gigantic rubbish heap of ill-digested and structureless learning, will be able to verify the judgment from his mental products, wherein sermons, lectures, valuable historical data and whole pages of names are jumbled together pell-mell like the scraps in the wallet of one of [Robert] Burns's Jolly Beggars.

It, therefore, devolved on me to shape up the clippings to snip off, insert and re-write many portions of them. All this wasn't by any means an easy task, and we had many an unvoiced conflict of opinion. Two or three times he had asked me in his innocence and wrath, "Who is the editor, you or I?" That was before he knew better. For I was getting $30 a week: whereas he was getting $25 — although I believe that he now gets 30. Gradually I got the strings of management in a letter to the printers which I dictated to [*the private* has been crossed out] a stenographer and had Mr. Garvey sign, making me the sole and final authority on matters relating to the admission of "copy" and to the "make-up" of the paper in form. I had to do this for the salvation of the paper: But, along with this has come a burdensome increase of work and responsibility. I have had to read again and re-shape every item of "copy" that came from his hand to mine — except his editorials and "Literary Mirror" articles.

Then there were the lucubrations of officials of the movement. Two especially have been veritable thorns in my side: the Rev. Mr. [H. M.] Mickens who has taken the place of "Prof." [B. C.] Buck as Secretary-General of the U.N.I.A., and the Rev. Mr. Gilliard, a divinity student. Both of these men work in the offices and, seemingly, when time hangs heavy on their hands they turn to the production of pronounciamentos for public consumption. To all such I am the mute with the bowstrings.

To add to my burdens, Ferris, who is now Chancellor of the Convention Fund, shirks his work as associate editor. By way of example: On Saturday I received from Mr. Garvey's office about 60 letters for the editors—an unusually heavy budget. I take a proper pride in seeing that every letter that is sent to my desk gets read and attended to on the same day. But, this batch, as I said before, was unusually large, I, therefore, divided up with Ferris by asking him to take a portion of them. He selected 24. I impressed on him the necessity of attending to them on that same day because some of them might contain timely matter of consequence. Yet, at six o'clock when I was getting ready to clean up and go home the letters were still there and Ferris was nowhere in sight. I was exasperated and sent the bundle to him by one of the messengers to Liberty Hall where he was to preside that night. On Sunday evening when I came in to work alone at my desk the letters were back on his desk unattended to. I had to go thru them, and it was well that I did so. One of them contained a letter from a Haytian (Schiller Nicholas) whose manuscript on American Rule In Hayti I have read, corrected and turned in to the printers to be set up. In this letter he requested that his name, for his own protection, should not appear as author of the article. I therefore had it deleted on Monday. But if I had not gone through Ferris' share of the mail it would have appeared, to our correspondent's injury, since Ferris did not touch those letters until today (Wednesday) and the paper, which came out yesterday was set up on Monday.

But crass and cowardly stupidity are even worse dangers than laziness. There is the case of Captain Cockburn's speech at Liberty Hall. Captain Joshua Cockburn commanded the "Yarmouth" (the first ship of the Black Star Line) on her first voyage under the Black, Red and Green. There seems to have been some underhanded business done to make the trip a failure and to prevent the ship from reaching port. At one time the Captain retired about midnight leaving explicit instructions, a man at the wheel, and the ship on a certain course. At four o'clock he awoke to find the fixes banked, the ship on a reef, wireless messages already sent out saying that the ship was sinking, life-belts distributed to passengers and crew and the boats being swung out from the davits— and all this done without any attempt being made to wake or call him. He had to threaten to shoot before he could get things again under control. Then, with the help of an officer who was not an engineer he got steam up and backed his ship off the reef. There was a white chief engineer and a white first mate on this trip and the treachery was generally supposed to have been the work of the engineer mainly.

All this Captain Cockburn told him in his speech at Liberty Hall the night after the ship docked on her return; although he told much of it indirectly and with an evident desire to suppress the more sensational aspects of the story. But as he told it the stenographers set it down. The Liberty Hall news story is generally set on the front page of the paper. On the night of Captain Cockburn's speech Mr. Garvey was away in Canada on his honeymoon, having left on the day after Christmas. I was present at the hall and took copious notes of the Captain's speech. But I was thunderstruck on Monday to find that Ferris had brought down the speech as reported by the stenographers and, after reading it, had given it to the printers to set, with all the unsavory details which, when read, would have destroyed the confidence of the public and stockholders and split the project of the Black Star Line wide open. I immediately, upon seeing the "proofs," ordered the story "killed" and re-wrote an account of the meeting and the speech from which these details were elided. This was one of the things which helped to induce Mr. Garvey to give me control of "copy" for the printers. So much for the paper.

And now Mr. Garvey has selected me to go to Liberia as chairman of a Commission of three (John E. Bruce and Mr. [Elie] Garcia are the other two) on a delicate diplomatic mission [The Liberian Commission] connected with the world-wide work of the U.N.I.A. He first broached the matter to me a month ago — to be exact, on Monday Feb. 16th. I advised him then against spreading the news of his intent until he had completed all his arrangements. But since it was announced at Liberty Hall about a week ago (although without announcement of the details) some people know of it in a vague and general way. It was I who mentioned it Saturday two weeks ago (Mar. 6th) to John E. Bruce, who, thereupon, expressed a wish to go as a member of the Commission. I told him then that I thought I could manage it, and advised him to write me a letter upon the receipt of which I would take the matter up with Mr. Garvey who, after selecting me as head, had not yet decided who the others should be. I waited for his letter until the following Wednesday and then, not having heard from him, I mentioned his request to Mr. Garvey and described his relations by correspondence and otherwise with the leading men of Liberia and other parts of West Africa. Mr. Garvey accepted the suggestion and told me to write him to that effect. Ten minutes later I got Bruce's letter.

Since then I have been trying to get Bruce up to dinner; but my wife's termagant temper has put obstacles in the way. Last Saturday (the 13th), after having invited him to dinner and a conference, I was forced by Madame's recalcitrance to phone him and cancel the engagement. However, we met last night. The dinner had to be given at Miss Julie Petersen's (670 Lenox Ave.) who took us in at moment's notice — for which I am very grateful to her. But, owing to the presence of the four other young women who live with Miss Petersen, and to the rush (I was to preside at Henry F. Downing's lecture on Liberia at Liberty Hall) we had neither privacy nor time enough to get down to an interchange of ideas. I had already shown him the notes which I had drawn up for Mr. Garvey's perusal, outlining the duties of the Commissioners, the principles which should guide their conduct, the results for which they were to work, and presenting a schedule of expenses involved.

Between these two happenings came a slight hitch. When I phoned Bruce on Saturday night he began to express doubts as to whether he could go. He had received, he said, a letter from Duse Mohammed who was coming to America and was to be his guest. Pressed for the details, he could not give me anything precise as to Mohammed's trip. I couldn't help thinking that since Bruce was sharing Arthur Schomburg's house and Schomburg was as well known to Mohammed as Bruce, that there was "a nigger in the woodpile" some-where. Therefore when I saw Bruce at Miss Petersen's I made it clear that "expenses" would be borne by the Association. As a consequence he has ceased to waver and today (18th) he sent me a letter asking, among other things, whether he would be paid for the time spent on the mission, since he was getting leave of absence "without pay." Here breaks thru one of the besetting sins of the American Negro — especially the male: they lack straightforwardness; that spiritual quality whose cruder form is known as courage. Why couldn't Bruce have spoken up like a man and said that he was financially unable to stand the strain of going unless his expenses were paid? I didn't keep Garvey guessing as to *my* financial status: I set it forth. Well; all's well that ends well, so far.

   61. On Garvey's Character and Abilities, May 24, 1920, HHHDI.

In the following diary entry from May 24, 1920, Harrison offers an extremely critical "general estimate of Mr. Garvey's character and abilities." He discusses Garvey's "bombastic blabbing," "autocratic interference," and "ignorance of ships and shipping matters," as well as how Garvey "lies to the people magniloquently" and prefers obedient followers to talented and independent thinking coworkers.

A remarkably similar appraisal of Garvey was offered three and a half years later by the Rev. E. Ethelred Brown, who had known Garvey since his Jamaica days. In a sermon on "Garvey-istic Devotion" Brown said of Garvey:

In the first place he is bombastic, conceited and arrogant. These qualities are too painfully obvious to call for further comment. Secondly, he has no regard whatever for exactness of statement and cares nothing for the character and reputation of other men. He lives in an atmosphere of exaggerations and falsehoods. He tells you of 50,000 delegates at a Convention attended by 200, and he makes it impossible by his exaggeration to know when his figures are true or near true or absolutely false. As to the reputation and character of men, almost every man who has left his association has been branded a thief and a liar and worse. He has prostituted the high uses of a newspaper to his own unscrupulous ends. And he has not changed. . . . Thirdly, Marcus Garvey cannot work with men. He gets on splendidly with tools but any man who dares to be a man becomes his enemy and is forthwith dismissed from his presence. On two succeeding conventions he has brought about the dismissal of men whom he himself at the preceding convention presented for election as efficient, loyal and honorable. They were too efficient, too loyal, too honorable to continue to be his tools, his phonograph — and they went.

Fourthly — he is a mean shifter of responsibilities. He claims all the honor and disowns all the blame.

Brown also considered Garvey "a coward President and a stubborn man — because of his cowardice to admit failure when failure was obvious, because of his remarkable stubbornness to carry through a scheme doomed for obvious reasons to failure from the start." Brown added that he was "responsible for the cruel willful waste of thousands and thousands of dollars." (It should be noted that after Brown delivered this sermon in January 1928, a listener, displeased with what was said, approached the pulpit, clubbed Brown over the head with a blackjack, and quickly departed.)[20]

May 24th 1920

It does not now appear that the "Commission" to Liberia will be allowed to materialize. I have been knocking at the door of the State Department for the past two months, but no passports have been forthcoming. The issue of the *Negro World* for [date not given — presumably c. March 10] will furnish a reason. In that issue will be found an insane collection of bombastic rantings as to what the "Commission" would do in Liberia, delivered in Liberty Hall by pin-headed preachers and other ignorant howlers — and all before the Rev. Mr. [James W. H.] Eason (vice-Bruce who had given up his chance on the doctor's advice) and I had got our passports. When [Hudson] Pryce, the new (third) editor was correcting the proofs at the printers' and came across this senseless slobber he called up Mr. Garvey on the phone and pointed out to him that if the stuff went in his "delegates" would hardly be able to get their passports. Garvey replied that he had heard it all spoken and had read it in type and that, in his opinion, it was "good propaganda" and should go in. So it went in.

In the meanwhile, as I have been credibly informed, Sam Duncan, who has two old scores to pay off and who is a mean dirty s. of-b. had written secretly to the State Dept. and set them on the trail just as he had previously done to the governors of the various British West Indian islands, resulting in the outlawing of the *Negro World* in those islands. So, there will be no passports for us. And it is mainly due to Marcus Garvey's prime defect, bombastic blabbing. He talks too much and too foolishly.

GARVEY'S CHARACTER

The last remarks may fittingly introduce a general estimate of Mr. Garvey's character and abilities.

When we had organized the Liberty League Garvey used to attend our meetings; at the same time he began to organize a branch of the Jamaica Improvement Association, which finally blossomed out into the U.N.I.A. and A.C.L. [African Communities

League]. Everything that I did he copied. Yet I was generous enough to introduce him to my audiences in New York at the Bethel meeting on the night of May [actually June] 12th 1917 and also at my lecture-forum in Lafayette Hall, as also in Brooklyn later. Sometimes, indeed, I would close my meeting in Lafayette Hall earlier than usual and ask my audience to go down to give him a crowd. Yet when Garvey had gone up in the world and the U.N.I.A. was "going strong" never a reciprocal courtesy was forthcoming from him.

Knowing that my work which had failed had laid the foundation for his success, I refrained from burdening his movement with my presence. Edgar Gray [Grey] has since told me that he again and again asked Garvey to call me in and utilize my abilities in counsel and service; but he would always refuse with the groundless excuse that "Harrison has his own propaganda," and that he was "dangerous," whereas at that time I had no propaganda of any sort except "Race First!" and was devoting my time to purely educational lectures outdoors and indoors.

The first big defect, then, in Mr. Garvey's make-up is a defect in the size of his soul. He is spiritually as well as intellectually a little man. That is why he doesn't want around him men who are of larger girth either way. Or if he gets them he does not utilize them in any way which would aid, amplify, or modify his chaotic plans and notions. If he can use them as his hired bravos, then so far, so good.

Today, most Negroes in and out of the U.N.I.A. who are interested in its work assume that the men of abilities like [Edward] Smith-Green, [William H.] Ferris and myself who are with Mr. Garvey, are, somehow, permitted to lend the aid of their knowledge and abilities to the work in hand. But it isn't so at all. Ferris is a mere pseudo-intellectual flunky with no more personality than a painted stick. I am only the editor of the Negro World and am in no way connected with either the U.N.I.A. the B.S.L. or the N.F.C. except as a dues-paying member of the first. Smith-Green has had to chafe against being over-reached, brow-beaten and superseded in his own department, and right now, Garvey is trying to make a scape-goat of him by a blanket-insinuation of malversation to cover up the snarled results of his own autocratic interference.

Since Jan. 1st there has been but one meeting of the Board of Directors (that of last Monday—the 17th May). Mr. Garvey, I learn from Smith-Green, Johnson (traffic and passenger agent) Cyril Henry, and others, has paid money on ships, published the news of the new acquisitions and *then* called the board to inform them that *he had done* this, and so. His ignorance of ships and shipping matters has resulted in his paying out tens of thousands of dollars unnecessarily and he has been victimized again and again by the white men from whom ships and ships' accessories were bought.

In the midst of all this he lies to the people magniloquently, bragging about impossible things while not owning the ships outright. The Yarmouth is at present lying at her pier at a cost I have been told of $150 a day while her black captain has been relieved of his command—although still in the company's service—and a white captain has been assigned to command her.

⚡⚡ 62. The UNIA Convention, August 28, 1920, HHHDI.
⚡⚡

The UNIA's "First International Convention of the Negro Peoples of the World" ran from
August 1 to August 31, 1920, in New York City. In discussing Harrison's participation in
the convention the *Negro World* of September 4 described him as "the most scholarly and
learned member of the convention." It added that "there is scarcely a man in all the race
whose learning is so profound, whose knowledge of economics, religion, sociology,
science, art, politics, literature is such as seems inexhaustible."[21]

This appraisal of Harrison was far different from Harrison's appraisal of Garvey. On
August 1, as the convention opened, Garvey announced that he was sending a telegram to
Eamon de Valera, president of the Irish Republic, with greetings from "25,000 Negro delegates assembled in Madison Square Garden in mass convention, representing 400,000,000
Negroes of the world." Such exaggeration (Harrison counted 103 delegates and there were
probably 260,000,000 Black people worldwide, almost all of whom were not represented)
was one of the factors that turned Harrison against Garvey.[22]

During the fourth week of the convention, as it wound to a close, Harrison recorded
several insider's commentaries in his diary. The two entries that follow provide a quite
different view from that which Garvey presented to the public. They are also quite un-
flattering to Garvey, whom Harrison describes as a "hypocrite" and a "mountebank."

Sat. Aug. 28th

On Wednesday night I delivered my address at Liberty Hall on "What Shall We
Do To Be Saved?" — (I shall insert the speech as reported at the end of this entry). [The
speech has not been found.]

The Convention has been in session since the 1st of the month. Garvey insisted on
presiding — as I have told Mr. [Francis Wilcum] Ellegor that he would — and has made
the welkin ring with his insane and bombastic rhodomontades. In plain English, he has
made an ass of himself and has made the movement a matter of ridicule. He has had not
the shadow of a program and when he was kept away from the meeting everything was
up in the air. He has plastered the air with lies. Imprimis, his circulars advertising the
Madison Square Garden meeting asserted that 25,000 (Twenty-Five Thousand) delegates were present from all parts of the world whereas the official balloting for the officers showed that Mr. Ellegor, who was the sole nominee for the office of Commissioner-
General, and presumably received the votes of all the delegates, received 103 (one
hundred and three) the highest number cast for any office. Garvey himself, sole nominee also, received 92 votes for President-General. Yet, despite such facts, he is again
declaring in circulars out today that there will be 20,000 delegates in the parade on
Tuesday.

The opening fanfarronade of the convention was the great-gathering at Madison
Square Garden on the evening of Monday the 2d inst. This was, from the standpoint of

members, a splendid success. The Garden was packed from top to bottom (15,000). But Garvey, instead of putting forth a constructive radical program, sank into silly rhodo-montades about ordering the white nations to "get out of here." (Africa). As a speaker he was a joke, and looked like a dog. It was [James W. H.] Eason who proved himself a splendid orator. When Garvey began to appeal for money the people went out ("walked out on him") by the thousands.

The first week of the Convention at Liberty Hall was taken up with the delegates' reports of conditions in their several sections. Most of the delegates were from the West Indies. At that, many of them were simply residents of New York whom he called in to pose as delegates *sent* from the West Indies and Africa. Such was the Rev. Mr. Maguire [Bishop Alexander McGuire] who represented Antigua and "Prince" Madarikan Den[i]yi of Lagos, Nigeria who has been in America for more than six years studying. Although my own credentials stated that I was the delegate of the Negro-Foreign-Born Citizens' Political Alliance Garvey insisted on recognizing me when I rose to speak as "the gentleman from the Virgin Islands"—which sent no delegates, although the Virgin Islanders among the Liberty Hall entourage had bought a banner (as those from the other islands and states had done) and marched behind it in the parade of Tuesday the 2nd inst.

63. Convention Bill of Rights and Elections, August 31, 1920, HHHDI.

In his diary entry of August 31, 1920, Harrison wrote about the last three weeks of the UNIA Convention and commented on the Bill of Rights, later called "The Declaration of Rights of the Negro Peoples of the World," as well as on the elections, salaries, and closing parade. The Bill of Rights drew the attention of the Bureau of Investigation (predecessor of the Federal Bureau of Investigation). On August 14, Herbert S. Boulin, the undercover special agent, known as P-138, who covered the Garvey movement for the Bureau, prepared his regular report covering August 12. He wrote that Harrison, "a Socialist and pronounced Negro agitator of the rabid type," had been "holding a series of meetings at 138th St. and Lenox Ave. every night." As the convention started "framing the Declaration of the Bill of Rights" on August 12, Harrison participated and reportedly "insisted that the majority of the bills were not strong and outspoken enough" and "on his suggestion, a number of them were sent back to the framers," and Harrison offered his help "to put the necessary 'kick' in them." Boulin correctly noted in his report, however, that "Garvey still rules with an iron hand." The following day, August 13, the "Declaration of Rights of the Negro Peoples of the World," with 122 signers, was completed. Harrison did not sign it.[23]

The [UNIA Convention's] second week's sessions were devoted to the formulation of a Bill of Rights, afterwards called a Declaration of Rights. One would have thought that the best brains would have been brought together in a committee to elaborate such a document. But this would not have suited Garvey's book. He is afraid of brains. He therefore put forth the silly proposal that each delegate should present resolutions from the floor, all resolutions to be worked up later by the Convention into the Declaration of Rights. In the meanwhile he had prepared his own D. R. and presented it from the chair (as a delegate). Consequently the other delegates' resolutions were brought forward as amendments and extensions of this document. Whenever anything was brought up that he didn't approve he ruled it "out of order." (And, incidentally, the man is such an ass that, although he has been presiding for 3 years he doesn't know enough to put the simple formula: "You have heard the motion; are you ready for the question?" but always gets it snarled up as "Yo'ave heard de motion: are yo' ready?) In this manner they evolved a document which he told them would make the white world tremble when given to the white papers. So far the papers have only laughed and jeered at his arrant imbecilities, altho' they began (the New York ones) with studious fairness — except the *Globe*. And although it was thus read in the presence of white reporters (who were admitted only to the evening sessions) Garvey hasn't given it to his own paper — to be published that Negroes may read it.

The man has a perfect mania for flamboyant publicity. And this, I think, will wind a rope around his neck later. The third week was taken up with aimless talks and the "election" of a "Provisional President of Africa." — himself; a leader of the American Negroes (Dr. Eason) to dwell in a "Black House" to be built in Washington, D.C., to hob-nob with "the other ambassadors" and draw, I think, $10,000 a year (The P.P. of A. is to draw $25,000). Two "leaders" of the West Indian Negroes were also "elected" and a leader for the Negroes of the world (400,000,000 according to him).

During the fourth week they elected "the high officers of the U.N.I.A." including a Potentate ([Gabriel M.] Johnson of Liberia, the only delegate elected in Africa) at $12,000 a year, a High Commissioner General (Ellegor), an International Organizer (Miss Henrietta Vinton Davis) at $6,000 a year, a Chaplain General (Maguire) [Bishop Alexander McGuire], a Minister of Legions at $3,000, a Surgeon General and other such high-sounding magnificos (The Chancellor's report showed that the organization has about $2,000). The election was the most shameless thing I have seen. Garvey shamelessly electioneered for the candidates whose names he had "suggested" to the Convention while condemning canvassing and electioneering for others. He sent people like Watkiss [Harry R. Watkis] — also [Henry V.] Plummer & [Arden A.] Bryan — from his office who were not delegates and they voted for his candidates. He even sent his mistress Miss Amy Jacques, but Arnold Ford, the Sergeant-at-Arms took the question up with him point-blank and he had to rule against her voting (This was done conversationally tete-a-tete, and not in public business). Several of his candidates were defeated on Thurs 26th and he ruled, therefore, that no one was elected who didn't have "a two-thirds majority." Then it was pointed out that "The Rev. Dr." [John Dawson] Gordon, his personal flunkey and not three weeks in the Association, was not elected either, not having received a 2/3 majority. This he fiercely debated but finally was forced to yield.

When the new election was held next day there was a tie on Gordon's office. Garvey had already voted, but he insisted that it was his right to cast another vote "as President General of the U.N.I.A." He did so and thus elected his henchman. But it revealed Garvey to the delegates and lined up much sentiment against him. I had been nominated for the office of Speaker In Convention, the last but one in the list. On the first ballot my vote was 39, [Frederick A.] Toote's 30 and Garvey's designee (a Rev. [B. F.] Smith of Philadelphia) 17. On the next morning (Friday) before the new elections I withdrew my name and while doing so asked all those who voted for me to cast their votes for Toote. Toote, on the balloting, (I stayed away from the hall) got 69 votes and was elected. Delegates are still asking why did I withdraw. Time will tell them: I won't.

Today was the day of the parade (the 3rd such). I did not march. Once may be a duty; but when it becomes a habit, I abstain. G[arvey] has declared Aug. 31st an international holiday for all the Negro peoples of the world; but the hypocrite kept the people employed at 54–56 W. 135th St. [site of the UNIA, the BSL, and the NFC] hard at work. This morning they gave the honors (The African Cross and D.S.O.E. [Distinguished Service Order of Ethiopia]) to the fortunate (I stayed away) and tonight they are having "a grand reception" and dance at 107th St, the New Star Casino.

Thus ends the most colossal joke in Negrodom, engineered and staged by its chief mountebank.

64. "Marcus Garvey at the Bar of United States Justice," *Associated Negro Press* (c. early July 1923): 2–4, HHHP Wr.

On May 21, 1923, the trial against Marcus Garvey and others for mail fraud opened before Judge Julian William Mack in U.S. district court in Manhattan. The prosecution charged that the Black Star Line had mailed circulars advertising sale of shares in a ship it did not own. The proof centered on a circular which contained a doctored photograph of a ship with the name *Phyllis Wheatley* superimposed over the original name, *Orion*—a ship that the BSL did not own. Garvey was found guilty on June 21, sentenced to five years in Atlanta penitentiary, and fined $1,000 and the costs of the lawsuit.

On the same day that Garvey was found guilty Harrison wrote in his diary that "Marcus Garvey was sentenced by Mr. Justice Mack to 5 years in a Federal prison for using the mails to defraud his 'fellow-men of the Negro race.'" Then, using a July 1 dateline, he wrote about Garvey and the case, and sent the article to Nahum Daniel Brascher, editor-in-chief of the *Associated Negro Press*, the country's leading Black press agency, who published it in the *ANP*. Drawing literary allusions from William Schwenck Gilbert's "The Yarn of the 'Nancy Bell'" and Eugene O'Neill's *The Emperor Jones* it offers a revealing and extremely critical look at Garvey and his activities.[25]

New York, N. Y. July [ ]. On Monday night in the Federal Court in New York presided over by Mr. Justice Mack, the curtain went down on the last act of the drama staged by Marcus Garvey, self-styled "Provisional President of Africa" and head of the "Distinguished Service Order of Ethiopia," president of the "Black Star Line," the Negro Factories Corporation and President-General of the Universal Negro Improvement Association and African Communities League, Managing Editor of the *Negro World*, the *Negro Times*, and the *Black Man*, etc., etc.,

"The man of many names went down
Pierced by the Sword of Peter Brown,"

who in this case was Maxwell Mattuck, assistant United States District Attorney for the second district of New York, who had conducted the government's side of the case with commendable zeal and skill. It was somewhat of a surprise to the score of people who were present in the court-room at half-past ten that all the other defendants who were represented by colored lawyers were acquitted while Garvey who had discharged his colored lawyer and retained two white ones "for advice" while he conducted his own case in the full glow of dramatic publicity, was convicted. Yet it might have been expected. All through his public career, Garvey has loved the limelight. He loved to be the center of everything. Like W. S. Gilbert's elderly naval man, he loved to say:

"Oh, I am a cook and a captain bold,
And the mate of the Nancy brig,
And a bo'sun tight
And a midshipmite
And the crew of the captain's gig."

He has always wanted to be the "whole cheese," and the jury took him at his own estimate.

GOT A FAIR TRIAL

No sane person who sat in the courtroom can deny that he got a fair trial. In fact, the judge strained both his temper and the court's rules of procedure to give him more leeway than had ever been granted to any lawyer. In his charge to the jury he was scrupulously fair and even fore-bore to press portions of the case which told against the defendant. When touching on the question of the credibility of Garvey, he drew the jury's attention to the fact that a bishop had testified that Garvey's reputation for veracity in the West Indies was "doubtful," he refrained from pointing out that it was Garvey himself who had subpoenaed the bishop as a character witness. But the Judge's fairness did not weigh with Garvey, who when he was ordered to be taken to the tombs, broke out into an undignified tirade of foul abuse and low language describing both Judge and district attorney as "damned dirty Jews" and threatened that he would make them suffer for his conviction.

Naturally, bail was denied; his motion for appeal was set aside and the ruler of over "400 million Negroes" was remanded to the Tombs prison to await his sentence to a term of years in a Federal penitentiary, having been convicted on the charge of swindling members of his race by means of the marine bucket-shop known as the "Black Star Line" whose fleet of ships to sail the seven seas existed mainly on paper and in the mind of Marcus Garvey. The S. S. Yarmouth which, in the words of the Rev'd Professor Sir William H. Ferris, M.A.K.C.O.N., was "soon to be rechristened" the "Frederick Douglass" was never rechristened, but went back to its original owners because it was not quite paid for; the "Shadyside" was a bluff, and the S. S. Phyllis Wheatley, a phantom ship which was never bought nor seen, but on which Garvey by false and misleading advertisements had collected thousands of dollars paid in as passage-money to Africa and as stock sales.

SAILING PUT OFF MONTHS

Nevertheless, that type of West-Indian peasant from the hoe-handle and cow tail brigade to whom Garvey is a god, and whose intolerant fanaticism may still compromise the thousands of intelligent and respectable West Indians in the United States; these people still believe that Garvey never did a crooked thing in his life. To them the receipts of the poor people for passage money, the advertisements in the *Negro World* of sailings of the Phyllis Wheatley, put off month by month from January to November 1921, the printed lies telling of 20,000 delegates to a convention in which anyone who could count would find only a hundred; to them these facts don't exist and they go about threatening to shoot even the lawyer whom Garvey discharged, as if McDougall [Cornelius W. McDougald] fired himself to injure Garvey, and making dangerous statements which, if the authorities choose to notice them, will cause the closing of Liberty Hall and the suppression of Garvey's African Legion as dangers to domestic tranquility. Indeed, the District Attorney of New York already has his eye on them and it is not by any means a loving glance.

PROGRAM A GOOD ONE

This colossal collapse is another striking illustration of the fact, so frequently ignored by our race in America, that wind is not always a good guarantee of worth, that noise and bluster are not the best foundations for anything permanent. The original program of the Universal Negro Improvement Association was a good one, and it is still good. That program was based on the belief that Negroes should finance the foundations of their future and not go begging to the white race either for help, leadership or a program. But this was not a novel contribution by Garvey. It had been the program of the Liberty League of which Garvey was a member in 1917 in New York. From that league

Garvey appropriated every feature that was worth while in his movement. His notion of a racial flag was one, and the flag of the Liberty League lies beside me as I write: black, brown, and yellow, symbolic of the three colors of the people of the Negro race in America. Red, black, and green were more discordant and bizarre and appealed to Garvey's cruder esthetic sense. Outdoor and indoor lectures, a newspaper, protests in terms of democracy — all these were adopted from the Liberty League. Garvey added an intensive propaganda more shrewdly adapted to the cruder psychology of the less intelligent masses, the sensationalism, self-glorification, and African liberation — although he knew next to nothing of Africa. But since Africa was far away and wild statements about its "400 millions" could not be disproved in New York that feature of it was a money-getter always. Then came the Black Star Line — an idea which Garvey took bodily from [Charles Christopher] Seifert, one of the original members of the Liberty League.

That the B. S. L. was designed as a money-getter for Garvey is proved by the fact that he "collected" money for it for many months without any legal safeguards until [Edwin P.] Kilroe, an assistant district attorney of New York got after him and he was forced to incorporate in due legal form. But he has never accounted for the monies which he "collected" before the incorporation. On the stand it was proved that the broken-down ships which he got were intended to seduce credulous Negroes who saw them into putting more of their money into Garvey's hands, and not as a bona-fide business procedure. He would let a cargo of perishable freight for New York rot while he paraded the Yarmouth in Philadelphia to catch more suckers. Then, instead of going to New York to unload it he would take the ship to Boston, declaring that it was "good propaganda." As a propagandist Garvey was without a peer; but, unfortunately most of his propaganda consisted of selling himself. He was the most valuable asset of the entire chain of enterprises — not one of which succeeded. That didn't phase him, however. He knew the value of appearances and, while a sane man would have finished paying for one ship before proclaiming a second, third and fourth, he flung himself from the unpaid "Yarmouth," to the rotten "Shadyside" which sunk at her moorings; then to the "Kanawha" whose machinery was a mess; finally to the phantom "Phyllis Wheatley." This flying Dutchman was advertised as sailing for Africa in January 1921. As she failed to materialize her sailing date was successively (and successfully) put off to February, March, April, May, etc. Pictures of her were faked in the office of the B.S.L. and printed in the *Negro Worlds*, each picture showing a different type of ship. But always he said he had her in possession and the Rev. Mr. [Frederick A.] Toote and Dr. [William H.] Ferris raised money from the people in Liberty Hall to pay for her "furnishings, linen, etc."

SOLD PASSAGE TO AFRICA

In the meanwhile he sold passage to Africa (receipts for such passage money were presented during the trial) on the ship which he knew didn't exist, and this was one of the things that got him in trouble. The fact that the jury convicted him on one count only doesn't mean that they found him guiltless on the others. They knew that a conviction on five counts would have made him liable to five years on each count and they had no desire to press him too hard. His trial was one of the fairest in the annals of New York. The Judge allowed him every latitude. Yet when the jury found him guilty he proceeded to accuse both the court and the public prosecutor of collusion with other dirty Jews — just as he had accused Kilroe, [Edgar M.] Grey, and [Richard E.] Warner in 1919 and 1920. Yet on the 21st of August, 1920, he published a retraction in the *Negro World* in which he admitted that he had lied about them.

Garvey has a great talent for lying. In 1920 when he attacked his first wife in Liberty Hall he said that if she had ever bought any houses he was absolutely ignorant of the transaction. But, on the stand, when shown a check of the B.S.L. for $5,000 made out to her and drawn and paid by him to a real estate agent for the purchase of a house for her, he "explained" that that was for a lien on the property. A check as a lien is a new thing in real estate deals.

GARVEY['S] AMERICAN ARRIVAL

When Garvey came to America in 1917 he was so poor that some of us had to give him food and clothes. He wouldn't work, not he. He had discovered a method of living without working. Today, he is well-fed, well-groomed, and well-off. In his flat for which he pays a rent of $150 a month, there are splendid couches swinging by chains from the ceiling. Yet this paranoiac has the nerve to talk about his "sacrifices for the race," although he refrains from telling what those sacrifices consist of.

Garvey is a worshiper of Garvey. On the "Yarmouth" he had two life-sized oil-paintings of himself. His office and his apartments contain dozens of such paintings. It was his instinct for self-worship that prompted him to appropriate the entire front page of the *Negro World* each week with his stupid declamations addressed to his "fellowmen of the Negro Race." It reduced the circulation of the paper from 50,000 to 3,000 copies; but Garvey didn't care. Instead of putting news in his paper he gave the readers his speeches. He quarreled with every person he ever worked with unless they were willing boot-lickers and glorifiers of himself. His insane egotism and jealousy were boundless. In 1920 he paid $100 *a day* for 31 days to [Cyril] Crichlow and [Isaac Newton] Brathwaite, stenographers, to report all the twaddle talked at the first convention. He promised to bring out the reports of that pow-wow in volumes that would startle the world. But although he started a fund for that purpose and said in his paper that the book was in the press, it never did come out. For months before every convention he would run a "Convention Fund" in the *Negro World*, which frequently ran to tens of thousands of dollars. Yet no visiting delegate ever got even a glass of lemonade that that delegate didn't pay for. What he did with the Convention funds is as much a mystery today as the Liberian Loan fund, the fund for "Certificates of Race Loyalty," the "African Redemption Fund," the money collected in 1918 to send delegates to the Peace Congress and the other bally-hoo devices by which money was extracted from his dupes while he prated of "dying for his race."

WHAT DOES THE PUBLIC WANT

The Garvey Case will go down in history as a splendid illustration of the race's gullibility. After all, it is not so much Garvey's fault, but his people's. A leader who would have made no promises that he couldn't keep, no statement that wasn't true, who always accounted for every penny and who made less "whoopin' and hollerin'" would not have appealed to them. He gave them what they wanted. And at this point I am reminded of "The Emperor Jones" — a fine picture of the psychology of the whole Garvey movement.

"Smithers — And I bet you got yer pile o' money in some safe place.

Jones — I sho' has! And it's in a foreign bank where no pusson don't ever git it out but me, no matter what come. You din't s'pose I was holdin' down dis Emperor job for de glory in it, did you? Sho'! De fuss and glory part of it, dat's only to turn de heads o' de low-flung bush niggers dat's here. Dey wants de big circus show for deir money. I gives it to 'em, an' I gits de money. De long green; dat's me every time."

And now, at the end of the spectacular career of *our* Emperor Jones, Judge Mack sticks up a sign marked "Five Years in Prison for Fraud." But will that be the end of it? I trow not. We may look forward confidently to some winter morning two or three years from now when Convict No. ( ) will point his finger majestically at a white warden and bellow, "Ho, there valet! Take a message to the Provisional Field Marshall of my African Legions and tell him to order out the Tenth and Eleventh Army Corps, for I have it in mind to hold a high field dry and general review. Quick, begone!" Then they will take that convict with the light of developed insanity in his eyes and put him in a room where he can't hurt his head when he hits it against the walls — because those walls will be padded. This may seem a bold prediction today. But wait three years and see.

65. "The Negro-American Speaks," *Boston Chronicle* (March 29, 1924), HHHP Wr.

In this March 29, 1924, "Trend of the Times" column, Harrison argued that "The American Negro is — after all — an American; and generally a deeper, truer American than nine-tenths of the whites." The "Negro Problem," he added, was "an American problem" that would be settled "here in America upon American lines." This position contrasted sharply with that of Garvey, whose program by 1924 centered on the notion of "African Redemption" and the building of an African empire.[26]

The American Negro is called to live as strange a life as the Christian pacifist who works in a munitions factory in war-time to support a large family. And like that pacifist he is driven to effect the best compromise that he can. The American Negro is — after all — an American; and generally a deeper, truer American than nine-tenths of the whites. So well is this known that when Woodrow Wilson was making the world safe for Something; when plots were rife, and explosions and murders, he put a guard around the White House made up *of Negro soldiers!* Down at Camp Upton on Long Island when our armies were being mobilized, every white person who sought admission to the camp was stopped by the sentry, questioned and searched. The only Negroes who were stopped and questioned were those who at first sight seemed white. All of which has a meaning.

And that meaning (running through every battlefield from Savannah and New Orleans to Kettle Hill and Flanders, shot through with the golden gleams of a million happy homes, blackened with the grime of slavery and lynching) is that while the Negro is no happier than the Jew, he, like the Jew, is here to stay and make the best of it. His problem is an American problem and he will settle it here in America upon American lines.

What the Negro needs in this new day is a Negro-American Messiah, a prince of promise who will gild his people's soul with the gleams of a glorious future — in America, who will show them how they can rise to heights hitherto undreamed of — in America, and help them to change proscription into power and salvation. It was Jesus who said "The kingdom of heaven is within you," while Lowell's Sir Launfal had to be taught that one need not mount and ride away to find the Holy Grail. If we flee from lions in our back yard be sure we shall not face them in their own jungles. Strength, courage and persistence will work wonders at home as well as elsewhere. We who have helped to build America with our blood and tears and sweat, who have eaten her bread and salt, and have looked the white man in the eye and lived and grown numerous and intelligent, we propose to reap the fruits of our labor and partake of the harvest which we have helped to produce.

And that is why twelve millions of us are still calling for a leader who will have some living message for us in terms of what we are — Americans!

7 Anti-imperialism and Internationalism

T o Harrison "the most dangerous phase of developed capitalism" was that of "imperialism — when, having subjugated its workers and exploited its natural resources at home, it turns with grim determination toward 'undeveloped' races and areas to renew the same process there." He was a staunch opponent of imperialist domination of the peoples and lands of Africa, Asia, and the Americas; he was well read on the histories and contemporary developments in the areas; and he often spoke and wrote on these subjects and included articles on them in his publications. One of his criticisms of the old-style Black leadership was that it was insular and knew little of world affairs. Harrison, in contrast, frequently started his analysis of problems from an international perspective and constantly sought to overcome ignorance of international events while building ties with the oppressed in other lands.[1]

The Great War

Harrison opposed the imperialist and white-supremacist aims of the Great War of 1914–18. He was especially critical of the imperial powers' plans for Africa, of their use of working people as soldiers for slaughter, and of the war's great human and material cost. He understood, however, that the conflict was also a "fratricidal strife" that burned and destroyed many resources of the "white world," that it facilitated contact between oppressed peoples, and that it provided an opportunity for the oppressed to press their demands.

The political climate for expressing such views was extremely harsh, particularly for noncitizens like Harrison (he did not become naturalized until 1922). Congress passed the First Espionage Act on June 15, 1917. It forbade obstruction of the draft and insubordination in the services and provided for penalties of up to twenty years and fines of up to $10,000. The Sedition Act of May 16, 1918, amended section 3 of the Espionage Act and called for a $5,000 fine, up to twelve years imprisonment, or both, for those who "willfully utter, print, write, or publish any disloyal, profane, scurrilous, or abusive language about the form of government of the United States" or in "support or favor [of] the cause of any country with which the United States is at war." It specifically warned against obstruction in the sale of war bonds, inciting insubordination in the services, and attempts to discourage recruiting, and it was made criminal to bring "into contempt, scorn, contumely, or disrepute" the United States or its constitution, armed forces, or flag. Some 2,168 persons were prosecuted under the Espionage Act, and 1,055 were convicted. On May 10, 1920, Congress would pass legislation providing for deportation of aliens convicted under the amended Espionage Act of 1917.[2]

Under these wartime conditions, as Harrison later explained, "those of us who saw unpalpable truths were compelled to do one of two things: either tell the truth as we saw it and go to jail, or camouflage that truth that we had to tell." He "told the truth for the most part, in so far as it related to our own race relations; but, in a few cases camouflage was safer and more effective." His camouflage, however, "was never of that truckling quality which was accepted by the average American editor to such a nauseating degree." As he explained: "I was well aware that Woodrow Wilson's protestations of democracy were lying protestations, consciously and deliberately designed to deceive," and "I chose to pretend that Woodrow Wilson meant what he said, because by so doing I safely held up to contempt and ridicule the undemocratic practices of his administration and the actions of his white countrymen in regard to the Negro." A prime example of this was Harrison's prominent display across the front page banner of *The Voice* of Woodrow Wilson's famous passage from his war message to Congress: "We will fight for the things we have held nearest our hearts — for the right of those who submit to authority to have a voice in their own government."[3]

Throughout the following articles Harrison's internationalism, anti-imperialism, and race consciousness emerge.

66. "The White War and the Colored World." *The Voice* (August 14, 1917), HHHP Wr, reprinted in *When Africa Awakes*, 96–98.

On August 11, 1917, *The Voice* came out with the first extra edition in Harlem newspaper history. The August 14 issue reported that sales were up to 11,000 and included the first publication of Harrison's important "The White War and the Colored World." This piece was based on his indoor and outdoor talks from the 1914–16 period, which emphasized how the fratricidal strife in Europe over the division of the nonwhite world was a self-destructive battle in which the white race would suffer.

> The newspapers which we read every day inform us that the world is at war. Searching the pages of the statisticians, we find that the world is made up of 17 hundred million people of which 12 hundred million are colored — black and brown and yellow. This vast majority is at peace and remains at peace until the white minority determines otherwise. The war in Europe is a war of the white race wherein the stakes of the con-

flict are the titles to possession of the lands and destinies of this colored majority in Asia, Africa, and the islands of the sea.

There can be no doubt that the white race as it exists today, is the superior race of the world. And it is superior, not because it has better manners more religion or a higher culture; these things are metaphysical and subject to dispute. The white race rests its claim to superiority on the frankly materialistic ground that it has the guns, soldiers, the money and resources to keep it in the position of the top-dog and to make its will go. This is what white men mean by civilization, disguise it how they may. This struggle is a conflict of wills and interests among the various nations which make up the white race, to determine whose will shall be accepted as the collective will of the white race; to decide, at least for this century, who shall be the inheritors of the lands of Africa and Asia and dictators of the lives and destinies of their colored inhabitants.

The peculiar feature of the conflict is that the white race in its fratricidal strife is burning up, eating up, consuming and destroying these very resources of ships, guns, men and money upon which its superiority is built. They are bent upon this form of self-destruction and nothing that we can say will stop them.

As a representative of one of the races constituting the colored majority of the world, we deplore the agony and blood-shed; but we find consolation in the hope that when this white world shall have been washed clean by its baptism of blood, the white race will be less able to thrust the strong hand of its sovereign will down the throats of the other races. We look for a free India and an independent Egypt; *for nationalities in Africa flying their own flags and dictating their own internal and foreign policies.* This is what we understand by "making the world safe for democracy." Anything less than this will fail to establish "peace on earth and good will toward men." For the majority races cannot be eternally coerced into accepting the sovereignty of the white race. They are willing to live in a world which is the equal possession of all peoples — white, black, brown and yellow. If the white race is willing, then, there will be such blood-shed later as this world has never seen. And there is no certainty that in such a conflict the white race will come out on top. Not the destinies of the world, but the destinies of the white race are in the hands of the white race.

67. "The White War and the Colored Races," (originally written in 1918) *New Negro* 4 (October 1919): 8–10, and reprinted in *When Africa Awakes*, 116–22.

In the October 1919 *New Negro* Harrison published "The White War and the Colored Races," his principal editorial on the war. He wrote it in 1918 ("when the Great War still raged") for "a certain well known radical magazine" (possibly a reference to Owen and Randolph's *Messenger*) which found it " 'too radical' for publication at that time." When he finally published it he explained that he did so "partly because the underlying explanation which it offers of the root-cause of the war has not yet received treatment (even among socialist radicals) and partly because recent events in China, India, Africa and the United States have proved the accuracy of its forecasts."[4]

Harrison's thesis — that the war in Europe was the result of the desire of the white governments of Europe to exploit the lands and labor of the darker races; that the war would decrease the white man's ability to do this successfully; and that this would result in the freedom from thralldom and the extension of political, social, and industrial democracy to the black, brown, and yellow peoples of the world — was indeed a "radical" analysis of events.

The Nineteenth Christian Century saw the international expansion of capitalism — the economic system of the white peoples of Western Europe and America — and its establishment by force and fraud over the lands of the colored races, black and brown and yellow. The opening years of the Twentieth Century present us with the sorry spectacle of these same white nations cutting each other's throats to determine which of them shall enjoy the property which has been acquired. For this is the real sum and substance of the original "war aims" of the belligerents; although in conformity with Christian cunning, this is one which is never frankly avowed. Instead, we are fed with the information that they are fighting for "*Kultur*" and "on behalf of small nationalities." Let us look carefully at this camouflage.

"The Sham of Democracy"

In the first place, we in America need not leave our own land to seek reasons for suspecting the sincerity of democratic professions. While we are waging war to establish democracy three thousand miles away, millions of Negroes are disfranchised in our own land by the "cracker" democracies of the southern states which are more intent upon making slaves of their black fellow-citizens than upon rescuing the French and Belgians from the similar brutalities of the German Junkers. The horrible holocaust of East St. Louis was possible only in three modern states — Russia of the Romanoffs, Turkey and the United States — and it ill becomes any one of them to point a critical finger at the others.

But East St. Louis was simply the climax of a long series of butcheries perpetrated on defenseless Negroes which has made the murder rate of Christian America higher than that of heathen Africa and of every other civilized land. And, although our government can order the execution of thirteen Negro soldiers for resenting the wholesale insults to the uniform of the United States and defending their lives from civilian aggressors, not one of the murderers of black men, women and children has been executed or even ferreted out. Nor has our war Congress seen fit as yet to make lynching a federal crime. What wonder that the Negro masses are insisting that before they can be expected to enthuse over the vague formula of making the world "safe for democracy" they must receive some assurance that their corner of the world — the South — shall first be made "safe for democracy!" Who knows but that perhaps the situation and treatment of the American Negro by our own government and people may have kept the Central Powers from believing that we mean to fight for democracy in Europe, and caused them to persist in a course which has driven us into this war in which we must spend billions of treasure and rivers of blood.

It should seem, then, that "democracy," like "*Kultur*," is more valuable as a battle-cry than as a real belief to be practised by those who profess it. And the plea of "small nationalities" is estopped by three facts: Ireland, Greece, and Egypt, whose Khedive, Abbas Hilmi, was tumbled off his throne for failing to enthuse over the claims of "civilization" as expounded by Lord [Edward] Grey.

SIR HARRY JOHNSTON SPEAKS

But this is merely disproof. The average American citizen needs some positive proof of the assertion that this war is being waged to determine who shall dictate the destinies of the darker peoples and enjoy the usufruct of their labor and their lands. For the average American citizen is blandly ignorant of the major facts of history and has to be told. For his benefit I present the following statement from Sir Harry Johnston, in *The Sphere* of London. Sir Harry Johnston is the foremost English authority on Africa and is in a position to know something of imperial aims.

> Rightly governed, I venture to predict that Africa will, if we are victorious, repay us and all our allies the cost of our struggle with Germany and Austria. The war, deny it who may, was really fought over African questions. The Germans wished, as the chief gain of victory, to wrest rich Morocco from French control, to take the French Congo from France, and the Portuguese Congo from Portugal, to secure from Belgium the richest and most extensive tract of alluvial goldfields as yet discovered. This is an auriferous region which, properly developed, will, when the war is over, repay the hardest hit of our allies (France) all that she has lost from the German devastation of her home lands. The mineral wealth of trans-Zambesian Africa — freed forever, we will hope, from the German menace — is gigantic; only slightly exploited so far. Wealth is hidden amid the seemingly unprofitable deserts of the Sahara, Nubia, Somaliland and Namaqua. Africa, I predict, will eventually show itself to be the most richly endowed of all the continents in valuable vegetable and mineral substances.

There is the sum and substance of what [Arthur] Schopenhauer would have called "the sufficient reason" for this war. No word of "democracy" there, but instead the easy assumption that, as a matter of course, the lands of black Africa belong to white Europe and must be apportioned on the good old principle: —

> "... the simple plan,
> That he shall take who hath the power,
> And he must keep who can."

THE ECONOMICS OF WAR

It is the same economic motive that has been back of every modern war since the merchant and trading classes secured control of the powers of the modern state from the battle of Plassy to the present world war. This is the natural and inevitable effect of the capitalist system, of what (for want of a worse name) we call "Christendom." For that system is based upon the wage relationship between those who own and those who operate the gigantic forces of land and machinery. Under this system no capitalist employs a worker for two dollars a day unless that worker creates more than two dollars worth of wealth for him. Only out of this surplus can profits come. If ten million workers should thus create one-hundred-million dollars' worth of wealth each day and get twenty five or fifty millions in wages, it is obvious that they can expend only what they have received, and that, therefore, every nation whose industrial system is organized on a capitalist basis must produce a mass of surplus products over and above, not the need, but the purchasing power of the nation's producers. Before these products can return to their owners as profits they must be sold somewhere. Hence the need for foreign markets, for fields of exploitation and "spheres of influence" in "undeveloped" countries whose virgin resources are exploited in their turn after the capitalist fashion. But, since every industrial nation is seeking the same outlet for its products, clashes are inevitable and in these clashes beaks and claws—armies and navies—must come into play. Hence beaks and claws must be provided beforehand against the day of conflict, and hence the exploitation of white men in Europe and America becomes the reason for the exploitation of black and brown and yellow men in Africa and Asia. And, therefore, it is hypocritical and absurd to pretend that the capitalist nations can ever intend to abolish wars. For, as long as black men are exploited by white men in Africa, so long must white men cut each other's throats over that exploitation. And thus, the selfish and ignorant white worker's destiny is determined by the hundreds of millions of those whom he calls "niggers." "The strong too often think that they have a mortgage upon the weak; but in the domain of morals it is the other way."

THE COLOR LINE

But economic motives have always their social side; and this exploitation of the lands and labor of colored folk expresses itself in the social theory of white domination; the theory that the worst human stocks of Montmarte, Seven Dials and the Bowery are superior to the best human stocks of Rajputana or Khartoum. And when these colored folk who make up the overwhelming majority of this world demand decent treatment for themselves, the proponents of this theory accuse them of seeking social equality. For white folk to insist upon the right to manage their own ancestral lands, free from the domination of tyrants, domestic and foreign, is variously described as "democracy" and "self-determination." For Negroes, Egyptians and Hindus to seek the same thing is impudence. What wonder, then, that the white man's rule is felt by them to rest upon a seething volcano whose slumbering fires are made up of the hundreds of millions of Chinese, Japanese, Hindus, and Africans! Truly has it been said that "the problem of the 20th Century is the problem of the Color Line." And wars are not likely to end; in fact, they are likely to be wider and more terrible — so long as this theory of white domination seeks to hold down the majority of the world's people under the iron heel of racial repression.

Of course, no sane person will deny that the white race is, at present, the superior race of the world. I use the word "superior" in no cloudy, metaphysical sense, but simply to mean that they are on top and their will goes — at present. Consider that fact as the pivotal fact of the war. Then, in the light of it, consider what is happening in Europe today. The white race is superior — its will goes — because it has invented and amassed greater means for the subjugation of nature and of man than any other race. It is the top dog by virtue of its soldiers, guns, ships, money, resources and brains. Yet there in Europe it is deliberately burning up, consuming and destroying these very soldiers, guns, ships, money, resources and brains, the very things upon which its supremacy rests. When the war is over, it will be less able to enforce its sovereign will upon the darker races of the world. Does any one believe that it will be as easy to hold down Egypt and India and Persia after the war as it was before? Hardly.

THE RACIAL RESULTS OF THE WAR

Not only will the white race be depleted in numbers, but its quality, physical and mental, will be considerably lowered for a time. War destroys first the strongest and the bravest, the best stocks, the young men who were to father the next generation. The next generation must, consequently, be fathered by the weaker stocks of the race. And thus, in physical stamina and in brain-power, they will be less equal to the task of holding down the darker millions of the world than their fathers were. This was the thought back of Mr. [William Randolph] Hearst's objection to our entering the war. He wanted the United States to stand as the white race's reserve of man-power when Europe had been bled white.

But what will be the effect of all this upon that colored majority whose preponderant existence our newspapers ignore? In the first place, it will feel the lifting of the pressure as the iron hand of "discipline" is relaxed. And it will expand, when that pressure is removed, to the point where it will first ask, then demand, and finally secure, the right of self-determination. It will insist that, not only the white world, but the whole world, be made "safe for democracy." This will mean a self-governing Egypt, a self-governing India, and independent African states as large as Germany and France — and larger. And, as a result, there will come a shifting of the basis of international politics and business and of international control. This is the living thought that comes to me from the newspapers and books that have been written and published by colored men in Africa and Asia during the past three years. It is what I have heard from their own lips as I have talked with them. And, yet, of this thought which is inflaming the international underworld, not a word appears in the parochial press of America, which seems to think that if it can keep its own Negroes down to servile lip-service, it need not face the worldwide problem of the "Conflict of Color," as Mr. Putnam-Weale [Bertram Lenox Simpson] calls it.

But that the more intelligent portions of the white world are becoming distressingly conscious of it, is evident from the first great manifesto of the Russian Bolsheviki last year when they asked about Britain's subject peoples.

And the British workingmen have evidently done some thinking in their turn. In their latest declarations they seem to see the ultimate necessity of compelling their own aristocrats to forego such imperial aspirations as that of Sir Harry Johnston, and of extending the principle of self-determination even to the black people of Central Africa. But eyes which for centuries have been behind the blinders of Race Prejudice cannot but blink and water when compelled to face the full sunlight. And Britain's workers insist that "No one will maintain that the Africans are fit for self-government." But no one has yet asked the Africans anything about it. And on the same principle (of excluding the opinion of those who are most vitally concerned) Britain's ruling class may tell them that "No one maintains that the laboring classes of Britain are fit for self-government." But their half-hearted demand that an international committee shall take over the British, German, French and Portuguese possessions in Africa and manage them as independent nationalities (?) until they can "go it alone," would suggest that their eyesight is improving.

To sum it all up, the war in Europe is the result of the desire of the white governments of Europe to exploit for their own benefit the lands and labor of the darker races, and, as the war continues, it must decrease the white man's stock of ability to do this successfully against the wishes of the inhabitants of those lands. This will result in their freedom from thralldom and the extension of political, social and industrial democracy to the twelve-hundred-million black and brown and yellow peoples of the world. This, I take it, is what President Wilson had in mind when he wished to make the world "safe for democracy." But, whether I am mistaken or not, it is the idea which dominates today the thought of those darker millions.

The Paris Peace Conference

68. "The Negro at the Peace Congress," *The Voice*[?] (prob. c. December 1918), reprinted in *When Africa Awakes*, 30–32.

After the armistice of November 11, 1918, plans were quickly made by the victors for a peace conference to begin in Paris in January 1919. When the first plenary session was held on January 18, delegates from twenty-seven countries attended, and Germany was excluded. The Conference lasted almost a year and formally ended with the formation of the League of Nations on January 10, 1920. The following article was written as preparations for the conference were under way and as Black leaders such as W. E. B. Du Bois, William Monroe Trotter, and Marcus Garvey were planning either to attend or to send representatives. To those with such plans Harrison advised that "Lynching, disfranchisement and segregation are evils HERE; and the place in which we must fight them is HERE."[5]

Now that they have helped to win the war against Germany, the Negro people in these United States feel the absurdity of the situation in which they find themselves. They have given lavishly of their blood and treasure. They have sent their young men overseas as soldiers, and were willing to send their young women overseas as nurses; but the innate race-prejudice of the American Red Cross prevented them. They have contributed millions of dollars to the funds of this same Red Cross and scores of millions to the four Liberty Loans; and they have done all this to help make the world "safe for democracy" even while in sixteen States of the south in which nine-tenths of them reside, they have no voice in their own government. Naturally they expect that something will have to be done to remove their civil and other disabilities. This expectation of theirs is a just and reasonable one. But—

Now that the world is getting ready for the Peace Congress which is expected to settle *the questions about which the war was fought* our Negroes want to know if the Peace Congress will settle such questions as those of lynching, disfranchisement and segregation. IT WILL NOT! And why? Simply because the war was not fought over these questions. Lynching, disfranchisement and Jim-crowing in America are questions of American domestic policy and can be regulated only by law-making and administrative bodies. Even a fool should be able to see this. And, since it was only by the military aid of the United States that the Allies were able to win the war, why should our people be stupid enough to think that the allied nations will aim a slap at the face of the United States (even if such things were customary) by attempting to interfere in her domestic arrangements and institutions?

We learn that various bodies of Negroes, who do not seem to understand the modern system of political government under which they live, are seeking to get money from the unsuspecting masses of our people "for the purpose of sending delegates to the Peace Congress." The project is sublimely silly. In the first place, the Peace Congress is not open to any body who chooses to be sent. A peep into any handbook of modern history would show that Peace Congresses are made up only of delegates chosen by the heads of the governments of the countries which have been at war, and never by civic, propaganda, or other bodies within those nations. Only the President of the United States has power to designate the American delegates to the Peace Congress.

Of course, if any body of people wish to send a visitor to Versailles or Paris *at their expense*, the government of the United States has nothing to do with that and would not prevent it. But such visitor, lacking credentials from the President, could not get within a block of the Peace Congress. They can (if they can read French) get from the papers published in the city where the Congress meets so much of the proceedings as the Congress may choose to give to the press. But that is all; and for that it is not necessary to go to France. Just send to France for copies of *Le Temps* or *Le Matin* and prevent a useless waste of the money of poor people who can ill afford it in any case.

"But," we are told, "such person or persons can make propaganda (in France) which will force the Peace Conference to consider American lynching, disfranchisement and segregation." Passing over the argument that such person or persons would have to be able to write French fluently, we wish to point out that the public sentiment of even one French city takes more than a month to work up; that the sentiment of one French city can have but slight weight with the Congress, and that, if it could rise to the height of embarrassing them, the French authorities would sternly put it down and banish the troublesome persons. Karl Marx, Prince [Pyotr Alekseyevich] Kropotkin, [Errico] Malatesta and [V.I.] Lenine are cases in point showing what France has done under less provoking circumstances.

Let us not try to play the part of silly fools. Lynching, disfranchisement and segregation are evils HERE; and the place in which we must fight them is HERE. If foolish would-be leaders have no plan to lay before our people for the fighting HERE, in God's name, let them say so, and stand out of the way! Let us gird up our loins for the stern tasks which lie before us HERE and address ourselves to them with courage and intelligence.

69. "Africa at the Peace Table," *The Voice* (December 26, 1918), HHHP Scr A, reprinted as "Africa and the Peace," in *When Africa Awakes*, 33–35.

In a second pre-Paris editorial Harrison emphasized that the war was really "fought over African questions" and that as "the mask is dropped" post-war the victorious nations would "disclose their real war aims." He advised that Black leaders from the United States, instead of elaborating plans on how to liberate Africa, would do better to learn from Africa.

The historian Winston James considers this attitude one of "the most distinctive features of Harrison's political thought." James explains that he had both "confidence in and humility before the peoples and cultures of Africa." Having studied the continent's history and culture, Harrison evidenced "none of the arrogant New World 'civilizationism' that one finds, for instance, in Garvey's pronouncements; none of the 'civilizing the backward tribes of Africa,'" as Garvey and the UNIA promised. To Harrison, "Africa was primarily a teacher; not a primitive unschooled child in need of 'civilization' and instruction."[6]

"This war, disguise it how we may, is really being fought over African questions." So said Sir Harry Johnston, one of the foremost authorities on Africa, in the *London Sphere* in June, 1917. We wonder if the Negroes of the Western world quite realize what this means. Wars are not fought for ideals but for lands whose populations can be put to work, for resources that can be minted into millions, for trade that can be made to enrich the privileged few. When King Leopold [II] of Belgium and Thomas Fortune Ryan of New York joined hands to exploit the wealth of the Congo they did it with the well oiled phrases on their lips. They called the land of horrors and of shame "The Congo FREE State!"

And, so, when Nations go to war, they never openly declare what they WANT. They must camouflage their sordid greed behind some sounding phrase like "freedom of the seas," "self-determination," "liberty" or "democracy." But only the ignorant millions ever think that those are the real objects of their bloody rivalries. When the war is over, the mask is dropped, and then they seek "how best to scramble at the shearers' feast." It is then that they disclose their real war aims.

One of the most striking cases in point is the present peace congress. Already President Wilson has had to go to look after democracy himself. Already responsible heads of the Allied governments are making it known that "freedom of the seas" means a benevolent naval despotism maintained by them, and that "democracy" means simply the transfer of Germany's African lands to England and the others. Africa at the peace table constitutes the real stakes which the winners will rake in. We may read in headlines the startling item "Negroes Ask For German Colonies," but Negroes of sense should not be deluded. They will not get them because they have no battleships, no guns, no force, military or financial. They are not a Power.

Despite the pious pittle of nice old gentlemen like Professor Kelly Miller, the King-word of modern nations is POWER. It is only Sunday school kids and people of child-races who take seriously such fables as that in the "Band of Hope Review" when we were children that "the secret of England's greatness is the Bible." The secret of England's greatness (as well as of any other great nation's) is not bibles but bayonets — bayonets, business and brains. As long as the white nations have a preponderance of these, so long will they rule. Ask Japan: she knows. And as long as the lands of Africa can yield billions of business, so long will white brains use bayonets to keep them — as the British government did last year in Nigeria.

Africa is turning over in her sleep, and this agitation now going on among American Negroes for the liberation of Africa is a healthy sign of her restlessness. But it is no more than that. Africa's hands are tied, and, so tied, she will be thrown upon the peace table. Let us study how to unloose her bonds later. Instead of futile expectations from the doubtful generosity of white land-grabbing, let us American Negroes go to Africa, live among the natives and LEARN WHAT THEY HAVE TO TEACH US (for they have much to teach us). Let us go there — not in the coastlands, — but in the interior, in Nigeria and Nyassaland; let us study engineering and physics, chemistry and commerce, agriculture and industry; let us learn more of nitrates, of copper, rubber and electricity; so we will know why Belgium, France, England and Germany want to be in Africa. Let us begin by studying the scientific world of the African explorers and stop reading and believing the silly slush which ignorant missionaries put into our heads about the alleged degradation of our people in Africa. Let us learn to know Africa and Africans so well that every educated Negro will be able at a glance to put his hands on the map of Africa and tell where to find the Jolofs, Ekois, Mandingoes, Yorubas, Bechuanas or Basutos and can tell something of their marriage customs, their property laws, their agriculture and systems of worship. For, not until we can do this will it be seemly for us to pretend to be anxious about their political welfare.

Indeed, it would be well now for us to establish friendly relations and correspondence with our brothers at home. For we don't know enough about them to be able to do them any good at THIS peace congress (even if we were graciously granted seats there); but fifty years from now — WHO KNOWS?

Anti-imperialism

U.S. capitalism expanded territorially through the first two-thirds of the nineteenth century. Then, between 1860 and 1900, as factory production of goods grew sixfold and annual capital investments grew ninefold, the United States was transformed from a predominantly agricultural country into the foremost industrial nation in the world. Industrial growth and desire to invest spurred an imperialist search for markets and outlets for capital, and this led, in 1898, to war with Spain and the annexation of Hawaii. Although these tendencies had been evidenced in earlier military and naval forays, the Spanish-American War marked a major turning point for U.S. imperialism. In consequence of that war, the United States annexed Guam, Samoa, the Philippines, and some fifty smaller Pacific islands; made a colony of Puerto Rico; and imposed political and economic domination on Cuba. The country's focus on the Caribbean quickly intensified: the United States seized Panama in 1903; applied a customs receivership to Santo Domingo in 1905; sent troops to Cuba in 1906 and Mexico in 1914 and 1916; occupied

Nicaragua (1909), Haiti (1915), and Santo Domingo (1916); and purchased the Virgin Islands in 1916–17.[7]

Years later, Harrison, referring in part to this era, described the "imperialist tendencies of American capitalism" as ones which impelled "capitalists to seek for investment outlets in the territories of the weaker neighbors in the West Indies, Central and South America." Throughout his life Harrison sought to expose and oppose imperialism, whether by the United States or by any other power. His aim was to get the oppressed darker millions and the workers of the imperial countries to join together in anti-imperialist effort. His writings on this subject covered imperialism in Africa, Asia, the Middle East, and the Americas.[8]

70. Sayid Muhammad Berghash (pseudonym), "Britain in India," *New Negro* 4, no. 1 (September 1919): 9–10, HHHP Scr A. [Barghash ibn Said (c. 1837–88) was a nineteenth-century ruler of Zanzibar.]

In the September 1919 *New Negro* Harrison's article "Britain in India," written under the pseudonym Sayid Muhammad Berghash, treated a familiar theme — the press. It also discussed the rebellion growing in opposition to British imperialism in India and elsewhere in Asia and called attention to the Rowlatt Bills which Harrison elsewhere described as "The rottenest legal terrorism that the modern world has yet seen." As this article suggests, Harrison was in the forefront in bringing matters pertaining to India, which he considered "the key-stone of the British imperial system," to the attention of the African American community.[9]

The international control of news to-day is in the hands of England's imperial Englishmen. How they can use this control to create current myths has been amply demonstrated during the World War. Now that the war is over, that control continues. This appears most strikingly in the case of India, whose 300,000,000 inhabitants are politically the serfs of the British Empire. Britain's international arm reaches out as far as France, Switzerland and the United States and gathers in for prison and transportation those Hindu exiles who have dared to tell the whole world the awful facts of Britain's bloody rule in India. Native newspapers are taken out from the mails so that they may not get out of India, and American books and pamphlets written by public men like [Theodore] Roosevelt and [William Jennings] Bryan and touching on the condition of India's peoples are taken out of American mail-bags and confiscated, so that they may not get to that six per cent of the population whom Britain has taught to read.

In spite of these strictly British tactics, however, some facts now and then escape to us. For instance, we learn from the *Daily Herald* of London that Sir Rabindranath Tagore [the 1913 Nobel Prize winner in literature] has resigned his knighthood as a protest against the awful orgy of brutality in which the British government of India is now indulging against a people whom they disarmed long ago. From the British Propaganda Service in the United States we learn some facts about the new budget for India which help to raise the curtain of secrecy still further. Bear in mind that Britain takes from India in taxes from 2 to 5 hundred millions of dollars every year; that India's people have so little to eat that, according to British official reports, more than 5 millions of them died of starvation in 1918; that, whereas in the territory of the Gaekwar of Baroda, an enlightened ruler of an Indian "native state," 85 per cent of the population can read and write, in British India 94 per cent of the population are illiterate after a hundred and sixty years of British rule. Then consider the figures of this budget. It allots 206 millions for the military machine that holds India by the throat; 121 millions for the railways owned by British capitalists and operated by the government for them; 2 millions and a half for agriculture and irrigation; four-fifths of a million for education — and nothing for Indian industries! Thus out of the taxes wrung from the starving ryots 40 per cent (four times the amount spent by Japan on her army and navy) is taken for the upkeep of an army in which no Indian is permitted to command even a regiment of infantry. Thousands of English troops are trained in India, and India is obliged to pay for their passage, and all military stores must be purchased in England.

Small wonder that the natives revolt. The Viceroy of India has officially declared that open rebellion exists and half of India's vast territory is under martial law. The all-India Congress has been insidiously suppressed; the Swadeshi Movement which was breaking down the walls of caste, race and sect, and drawing the Indians together in the work of self-regeneration has been outlawed; and the English in India, by their own declarations, are ruling by sheer brute force. During the past three months, Delhi, Lucknow and other Indian cities have been raided (in the native quarters) by huge bombing aeroplanes, and every barbarity which the British and American press denounced when done by Germany in time of war, has been perpetrated on these unarmed Hindus in time of peace.

The Rowlatt Bills have been enacted into law. According to this new law, a copy of Edmund Burke's speeches on the trial of Warren Hastings, found on the person of a young Hindu student has sufficed to send him to the Andaman Islands for 12 years! The law expressly provides that the accused shall neither be represented by counsel nor have the right to be confronted with his alleged accusers. He may be arrested on one charge and tried on another. And no native paper may publish the proceedings on pain of instant suppression.

It is expressly announced in Bengal that "not to be in favor of the government is as much a crime as being opposed to it" — and this pure negation may be punished by a term in jail. The result of all this is that Rebellion stalks stealthily through the length and breadth of British India. In the north secret missions have been despatched to Russia while it was rumored that in the south and east communications have been opened up with Japan through the medium of hundreds of Japanese commercial travelers who flocked to India during the war period to sell Japanese goods. The fact that the number of these drummers has shrunk considerably during the past four months suggest that it was this "spectre" which forced the British at the Peace Congress to grant Shantung to Japan which thereupon withdrew its "commercial agents" from British India.

But the most significant result of all is the consolidation of the Indian patriotic parties. There are now no moderates, conservatives and liberals; there are only patriots and traitors. So far, the latter are restricted to the Rajahs and their circles, the decorated decoys. There is also noticeable a consolidation of anti-British and anti-European sentiment all over Asia, from Persia to Peking.

 71. "When Might Makes Right," *When Africa Awakes*, 108–110.

The editorial "When Might Makes Right" discusses how the white race preaches "goodness," "right," and "justice" to those over whom they rule, but uses "force without stint" in order "to establish 'rights' which they claim over territories, peoples, commerce and the high seas." Harrison believed that the exposure of such hypocrisy would help weaken the ability of the white race to rule and strengthened the resolve of the oppressed to resist.

A correspondent whose letter appears elsewhere raises the question of the relation between mental competence and property rights. "Does inability to govern destroy title to ownership?" he asks. The white race assumes an affirmative answer in every case in which the national property of darker and weaker races are concerned and deny it in cases in which their own national property rights are involved. It seems strange that whereas the disturbances occurring in our own southern states are never considered sufficient to justify the destruction of their sovereignty, on the one hand, such disturbances occurring in Hayti or Mexico are considered a sufficient reason for invasion and conquest by white Americans. The same is true of England, France and Italy. A disturbance in Alexandria, Delhi, Ashanti or the Cameroons suffices to fix upon those territories and cities the badge of inferiority and incompetence to rule themselves. The conclusion is always drawn in such cases that the white race has been called by this fortunate combination of circumstances to do the ruling for them. But similar disturbances occurring in Wales, Essen or Marseilles would never be considered as sufficient to justify the dictatorship of foreign powers in the interest of "law and order."

The truth is that "might makes right" in all these cases. White statesmen, however, often deny this at the very moment when they are using "force without stint, force to the utmost" to establish "rights" which they claim over territories, peoples, commerce and the high seas. Their characteristic hypocrisy keeps them from telling the truth as plainly as [Friederich A. J.] Von Bernhardi did in his now famous book, *Germany and the Next War*. The "sociological" reason for this hypocrisy is the fact that they need to preach "goodness," "right" and "justice" to those over whom they rule in order that their ruling may be made easy by the consequent good behavior of the ruled. But they themselves, however good, must practice ruthlessness, injustice and the rule of the strong hand to make their governance go. It is this fact which causes intelligent Negroes, Filipinos, Chinese and Egyptians to spurn with contempt the claims which Caucasian diplomats, statesmen, writers and missionaries make on behalf of their moral superiority. They lie; they know that they lie, and now they're beginning to know that we know it also. This knowledge on our part is a loss of prestige for them, and our actions in the future, based upon this knowledge, must needs mean a loss of power for them. Which is, after all, the essential fact.

72. "The Line-Up on the Color Line," *Negro World* (December 4, 1920), HHHP Scr B.

"The Line-Up on the Color Line" appeared in the December 4, 1920, *Negro World* and was written by Harrison, though his identifying initials were absent. After presenting a revealing story on one of the formative meetings of the NAACP, Harrison displayed a broad grasp of international affairs as he reviewed the grievances of people of color worldwide. He then urged that "the first great international duty" of African Americans was "to get in international touch" with "the downtrodden section of the human population of the globe and establish business, industrial and commercial relations with them." The internationalist themes are compelling, though at key points Harrison's language is male-oriented.

[The *Negro World* article contained the concluding clause "and the U.N.I.A. is the instrument which the Negroes must use in that conflict for his own liberation." Harrison, however, crossed this out in his scrapbook, indicating that this last line was not his.]

About 1909 or 1908 there was organized in New York what was known as the National Negro Committee. I went down to the United Charities Building and listened to the speeches of the great defenders of our race. One of the striking speeches that appealed to me was that of Mrs. Celia Parker Wooley, of Boston, Mass. Mrs. Wooley pointed out in a ten-minute talk that whereas the white press, the publicists and writers of books, and politicians generally, were talking and expatiating about the race hatred of the Caucasian, it was a most sinister fact that, unrecorded and unexpressed by them, there had grown up and was growing up, on the part of black folk in America, a corresponding and countervailing race hatred. That was a fact which it was important to bring out. It was reported in the *Evening Post* of that particular date. But when the National Negro Committee (which later grew into the N.A.A.C.P.) came to print the proceedings of that conference those words of Mrs. Celia Parker Wooley were elided from the records.

What does it all mean? It means that some white people seem to think a certain public attitude towards white people to be fit and proper, and a certain other attitude—an attitude which white people would maintain if they were in the same situation — as unbecoming to black people. And so the white man has gone along discussing the race problems and attempting to solve them from this point of view: That the race question for him was: "What would be done with the Negro?" without asking what the Negro himself thinks of it. It was to be settled by the words, the mandates, the principles, the judgments and the opinions coming from one side only. As in the case of the Negro in America, so with the case of the Egyptian, of the South African and the West African, the Hindu and the Chinamen.

The dominant race has been walking rough-shod over the hearts, the sentiments, the feelings, the rights, the riches of the black, brown, and the yellow peoples of the world. And they have thought heretofore that the only question for them to decide was: "What shall we do with them?" Now the big, sinister fact of international politics dimly recognized by such writers as Mr. [T. Lothrop] Stoddard and Mr. Putnam Weale [Bertram Lenox Simpson] — is the demand on the part of black, brown and yellow people, that their voices shall be heard in any solution affecting their welfare and their future.

The world conflict of color carries a very definite danger to the present supremacy of the white races. By keeping in touch with the thought and the movements of the colored races we will learn that these people do not propose merely to open their mouths and talk. They do not propose to be satisfied with protest. The young Turk movement; the young Egypt movement; the Swadesh movement; the All-India Congress movement, and the radical movement led by the second Chinese president, Sun Yat Sen, in China, all mean that these people intend and desire to take their destinies out of the hands of the white lords of misrule.

They do not say — any particular group of them — that singly they are competent to meet in arms and to overthrow the white nations of the world now, but Japan says that she is. China, under the tutelage of Japan, is coming to the point where she is beginning to grumble that she thinks she will be, India is a sort of seething, raging, but suppressed volcano, with a cover on which the Englishman sits, believing that if he but sits there the fires will no longer burn. But the Hindus believe that some day the wooden cover will burn through and something will get scorched.

That is why the Maharajah of Baroda, the most enlightened Indian prince in all India today, at the Durbar a few years ago, turned his back upon the British king and walked away. Another Hindu who is a quietist — a man whom the British Rajah had gone out of his way to honor by recommending that he should get the Nobel prize for literature, a man whom the British had decorated with medals and titles of knighthood — Rabindranath Tagore — tore off the decorations and sent them back to the British king, saying that "the blood you are spilling in India will be upon my hands if I accept any decoration from you." That is why men in India today are fighting for Swadesha and Swaraj, which is home rule for them — those people are being sent to the Andaman

Islands exiled for twenty years and more, but they are still at it. And what the English are doing in the dominions, the Belgians have done in theirs.

In the section of Africa known as the Congo, in about three decades, the Belgians reduced the population of that most prolific area from 20,000,000 to 8,000,000. Read the records of Sir Arthur Conan Doyle in his little book, *The Crime of the Congo*, or the writings of Mr. E. D. Morel, who has made himself an English authority on that question, or the reports of the consul general, the great, glorious, lamented and martyred Sir Roger Casement, and you will find the photographs of hands chopped off, legs and feet chopped off by bunches, bundles, barrels full, when the Belgian king could not get those Congo people to make rubber enough for him.

The International Association for the Exploitation of the Congo got its grant under the most sweeping and assuring statements about the goodness of their hearts and the sincerity of their minds. They wanted to save Africa, Christianize and civilize it. But the first thing that King Leopold did was to pass a law saying that all the land belonged to the State; a poor Kongolese had no right even to go out and gather firewood because the land was the State's.

The United States that was so long in recognizing the independence of Hayti and so quick to jump in now to destroy the reality of Haytian independence — the United States that was so long in recognizing the independence of Liberia, her own foster child, was the first to recognize the independence of the Congo Free State.

In Nigeria today when black meets white — in black's ancestral land — black must go down on his knees and wait until white goes by in a palanquin, and if he does not he will go to jail or will be beaten with many stripes.

In the civilized section of Southern Nigeria you will find that the white English Christian minister who goes there gets the people together in church, and after he has drunk enough champagne to make sure he can stand the climate he proceeds to settle down and organize a Negro church. At present they have Negro graveyards and all the separatist things that we have got here, including the Jim Crow car.

Finally in this summary of the series of grievances which black men, brown men and yellow men have against white there is the question of sex. How the white men with millions of Urasians whom they have produced in India and whom they despise after having created them — the millions of mullatoes and interbloods that they have created in the United States, the West Indies and elsewhere — can look themselves in the face and talk about the sexual criminality of the black man is more than I can understand. They have gone all over the world using up the womanhood of the other races — dividing up with them — lightening them up. And now when the other races stand up and say, "If you have divided with us we are going to divide with you," their answer is the lynching bee. That answer cannot stand in terms of the facts of today. We breed faster than they do. We double our population in forty years, when they take eighty years to double theirs. We breed so fast that the white doctors in their hospitals from the South to Harlem are driven to perform operations upon colored women — unbeknown to them — to be sure that they will not be breeders of men. But we will survive, although some of us who study too hard and drink too hard and do some other things too hard may go crazy once in a while. But we do not go crazy one-tenth as fast as they do. Statistics show that in England, France, the United States and Canada, they go crazy faster than we do. That means that their physiological organization — the structure by which they live and function — their nervous structure in particular — breaks down under the weight of the burdens they have gone out and shouldered for themselves.

In the face of these facts the first great international duty of the black man in America is to get in international touch with his fellows of the downtrodden section of the human population of the globe and establish business, industrial and commercial relations with them. We need to join hands across the sea. We need to know what they are doing in India; we need to know what they are doing in China; we need to know what they are doing in Africa, and we need to let [*make* has been crossed out] them know what we are doing over here. We must link up with the other colored races of the world, beginning with our own, and after we have linked up the various sections of the black race the black race will see that it is in its interest and advantage to link up with the yellow and the brown races. We must establish friendly relations with each other because the white man is at present more powerful than we are, and we must do this to help us in deciding what our section shall do to avail itself of the power of the white man to be used against the white man. The conflict of color is the call to the black race, the brown race, the yellow race today. It is a bid for their self-emancipation. . . .

 73. "On 'Civilizing' Africa," *Negro World* (December 18, 1920), HHHP Scr B.

In this *Negro World* piece Harrison discusses how "white people" arrogantly talk "of civilizing Africa and assert that the Africans are uncivilized" and in so doing he casts serious doubt on their understanding of the terms. He characterizes their civilization as that "system which produces profits by taking the land from under the feet of the workers, producing a propertyless, landless proletarian class which must either work (for wages) or starve." Harrison displays his exceptional knowledge of African history and societies, discusses various African civilizations, and contrasts these civilizations with "that particular brand which white people" brought to Africa "in exchange for the untold millions of dollars," labor, and resources that they took.

When white people today talk of civilizing Africa and assert that the Africans are uncivilized [they] awaken in the minds of well-informed Africans a doubt as to whether white people know what is meant by the term. For, no matter how it may be defined, it is clear to the instructed that various "civilizations" not only have existed in Africa, but do exist there today, independently of that particular brand which white people are taking there in exchange for the untold millions of dollars which they take from there.

If by civilization we mean a stable society which supports itself and maintains a system of government and laws, industry and commerce, then the Hausas and Mandingoes, the people of the Ashanti and Dahomey, and the Yorubas of the Gold Coast had and have all these, and they are consequently civilized. So were the Zulus and Bechuanas, the Swazis and Mashonas of South Africa, as well as the Baganda [Buganda] people of Uganda. According to [Hermann] Staudinger, [Georg] Schweinfurth, [Heinrich] Barth and [Franz] Boas, smithwork and the smelting or iron were original with some of the West African peoples. The weaving of cotton was known in the Sudan as early as the eleventh century, and is known there today.

In a recent work of anthropological research [Jerome] Dowd, a southern savant, says: "It is not altogether pleasant to have to admit that some of the most important medical discoveries of modern times were first made in Africa: for example, the fact that flies and mosquitoes are the purveyors of disease. While this fact has been announced in Europe and America with a flourish of trumpets as if it were something new, it has been known for many centuries by the medical men of Yoruba. They do not always resort to magic or rely upon spirits and deities, but have a considerable knowledge of *materia medica*, and treat disease upon purely scientific principles; that is to say, they examine the patient locate the seat of the disease and prescribe certain diet and medicines." Long before [Edward] Jenner lived black African doctors were inoculating as a preventive against smallpox, and white residents of South Africa often take today the cures prescribed by Negro physicians for the African fever. Many of these physicians without knowing anything of the white man's medical science, possess an intelligent knowledge of the pathology of the disease and use a variety of efficacious medicines. On this point, then, Europeans who go to Africa are not entitled to maintain that there is no civilization already there, any more than Dr. Alexis Carrel would be entitled to say that he found none in the Balkans.

But here the missionary-minded steps in with his blind-belief that his particular "faith" is the only one entitled to respect (although in his own mind the jails are still full, as well as the bawdy houses and rumshops), and tells us that the Africans have no knowledge of God. One of the most learned Egyptologists, Dr. Wallis Budge, curator of Egyptian antiques in the British Museum, gives the lie to that flattering assumption. In his *Osiris and the Egyptian Resurrection* after dealing in scholarly fashion with the religion of ancient Egypt he summarizes the testimony of dozens of scientists and travelers from all countries of Africa, and shows that not only do Africans believe in Gods, but that under many names and forms from the Bobowissi of the Ashanti, the Mawa of Dahomey, the Olorun of the Yoruba, down to the Umkulunkulu of the Zulus, most of them have a more or less clear perception of what Mr. [H. G.] Wells calls God, "the Invisible King." Bishop [Henry] Calloway established this fact for the Bantus of South Africa and Dr. Duff MacDonald for the Bantus of the Shire Region. But most religious enthusiasts were neither so candid nor so well informed.

Then, too, the Africans' religion works. In a Christian country where to have a pile of provisions at the open door of a Christian church and place a sacred crucifix on the pile for protection without any watchmen or police his fellow Christians who know the value of their religion would call him a fool. And if his gods had not entirely disappeared by the next day it would be accounted a miracle. Yet the miracle happens every day in Northern Nigeria, among the Vais of Liberia and in Congoland whenever the holy symbol of their religion (i.e. fetish) is left to protect goods. For these people really *believe* their religion while we only *believe in* ours. On the religious test, then there is *seen* to be civilization in Africa.

The real civilization meant by most whites who talk of civilizing Africa is the system which produces profits by taking the land from under the feet of the workers, producing a propertyless, landless proletarian class which must either work (for wages) or starve. Such a class doesn't exist anywhere among black Africans except where white peoples have robbed them of their lands by force direct, as in Rhodesia and the Cape. In either case the "civilizing" of Africa means the establishment of the European system, of "concessions" for rubber, railroads, factories and mines, whereby the labor of the native population and the new tastes developed in their minds yield enormous revenues to the white people who rule these lands. And all their resources of reasoning, rhetoric and sentence are directed to the end of convincing the world that the African, like the boy in the Pear's soap advertisement, "won't be happy till he gets it."

74. "Imperialist America," review of *The American Empire* by Scott Nearing, HHHP Wr, reprinted in *Negro World* (April 30, 1921): 5, HHHP Scr B.

In the *Negro World* of April 30, 1921, Harrison reviewed *The American Empire* by Scott Nearing (1883–1983), a prominent socialist and economist who had been indicted for treason in 1918 for his forty-four-page pamphlet *The Great Madness*. In this insightful review, Harrison displayed his familiarity with radical economic thought and offered one of his clearest and most forceful descriptions of the workings of imperialism.

The most dangerous phase of developed capitalism is that of imperialism—when, having subjugated its workers and exploited its natural resources at home, it turns with grim determination toward "undeveloped" races and areas to renew the same process there. This is the phase in which militarism and navalism develop with dizzying speed with their accumulating burden of taxation for "preparedness" against the day when the capitalist class of the nation must use the final argument of force against its foreign competitor for markets. These markets change their character under the impact of international trade and are no longer simply markets for the absorption of finished products, but become fields for the investment of accumulated surplus profits, in which process they are transformed into original sources for the production of profits by the opening up of mines, railroads and other large scale capitalist enterprises. It becomes necessary to take over the government of the selected areas in order that the profits may be effectually guaranteed; and "spheres of interest," "protectorates" and "mandates" are set up.

Thus the lands of "backward" peoples are brought within the central influence of the capitalist economic system and the subjection of black, brown and other colored workers to the rigors of "the white man's burden" comes as a consequence of the successful exploitation of white workers at home, and binds them both in an international of opposition to the continuance of the capitalist regime. Most Americans who are able to see this process more or less clearly in the case of other nations are unable to see the same process implicit and explicit in the career of their own country. Professor Scott Nearing in *The American Empire* endeavors to open their eyes. He has written a book which is timely and serviceable. He makes clear some of the political implications of our "manifest destiny" in extending the mantle of our own imperialism over Hawaii, Cuba, Hayti, Porto Rico and the Philippines and shows the trend of the same commercial purpose toward our weaker neighbors to the south of us. He follows the history of the American capitalist class marching on its career of conquest with gigantic strides and involving itself in the same contradictions as the imperial plunderbund of England, Germany and France, and without any special parade of propagandist phrases he shows what the mass of workers are "up against."

Professor Nearing cleverly combines in this book the aims and methods of the historian, the economist and the propagandist. As a historian of the imperial process in American affairs his work is of uneven merit. He evidently takes the claims advanced on behalf of the high motives of the early fathers at their full face value. The mass of material which invalidates these claims has been well set forth and properly documented by original scholars like Gustavus Myers (*History of the Great American Fortunes*, *History of the U.S. Supreme Court*, and *History of Tammany Hall*), [John Bach] McMaster (*History of the People of the United States*) and [Sydney G.] Fisher (*The True American Revolution*); but Professor Nearing appears to be unacquainted with the work that has been done in that field, and still shares the illusions of "the Golden Age." He is evidently unacquainted with the deep-seated disease of the system of "indentured servants" which was the name given to the chattel-slavery of white men and women in America which for more than two centuries, was substantially on all-fours with the chattel slavery of black men and women. This is all the more strange when one recalls that James Oneal's book *Workers In American History*, the best authority at second hand on this significant phase of our early industrial life, is sold at the Rand School Book Store. Yet in regard to some of the later phases and incidents of American history his grip is sure and his presentation of the facts is illuminating. This is especially true of his treatment of Negro slavery and the slave-trade, the acquisition of Texas, the Spanish-American War, and the suppression of Hawaiian and Philippine independence.

As an economist, he is well-fitted for the task of opening the eyes of our economic illiterates to the nature and meaning of the economic processes that are going on all around us. His implicit indictment of the crumbling system of capitalist exploitation at home and abroad is put with a fine reasonableness and good temper which should gain him many readers from among that inert mass which is impervious to ordinary Socialist propaganda. And, after all, it is for those "outsiders" that such works are primarily written. Professor Nearing, in making his program implicit rather than explicit, shows that he sets a proper valuation upon missionary success. He avoids disturbing technical discussion, such as that on the fall of the *rate* of profits which is simultaneous with the increase in the *amount* of profits, and even preserves the simple outlines of a few proven economic fallacies of an earlier day, like that of the concentration of property *titles* in fewer and fewer hands; and this, despite the fact that he himself shows in an earlier chapter what the fact of real significance is, viz; the concentration of *Control* (pp. 90 to 94).

On the whole, however, his grip on the mechanics of imperialism is firm and his exposition of its methods is always clear and sound. His book is a worthy contribution to the literature of radical economic thought.

75. "Wanted — A Colored International," *Negro World* (May 28, 1921), HHHP Scr B.

In early 1921 Harrison reportedly rejected an offer of financial support from the Communist Party of the United States, which was affiliated with the Third (Communist) International (or Comintern) headed by the Bolshevik party of Russia. According to Bureau of Investigation special agent P-138 (Herbert Simeon Boulin), Edgar M. Grey, secretary of the Liberty League, had said "in confidence" that Cyril Briggs's periodical, the *Crusader*, was subsidized by the Communists and that toward the end of May, party member Rose Pastor Stokes had offered party support to Harrison "so that he could use the LIBERTY LEAGUE as a branch of spreading communism among negroes." Harrison reportedly refused the proposition because he preferred "to make the Liberty League a purely negro organization, fighting for the negro cause." According to historian Robert A. Hill, Harrison's rejection of the overture showed he would not be the Communists' "stalking horse against Garvey." Hill adds that Briggs, on the other hand, joined the Communist Workers Party around this time.[10]

The Communists were attempting to pay attention to the "Negro Problem" and wanted radical propagandists like Harrison. A section of the "Program of the United Communist

Party," on the "Negro Question," reprinted in the *Toiler* of February 12, 1921, described "The negro population of the United States" as an "outlaw race" and "the most exploited people in America." The UCP emphasized that "the only possible solution of the negro problem" was "through the overthrow of the capitalist State and the erection of the Communist society." In order "to break down the barrier of race prejudice that separates and keeps apart the white and the negro workers, and to bind them into a union of revolutionary forces for the overthrow of their common enemy," the UCP aimed to "find the revolutionary and potential revolutionary elements among the negroes and select those most likely to develop into revolutionary propagandists" for training in "revolutionary work."[11]

Around the time that he reportedly rejected the Communists' offer, Harrison wrote a call for a "Colored International" which appeared in the May 28, 1921, *Negro World*. It was based, in part, on his "The New International," which had appeared in the *Negro World* of May 15, 1920. Harrison's "call" reflected the fact that he was not only distancing himself from Garvey, but that with his class-conscious and anti-imperialist views he was also posing an alternative to the communists while trying to resurrect the Liberty League. This article, with its perceptive explanation of the cause of modern war and its call for an anti-imperialist "congress of the darker races," was Harrison's clearest alternative response to communist efforts to woo him and other African Americans. He advised that the "revolutionists" should "show their sincerity by first breaking down the exclusion walls of white workingmen before they ask us to demolish our own defensive structures of racial self-protection." Overall it is a cogent and powerful plan for action.[12]

All over the world today the subject peoples of all colors are rising to the call of democracy, to formulate their grievances and plan their own enfranchisement from the chains of slavery, social, political and economic. From Ireland and Armenia, from Russia and Finland, from India, Egypt and West Africa, efforts have come looking for their relief from the thralldom of centuries of oppression.

Of all those peoples the darker races are the ones who have suffered most. In addition to the economic evils under which the others suffer they must endure those which flow from the degrading dogma of the color line; that dogma which has been set up by the Anglo-Saxon peoples and adopted in varying degrees by other white peoples who have followed their footsteps in the path of capitalistic imperialism; that dogma which declares that the lands and labors of colored races everywhere shall be the legitimate prey of white peoples and that the Negro, the Hindu, the Chinese and Japanese must endure insult and contumely in a world that was made for all.

Here in America, we who are of African ancestry and Negro blood have drunk this cup of gall and wormwood to the bitter dregs. Our labor built the greatness of this land in which we are shut out from places of public accommodation: from the church, the ballot and the laws' protection. We are Jim-Crowed, disfranchised and lynched without redress from law or public sentiment, which vigorously exercises its humanity on behalf of the Irish, Armenians and Germans thousands of miles away, but can find no time to concern itself with the barbarism and savagery perpetrated on black fellow citizens in its very midst.

This cynical indifference extends to the leaders of the Christian Church, the high-priests of democracy and the conservative [*conservative* is crossed out in the scrapbook] exponents of the aims of labor. Thus the Negro is left out of the plans being put forward by these groups for the reorganization and reconstruction of American affairs on the basis of "democracy."

We Negroes have no faith in American democracy, and can have none so long as lynching, economic and social serfdom lie in the dark alleys of its mental reservations. When a president of this country [Woodrow Wilson] can become famous abroad for his preachments on "The New Freedom" while pregnant Negro women are roasted by white savages in his section of the South with not one word of protest coming from his lips; when a church which calls itself Christian can grow hysterically "alarmed" over the souls of savages in Central Africa, while it sees everyday the bodies of its black fellow Christians brutalized and their souls blasted while it [HH changed *while it* to *and*] smirks in gleeful acquiescence; when the "aims of labor" on its march to justice exclude all reference to the masses of black workers whom conservative labor leaders would condemn in America to the shards and sweepings of economic existence—when such things represent what happens every day in a "sweet land of liberty" where "democracy" is the great watchword, then we Negroes must be excused for feeling neither love nor respect for the rotten hypocrisy which masquerades as democracy in America.

When we look upon the Negro republics of Hayti and Santo Domingo where American marines murder and rape at their pleasure while the financial vultures of Wall Street scream with joy over the bloody execution which brings the wealth of these countries under their control; when we see the Virgin Islanders in the deadly coils of American capitalism gasping for a breath of liberty, and Mexico menaced by the same monster, we begin to realize that we must organize our forces to save ourselves from further degradation and ultimate extinction.

We have appealed to the common Christian sentiment of the white people for justice, but we have been told that with the white people of this country race is more powerful than religion. We have appealed to the common patriotism which should bind us together in a common loyalty to the practice rather than the preachments of democracy, and in every case we have been rebuffed and spurned. We have depended on protest and publicity, and protest and publicity addressed to the humane sentiments of white America have availed us nothing. We are too weak to wage war against these evil conditions with force, yet we cannot afford to wait for help to come to us from those who are our oppressors. We must, therefore, learn a lesson from those others who suffer elsewhere from evils similar to ours. Whether it be Sinn Fein or Swadesha, their experiences should be serviceable for us.

Our first duty is to come together in mind as well as in mass; to take counsel from each other and to gather strength from contact; to organize and plan effective resistance to race prejudice wherever it may raise its head; to attract the attention of all possible friends whose circumstances may have put them in the same plight and whose program may involve the same way of escape. We must organize, plan and act, and the time for the action is now. A call should be issued for a congress of the darker races, which should be frankly anti-imperialistic and should serve as an international center of co-operation from which strength may be drawn for the several sections of the world of color. Such a congress should be worldwide in scope; it should include representatives and spokesmen of the oppressed peoples of India, Egypt, China, West and South Africa, and the West Indies, Hawaii, the Phillipines, Afghanistan, Algeria and Morocco. It should be made up of those who realize that capitalist imperialism which mercilessly exploits the darker races for its own financial purposes is the enemy which we must combine to fight with arms as varied as those by which it is fighting to destroy our manhood, independence and self-respect. Against the pseudo-internationalism of the short-sighted savants who are posturing on the stage of capitalist culture it should op-pose the stark internationalism of clear vision which sees that capitalism means conflict of races and nations, and that war and oppression of the weak spring from the same economic motive — which is at the very root of capitalist culture.

It is the same economic motive that has been back of every modern war since the merchant and trading classes secured control of the powers of the modern state from the battle of Plassy to the present world war. This is the natural and inevitable effect of the capitalist system. For that system is based upon the wage relationship between those who own and those who operate the gigantic forces of land and machinery. Under this system no capitalist employs a worker for two dollars a day unless the worker creates more than two dollars worth of wealth for him. Only out of this surplus can profits come. If ten million workers should thus create one hundred million dollars worth of wealth each day and get twenty or fifty millions in wages it is obvious that they can ex-pend only what they have received, and that, therefore, every nation whose industrial system is organized on a capitalist basis must produce a mass of surplus products over and above, not the need, but the purchasing power of the nation's producers. Before these products can return to their owners as profits they must be sold somewhere. Hence the need for foreign markets, for fields of exploitation and "spheres of influence" in "undeveloped" countries whose virgin resources are exploited in their turn after the capitalist fashion. But since every industrial nation is seeking the same outlet for its products clashes are inevitable, and in these clashes beaks and claws — must come into play. Hence beaks and claws must be provided beforehand against the day of conflict, and hence the exploitation of white men in Europe and America becomes the reason for the exploitation of black and brown and yellow men in Africa and Asia. Just as long as black men are exploited by white men in Africa, so long must white men cut each other's throats over that exploitation.

Thus the subject races and the subject classes are tied to each other like Kilkenny cats in a conundrum of conflict which they cannot escape until the system which so binds them both is smashed beyond possibility of "reconstruction." And thus it becomes the duty of the darker races to fight against the continuance of this system from without and within. The international of the darker races must avail itself of whatever help it can get from those groups within the white race which are seeking to destroy the capitalist international of race prejudice and exploitation which is known as bourgeois "democracy" at home and colonial imperialism abroad.

And here we meet our oppressors upon their own ground — a fact which can be readily appreciated. When Mr. [J. P.] Morgan wants to float a French or British loan in the United States; when Messrs. [Woodrow] Wilson, [Georges] Clemenceau and [David] Lloyd George want to stabilize their joint credit and commerce or to wage war on Germany or Russia; when areas like the Belgian Congo are to be handed over to certain capitalist cliques without the consent of their inhabitants — then the paeans of praise go to the god of "internationalism" in the temple of "civilization." But when any portion of the world's disinherited (whether white or black) seeks to join hands with any other group in the same condition, then the lords of misrule denounce the idea of internationalism as anarchy, sedition, Bolshevism and "disruptive propaganda," because the international linking up of peoples is a source of strength to those who are linked up. Naturally, our overlords want to strengthen themselves. And, quite as naturally, they wish to keep their various victims from strengthening themselves in the same way.

Today the great world majority, made up of black, brown and yellow peoples, are stretching out their hands to each other and developing a "consciousness of kind." They are seeking to establish their own centers of diffusion of their own internationalism, and this fact is giving nightmares to Downing Street, the Quai d'Orsay and the other centers of white capitalist internationalism.

The object of the capitalist international is to unify and standardize the exploitation of black, brown and yellow peoples in such a way that the danger to the exploiting groups of cutting each other's throats over the spoils may be reduced to a minimum. Hence the various agreements, mandates and spheres of influence. Hence the League of Nations, which is notoriously not a league of the white masses, but of their gold-brained governors. Freed by such a tendency on the part of those who bear the white man's burden for what they can get out of it, the darker peoples of the world have begun to realize that their first duty is to themselves. A similarity of suffering is producing in them a similarity of sentiment, and the temper of that sentiment is not to be mistaken.

We in America, in attempting to win life, liberty and happiness for ourselves, must utilize this sentiment to strengthen our position. Our enforced participation in the first World War brought us into contact with the wider world of color, and we have learned from that contact much that has enlightened us. We have learned that American race prejudice was not willing to stay at home, but insisted on pursuing us as far as France, where it sought to establish itself in the hearts of a European people to whom it was previously unknown. We have learned that capitalist America was quite willing to co-operate with Bolshevik Russia when it thought that its own ends could be served by so doing. We have learned that jim-crow cars exist in Nigeria, India and Egypt, and that lynching, disfranchisement and segregation are current practices in the French Congo and in South and East Africa. And, having learned these things, we have done our own thinking, and reached our own decision to avail ourselves of the international forces and factors which will aid us to work out for ourselves a fairer destiny than the doom which threatens us if we submit supinely to the forces of racial aggression.

We should, therefore, take the lead in linking up with those agencies and groups which tend to disrupt the white man's world as at present constituted, because it is from its present constitution that we chiefly suffer to pull chestnuts from the fire for either radical or conservative groups. Until we can co-operate with them on our own terms we choose not to co-operate at all, but to pursue our own way of salvation. We will not allow either communists or Quakers to break down our developing racial solidarity, and we shall denounce every attempt to stampede us into their camps on their terms until they shall have first succeeded in breaking down the opposing racial solidarity of the ranks of white labor in the lands in which we live. Sauce for the black goose ought to be sauce for the white gander, and the temporary revolutionists of today should show their sincerity by first breaking down the exclusion walls of white workingmen before they ask us to demolish our own defensive structures of racial self-protection. The latter arose as a consequence of the former and the cause should be removed before the consequence can fairly be expected to disappear.

But those who will meet us on our own ground will find that we recognize a common enemy in the present world order and are willing to advance to attack it in our joint behalf.

Disarmament and the Washington Conference

The Washington Conference on disarmament was held from November 12, 1921, to February 6, 1922. It grew out of the naval race that developed between the United States, Great Britain, and Japan after World War I and the Paris Peace Conference. This race intensified after the United States passed legislation for a strengthening of the navy and stationed a large fleet in the Pacific in response to similar actions by Britain and Japan and the threat of a renewed Anglo-Japanese alliance. The Conference was called at the urging of President Warren G. Harding who sought an alternative to U.S. participation in the League of Nations.

The Disarmament Conference was attended by delegations from the United States, Great Britain, Japan, Italy, and France, as well as representatives from China, Belgium, Portugal and the Netherlands, who met on Far Eastern questions. When it opened on November 12, Secretary of State Charles Evans Hughes and President Harding proposed that the United States scrap thirty ships weighing a total of 845,000 tons, Britain 19 ships weighing 583,375 tons, and Japan 17 ships weighing 448,928 tons. The conference ultimately agreed on a ratio of naval tonnage for the major powers in which Britain conceded superiority to the United States. It also called for an end to the Anglo-Japanese alliance and recognized colonial possessions in the Far East as well as Japan's role as an international power.[13]

In the following two articles Harrison analyzes the Washington Conference and pays particular attention to Japan and the "darker races," whose land, labor, and resources were at stake. He points out that India was the real key to the Anglo-Japanese alliance and that there would be no real disarmament "So long as the will-to-be-free of these darker millions" could be "limited by the will-to-power of the white people of Europe and America."

76. "The Washington Conference," *Negro World* 11 (November 19, 1921): 4, HHHP Scr B.

A consideration of what is called the Disarmament Conference properly begins with Japan. And it is significant that in every weighty pronouncement recently made by experts on international tensions Japan has been set up as the main target in the discussion. A few of these statements may properly precede our own interpretation.

Mr. Lothrop Stoddard's recent book on *The New World of Islam* has caused as much disquietude as his earlier work. In its issue of October 23 the *New York Times* endeavors to dispel this disquietude by carrying a long article by General [Charles-Marie-Emmanuel] Mangin of France which attempts to argue away the impression left by Stoddard's book, viz., that the darker peoples of Near, Middle and Far East are preparing to challenge the supremacy of the whites in Asia and North Africa. It is a fact to be noted that General Mangin in his answer, which follows step by step the plan of Stoddard's book, never mentions that volume once. But he drags Japan into it; and gets off the following remarkable dictum:

A small amount of wisdom will be sufficient to enable her (Japan) to assure herself and to demonstrate to the eyes of the world that she repudiates the idea of entering into rivalry with the European powers in Asia or of nursing a latent and dangerous hostility against the United States in the Pacific.

In *Le Matin* for October 7, Jules Sauerwein, its foreign editor, in a summary of the international situation, uttered this pregnant sentence: "Popular excitation and race hatred are increasing every day between America and Japan."

At the recent Press Congress held in Honolulu, Mr. M[otosada]. Zumoto, editor of *The Herald* of Asia and formerly secretary to Marquis [Hirobumi] Itō, told the white men there assembled what all Japanese felt, but no Japanese diplomat cared to express in public when he said:

> If the West persistently refuses to listen to the voice of reason and justice and aggravates the antagonism of culture by injecting race prejudice, it is not inconceivable that the result may possibly be war between the races incomparably more calamitous than the last great war and wider in extent. . . . The question of cultural antagonism cannot be settled by official conventions. . . . Japan and America are the respective vanguards of two civilizations, expressing temperaments and modes of thought so different that when they come into contact the shock is bound to be unpleasant and disconcerting.

In a Washington Dispatch to the *Evening Post* dated November 5 the correspondent of that paper states that "official Washington is trying to get a line on the leading Asiatic statesmen upon whose attitude to a large extent depends the success of the world's greatest peace parley." And recently General Sir Ian Hamilton told the members of the London Press Club that—

> The Japanese know that if battleships should cross the Pacific to attack them they would never get back, because of lack of adequate naval bases. If we had trouble with the Japanese they would be able to take Hong Kong and the Philppines and it would be a long time before they could be ousted.
>
> The facts in the situation should be realized in connection with the Washington conference, which is something like a smoking concert in a powder machine.

To any one who will think these quotations will definitely indicate both the drift and the intent of the Peace Congress (for that is what it is) now assembled in Washington. The Wilson Peace Congress and its resultant fake League of Nations were flat failures. There are twice as many soldiers now under arms as there were in 1914, and the burden of taxation presses heavily on the purses of white nations. While millions are out of work and starving shells and bombs are going up (and down) in tests. Some of them cost as much as the food which would feed a village for a year. Manifestly, something must be done. And those whom Mr. [H. G.] Wells described some years ago as "Gawd-sakers" have begun to squawk, "For Gawd's sake, let's do something." But Banquo's ghost sits with them. Their overlordship entails the maintenance of "white supremacy." And since some of the darker peoples have arms it is obvious that the white powers must first disarm them before they themselves can disarm. Of these darker nations Japan is the most powerful. She alone has "entered into rivalry with the European powers in Asia." Therefore their main concern is Japan at the second Peace Congress.

But Japan is only an index. Hundreds of millions in Asia and Africa are restive under white control. If Japan should take up arms against any white nation at this time it would be "all Hell let loose" — and they know it. Hence the main business of the bearers of "the white man's burden" is to trick Japan into a position where she can be prevented from fighting — except at a great disadvantage. Yet, with all this talk of disarmament, the white nations do not intend to forego "white supremacy," the power of the white nations of Europe and America to interfere in the affairs of Africa and Asia. The white man must bar the Asiatic who is his superior in courage and industry from the Western world; but no white nation will agree to let itself be barred from the Orient. Under these circumstances the Washington Conference is a patent fraud. As Ido Fimmen said last month at The Hague: "I do not believe for an instant that the gentlemen are serious in their talk of disarmament. The most important delegates are military chiefs from the recent war — [Ferdinand] Foch, [Douglas] Haig, [David] Beatty, [Armando] Diaz, etc."

And there is another reason for restraint. Conceding that no nation wars except in self-defense, its safety must depend upon its military might. Since it cannot know how many nations may attack it at once, how can any one expect it to voluntarily decrease its powers of resistance? The thing is too ridiculous. Therefore, we may expect the usual crookedness and lying, the secret treaties and reservations and all the paraphernalia of "diplomacy." "Civilization" as determined by the white race, sees itself on the toboggan slide, knows where it is going, but can not stop nor deflect its course. This thing in Washington is simply one of its last heroic gestures. The only man of them all who seems to know what's what will be in the press gallery — Herbert George Wells. If one wants to know just how hopeless is the case for white civilization — Japan or no Japan — let him read Mr. Wells' recent book, *The Salvaging of Civilization* in which it is pathetically set forth. And we might remark in closing that secretary [of state Charles Evans] Hughes' grand offer of last week was only America's big bluff.

77. "Disarmament and the Darker Races," *Negro World* 11 (December 31, 1921): 3 (based on the handwritten article "Disarmament and the Darker Races" by Hira Lal Ganesha [pseudonym], probably December 4, 1921), HHHP Wr.

Harrison handwrote his December 4, 1921, talk on "Disarmament and the Darker Races" and, later in the month, wrote a three-page piece with the same title under the pseudonym "Hira Lal Ganesha." (Ganesha is the Hindu god of wisdom.) In the *Negro World* of December 31, he published the article in a modified form. The core message of all three pieces was similar: "So long as the will-to-be-free of these darker millions is limited by the will-to-power of the white people of Europe and America, just so long must these white people stay armed"; "out of the colonial and imperial control springs . . . the need for armaments."

At one of the sessions of the butchers' convention an orphaned calf strayed in through the open door and created a considerable commotion. He was finally shooed out, however; and amid the laughter that ensued one humorous delegate suggested that perhaps the calf had had something to say. This caused a titter of amusement. "But," said another delegate, "who cares to hear what a calf has to say?" And, the incident closed in a burst of hilarity.

The present population of the earth numbers more than seventeen hundred million, of which over twelve hundred million are colored people. The white populations of Great Britain, France, Italy, the United States, Belgium, Holland and Spain amount to approximately [220,000,000]. [The number was left blank in the *Negro World* article, and Harrison wrote *220,000,000* on his copy. He also wrote "do not exceed two hundred and eighty-three million" on the handwritten article.]

Yet, in the publicly expressed opinion of these latter when they meet "to settle world affairs," including that of disarmament, the reaction of the hundreds of millions to the program put forward are worth as little consideration as those of so many calves would be worth at a butchers' convention. Nothing reveals crass inadequacy of statesmanship, and the futility of the present mode of managing world affairs as does this singular fact. For, without putting in any humanitarian pleas, it is easy to show that explosive possibilities lurk in every dumb and suppressed minority. How much more explosive must be these possibilities when what is suppressed is an overwhelming majority linked unwillingly in a state of unstable subordination to a permanent ruling minority. Out of a similar unstable subordination in domestic affairs springs the permanent need of the police machinery of the State, with its consequent burden to the taxpayers. And out of the colonial and imperial control springs as a pragmatic fact the greater portion of the need for armaments.

At the Disarmament Conference now being held in Washington the French delegates demurred to the demand for reductions in the size of the French Navy, and the main ground of their objection was stated by Stephane Luzanne:

> If one takes into consideration the length of the French coasts and the importance of the French Colonial Empire, which by its size is the second greatest colonial empire in the world, one will easily admit that these demands [for special consideration of the French Navy] are far from being exaggerated.

And what is true of France is equally true of the other Great Powers. Now it happens that, with the sole exception of Japan, the Great Powers are white and their imperial dominion is a dominion over colored people: "the lesser breeds without the law," as [Rudyard] Kipling calls them. It is the land, labor and resources of these backward and weaker peoples which constitute the stakes of diplomacy and war today. A glance at the map of the world will show that the danger points are those places where white nations have staked out competing claims to the ownership, control and "development" of the lands of colored peoples — mainly in Africa and Asia. Britain, Belgium and France having absorbed most of Africa, Asia remains as the prolific center of future troubles. And just as the "inferior" blacks of four Southern States dominate the domestic policies of those States, so do the "inferior" Asiatic groups dominate the international policies of white Europe and America.

In America our white political experts have managed to dodge the real inner reason for England's Asiatic alliance with Japan. That reason is—India, which is the key-stone of the British imperial system. The mere existence of a colored great power in Asia is a tremendous stimulant to Asiatic self-assertion. Add to this the fact that this colored power has defeated successively two white powers and driven them from Asia's eastern front, and it will be seen what trouble it could stir up in India with its 150,000,000 people if it should, in a spirit of unfriendliness assume the role of liberator or leader.

Then there is China. In a recent article in the *Times' Current History Magazine* Mr. Stephen Bosnal tells us that "China is a market which . . . we cannot afford to lose," and goes on to paint a beautiful ethical picture of the United States as the champion of China against Japanese aggression. But here again the white publicist deliberately covers up and hides away the racial implication of his thesis. "Our pledge to support China against outside aggression," he says, "goes back to the treaty of 1858." Yet since that time large slices of China have been taken by England, Germany, France and Russia, and the fact remains that against these aggressions the United States made no protest, did not assume the role of ethical champion.

In 1894, when the rising empire of Japan defeated the empire of China, the Japanese attempted to do what England did after she had defeated Germany—to take some of the territory of the conquered. At that time Russia presented a note to the powers in which it was maintained that any taking of territory of Japan would be opposed by the armed forces of Russia, England, Germany and France. When the joint note was presented to Japan her hand was stayed, for she could not fight these four powers. But they proceeded to take what they had denied Japan. England took Wei Hai Wei, Germany took Shantung, Russia took Port Arthur, and France also took her slice. All this showed the Japanese that strong armies and navies were the only things respected by the righteous powers. These she proceeded to develop. And it was only because of these that she ousted Russia in 1905, and Germany in 1915. While the white powers were stripping China the United States did not assume any ethical role. And to men of color it seems that she does so now only because Japan, as a colored nation, has assumed in China a prerogative exclusively appropriated hitherto by the dominant and superior whites.

Of course this is quite natural. And thoughtful men of color do not blame the whites for wishing to have their own stock eternally on top. But they could wish that those who act as spokesmen for the enlightened sections of the white world could be candid enough to admit openly this fundamental dictum of their present political philosophy. This philosophy of the White Man's Burden may be justified on pragmatic grounds which may be left for formulation to white statesmen and publicists. But yellow, brown and black men all over the world are laughing lightly in their sleeves at the thought that the white men can hold firmly by that philosophy and still talk of disarmament. So long as the will-to-be-free of these darker millions is limited by the will-to-power of the white people of Europe and America, just so long must these white people stay armed.

But fate's Gargantuan jest lies in another aspect of the international situation. When the next great war breaks out the nations involved will be divided into two groups — those fighting and those being fought for. With the tremendously increased destructiveness of chemical warfare the amount and range of the destruction wrought will be far greater than that of the first great war. It seems a safe guess that the greater the technical development of the nations in the first group the greater will be the destruction which they will wreak upon each other. Perhaps civilization (as they know it) will be wiped out. The nations which will escape destruction will be those that are being fought for. So the doctrine of domination will end its cycle of extinction and "they that take the sword shall perish by the sword."

The Caribbean

Harrison was an extremely knowledgeable commentator on events in the Caribbean in the 1920s. One of his major contributions to the *Negro World* was his pioneering "West Indian News Notes" column, which ran, often on page 6 of the publication, from 1920 to 1922. In a typical column from March 25, 1922, developments relating to Guadeloupe, Dominica, Jamaica, Demerara, Trinidad, and a West Indian Federation were discussed. Harrison's "Notes" column attracted the attention of British military intelligence officials who contacted the New York office of U.S. military intelligence about his writings.[14]

The three pieces that follow were all probably written in 1920. The first discusses the U.S. occupation of Haiti, the second treats U.S. involvement in the entire Caribbean region, and the third provides one of Harrison's most forceful critiques of imperialism as well as a moving plea to action on behalf of the Haitian people.

78. "Help Wanted for Hayti," *Negro World* [?] (c. July 1920), reprinted in *When Africa Awakes*, 104–5.

The United States occupied Haiti from 1915 to 1934, and it occupied Santo Domingo in 1916 and again in 1920. In each case the troops unleashed reigns of terror. After being severely criticized for the Santo Domingo occupation, President Woodrow Wilson agreed to withdraw U.S. forces. This was not done, however, until 1922, under President Warren G. Harding, when a new provisional government was established and election plans announced.

The activities of the Wilson administration in Haiti drew increased national attention after the 1920 Democratic vice-presidential nominee, and former assistant secretary of the navy, Franklin Delano Roosevelt, in a campaign statement declared: "I have had something to do with the running of a couple of little republics. . . . I wrote Haiti's Constitution myself, and, if I do say it, I think it is a pretty good Constitution." Roosevelt was referring to the constitution written under the U.S. Navy's occupation. In a subsequent campaign speech, Warren G. Harding, the 1920 Republican presidential nominee, spoke of the "rape of Haiti" and charged that "thousands of natives have been killed by American marines." Harding's comments greatly fueled anti-occupation sentiment, which had been spearheaded by efforts from people such as Ernest Gruening of *The Nation*, James Weldon Johnson and Herbert J. Seligmann of the NAACP, and Harrison of the *Negro World*, and which had included editorials like Harrison's "Help Wanted for Hayti."[15]

While we were at war our President declared, over and over again, that we were calling upon the flower of our manhood to go to France and make itself into manure in order that the world might be made safe for democracy. Today the deluded people of the earth realize that the accent is on the "moc(k)." Ireland, India and Egypt are living proofs that the world has been lied to. We need not bite our tongues about it. Those who told us that the world would be made safe for democracy have lied to us. All over the world men and women are finding out that when an American President, a British Premier or a French "tiger" speaks of "the world," he does not include the black and brown and yellow millions, who make up the vast majority of the earth's population. And now the sheeted ghost of the black republic rises above the tomb where its bones lie buried and points its silent but accusing finger at American democracy. What can we answer in the case of Hayti? British India and Ireland, Turkish Armenia or Russian Poland have never presented such ruthless savagery as has been let loose in Hayti in a private war for which President Wilson has never had the consent of Congress. The white daily newspapers speak complacently about the repulse of "bandits." What is this but a developing disease of the American conscience, to put the blinkers of a catchword over the eyes of the spirit?

The people of Hayti are being shot, sabred and bombed, while resisting an illegal invasion of their homes, and, if public decency is not dead in America white and black men and women will insist that Congress investigate this American Ireland.

When Ireland feels the pressure of the English heel, the Irish in America make their voices heard and help to line up American public opinion on their side. When [Ignacy Jan] Paderewski's government massacres Jews in Poland, the Jews of America raise money, organize committees, put the U.S. Government on the job—and get results. But when Negroes are massacred—not in Africa, but in Hayti, under American control—what do we American Negroes do? So far, nothing. But that inaction will not last. Negroes must write their Congressmen and Senators concerning the atrocity perpetrated at Port au Prince last week. They should organize committees to go before Congress and put the pitiful facts, demanding investigation, redress and punishment.

For as long as such things can be done without effective protest or redress, black people every where will refuse to believe that the democracy advertised by lying white politicians can be anything but a ghastly joke.

79. "The Cracker in the Caribbean," *Negro World* [?] (c. 1920), reprinted in *When Africa Awakes*, 105–8.

The U.S. occupation of Haiti by Marines and sailors began on July 28, 1915, and was quickly reinforced by troops dispatched from the Guantánamo Bay naval base in Cuba. The navy imposed authoritarian control and racial segregation on the islanders and aggressively suppressed democratic institutions and the press. The Haitian people responded with widespread opposition that included militant armed resistance from *cacos*, peasants who served as part-time soldiers in military units of local rulers. In 1918 Major Smedley D. Butler implemented a forced-labor road-building program, under which Haitians were taken from their homes by armed guards, roped together, marched out of their local districts, and subjected to assorted brutalities. Haitians responded to the occupation and forced labor with massive resistance, which the American troops brutally repressed. Prisoners were often murdered, and in March 1919 *cacos* units were subjected to aerial bombings in the first recorded instance of coordinated air-ground combat. Some 1,861 Haitians were killed in 1919 alone; 2,250 were killed in the first five years of the occupation. The brutality of the U.S. occupation of Haiti was a theme that Harrison frequently addressed.[16]

> "Meanwhile the feet of civilized slayers have woven across the fair face of the earth a crimson mesh of murder and rapine. The smoke of blazing villages ascends in lurid holocaust to the bloody god of battles from the altar of human hate in the obscene temple of race prejudice."

These words, which we wrote in 1912, come back to our mind eight years later with no abatement of the awful horror which they express. And what gives a special point to them at this moment is the bloody rape of the republics of Hayti and Santo Domingo which is being perpetrated by the bayonets of American sailors and marines, with the silent and shameful acquiescence of 12,000,000 American Negroes too cowardly to lift a voice in effective protest or too ignorant of political affairs to know what is taking place. What boots it is that we strike heroic attitudes and talk grandiloquently of Ethiopia stretching forth her hands when we Africans of the dispersion can let the land of L'Overture [Toussaint Louverture] lie like a fallen flower beneath the feet of swine?

The facts of the present situation in that hapless land are given in the current issue of *The Nation* (a white American weekly). Taken together with the accounts which we have printed from time to time, it tells a tale of shuddering horror in comparison with which the Putumayo pales into insignificance and the Congo atrocities of Belgium are tame. The two West Indian republics have been murderously assaulted; their citizens have been shot down by armed ruffians, bombed by aeroplanes, hunted into concentration camps and there starved to death. In their own land their civil liberties have been taken away, their governments have been blackjacked and their property stolen. And all this by the "cracker" statesmanship of "the South," without one word of protest from that defunct department, the Congress of the United States!

The Constitution of the United States says that the power to declare war shall belong exclusively to the Congress of the United States. But the Congress of the United States has been shamelessly ignored. In furtherance of the God-given "cracker" mandate to "keep the nigger in his place," a mere Secretary of the Navy [Josephus Daniels] has assumed over the head of Congress the right to conquer and annex two nations and to establish on their shores the "cracker-democracy" of his native Carolina slave-runs.

It is high time that the Negro people of the United States call the hand of Joseph[us] Daniels by appealing to the Legislature of the United States to resume its political functions, investigate this high-handed outrage and impeach the Secretary of the Navy of high crimes and misdemeanors against the peace and good name of the United States. The ordinary excuse of cowards will not obtain in this case. We would not be violating any law — wartime or other — but, on the contrary, we should be striving to put an end to a flagrant violation of the Constitution itself on the part of a high officer, who took an oath to maintain, support and defend it. That is our right and our duty. Irishmen, on behalf of Ireland, sell the bonds of an Irish loan to free Ireland from the tyranny of Britain — with whom we are on friendly terms — on the very steps of New York's City Hall, while we black people are not manly enough to get up even a petition on behalf of our brothers in Hayti.

Out upon such crawling cowardice! Rouse, ye slaves, and show the spirit of liberty is not quite dead among you! You who elected "delegates" to go to a Peace Conference to which you had neither passport nor invitation, on behalf of bleeding Africa, get together and present a monster petition to the American Congress, over which you have some control. Remember that George the Third engaged in a contest with the colonies because he had trouble at home. He could not defeat the Pitts, Burkes and Foxes at home, and wanted to win prestige from the colonials. Had he succeeded in setting his foot on their necks he would have returned home with increased prestige and power to bend the free spirits of England to his will. [William] Pitt knew this, and so did [Charles James] Fox and [Edmund] Burke. That is why they took the side of their distant cousins against the British kings. And the British liberals of today thank their memories for it. If the "crackers" of the South can fasten their yoke on the necks of our brothers overseas, then God help us Negroes in America in the years to come!

If we were now appealing directly to the white men of America we might dwell upon the moral aspects of the question. But we must leave that to others. Yet we cannot do so without recalling the words of a great poet:

> "But man, proud man,
>
> Drest in a little brief authority,
>
> Most ignorant of what he's most assured —
>
> His glassy essence — like an angry ape,
>
> Plays such fantastic tricks before high heaven
>
> And make the angels weep."

And we draw some slight consolation from the fact that, even if he should escape impeachment, Josephus Daniels must surrender up his "brief authority" in another twelvemonth.

But we who are still free in a measure must not wait twelve months to act. We could not do that and preserve our racial self-respect. For —

> "Whether conscious or unconscious, yet Humanity's vast
>
> frame
>
> Through its ocean-sundered fibres feels the gush of joy
>
> or shame;
>
> In the gain or loss of one race all the rest have equal
>
> claim."

80. "Hands across the Sea," *Negro World* (September 10, 1921), HHHP Scr B.

In this forceful *Negro World* piece Harrison offers a concise explanation on how imperialism, the "most dangerous stage of developed capitalism," turns to "the subjection of black, brown and colored workers." In the process he offers concrete suggestions for action in opposition to U.S. imperialism in Haiti.

The most dangerous phase of developed capitalism is that of imperialism — when having subjugated its workers and exploited its natural resources at home, it turns with grim determination toward "undeveloped" races and areas to renew the same process there. This is the phase in which militarism and navalism develop with dizzying speed with their accumulating burden of taxation for "preparedness" against the day when the capitalist class of the nation must use the final argument of force against its foreign competitors for markets. These markets change their character under the impact of international trade, and are no longer simply markets for the absorption of finished products, but become fields for the investment of accumulated surplus profits, in which process they are transformed into original sources for the production of surplus profits by the opening up of mines, railroads and other large-scale capitalist enterprises. It becomes necessary to take over the government of the selected areas in order that the profits may be effectually guaranteed, and "spheres of influence," "protectorates," and "mandates" are set up.

Thus the lands of "backward" people are brought within the central influence of the capitalist economic system and the subjection of black, brown and other colored workers to the rigors of "the white man's burden" comes as a consequence of the successful exploitation of white workers at home, and binds them both in an international opposition to the continuance of the capitalist regime. Most Americans who are able to see this process more or less clearly in the case of other nations are unable to see the same process implicit and explicit in the career of their own.

The case of Hayti and the present plight of the Haytian people helps us to see the aims of our own American imperialists in the white light of pitiless publicity. A people of African descent, scarcely seven hundred miles from our own shores, with a government of their own, have had their government suppressed and their liberties destroyed by the Navy Department of the United States without even the slightest formality of a declaration of war by the United States Congress as required by the Constitution. In the presidential chair our "cracker" marines have installed a puppet in the person of Monsieur [President Phillipe Sudre] D'Artiguenave to carry out their will; the legislative bodies of the erstwhile republic have been either suppressed or degraded; unoffending black citizens have been wantonly butchered in cold blood, and thousands have been forced into slavery to labor on the military roads without pay. Here is American imperialism in its stark, repulsive nakedness. And what are we going to do about it?

The fight which will soon be waged in Congress for the restoration of Haytian rights is receiving no help from the millions of Negroes who are presumably interested in the international movement for the practical advancement of people of Negro blood. It is high time that it should. This is an opportunity that lies ready to our hands. And if we would use our votes here in an intelligent, purposeful way we could at least make our voices heard and heeded in Washington on behalf of our brothers in black who are suffering seven hundred miles away. Pending this, we could inaugurate gigantic propaganda meetings in such places as Faneuil Hall, Madison Square Garden and the Negro churches; we could in our newspapers and magazines agitate for the withdrawal of the forces of the American occupation, as the Irish did on behalf of Ireland; we could, at least, get up a gigantic petition with a million signatures and carry it to Congress. Even a "silent protest parade" would become us better than this slavish apathy and servile acquiescence in which we are now sunk.

Believe it or not as we will, the Negro American is now on trial before the eyes of the world and if he fails to act he may yet hear the God of opportunity utter those fateful words recorded in the third chapter of Revelations concerning the angel of the church of the Laodiceans. For we may be sure that French, British and Belgian imperialism is a limb of the same tree of white domination on which our home-made branch grows.

The Virgin Islands

Although Harrison never returned to the land of his birth, he kept St. Croix and the Virgin Islands close to his heart and in his thoughts. Over the years he would write about island developments and lecture in support of Virgin Islander organizations such as the Virgin Island Congressional Council, the Virgin Islands Committee, and the Virgin Islands Protective League. He maintained close ties with a number of Virgin Islanders including his boyhood classmate D. Hamilton Jackson (a prominent labor and political leader on St. Croix and editor of the *Herald*); Harlem activists such as James C. Canegata (the father of the actor Canada Lee), Frank Crosswaith (a leading Socialist Party member and trade union organizer), and Casper Holstein (a major contributor to island and civil rights causes); Virgin Islands activists Elizabeth Hendrickson and Rothschild Francis (editor of the *Emancipator*); and bibliophile Arthur Schomburg (whose mother was a Crucian and who spent his early years on the island). In the first of the following two pieces Harrison defends Jackson, in the second, he provides a fascinating and informative overview of the Virgin Islands.

81. "A St. Croix Creole" (pseudonym), letter to the editor, *New York Evening Post*, May 15, 1922.

On May 7, 1922, Harrison responded to a letter by Thomas S. Stribling (the author of *Birthright*) that appeared in the previous day's *New York Evening Post*. Harrison's response was written under the pseudonym "A St. Croix Creole." This was done probably because the letter called attention to the noncitizen status of Crucians in the United States, and Harrison was not yet a citizen. (He became a naturalized United States citizen on September 26, 1922.)[17]

> To the Editors of the *New York Evening Post*:
> The article on "Dumb St. Croix" by Mr. Stribling in last Saturday's *Post* leaves at least one reader in a state of bewilderment. The writer was born in St. Croix, has taught in its largest rural school, the one at Friedensfeld — and is at present a lecturer for the Board of Education of this city, as well as a regular contributor (under other names) to some of the better known periodicals.
> Let me merely indicate the fictional quality of Mr. Stribling's picture of St. Croix. D. Hamilton Jackson (a former classmate of the writer) is at present a lawyer, having received his legal training in the United States. His father was the most prominent teacher, white or black, in the three islands, and presided over the Danish school in Christiansted. When Jackson started out to regenerate the Negro laborers they were dispirited and hopeless on a daily wage of 20 cents. He has licked them into such co-operative shape that they now own eight of the "estates" on which they formerly worked for hire; they have a newspaper, a warehouse, and a bank. And they got these

things only by banding together. Let me add that it was the success of this cooperative labor movement which, more than anything else, disposed the Danes to sell the islands, in order that resident whites could control their black labor problem in approved American fashion.

When Mr. Stribling says that Jackson teaches his people to hate whites, he substitutes fiction for fact. Jackson is now in trouble with his own group because he refuses to exploit race hatred in their behalf.

Virgin Islanders occupy a most anomalous position. In consequence of the dodging tactics of the State Department the 20,000 of them living in New York City are neither citizens nor aliens. They cannot vote and they cannot get naturalized because they have no "allegiance" to forswear. Their status is a standing disgrace to democracy and ought to be speedily changed. But there has been no discussion of the facts before the American people.

A St. Croix Creole
New York, May 7

82. "The Virgin Islands: A Colonial Problem," October 31, 1923, HHHP Wr.

While serving as a lecturer for the New York City Board of Education, Harrison finished a lengthy nineteen-page article, "The Virgin Islands: A Colonial Problem," for *The Nation* magazine. The completed article was to be one in a series of articles entitled "These United States," which were to appear on alternate weeks. Though *The Nation* ultimately did such a series (later republished in part as *These "Colored" United States*) that included a piece on St. Croix by Ashley Totten, Harrison's far superior piece was never published. Harrison's article is a fascinating and informative depiction of the island, its people and history, and conditions under the current naval occupation.[18]

It is possible to write an account of Louisiana, Mississippi, Virginia or any other southern state without mentioning its Negro population; and indeed most of the popular school histories of these states have been written in that way. But this is hardly possible in the case of the Virgin Islands whose population is 93 per cent Negro. For weal or woe, these islands (St. Croix, St. Thomas and St. John's) are now a part of our far-flung colonial empire and represent one portion of "the white man's burden" which our republic has been driven by "manifest destiny" to assume. But this assumption of sovereignty over darker peoples carries with it the obligation to know something of them. Unfortunately, most Americans—from our statesman up—believe that they can manage to dispense with this obligation; and this happy-go-lucky attitude results in the production of some singular anomalies, as for instance:

Our Navy is our right arm of war and was never intended as a co-ordinate branch of our own government which has so far consisted of the Executive, Legislative and Judicial departments. It is true that since the opening of the 20th century we have used it to hold Hayti, Santo Domingo and Nicaragua in thrall; but these people are all foreigners who had to be either subjugated or intimidated. Their lands constitute no portion of the United States; whereas the Virgin Islands were peaceably purchased from Denmark. Yet they are administered entirely by the officials of the Navy Department instead of the Bureau of Insular Affairs, the Department of State or the Department of the Interior.

Again: In the United States we incline towards a government by law and the Fathers of that country laid it down as a primary principle of government that the executive, legislative and judicial functions should never be united in any one person or, to put it in plainer English, that no person, however great he might be, should at the same time make the law, interpret the law and apply the law; because they seemed to think that in such a case that person would be the law — which is the very essence of autocracy as opposed to democracy. Yet what the wisdom of the American people with-held from Washington, Lincoln and Roosevelt is conceded by the carelessness of Congress not only to every naval Jack-in-office who may be temporarily promoted to the governorship of the Virgin Islands but even to official underlings, like Mr. George Washington Williams, a gentleman from the South, who is at the same time district attorney, magistrate, police commissioner and quite a few other things.

A captious outsider might be moved to enquire why our nation should take on more of these darker peoples when we find our present freightage too big a burden for our Christianity, democracy and humanity. Our limitations in the matter are painfully obvious even to ourselves. But the imperialistic urge is not to be stayed by such simple considerations and it suffices to argue that "we're here because we're here — and what are you going to do about it?"

In the case of the Virgin Islands their geographic position and consequent strategic importance [HH crossed out *were the foundation reasons that*] urged us to acquire them and these same considerations may in time bring the entire West Indian group under our control. In the roaring days of [Henry] Morgan, [Edward "Blackbeard"] Teach and the other pirates and buccaneers the strategic and commercial importance of St. Thomas had exalted the port of that island into a position of unrivalled supremacy over all the other West Indian islands. Even down to the middle of the last century it could challenge commercial comparison with the best of them; and at that the number of ships that called there exceeded twenty five hundred annually.

St. John's, the smallest of the three islands, has a wonderful harbor in which an entire fleet might maneuver. At one time it was dotted with scores of plantations which produced sugar, rum and molasses. St. Croix or Santa Cruz, is the largest, most important and most beautiful of the three. It was acquired by Denmark much later than the other two and very soon outdistanced them in the production of sugar and rum. For more than two centuries Santa Cruz rum was the most famous of West Indian spirits. In 1810 this island alone exported forty-six million pounds of sugar. The production of cotton has been attempted several times and in the last decade of the 18th century 157000 bales was the amount of the annual crop.

The tourist in search of romance can find its footprints in the Virgin Islands. The grim walls of Bluebeard's Castle on the heights overlooking the town of Charlotte Amelia [Amalie] recall the days when the black flag with its skull and cross-bones threw terror into the hearts of peaceful merchants. The Salt River plantation still stands at the mouth of a lagoon in which tradition says Columbus landed on St. Ursula's day when he named the group of islands in honor of her and her eleven thousand virgins. It was in the little town of Bass End or Christiansted that Alexander Hamilton labored as a clerk and first exhibited those remarkable mental powers that took him through Columbia College in New York at the age of [about nineteen; Harrison left this blank] and made him the active genius of the American Constitution. And here, on this same island slavery was abolished by the slaves themselves after a bloody uprising in 1848. But long before this the fierce love of freedom characteristic of the Danish blacks had blown a spark over on the mainland where in 1822 one of them by the name of Denmark Vesey had organized a slave revolt in Charleston, South Carolina which all but succeeded.

These black people of the Virgin Islands are an interesting race. They are almost entirely of African extraction, the few Carib Indians who were found there in the 16th century having died off very quickly upon contact with the first white men. The social characteristics of the Negro populations of the Virgin Islands are only to be adequately understood and appreciated by reference to similar characteristics to be found in the West African Negroes from among whom the slaves for the Danish Islands were mainly drawn — the locale extending from the Upper Gold Coast to the south-eastern limits of Nigeria. Their customs are rooted in the African communal system; and the planters of the Danish islands left these inherited customs generally undisturbed. Down to twenty years ago there was a free public garden on every plantation which was stocked with fruit trees: mangoes, mammy-apples, sour-sops, avocado-pears, sugar-apples, and bananas. These were to be had for the picking not only by every person resident on such plantations (or "estates," as they were called) but also by any stranger who happened to pass by. The fishes and shrimps in any "glut" or stream were just as free to everyone, and the most popular method of taking them was that of throwing buckets of lees or liquid sugar-cane refuse into a small stream and picking out the intoxicated fish as they floated helplessly to the shore. Every family of agricultural laborers (like the English white slaves of the 13th century) had its own half-acre of provision land on which yams, tannias, okra, sago and potatoes were produced as additions to the regular dietary, the surplus being regularly disposed of in the towns on Saturday (which was a weekly holiday) in markets that exactly reproduced those to be found in the hinterlands of Sierra Leone, Liberia, the Cameroons and Yoruba. Because of these communal extensions of individual economics the agricultural laborer under Danish rules could keep himself and his family healthy and well-dressed, and send some of the children to private school on 20 cents a day where today under the rigid American economic system a dollar and a half a day (which he doesn't get) would be insufficient to give him one-half the well being which he formerly enjoyed.

There are certain well-defined economic limits to the prosperity of the islands: the thinness of the soil on a volcanic foundation and the frequent disappointing fluctuations in the rainfall are among the most important. But despite these limits their actual and potential resources include sugar-cane, from which sugar rum and molasses are made, bay rum furnished by the bay-tree, cotton, mahogany, logwood, mangineel (a sort of vegetable carbolic acid), the cashew, valuable for dyeing, and pigs and oxen which can be raised with little expense. Despite the present deplorable economic depression there still is an opening for any ambitious American whose capital does not exceed five thousand dollars.

American efforts to possess this "key to the Carribean" [*sic*] date back to 1867 when the proceedings went as far as the taking of a plebiscite by the Danish colonial officials, the result of which was favorable to the transfer which could then have been effected for the sum of fifteen million dollars. But ratification by the United States Senate was blocked by the spitefulness of Charles Sumner who used his position as Chairman of the Senate Committee on Foreign Relations to pay off his personal scores against the administrations of [Andrew] Johnson and [Ulysses S.] Grant. For the next half a century the acquisition of the islands remained just on the margin of our political field of vision, occasionally projecting itself into focus. But it required a European War to rush our conglomerate Congress into doing that which, as a necessity of our new imperialism, should have been done at leisure long ago. [Harrison crossed out "(It is to this gawd-sakers' mood of precipitation that the present political anomalies in the government of this Carribean [*sic*] dependency are largely due.)"] Our final reasons for the acquisition were, like our first, almost entirely strategic, and need not be gone into here except so far as to say that this strategy implied an intention on the part of the Wilson Administration to get us into the war as an opponent of Germany as early as 1916.

During the sixty years between Johnson and Wilson the sugar-industry in the West Indies, under the fierce competition of German and American sugar, had shrunk disastrously; and the black West Indian laborers had begun to pour into the cities of our North Atlantic states in numbers that steadily increased as the years rolled by. In the British West Indies the conditions were intensified by the fact that the younger sons of the English upper classes descended like a swarm of hungry locusts on the already impoverished colonies. It is not generally known that the governor of the island of Jamaica not only receives a salary which was, down to 15 years ago, as large as that of the governor of the richest state in our Union, but when the term of office is ended he goes home to England to receive for the rest of his natural life a pension drawn from the revenues of that poverty-stricken place. Similar provisions are made in the other British islands for all the higher officials of their governments. The pinch of poverty was felt, in consequence, by the masses of the West Indian people. But the main source of the pressure was economic rather than bureaucratic. Of this economic pressure the Virgin Islands, though Danish, had their full share; and out of it there developed in course of time a definite labor movement with clear-cut radical aims.

It was the rise and potency of this labor-movement as expressed mainly in the St. Croix Labor Union which determined the planter-element in the islands to revive and support the movement for the transfer of the Virgin Islands to the United States. In the days before the union the regular wage of an agricultural worker was twenty cents a day. By organizing the workers the union was soon able to pull up wages to fifty cents, seventy-five, and finally a dollar a day. Nor was this all. These black Danish workers began to give evidence of a social vision far in advance of that which was being exhibited by white workers in the United States. They organized a bank of their own, secured a printing-press, published a newspaper and bought up seven of the estates on which they had formerly been employed. It became evident that they meant to try conclusions with the capitalists of the islands on their own ground. Against such organized economic co-operation the planters could not hope to compete successfully. They realized that transfer to the United States, in which racial subordination was most effectively organized and intrenched in the politico-economic structure of the actual government, would redress the balance and restore their effective control over wages and working conditions. Their propaganda for the sale happened to coincide with the urgent strategic needs of the United States and the financial embarrassments of the Danish Colonial office. The voice of the planters could make itself heard more effectively in Copenhagen than that of the laborers and its influence percolated easily enough through the capillaries of officialdom and the press in Denmark — not of course on these realistic grounds, but on the others more seemly to the minds of party-leaders in the Danish parliament who were faced on the other hand with a secret and sinister ultimatum that would have left their government no choice in any case. Under these convergent pressures the sale was consummated on the 31st of March 1917; and, having perfected all his preliminary arrangements, the president who had "kept us out of war" went before Congress and ordered us in.

Mr. [David] Lloyd George, commenting on the German situation during his recent tour of the States, justified his demand for a dictatorship in Germany with the remark that both England and America had had "a practical dictatorship" during the war. During our dictatorship most of the functions of Congress were taken over by the Executive; and it was in that very period that the Virgin Islands came into our hands. It was perfectly natural, therefore, that the administration then set up should have followed the fashion of autocracy rather than that of democracy. And the present government of the Virgin Islands is that of a naval autocracy responsible not to the Congress of the United States but, in a dim and remote way, to the President alone. For instance,

The naval commandant and the governor are one and the same person; the lieutenant-commander of the Signal Corps is the Government Secretary, the Captain of the Marine Corps is head of the Legal Department, the aide to the Naval Chief of Staff is the head of the Department of Public Works, and the head of the naval hospital Director of Health for the islands. These are but a few of the official identities which exist to prove that the government of the Virgin Islands is a naval government. The point is of vital importance and the naval officials, realizing this, have been busy explaining it away. During his two-day visit to the islands in April last Secretary [of the Navy Edwin] Denby in the first two sentences of his address delivered in St. Thomas declared, "I am only a visitor here. The administration of these islands is a civil administration which the Navy furnishes with men to carry on." Then he immediately explained that "I have no authority here *outside of a strictly military authority*" — which, of course, gave the whole show away.

Meanwhile the inhabitants continue to protest against the hitherto unheard of theory of political serfdom which puts the government of an American colony into the hands of the Navy Department. Virgin Islanders can readily understand how *a conquered territory*, prior to the setting-up of civil government, can be administered by those having only "a strictly military authority" by which its subjugation had been effected, but they fail to find any precedent in the history and laws of the United States, or those of any other English-speaking country, for the present arrangement which turns over the civil rights of a free people whose territory has been peacefully acquired by treaty and purchase to the by no means tender mercies of that same Navy Department which has already achieved such an unsavory reputation in Haiti; and insist that the dignity, self-respect and good faith of the United States are involved until such time as the government of the Virgin Islands shall be put under the appropriate department of the United States government.

But the objections to the naval regime goes deeper than the question of political form. It is a notorious fact, known in every seaport of the world, that the behavior of our seamen when on shore is more unruly than that of the seamen of any other great nation. Especially is this so when they have to deal with colored inhabitants. It was their record in Kingston, Jamaica, which was responsible for the drastic order of Governor Sir Alexander Swettenham during the Jamaica earthquake sending them back to their ships and refusing the aid of American marines in policing Kingston. In explanation of his unauthorized landing the American admiral had declared, "You know, niggers will loot." The wrathful Swettenham retorted, "Sir, we have no 'niggers' in Jamaica — only black and white citizens. Take your men off at once." These things, of course, are not known in America: we have a national preference for knowing only the good things about ourselves. They are well known, however, all over the Carribean [sic] and also in South and Central America. And, whatever may be said of the American army, it has less race-prejudice than the navy—in which "Southernism" runs riot. Under these circumstances, control of a Negro community by the Navy Department is seen to be nothing short of a social and civic calamity. During the Danish days there were "superior" and "inferior" people on the islands; but in no instance were they made so by the color of their skin. This doctrine of chromatic inferiors and superiors has been violently thrust upon the islanders by the personnel of the naval administration. In his official report for 1920–1921 one governor ([Sumner] Kittelle) attempts to create "a Negro class" while other Americans have gone even further like the Rev. Mr. [John] Whitehead and Mr. [Thomas] Stribling who (letting the wish illegitimately father the thought) strive to make it appear that the darker people are laborers and the lighter ones middle class. If the lines of social and economic cleavage had at anytime followed those of chromatics some knowledge of this fact might well have been vouchsafed by divine providence to one who, like myself, grew up in the islands. But I know of no such thing.

With such notions it is easy for our naval Americans to believe that *all* white people are fore-ordained to enjoy the prerogatives of rulership while *all* black or mixed-blood people are pre-ordained to obey their orders and serve them to the end of time. This is a rational and defensible doctrine, like that of a war to end war; but then, it must be conceded that it is better suited to sailors and soldiers than to those who administer governments: in that sphere it provokes fiction and causes no end of trouble. And from the very first there has been friction over its application in the former Danish Islands. In the very first week of the American occupation marines and sailors began to assault citizens and shoot up the town.

Perhaps the presentation of one typical case may be valuable as a bird's-eye view of what marine brutality means to the Virgin Islanders. I quote from a St. Thomas newspaper of April 10th 1921.

> The peaceful inhabitants here were treated to another sample of the bravery and soldierly conduct of United States marines stationed here when on the eve of the fourth anniversary of American occupation of the island, a gang of marines went on a rampage for several days, shooting at defenseless citizens indiscriminately.
>
> These disreputable law-breakers went through the streets the first night, assaulting civilians, and badly injuring two.
>
> They were rounded up by Director of Police Nolan and District Chief O'Leary and marched off to the barracks. About two hours later they left the barracks again, armed this time with rifles, bayonets and clubs, evidently bent upon attacking the defenseless men, women and children on the island. They marched through the

streets attacking everything in sight, and when they reached the house of a Mr. J. Gimenez about eleven o'clock that night, the leader, upon seeing Mr. Gimenez's brother-in-law's head in the window, shouted, "Shoot that nigger." Immediately a shot was fired through the window at him.

After terrorizing men, women and children in the downtown section, the marines directed their activities to the Garden, where they let loose a veritable reign of terror.

The Salvation Army, which was holding a revival meeting in the Savanne, were routed by the attacking marines, who threw stones and other missiles at them. After the attacks, civilians picked up clips of loaded cartridges as well as empty shells in several parts of the town. The people here are at a loss to understand what caused this riotous outbreak on the part of the marines. Some attribute it to the fact that the marines feel they can attack Negroes with impunity: others think that it was due to the fact that Governor Oman proposed leaving the island and that there was no restraint exercised over the marines.

According to reports, the casualties amount to nearly a score of severely injured civilians and several who received minor injuries and a number of houses damaged by rifle fire.

None of these marauders have been punished so far, [HH crossed out *and these marauders have been of distressing frequency,*] as they undoubtedly would have been punished had this taken place in the United States—as the Negro soldiers now in Leavenworth prison can testify. But the brutality which is consequent upon helplessness has not been restricted to shooting. Rape, a serious crime hitherto unknown to the islands, began to appear with distressing frequency—the offenders being in every case white. Today the number of illegitimate children is astonishing. Colored girls are insulted with impunity, marines, in many instances, invading the sanctity of respectable private homes. Some of the social consequences are referred to in the official report of ex-Governor [Sumner] Kittelle cited above. He declared that "venereal diseases are [now] very prevalent . . . statistics for several years back show that this increase . . . appeared first in the figures for 1917, co-incident with the arrival of the Americans." Concretely, this is what a naval autocracy must of necessity mean; and this is only one of the reasons why Virgin Islanders want Congress to abolish the naval rule under which they are suffering. They want *responsible* government—responsible to themselves, if possible, and if not, then responsible at least to the United States Congress.

The Congressional Council of the Virgin Islands, recently declared that "we naturally feel civic bewilderment and political uncertainty as to our status. Are we American citizens or American subjects? Until Congress decides we remain mere subjects, suffering from the same civic disabilities as the subjects of Europe's Kings and Asia's Emperors—a status not at all creditable to the democratic integrity of the *republic* which rules our destinies."

Under the present regime criticism of naval autocracy is tantamount to the crime of *lese majestatis beleidigung* as it was understood in Prussia in the days of "the Kopenick Captain." And the Navy frowns upon that crime. Already there have been two deportations on that ground, the [Rev. Reginald G.] Barrow and [G. H.] Morenga-Bonaparte cases, in the latter of which a Negro editor had ventured to reprint a mildly critical quotation from the report of that Congressional Commission which went out to whitewash the Navy in 1921. Meanwhile, out of a population of 26,000, 424 are permitted to vote: neither the 15th nor the 19th Amendment applies to them, although the 18th is in all its rigor and at the cost of tremendous economic suffering. This voting arrangement is the expression of an old Danish law placing a property limitation on the suffrage, which limitation was lifted in Denmark itself many years ago but remained in force in the colony. So, the bulk of the people were denied the right of adult suffrage because American officials, paid from the taxes of the American people are administering the laws of the foreign country (Denmark)—a situation without parallel on earth today. Yet the welcome which the inhabitants gave the Americans when they took over the islands was genuine and sincere enough. Not knowing any better, they expected friendship and co-operation. They had had no previous acquaintance with the psychology of race-prejudice and the harsh superciliousness of the Navy officials has done much to disillusion them.

To this disillusionment the horrors of quasi starvation have now been added. There has been practically no rain during the last three years; the crops have failed in consequence; work has fallen off and wages have declined below the subsistence level. Agricultural laborers find it hard to keep body and soul together on two days work a week at thirty cents a day with the prices of staples as high as they are in the United States. The present distressing poverty and semi-starvation has become a scandal all over the West Indies, and in the British, French and Dutch Islands they are pointed to as an earnest of what may be expected under American rule. Nor is this wholly unjust. For while a part of the present distress may be fairly set down as hard luck and charged to uncontrollable natural conditions a fairly large part of it is due to callous indifference on the part of the American overlords. The manufacture of rum is prohibited here where much of the economic welfare of the people depends upon it, while the prosperous Phillipine Islands are exempted from the operation of the Prohibition Amendment. As if this were not enough, the Navy Department has imposed a number of troublesome port-regulations which have had the effect of driving away four-fifths of the shipping that brought work and wages to the islands. Tariff restrictions on American imports and insular exports are another preventable root of the present depression. Instead of purchasing in the islands such supplies as are available there the Navy imports most of it from the United States and the rest (including fresh vegetables and fruits) from the British islands. Governor [Sumner] Kittelle's report says explicitly that "fruits and vegetables are imported in large quantities from Tortola and other British islands and from Porto Rico where conditions of growth are not markedly more favorable."

The land from which the overwhelming majority of the people must get their living is overburdened with new taxes. While the land-tax in prosperous Porto Rico is $2.50 an acre it is set at $8.27 cents an acre in the impoverished Virgin Islands. And the direct consequence of such preventable conditions is barely hinted at in the ex-governor's report when he says that "deaths of children under one year comprise 25 per cent of all deaths in the Virgin Islands."

Any one who reads intelligently this official record of American rule as administered by the Navy Department (reprinted in *Lightbournes's Annual of the Virgin Islands*, 1923) must be struck at once by the accumulated evidence of a vast disaster that has come upon the islanders "co-incident with the arrival of the Americans," to use the ex-governor's phraseology. Again and again the official figures show that the social conditions of today are worse than those of 1915. Everywhere we hear the melancholy refrain of the recorded facts which tell us that bad as the Danes were painted they never sponsored so much social misery as the unfortunate representatives in mis-management of the Navy Department.

It almost seems as if the present policy of the Navy is to depopulate the Virgin Islands. Faced with starvation if they stay, those working people who can get their passage-money from friends abroad are leaving the islands in droves. If the present conditions and the exodus should continue for two years longer it is hard to see what the Naval Administration will have left to govern except goats, sheep and cattle.

Caribbean Peoples in the United States

83. "Prejudice Growing Less and Co-Operation More, Says Student of Question: Writer of Special Article for Courier Readers Says Immigrants Are Becoming Americanized and Naturalized — Garveyism Has Had Little Effect on Mental Outlook," *Pittsburgh Courier*, January 29, 1927, 2:7.

In this brief overview of West Indian immigration and contributions to America, Harrison points out that "the mingling of West Indian with American Negro has been highly beneficial to Harlem — and to America at large." He also offers an explanation for why West Indian immigrants were becoming Americanized and naturalized and why Garveyism had little effect on their mental outlook.

NEW YORK, Jan. 27. — The destinies of the Negro-American and the Negro West Indians have been tangled and twisted together from the very beginning in this Western world. Too many people forget that what Columbus discovered was the West Indies —

long before anybody discovered America. And African slaves were first imported into the West Indian islands from which practice spread by the Spanish, Dutch, French and English colonies on the mainland. So that the West Indies Negro is an earlier product of Christian civilization than the American Negro.

Back and forth the currents of contact have flowed, now from this side, now from the other, sometimes Negro-American slaves who showed too stubborn a spirit were sold into the West Indies, and sometimes West Indian slaves were sold in southern slave-markets. And at one remove we have a black Santo Domingo regiment saving the white American patriots at the siege of Savannah in our Revolutionary War and hundreds of black American colonists who have settled in Hayti and elsewhere, and have been absorbed into the general West Indian population.

Individually the West Indian Negro has often played a great part in the drama of Negro development here in America. It is exactly one hundred years since the first Negro newspaper was published in America. This was *Freedom's Journal* which was domiciled in New York and edited by John Brown Russwurm, a West Indian and the first Negro graduate of Dartmouth College. But before this time there was Alexander Hamilton, who "passed for white" successfully after coming to America and became one of the Fathers of the country. At a later date there was Denmark Vesey, a Danish West Indian Negro who, although a freeman and property holder, risked and lost freedom, property and his life itself in a slave rebellion which he had organized in Charleston, S.C., in 1822. And more recently, West Indian Negro blood has flowed in the veins of at least one President of the United States.[19]

Today there are more than forty thousand West Indians in the United States of which about seven-tenths live in New York City alone. The concentration has resulted in intensifying the strains and problems of adjustment. The relations between them and their colored neighbors have changed and developed with the kinds and quantity of social control and effective cooperation. In the first period of West Indian immigration, when those who came here were mainly students and scholars seeking wider fields of usefulness, the Negroes of America drew from these some of their first and most favorable estimates of West Indian character, it was taken for granted that every West Indian immigrant was a paragon of intelligence and a man of birth and breeding.

Then came the slump in West Indian sugar, caused by German and American competition and the impoverished islands began to decant upon the mainland their working population, laborers, mechanics, peasants, ambitious enough to be discontented with conditions at home and eager to improve their lot by seeking success in the land of Uncle Sam. At first they furnished the elevator operators, bellboys and porters, maids and washerwomen of upper Manhattan almost exclusively, with a few tradesmen and skilled workers thrusting themselves forward into better positions and breaking the trail for the Negro-Americans to follow. But during the last two decades they have won their way in New York as business men, lawyers, doctors, school teachers, musicians and journalists. Besides, there is the significant fact that almost every important development originating in Negro Harlem — from the Negro Manhood Movement to political representation in public office, from collecting Negro books to speaking on the streets, from demanding Federal control over lynching to agitation for Negroes on the police force — every one of these has either been fathered by West Indians or can count them among its originators. And today the only Negro patron of art and letters in New York is Casper Holstein, a Negro from the Virgin Islands.

Of course it has not always been easy sledding for the West Indian. There has been some prejudice. But that prejudice had worn so thin by 1917 that in the political campaign of that year West Indian and American Negroes were pulling together like two horses in a team, working for the election of James C. Thomas, Jr., to the Aldermanic Board and for the principles of elective representation which has since been accepted by all political parties in Negro Harlem. It was the Liberty League under whose banner the West Indian and American Negroes first cooperated on anything like a large scale; although in St. Mark's and St. Benedict's lyceums in West 53rd street they effected literary combination some years before and in the Equity Congress such stalwarts as Captain Blount, Prof. [David E.] Tobias and Louis Leavelle could always count upon their support in that great movement which gave birth to the "Fighting Fifteenth" [National Guard of New York and Fifteenth Regiment, New York, which became the 369th Infantry Regiment, known in France as the "Harlem Hellfighters," and which won the Croix de Guerre].

It may sound strange to outsiders, but it is my firm belief that, between the ordinary Negro American who lives by working and the ordinary West Indian in America there is not the least prejudice in the world. The working Negro American who lives by work gets that work from the white man, and, as he figures it, the white man has work enough for both. But with the Negro American who lives on prestige the case is different. It is to him a matter of life and death that the Negro masses should look up to him with reverence for the superiority vested in him by virtue of something called "education." He meets the West Indian similarly situated, and finds that whether that educated West Indian be Danish, Dutch, French, Spanish or English, he has been furnished by Denmark, Holland, France, Spain or England with a more thorough and competent intellectual equipment than race-prejudiced America has given to the Negro-American. Naturally, since it is to him a matter of life and death, we find that prejudices take shape in such a situation. But these prejudices seem restricted to the intelligentsia on both sides. I speak, of course, of the men. The cause of the West Indian woman is one which I shall not touch upon just now.

In the meanwhile, West Indian men are marrying Negro-American women in ever-increasing numbers and rearing children who are American Negroes. These are indistinguishable from other Negro-Americans. I presume that most Negro-Americans know of the West Indian ancestry of such well-known Negro-Americans as W. E. B. Du Bois, Charles W. Anderson, collector of Internal Revenue in New York City; of George E. Wibecan of Brooklyn and William Stanley Braithwaite (pronounced in English "Braf-fit").

Despite the general belief, British West Indians are becoming naturalized Negro Americans at a fairly rapid rate. But, whether naturalized or not they certainly do become Americanized — even despite the Garvey movement. They grow into spiritual participation with Negro-America and exchange cultural gifts with increasing facility. If the West Indian brings to the market a certain out-spoken and downright courage, he gains there a certain flexibility and tact which is necessary both for survival and success in the American atmosphere. And when the years bring their harvest it will be found that the mingling of West Indian with American Negro has been highly beneficial to Harlem — and to America at large.

84. "Hubert Harrison Answers Malliet: Replies to Malliet Saying He Did Freely What Other Islanders May Be Forced To: Likes America Because Country Is Democratic; Has 'Fighting Chance' Here Which Is Denied 'Subjects' in Crown Countries," *Pittsburgh Courier*, October 22, 1927, 1:3.

In this *Pittsburgh Courier* feature, Harrison responds to Arnold Mahew Wendell Malliet, a Jamaican writer, who had founded the *British West Indian Review* in 1923. Malliet had written an article in the July 2, 1927, *Courier* emphasizing the relative absence of race prejudice in Jamaica as opposed to the strong prejudice in the United States. Malliet's article was the first in a series of articles written on "Why I Cannot Become Americanized." His series ran until August 13 and centered on a theme he developed in the July 9 issue — that he "came to the U.S. [in September 1917] with high hopes but found race prejudice barring him at every turn."[20]

In the final installment in his series, Malliet argued that "so long as the dominating race philosophy of America remains what it is, so long will I refuse to become Americanized." He thought it "unthinkable that a colored man born outside of the United States of America could enter the country and assimilate American ideas, customs, etc." and "take unto himself the characteristics of white Americans without possessing a mind morbidly obtuse to a proper appreciation of the eternal principles of Justice, Liberty and Fraternity."

Towards the end of his article, Malliet paid his respects to his "scholarly friend, Dr. Hubert H. Harrison" and pointed out that when he consented to write on the subject "Why I Cannot Become Americanized" he did not intend to "open up a controversy." He stressed that "Americanization" had a totally different meaning from "Naturalization," which was not the subject of the discussion. He also conceded that "the economic and educational opportunities offered by America are far greater than those to be enjoyed in the West Indies" and were "sufficient to induce West Indians to come to America." Malliet also wanted it "clearly understood" that he "advocate[d] the most friendly relationship between West Indians and Afro-Americans" and "believe[d] that whatever the attitude of West Indians may be on Americanization they owe it to the welfare of the race to co-operate to the fullest extent with their colored American cousins in their fight for Liberty, Justice and Equality."[21]

On August 13 the *Courier* editors announced, as they had when Malliet's series was set to begin, that Harrison would reply with "Why I Became Americanized." They did not know how long it would take for Harrison to frame his reply, but they imagined it would be "before Christmas," and they would announce his article a week in advance.[22]

In his reply Harrison referred to the United States as "the greatest democratic experiment that the world has ever seen," described the American as a person who was still "evolving," and offered the revealing comment that during the current period of change and unrest he "would not have been satisfied" wherever he lived.

NEW YORK, Oct. 20. — After the Malliet series, which is expositive, we will present the opposite point of view from Dr. Hubert H. Harrison, noted West Indian lecturer for the New York Board of Education who will write on the subject "Why I Became Americanized."

From the above statement in *The Courier* of July 23 I received my first intimation exactly a week later that *The Courier* had matched me to go four rounds with Mr. A. M. Wendell Malliet, no decision. Then, on August 27, I learned that Mr. Malliet's series had come to an end on August 13. All of which goes to prove my own original innocence of any evil intent. I suppose that my own controversial make-up is very highly developed; nevertheless, I do prefer to pick my own fights. Wherefore I beg to remind the reader — if *The Courier* will permit — that I am not engaging in any controversy with Mr. Malliet, but shall leave his friendly presentation of the points at issue between him and American "civilization" to some of those remaining writers for *The Courier* who detest West Indians on principle. I think this a good opportunity to put in evidence that "clannishness" so often ascribed to us, and to suggest that West Indians may be too "canny" (not "clanny") to stage a dog-fight for the enjoyment of the spectators. I shall, therefore, confine myself simply to a presentation, to "the opposite point of view" — in a single brief article.

And, in the first place, please give me leave to wonder whether I am a West Indian at all. Both Mr. Malliet and most Americans assume that a West Indian is a "Britisher," owing allegiance to a British King, and chock-full of British culture; whereas there are Spanish, French, Dutch, Danish and (now American) West Indians. Personally, I have never been British. I was born Danish and am now twice an American; first by my own free choice and next by Uncle Sam's purchase of the Danish islands. I left those islands, finally, at the age of 17 and have lived in New York for 27 years. Here I printed into manhood, became in course of time, the kind of American which I am at present.

I have found here all sorts of Americans. I have found white people who have the usual "cracker" attitude of the British white man in South Africa, smooth white hypocrites like the British white man in Jamaica who pretend and patronize, and white men without a trace of race-prejudice. I have found Negroes who are fawning, docile and slavish, Negroes who "draw the color line," and Negroes who are manly as Mr. Malliet. I have had to contend against black, white and colored people for my place in the sun, and often I have found the whites eager to extend me welcome and recognition where Negroes have not. I have watched American race prejudice fluctuate in its incidence; have seen lynchings decrease, and inter-racial committees increase even in the South, have observed the multiplication of social contacts between black and white people from North Carolina to New York, from Atlanta to Chicago; have seen the strivings of black men — and women, too — from bootblacks to bankers, from coal-heavers, to college presidents; and, after looking the whole scene over, I am more in love with America than with any other place on earth.

I have found here the full measure of manhood not in a nice, fat place prepared for me, but in the opportunity to battle for any place. And although I cannot be President of the United States, I can be what men of my race have been and may be again, Senator, Congressmen, Registrar of the Treasury, Assistant Attorney-General or Minister to Hayti or Liberia. Lawyer, doctor, dentist, teacher, legislator, financier — all these are open to me and to my children, if we care to strive for them, and the future opens before us. And in the meanwhile we are participants in the greatest democratic experiment that the world has ever seen. It is not the American of today that fascinates me, but the American which is evolving out of it. The "cracker" may yelp as much as he pleases, but his descendants and mine will make the future America; they will either live together in peace and prosperity or their conflicts will crack both democracy and America wide open in the presence of the enemies of both. Personally, I bet on democracy — and that's why I prefer to be here. I am so far American psychologically that the mere thought of being a *subject* (however kindly treated) of *belonging* to any human being, be he King or Emperor really fills me with disgust. I like to play my part when voters are being registered and enrolled, to go to the polls on Election Day with the consciousness that my vote is the equal of any other man's in determining the issues of an election and the policies of government. I realize, of course, that there are limitations — just as the magazine called *The Jamaica Critic* informs me that there are for black men in Jamaica, just as there are for the black people in St. Kitts who are not free either to organize a labor-union or run a newspaper of their own, just as there are for the millions of underpaid, down-trodden black people in South Africa. But I realize that, like the white people of England four-fifths of whom were slaves (serfs) down to the 18th century, I and these darker millions must take our places in the rising ranks of color and carry on as we have been doing, striving for, and achieving by our struggles, an increasing measure of the world's respect and consideration. We will not expect anything to be given to us, but mean to fight for what we want.

Of course, we expect to be handicapped by our own ignorance, stupidity and cowardice, by our own inferiority complex and the snobbishness of some of our own people. But I understand that these handicaps also exist in Jamaica and elsewhere, so I doubt that remaining a West Indian would remove them anywhere from my path. And then, too, as a purely sporting proposition, consider that I make my living among these people, that, in some sense, I eat their bread; I partake of their spiritual nourishment such as books and free libraries, free schools, museums, parks, public gardens and recreations. Surely if these things are good enough for me to enjoy they are good enough for me to join in preserving and to give my assistance to the fight against lynching, Jim-Crow, segregation, bad leadership and stupidity. Becoming an American doesn't commit me to the upholding of these baser elements in American life, and if I were to wait until Denmark or any other country had lost all of them I should now be playing pushball in the New Jerusalem.

So I became Americanized (whatever that may mean) — I became an American because I was eager to be counted in the fight wherever I happened to be, to bear the burden and heat of the day in helping to make conditions better in this great land for the children who will come after me. And although I am not SATISFIED with American conditions as they now are, I realize that in these days of change and unrest I would not have been satisfied anywhere else. In China I would be fighting against foreign domination, in Egypt, India, South Africa or West Africa I would be fighting against the British oligarchs, in Jamaica against the sinister repression of black people practiced by both whites and mulattoes, and in the Dutch, French or American West Indies against crackerism, stupidity or cowardice.

BESIDES — when America gets ready to buy the West Indian islands of any European Power the inhabitants, as people who are OWNED, are not going to have any final voice in determining there destiny — any more than the Porto Ricans or Virgin Islanders had. And that is something which they may face in the next thirty years — as I see it. So that I suspect that all the other West Indians will ultimately be forced to do what I did without being forced.

Meditations

Despite a life of extraordinary activity, Harrison was much given to meditative and reflective thought. Sometimes his meditations merely commented on phenomena of life. At other times more careful reflections aimed at deeper understanding of events or concepts. At still other times he entered pithy sayings in an aphorism section of his diary.

In revealing diary entries from 1907 and 1908 Harrison wrote that he preferred "to go to the grave" with his "eyes open" and that if his life was simply one of "eat and sleep and rise again to procure the wherewithal to eat and sleep" he "wouldn't hesitate two hours to put an end" to it. He also commented that "The infinite sorrow in the face of the Christ-man, deeper than unfathomable seas, the face of [Thomas] Carlyle, ridged with the furrows of travail and turmoil; the fire-chastened face of Dante [Alighieri] that bearer of an immortal grief to the regions of underlying woe — these have always had a strange attraction for me."[1]

The following entries are some samples of Harrison's published "Meditations."

 85. "Goodwill toward Men," *The Voice* (December 26, 1918), HHHP Scr A.

Shortly after the November 11, 1918, armistice that ended World War I, Harrison offered an editorial entitled "Goodwill toward Men." It alluded to a lynching — probably that of Mary Turner, which had been reported in the May 18 *New York Times*. Turner, a Black woman from Valdosta, Georgia, was eight months pregnant when she was brutally murdered. The lynch mob had already killed her husband when it took her down an abandoned road, tied her upside down from an oak tree, poured gasoline and oil on her, and burned her clothes off her while she was still alive. The mob then cut open Mrs. Turner, and her premature baby fell to the ground, offering two weak cries before being crushed by the heel of a member of the mob. Hundreds of bullets were then fired into Mrs. Turner's body.[2]

According to the Scriptures the first Christmas Day was ushered in by a chorus of angels singing, "Glory to God in the highest, and on earth Peace and Goodwill toward men!" Peace and goodwill stood always in the forefront of the doctrine of Christ. But the "Christian" nations of today don't seem to care much about the doctrine of Christ. The centers of "white Christianity" are the centers of organized bloodshed and permanent preparation for perpetual war. Beneath the banners of Christendom the fair feet of civilized slayers haven woven across the fair face of the earth a crimson mesh of murder and rapine. Five hundred million Chinese have been driven from their calm and quiet and compelled to arm themselves with Krupp guns to stand off the followers of the Prince of Peace!

And what of Goodwill? Here in our own land, the hook-wormed helots of the Anglo-Saxon south drop into Africa to mark their belief in the brotherhood of man, and then go out to roast a gravid Negro woman, to chop off her fingers and toes to serve as souvenirs, to rip her body open and trample the unborn babe beneath their cow-hide boots by way of proving how well the religion of Christ has sweetened their souls. The meek and lowly Nazarene loved even those who murdered Him; but the Anglo-Saxon race in this country has neither love nor goodwill for its fellow-citizens — when they are of Negro blood.

The coming of Christmas helped to make us see the great gulf fixed between Christianity and Christ, between the all-embracing charity of the carpenter of Nazareth and the cruel, stubborn pride, the vicious race-prejudice, the hatred and intolerance of the white savages who take His name in vain in the twentieth century of the "Christian" era.

It was said of Jesus that "He was despised and rejected of men, a man of sorrows and acquainted with grief"; and if there is again value in this fact then is Christ nearer this Christmas Day to the despised and down-trodden Negro than to his haughty Anglo-Saxon oppressor. And the Negro people may find some consolation in the fact that it is the custom of the Destiny that governs in the affairs of men to put down the mighty from their seats and to exalt them of low degree.

Ethiopia shall stretch forth her hands, and the Negro, stolen from his Fatherland, degraded by his oppressors, may (when the wheel of fortune turns) be again the companion of the gods and the chief of Heaven's favorites.

86. "Meditation: 'Heroes and Hero-Worship, and the Heroic in Human History,'" *Negro World* (October 16, 1920), HHHP Scr B.

In this insightful *Negro World* "Meditation" Harrison builds on the work of the Scottish essayist and historian Thomas Carlyle's *On Heroes, Hero-Worship, and the Heroic in History* (1841). Harrison offers that heroes are looked to for shaping and guidance that leads the world to "fuller realization of its latent powers and hidden inclinations." Heroes have stern responsibilities and must follow the bent of their own natures, not "the course mapped out . . . by the multitude." They should, adds Harrison, be willing to incur the "hounds of slander and the curs of foul abuse."[3]

At sundry times and in diverse manners man has made God in his own image. From the beginning until now most men have worshipped something set above themselves in honor and dignity and power. Sometimes this god-like glory burned in the blue sky above them; sometimes it was a divinity dwelling beyond the stars in a temple made without hands; sometimes it took visible form in idols of silver and gold, or even of wood and stone; sometimes it blossomed in their loftiest thought as "God the Invisible King." But whatever form it took its substance was the same: It was the best that man could see in himself. This he abstracted and offered homage to. Thus, the best in him, thrown bravely in advance, tugged at the lagging rear guards of his soul and dragged them ever onward. And thus his god (or good) has nearly always served as a dynamic ideal to lift man further from the mud and nearer to the stars.

Viewed in this light the doctrine of the incarnation, shared by many religions, is a tribute to the deepest truth and the most ancient spiritual fact. For the divinity that dreams within us often awakes to reality in the life of some other person in whom we perceive a greater measure of the same effulgence. As old [Thomas] Carlyle put it:

> Know that there is in man a quite indestructible reverence for whatsoever holds of Heaven, or even plausibly counterfeits such holding. Show the dullest clodpole, show the haughtiest featherhead, that a soul higher than himself is actually here: were his knees stiffened into brass, he must down and worship.

Hero worship is a tribute which humanity pays to its better nature. It changes with the stress of times and circumstance, and the Hero bears always the imprint of the age that brought him forth. The Christ of Calvary makes no great impression in a world of willful murder nor the bloody God of Battles in a period of peace. The jealous Jehovah thundering from the clouds of Sinai is a fit deity to preside over the dark destiny of a robber race which was dispossessing peaceful pagans from their native lands. And as with gods even so it is with heroes. Buddha, Mohammed and Cromwell; Caesar, St. Francis and Charles Darwin are all the embodiments of social tendencies peculiar to particular ages. Each in his own way and for his own time led the world to a fuller realization of its latent powers and hidden inclinations. Their own humanity looked up to them for guidance, shaping and control.

But such leadership carries its own stern necessities of duty and responsibility. Truly has Milton told us that "he who would write a heroic poem must be himself a true heroic poem." He who would be a Hero must be a true heroic soul, rising like a mountain-peak into the circumambient air dwarfing the common hilltops by the very majesty of its elevation. And this is no idle figure; for the Hero must rise to heights of spiritual grandeur in which he will have perhaps no cheering companionship. He must follow the bent of his own nature and not the course mapped out for him by the multitude. So only can he dwell with God above the clouds "in private duty and in public thinking."

And that is one reason why Heroes are so very rare. For it is the virtue of the crowd to be crowd-minded, and the hounds of slander and the curs of foul abuse often follow yelping at the heels of him who dares to venture on the Better way. It is humanity's eternal tragedy that its Heroes who were worshipped after death were most often in life the very

> "souls that stood alone
> While the men they agonized for
> hurled the cotumelious stone."

But,

> "Humanity sweeps onward: Where
> today the martyr stands,
> On the morrow crouches Judas with
> the silver in his hands;
> Far in front the cross stands ready
> and the cracking fagots burn.
> While the hooting mob of yesterday
> in silent awe return
> To glean up the scattered ashes into
> History's golden urn."

But that imminent tragedy deters no high heroic soul from pursuing that straight and narrow way in which we travel only single file. And, after all, this is humanity's costlier process of learning by experience. The love which they lavish on those who have borne the burden and the heat of the day is but their little alter to the Unknown God whom, therefore, they ignorantly worship.

87. "The Meditations of Mustapha: A Soul in Search of Itself," *Negro World* [?] (c. October 23, 1920), HHHP Wr.

Around October 23, 1920, Harrison handwrote the self-revealing piece, "The Meditations of Mustapha: A Soul in Search of Itself," which opened with lines from Tennyson's *In Memoriam* (XCVI). This material, prepared for a talk to be delivered at the People's Forum, is as close to offering a personal creed as Harrison came. In it he puts forth his beliefs and describes his approach which, while seeking "to prove all things where proof is possible," is also willing "to suspend judgement where there is no proof."

> "Perplext in faith, but pure in deeds,
>   At last he beat his music out.
>   There lies more faith in honest doubt,
> Believe me, than in half the creeds."
>
> *In Memoriam.*

Kind Christian friends are wont to assume that all those who fail to share their faith disbelieve also in goodness and give up those virtues which help to lift us all higher when they give up the ancient dogmas; and they firmly believe that all those outside the shelter of their fold are bound to a sad and sordid materialism of the flesh. Yet the examples of great and good men in all times, from Socrates to Spencer and from Hadrian to Huxley, might plead for a more neighborly estimate. It would be pushing the point too far to insinuate that a good pagan may be better than a good Christian, but surely it is safe to say that he is no worse. In the humble words of Thomas Atkins:

> "We ain't no thin red 'eroes
> And we ain't no blackguards too,
> But single men in barricks
> Most uncommonly like you."

And, perhaps, if we could see into one another's souls we might find that we could respect each other even "across the gleaming gateways of the morn." But it does require something of nobility to be able to do this; something of that spiritual self-respect which stands at salute in the presence of respect in others.

> "Be noble; and the nobleness that lies
> In other men, sleeping, but never dead,
> Shall rise in majesty to meet thine own."

To help in forwarding the dawning of the larger day one of these souls who have wandered in search of themselves (because such was their destiny) has presumed to set forth something of its find of faith and unfaith, of strange desire and desperate opinion on the primal problems of the meaning and the mystery of this life to which no traveler from the great beyond has yet brought back a key.

I believe in Man my brother, his duties and his rights. I believe in the sacrament of sacrifice in giving myself in varying degrees to those who are about me; first to my friends, secondly to my race, next to my country, and lastly to Humanity. I believe that man should not live by bread alone. If to eat and sleep and dress, to run the gamut of selfish success and to play at precedence with a next-door neighbor were all that there was to live and labor for I would as lief be dead. For if these were the ends of life wherein would man be higher than the brutes?

. . . to be tolerant of all men's honest opinions while holding by my own; to follow after the truth as it is given me to see the truth; to prove all things where proof is possible and to suspend judgement where there is no proof; to continually diminish by knowledge the number of my prejudices and to give even the devil a hearing before condemning him; to live my own life in my own way, with pleasure to myself if possible and if not, with satisfaction at least; to try my best to make this world a little better for my being in it, and to pay back to Nature something of what was expended in putting me here; to keep my face toward the light and my feet in the way of that Nobler Life — these are my principles which if I fail to keep I hope for the charitable forgiveness of mankind, since no man was ever as good as his creed.

To subsist in the grave — or elsewhere — until the day of resurrection, or to live on forever and from everlasting unto everlasting, is something for which I have had no relish even as a child. To live for a few hundred years beyond my mortal term might indeed engage my thoughts and win me to seeming assent. But, however the poet may sing, the heart of man, undriven by the dogmas of his creed, longs for some *final* resting place and finds it not in the grave which opes again. To lay down once for all the burden not of life but of *existence*; to make an end of being; to be done with life, its sorrows and elations, its golden tints and deeper shadows; to be done with pain and pleasure, good and evil, contentment and care; to quaff the cup of Lethe and decline into an endless oblivion — this is, to me, a blessed boon and privilege greater than all the blessings of an immortal life.

> "From too much love of living,
> From hope and fear set free,
> We thank with brief thanksgiving
> Whatever gods may be
> That no life lives forever;
> That dead men rise up never;
> That even the weariest river
> Winds somewhere safe to sea.
>
> Then star nor sun shall waken,
> Nor any change of light;
> Nor sound of waters shaken,
> Nor any sound or sight;
> Nor wintry leaves nor vernal,
> Nor days nor things diurnal;

> Only the sleep eternal
> In an eternal night."

 88. "On Praise: From the Arabic of Abulfeda, Prince of Humah (in Syria), 1328. Done into Modern English by Hubert H. Harrison," *Negro World* (January 1, 1921), HHHP Scr 35. [Abū al-Fidā (1273–1331), also called Abulfeda, was an Arab historian and geographer who fought against crusaders (1285–98) and was the Prince of Hamāh (1310–30).][4]

On January 1, 1921, Harrison, as associate editor of the *Negro World*, used his Contributing Editor column to open the year with "On Praise." This commentary brings to mind Harrison's criticism of Garvey for preferring fawning followers over critically thinking associates as well as his own dislike of cajolery and wheedling. It suggests why Harrison's intellectual bent and personality characteristics may have placed limits on his becoming a mass leader in the style of Garvey.[5]

If there is one thing I hate next to lying and hypocrisy in human beings it is praise coming from human beings. Through most of life it has been a hard medicine to swallow. The first dose bewilders, the next annoys, the third irritates and the added installments make me feel murderous. And yet I believe I am quite human. I do enjoy the kindly appreciation of my elders and the critical appreciation of my equals. But this spiritual pawing over one's soul by the soiled hands of every chance comer is a thing abhorrent to me.

Why will people obtrude their praise on one? Why should they be so silly? Do they think that (outside of artists, poets and women) people do worthwhile things for praise? I really think that if most of them could know how it nauseates they might be induced to withhold their sentimental slobberings over the thing that they like to enjoy.

I understand, of course, that most people are different. Well, I am what I am and I don't want to be different. I therefore have no apologies to offer on the point. I hate the praise of people because I look upon nine-tenths of it as sniffling insincerity, and therefore an insult to my intelligence. And then, too, I despise it when it takes the form of crowd approbation because I appraise it at its true value and recognize it as merely a momentary mood and fashion of their shallow souls. And I can understand now how a beautiful and clever woman must despise men.

Lynching, the Klan, "Race Relations," and "Democracy" in America

During the early twentieth century lynching was unquestionably one of the issues of most concern to the African American community. Lynching figures compiled by Tuskegee Institute indicate that the number of African Americans lynched was more than 100 in 1900, the year that Harrison arrived in the United States, and still stood at 60 in 1918 and 76 in 1919. Harrison was convinced that militant direct action "at the places where lynchings occur" and "at the times when they are attempted" and the withholding of labor power through migration were key steps to ending the brutal horror. He also consistently advocated enactment of federal antilynching legislation and enforcement of the Fourteenth and Fifteenth Amendments.[1]

Lynching and the Ku Klux Klan

The Ku Klux Klan was started in Pulaski, Tennessee, in late 1865. It served as a local regulator of white vigilante organizations that sought to maintain white supremacy and often functioned disguised and in secrecy. The Klan terrorized, often through lynching, recently emancipated African Americans in the South. Federal intervention supressed the Klan in the 1870s, but it was revived in 1915 by William J. Simmons (the son of an original Klan leader) who served as imperial wizard until 1922. The revived Klan grew slowly in the South until 1920 and then became a nationwide phenomenon with significant influence in Oregon, Texas, Indiana, Wisconsin, and other states. It was also active in New York and New Jersey. By 1924 the Klan, with a program of white supremacy and opposition to African Americans, immigrants, Jews, Catholics, radicals, and trade unions, was positioned to make a major, though unsuccessful, effort at determining the Democratic party's presidential candidate.[2]

As the new Klan grew and lynchings increased, Harrison directly challenged it in his writings and in his public talks. He thought that it was important to expose Klan history and practices and to urge direct action and militant self-defense as a means of ending lynching and Klan terror.

89. "A Cure for the Ku-Klux," *The Voice* (January 30, 1919), HHHP Scr A, reprinted in *When Africa Awakes*, 36–38.

In its *Tenth Annual Report* for the year 1919, the National Association for the Advanced of Colored People outlined the areas on which it planned to undertake work. It emphasized that "lynching must be stopped" and explained that "Many Americans do not believe that such horrible things happen as do happen when Negroes are lynched and burned at the stake. Lynching can be stopped when we can reach the heart and conscience of the American people. Again, money is needed."[3]

As the Ku Klux Klan grew and lynchings continued, Harrison became utterly dissatisfied with such an approach. He believed it was necessary for African Americans to take direct armed action and to meet the KKK on its own ground. In the following *Voice* editorial, written in January 1919, he offers "A Cure for the Ku Klux."

It was in the city of Pulaski in Giles County, Tennessee, that the original Ku-Klux Klan was organized in the latter part of 1865. The war had hardly been declared officially at an end when the cowardly "crackers" who couldn't lick the Yankees began organizing to take it out on the Negroes. They passed laws declaring that any black man who couldn't show three hundred dollars should be declared a vagrant; that every vagrant should be put to work in the chain-gang on the public works of their cities; that three Negroes should not gather together unless a white man was with them, and other such methods were used as were found necessary to maintain "white supremacy." When the national Congress met in December, 1865, it looked upon these light diversions with an unfriendly eye and, noting that nothing short of the re-enslavement of the Negroes would satisfy the "crackers," it kept them out of Congress until they would agree to do better. Finding that they were stiff-necked, Congress passed the 14th and 15th amendments and put the "cracker" states under military rule until they accepted the amendments. The result was that the Negro got the ballot as a protection from "the people who know him best."

In the meanwhile, the Ku-Klux after rampaging around under the leadership of that traitor, General Nathaniel B. Forrest, was put down—for good, as it was thought. To-day, after the Negro has been stripped of the ballot's protection by the connivance of white Republicans in Washington and white Democrats at the South, the Ku-Klux dares to raise its ugly head in its ancestral state of Tennessee. This time they want to increase that fine brand of democracy which every coward editor knows that Negroes were getting when they were bidding them to be patriotic. The Ku-Klux means to shoot them into submission and torture them into terror before they get to showing their wounds and asking for the ballot as a recompense.

In this crisis what have the Negro "leaders" got to say on their people's behalf? Where is Emmett Scott? Where are Mr. [Robert Russa] Moton and Dr. Du Bois? What will the N. A. A. C. P. do besides writing frantic letters. We fear that they can never rise above the level of appeals. But suppose the common Negro in Tennessee decides to take a hand in the game? Suppose he lets it be known that for the life of every Negro soldier or civilian, two "crackers" will die? Suppose he lets them know that it will be as costly to kill Negroes as it would be to kill real people? Then indeed the Ku-Klux would be met upon its own ground. And why not?

All our laws, even in Tennessee, declare that lynching and white-capping are crimes against the person. All our laws declare that people singly or in groups have the right to kill in defense of their lives. And if the Ku-Klux prevents the officers of the law from enforcing that law, then it is up to Negroes to help the officers by enforcing the law on their own account. Why shouldn't they do it? Lead and steel, fire and poison are just as potent against "crackers" as they were against Germans, and democracy is as well worth fighting for in Tennessee as ever it was on the plains of France. Not until the Negroes of the south recognize this truth will anybody else recognize it for them.

> "Hereditary bondmen, know ye not
> Who would be free themselves must strike the blow?"

90. "Ku Klux Klan in the Past," *Negro World* (September 24, 1921), HHHP Scr B.

On September 6, 1921, the *New York World* began a three-week exposé of the Ku Klux Klan that was researched by Rowland Thomas. The series focused on Klan violence, estimated Klan strength at half a million, and was carried by eighteen leading papers around the country. While the report was partly responsible for an investigation of the KKK by the Committee on Rules of the House of Representatives, it and the hearings also helped to publicize the Klan. In the September 24, 1921, *Negro World* Harrison applauded the "good work" of the *World* "in exposing the Ku Klux Klan of today," but pointed out that the paper's editorial writers were "just as ill-informed concerning the facts of American history as most educated Americans are."[4]

While the *New York World* is doing good work in exposing the Ku Klux Klan of today, we fear that the writers of its editorials are just as ill-informed concerning the facts of American history as most educated Americans are. Their justification by concession of that band of bloody midnight assassins which terrorized Negroes in the South from 1865 to 1870 reveals an abysmal ignorance of the proven facts of that period and causes educated black men to wonder whether educated American whites ever read any source-books of information on American history. To come straight to the point. Speaking of that earlier band of bloody brothers, the *World* says:

Nobody familiar with reconstruction legislation will deny that there was justification for the Klan's political activities, although its methods in innumerable cases were brutal, criminal and indefensible. Its practices of intimidation were uniformly cowardly, and it was tolerated by decent Southerners only because they were living under an autocratic government imposed upon them by Federal bayonets and were ready to use any weapon on which they could lay their hands. . . . The Ku Klux Klan of Reconstruction days even at its worst represented an organized resistance to political oppression only.

We do not argue that this view is either unjust or dishonest, we merely insist that it isn't true. The facts are recorded in that very report of the Congressional Committee of Investigation to which the *World* makes reference, but which we sadly conclude that it has never read. We do not wonder at this for the collection of ponderous tomes dealing with the different States is indeed a formidable thing to tackle. However, there are other records in print which are easier of access. We name the following at random: James G. Blaine's *Twenty Years of Congress*, volume 2; William Garrott Brown's *The Lower South in the Civil War*; Alexander Johnson's article in *Labor's Cyclopedia of American History*; Carl Schurz's Report; the series of articles in *The Nation* in 1865 and 1866 contributed by its then editor, Edwin Lawrence Godkind, and the third volume of Prof. Albert Bushnell Hart's *American History Told by Contemporaries.*

A perusal of these volumes will show that the Ku Klux Klan was organized in 1865 (the date *is* very important), during the interregnum between the dastardly murder of Abraham Lincoln and the convening of Congress which took place in December of that year. During that period the people of the South were given an absolutely free hand to deal with the Negro and their other domestic problems as they should see fit. And this is what they did:

They (who had been defeated) proceeded to pass laws reducing the Negroes to a new condition of serfdom more galling and hopeless than slavery had been. For instance, in Alabama and elsewhere it was decreed that any slave who did not possess $350 cash should be declared a vagrant, taken into custody and sentenced to hard labor on the public works for six months. Blaine described this as "the meanest piece of legislation on the statute books of any civilized State." By this labor the city of Mobile was rebuilt, and many another southern city. Negro children were ordered "bound out" to their former masters to work without pay until they were twenty-one. It was made a crime for three Negroes to converse together; they were ordered not to practice the trades of carpenter, wheelright, blacksmith, etc., unless they could first pay to the state several hundred dollars.

All these things were done during the summer, fall and winter of 1865. And it was during that period that the Ku Klux Klan was organized. The date is approximately fixed by the testimony of Gen. Nathaniel B. Forrest, who became its head upon the first general reorganization of the Klan. There is also the testimony of William Garrott Brown in his book mentioned above, and that of [John C.] Lester and [D. L.] Wilson, two Klansmen, in their book on the Ku Klux Klan [*Ku Klux Klan: Its Origin, Growth and Disbandment*].

But if we have the date of its organization thus fixed, it is an evident absurdity to argue, as *The World* and so many others do today, that the Klan was organized to put down "black supremacy," or to keep the Negroes from the ballot box. For the Southern Negro was not given the ballot box until 1866 [HH changed this to *1868*]! Indeed, it was the attitude of the South toward the Negro as illustrated by the Ku Klux killings and whippings, and the legislation above described (the celebrated Black Code), which forced Congress to give the ballot to the Negro in order that he might be able to protect himself from the unreconstructed slavists.

When Congress met in December, 1865, it considered the Black Code and the other facts of the situation. It found that, if the fruits of victory were not to go to the losers in the conflict, it had to take some drastic steps. The first of these steps was the passing of the Thirteenth Amendment to the United States Constitution, forever abolishing slavery; since Lincoln's proclamation was only a war measure and did not free all the slaves. It made the acceptance of this amendment a condition precedent to re-entry into the union and submitted it as such to the conquered Confederacy. But the South would not accept it. As Congressman James A. Garfield said, "The last one of the sinful ten, (I quote from memory) has flung back into our teeth with scorn the magnanimous offer of a generous nation."

There could be no better indication of the rebels' intentions toward the Negro. Congress thereupon divided the South into military districts, each of which was under the command of a major-general of the United States Army, and proceeded to elaborate and enact the Fourteenth and Fifteenth Amendments, and to govern the rebellious States under martial law until they should accept the three war amendments. And, in the meanwhile, the government strove to effect civil reconstruction. When, finally, in 1868, the South was reconstructed, the Negroes, as the largest body of people who were loyal to the United States, aided by white ex-soldiers from the North and a handful of white Southerners played, of necessity, a large part in that process, and it is noteworthy that, within less than two years from the time that the Negro got the ballot, the Ku Klux was disbanded.

Such are the essential facts of history as they relate to the Ku Klux of the past. In *The World* of last Sunday (11th inst.) Col. N. F. Thompson, a former Klansman, tells us that "I became a member of the Klan in 1866, as did nearly every Confederate soldier." And yet white Americans of education, as ignorant of their country's history as "Colonel" [William J.] Simmons and Tom Dixon, keep repeating that the earlier Klan was really organized "to save white civilization from the domination of ignorance." Isn't it high time that white Americans cease being so grossly ignorant of the facts of their history? I submit that the substantial truth of the account given above can not be controverted except by those fanatics who improvise their facts.

And now what of our Negro "scholars" and near-scholars, professors, educators and journalists? How is it that they have never set forth these facts, but have accepted instead the historical glosses of white people from James Ford Rhodes to *The World's* writers and readers? We can only conclude that they themselves are grossly ignorant and have never done any independent study of the original sources of American history as it affects their race. What is the use of prating about "alien education" when we are either too lazy or too monkeyfied to sift facts for ourselves? The Negro race needs real scholars and real students now as it never did before, and they must come from this generation of Negroes. Let us hope that they will take the hint.

And in the meanwhile let us remember that if the revived Ku Klux had not gone out and meddled with Catholics, Jews and other foreigners no great newspaper would ever have organized its forces to hunt them down. It is the duty of our editors and publicists to point out now that in regard to disfranchisement and other things, if white Americans ignore them because they only affect Negroes, the time must come, sooner or later, when these things will also be set in motion against whites. On that basis we can enlist their self-interest to investigate and squelch those other things now. Intelligent statesmanship for the weak consists in making allies of the strong who stand within the same danger.

91. "How to End Lynching," *Boston Chronicle* (June 28, 1924), HHHP Wr.

In the first half of 1924 Harrison wrote a "Trend of the Times" column for the *Boston Chronicle* while he sought to build his new organization, the International Colored Unity League. His June 28 column on "How to End Lynching" reflected his belief in the need for direct action when and where it occurred. The action could be armed, it could be the action of withholding labor power, or it could be the action of migrating. He also saw little prospect in appealing to the kindness or Christianity of whites, and, in something of a departure from his Liberty League days, he urged African Americans outside the South to focus on enforcement of the Fourteenth and Fifteenth Amendments rather than on any new legislation.

Lynching is the greatest of our outdoor sports for just one reason: it is the safest. Any decrease in the safety of it must inevitably decrease its attractiveness and popularity. The Negroes have the greatest stake in the reduction of lynching; and any steps toward its decrease must therefore be initiated by us. Most lynchings occur in the South and it is to the Southern Negro that we must look for direction against lynching. We in the North can only help indirectly, and to pretend otherwise is only to deceive our Southern brothers and delude ourselves.

But how can lynching be abolished? First by direct action: That is, action on the job — at the places where lynchings occur; at the times when they are attempted. The Southern Negro has already decreased lynchings by more than 50 percent by the action involved in migration from the places where most lynchings occurred. By migration from those places he has utilized a power absolutely within his own control. By affecting the production of wealth he has struck a body blow at the most powerful interests in the South and has compelled them to exert their influence against lynching. And he has done this without a single petition or appeal to the kindness, the Christianity, or the democracy of the white folk.

Not that there have not been such appeals. But those appeals were always the product of certain groups of Northern Negroes. Yet it is clear that lynching cannot be stopped from a distance. Certainly it can never be stopped by wasting money on "publicity" whether that "publicity" takes the form of fervid appeals to a moral sense which exists only on paper, of indignant protests, or bombastic ravings. Neither can lynching be stopped by national legislation. The 14th and 15th Amendments are portions of the United States Constitution — infinitely more sacred and powerful than statutes-at-large. If they cannot be enforced what chance has any mere Congressional enactment?

When the Ku Klux Klan of the nineties rampaged in West Virginia the Federal Government sent soldiers and put them out of business. Only the revenue from whiskey was involved; but the Government found that it had an interest in law-enforcement then. If we Northern Negroes were really sincere in the desire to give genuine though indirect help to our Southern brothers in putting down lynching, we would so use our votes in [HH has crossed out *Virginia*] Ohio, Indiana, Pennsylvania and New York, as to make the administration find an interest in enforcing the 14th and 15th amendments. And until we develop courage enough to do that we shall ourselves be the political monkeys that we are at present. We don't need a single new law: only the enactment of what we already have. For with the two amendments enforced either the South will become so weak politically that it will be unable to oppose liberal legislation from the North; or the Southern Negro, having won the ballot, with Southern governors, judges, sheriffs and militia responsive to their votes, will be able to solve for themselves the problems of lynchings, Jim Crow, Education and all other problems that some of us in the North make a living by pretending to solve for them. In any case our one best bet is to concentrate on the enforcement of the 14th and 15th Amendments.

"Race Relations"

Throughout the 1920s Harrison wrote pieces commenting on aspects of race relations in the United States. Though he recognized that "race" was a "shifting reality," and though he favored a scientific approach to problems, he also realized that on the subjects of "race" and "race relations" even science could reflect bias and be used to lie and deceive. His efforts were directed at exposing falsehoods and at breaking from existing race-relation patterns under which African Americans were expected to act in subordinate ways. One step in this process was to end the practice of having a selected African American serve a white or whites as an "index" of Black thought. The following pieces are examples of Harrison's writings in these areas.

92. "The Negro and the Census," *Negro World* (August 27, 1921), HHHP Scr B.

Harrison was particularly critical of the United States Census, which he considered "a lying document so far . . . as the Negro population is concerned." In the following editorial he cites the 1850 census which was used to argue that the African American population would die out by 1922 as part of a larger effort at "subverting the spirit of the subject races and classes."[5]

The recent letter of Professor Kelly Miller to the Director of the Census, which was published in the *New York Age*, brings again to our attention the fact that the white men of America habitually tell lies about the Negro people.

It is said that figures don't lie; but it is a notorious fact that liars do figure — especially in the census office. As far back as 1850 this falsification of figures will be found. If Professor Miller will consult Mrs. Stowe's greatest book, *The Key to Uncle Tom's Cabin*, he will see there detailed proof of this falsifying. The case was brought up in the United States Senate at the urgent request of the American Statistical Association. But despite the revelations of deliberate lying, these errors were not corrected and the controversy [was] forgotten. The present Director's aversion to correcting the errors is thus seen to be part and parcel of a definite purpose historically established.

Of all the available instruments of control in the hands of the white overlords the lie is the most effective for subverting the spirit of the subject races and classes. And in the case of the English-speaking Negroes it has been used with deadly effect. In the case of the census it is obvious that the people classed as Negroes have increased and are increasing far beyond the comfortable expectations of the whites. In *DeBow's Review*, on the basis of the census of 1850, it had been prophesied that the Negro in America would have died out by 1922. Here, as in so much American "science," the wish was father to the thought. Now, as a matter of fact, if it had not been for the great tide of white immigrants into America from 1800 to 1921, this country would have had a population largely Negroid. It is said that the breeding powers of the Negro are so great that he can double his own population in half the time required by the whites. Therefore the whites who are in authority are worried at this power of expansion, especially in the face of the shrinkage in the birth-rate of the American whites.

Lynching, race riots, degradation and slums having failed to decrease their numbers, white physicians have had to do their share in recommending operations which leave Negro women incapable of child-bearing. But the increasing host of Negro physicians defeats that move and the whites must fall back upon their great [HH crossed out *god*] Lie, to help them to a spurious appearance of triumph. Hence the census figures.

But we Negroes must let it be known that the great U.S. census is a lying document so far, at least, as the Negro population is concerned, and that it stands discredited.

 93. "Bridging the Gulf of Color," c. April 22, 1922, HHHP Wr.

Around April 1922 Harrison prepared a lecture, "Bridging the Gulf of Color," which he sent to Ernest Crandall of the New York City Board of Education in support of his desire to be hired on a regular basis as a lecturer. The talk discussed the inadequate "social contact" between Blacks and whites and how the gulf between them worked against "adequate exchange of correct information," which was a "first desideratum" for improved "race relations." Harrison argued that "until white and black know each other better there can be no bridging of the gulf that divides them." On April 22 Crandall wrote to Harrison that the piece was "startlingly illuminating" and its "conclusion inescapable." He was hired as a staff lecturer for the Board of Education later that year.[6]

One of the most regrettable features of the great American race-problem today is the wide gulf existing between the mind of the Negro and the mind of the Caucasian. When we consider that the existing relations between white and black are far from satisfactory and that any improvement in these relations must be the joint product of the better minds of both groups, the permanent existence of such a gulf seems little short of disastrous. If we could throw a bridge across this gulf the tides of mental traffic that would flow over it in both directions would tend to improve and stabilize the relations between the two races and reduce to a minimum the friction of new and necessary adjustments.

At present the lack of such a bridge is felt on both sides. White investigators of interracial matters are often amazed at the great differences in quality between the standards of their own race's output and those of the Negro's. They find classes in Howard University taking elementary lessons in civics and calling them courses in sociology. They find Negro sociologists and economists restricting their "science" to the compilation of tables of statistics in proof of Negro progress, and Negro "scholars" still expressing the intellectual viewpoints of the eighteenth century. They read Negro newspapers and like Stephen Graham, they find school-boy errors in English in every paragraph and bushels of "poetry" like the following which was approved by a colored graduate of Yale and Harvard:

> "Lord God do thou arise
> And let us all unite
> with one accord.
> Jesus doth thou adore
> And bless us Evermore
> Sing praises and sing prayers
> Let freedom Reign."

And they wonder at these things. But it is easy to account for them. Christian America created the Color Line; and all the great currents of culture and ideas which have been making for self-criticism, from the 18th century to our own time have found that great gap impassable. Behind the Color Line one has to think perpetually of the Color Line, and most of those who grow up behind it can think of nothing else. Even when one essays to think of other things that thinking is tinged with the shades of the environment. Add to this the fact that in South Carolina, which is a typical Southern state, each Negro child gets in Lawrence county 97 cents worth of education a year; in Bamberg, 89; in Saluda, 68; and in Calhoun, 58 cents worth—and the differences in quality of output between the higher levels of both races will be easy to understand. Unless the stream of modern ideas can flow unhindered through such a mass it will continue to be a backwater in which cultural crudities take root; and when able intellects arise among Negroes, like Alain Leroy Locke, the scholar, William Browne, the mathematician, and Ernest Just, the biologist, their superiority, unperceived by their own race, escapes the assessing observation of the whites; and so, lack of proper recognition, fails to exert its full force as standard and example.

But the white race also suffers. In the good old days white people derived their knowledge of what Negroes were doing from those Negroes who were nearest to them; generally, their own selected exponents of Negro activity or of their own white point of view. A classic illustration of this mode of "Knowing the Negro" is afforded by the Republican Party—which is now paying the penalty by losing the Negro vote in New York, New Jersey, Maryland and other states. But the Episcopal and Methodist churches, the Urban League, the white heads of the N.A.A.C.P. or the United States government would serve as equally good examples. Today the white world is vaguely but disquietingly aware that Negroes are awake, different, and perplexingly uncertain. Yet it retains its traditional method of interpreting the mass of Negroes by the one nearest to itself. The results so far are not encouraging. White publicists in magazines and the daily press seem to alternate between bovine placidity in the face of developing dangers and recurrent fits of the jumps when they see their own shadow. It is amusing to well-informed Negroes to observe the gullibility of which news-gatherers in the presence of hysterical developments on the other side of the Color Line. It so often happens that their Brocken specter is but the magnified and distorted shadow of their own ignorance and fears.

But this is not all. There is such a thing as the wiliness of the weak. It is easy for those who have learnt wisdom in the school of slavery to play up to the racial egotism of the Caucasian. Subserviency is often the goats-horn on which the fox climbs out of the well. And the Negroes who know this are not all on the lower levels. Booker Washington was a case in point. Undoubtedly he was a great man. But he was also astute. It was his astuteness which pointed out the way to greatness; by fawning and flattering the whites he got their assistance and so was able to serve his race successfully.

Then there is the case of Bert Williams, the actor. It is hardly reasonable to expect, when we take a people as inferiors, as the butt of our jokes, that we should allow representatives of that people to become the recipients of our serious admiration and applause unmodified by a due sense of our own superiority. The comedian ministers to our own enjoyment in the capacity of an inferior — as: mountebank. Wherefore we will accept Negro comedians, but hardly Negro actors in the legitimate drama. For Bert Williams the way to personal success lay in flattering the white people's sense of superiority by always playing the clown. Had he done otherwise the tens of thousands of dollars which finally found their way to his pocket would have remained in the pockets of the whites. When Cole and Johnson at the Fifth Avenue Theater in the fall of 1910 appeared before white audiences in unobtrusive evening dress with an act of "high class" singing, piano playing and clever dialogue their audiences fell off suddenly. It didn't pay. Then they made a quick change back to the standard of "A Trip to Coontown" — fair part: Success.

All this was done on the level of honesty. But below that level the thing is done by millions every day. If white people could overhear the opinion of their sapience expressed by their colored servants and henchmen in the privacy of their homes they might soon realize that "inferiors" may dupe and despise their "superiors" — and "work" them for "a good thing." In this atmosphere of deception and ignorance mistrust maintains herself and the seeds of race-hatred and race-riots spring up in her footsteps to embitter the permanent relations between the two races.

"The fathers have eaten sour-grapes, and the children's teeth are set on edge" and we of today must straighten the racial tangles which our fathers have bequeathed to us. In the first place there should be some way in which Black men can speak to white men across this gulf before either or both can hope to bridge it. Correct information must somehow come across from the black man's world. It hardly seems much to concede, yet white men must be willing to let unfettered black people interpret to them the facts and situations of the black world. Whether it be Ray Stannard Baker, Carl Sandburg, Mr. [Herbert] Seligmann or Professor [Robert] Kerlin, no white man can understand and interpret the Negroes to white people as well as black men who live behind the Veil. Provided of course, that the black men are as well-equipped as the whites. And white America would do well to realize that, here and there, there are black men in our country as well-equipped mentally as any of the white men mentioned. But these men have not in their past been free to function as interpreters of their world. Before a Black man could get a hearing he had to be somebody's man, whether that somebody was a Vesey Street Liberal, or Northern millionaire or a powerful politician; and as somebody's man he could only tell somebody's truth — not the truth which is now necessary to a better understanding. (If American newspapers and magazines want this truth they should assign Negroes to the task of interpreting for their reader the trend of events among Negroes and the drift of the current of Negro thought and feeling. But these Negroes must be free. That is the only guarantee which the whites can have that these blacks are *not lying to them* for their own advantage.)

And in the meanwhile, white America must be willing to make a genuine gesture of friendship to the Negro people, not as a mawkish condescension but as a human investment for safety sake. When Southern white men burn to death a gravid Negro woman and trample to a pulp her unborn babe do white Americans know that thousands of Negro mothers pledge their children to purposes as far from playful as was that of Hannibal's youthful oath? When Negroes who fought in France for a democracy denied them on their return to Florida, do white Americans know anything of their deep and dark resolutions in the event of war with a nation that isn't white? It is a visiting Englishman who points out for them the truth which they ignore when he says: "Destiny is being shaped in this race and white men are the instruments who are shaping it. May it not emerge eventually as a sword, the sword of the wrath of the Lord?" Suppose that revolutionary disturbances among them should synchronize with revolutionary disturbance among the whites themselves, or with a foreign war? Surely these matters are worth serious thought and earnest efforts toward some bridging of the gulf.

At present such social contact as exists between both people is furtive and surreptitious except on the lower levels as in the dives of northern cities and the plantations of the south where white men who have "an instinctive aversion against compromising the purity of their race" manufacture the millions of mulattoes who testify against them. On the higher levels the social approach is a thing of diffidence. One may sometimes find Negroes and white commingling on temporary terms of social and intellectual equality at the Sunrise Club in New York and in a few radical organizations in some of the Northern cities, notably in Boston and Chicago. And as late as six years ago there met every Sunday at Lenox Casino in New York a lecture forum made up of hundreds of cultivated whites who had selected as the leader and teacher a man of undiluted Negro blood. Here and there one finds black doctors who have white patients, black lawyers with white clients and black teachers with white pupils. But, on the whole, the amount of social contact is not extreme enough to guarantee any adequate exchange of correct information. And correct information however it may come is still the first desideratum. For whatever theory of racial relations may be the correct one, it is only by the fruits of knowledge that the correctness of such theory can be tested. And until white and black know each other better there can be no bridging of the gulf that divides them.[7]

94. "At the Back of the Black Man's Mind," submitted to *New Republic*, c. November 1922, HHHP Wr.

Around November 1922 Harrison wrote "At the Back of the Black Man's Mind," prompted by a casual conversation with Robert Littell, editor of the *New Republic*. The article "rushed in where angels feared to tread," discussing such topics as "the undivulged pretense," the "slave inheritance," the inferiority complex, color prejudice, lying and laughter, playing to racial egoism, the "spot-light artist," and "the exclusive exponent."

Of particular interest is Harrison's depiction of the two large mass meetings at the UNIA's Liberty Hall during the 1921 New York City municipal campaign. On November 3, John F. Hylan, the Democratic mayoral candidate and eventual victor, addressed a crowd at Liberty Hall. The following night the Fusion party candidate, Henry H. Curran, a Republican lawyer, former alderman, magistrate, borough president, and reporter for the *New York Tribune*, spoke at Liberty Hall. The *New York Times* and the *New York World* reported the crowd to be thirty-five hundred people. At that event, sponsored by the Manhattan Republican Club, Curran attacked William Randolph Hearst and criticized Hylan for his "subserviency" to Hearst. The audience cheered Hylan and hissed, screamed, catcalled, and threw fists and chairs after Curran's comments. In his official statement after the event Curran praised the "colored men and women of Harlem" as "orderly, good and patriotic citizens" and blamed the disorder on "a few Hylan agents" in the crowd. Harrison describes both events as "cases of political thimble-rigging."[8]

The quixotic idea implied in the title of this article emerged from a casual conversation with the editor of the *New Republic*; although my memory is not quite clear as to whether the initial impulse toward this indiscretion came from him or from me. I only recall that when I left the office I stood committed to this project of rushing in where angels feared to tread. And I remember pleading in deprecation that the people of my putative race (I am black) would tear the scalp from my quivering cranium if they should see this thing in print. I think I was assured that the white race (among whom I have many thousands of friends) would protect me in such an event. But when I intimated that it was my intention to be no less disrespectful to certain subliminal certitudes of white people than to those of Negroes, the editor threw up his hands and commended me to the care of that kindly Providence which always looks after little children, drunken men and fools. And so, like Banquo:

> "In the great hand of God I stand, and thence
> Against *the undivulged pretence* I fight."

Those who would feel better for not believing any of "the secrets of the prison house" which I may reveal are respectfully admonished in advance that they need not. An opportunity to tell the truth is a privilege so rarely proffered to a black writer that I gladly dare even the damnations of the professional colored men for the sake of the luxury. For, let it be said in the first place that the professional colored man always maintains "the undivulged pretence" as against any white friend or foe. Always his soul is on parade, dressed up for inspection, like the belle at a ball who maintains a simulated unconsciousness of the "Killing" effect of her silks and laces or the "fetching" qualities of her powder and paint. In short, the individual Negro when under inspection maintains a pose through which very few of his white friends can pierce. This pose, however, is no bar to an adequate comprehension of the "race problem," which concerns the relation between white people on the one hand, and black and colored people on the other and which need take no note of the essential nature of the souls of either. And that is why some white *simpaticos* who understand the Negro problem assume that they understand the Negro. I trust that before I get through I may satisfy even these that they don't.

In setting out on what may prove to be a perilous expedition to the Lares of logic; and before getting to the back of the black man's mind I shall first explain what that mind is. The first obstacle in the way is that of the kind-headed people who imagine that race is not a [HH crossed out *social and*] psychic reality just because there is no point at which one can say: "here is the true dividing line, on the one side of which you have one thing for certain and on the other something different." But that position is easily turned; as for instance: Between 4 and 9 a.m. there isn't a single second of which anyone can truthfully say: "This is the precise point at which night ends and day begins." Yet the difference between day and night is a very obvious reality. True, the difficulties of the very queer thing called "social psychology" are misused by those other extremists who talk about "the Teutonic mentality," "the race-mind of the Anglo-Saxon" and the "Aryan consciousness." But we leave them to [Jean] Finot and [John] Oakesmith and [Alexander A.] Goldenweiser, and proceed on our way—

In the first place, then, the "mind" of the American Negro of today is largely embryonic; a great psychic smear, as of something rubbed out or rubbed off with nothing to replace it except the other fellow's mental furniture to which the rooms are not yet quite adjusted. For instance: it always happens that the gods that men make are made in their images: the gods of yellow men are always yellow; of brown men, brown; of white men, white; and of black men (in Africa), black. The only racial group of whom this is not true is the Westernized Negro of the United States and the West Indies. It has always made me laugh to hear them singing: "Wash me and I shall be whiter than snow." But it is a bit tragic when that same subversion of an ethnic ideal works itself out in the forms of "Kongolene Knocks Kinks," "Bleach Your Black Skin" and those ghastly advertisements of a similar sort with which Negro newspapers are replete—in America. Let the *reason* be what it may, the *fact* remains that the Westernized Negro (of whatever nationality) is what the white man has made him—a psychic hybrid—and his struggle for self-expression must take place in a house spiritually divided against itself. [HH has deleted a substantial section]

No matter how it was made to happen, the fish swims because it must move about in water and the bird flies because it must move about in the air. Our environment develops in us characters to suit. The environment which the white man provided for the black was that of slavery and subjection. After three hundred and fifty years the slavery was removed: the subjection remained. If social environments shape psychic characters then it is non-sense to suppose that there has been no slave-inheritance for the Western Negro. Ask yourself why was John Brown overpowered? Because the Virginia slaves did not rise as he expected. And why didn't they rise? Because the whips of slavery had beaten the heart out of them. Again, what is the greatest *moral* claim of American Negroes? That, even after Lincoln had issued a proclamation declaring them free and specifically calling on them to rise and do something; when their masters were at the front fighting to keep them in slavery—the slaves of the South never struck *one* violent blow in their own behalf. That is the *boast*! Would the Irish, Greek, English or any other white group *boast* about such a thing? They have never done so. *The Slave Inheritance, then, is a substratum of Negro consciousness.*

Now, it is obvious, that those who are robbed of rights and power turn to guile and deceit. That is why most judges won't believe women on the witness-stand. The Negro is no exception, and it is here that his strength lies. He had to pretend and pose and express everything but his real thoughts and feelings; and it has now become a second nature to him. The particular individual may have studied at Oxford, Yale or Gottingen; he may be a "scientific radical"; a suave symbol of pseudo-culture, or a New York legislator—if he is of the stock that Lincoln freed, it is ten to one that he will always pretend and never own up to the freightage of original evil which he now knows is in his cargo.

But there are other products of the slave-psychology besides those already mentioned. For instance, there is no color prejudice in America—except among colored people. The writer of this article writes for the *New York World*, the *Tribune*, and *The Nation*. The editors of those journals, like the editor of the *New Republic*, require assurances only on the two points immediately germane. Does he know? Can he write? They care nothing about my color. Even if they had race-prejudice they would then refuse my writings altogether because of my being a Negro. They wouldn't care whether I was a light one or a dark one. But I would be "too dark" to get employment at any but one Negro paper or periodical in New York. There are Negroes who keep the white newspapers warm with their protests against what they call, with unconscious humor, the color-prejudice of the whites. Some of them make very good livings at this sort of thing. In their published writings they are as black as the proverbial ace of spades. But you will find that they have their own "light" churches as in Washington, "light" graveyards as in Charleston and "light" social sets as in New York. And it may as well be said here that this contempt for the Negro's characteristic color is fully shared by the black people themselves. Yet one will find no reference to this dominant obsession in the writings or speeches of those who "represent" the race. It is considered very bad form to see the grinning head of the skeleton in the closet.

Another slave-product is the inferiority complex — that consciousness of unimportance which needs the aid of garish uniforms, swords, strutting and "big-talk" for its temporary suppression. This connects with a somewhat distorted sense of reality which makes "supposed to be" the most frequently-recurring phrase in any discussion between Negroes dealing discursively with allegations of fact —

But all this is not to be taken as evil. Far from it. We have the twin gifts of lying and of laughter; of pretence and poetry wherein consists our real claim to consideration. For always, side by side with developing civilization, there has developed some means of escape from the pressure of present reality; whether rum, reason, religion or morality; which latter does not consist so much in doing the right thing as in telling the right lie. The Negro, like any other eastern race, has what the cold and critical western white calls "a vivid imagination." And this, when the western Negro shall have developed self-reliance and a soul of his own, will count for much. At present, even with what he has he manages, in the expressive vernacular of the day, to "put it all over" the white man. How? In this way:

The white man — especially the Anglo-Saxon — is keen on the assertion of his own superiority. The Negro has learnt how to play up to this racial egotism of the white, by flattering which he often gets some of the durable satisfactions of life. A few, striking illustrations should occur readily to the American reader. Such things are rendered easy by the traditional methods of inter-racial contact. When the uplifting agencies, rich philanthropists, big politicians or professional "friends of the Negro" wish to establish contacts with the race in America they select one Negro to serve as the exclusive exponent of Negro activities. These are always pre-digested in his own consciousness before he passes them on into theirs. As a "spot-light artist" it is not to his interest to reveal to them the existence of any other personality in the background or any disturbing element in the order of things which they have complacently schematized by multiplying him ten million times to represent "the Negro." If such white people could overhear the opinion of their sapience which is expressed everyday by their colored savants and henchmen in the privacy of their own homes they would soon realize that "inferiors" may dupe and despise their "superiors" and "work them for a good thing." But they never venture to "check-up" on their bell-weathers; and, consequently remain blind—and workable. Politics will furnish many amusing illustrations. For instance:

During the last week of the municipal campaign of 1921 in New York the two largest mass-meetings ever held among Negroes in America were held in Liberty Hall, the home of the adherents of the Back-to-Africa movement. In both cases the hall had been hired by politicians; the Democrats held their meeting on Thursday night [November 3], the Republicans on Friday night. Both were cases of political thimble-rigging. The hall holds three thousand people and is filled nearly every night in the week by Garvey's crowd—who have no votes, being for the most part aliens. It was this same crowd, plus about 400 possible voters, who filled the house on both nights. But this, although known to the canny colored local leaders, was not even suspected by the white politicians who naturally gave great credit to the local party-riggers for turning out such a multitude of voters to listen to them. But although the Garvey people hadn't votes, they had plenty of the local feeling in regard to politics. So they applauded the Democrats with enthusiasm on Thursday night and Garvey himself spoke in their behalf. But when Major [Henry H.] Curran and his Republican team-mates attempted to speak for their ticket the next night they were heckled, hissed jeered and booed. The reserves were called out and the meeting broke up in disorder. The audience was expressing the deep detestation in which the Republican Party is held in Negro Harlem. But of this detestation—which was wide enough to reach even the remote non-voters—the official Republican Party hadn't an inkling. They had been successfully duped by their dark "inferiors" whose cleverness they had held in collective contempt. And let it not be supposed for a moment that the Republicans are alone in this matter. There are others—although *they* have not yet discovered themselves.

Even our dear old Uncle Sam is not exempt from this exploitation from below. For he (or the Republicans for him) maintains in Washington a "kitchen cabinet" of three colored appointees who act as almoners for the distribution of such crumbs of patronage as may be left over for Negro uses. These men are generally selected from those sections of the south in which the Negro is not permitted to cast his vote; to the end that they may be doubly dutiful, subservient—and despised. Yet when a well-known black Boanerges [Marcus Garvey] wished to return to this Land of Easy Pickings, and the white man's government held him at arm's length away from is shores, it was these three that (unbeknown to Uncle Sam) heard the tempting tinkle coming from the royal mountebank's coffers, hurried to get some golden grease on their hands and wrought so connivingly at the office of State that orders were issued to let him in. And to this day those same men have been able to baffle all the special agents of a certain department and to keep their private provider from coming to trial. So that, on the whole, the white man can hold the black man to be a fool only at the risk of becoming himself the fool of this fool. And in America today the black man finds the white man such an "easy mark" that it is small wonder when the white man wakes up and discovers what really is at the back of the black man's mind that he rushes out in a red rage and kills him. And that is when the high gods really laugh.[9]

"Democracy" in America

As a Socialist, Harrison considered "the Negro the touchstone of the modern democratic idea" and suggested that true democracy for African Americans would imply "a revolution startling even to think of" (selection 8). In 1920 he described the "cant of democracy" during World War I as "a convenient camouflage behind which competing imperialists masked their sordid aims," as "dust in the eyes of the white voters," and as "bait for the clever statesmen" who were "fishing for suckers." He emphasized that those who proclaimed the new democratic demands never had any intention of extending "democracy," but, their slogan came back to "plague" them as the oppressed millions demanded that democracy "be made safe for them."[10]

Several years later, in a July 28, 1926, speech before the Bronx Rotary Club on the "New Americanism," Harrison again insisted (as he had for his entire adult life) that "the Negro is the touchstone of all our democratic pretensions in America." He described America as a "great experiment in democracy," "unique in the history of the world," and he predicted that "the great American experiment" would determine "whether we can make out of the welter of races and nations one people, one culture, one democracy." He thought it possible, and his remarks received thunderous applause.[11]

This dual awareness—of the misuse of "democracy" and of democracy's great potential—is evident in Harrison's writings on the subject and emerges in the articles that follow.

95. "'Democracy' in America," *Negro World* 11 (October 8, 1921): 3, HHHP Scr B.

In an October 1921 letter to the editor of the *Negro World* Harrison commented that "white [capitalist] civilization" oppresses laborers and "deserves to die." Developing this theme further, one week later he wrote "'Democracy' in America" in his column. It expresses a lack of faith in American democracy and contains one of his most powerful critiques of "capitalist imperialism" and the "color line." The analysis also contains strong criticism of the "cynical indifference" of the leaders of the Christian church.[12]

All over the world today the subject peoples of all colors are rising to the call of democracy to formulate their grievances and plan their own enfranchisement from the chains of slavery—social, political and economic. From Ireland and Armenia, from Russia and Finland, from India, Egypt and West Africa efforts have come looking for their relief from the thralldom of centuries of oppression. Of all these peoples the darker races are the ones who have suffered most. In addition to the economic evils under which the others suffer they must endure those which flow from the degrading dogma of the color line, that dogma which has been set up by the Anglo-Saxon peoples and adopted in varying degrees by other white peoples who have followed their footsteps in the path of capitalist imperialism; that dogma which declares that the lands and labors of colored races everywhere shall be the legitimate prey of white peoples and that the Negro, the Hindu, the Chinese and Japanese must endure insult and contumely in a world that was made for all.

Here in America we who are of African ancestry and Negro blood have drunk this cup of gall and wormwood to the bitter dregs. Our labor built the greatness of this land in which we are shut out from places of public accommodation; from the church, the ballot and the law's protection. We are jim crowed, disfranchised and lynched without redress from law or public sentiment which vigorously exercises its humanity on behalf of the Irish, Armenians and Germans thousands of miles away, but can find no time to concern itself with the barbarism and savagery perpetrated on black fellow citizens in their very midst. This cynical indifference extends to the leaders of the Christian Church, the high priests of democracy and the conservative exponents of the aims of labor. Thus, the Negro is left out from the plans being put forward by these groups for the reorganization and reconstruction of American affairs on the basis of "democracy."

We Negroes have no faith in American democracy and can have none so long as lynching, economic and social serfdom lie in the dark alleys of its mental reservations. When a President of this country can become famous abroad for his preachments on "The New Freedom," while pregnant Negro women are roasted by white savages in his section of the South with not one word of protest coming from his lips; when a church which calls itself Christian can grow hysterically "alarmed" over the souls of Christians brutalized and their souls blasted while it smirks in gleeful acquiescence; when "the aims of labor" on its march to justice exclude all reference to the masses of black workers whom conservative labor leaders would condemn in America to the shards and sweepings of economic existence—when such things represent what happens every day in a "sweet land of liberty" where "democracy" is the great watchword, then we Negroes must be excused for feeling neither love nor respect for the rotten hypocrisy which masquerades as democracy in America.

Miss Mary Kingsley used to say that she did not believe that Christianity could be a solution of the African's problem "because, while it may be possible to convert Africans *en masse* to Christianity, it is not possible to so convert Europeans." This still remains substantially true. But since Europeans insist that the religious system which they preach and practice must be called Christianity, we who regard it with unfriendly eyes must make a distinction between the religion of Jesus Christ and Christianity. We venture to believe that the religion of Jesus Christ would be a good thing not only for Africa, but also for Europe. But this queer thing called Christianity does not benefit Europe and America and is considerable of a curse to Africa. It is in Christian Europe and America that we find most hatred and race prejudice, greed, obscenity, drunkenness and organized bloodshed and banditry.

Why, then, will Christian ministers turn their backs upon iniquity at home and have such a fine eye for it in Africa? If they really wanted to preach Christ it seems to us that there is room enough and need enough in Christian lands.

The African Negro who is not quite the fool that some of his kind friends think, knows, as they know, that it is only when Christianity comes into his continent that gin comes with its blight and degradation; that it is only where Christianity goes that prostitution finds an entrance with its dirty diseases that destroy life or make it a living curse; he knows that when Christianity reaches him he loses the land on which he lives and must become a landless legal bondservant to the white Christians of all sorts; he knows that whereas all true believers are equal under Islam not only "in the sight of God," but in the sight of the magistrate, and in every civil right, Christianity, as organized and made effective in all her institutions, from the church to the jail, insists that only white men are men and that Negroes especially must be treated like dogs, whether kindly or cruelly. The African Negro knows this; the missionary and his friends know it; and the African knows that they know it. Is it any wonder, then, that when the missionary and his fellow Christians speak to the African at home of "the stability of the Christian Church" and her intention "to establish herself *permanently* as the *consistent* guide in the evolution of the higher African civilization," the African answers in the words of one whom the Christian Church crucifies anew each day by its deeds: "Thou hypocrite! first cast out the beam from thine own eye, and then shalt thou see clearly to cast out the mote from thy brother's."

We cannot quite understand the ground on which white Christians offer Christianity to the black African. We *can* understand why white capitalists insist on taking capitalism to him. It is something at least which they have tried. It *works* among them and since they like its products there they are willing to take the same system elsewhere in expectation of the same products. But can the white missionary justify his religion in the same way? Does not charity begin at home? And how are things at home? Have white women in Europe (including the queens) stopped smoking cigarettes and drinking cocktails? Do they still snatch each other's husbands as a pastime in the upper classes, as the newspapers daily tell us? Isn't there still a jail population in every Christian country? And do not the atheists and agnostics and rationalists exist by the millions at home? The legislators like [David] Lloyd George and the "sinister liars" like Lord [Edward] Grey who plunged millions of British Christians into a bath of blood — have the missionaries yet succeeded in teaching them "the love of Christ, who dies to save all men?" Has Christian love at home been strong enough yet to reach the suffering children of Russia and include the Soviet ruler, Lenine, in its ample bosom? And if these questions disturb and trouble the hearts of honest men "at home" what can be the reason for this fervor of faith in behalf of the conquest of pagan lands by the creed of Christiandom?

The truth is that the work of the white missionary, like that of the white soldier is dirty work. We will be told that there are and have been noble missionaries like [David] Livingstone and Dan Crawford. We admit it. And there are and have been noble soldiers like [Thomas J.] Stonewall Jackson and [Charles George] Chinese Gordon. But that fact has not altered the character of the work of the soldier, which is to carry destruction wherever he may be sent to carry it irregardless of the innocence of the "enemy" or the guilt of their own government. In the modern European state every institution is used by the dominant class to some end which contributes to the general social purpose of that class. It is not necessary that any personal part of such institution should understand the purpose of his calling. Quite possibly he may idealize his own intents and aims; indeed, it is better for his masters that he should not see them as his masters. Then he can be quite "sincere," earnest and spiritually-minded. But the facts remain. The missionary's function is to spread what form of religion which will soft-soap the soul of black Africa so that the business of robbing and ruling it shall become less costly and less dangerous to those who do the robbing and the ruling. That such work is necessary is especially conceded by "liberals" like Sir Sydney Olivier, Sir Harry Johnston, the Liverpool Chamber of Commerce and a certain wing of the Aborigines' Protective Society.

For this purpose the "infidels" like Johnson, Olivier and Putnam Weale [Bertram Lenox Simpson] join hands with the fervid believers of the National Liberal Club to missionarize the African into contentment and submission while the robbing and ruling go forward. In his book, "*The Conflict of Color*," Mr. Putnam Weale states the naked truth nakedly and explains why "infidels" like himself and Sir Harry Johnson are so keen on backing the Cross against the Crescent. And, finally, the Secretary of the American Board of Foreign Missions, the Rev. Dr. [Cornelius Howard] Patton, tells us in his missionary handbook, "*The Lure of Africa*," just what we might have expected after studying the political work of the missionaries in Uganda and Lubaland, namely, that one missionary is worth more than a battalion of soldiers to the white government inasmuch as he keeps the black African from organizing his discontent in ways that endanger the permanency of the white man's rule. And he explains that that is the express reason why the British government is putting the education of the black African more and more into the hands of the white Christian missionary. The African knows this and that knowledge explains why, after five hundred years of Christian contact with Africa, only four million of its two hundred million inhabitants are nominally Christians — from which number we must deduct a million and a half white Afrikaners in South Africa.

96. "The Negro and the Nation," Address by Dr. Hubert H. Harrison of the Lecture Bureau, Dept. of Education, New York City, Thurs. June 21st, 1923 — By Radio Broadcasting of American Telephone Telegraphic Co., HHHP Wr.

On June 21, 1923, Harrison lectured from handwritten notes on "The Negro and the Nation" over the radio for the Lecture Bureau of the Department of Education (which frequently referred to him as "Dr.," though he had earned no such degree). In his diary he noted that this "unique" talk was on the most powerful radio station in the Eastern United States, the American Telephone and Telegraph Company's WEAF. In the lecture Harrison argued that the "destiny of the American Negro lies in the future of America," a nation whose physical and spiritual chararcter was still emerging, and, in a direct challenge to Garvey and others, he added that the strands of the Negro's soul "are woven into the fabric of our national existence and no mere demagogue can untwist them."[13]

We Americans are a composite people and have been from the beginning, when Swede and Spaniard, Dutch and English, German, French and Irish were helping to make the country in which we now live. And today the melting-pot includes men of many races: Nordic, Slav, Latin, Celt, Jew, Negro and Red Indian. All these and their descendants have fought at various times to keep this country free and to make it great and united. All these things involve mutual forbearance, the endeavor to understand and be understood by one another, the practice of the great democratic principle of "live and let live." For all these different stocks came trailing clouds of custom and tradition from other climes, with different habits of thought and feeling which had been built up into the spiritual fabric of their lives.

Did all these have to be whittled down to one common standard quality, or did they persist to contribute their special values to the composite American character? The simple truth is that both processes are and have been at work. An American character, physically and spiritually one, is emerging from this complex of cultural forces; while at the same time each contributes its special gifts toward the building of that national character. The Irish, the Jew, the Italian have enriched America by being what they are and have themselves gained from the normal interplay of forces which have been at work on them and around them. Thus the fingers of Fate have been shaping us on the iron anvil of necessity into the outline of a great experiment in democracy that will yet make these United States the herald of the Dawn that is to be.

It is from this point of view that I shall endeavor to present the subject of "The Negro and the Nation." It is not my intention to discuss "the Negro Problem" in the traditional manner. For such a discussion must of necessity involve and evoke sentiments and feelings which may stand in the way of that wider appeal which I wish to make. The point of easiest penetration is not always the point of most effective entrance. So we must consider the question of the relations between black and white in America like neighbors who realize that they must live together and are willing to take counsel together in a neighborhood spirit as to the ways in which they may get the greatest value out of their relationship. And perhaps it would be well for us to begin at the beginning.

The American Negro antedates American democracy. When the Pilgrim Fathers arrived in the Mayflower the Negro had been here for more than a year. He had come to America on the most pressingly urgent invitation that would not be denied, and when he reached these shores the first Virginia Assembly had not yet begun to legislate. Indeed, under the Spanish *conquistadores*, the Negro was here long before any of the people of Anglo-Saxon stock. So that the Negro is very near to being the oldest American in our melting pot. And if length of residence can strengthen a claim to consideration then the Negro should seem to deserve more from America than most of the other Americans. Unfortunately, he had come here as a bond-servant, as the man farthest down, who had to do the nation's dirtiest work and get for it no more than food and blows. Nor was this unfortunate for the black man alone; it was even more unfortunate for the white men who took part in that social evil and its tragic consequences. Because the white Americans of 1791 acquiesced in the slavery of black Americans, white Americans in 1861 had to slay each other by hundreds of thousands. This was the moral retribution for "following a multitude to do evil" — and our account is not yet closed: It was Abraham Lincoln who told us that "If God wills that [the war should] continue until all the wealth piled by the bondman's 250 years of unrequited toil shall be sunk, and until every drop of blood drawn by the lash shall be paid by another drawn with the sword, as was said 3000 years ago, so still it must be said, 'The judgments of the Lord are true and righteous altogether.'"

America will never forget that great Civil War. But America sometimes forgets the part which the Negro played in that conflict. 180,000 Negroes volunteered "to help keep the jewel of liberty in the diadem of freedom" and gave their blood and bodies to cement the bonds of union. In a letter to Charles D. Robinson of Washington, dated August 17th 1864 Lincoln said, "Drive back to the support of the rebellion the physical force which the colored people now give and promise us, and neither the present nor any coming administration can save the Union. Take from us and give to the enemy the hundred and eighty thousand colored persons now serving us as soldiers, seamen and laborers, and we cannot longer maintain the contest. The party which could elect a President on a War and Slavery Restoration platform would, of necessity, lose the colored force; and that force being lost, would be as powerless to save the Union as to do any other impossible thing."

If Lincoln's words were true, then America would seem to owe a tremendous debt of gratitude to the Negro; and the Negro's long record of loyalty and patriotism has been added to that debt. His blood has dyed the battlefields of the Revolutionary War, the War of 1812, the Civil War, the Spanish-American and that other war in which he went 3000 miles across the ocean to help "make the world safe for Democracy." No white soldier who fought in the World War will forget the record of Colonel [William] Hayward's regiment, "The Fighting Fifteenth," or that of the 8th Illinois, under [Otis] Duncan, its Negro Colonel. For these regiments were decorated with the Croix de Guerre, as military units, on the fields of France by those who had seen them fight.

But the record of the Negro's co-operation with his white fellow-citizens has not been restricted to the work of War. "Peace hath her victories no less renowned than war," and in these victories too the black man has played his part. He has given us our only bona-fide American music; our world-beating cotton crop is raised by his labor and for the most part on his land. The lines of his economic advance since slavery show us a commendable industrial activity, an increasing ownership of homes, scores of banks and life-insurance companies, many of them doing a business of more than a million dollars a year. Along cultural lines we see him represented in education, religion, art, science and the professions. He has created out of the hidden forces of his nature, at the call of need, his own group-organizations: churches and church schools, law-and-order leagues, fraternal-bodies and that greatest of Negro civic bodies, the National Federation of Colored Women's Clubs.

And all this has been achieved in the face of repressions, restrictions and handicaps such as are imposed on no other race in America. Jim-Crow cars still mock his attempts to assume that dignity and self-respect which should characterize the bearing of every man who calls himself by the proud title of American. A policy of educational starvation in certain parts of our country condemns his children to 89 cents worth of education a year. Disfranchisement crushes his political aspirations, while the odor of fricasseed freemen go up in daily offering to the unwinking skies. This is not as it should be. There is an eternal obligation resting on the white man of America to help and not hinder the black man in his efforts to make the best of himself. And this is not an obligation of charity but one of self-protection. "The strong imagine that they have a mortgage upon the weak, but in the domain of morals it is the other way. We so often complain that virtue and intelligence are not safe in the neighborhood of ignorance and vice. God means that it should be so. So only does he take bonds of the mighty to do justice to the weak." The white man brought the Negro here against his will and all the Negro's problems are, therefore, of the white man's making. Not until the white man has spent his last surplus dollar and exhausted the last faculty of his brain in the effort to lift up his weaker brother can he stand in the presence of infinite justice and complain of the ignorance of the black.

And yet it is not all dark on that side of the scene. Even in Dixie the day is beginning to dawn, and in the southern cities and colleges the better minds of that section are coming together in the new spirit of neighbors rather than masters of plan to make America better by making that American better who is their nearest neighbor. In the presence of these indications it becomes the duty of the white man of the north to set his face like flint against any attempt to make him give ground against invading prejudice; for thereby he will be helping to hold up the hands of that better element in the south which serves as the keepers of its nascent conscience. At the present time the North offers to the Negro better opportunities of civic advancement than the South does: the effect of this appears in the migration in ever-increasing members from the South, which must eventually compete with the North for Negro labor by offering better opportunities in turn.

The northern cities afford the Negro all available facilities for education, opportunities for civic advancement, respect for his manhood and citizenship and safeguards for decency. Northern philanthropy even reaches down into the south to help the Negroes there, as the Jeannes, Stokes and Carnegie funds have shown. The Roman Catholic Church has also begun to send teachers among them to build schools, industrial schools and colleges while individual Catholics like Sister [Katherine Mary] Drexel of Philadelphia and Monsignor [John J.] Burke of New York are spending themselves heroically in the service of the Brother in Black.

Typical among Northern cities in its treatment of the Negro is our great metropolis of New York. There, the public schools offer to his children the same high grade of education which they offer to other children — not in segregated buildings but in the same class-rooms where early contact breeds civic good-will and inter-racial tolerance and appreciation. The two great free colleges, City and Hunter College, are open to his sons and daughters, who, on completion of the prescribed courses, may teach in the city's public schools. New York's dental and other clinics under the efficient management of the Board of Health are available to Negro children as to others, and the free milk stations which are maintained by the municipal authorities and by public-spirited citizens like Nathan Strauss and Mrs. William Randolph Hearst, conserve the health and save the lives of black babies as well as white ones.

The rights of civic participation; the ballot and elective representation, are enjoyed by the Negro in New York. They have a representative — their third — in the state Assembly, they are represented in the Board of Alderman. One of the Civil Service Commissioners [Ferdinand Q. Morton] is a Negro and one of the Assistants to the Corporation Counsel. There are over 40 Negro policemen and two detective sergeants, scores of school-teachers, and hundreds of Negro employees in the Municipal Civil Service. Dr. Earnest L. Crandall, Supervisor of Lectures of the Department of Education has placed on his staff of lecturers the black man who writes these words. In our city the average Negro gets justice in the courts, freedom from mob-violence, freedom to work out his own salvation and the opportunity to rise in the world to the measure of his own abilities. The New York doctrine is the democratic doctrine: not grudging justice but helpful co-operation to the end that the Negro American may always have more to give whenever America calls.

What is the significance of all this? It is that the Negro is an integral part of the American nation: not a mere incident or problem. The strands of his soul are woven into the fabric of our national existence and no mere demagogue can untwist them. The destiny of the American Negro lies in the future of America and no one need think that he will mortgage that future for the sake of a barbaric dream of African Empire with Dukes of Uganda and Ladies of the Nile. The present Negro population of Africa is quite able to work out its own salvation on the spot. And while the racial heart of the American Negro will always beat in response to the call of the blood, he recognizes that he is part and parcel of the American civilization. It is here that he has been the burden-bearer; having borne the burden and heat of the day he intends to receive the wages due him here for that work. He has endured through slavery and serfdom, has survived Jim Crow, lynching and lies.

But these are changing times, and the burden bearer has lifted up his eyes to behold in the east the dawning of a better day. As he gazes, the pink shimmer of the dawn gives place to the golden glow of sunlight which suffuses the morning sky with the promise of enlightenment. And in the sunshine of that promise he prepares to slip his burden and to run with freed feet in that great race where nations and races strain toward the glorious goal of Liberty. Let me conclude with a few verses from the late Mrs. [Ella] Wilcox who has so eloquently summarized the moral obligations of the white race in America and the spiritual strivings of the Negro. . . .

10

Literary Criticism, Book Reviews, and Book Reviewing

A major venue for African American criticism in the 1920s was the NAACP's *Crisis* magazine. Reviews and criticism were provided by editor W. E. B. Du Bois with additional contributions offered by Jessie Redmond Fauset and William Stanley Braithwaite. In his 1921 article "Negro Art," Du Bois articulated his influential position on the merging of aesthetics and politics, arguing, "We want everything that is said about us to tell of the best and highest and noblest in us. We insist that our Art and Propaganda be one." Related to this was his notion that the more intelligent and advanced leadership class in the African American community was that represented by the Talented Tenth.[2]

Harrison contested these positions. He challenged the idea that art had to elevate and repeatedly claimed that he viewed drama as a mirror of the social soul. He saw the masses and the audience helping to shape the art, and, as Alain Locke would later say in the *New Negro*, "In a real sense it is the rank and file who are leading, and the leaders who are following." Harrison was also critical of Black leaders who didn't form their own judgments, but instead relied on whites for the development of their critical opinions.[3]

The following selections demonstrate that Harrison is truly an important, though neglected, figure in the history of African American literary criticism.

On Criticism and Book Reviewing

Harrison offered his first comments on book reviewing and on theories of literary criticism in 1907 in the *New York Times Saturday Review of Books*. He wrote occasional book and theater reviews over the next decade and in *The Voice* he began plying the trade professionally in 1917. In 1920 he started the "first regular book-review section known to Negro newspaperdom" in the *Negro World*. Harrison was an avid book reader and in every publication that he edited he included book reviews. His reviews were wide-ranging and the following samples are drawn from among the approximately seventy reviews that have been located.[1]

97. "Views of Readers on Criticism: Mr. H. H. Harrison Reiterates His Theories," letter to the editor, *New York Times Saturday Review of Books*, April 27, 1907.

In April 1907, at age twenty-three, Harrison had his first of two letters on literary criticism published on the front page of the *New York Times Saturday Review of Books* Literary Section. That letter, in the April 13 issue, excoriated the previous week's reviews as being "void of any sense" and described a piece by Hildegarde Hawthorne on intellectual women in ancient Greece and Rome as "the merest buncombe" complete with "a schoolgirl's giggle" and "a boarding school rehash of two or three facts in Greek history." These comments provoked a series of responses in her defense including one by Mary Hamlin Ashman, who decried Harrison's "altogether ungracious summary," argued that it was "the essence of femininity which Mr. Harrison does not understand," and maintained that a reviewer need not specifically describe the book being reviewed.

Harrison responded to Ashman's letter with a second letter that appeared on April 27, his twenty-fourth birthday, and propounded his theory of literary criticism. He described four different types of criticism ranging from simple impressionism to what he termed "creative criticism" (which "creates new current of thought"). He also described the characteristics of a competent book review and exhibited his willingness to forthrightly offer criticism. This interest in, and willingness to offer, criticism would continue for the rest of his life and views articulated in these letters remained an important part of his intellectual arsenal.

To: *New York Times Saturday Review of Books*:

I beg leave to trouble once more your editorial ear. While I have no quarrel with "admirers" or with charming writers I must demur to all sentimental considerations in the matter of literary criticism. Criticism may be regarded either as a science or as an art. In either case it has its laws and methods which must be followed if any good results are to be obtained. From the days of [Dionysius Cassius] Longinus, the unknown Alexandrian, to our own time critics have agreed that literary criticism involves an estimate of literary productions. All criticism is judgment of one sort or another. Even in the darkest period of English criticism — from Colley Cibber to Jeffries [Francis, Lord Jeffrey] of *The Edinburgh Review* — when laws were thrown to the winds and dogmatism was supreme, even then criticism was held to be judgment. Let us remember this that we may not stray too far. Now there are several sorts of criticism. The first and lowest is impressionism. In this the critic consults no general principle of the art, (or science,) but receives an impression. The method is subjective; it is the method of the man in the street, the "admirer," the essentially uncritical mind. Then there is comparative criticism. In this the critic compares one literary production with another, (usually one already acknowledged by time and common consent to be good) and depends on the results. Again we have interpretive criticism, in which the critic expounds the work of an author, gives that which is written between the lines, and helps the reader to understand more readily. The highest of all is creative criticism, which — to crib an expression from Matthew Arnold — creates new currents of thought to act as points of departure. There are others, but these are enough for our purposes. And now I shall give an example of each kind: (1) [Robert G.] Ingersoll's Lecture on Shakespeare; (2) Longinus on the Sublime, e.g., chapters on Sappho's poetry; (3) [Thomas] Carlyle's essay on [Robert] Burns, and (4) [Thomas] De Quincey on The Knocking at the Gate in *Macbeth*.

In *The New York Times Saturday Review of Books* we often meet one or other of the first three (it would be unfair to expect the fourth) in letters, in notices, and reviews. Are we forbidden to judge them by the same standard which we elsewhere apply? I think not. And here, as elsewhere, charm of style is an inadequate substitute for criticism or reviewing. And what are the characteristics of a competent review of any book? These: It must explain the purpose of the author, tell whether he attains it, it must reproduce his thesis in little, or the plot, if a novel; it must tell in what spirit the author's work is done — in short, it must tell what the book is so that the casual reader may know whether it is worth his while to read it. These are the essentials which a good review must have.

If it has them not it is not a good review, no matter what else it may have. In our day ignorance sits enthroned in high places, and as long as this world approximates to Carlyle's contemptuous estimate of it so long shall she so sit. But in the meanwhile there are still some of us who, to use [Theodor] Mommsen's phrase, "stand aloof from all ideology and everything fanciful," and dare to make known our belief that there is nothing essentially sacred or immune in feministic criticism.

98. "On a Certain Condescension in White Publishers [Part I]," *Negro World* 12 (March 4, 1922): 7, HHHP Scr B.

In the March 4 and 11, 1922, *Negro World* issues Harrison offered a two-part article "On a Certain Condescension in White Publishers." In the first part Harrison explained that his twofold aim as a reviewer was to inform the Black reading public what the white world was thinking about it and to bring the white publishers' wares to the African American community. In attempting to do this he encountered white publishers who took neither the Black reading public nor a Black reviewer seriously.

It is an undoubted, if ignored, truth that in the arts of buying and selling the black brother is the equal of the whites. I mean not here to challenge that fine fiction to which we in America have dedicated our lives, but simply to insist that when the American farmer wants to get pennies for his pumpkins the color of the hands from which those pennies fall is of little concern to him. And we may safely presume that what is true of farmers is true also of most other men who have something to sell.

In my mind's eye there lurks a light similitude between the tiller of the agricultural soil and his more pretentious brother who tills and traffics in the product of the intellectual soil. These also "raise their crop," deciding at their own risks what weeds shall grow or what goodly harvests shall come up. But the point of chief importance in our comparison lies in the fact that publishers as well as farmers do finally bring or send their crops to market, where the bane or blessing rests with the hands from which must roll in either case the pennies that pay for pumpkins. Now, out of this necessity there springs a certain rough democracy of dealing; since we must sell, and all buyers' coins are equal, let us extend the courtesies of the market in equal measure to all prospective purchasers. It is this courtesy of trade which helps to reconcile the brother in black to the capitalist system of the brother in white; if all men are not equal, at least all moneys are. One dollar from Sam Jones will buy as much social service as one dollar from Lloyd George—and trade courtesy is a social service.

But life, alas, has some hard shocks for logic, and the white publishers of America have given me many such. It is now two years since I inaugurated in this newspaper the first (and up to now the only) regular book-review section known to Negro newspaperdom. Since that time I have observed that the magazine called *The Crisis* has been attempting to follow my footsteps in the trail—with such success as was achievable by youth and inexperience.

When the book reviews were begun it was with this two-fold aim: to bring to the knowledge of the Negro reading public those books which were necessary if he would know what the white world was thinking and planning and doing in regard to the colored world; and to bring the white publisher and his wares to a market which needed those wares. Sometimes the books had been written by Negro authors with whose works Negro readers were thus made acquainted. I aimed to render a common service and to a certain extent I succeeded. But one would have thought that the white publishers would be eager to avail themselves of the novel opportunity thus offered to get some more pennies for their pumpkins. But it was not to be.

I recall my humorous amazement when, after writing to Boni & Liveright for a review copy of a book dealing with the anthropology of colored peoples, I received and read their reply. The supercilious magnificence of that reply was regal in its sweep. They wanted me to supply them with back numbers of the journal—and even then they simply subsided into silence. What could Negroes know of anthropology, whether as critics or simple readers? It reminded me so much of the outraged dowager's dignity of Mrs. Elsie Clews Parsons when a black man in West Africa wrote her some years ago for an exchange copy of *The Family*. She wrote to tell him in reply to his courteous request that the book was not of a sort to interest him and that, perhaps, he had been misled. It created laughter from Lagos to Sierra Leone because the man who had written was John Mensah Sarbah, the illustrious author of the *Fanti Customary Laws* [1904], who knew just about five times as much of social anthropology as Mrs. Parsons.

So I laughed at the top-lofty airs of Boni and Liveright at that time. The readers of this journal will recall that *The Story of Mankind*, by Hendrik Willem Van Loon, was published by Boni and Liveright and was recently reviewed by me. All things change and white publishers may change also.

But Boni and Liveright were only an index. To this day I cannot get the New York representatives of Macmillan and Company to take the Negro reading public seriously. It is more than three months since I wrote for a review copy of *A Social History of the American Negro*, by Benjamin Brawley—and up to now they have not even deigned to reply. Of course one might raise the question of the intrinsic quality of the literary criticism done in this section. And that is fair enough, although I am estopped from taking the stand to testify. But other witnesses are not lacking. Eugene O'Neill, author of *The Emperor Jones*, has written to say that the review of that work done in this paper was one of the two or three best that had come from any source. The publishers of [William Bayard] Hale's *Story of a Style*, [Edmund D.] Morel's *The Black Man's Burden*, [John H.] Harris' *Africa, Slave or Free?* and [Ambrose] Pratt's *Real South Africa*, have found, to their surprise, (and profit) that we can do workman-like work in book-reviewing.

99. "On a Certain Condescension in White Publishers (Concluded) [Part II]," *Negro World* 12 (March 11, 1922): 7, HHHP Scr B.

In the second part of his commentary on the publishing industry, Harrison again criticizes the condescension which leads white publishers to ignore the Black reading public. Then, aware of his pioneering role as a book reviewer, he offers advice to those Black writers who will follow in his wake.

The publishers of Mr. [Theodore] Lothrop Stoddard's two books, *The Rising Tide of Color* and *The New World of Islam*, have had occasion to commend the thoroughness of our literary criticism of those two books; and Mr. Stoddard himself entered into friendly and faithful correspondence with us. Huebsch, Scribner, Doran and Dutton have had the product of their presses properly presented to our readers—to their [HH crossed out *mutual*] profit. And even the Macmillans have had *The Soul of John Brown*, by Stephen Graham, and *The Influence of Animism on Islam* by Dr. [Samuel M.] Zwemer, reviewed by us. Yet the force of an ancient attitude is strong, and this and other publishing houses still seem unaware of the fact that many of the 12,000,000 Negroes in this country do buy and read not only books on the Negro but other literary and scientific works.

As the only "certified" Negro book-reviewer in captivity I feel the onus of this backward view which white publishers take of the market which the Negro reading public furnishes for their wares. It is not complimentary to us; it is short-sighted and unsound. After all, pennies are pennies, and books are published to be sold. We believe that the Negro reading public will buy books — when they know of their existence. One sees proof of this in the amazing stream of letters and money orders which flow in to Mr. [J.A.] Rogers at 513 Lenox avenue for his books, *From Superman to Man* and *As Nature Leads*. This young Negro author's continued success is also proof of the great intellectual awakening which has been brought about by the forces of the last decade.

And now, a word to our own. I foresee that in the near future there will be many book reviewers (which is the name for literary critics in their working clothes) among us. Indeed, they are already treading on my heels in this paper. May one veteran (since my book reviewing began in the *New York Times* in 1906) offer a word of advice to the new recruits? In the first place, remember that in a book review you are writing for a public who want to know whether it is worth their while to read the book about which you are writing. They are primarily interested more in what the author set himself to do and how he does it than in your own private loves and hates. Not that these are without value, but they are strictly secondary. In the next place, respect yourself and your office so much that you will not complacently pass and praise drivel and rubbish. Grant that you don't know everything; you still must steer true to the lights of your knowledge. Give honest service; only so will your opinion come to have weight with your readers. Remember, too, that you can not well review a work on African history, for instance, if that is the only work on the subject that you have read. Therefore, read widely and be well informed. Get the widest basis of knowledge for your judgment; then back your judgment to the limit. Here endeth the First Encyclical.

A. Philip Randolph and Chandler Owen

Asa Philip Randolph (1889–1979), the son of an African Methodist Episcopal minister, was born in Jacksonville, Florida, and arrived in Harlem in 1911. He worked menial jobs and enrolled in City College at night. Chandler Owen (1889–1967) was born in Warrentown, North Carolina, and graduated from Virginia Union before entering Columbia University in 1913. The two became friends in early 1916 and around that time also "learned of the radical ideas of Hubert H. Harrison" whose talks at 135th Street and Lenox Avenue they regularly attended. In the spring of 1916 they organized the Independent Political Council in Harlem and, after exploring possibilities with the Republicans and Democrats, joined the Socialist Party, founded the Brotherhood of Labor and the *Hotel Messenger,* which became the *Messenger* magazine, and received financing from the Socialist Party and from Randolph's wife, Lucille E. Green Randolph, who had a prosperous hair styling business. During World War I they emerged as critical opponents of U. S. involvement.

By 1920 Randolph and Owen would be the two most prominent Black Socialists in

America. In 1920 Randolph won more than 200,000 votes as the Socialist candidate for New York state comptroller; in 1925 he was instrumental in founding the Brotherhood of Sleeping Car Porters (BSCP), which gained AFL recognition in 1929 and signed a collective bargaining agreement with the Pullman Company in 1937. Randolph served as BSCP president from 1925 to 1968 and headed the leftist National Negro Congress. He broke with the NNLC in 1940 and served as the principal organizer of the March on Washington Movement (MOWM) during World War II. Randolph was elected a vice-president and member of the executive council of the American Federation of Labor–Congress of Industrial Organizations at its founding meeting in 1955, and he served, along with Dr. Martin Luther King Jr., as one of the principal organizers of the August 28, 1963, March on Washington for Jobs and Freedom. While Randolph is generally recognized as the most famous Black labor organizer of the twentieth century and a leading civil rights activist, Owen moved away from socialism and from Randolph in the early 1920s and became active with the Republican Party.[4]

100. Review of *Terms of Peace and the Darker Races* by A. Philip Randolph and Chandler Owen, *The Voice* (September 19, 1917), reprinted in *Messenger* 1, no. 11 (November 1917): 33.

In September 1917 Harrison offered favorable comments on the antiwar pamphlet *Terms of Peace and the Darker Races* by A. Philip Randolph and Chandler Owen of the Independent Political Council (IPC). According to later writings in which Harrison was far more critical of them, Owen and Randolph had previously sought both Republican and Democratic backing. Owen made weekly visits to Tammany chief Charles Murphy from June to August 1917 seeking to be put on the Democratic party payroll, and he met with Ferdinand Q. Morton, head of the United Colored Democracy, who also refused to provide him the backing he sought. Despite such political wanderings, Harrison supported the antiwar message of these two developing activists and helped to promote their pamphlet.[5]

Shortly after Harrison's influential review, Owen and Randolph, representing the "Independent Political League of Harlem," appeared before the Executive Committee of the Socialist Party of Local New York and said that they were eager to work for the SP during the campaign. They indicated that the IPC's "primary, sole and immediate aim" was "to fight for a progressive, clean and honest government" and to use the ballot (the "mightiest weapon of the ages") to obtain "a just political status for the colored people in particular." They also offered to rally Harlem behind the Socialist candidate for mayor, Morris Hillquit. Their plan was accepted and with Socialist assistance they established a Socialist club in the Twenty-first Assembly District and helped Hillquit to receive 145,332 votes (four times more than the party received in 1912) and to finish third behind Tammany's John F. Hylan and the Fusion Party's John Purroy Mitchel. The Socialists received one-quarter of the Black vote and elected ten Socialist state assemblymen, seven alderman, and one municipal judge. In November 1917 Randolph and Owen also organized The Messenger Publishing Company and put out the first volume of the *Messenger*. The following November they both ran for office on the Socialist ticket, and in December 1918, along with other Black Socialists in New York including W. A. Domingo, Lovett Fort-Whiteman, and Charles Moore, they published *The Negro Worker*.[6]

Harrison's early influence on Randolph and Owen is clear. They attended his talks and, according to J. A. Rogers, were "profoundly influenced" by him. *The Voice*, according to historian Robert A. Hill, was the "radical forerunner" of their November 1917 *Messenger* (as well as of other New Negro publications including Cyril Briggs's *Crusader* and Marcus Garvey's *Negro World*). In December 1917 they organized "a club for the purpose of introducing socialism among the colored people" of Harlem, a clear imitation of Harrison's effort with the Colored Socialist Club six years earlier.[7]

When Randolph and Owen undertook Socialist organizing in 1917–18, conditions were objectively different from those faced by Harrison in 1912. The growth of the Harlem community, the more favorable wartime employment possibilities, and the awakened race consciousness sparked by the war and by an autonomous African American movement led by Harrison had created a very different climate. The Socialist Party was able to recruit one hundred Black members in New York City in 1917, and, while the Party thought this was due to its message, Harrison felt that it "took credit for an upsurge due to race."[8]

Randolph and Owen projected themselves as "class first" socialists, however, and downplayed the race question in this period. By 1925, however, Randolph would significantly change course. In a major re-evaluation he concluded that left with pure socialist propaganda, the Messenger people "alienated the very group" they wanted to reach. They then "eliminated all definite Socialist propaganda," declared their opposition to communism, and focused their efforts on Black workers in general and sleeping car porters in particular. The change was "based upon the belief that it is more important that Negro workers be organized into trade unions than that they vote the Socialist ticket or that they be organized only as Socialist workers."[9]

In the review that follows, Harrison focuses on the 1917 pamphlet and praises the antiwar position of the two young radicals.

These two brilliant young leaders of the Independent Political Council have given us a pamphlet that is unique. We often find Negro leaders who are radical — on the subject of their race. But frequently they know so little of anything else that they have no radical attitude, no opinions worth while on anything else. These two companions-in-arms have knowledge and opinions well worth the getting. Knowledge of modern world-politics and history, economics and finance, and opinions on the twisted tricky course of war-time diplomacy and lying. This knowledge and these opinions are on tap in this little book, and they make good reading. The authors are bold — perhaps too bold for safety's sake — but in these days of cowardly compromise and shifting surrender we cannot find it in our heart to condemn the opposite qualities. The pamphlet brings to the judgment-seat of reason and information the clashing claims of the two groups of combatants in the present world-war. It analyzes their motives and their methods and makes a bold bid for the President's first demand for "peace without victory." It then goes on to consider the claims of the darker races for the possession of whose lands the war is being waged. And it demands, for their protection an International Council on the Coalition of the Darker Races on which their representatives shall sit and in which they shall voice their demands for a democracy big enough to include them; for free scientific education for their boys and girls; for a right for their place in the sun.

For, "so long as African territory is the object of unstinted avarice, greed and robbery, while its people with dark skins are considered as just subjects of exploitation — now here and now there in slavery, enforced labor, peonage and wage-slavery — just so long will the conditions smolder and brew which must inevitably produce future war."

This is a pamphlet well worth reading by both the white and colored people — not only of America, but also of the civilized world. It is published by the Poole Press Association of No. 57 Ann Street, New York City, and we are glad to learn that the first edition is going rapidly.

J. A. Rogers

Joel Augustus Rogers (1880–1966) was born in Negril, Jamaica and migrated to the United States in 1911. He worked as a Pullman porter while pursuing a career as a journalist and lay historian of Black history, biography, and race relations. His first book, From "Superman" to Man (1917), attacked racist assumptions of Black inferiority and, like many of his subsequent publications, was self-published. In the 1920s Rogers wrote a weekly column for the *Pittsburgh Courier*, served as contributing editor to the *Chicago Enterprise*, and was sub-editor of Marcus Garvey's short-lived *Daily Negro Times* (1922). He also wrote occasional pieces for the *Negro World*. In 1924 he started a series of biographical sketches on Black historical figures which he completed in 1947 as the two-volume *World's Great Men of Color*. That book includes an extremely laudatory portrait of Harrison. Rogers authored a number of other volumes and his work attained much posthumous popularity as many of the books went through numerous editions and reprints.[10]

 101. Ignacio Sanchez (pseudonym), "The Negro in History and Civilization," *New Negro* 4 (October 1919): 15–16; reprinted as "The Negro in History and Civilization: *From Superman to Man* by J. A. Rogers," *Negro World* 8 (July 31, 1920): 8; and reprinted in *When Africa Awakes*, 135–36. [Ignatius Sancho (1729–1780) was an African former slave who became an outstanding composer, musician, artist, playwright, and pamphleteer in England.][11]

In the "Our Book Review" section of the September *New Negro*, Harrison, under the pseudonym Ignacio Sanchez, published his review of Rogers's *From Superman to Man*. He described the 1917 publication as "the greatest little book on the Negro that we remember to have read." Rogers greatly appreciated Harrison's support of his writing, and around 1921 he wrote to Harrison that "it was due to your stimulation that I made the effort to get out F. S. to M." He added that he was "much indebted" and would never be able to thank Harrison enough "for the publicity given 'F.S. to M.' in *When Africa Awakes*," where Harrison reprinted his laudatory review. Long after Harrison's death, his comments continued to adorn the dust jacket of subsequent reprints of *From Superman to Man*—a fact which suggests both the respect and friendship (at times Rogers lived with Harrison and his family) between the two outstanding lay intellectuals.[12]

This volume by Mr. Rogers is the greatest little book on the Negro that we remember to have read. It makes no great parade of being "scientific," as so many of our young writers do who seem to think that science consists solely in logical analysis. If science consists fundamentally of facts, of information and of principles derived from those facts, then the volume before us is one of the most scientific that has been produced by a Negro writer. It sweeps the circle of all social sciences. History, sociology, anthropology, psychology, economics and politics—even theology—are laid under contribution and yield a store of information which is worked up into a presentation so plain and clear that the simplest can read and understand it, and yet so fortified by proofs from the greatest standard authorities of the past and present that there is no joint in its armor in which the keenest spear of a white scientist may enter.

Unlike an older type of scholar (now almost extinct) the author does not go to vapid verbal philosophers or devotional dreamers for the facts of history and ethnology. He goes to historians and ethnologists for them, and to anthropologists for his anthropology. The result is information which stands the searching tests of any enquirer who chooses to doubt and investigate from accepting what is set before him.

From this book the unlearned reader of the African race can gather proof that his race has not always been a subject or inferior race. He has the authority of Professor [George Andrew] Reisner, of Harvard; of Felix Dubois, Volney, Herodotus, Finot, [Guiseppe] Sergi, the modern Egyptologists and the scholars of the white world who assembled at the Universal Race Congress in London in 1911, for the belief that his race has founded great civilizations, has ruled over areas as large as all Europe, and was prolific in statesmen, scientists, poets, conquerors, religious and political leaders, arts and crafts, industry and commerce when the white race was wallowing in barbarism or sunk in savagery. Here he can learn on good authority from St. Jerome and Cicero, Herodotus and Homer down to the modern student of race-history, that cannibalism has been a practise among white populations like the Scythians, Scots and Britons; that the white races have been slaves; that here in America the slavery of white men was a fact as late as the 19th century, and "according to Professor [Bernard John] Cigrand, Grover Cleveland's grandfather, Richard Falley, was an Irish slave in Connecticut." In short, he will learn here, not that newspaper science which keeps even "educated"

Americans so complacently ignorant, but the science of the scientists themselves. He will learn all that this kind of science has to tell of the relative capacity and standing of the black and white races — and much of it will surprise him. But all of it will please and instruct.

The book also deals with the facts of the present position of the Negro in America and the West Indies; with questions of religion, education, politics and political parties, war work, lynching, miscegenation on both sides, the beauty of Negro women and race prejudice. And on every one of these topics it gives a maximum of information. This information flows forth during the course of a series of discussions between an educated Negro Pullman porter and a Southern white statesman on a train running between Chicago and San Francisco. The superior urbanity of the Negro, coupled with his wider information and higher intelligence, eventually wins over the Caucasian to admit that the whole mental attitude of himself and his race in regard to the Negro was wrong and based on nothing better than prejudice.

This conversational device gives the author an opportunity to present all the conflicting views on both sides of the Color Line, and the result is a wealth of information which makes this book a necessity on the bookshelf of everyone, Negro or Caucasian, who has some use for knowledge on the subject of the Negro. [In the two reprints, Harrison adds, "The book is published by the author at 4700 State Street, Chicago."]

102. "White People versus Negroes: Being the Story of a Great Book [*From Superman to Man* by J. A. Rogers] *Negro World* 11 (January 7, 1922): 10, HHHP Scr B.

In the January 7, 1922, *Negro World* Harrison discussed the history of Rogers's *From Superman to Man* from when he first picked up the book in August 1917 "in a Negro book shop" (probably that of George Young). In the course of his discussion Harrison offers criticism and observations regarding how the book was reviewed and publicized by others. In particular, he takes to task prominent Black writers and editors for their reluctance to call attention to a work by an unknown Black writer and for the failure to develop critical intellects of their own.

Some time in August 1917 I picked up in a Negro book shop a book entitled, *From Superman to Man*, by J. A. Rogers. I sat down to read it and did not rise from my seat until I had read it through. Then I paid for it and took it home, realizing that I had found a genuine treasure. Of the author I could learn nothing, as there was no publisher's name and address in the volume, which had been published by the author at his own expense. Two years later, while in Washington, I came across a second edition of the book, bearing this time the imprint of "The Goodspeed Press." I wrote them at once, got the author's address, and wrote to tell him how highly I thought of his book. Since then I have reviewed it in the *Negro World* and elsewhere. I still insist that it is the greatest book ever written in English on the Negro by a Negro, and I am glad to know that increasing thousands of black and white readers re-echo the high opinion of it which I have expressed.

During the period from 1917 to the present time this book has made its way to success without one word of encouragement or praise from any of the more prominent Negro writers or editors except Mr. [William H.] Ferris and myself, although free copies had been sent to Dr. [W. E. B.] Du Bois, Kelly Miller, Benjamin Brawley, Monroe Trotter, Prof. [William Sanders] Scarborough, [William Stanley] Braithwaite, and many others, including the National Association for the Advancement of Colored People. Almost the only colored people who helped to spread its fame were the lesser known and humble classes, who still pilgrimage to 513 Lenox Avenue in quest of it. The best known Negroes have failed to notice it.

What the Whites Did

It was a colored woman who used to do day's work at the University of Chicago who showed a copy to one of the university professors, Professor [Zonia] Baber, a southern white woman. She read it and at once wrote Mr. Rogers to say that she considered it to be "the finest bit of literature she had read on the subject," and that she had placed it on the required reading list for her classes. In addition, she had it placed in the university library. Some time later she gave a reception at her home to her students (all white) and invited the author (a Negro) to come and speak to them on the subject of the book — the Negro in history and civilization. She bought fourteen copies and sent them to leading white educators at such leading universities as Minnesota and Michigan, and to librarians at the leading scientific libraries.

A colored Catholic got hold of the book by accident. It was then passed on to the Catholic Board for Mission Work Among Colored People. They sent a white priest to Chicago to look up the author; but this man failed to find Rogers, who was away from home working as a Pullman porter. So they sent a letter saying that: "The members of the board have read with much interest and pleasure your book, *From Superman to Man.* There are more objections against the colored race answered satisfactorily and convincingly in this book than in any book we have read upon the question. We intend using it as a textbook for the advancement of our students in the knowledge of the race question." The letter ended with an immediate order for twenty-five copies. The Catholic College in Greensburg, Pa., followed with an order for ten copies for use in their sociology class.

Since then they have asked Mr. Rogers to write for them a catechism on the race question for use in their schools, to be printed first in their magazine of 60,000 circulation. Later they sent him a present of $200 for Christmas as a recognition of genius and encouragement of the same. Mr. Rogers, by the way, is not a Catholic. These two cases are just samples.

What the Big Negroes Didn't

In the meanwhile he had sent a copy of the book to every leading Negro college in the country, to Atlanta, Fiske, Wilberforce, Howard, Tuskegee, Shaw; to Dr. Du Bois, Dr. [Joel E.] Spingarn and Dr. [Charles E.] Bentley, head of the N.A.A.C.P. in Chicago, and to the N.A.A.C.P. in New York, under the curious delusion that an Association for the Advancement of Colored People would like to hear of a book in which the cause of colored people was so well advanced. He also mailed them letters. But they were too ill-bred and unmannerly to vouchsafe him a reply. Copies of the book, accompanied by letters, were also sent to Kelly Miller, [William Stanley] Braithwaite, [William Sanders] Scarborough, Isaac Fisher, of Tuskegee; [Benjamin] Brawley, of Morehouse College; [Charles] Banks of Mound Bayou, and many others. Kelly Miller and Isaac Fisher acknowledged receipt but made no comments. The lady-like Brawley opined that the book was "rather interesting," but that the author made a great error in putting philosophy in the form of fiction, and hoped that if he ever wrote again he wouldn't commit the same grave error against the transcendental technics of the exalted act of saying nothing. The book, by the way, is no more a work of fiction than is [Thomas] Carlyle's *Sartor Resartus*, or the *Dialogues of Plato*. The truth is that Brawley, as usual, was too stupid too form any critical opinion worth a tinker's damn — as Brander Matthews, of Columbia, gently hinted a short while ago.

The others didn't answer. But [James K.] Vardaman, of Mississippi, whom the book attacked, sent a courteous note of acknowledgement. The leading Negro journals like the *Chicago Defender*, the *Boston Guardian*, the *Crisis*, the *Christian Recorder*, all got copies but took no notice of it. The *Indianapolis Freemen* wrote an article on it — and the writer sent Rogers a bill for that! Three years later the *Defender* carried a notice of the book, and charged him $28. The *Journal of Negro History*, as well as the *Crisis* have also received copies of Rogers' second book, *As Nature Leads*, but they have taken no notice so far.

What the Little Negroes Did

"On the other hand," Mr. Rogers says, "Negroes to whom the book was not sent recognized it for themselves and sought me out with helpful greetings and generous praise. Among these were the Rev. George Frazier Miller, of St. Augustine Church, Brooklyn; Messrs. Arthur Schomburg, Wm. H. Ferris, John E. Bruce and Hubert Harrison. None of them knew me personally except Ferris. Harrison wrote me a warm letter of congratulation in 1919 and reviewed the book in a magazine and later in the *Negro World*. He also suggested that I send a copy to the *Crisis*, "but don't let them know that you are colored or they'll never publish you." They are somewhat color-blind on genius. Harrison's belief was confirmed beforehand, as the book had been sent two years before, and no notice had been taken of it. . . . But two colored school teachers of Washington — Mrs. N. T. Myers and Mrs. R. G. Moore — sold hundreds of copies refusing any remuneration, and Mr. Nathaniel Guy sent a copy at his own expense to every judge and truant officer in the District of Columbia. The book is now in its third edition."

Can We Explain?

Such is the history of a masterpiece of literature. How can we explain the conduct of the colored big-wigs? Perhaps there are two explanations. The Negroes whom Christian slavery reduced to the social level of brutes still have today some of the traits of the slave. And one of these finds continuous expression in our "big Negroes" namely, "Don't help to push any other Negro into notice if you have won notice yourself. Notice for them detracts from your notice." So, we find that "big Negroes" prefer to advance ignoramuses since their own superiority will be thereby enhanced. To advance a "comer" might abate their own brilliance. God help us as a race, so long as this contemptible trait shall flourish among us!

But I don't think that this explains all of it. There is another reason which will shock many. The truth is that many of our "brightest" minds have not yet developed any intellect of their own. They can give you the most brilliant expositions of [George Bernard] Shaw, [Paul Laurence] Dunbar or [John Cheri] Marin — provided he has been previously explained for them. But when they are asked to explain a new writer whom no one from whom they draw their opinions has yet seen or sampled, they are "stuck." I know young men like Mr. [Willis] King and Mr. Sunday [HH changed *Sunday* to (Hodge) *Kirnon*] who can do it. But they are not prominent yet. No one knows them. Du Bois and Owen, Brawley and Randolph, [James Weldon] Johnson and Kelly Miller can't do it. It requires a quality of independent judgement that is certain of itself and sure of its ground. Herein "education" (which can be poured into a person) is no substitute for intellect, which is one's own. The men whom I have named are men of "education" — some of them men of culture. But Ernest Just, Alain Leroy Locke, [Willis J.] King and Kirnon are men of intellect. They can think for themselves in the face of a brand-new fact. The others can't. Yet it is these others that our black world mistakes for men of light and leading.

When Claude McKay erupted into notice these colored pseudo-intellectuals couldn't tell from reading his poems that he was worth noticing. But now that their superiors have spoken they take Claude out to lunch and lionize him "most much." As with McKay, so with Rogers. As soon as these copy cats shall have learned from their teachers how great is *From Superman to Man*, they will slobber over him and give space to his book. In the meanwhile it is well that they should know how those of us who have eyes to see have taken their tiny measure. "*Quis custodiest ipsos custodes?*" asks the old Vulgate, and we of today re-echo it in modern terms: "Who shall put brains in our brainy men?"

T. Lothrop Stoddard

In August 1920 Harrison completed his second book, *When Africa Awakes.* In it he explained that "as early as 1915," in indoor and outdoor lectures, he had offered an "explanation of the racial significance of the whole process of the war" which preceded "the sweeping tide of racial consciousness which found expression subsequently in those Negro newspapers and magazines . . . called radical." Harrison stressed this "point of priority" because in 1920 a "remarkable book" by Theodore Lothrop Stoddard, *The Rising Tide of Color against White World-Supremacy*, became "an instant success."[13]

The Harvard-educated Stoddard (1883–1950), grandson of the wealthy abolitionist Lewis Tappan, became convinced around 1910 that "the key-note of the twentieth century world politics would be the relations between the primary races of mankind." Over the next two decades he became one of the nation's most influential writers on race. His book, the first he wrote on this and related subjects, propounded the thesis that the white race, particularly the "Nordics," were in danger of being inundated by inferior races with higher birthrates. *The Rising Tide of Color* was published in April and Harrison responded with a review in the May 29, 1920, *Negro World.*[14]

On June 17 Stoddard wrote to Harrison asking him to send one or two copies of the "extremely interesting review." That letter initiated a correspondence between the two men which was carried on over the next few years. In his response Harrison enclosed a copy of his article on "The White War and the Colored Races," written in 1918 and reprinted in the *Negro World* in February 1920. It was based on his talks "to white audiences during 1915 and 1916" and he thought it would help Stoddard "to realize that some black men, unknown and unnoticed by the white world in America, have been thinking their thoughts on this subject without waiting for the 'lead.'" Harrison saw fit to add, "since I am a Negro, my sympathies are not at all with you: that which you fear, I naturally hope for."[15]

103. "*The Rising Tide of Color against White World-Supremacy* by Lothrop Stoddard," *Negro World* (May 29, 1920); HHHP Scr B; reprinted in *When Africa Awakes*, 140–44.

In his *Negro World* review of T. Lothrop Stoddard's popular book, *The Rising Tide of Color against White World-Supremacy*, Harrison offered some insights into his sociohistorical understanding of race. He called attention to white civilization's "mad dance of death," offered critical comments on Madison Grant's introduction, which "reads back into history the racial values of today," and discussed Stoddard's gradation of races based in large part on military might. Harrison made a distinction between Stoddard's serious effort at scholarship and Madison Grant's pseudoscience, and, unlike those who would criticize Stoddard's book because it doesn't elevate, he encourages Black readers worldwide to read it.

About ten years ago Mr. B. L. Putnam Weale [Bertram Lenox Simpson] in *The Conflict of Color* tried to open the eyes of the white men of the world to the fact that they were acting as their own grave diggers. About the same time Mr. Melville E. Stone, president of the Associated Press, in an address before the Quill Club on "Race Prejudice in the Far East" reinforced the same grisly truth. Five years later T. Shirby Hodge wrote *The White Man's Burden: A Satirical Forecast*, and ended it with these pregnant words: "The white man's burden is—himself." His publishers practically suppressed his book, which, by the way, should have been in the library of every intelligent Negro. The white world was indisposed then to listen to its voices of warning. But today the physical, economic and racial ravages of the World War have so changed the white world's mind that within four weeks of its appearance *The Rising Tide of Color Against White World Supremacy*, by Lothrop Stoddard, has struck the bull's-eye of attention and has already become the most widely talked-of book of the year. White men of power are discussing its facts and its conclusions with bated breath and considerable disquietude.

Here is a book written by a white man which causes white men to shiver. For it calls their attention to the writing on the wall. It proves that the white race in its mad struggle for dominion over others has been exhausting its vital resources and is exhausting them further. It proves to the hilt the thesis advanced in 1917 in my brief essay on "The White War and the Colored Races" that, whereas the white race was on top by virtue of its guns, ships, money, intellect and massed man-power, in the World War it was busy burning up, depleting and destroying these very resources on which its primacy depended. But even though the white capitalists knew all this their mad greed was still their master. This great race is still so low spiritually that it sells even its racial integrity for dollars and cents. Mr. Stoddard's book may disturb its sense of security for a brief space, but it cannot keep white "civilization" from its mad dance of death. "What shall it profit a man if he gain the whole world and lose his own soul?" And the white race will finally find that this is even more true racially than individually.

We have noticed for many years that whereas domestic journalism was merely journalism—the passing register of parochial sensations—the journalism of the international publicists like Lord [James] Bryce, Meredith Townsend, Archibald Colquhoon, Putnam Weale and [Henry Mayers] Hyndman was something more solid than journalism. In the writings of these men hard fact and stark reality are wedded to wide reading and deep thinking. They are the real social scientists rather than the stay-at-home, cloistered sociologists who, presuming to know everything, have seen nothing. The present volume is one of the best of the former and is full of the qualities of its class.

But at the very outset it suffers from the unwelcome assistance of Dr. Madison Grant, "chairman of the New York Zoological Society and trustee of the American Museum of Natural History." Dr. Grant has accumulated a large stock of many ethnological ideas of which he unburdens himself in what he evidently intends as a "learned" introduction, without which freightage the book would be much better. The difference in value and accuracy between Mr. Stoddard's text and the pseudo-scientific introduction of Dr. Grant would furnish material for philosophic satire. Unfortunately we cannot indulge the inclination in the columns of a weekly newspaper.

Dr. Grant, in owlish innocence, splutters out the usual futile folly which (in other domains) has brought the white race to the frontiers of the present crisis. He reads back into history the racial values of today and trails the Anglo-Saxon's crass conceit and arrogance across the pages of its record, finding "contrast of mental and spiritual endowments . . . elusive of definition," and other racial clap-trap whose falsity has been demonstrated again and again by warm-hearted enthusiasts like Jean Finot and coldly critical and scientific scholars like Dr. [Isaac] Taylor (*Origin of the Aryans*), [Giuseppe] Sergi (*The Mediterranean Race*) and J. M. Robertson (*The Evolution of States*). But one can forgive Dr. Grant; he is a good American, and good Americans (especially "scientists" on race) are usually fifty years behind the English, who, in turn, are usually twenty years behind the Germans. Dr. Grant's annexation of the past history of human culture to the swollen record of the whites sounds good — even if it smells bad. And he is in good Anglo-Saxon company. Sir Harry Johnston does the same thing and gets titles (scientific and other) by so doing. The Englishman takes the very Egyptians, Hindus and tribal Liberians, whom he would call "niggers" in New York and London, and as soon as he finds that they have done anything worth while he tags them with a "white" tag. Thus, to the professional "scientist" like Dr. Grant, living in the parochial atmosphere of the United States, science is something arcane, recondite and off the earth; while to the American like Mr. Stoddard, who has been broadened by travel and contact with the wider world, science, is, as it should be, organized daily knowledge and common sense. Thus journalists, good and bad, are the ones who form opinion in America, because "scientists" are so distressingly stupid.

Mr. Stoddard's thesis starts from the proposition that of the seventeen hundred million people on our earth today the great majority is made up of black, brown, red and yellow people. The white race, being in the minority, still dominates over the lands of black, brown, red and (in the case of China) has assumed a right of dictatorship and disposal even in the yellow man's lands. In the course of this dictatorship and domination the white race has erected the barrier of the color line to keep the other races in their place. But this barrier is cracking and giving way at many points and the flood of racial self-assertion, hitherto damned up, threatens to overflow the outer and inner dikes and sweep away the domination of the whites.

The author approaches his theme with a curiously graduated respect for other races. This respect, while it is a novelty in the attitude of the blond overlords, is always in direct proportion to the present power and discernible potentialities of the races discussed. For the yellow man of Japan and China he shows the greatest deference. The browns (of India, Persia, Afghanistan, Egypt and the Mohammedan world in general) are, of course, inferior, but must be respected for their militancy. The reds (the original American stock which is the backbone of the population of Mexico, Central and South America) are a source of contamination for white blood and an infernal nuisance, capable of uniting with Japan and China in an onslaught on the land areas reserved for white exploitation in the western world; while the blacks, at the foot of the ladder, have never amounted to anything, don't amount to anything now, and can never seriously menace the superiority of the whites.

The gradation is full of meaning, especially to those fervid theorists who affect to believe the religion, morality, loyalty and good citizenship constitute a good claim to the white man's respect. For it is Japan's actual military might and China's impending military might which have put them in Grade A, while the brown man's show of resistance in Egypt, India, and elsewhere under Islam, and his general physical unrest and active discontent have secured for him a classification in Grade B. The American in Mexico and South America keeps his window open toward the east; but the black man still seems, in our author's eyes, to be the same loyal, gentle, stupid beast of burden that the white man's history has known — except in those parts of Africa in which he has accepted the Mohammedan religion and thus become a part of the potential terror of the Moslem world. In this we think our author mistaken; but, after all, it is neither arguments nor logic that will determine these matters, but deeds and accomplishments.

But, however his racial aspect may be apportioned, Mr. Stoddard holds that his race is doomed. "If the present drift be not changed we whites are ultimately doomed. Unless we set our house in order the doom will sooner or later overtake us all." The present reviewer stakes his money on "the doom," for the white race's disease is an ingrowing one whose development inheres in their very nature. They are so singularly constituted that they would rather tear themselves to pieces parading as the lords of creation than see any other people achieve an equal favor of fortune.

In the pages of this book the author presents many chastening truths and wide vistas of international politics which are enlightening when carefully studied. But it is not our intent to cover the entire field of this work, and we think we have said enough to indicate the high value and suggestiveness of the work. But we may be allowed to point out that all the way through the author, though clear and enlightened, remains an unreconstructed Anglo-Saxon, desirous of opening the eyes of his race to the dangers which beset them through their racial injustice and arrogance; but sternly, resolutely, intent that they shall not share their overlordship with any other of the sons of the earth. His book is written in a clear and commendable style; he shows but few defects of temper and a shrewd mastery of his materials. The book should be widely read by intelligent men of color from Tokio to Tallahassee. It is published by Charles Scribner's Sons at $3 and is well worth the price.

104. "The Rising Tide of Color," *Negro World* [?] (June 12, 1920), reprinted in *When Africa Awakes*, 113–15.

In the summer of 1920 Harrison discussed editorial comments on Stoddard's book made by William Randolph Hearst (1863–1951), the most powerful newspaper publisher in America. Hearst's chain of papers, known for their sensationalist reporting, included the *San Francisco Examiner*, the *New York Journal*, and the *New York Evening Journal*. This publishing base was used to support Hearst's political career which included service as a member of the House of Representatives (1903–1907) and unsuccessful campaigns for mayor of New York City (1905, 1909), governor of New York (1906), and president of the United States (1904). Since Hearst was not a friend of the darker races, Harrison considered his interest in Stoddard's book as a sign of the impending danger to the white race.[16]

Mr. William Randolph Hearst, the ablest white publicist in America, has broken loose, and, in a recent editorial in the New York *American*, has absolutely endorsed every word of the warning recently issued by Lothrop Stoddard in his book, *The Rising Tide of Color*. In justice to Mr. Hearst it must be pointed out (as we ourselves did in 1916) that he saw this handwriting on the wall long ago. Mr. Hearst is not particularly famous as a friend of the darker races; but one must give him credit for having seen what was involved in the war between the white nations of Europe and America. As far back as 1915, the present writer was engaged in pointing out to white people that the racial aspect of the war in Europe was easily the most important, despite the fact that no American paper, not even Mr. Hearst's, would present that side of the matter for the consideration of its readers. Now, however, they are beginning to wake up — as people generally do when disaster is upon them — frantically with much screaming and flapping of arms. But, in such cases, the doom approaching is but the ripened result of deeds that have been done, and is, therefore, absolutely inescapable.

The white race has lied and strutted its way to greatness and prominence over the corpses of other peoples. It has capitalized, Christianized, and made respectable, "scientific," and "natural," the fact of its dominion. It has read back into history the race relations of today, striving to make the point that previous to its advent on the stage of human history, there was no civilization or culture worthy of the name. And with minatory finger it admonishes us that if it were to pass off the stage as the controlling factor in the World's destiny, there would be no civilization or culture remaining. Naturally, we take exemption to both these views, because, for the past, we know better and, for the future, we think better of the many peoples who make up the cycle of civilization.

But these conditions are not the gravest at present. The fact of most tremendous import is that the white race in trying to settle its own quarrels has called in black, brown and yellow to do its fighting for it, with the result that black, brown and yellow will learn thereby how to fight for themselves, even against those whom they were called in to assist. The white race cannot escape from its dilemma, however. If it were to decree hereafter that wars between whites should be restricted to whites alone, then we should be given the poignant spectacle of the white race continuing to cut its own throat while the increasing masses of black, brown and yellow remained unaffected by that process. "It is to laugh," as the cynical gods would say. Or, to use a trite Americanism, it is, "heads I win, tails you lose." It is thumbs down for the white race in the world's arena, and they are to be the dealers of their own death blow. Such are the consequences of conquest!

The analogies between the present situation of the white race and the situation of the Roman Empire in the fourth century of the Christian era are too many and too striking to be easily ignored. Now, as then, we have "barbarians" and "super-men." Now, as then, the super-men are such in their own estimation. Now, as then, they have, as they fondly think, a monopoly of the money power, brain power and political power of the world. Now, as then, the necessities of their own selfishness and greed, constrain and compel them to share their education and their culture with the races whom they exploit. Now, as then, in the crisis of their fortunes, they must utilize the knowledge and abilities of these barbarian folk, and now, as then, this exercising of abilities on behalf of the overlord develops abilities and ambition at an equal rate; and, having given the barbarian tiger its first taste of blood, the unleashed results can not now be restrained.

In the Roman days, as in the days of Charlemagne's successors, those who hold the balances generally also wield the sword; and if *their* blood and sand determine which among the rulers shall get the prizes of victory, then these same qualities must needs urge them to take from such victors-by-proxy so much of the fruits of victory as their own needs may suggest or their power maintain. Truly "they that take the sword shall perish by the sword."

105. "The Brown Man Leads the Way, Part 1, review of *The New World of Islam* by Lothrop Stoddard," *Negro World* 11 (October 29, 1921): 8, HHHP Scr B.

On August 1, 1921, T. Lothrop Stoddard wrote to Harrison informing him that he had requested that Scribner's send him copies of his recent book *The New World of Islam*.[17] Harrison responded by sending Stoddard a copy of his review of October 29 which was reprinted in the November 5 *Negro World* (with corrections made on "14 glaring typographical errors") along with its concluding part. The two-part review offers an instructive look at the last several centuries of developments of international Islam. Harrison discusses the work of leaders and movements with confidence and in the first part also praises the non-Islamic leader Mohandas Gandhi.

Mr. Lothrop Stoddard has maintained his interest in colored people and their recent history for a fairly long period. He gave us quite a respectable and well-documented study in *The French Revolution in San Domingo*. Only last year, in *The Rising Tide Of Color Against White World-Supremacy*, he plotted the descending curve of the white race's contacts with the colored races in Asia, Africa and America. A little more than a month ago Scribners brought out *The New World of Islam*, an intensive and detailed study of the various ferments at work in the Near and Middle East, where the brown Mohammedan millions are lining up for the final struggle against the domination of the white men of the Western world. And he is already engaged in the preparatory work for a study of the Pan-African movement in Africa. From such industry and zeal we should expect increasing accuracy, sympathy and comprehension. And we find in Mr. Stoddard's later work an increasing measure of respect for the ideas and institutions of men of color, which keeps pace with his increasing knowledge of their activities and purposes.

The present volume presents a bird's eye view of that series of movements which may be said to have started with Mohammed ibn Abd-al-Wahhab in the first half of the eighteenth century, rising to grave and disquieting proportions under Seyid Mohammed ben Senussi and Djemal-el-Din Sherif and Sir Syed Ahmed Khan in the early part of the nineteenth century, and now, under a variety of forms and under many different leaders like the Emir Feisal, Mohammed Farid Bey, Yahya Siddik, Ahmend el Sherif and Sir Sed Ahmed Khan, comes to a dangerous and revolutionary head in this revolutionary century of ours. The geographic and racial scope of these movements will be appreciated when it is recalled that Abd-el-Wahab was born and bred in the heart of the Arabian desert, and Feisal [King Faisal I] in Mecca; ben Senussi and his grandson, el Sherif, in Algeria; Djemal-el-Din, in Persia; Siddik and Farid Bey, in Egypt, and Sir Syed Ahmed Khan in India. In fact this "far flung battle line" stretched clear across Northern Africa from West to East, runs through Asia Minor, the Arab peninsula, Persia, Afghanistan, Turkestan and India, and goes right through into China. Adequately to trace such a movement through one hundred degrees of latitude and two centuries of time, one must be a competent historian as well as a publicist; and Mr. Stoddard as a historian is quite competent. The historical preparation of his earlier period in which he learned how to handle records and out of them to construct a living past, stands him in good stead in this, his middle period in which he makes of the distant present a near and visible reality.

Our readers, however, will be more interested in the present than in the past. Yet in order that they may understand the full meaning of the Islamic ferment of today, a word must be said of the Mohammedan world of yesterday and the day before.

It was in the seventh century that there erupted out of the back yard of Africa a race of fighting brown men with a new religion, a genius for democracy and civilizing gifts of a high order. In less than a hundred years they had spread that religion over half the earth —

> "Shattering great empires, over-throwing long established religions, remolding the souls of races and building up a whole new world — the world of Islam . . . Inter-marrying freely and professing a common belief; conquerors and conquered rapidly fused, and from this fusion arose a new civilization — the Saracenic civilization in which the ancient cultures of Greece, Rome and Persia were revitalized by Arab vigor . . . Arab genius and the Islamic spirit . . . Studded with splendid cities, gracious mosques and quiet universities where the wisdom of the ancient world was preserved and appreciated; the Moslem East offered a striking contrast to the Christian West (which was) then sunk in the night of the Dark Ages."

But as Tennyson tells us:

> "Our little systems have their day;
> They have their day and cease to be."

and the glory of Islam was dimmed when the seat of government was shifted to Baghdad on the Tigris, and its democracy dampened under the influence of Persian despotism. "The fierce, free-born Arabs of the desert," says Mr. Stoddard, "would tolerate no master, and their innate democracy had been sanctioned by the prophet who had explicitly declared that all believers were brothers." Persian primacy in the affairs of Islam was the beginning of the downfall of imperial Islam. When the Turanian Turks fell upon the luxurious Iranians they crumbled before a more vigorous people whose barbarian brutality has been the continuing cloud in the Mohammedan sky. For the Turk was a barbarian then and, despite his commendable transformation, he remains substantially a barbarian today, and almost as brutish as the British in Ireland.

In the meanwhile the Western nations of Europe had come into possession of gunpowder and a thirst for wealth. These white barbarians, like the yellow ones on the Eastern front, had one great advantage in common with all other barbarians — constant fighting had made them harder fighters than the more civilized people who fought less frequently. Therefore, when by the crusades they had been brought into contact with the higher civilization and culture of the Saracenic world and had come into their own period of renascence, their expanding powers were set to serve an awakening greed for gold. Commerce and discovery were the two handmaidens of the new desire. Fronting on the sea, as they did, they evolved into maritime powers at the time when the Mohammedan lands had lost their central unity and the powers of further propagation. Thus the sceptre of sovereignty which fell from the weakened grasp of the followers of Mohammed was seized by the newer nations of the Christian world. It is hardly six hundred years since the Turks were thundering at the gates of Vienna, and not quite twelve hundred since Moslems were arrayed against all Europe on the battlefields of Spain and Southern France, and Moslem armies were encamped before Lyons and Besancon. Yet in the few centuries since the white man has risen to the heights of rulership from which he looks down with flattering self-complacency on all the rest of the world.

And yet, that earlier world-domination of Islam was in many respects superior in moral and spiritual values to that of the white man. In the first place it was not eaten by the corroding canker of race prejudice. In political and civic matters character counted for much; color and race for nothing at all. As Mr. Stoddard remarks, "All true believers were brothers." Black and brown and yellow were not, as in the Christian system, brothers in theology only, but they were genuinely so in practice before the magistrates and in all the relations of daily life. As Shaikh Mushir Hosain Kidwai, himself a dark son of India, tells us in his little book on "Pan Islam" —

> It is the Christian white, "dis-colored" European people who are fanatically prejudiced against the "colored" and Asiatic races . . . It is they who constantly disturb the amity and fraternity that should exist and which did exist under the true Islamic civilization. The black men of Abyssiania, the white of Spain, the yellow of China and the brown of Asiatic countries loved one another like brothers and treated each other on terms of perfect equality — and so they do even today if they are Mohammedans . . . Christianity has also (on this account) failed altogether in bringing peace (on earth). It is the Christian people who have shed the greatest quantity of human blood in the past and who are still bent on their bloody pursuits.

In the next place those who profess Mohammedanism practice what they preach. If it is true that "by their fruits ye shall know them," then the sons of the Prophet are nearer to "the kingdom of Heaven" than those who parade the principle of the Judean carpenter, yet never put them into practice. "Wine, women of ill-fame and gambling are the three great curses of Christian countries," as Shaikh Housin Kidwai points out, while to read the polemics of Christian writers one would think that these things existed only in "heathen Africa" or "Backward Asia." In diplomacy, politics, war propaganda, business and family life the Lie is regent in all Christian lands.

But it is in another and no less important respect that Islam's superiority is demonstrated. It is a fact known to all students of history except those whose collars button in the back that, while Christianity as an ecclesiastical system controlled Europe's educational systems and institutions, no thinker dared to think a new thought. The inquisition and the lesser tribunals sat cross-legged at the birth of every scientific idea to insure that it would be stillborn. The facts of science upon which Christian civilization now besets its claim to intellectual supremacy had to fight for their lives in the teeth of that Christian bigotry and ignorance that made the Dark Ages dark. And if that bigotry and ignorance had prevailed the telephone, wireless, steamship and traction plow would still exist only in the womb of the future. On the conceded facts of history the Christian system was in its own domain incompatible with knowledge and free inquiry.

On the other hand, despite the huge cairn of lies that have risen on the graves of Islam's reputation in the Western world, the Mohammedan system from its very beginning strove to promote knowledge and free inquiry. For the proof of this we need go no further than the admissions of Western scholars like John William Draper, in *The Conflict Between Religion and Science*. But Mr. Stoddard brings even better testimony when he tells us that, "As a matter of fact Mohammed reverenced knowledge," and cites Mohammed's own words in the *Koran*:

"Seek Knowledge even if it be on the borders of China."

"Seek Knowledge from the cradle to the grave."

"One work of Knowledge is of more value than the reciting of a hundred prayers."

"God has created nothing better than reason."

"The ink of sages is more precious than the blood of martyrs."

"In truth, a man may have prayed, fasted, given alms, made pilgrimage, and all other good works; nevertheless he shall be rewarded only in the measure that he has used his common-sense."

What a harvest of good we, who hate knowledge and despise the warnings of wisdom, might have reaped if we had considered such precepts as a necessary part of our religion!

Such was the religion which linked together and still links the souls of hundreds of millions of black, brown and yellow peoples from the Senegal to the shores of the Yellow Sea. And it is this multitudinous mass which is now on the move, struggling upward to their "place in the sun," under the impact of white arrogance, greed and race-prejudice which call to their aid the forces of religion, business, imperialism and war.

But, in truth, the line-up is not as simple as it seems. The racial element, though complex, overbears the religious. For Mr. Stoddard's study includes the purely Hindu movement of Mr. Gandhi, the people of Turkestan (who are not brown in any sense of the word) the black populations of portions of India and Africa; and his map at the end of the volume (which is the only crude thing in his book) shows as his test does, that the present unrest is discernible among the Moslem part of the population of Yellow China. In India the brunt of the struggle for liberation has been borne mainly by the non-Moslem Hindus whose leader, M. K. Gandhi, stands out among men of all colors today as the greatest, most unselfish and powerful leader of the modern world. But Mr. Stoddard planned his book as a study of the unrest in the Islamic world and, although he notes the extension of the international impulse to the Hindus and some other peoples who are not Mohammedans, he sticks valiantly to the distinction laid down in his main thesis. There is a justification for this in terms of Weltpolitik, for it is the Moslem movement which is the chief disquieting feature of the Eastern problem today. Japanese aspiration being dangerous rather for what it may evoke out of this ferment.

The Islamic world which has sunk into somnolence is awakening. This awakening takes many forms. One of the most significant of these is the conversion of new millions to the religious tents of Mohammedanism. Of its progress in Africa Mr. Threlfall told us in 1900 that it "is making marvelous progress in the interior of Africa. It is crushing paganism out. Against it the Christian propaganda is a myth." Mr. Stoddard quotes [D. A.] Forget, a French Protestant missionary, as saying: "We see Islam on its march, sometimes slowed down but never stopped, toward the heart of Africa . . . Even Christianity, its most serious rival, Islam regards without hate, so sure is it of victory. While Christians dream of the conquest of Africa, the Mohammedans accomplish it."

> "And these gains are not made solely against paganism (says our author). They are being won at the expense of African (?) Christianity as well. In West Africa the European missionaries lose many of their converts to Islam, while across the continent the ancient Abyssinian Church, so long an outpost against Islam, seems in danger of submersion by the rising Moslem tide. Tribes which fifty or sixty years ago counted hardly a Mohammedan among them, today live partly or wholly according to the precepts of Islam."

The Russian Tartars, despite the persistent efforts of the Orthodox Russian Church to convert them to Christianity, reverted to Islam; and the Chinese in Yunan province and its hinterland have come under the Crescent, as well as the population of Chinese Turkestan. India, the Dutch East Indies and the Philppines tell the same story.

What is the source of this new strength and what is the machinery by which it expresses itself? The answer to this question is of the very highest importance to us Negroes of the western world engaged as we are in a similar movement of release: it may give us guidance and inspiration and something of clear vision. That answer and the concluding portion of this review will be given in the next issue, if the printers (who made Mr. Ferris talk of "surpliced chairs" and who slipped a "not" last week into my statement that thousands of white men could answer the questionnaire off-hand) will permit.

106. "The Brown Man Leads the Way, review of *The New World of Islam* by Lothrop Stoddard (concluding Part)," *Negro World* 11 (November 5, 1921): 5.

In the second part of his review of T. Lothrop Stoddard's *The New World of Islam* Harrison emphasizes how the Islamic world, conscious of humiliation from its subjection to white

Christian Europe, responded by stressing learning, by a willingness to look inside their own world for weaknesses which held them back, and by encouragement of group responses based on their own needs. In the course of his review Harrison offers thought-provoking comments on "the shifting reality of race" and on those shortsighted leaders who had eagerly urged support of the Allies in the First World War. He points out that if the Allies had lost before America went in, Britain's colored subjects in Africa and Asia would have won their freedom.

The new and awakened Islam had its roots in the consciousness of humiliation with which the leaders of the people faced the fact of subjection to white Christian Europe. This subjection was not only political: there was also the cultural superiority of the European peoples. Theirs were the new advances on the older knowledge, the inventions and improvements by which they had harnessed up the mighty forces of earth and air and sky and converted them into servants of their "will to power" over other human beings. The leaders of the brown man's world foresaw that truth which has been stated in *When Africa Awakes*, namely that "never until the black man's knowledge of nitrates, machinery, textiles, engineering, etc. shall at least equal that of the white will the black man be able to measure arms successfully with him." They made up their minds that the brown man must go to school — even if he had to learn from the white.

But they also perceived that a part of the difficulty lay inside their world and that its removal must precede the removal of that part which lay outside of it. Selfishness, greed, fanaticism, and ignorance — these must be grappled with. The first great necessity, therefore, was one of Regeneration. And to this task of regeneration they first addressed themselves. "The messianic hope of Mahdism" and its bloody but abortive uprisings accomplished nothing whether in the Egyptian Sudan or under the powerful Makechabendlya in Turkestan and China.

It was a mere straw fire; flaring up lively here and there, then dying down, leaving the disillusioned masses more discouraged and apathetic than before. . . . The importance of the wildest outbursts of local fanaticism against the methodological might of Europe convinced thinking Moslems that long preparation and complete coordination of effort were necessary if Islam was to have any chance of throwing off the European yoke. Such men also realized that they must study Western methods and adopt much of the Western technic of power.

This new realization expressed itself on the one hand through the new type of religious fraternities like the Senussiya, in Algeria, the Ikhwan in Arabia and the Saiafi movement in India, and, on the other, through the propaganda of a new group of thinkers like Djemal-ed-Din, Mustapha Kamil, Kheir-ed-Din and Ahmed bey Agayeff. The new fraternities, of which the Senuissiya is a fair type, devoted themselves to elevating the morals of the people, giving them education and enlightenment, uplifting their souls and welding them together in a discipline inner and outer, which is as great as it is unprecedented. Mr. Stoddard describes these organizations with sympathetic comprehension. But he makes no mention of the Bahai Movement—a most significant offshoot of the Mohammedan reformation. For, even though the Bab and his successor, Baba'ollah suffered martyrdom at the hands of Moslem tyrants, they and their more famous successor Abbas Effendi (better known as Abduh Baha) must still be reckoned as Moslem reformers. And the increasing number of the truly spiritual who follow the Bahai teachings in Western lands are a living proof of the spiritual superiority of rejuvenated Islam over obsolescent Christianity.

The work of the thinkers and scholars has been manifold. In all the Islamic countries they have striven to evoke a group response to their native cultural needs. Sometimes the appeal was put in terms of religion, sometimes in terms of that shifting reality called race; but always it was in terms of themselves. And this has borne fruit in the present Pan-Islamic movement and in the various movements of Islamic nationalism in Egypt, Turkey, Persia, Turkestan and elsewhere. The joint result of this is a very real "International" of Islamic peoples (mainly brown, but also black and yellow) which keeps England and France in a perpetual fit of the jumps at the thought of what might happen should Japan, the foremost colored nation and the only colored Power, assumes the leadership of this group or cast in her lot with it.

Every Moslem country is in communication with every other Moslem country; directly, by means of special emissaries, pilgrims, travelers and postal exchanges; indirectly, by means of Mohammedan newspapers, book, pamphlets, leaflets and periodicals. I have met with Cairo newspapers in Baghdad, Teheran and Pashawar; Constantinople newspapers in Basra and Bombay; Calcutta newspapers in Mohammerah, Kerbela and Port Said.

All of which gives point to the thesis which I expounded in this column some time ago on "The Theory and the Practice of International Relations among Negro-Americans." And, in spite of mulish ignoramuses it still remains a necessary part of our preparation for ultimate "redemption."

The late war has intensified under the unrest in the Islamic world, as Mr. Stoddard abundantly proves. In the first place, when the Sultan Abdul Hamid—who was also the Caliph of Islam—issued the call for a Jehad or Holy War.

It was not the flat failure which allied reports led the West to believe at the time. As a matter of fact, there was trouble in practically every Mohammedan land under Allied control. Egypt broke into a tumult smothered only by overwhelming British reinforcements; Tripoli burst into a flame of insurrection that drove the Italians headlong to the coast; Persia was prevented from joining Turkey only by prompt Russo-British intervention; while the Indian northwest frontier was the scene of fighting that required the presence of a quarter of a million Anglo-Indian troops. The British government has officially admitted that during 1915 the Allies' Asiatic and African possessions stood within a hand's breadth of a cataclysmic insurrection.

Colored men of common sense can now see how silly and shortsighted was the advice given by our educated but ignorant editor-leaders when they asked their befuddled followers to work, fight and pray for Allied success. For it is obvious that if the Allies had lost before America went in the colored peoples now under British subjection in Africa and Asia would have won their freedom at the same time.

In another way the war made for a tightening of the strings of Islam's resolution to be free. The democratic pretense of the Allies furnished a ferment which is still at work.

During the war years the Allied statesmanship had officially proclaimed times without number that the war was being fought to establish a new world order based on such principles as the rights of small nations and the liberty of all peoples. These pronouncements had been treasured and memorized throughout the East. When therefore, the East saw a peace settlement, based upon the imperialistic secret treaties, it was fired with a moral indignation and sense of outraged justice never known before. A tide of impassioned determination began rising which has already set the entire East in tumultuous ferment, and which seems merely the premonitory ground swell of a greater storm. . . . The great war has shattered European prestige in the East and has opened the eyes of Orientals to the weaknesses of the West. . . . Asia and Africa today know Europe as they never knew it before, and we may be sure that they will make use of that knowledge.

Our author makes some comprehensive analyses of the present effects of Western contacts on the structure and institutions of the Mohammedan world. The chapters on "The Influence of the West," "Political Change," "Nationalism in India," "Economic Change," and "Social Change" will prove a liberal education to the Negro-American who may wish to know what's what in the international world of color. The book has a broad sweep; yet, unlike Mr. [Isaac F.] Marcosson's *An African Adventure*, it is not at all superficial in its treatment. Mr. Stoddard's errors are few and venial. He fails to consider the significance of the wide social scope of the Swadeshi movement in India and unfairly limits his criticism of it to its economic program—which is far from being the gist of the thing—as his cited authorities must have shown him. He sometimes minimizes European moral turpitude as when he ignores the deliberate "fakery" of the [Alfred] Milner commission to Egypt. While Lord Milner's sincerity is vouched for, as we know on independent grounds, by Mohammed Abdou, the rector of Al Hazar, yet those who sent him to delude the Egyptians with false hopes while they settled with India and Russia well know that they were using his sincerity as they had previously used that of Colonel [Thomas Edward] Lawrence with the Arabs. The fact that the Egyptian leader now in England is likely to get a qualified "independence" for Egypt is not due to any original sincerity of the English Government, but rather to the popular strength of that other Egyptian leader whom the British rejected because he really wanted independence unqualified.

Homer sometimes nods, and once in a while Mr. Stoddard trips on a fact. There was no massacre in Alexandria before the British bombarded that city in the eighties. This has been established on French and Egyptian authorities on the spot and on some unimpeachable British authorities like that of Wilfrid Scawen Blunt. But, at the worst, this is a small peck of "errors" in a granary of good wheat. Mr. Stoddard's book is a masterly epic of the facts of international Islam and as such is a welcome handbook into which the readers of *The Negro World* can devise with pleasure and profit.

W. E. B. Du Bois

107. "Review of *Darkwater* by W. E. B. Du Bois," *Negro World* (April 17, 1920); HHHP Scr B; reprinted in *When Africa Awakes*, 137–40.

In the April 17, 1920, *Negro World* Harrison reviewed W. E. B. Du Bois's *Darkwater* and perceptively called attention to Du Bois's great skill as a "splendid literary artist" while offering insightful comments on African Americans and book reviewing. Interestingly, Harrison's appraisal of Du Bois's strength anticipated comments by Claude McKay and Arnold Rampersad. McKay wrote that Du Bois's "purely academic intellect kept him within the bounds of political opportunism and reformism" and limited him as a leader, but he "nonetheless deserves first place in the field of literature, unsurpassed by anyone else." Rampersad added that Du Bois's "greatest gift was poetic in nature, and that his scholarship, propaganda, and political activism drew their ultimate power from his essentially poetic vision of human experience and from his equally poetic reverence for the word."[18]

An unwritten law has existed for a long time to the effect that the critical estimates which fix the status of a book by a Negro author shall be written by white men. Praise or blame—the elementary criticism which expresses only the reviewer's feelings in reference to the book—has generally been the sole function of the Negro critic. And the results have not been good. For, in the first place, white critics (except in music) have been too prone to judge the product of a Negro author as Dr. Johnson judged the dancing dog: "It isn't at all like dancing; but then one shouldn't expect more from a dog." That is why many Negro poets of fifth grade merit are able to marshal encomiums by the bushel from friendly white critics who ought to know better. On the other hand, there is a danger of disparagement arising solely from racial prejudice and the Caucasian refusal to take Negro literary products seriously.

In either case the work fails to secure consideration solely on its merits. Wherefore, it is high time that competent appraisal of Negro books should come from "our side of the street." But, then, the Negro reading public should be taught what to expect, viz., that criticism is neither "knocking" nor "boosting"; but an attempt, in the first place, to furnish a correct and adequate idea of the scope and literary method of the book under review, of the author's success in realizing his objects, and of the spirit in which he does his work. In the second place, the critic should be expected to bring his own understanding of the subject matter of the book to bear upon the problem of enlightening the readers' understanding, that at the end the reader may decide whether the work is worth his particular while.

This book of Dr. Du Bois' is one which challenges the swing of seasoned judgment and appraisal. It challenges also free thinking and plain speaking. For, at the very outset, we find ourselves forced to demur to the publishers' assumptions as to its author's status. "Even more than the late Booker Washington, Mr. Du Bois is now chief spokesman of the two hundred million men and women of African blood." So say the publishers—or the author. But this is outrageously untrue. Once upon a time Dr. Du Bois held a sort of spiritual primacy among The Talented Tenth, not at all comparable to that of Booker Washington in scope, but vital and compelling for all that. The power of that leadership, however, instead of increasing since Mr. Washington's death, has decreased, and is now openly flouted by the most active and outspoken members of The Talented Tenth in Negro America. And, outside of the twelve or fifteen millions "of African blood" in the United States, the mass of that race in South and West Africa, Egypt and the Philippines know, unfortunately, very little of Dr. Du Bois. It may be, however, that this is merely a publisher's rhodomontade.

And it is the publishers themselves who challenge for this volume a comparison with *The Souls of Black Folk*, which was published by McClurg in 1903. It is regrettable that they should force the issue, for *The Souls of Black Folk* is a greater book than *Darkwater* in many ways. In the first place, its high standard of craftsmanship is maintained through every chapter and page. There are no fag-ends, as in the chapter "Of Beauty and Death" in the present volume, where the rhetoric bogs down, the author loses the thread of his purpose and goes spieling off into space, spinning a series of incongruous purple patches whose tawdry glitter shows the same reversion to crude barbarism in taste which leads a Florida fieldhand to don opal-colored trousers, a pink tie, parti-colored shirt and yellow shoes. Artistically, the chapter is an awful thing, and I trust that the author is artist enough to be ashamed of it.

And, though it may savor of anti-climax, *The Souls of Black Folk* was more artistically "gotten" up—to use the grammar of its author. *Darkwater* is cheaply bound and cheaply printed on paper which is almost down to the level of the Seaside Library. Neither in mechanical nor mental quality does the book of 1920 come up to the level of that of 1903.

Yet, in spite of some defects, *Darkwater* (with the exception of chapters six, seven, eight and nine) is a book well worth reading. It is a collection of papers written at different times, between 1908 and 1920, and strung loosely on the string of race. One wishes that the author could have included his earlier essay on The Talented Tenth and his address on the aims and ideals of modern education, delivered some twelve years ago to the colored school children of Washington, D.C.

Each paper makes a separate chapter, and each chapter is followed by a rhetorical sprig of symbolism in prose or verse in which the tone-color of the preceding piece is made manifest to the reader. Of these tone-poems in prose and verse, the best are the Credo; A Litany at Atlanta; The Riddle of the Sphinx, and Jesus Christ in Texas. In these the lyrical quality of the author's prose is lifted to high levels. In these elegance does not slop over into turgid declamation and rhetorical claptrap—which has become a common fault of the author's recent prose as shown in *The Crisis*. In this, the first part of the book, the work is genuine and its rhetoric rings true. Nevertheless, the sustained artistic swing of *The Souls of Black Folk*, which placed that work (as a matter of form and style) on the level of Edgar Saltus' *Imperial Purple*—this is not attained in *Darkwater*.

The book may be said to deal largely with the broad international aspects of the problem of the color line and its reactions on statecraft, *welt-politik*, international peace and international trade, industry, education and the brotherhood of man. Each chapter, or paper, is devoted to one of these reactions. Then there is a charming autobiographical paper, "The Shadow of Years," which first appeared in *The Crisis* about three years ago, in which we have the study of a soul by itself. The growth of the author's mind under the bewildering shadow cast by the color line is tragically set forth. I say tragically with deliberation; for what we see here, despite its fine disguise, is the smoldering resentment of the mulatto who finds the beckoning white doors of the world barred on his approach. One senses the thought that, if they had remained open, the gifted spirit would have entered and made his home within them. *Mais, chacun a son gout*, and no one has the right to quarrel with the author on that doubtful score.

In the chapter on "The Souls of White Folk" we have a fine piece, not so much of analysis, as of exposition. The author puts his best into it. And yet that best seems to have failed to bite with acid brutality into the essential iron of the white man's soul. For the basic elements of that soul are Hypocrisy, Greed and Cruelty. True, the author brings this out; but he doesn't burn it in. The indictment is presented in terms of an appeal to shocked sensibilities and amoral sense which exists, for the white man, only in print; whereas it might have been made in other terms which come nearer to his self-love. Nevertheless it is unanswerable in its logic.

In "The Hands of Ethiopia," as in "The Souls of White Folk," we catch the stern note of that threat which (disguise it as our journals will), the colored races are making, of an ultimate appeal in terms of color and race to the white man's only God—the God of Armed Force. But the author never reaches the height of that newer thought — an international alliance of Black, Brown and Yellow against the arrogance of White.

In "Work and Wealth" and "The Servant in the House" the problems of work and its reward, and the tragedy of that reward, are grippingly set forth in relation to the Negro in America and in the civilized world. The "Ruling of Men" is followed by three papers of very inferior merit and the book ends with a fantastic short story, "The Comet" which, like "The Coming of John" in "The Souls of Black Folk," suggests that Dr. Du Bois could be a compelling writer of this shorter form of fiction. The touch in this story of incident is light, but arresting.

Dr. Du Bois, in the looseness of phrase current in our time in America, is called a scholar — on what grounds we are not informed. But Dr. Du Bois is not a scholar; his claim to consideration rests upon a different basis, but one no less high. And when the Negro culture of the next century shall assay the products of its own it will seem remarkable that this supreme wizard of words, this splendid literary artist, should have left his own demesne to claim the crown of scholarship. Surely, there is honest credit enough in being what he is, our foremost man of culture. And this *Darkwater*, despite its lapses from artistic grace, helps to rivet his claim to that consideration. It is a book which will well repay reading.

Monroe Nathan Work

108. "Review of *The Negro Year Book*, 1918–1919, edited by Monroe N. Work," *Negro World* (April 17, 1920), HHHP Scr B.

Monroe Nathan Work (1866–1945) was the director of records and research at Tuskegee Institute in Alabama and a lifelong recorder of the Black experience. He started at Tuskegee under Booker T. Washington in 1908 and began publishing the *Negro Year Book* in 1912. Harrison judged the 1918–19 edition "the most serviceable" of "all the books produced in Negro America" and "an indispensable necessity, with no rival in its field."[19]

Of all the books produced in Negro America this volume of 500 pages is the most serviceable. It covers every department of Negro activity, from banking to radicalism. It deals, among other things, with Racial Co-operation, Education, Religion, the War, Riots, Lynching, Politics, Literature, Science and History, Abyssinia, Haiti, Liberia, Sports, Population, Office Holding and Music. It also contains many lists of books on various aspects of race relations here and abroad. It is truly "an annual encyclopedia of the Negro" and all those who want information of any sort on that subject must "pass up" the big encyclopedias and go to this one. A convenient index makes it easy to look up any fact which one may need without loss of time.

There are a few minor defects—mainly of omission—and many typographical errors due to inefficient proofreading. We hope that these will be eliminated in the next issue. But the book remains an indispensable necessity, with no rival in its field.

Thorstein Veblen

 109. "The Superscientist," review of *The Place of Science in Modern Civilization and Other Essays* by Thorstein Veblen, *Negro World* (September 11, 1920), HHHP Scr B. [Harrison's corrections have been incorporated.]

Thorstein Bunde Veblen (1857–1929) was an original-thinking and influential early-twentieth–century American sociologist and economist. His work introduced such concepts as "conspicuous consumption" and "wasteful" extravagance and challenged social-Darwinist theories by arguing that the practices of the class on top were atavistic "throwbacks" to earlier, plundering, barbarian tribes and a hindrance to human development. His writings include *The Theory of the Leisure Class* (1899), *The Theory of Business Enterprise* (1904), *The Instinct of Workmanship*, (1914), *The Higher Learning in America* (1918), and *Absentee Ownership and Business Enterprise in Recent Times*. In the September 4, 1920, *Negro World* Harrison offered the following, extremely laudatory review of Veblen's *Place of Science in Modern Civilization and Other Essays* (1919) and his other works. He calls particular attention to Veblen's work on the evolution of the scientific point of view, a subject he considers to be of special value to those who have suffered from pseudo-science masquerading as science.[20]

It is some time since Professor Thorstein Veblen (Danish in name as in thoroughness of thought) burst upon our jaded world with a new and thought-compelling vocabulary of his own. And, as in the case of [Thomas] Carlyle and [Herbert] Spencer, this unique vocabulary was itself an index to a new and unique method of looking at things. In the first place, it was like a blistering blaze of truth; it sacrificed. Then it provoked thought; it shocked our jaded sensibilities. But, over and above all these, it was ironical with the irony of superior perception; it was neither wit, humor nor cynicism; yet it partook of the nature of all three. When the reader ran across such phrases as "the pecuniary canons of taste," the "feudalistic hierarchy of agents and elements," "exploit and industry," "vicarious consumption," "conspicuous consumption," "the requirements of conspicuous waste" or "the requirements of pecuniary decency"—he was compelled to feel the vigor of an alert and critical intelligence that had worked out not merely words for itself but standards of judgment and interpretation which challenged serious attention and respect.

This attention and respect have come now to Professor Veblen and his work in the field of economic and institutional science which we think was fertilely tilled by the late Nathaniel S. Shaler with an equipment vastly inferior in scientific scope and power to that of our brilliant Danish-American. We think it high time that Professor Veblen's work should be recommended to the intellectual leaders of Negro America for their instruction and enjoyment. For years it has been notorious among us that our leaders of thought, whether selected by us or by others, have been playing at a child's game of imitation scholarship, and the increasing number of educated Negro laymen are demanding more and more that the intellectual furniture of their leaders' minds shall approximate more nearly to the accepted standards of those of the white world by which they are surrounded.

That is why I take this opportunity afforded by Huebsch to introduce Negro America to Professor Veblen. Yet, in spite of a good resolution, I find it somewhat difficult to review even in the pages of the *Negro World* Professor Veblen's *The Place of Science in Modern Civilization*. For Veblen's books are notoriously hard to read and the latest book of his is one of the hardest. The reviewer must, of necessity, write on the level of his medium as well as the level of his theme and when the two levels diverge he has indeed a hard task. The most he can do, therefore, is to indicate values as in the present case.

The present collection of essays is concerned mostly with criticism of the claims and conduct of the higher intellectual science. Of 18 essays, 14 are devoted to this, and the limitations of our medium constrain us to pass over these 14 scholastic achievements. But the first two on the title subject and "The Evolution of the Scientific Point of View" may be recommended for reading by people who have been steeped in "literary" culture and who know only from hearsay of the claims of science with a capital S. Professor Veblen in these two essays as well as in the two toward the end of the book on "The Blond Race" and "Aryan Culture" not merely shows the drift and intent of scientific spirit but, as a critic of that spirit who shares its general mental attitude, he stands revealed as a super-scientist; hence his value to us who have suffered so much from pseudo-science masquerading as science. There is striking comparison made in the first two essays between the present animus of the "idle curiosity" of the "up-to-date" scientist of today and his brothers of the medieval and pre-historic barbarisms that is highly diverting—to those who can appreciate it. For the rest we recommend our young and enthusiastic Socialists to a careful study on "The Nature of Capital" and "The Socialist Economics of Karl Marx" from which they may learn a great deal.

But we do not expect that very many "educated" Negroes will want to read *The Place of Science in Modern Civilization*. More's the pity. The same cannot be said of *The Theory of the Leisure Class*. This is a work which should be on the bookshelf of every cultivated liberal and radical, white or black. It calls itself "an economic study of institutions" and it is that, and more. Those who want to see how philosophy can come down to earth and do splendid journeyman's work are advised to get it. Such institutions as leisure class, political government, manners, press, the higher learning and religion are brilliantly interpreted here from the standpoint of the highest and deepest modern standards of evaluation. The critical comments on Religious Mummery are highly diverting and instructive. In *The Place of Science*, Prof. Veblen describes the pulpit as "the accredited vent for the exudation of effete matter from the cultural organism" and in *The Theory of the Leisure Class* he analyzes in a similar spirit "the shaven face of the priest," "his livery of a very expensive character," "his wasteful expenditure," and the other ear-marks of devout ceremonial. His discussion of women's dress, particularly the corset, introduces and illustrates a theory of economic values and their function in a class of society which contains the key to a new world of thought. No preliminary study of sociology and economics can be said to be complete without this work of Veblen. Besides these two books his work on *The Instinct of Workmanship*, *The Theory of Business Enterprise* and *The Higher Learning in America* are especially to be recommended. And we feel sure that whoever may get acquainted with any of Prof. Veblen's books through our recommendation will live to thank us for it.

Africa

Harrison read widely on Africa and in his writing, speaking, and teaching he repeatedly urged his audiences to learn about Africa's history, cultures, and peoples. He served as secretary for the Negro Society for Historical Research (founded by lay scholars Arthur Schomburg and John Bruce) which sought "to instruct our people in Negro history and achievement" and to "inspire love and veneration" for the race's "men and women of mark." Harrison also wrote numerous reviews in the *Negro World* and the *New York World* (as well as others in *The Nation* and *Opportunity*) on Africa; he developed a fifteen lecture series on African culture which he delivered in Brooklyn; and he played a founding role in establishing the "Department of Negro Literature and History" of the 135th Street Public Library which later developed into the Schomburg Center for Research in Black Culture, one of the international centers for research on peoples and cultures of Africa and African descent. Harrison had none of the condescending attitude toward Africans that many of his American contemporaries evidenced and he considered West African leaders such as Casely Hayford and John Mensah Sarbah to be "at the very tiptop of Negro intellect, enterprise and achievement." His core message, reflected in the writings that follow, was to learn about Africa, to establish contacts with and learn from Africans, and to realize "that African Negroes," not "American Negroes," would lead struggles in Africa.[21]

110. "The Black Man's Burden," (review of *The Black Man's Burden* by E. D. Morel), handwritten manuscript; reprinted in *Negro World* (December 11, 1920); HHHP Wr.[22]

In the December 11, 1920, *Negro World* Harrison reviewed *The Black Man's Burden* by the British Socialist Edmund D. Morel (1873–1924). Harrison considered Morel to be one of those "white men who will befriend the Negro, who will give their dollars to his comfort and welfare, so long as the idea of what constitutes the comfort and welfare comes entirely from the white man's mind." Nevertheless, in this review he found that Morel furnished "the facts on which we rest our case against the white man's domination of our own motherland." For that reason he judged the work deserving of "the serious attention of intelligent Negroes."[23]

The present volume of 241 pages is the American edition of an English book that is hardly a year old. This in itself is significant. The volumes have been eagerly awaited by those among us who have been long familiar with the monuments of Mr. Morel's industry in the field of African history and social science in which he has won for himself an enviable place as an authority of the very first rank. He has been for many years a most prolific writer on Africa, and his published works include many valuable contributions, such as *The Affairs of West Africa, King Leopold's Rule in Africa, The Congo Slave State, Trading Monopolies in West Africa, Nigeria, Its People and Its Problems, Red Rubber, Africa and the Prince of Europe*, and a host of lesser writings, besides a staggering quantity of contributions to periodicals and much controversial literature. Whatever we may think of his defects and limitations such a writer is worthy of serious attention. And *The Black Man's Burden* especially deserves the serious attention of intelligent Negroes here and in Africa.

For it is the summary of the history of the white Christian's attempt to take to the African peoples his own peculiar brand of civilization and culture — and it makes particularly nasty reading. If any servile Negro wants to preserve his traditional love and respect for the white race he had better not read this book. For in its pages he will find that the best and highest of that race — its king and queens, its statesmen, generals, editors and industrial magnates — are, in plain English, professional liars, slimy hypocrites, and blood-thirsty thieves. England, France, Italy, Germany, Portugal and Belgium have blackened themselves with the same brush in their game of African expansion. Lying, cunning, brute force and slavery have been and still are the main methods of controlling the destinies of the unhappy people of the African continent. No story of marauding buccaneers rivals in brutal blood-lust the history of these six Christian nations in their dealings with the black Africans. The recorded deeds of [Captain William] Kidd, [George] Watling and [Edward "Blackbeard"] Teach and the pirates of the Spanish Main pale into insignificance beside the deliberate and atrocious butcheries engineered and carried out by Dr. [Leander] Jameson in Rhodesia, [General] Lothar von Trotha in Damaraland, [King] Leopold [II] in the Congo, and bearers of "the white man's burden" everywhere in Africa. Indeed, if all the African blood that has been shed by white men in the past fifty years could be made to come in one place it would drown the dwellers in London.

So long as effeminate fools on our side descant on the "reconciliation of the races" and persist in preaching "love" to the lamb rather than to the lion, books like this one of Mr. Morel will serve a useful purpose among us. Not indeed, that the purpose coincides with Mr. Morel's. It is far otherwise. He "seeks to lay down the fundamental principles of a human and practical policy for the government of Africa *by white men*," and his emotions are limited to the philanthropic round. As long as the African can furnish fit scope for Mr. Morel's sympathies as an object of compassion so long and so far is Mr. Morel his champion and defender. But he refuses to rise above that philanthropic role and consider the black race as humanly the equal of his race in rights, or as an independent shaper of its own destiny. "The actual *government* of tropical Africa in the proper sense of the term, *by the white man*, is only beginning, according to our author, and his terribly straight-forward arraignment of the past and present brutalities of the white man's rule in that continent is made in an earnest and sincere effort to abate the *brutalities*, not the *rule*. "The real problem," according to him "is to insure that a material relationship, which is inevitable, shall not preclude just, humane, and enlightened government of tropical African peoples *by European States*." As a struggling, handicapped race, we should be foolishly shortsighted if we failed to accept the friendly gestures of Mr. Morel and his congeners of the Aborigines' Protection Society, so far as they go. But as critics of our own condition we must take the opportunity to tell them that it doesn't go very far—with us. Doubtless that will genuinely surprise them. But that is their business, not ours. They can afford the fatuous conclusion (after all that they have seen) that the rule of white men and brutality to us are inseparable. We can not, and we have *all* the past experience in the case on our side. They have none. But even if the separation of the two were possible we should still prefer (as they would in our place) our own rule over ourselves to their rule over us. And since the areas are ours, they can only justify the over-riding of theirs under similar circumstances, namely; superior brute force. And there is the final term in these questions of international and inter-racial political philosophy, whether Mr. Morel sees it or not.

The Black Man's Burden begins with an account of the slave trade in which the Portuguese and Spaniards led, with unctuous phrases of religion on their lips. They were quickly followed by the English, Dutch, Danish, French and others. Of these the English, especially after the Treaty of Utrecht became the most notorious both for the extent of their traffic and its savage brutality. Back in the sixteenth century the great Queen Elizabeth was the silent partner of the infamous John Hawkins, whom she sent out on the good ship Jesus to burn peaceful towns and villages on the Guinea coast and seize the inhabitants as slaves. Later in the seventeenth century Queen Anne added to her private income in the same way. By the Treaty of Utrecht England forced the Spaniards to give her the monopoly of supplying slaves to the Spanish colonies, and the wealth which flowed from this source was used to pay the expense of the war with Spain which had just ended. Thus, as early as 1713 the white Christians of England had already adopted the pernicious principle which Sir Harry Johnston announced in 1914 and the Colonial Office is now living up to: that the costs of white Christian warfare must be paid by black "heathen" Africa. Both the elder and the younger [William] Pitt proceeded on this principle, as a result of which the English government persisted in forcing the slave trade upon the American colonies—a fact not generally known by "educated" and loyal British Negroes.

But the nineteenth century brought this traffic to an end. Yet it was in the nineteenth century that the other form of slavery was established: the slavery of entire peoples and lands to the armed buccaneers of imperial expansion. The account of this new horror, with its horde of suave and subtle missionaries in front, its traders and concessionaires in the middle, and its legions of licentious soldiery behind, is given by Mr. Morel in seven significant episodes which are intended as "samples": The British acquisition of Rhodesia, the German conquest of the Hereros, France's seizure of Morocco, Italy's grab at Tripoli, Belgium's Congo horror and France's similar hell in the French Congo, and the Portuguese slave raid on Angola and the Cocoa Islands, where one-tenth of the male population is worked, beaten and starved to death every year. It is hardly necessary to pick any particular one of these for excoriation. For there isn't a pin to choose between them. And if the English-speaking public still thinks of Belgium's Congo as the supreme atrocity, it must be remembered that Belgium had in the Congo a great economic advantage over England at that time: that England, by its cable monopoly, controlled the news of the world and Belgium did not. The English (and Americans) could, therefore, "play up" the Congo atrocities to a gasping world while the Belgians couldn't "play up" theirs. As Mr. Morel points out, each one of the imperialist groups can be perfectly trusted to tell the full and complete truth *about the other*. By collating these several national truths we can get the entire international story.

Yet we cannot refrain from adverting to our author's account of the British robbery of Rhodesia, since the lying account of native conditions in that country given in 1895 by Mr. E. F. Knight in his book *Rhodesia of Today*, is still to be found in our local public library. Mr. Knight went to Rhodesia, as a half-baked literary tout of the Rhodes-Rudd interests and was chaperoned by that notorious and discredited thief, Dr. [Leander Starr] Jameson. According to him, the Chartered Company was the soul of honesty and trusted in every way by the Mashonas and Matabele who were always so eager to work that they would stay six months when their contract called for only one. Mr. Morel's account gives the facts of seizure and occupation of this country three times the size of England. It was the son of the missionary, [Robert] Moffat, who acted the congenial role of decoy or "come-on" to poor old Lobengula [king of the Matabele]. This misguided monarch trusted too much to "the word of God" as interpreted by Christian Englishmen. And this is the way he was "worked": While the Duke of Fife [Alexander William George], King Edward's son-in-law, Earl Grey [Alfred Henry George], Lord [Hugh Charles] Clifford and a few more lordly land sharks, secured a royal charter at the Colonial Office, Cecil Rhodes and Alfred Belt worked the South African end of the wire and got Moffat to induce Lobongula to sign away the land to their company by lying to him as to the nature and purport of that treaty. As soon as the African king learned the full meaning of the document he protested to Queen Victoria and the Colonial Office. But the great Queen's relatives and the Colonial clique were too deeply involved and she herself could offer only cold comfort.

Meanwhile Dr. Jameson, as the African manager of the Chartered Company, worked out a plan of armed invasion. With this in his pocket he egged on his gang of freebooters to raid cattle in Lobengula's territory, to murder his indunas and stake out land claims. He offered £9000 worth of land and twenty claims in addition to each marauder, and when everything was ready they rushed Lobengula. The "uprising" which was provoked in this manner was drowned in the blood of the Matabeles and Mashonas, thousands of whom were butchered as they fled. At present the remainder are permitted, by grace of the English, to live on reservations in one corner of the country—the bleakest and least productive—while the good white people have instituted a collective slavery which compels the former owners of the soil to labor for next to nothing in the mines and on the farms of their masters. Any white settler may take up land occupied by natives who are then compelled to pay him $5 a year for the privilege of living on that land and $5 more to the Chartered Company. This money must be earned by working for the invaders who have now succeeded in bringing into existence in that part of Africa one of the chief blessings of that part of Africa one of the chief blessings of Christian capitalist civilization; a propertyless, landless, proletarian class. In this spoliation of Mashona and Matabele people it was the official and responsible arm of collective English Christianity which was unable to protect the duped king from his own landsharks; but as soon as they had attacked him it sent its soldiers to slay him and his people and seize their lands.

What then, must black people conclude, is the collective character of white Christians? The facts here given as a small slice of the imperialistic record show them to be crooked and contemptible liars, cold-blooded bandits and canting, psalm-singing hypocrites. Doubtless Mr. Morel would say that there is another Europe. We confess inability to see this. If nine-tenths of us black people are servile and ignorant, both Mr. Morel and his countrymen would swear by all the gods of reason and logic that Negroes, as such, were servile and ignorant! And we, the one-tenth, couldn't contradict this by offering ourselves as evidence to the contrary. Sauce for the goose is sauce for the gander, both in life and logic, we Negroes cannot forget this fact.

One of Mr. Morel's pet horrors is the danger (to Europe) of armed Africans enrolled in the military service of white nations. It seems to give him scant sleep o' nights. We, on the contrary, desire that very consummation. For we can't forget that Rome came to an end in that way, and we are hoping that the white man's blind and greedy imperialism will meet the same fate by the very products of its own rapacity. "Africa has always repaid her exploiters," and already Nemesis has begun to write upon the wall. We quote from Mr. Morel:

> The narrow, irregular streets of a Moorish town, into which shells from warships riding on the sparkling blue waters of the western Atlantic are falling in an incessant and murderous hail, smashing the white-walled, flat roofed houses and splashing them all over with the blood of the white-clad inhabitants who sprawl in mangled heaps at the doors of their homes—between such a scene as this and the pitted, scarred battlefields of Europe, today with the blasted stumps which were once trees, and the piles of masonry and timber which were once towns and villages, there appears at first thought no connecting link of circumstance.

> "Whatsoever a man soweth, that also shall he reap," is as true of nations as of individuals; and even as Belgium between 1914 and 1918 reaped in disaster and destruction some fruits of her sowing in Africa, so also may England reap her whirlwind of destruction in the days to come. And so may all the others. In the meanwhile Mr. Morel's book should be sought after by everyone who can afford a copy. It will furnish the facts on which we rest our case against the white man's domination of our own motherland.

111. "The Caucasian Canker in South Africa," review of *The Real South Africa* by Ambrose Pratt, *Negro World* (May 14, 1921), HHHP Scr B.

In the May 14, 1921, *Negro World* Harrison reviewed *The Real South Africa* (London, 1913) by Ambrose Pratt (1874–1944), an Australian journalist who visited South Africa in 1910. He considered the work, which discusses the attempt at settlement over colonization by whites in South Africa, to be "one of the most informing," "courageous," and well-documented books on the subject. In the course of the review Harrison elaborates on the thesis that "wherever the white race enslaves and oppresses the black, the white shall sink and the black shall rise."

> Mr. Pratt is an Australian journalist who visited South Africa in 1910 in the company of Andrew Fisher, who was then Prime Minister of the Australian commonwealth. While in the Union he made such good use of his time that the book which he gives us as the

result of his observations is one of the most informing and courageous books that have been written about South Africa. It is packed full of facts, most of which have been directly observed or culled from public and official documents. The story which he tells is both well documented and well attested. It is a story which the whites of South Africa would rather not see in print. For it tears the bandage of suppression from the ulcer of their lives and leaves it open to the eyes — and the nostrils — of a contemptuous world. Instead of an earthly paradise for the white race we see an imposing edifice, gorgeously gilt on the outside but reeking with the stenches of decay on the inside. Here is the sinister spectacle of a race in the process of collapsing under the weight of "the white man's burden" which it was driven by greed and pride to assume in the course of capitalistic expansion and imperial conquest. Here is the story of a "superior" race, with laziness, crime, disease and arrogance eating its very vitals out. Here we see the white man, with all his parade of "civilization," wilting under the fierce sun of Africa, while the dominated black increases in numbers, strength, solidarity and the sense of power — in spite of oppression, subjection and outrage. Between the wind that he has sown and the whirlwind which he must reap the South African white is in an unenviable position. But the story is worth re-telling.

South Africa, between the Zambesi and the Cape of Good Hope is an enormous stretch of territory (1,250,000 square miles) thinly populated by Bantus, Bushmen and Hottentots. Boers and British, Dutch, German, French and Portuguese have during four centuries endeavored to subjugate and exploit various portions of this immense area. The British, who beat the world in swiping everything which has not been nailed down — and most things that are — have finally succeeded in ousting from political control all the other Europeans and have now consolidated the sub-continent under the title of the Union of South Africa, in which Boers and Britons subsist upon the underpaid labor of millions of aborigines.

The significance of this experiment lies in the fact that it is the first attempt made by a white European population in historic times to establish themselves as denizens of the Black Continent. Hitherto white men have confined their control over Africans in Africa to the administration of government and the control of trade and commerce. Overlordship, not settlement, has been the only practicable form of exploiting African resources. In the South African Union, however, the European believed that he had found a section of the continent suitable for his habitation where he could live and rear his children, duplicate his peculiar form of civilization, and add another permanent extension to the white areas of the world.

But it seems that God or nature has established metes and bounds even to the vaulting ambition of the whites. For we find that they have been "corrupted and enervated by their long and uninterrupted dependence on the blacks. . . . South Africa has been settled for several hundred of years; it has been fought and bled for by many peoples;

today its total white population scarcely exceeds 1,200,000 souls. Here is a truth which tells its own tale. . . . The natives are so physically vigorous and mentally virile, their numbers are so vast, their rate of natural increase is so great and rapid, and their desire to exceed the bounds of the white man's caste prejudice is so keen that it is staringly obvious that their aspirations must be restricted and repressed as a condition precedent to the preservation of white supremacy. Undoubtedly the time will come when they will try conclusions with their present masters and put to some final test the white man's ancient claim to be their overlord and governor."

It is the recognition of white dependence and black strength which overcasts the white man's sky in South Africa and gives rise to a policy of brutal repression which, curiously enough, parallels in almost every respect that of the "crackers" of the southern United States. Lynching, segregation disfranchisement and educational starvation are rampant there as here. Yet, the South African "cracker," like our domestic [HH changed this to *the American*] variety, declines in physical and mental vigor, becomes increasingly lazy, vicious, degenerate and washed-out. His children grow up illiterate and shiftless and his women fail to breed as they should. It seems as if fate had decreed as a law of inexorable retribution that wherever the white race enslaves and oppresses the black the white shall sink and the black shall rise.

Mr. Pratt's book lends itself so readily to quotation that it is difficult to refrain from reproducing portions of it.

> Let those blink the fact who choose or can (he tells us), South Africa is a black man's country. It belongs of natural right to the Negroid races. The white man is its overlord, has been for centuries, but its owner and enduring occupant, no — at least, not yet. Natural forces are massed and ranged against him, of which he is only now beginning to acquire an adequate conception. Climate, Disease, Increase — so are the forces named. . . . The blacks are increasing at a more rapid rate than the whites. . . . The white man has a natural instinct that he is superior to the uneducated native. But the white man's higher plane cannot possibly subsist any longer than he can prevent the native from developing the qualities of intellect, initiative and resource which have given the former the mastery. The white man's rule depends on keeping the blacks ignorant and mentally benighted. Yet this cannot be done forever. Just now the native is doing all the rough and unskilled work in South Africa. The whites are merely overseers. . . . The practice is injurious and short-sighted to the last degree. It undermines and diminishes the white man's industrial efficiency and it trains the native to supplant him. But it is the iron custom of South Africa, and nobody dares to break it.

We learn from Mr. Pratt's book that, whereas the native miner receives two and a half shillings a day in the mines, the white miner gets twenty-two and a half. Even in the ordinary industrial occupations the "superior" white laborer plays the part of a racial aristocrat. The black worker must carry his tools and every white bricklayer must be attended by natives, who hand him the bricks which he lays. A deadline is drawn between "white man's work" and "Kaffir's work" and no white man must soil his hands with the latter, or white supremacy is done for.

Premier Fisher, who penned the introduction to the book, insists that, for the salvation of the white man's prestige, "there must be a line of demarcation between white and colored labor." But Mr. Pratt takes occasion in a special chapter addressed to "Englishmen, etc.," to warn white men of the working classes that they should shun South Africa as they would the plague because there is no work there for them, as a result of this very attitude on the part of the white man. And the effects are far-reaching. Unless white men are willing to work in competition with Negroes in South Africa they must get jobs as overseers. Now it is clear that profitable industry cannot be made to support an excess number of overseers whose salaries are a charge against the profits of production. Capitalists will not knowingly forego their profits for racial reasons — and the work of production must go forward. They, therefore, employ the black laborers, who "increase and multiply and replenish the earth," on the wages which they get. This the white laborer cannot do on anything like the same wage; and the result in South Africa must eventually be that the white working class will be squeezed out in the contest, and instead of South Africa becoming a white workers paradise it will be, for weal or woe, the heaven of black workers. Africa always pays — for wars and other things; but the catastrophic fact remains that, as Morel puts it, "Africa always repays."

"This attitude of the white man has greatly affected his efficiency as a laborer. . . . The standard of efficiency of white unskilled labor in South Africa has fallen very much lower than in countries where there is no colored labor." The Royal Commission informs us that 85 per cent. of the mechanics employed in the building trades in Kimberly are colored; that the wagon building industry has fallen almost completely into the hands of the Negro; that 30 per cent. of those engaged in the printing trade are Negroes; and that black competition is already acute in the trades of carpentering, plastering, saddlery, painting, tailoring and bricklaying. Thus even if the prejudice against Kaffir's work were broken down completely and universally tomorrow the position would hardly be one whit altered; for there would be little or no unskilled work for the white man to do, since the black man does it better and much cheaper. The Royal Commission found, in consequence, "that there is an immense amount of white indigency prevailing in all parts of South Africa. Many thousands of white men are living as vagrants on charity. Thousands more live by vice and crime. The country is cursed with a large pauper population of unskilled white workers. And there is no immediate hope or prospect of relief." There are special settlements of these people, subsidized by the Union government, notably at Goedodorp, Donkey Camp and Vrededorp. The "poor whites," in the commissioner's report, "are neither willing nor able to do a hard day's work." Thus the crime which the white people have perpetrated on the Negroes of South Africa recoil upon their own hands [HH changed this to *head*].

Space [HH changed this to *Time*] will not permit us to summarize the whole story of white degeneracy in that country as Mr. Pratt tells it. We can merely insist that it is well told. Mr. Pratt shows the Negroes as climbing steadily and making great gains in education and enlightment in spite of their severe handicaps. The chapters entitled "The Black Man," "The Black Menace," "The Boer and the Rand," are replete with information which is valuable to all thinking Negroes and our thanks are due to Mr. George Young [of Young's Book Exchange] for making it available to the Negro people of America.

112. "M. Maran's *Batouala*, a French-African Tale: Work of a Negro Novelist as It Impresses a Negro Reviewer — Prize Story of a Land That Has Known the Abuses of Civilization," *New York World* (August 20, 1922).

In the August 20, 1922, *New York World* Harrison reviewed *Batouala* by the Martinique native René Maran (1887–1960), which was set in Ubangui-Shari in French Equatorial Africa (later the Central African Republic) under French colonialism. Maran's work initiated considerable intellectual criticism of colonialism in Africa and won the Goncourt prize, the most sought-after prize in French literature. Maran was the first Black writer to win the prize, and his preface, in particular, caused considerble debate because it openly criticized the social and economic conditions of the inhabitants of French Equatorial Africa, the forced labor imposed in the region, and French colonial policy. In July Ernest Hemingway declared it a great novel, and in September *The Crisis* claimed "the whole world [was] reading it."[24]

Maran read Harrison's review and wrote from his home in Fort Achambault, French Equatorial Africa, saying he had received little financial profit from *Batouala*. He asked that Harrison make known his financial situation in the hope that readers could offer some financial assistance. In one of his many efforts to help a struggling Black artist, Harrison had this information publicized in the April 5, 1923, *Chicago Defender*.[25]

RENE MARAN'S *"veritable roman Negre"* which won the Goncourt last winter and created an unusual furore in French literary and administrative circles is now presented to us in an English dress. Despite its stark and sombre realism, it is a book of atmosphere and flavors — and these are precisely the things which it is most difficult to transfer from one language to another.

We cannot quite blame Mrs. Adele Szold Seltzer for the undoubted fact that the fine Gallic flavor of *Batouala* has evaporated from the English version. But enough of the basic quality of the book survives to justify its claims to special consideration.

Batouala is not exactly a novel, as understood either in English or in French, but rather a series of sketches of the inner and outer life of the degraded natives of the section of the French Congo which lies between three different culture-areas; the Egyptian Soudan, Soudanic and Bantu Africa. The people whom Maran depicts constitute a branch of the cannibal group known as the Nyam-Nyam, which has been elaborately described by [Georg August] Schweinfurth.

It happens that these people are no more representative of the average African cultures surrounding them than the Basques of the Cantabrian Mountains are representative of the average culture of England, France or Germany. But on their original degradation has been superimposed an additional degradation by the tax gatherers of French imperialism, and M. Maran even charges, through the medium of his characters, that the vices of Europe have been deliberately imported among them.

But *Batoula*, as Maran insists, is not a polemic. "It happens, by pure chance, to be 'timely.' The Negro question is a present reality. It has been made so by the Americans and by the newspaper campaign from the other side of the Rhine." Yet, oddly enough, there is no "defense of the Negro" in the book. On the contrary, the objective, artistic conscience of this Negro realist makes him paint the Negro before him as he really is in that particular section of Central Africa—a stark and brutal savage without a single glimmer of uplifting hope. But the picture could have been worse in its brutal savagery. For instance, there is no direct description of these orgies of ceremonial cannibalism for which that neighborhood was long famous. This is one of the things which French rule has suppressed, although, like the ga'nza, it crops up from time to time in those sections which are not effectively supervised.

Maran introduces us to some genuine Congolese characters: Batouala, the headman of the district, Yassiguindja, the chief wife (of nine), Indouboura, another wife, Bissibingui, a gay Lothario whose "affairs" with Yassiguindja furnished the lurid flare of primeval passions that lights up the corners of the African triangle, and Batouala's father, a wise old rip who serves as a sort of African Polonious.

The love affair is not as simple as it seems at first sight; for the young Bissibingui has been unofficial husband to the nine wives of his chief—and to many others. Eventually his amour with Yassiguindja is revealed at the great ga'nza and Batouala's jealousy is aroused. But he hides it under a specious mask of friendship which deceives no one, and least of all Bissibingui, who plans to do away with the old chief at the next "burning of the bush," which is the symbol of the great seasoned hunt.

Batouala has similar kindly intentions; but when he attempts the life of his rival he misses his spear-cast and is ripped open by a leopard. After lingering many days in agony, he dies in his hut, abandoned by all but Bissibingui and Yassiguinda, who have foregathered there to embrace each other in frank Congolese fashion.

The story is as sordidly primitive as the natural surroundings which M. Maran describes with a power and poignancy that it would be hard to match. Some of the details are a bit too strong for American stomachs. These have been omitted in the translation. But they are only a few, and they hardly amount to more than a couple of pages altogether.

This book marks M. Maran as a great artist who, if he should stick to this field of French Colonial Africa, will enjoy a primacy all his own. He has the seeing eye and the understanding mind and he draws with a hand that is steady and true. Any one who wishes to get the genuine atmosphere of the French section of Congoland may feel assured that he will get it in this book, which is, as its author describes it, "*un veritable roman Negre.*"

Octavus Roy Cohen

 113. "The Southern Black — As Seen by the Eye of Fiction," review of *Highly Colored* by Octavus Roy Cohen, *Negro World* (December 10, 1921): 8, HHHP Scr B.

Octavus Roy Cohen (1891–1959), born in South Carolina, was a prolific humorist, short story writer, playwright, screenwriter, and novelist whose stories often included characters of pronounced stereotypes. Cohen always maintained that he portrayed southern Blacks knowledgeably, with affection, and without bias, but his stylized characters, his subsequent writings (some of which were used in the "Amos 'n' Andy" radio show), and some of his titles (including *Polished Ebony* [1919], *Assorted Chocolates* [1922], and *Carbon Copies* [1932]) received strong criticism. In the *Negro World* of December 10 Harrison reviewed Cohen's *Highly Colored* and observed that the social life of Black Americans offered many social types of interest to the true fictionalist. He regretted that Black writers were not preserving these characters, and he praised Cohen's effort and "delightful stories."[26]

The highly specialized life which the Negro lives in his highly specialized American world has produced many interesting social types which are tempting to the true fictionalist. It is to be regretted that the Negro writers since [Paul Laurence] Dunbar and [Charles Waddell] Chesnutt have not seen fit to limn the larger number of these types for posterity. Just as the callow representatives of "culture" turned in top-lofty disdain from the hymns of the colored Baptists and Methodists of the plantation South until white men like [Antonín Leopold] Dvorak and [Henry Edward] Krehbiel pointed out to white and black that these were the only genuine music produced in America, so, the dress-coated devotees of a hand-me-down elegance have refused to deal with the rich mine of human material to be found in the daily lives lived by nine-tenths of our people, North and South.

Today, when a young Negro college graduate puts pen to paper to portray imaginatively the life of the American Negro he either produces a propaganda pamphlet in the guise of "a story," or he writes almost exclusively of the upper-class Negro types and pushes the lives below that level into the background of obscurity.

We can hardly condemn this tendency; indeed it is quite natural. It is the way in which all literatures begin. But it is well to insist that we need not stop at the beginning stage forever. A time comes when we must say, "Let's go!" And that time has come for Negro writers of fiction. For the white man is already exploiting the field which should be theirs. And the results are not always to our liking.

How Negroes will take the brilliant short stories of Mr. Cohen will depend upon their sense of humor. We are still touchy about our tribe and tend to get huffy when the type that is amusing happens to be "colored." Yet we boast at the same time of the Negro's "unfailing humor" as a godsend! But then there is the humor of malice and the humor of sympathy as well as the humor of sheer pleasure without any ulterior purpose. Mr. Cohen's humor in this book is of the latter sort. I think that the supreme dandy and man-about town, Mr. Florian Slappey, Lawyer Evans Chew and that close-fisted man of money, Mr. Semore Mashby, will live in the memory as outstanding types together with the stalwart society known as "The Sons and Daughters of I Will Arise." Of course they are drawn to the scale of humor, and on that scale they bulk large — even for Birmingham, Alabama.

Mr. Cohen sticks to "Bumminghum," although the types which he draws would be just as representative of Norfolk or any other large Southern city. No normal human can read these delightful stories without bubbling over with enjoyment. Book-hardened reviewers don't read a book over as a rule; but I must confess that as soon as I lay down the pen I shall take up for a second reading the book which lies beside me. The short stories are shaped to perfection — all but one — and the dialect is lovingly chisselled to a high and fine finish. My one regret is that the book has only one illustration.

It is worthy of special remark that no criminal or contemptible types are represented in this book — "just folks."

114. "The Real Negro Humor: Brought Out, Says a Writer of the Race, in Octavus Roy Cohen's Tales," *New York World* (October 23, 1923), HHHP Wr.

In this review of a second book by the humorist Octavus Roy Cohen, Harrison calls the attention of Black writers to the "inexhaustible veins of humor" available to them. He also observes that an intellect above average, a deep knowledge of humanity, and sympathetic comprehension are crucial for the humorist.

Octavus Roy Cohen has carved for himself a little corner in our contemporary literature, thanks to the inferiority-complex which seems to keep Negro writers of fiction from utilizing the inexhaustible veins of humor and comic value which run under their racial sod. The existence of these riches is known far and near, yet no one would ever suspect it from any indication in the works of the representative Negro writer of to-day.

When a young Negro college graduate puts pen to paper to portray imaginatively the life and soul of his people he either produces a propaganda pamphlet in the guise of a "story" or he writes as if his race consisted exclusively of lawyers, doctors, savants and millionaires. The rich human values that lie in the lives of the rank and file are surrendered to the pens of white writers. And when they are concentrated on the humorous aspects of the material "the talented tenth" gets touchy.

But, as Mr. Mencken recently remarked, it is the man with a sense of adequacy who can find humor in a situation of conflict, while the man with a sense of inferiority quickly goes "up in the air." The English, the Irish, the American have all been served up to us in literary dishes highly spiced with humor, and no one was injured thereby. Now it is the Negro's turn. But, then, there are the humor of malice and the humor of sympathy, as well as the humor of sheer pleasure without any ulterior purpose. Mr. Cohen's humor is of the last sort. What he gives us in *Dark Days and Black Knights* (Dodd-Mead) is a gallery of outstanding Negro types around which he develops comic situations of amazing fidelity to fact.

Florian Slappey, that supreme dandy and the man-about-town; Lawyer Evans Chew, Rev. Plato Tubb, Sis Callie, Flukers, Gussie Muck, Eli Gouch and that close-fisted man of money, Mr. Semore Mashby, together with the stalwart society, Known as "The Sons and Daughters of I Will Arise" — all these can find their counterparts in Negro life as it is lived to-day in any large city. Of course, they are drawn to the scale of humor, and on that scale they bulk large — even for Birmingham, Ala., where the scene is laid.

To one who lives on the inside of Negro life it is obvious that Mr. Cohen is not so much creating characters as transcribing them from life. Of the inner motives and springs of character to be found in the Negro society of a large Southern city, he has a thoroughness of comprehension which no [HH crossed out *other*] white man ever had. True, he purposely distorts it in his magic-lantern, but no amount of distortion can disguise the intimate accuracy of his knoweldge.

Besides, Mr. Cohen's humor is not of the sharpest sort. He has no conventional lay figure like those of the "good old darky" and "Massa John's man," the latter helpless apart from the kickings and crusts of some bogus "Kunnel," "Jedge" or "Gin'ral." These colored people are individualized and self-sufficing. The rich and rollicking humor grows out of their changing relations to each other and to organic social situations, and is not inconsistent with patches of the pathetic, ironic insight and the flavor of romance. This is the broad essential difference between Cohen and a whole raft of writers like [Hugh] Wiley and "Judge" [Thomas] Dixon who have used the Negro as humorous material. They produce "slapstick commedy" while he produces humor. And after all (as Mark Twain, [François] Rabelais and Anatole France, have shown us), an intellect above the average, a deep knowledge of humanity and the sympathy of perfect comprehension are necessary for the finest flavors of the humorist.

Carter G. Woodson

Carter G. Woodson (1875–1950) has been called "the father of Negro history." A son of former slaves, he earned bachelor's and master's degrees from the University of Chicago and a Ph.D. from Harvard before teaching in Washington, D.C. (1909–1918), serving as dean at Howard University (1919–1920), and teaching at West Virginia State College (1920–1922). In 1915 Woodson founded the Association for the Study of Negro Life and History and the *Journal of Negro History* and he later started the *Negro History Bulletin.* Among his major other writings are *A Century of Negro Migration* (1915), *The Negro in Our History* (1922), and *The Mis-Education of the Negro* (1933).[27]

In the following two reviews Harrison, seeking to judge Woodson's efforts on their merits, offers strong criticism in the first and lavish praise in the second.

 115. "Negro Church History: A Book of It Badly Marred by Neglect of the Race Foundation," review of *The History of the Negro Church* by Carter G. Woodson, *New York World* (July 23, 1922), HHHP Wr.

As to *The History of the Negro Church*, by Carter G. Woodson, Ph. D. (Associated Publishers, Washington, D.C.), it is unfortunate that this book of a Negro scholar should succumb, as it does, to the passion of the propagandist. The author tells us that "the church has surrendered to the capitalistic system and developed into an agency seeking to assuage the pains of those suffering from the very economic evils which the institution has not the courage to attack." And in the meanwhile he overlooks obvious points of scholarship of which his work stands in need.

For instance, every scholarly historian should know that when the Negro slaves were brought to the Western world they had been uprooted from a culture of their own in which were embedded their own religious habits and institutions. These constituted the new religious foundations upon which Christianity was set, and these foundations determine even in our own day the form which the religious consciousness of the Negro takes. But no attempt is made by Dr. Woodson even to sketch these African foundations of his theme, consequently no one will learn from his work how differently Negroes worship God, or anything of their emotionalism, or of their age-long divorce of practical ethics from religious preachments under Christian teaching and example.

Dr. Woodson tells the story of the Christian Church in America so far as it is recoverable from the records and proceedings of the various church bodies. His range of documents is narrow and he nowhere rises to more than mediocre respectability. The story which he tells is itself highly interesting, but his telling serves to lower that interest to the point of dullness. Nor does the slovenly English in which the book abounds add to its value. As a piece of historical scholarship it is distinctly disappointing and far inferior to the author's other works.

116. "Negro's Part in History," review of *The Negro in Our History* by Dr. Carter G. Woodson, *New York Tribune* (January 7, 1923): 6:18. [The *N* in *Negro* was not capitalized in the original.]

Here at last is a history of the American Negro in succinct and readable form, suitable as a text book for high school or college and for the general reader who wishes to acquaint himself with the ways in which the presence of the Negro population has influenced the march of great events in the United States. It hasn't the range and sweep of Benjamin Brawley's *Social History of the American Negro*, but its compressed materials and the fine illustrations, which its great rival lacks, makes it a more handy work of reference.

Dr. Woodson is the editor of the *Journal of Negro History*, the only learned periodical published by American Negroes. He has assumed the role of professional historian of the Negro and he brings to that task considerable erudition and remarkable industry. *The Education of the Negro Prior to 1861, A Century of Negro Migration*, and *The History of the Negro Church* have already appeared as products of his learning and industry, and the present volume clinches his claim to consideration. It is unfortunate that Dr. Woodson's style is cramped and slovenly in all these volumes, but the interest of the subject matter in the volume now before us is so compelling that it enables us to overlook this prime defect.

The various form of Americas slavery are clearly exhibited: the first soul-grinding phase which changed to a mild patriarchal form as the South became saturated, changing again to intensified exploitation as Crompton's "mule" and Whitney's cotton-gin made cotton king and dictated the extension of slavery with its consequent political conflict which gradually estranged the two great sections of the country from each other and led to the Civil War. Freedom and reconstruction and the rise of the freedmen to their present status are graphically treated, and a wealth of material is presented which will open the eyes of many American readers whose knowledge of their darker fellow citizens rests mainly on a mass of myths.

Carl Van Vechten

Carl Van Vechten (1880–1964), a novelist, photographer, and the former assistant music critic of the *New York Times* and drama critic of the *New York Press*, was an enthusiast of Black culture and a controversial white figure associated with the "Harlem Renaissance" in the 1920s. As Harlem became a national and international center of Black thought, writers worked at poetry, fiction, drama, and essays while artists worked with new confidence in music, dance, painting, and sculpture. In the course of this outpouring, concern emerged over the role of white patrons and friends, over the authenticity of the works that were produced, and over whether what was being produced was serious effort related to the masses. These issues concerned Harrison and he addressed them in the following articles on Van Vechten's controversial 1926 novel *Nigger Heaven*.[28]

 117. "Homo Africanus Harlemi," review of *Nigger Heaven* by Carl Van Vechten, *Amsterdam News* (September 1, 1926), HHHP Wr.

Harrison offered his first review of Van Vechten's *Nigger Heaven* under the title "Homo Africanus Harlemi" in the September 1, 1926, *Amsterdam News*. Van Vechten's book had stirred quite a controversy and, according to Robert Worth, "Never again would white writers roar uptown with such feckless glee, and never would blacks admit them again so freely." Harrison criticized the work based on the fact that he considered it to be an inferior product. The phrase "Homo Africanus" had been used by L. M. Hussey in a 1925 *American Mercury* piece which discussed how African Americans had learned to survive by wearing the mask and playing roles that made whites feel comfortable. Harrison likely chose the title to offer comment on some of Van Vechten's friends.[29] [The article includes Harrison's corrections.]

The author of this breach of the peace has been well and favorably known to Harlem's new and nocturnal aristocracy of "brains" and booze. He has been wined and dined by the seekers after salvation by publicity, by the pundits of "advancement" and by the white pen-pushers who manufacture retail prominence for the smart snotties of the New Renaissance — Negro type, Model 1926.

Nigger Heaven — the title and the theme should be highly appreciated by Van Vechten's dusky hosts — and hostesses — over whose bottles he imbibed the conception of Harlem, which is here exhibited. To the rest of us it seems strange that one of the professional experts on the Negro should select a selling title which gives such offence to all self-respecting Negroes that even a Southerner like Octavus Roy Cohen eschews it from all his writings.

Our main concern, however, is not with the book's title but with its theme and treatment; and we are forced to reflect at the outset that two dollars and a half is a pretty stiff price to pay for piffle. But we must presume that the publishers, like [P. T.] Barnum, knew their public. Else why should they tell them opposite the last page that the book is set to Caslon type, when it quite obviously isn't?

As far back as 1923, in more than one review in *The New York World*, I warned "our young writers" that if they persisted in neglecting the rich human and literary values which lie all around them they would be estopped from crying out loud when white writers dished up these viands spiced with the sauces of their own mental distortions. Well, Mr. Van Vechten has done it!

Nigger Heaven is an "atmosphere" story of Harlem, flanked by tone-sketches and garnished with a vicious "nigger dialect" whose sole source must be the author's mind at 4 a.m. after supping—and something else. Having lived nineteen years in Harlem, roamed all its streets unchaperoned, and been at home with all its varied human types I can speak, I think, with some authority when I say that Van Vechten's dialect doesn't exist up here.

Frankly, I have never heard a Negro say "leab." "Ah doan perzackly recerlec' duh name" (182) is equally alien to me and Harlem. But V. V. is young yet. He seems to think that "the berries" is Negro, while we know that it came up from the Jewish East Side. He also tries to father "Counsellor" on us; but if he had turned to a real student of language like Mr. Mencken, he might have been better informed. He had heard "spagingy-spagade" and guesses that it means Negro, but doesn't dream that it says "spade." Our "copastettick" which came from down South, he gets "kopasettee"—etc., etc.

The story in *Nigger Heaven* is not easy to summarize, because the book is so much else besides the story in it. The author sets out to paint Negro Harlem society; and his first exhibit is an impossible figure of a ruttish female who goes out to buy a pimp with as little tact and "romance" as one exhibits in buying apples.

Some years ago the Maharani of Barodi, in a last interview before she left these shores did declare that the white American woman's way with a man was as crude as her brother's approach to a football in a game; but she didn't mean this sort of thing. There is only one sort of woman who pursues her prey in the Van Vechten manner—and she never, never does it when she goes after a "p. i."

After this false start, our author begins his story up among the leisure class Harlemites, develops a love-story with a spoilt rah-rah boy and a sweet little girl as protagonists, curses him with a college "education" and an itch to write, and finally whelms him in the rotten results of his own waywardness and asinine incompetence.

From the first page to the last one brilliant quality of Van Vechten spills itself over this book, as it does in *The Blind Bow Boy*. He can describe furniture and its accessories, female clothes and fripperies with all the ecstatic abandon of a maiden lady at a wedding and the self-satisfaction of a man-milliner toying with a pink powder-puff. In that domain, I think, he hasn't his equal—among men.

Mr. Van Vechten can write, or, I should say, he could. This is sufficiently attested by

The Blind Bow Boy, a novel of luxurious New York and Long Island in which character and atmosphere, vice and refinement, combine in an organized unity of literary presentation which is worthy of a better cause. But writers sometimes "fall down," Shakespeare wrote *Andronicus*, [Guy] de Maupassant went insane, and Van Vechten wrote *Nigger Heaven*. *The Blind Bow Boy* had indubitable atmosphere: it was genuine. This piece of cheap shoddy has neither atmosphere, depth nor character. The poor putty figures in it are jerked by visible wires that are visibly rusty—and they creak so!

As literature—as art—it is condemned, not in reference to any standard of literary excellence assumed by me, but in reference to its author's previous capacity for worthwhile work, as shown in *Peter Whiffle*, *The Tatooed Countess* and *The Blind Bow Boy*.

And while the present writer hasn't the proper flair for sexual slobber, he would lift a timid voice to point out that some of the words in the "Glossary of Negro Words and Phrases" are filthy to the last degree. Had he used here the same freedom of invention shown in the selection of fantastic cognomens (like Arabia Scribner, Anatole Longfellow and Russia Cloudcroft), he might not have made a worse book, but it might have smelt less like a stable.

In the last four chapters of the book the author becomes painfully aware that the carpentry of it is crude, becomes conscious that he has been turning out superficial trash, and tries to compensate therefore by speeding up the pace of his approaching crisis. But even that fails to rescue the thing.

Yet I am not one of those who believe in absolute goodness or badness, and I can even find a few good things to say of Van Vechten's novel of Harlem life. He does show up the present worthlessness of what passes for colored "society" in Harlem. Its cheap and tawdry assumptions of aristocracy, its reeking but camouflaged color prejudice and its collective crab-barrel tactics are revealed quite as effectively by means of Van Vechten's lay-figures as they would be by genuine characters. In this respect the book is a thinly disguised homily. And, indeed, there is a singular appropriateness in the shoddy quality of this book—a sort of argument-by-example—for it deals with a shoddy social set.

The futile footing of our "intellectual" ephemeridae is fairly well indicated in the character of Bryan Kason, which is (like the other chief characters), a composite of elements to be found in the real Harlem.

Mary Love stands out like a gleaming violet on a dunghill, while Lasco Sartoris, the social leper, and Adora Boniface, the black millionaire who hates "the damn black niggers," are almost memorable. His sly, satiric digs at certain features of our social scene will make some wish that he had planned the whole thing as forthright satire instead of complicating the involved ironies with piffling sentimentality and unreal "atmosphere."

One thing, however, Van Vechten has achieved and we thank him for it—he has risen up like a German submarine to throw the fear of *Nigger Heaven* into "the whole crowd of timorous and flocking birds" who hover around in Harlem dreaming that they are writing "Negro" literature, because Van Vechten's kind has coddled them at pink-tea and literary contests. May this brutal and bungling book serve as a spur to make them take the leap over the wall of weakness with which they are surrounded and write (with the virile power of Walter White), of the actual lives of actual Negroes in this Harlem, which has been suffering for six years from blase neurotics whose Caucasian culture has petered out and who come to this corner of Manhattan for pungent doses of unreality, such as we get in *Nigger Heaven*.

118. "*Nigger Heaven* — A Review of the Reviews," *Amsterdam News* (November 13, 1926).

Harrison's early review of *Nigger Heaven* preceded numerous other reviews by supporters and critics of Van Vechten's book. In the following review of reviews he makes clear that he did not base his unfavorable opinion "on the popular ground that it doesn't present the Negro in favorable light" — a view he had "always repudiated." He emphasizes that the critic has no right "to dictate to the creative artist what aspects of life" to "select for representation." His criticism of the work was because it was "a poor specimen of literary craftsmanship" and "a viciously false picture of the life" it pretended to depict.

The review of *Nigger Heaven* which appeared under my name in *The Amsterdam News* for September 1, seems to have released the rush of Negro writers and set the pace for the expressions of critical (and other) condemnation of that book which I had prophetically described as a "breach of the peace." It has also provoked Mr. Van Vechten's Negro friends to fly to his relief — which is as it should be.

I should have been genuinely surprised if my own estimate of the book had proved to be the only estimate, and I set out now to summarize the critical output of its friends and foes without feeling any special animus against the former or any special friendship for the latter. I shall try, at any rate, not to misrepresent, not to falsify. My main motive is to shed some light on the character and quality of the numerous critical and pseudo-critical comments on the book and to assess their merit in the light of reason and the sociologic background on which alone literature and literary judgements must rest their claims to validity.

But I must make it clear at the outset — in the face of much fog that has been raised — that in my review I did not base my unfavorable opinion of *Nigger Heaven* on the popular ground that it doesn't present the Negro in favorable light. I have always repudiated that point of view, and I do so now. It is no part of the critic's right to dictate to the creative artist what aspects of life he should select for representation.

When I read the "Sixth Satire" of [Decimus Junius] Juvenal I rest my critical opinion of its literary merits on its artistic excellence, as form, and on its sociologic truth, or lack of it; and this must be buttressed by my own independent knowledge of the state of Roman society when Juvenal penned his indictment of it.

I condemned Van Vechten's book as a poor specimen of literary craftsmanship, and on the further ground that it is a viciously false picture of the life which he pretends to depict. Had its characters been more than mere lay-figures, lacking the breath of life, I should have praised it for that—no matter how it might have "shown up" Harlem Negro society. And, indeed, so far as it did that very thing—in spots—I gave it a modicum of compensating commendation.

We come now to the summary of the opinions which it evoked. Some of these opinions proceeded from white writers and appeared exclusively in the white press. These I shall pass over—for obvious reasons. But I may consider two by way of examples. Mr. Heywood Broun has guaranteed the artistic, literary and sociological merits of the book. But, then, Mr. Broun is a "columnist," not a critic. His naive, emotional reactions have not yet given any recognized critical value to his pontifical pronouncements and, except as evidences of friendship, or back-scratching, they remain critically out of court. Then there is Mr. Harry Hansen's writing in the *New York World*. His validation of Van Vechten's book was, however, a curious contradiction in terms. He admits near the end of his review that he himself is unacquainted with Negro Harlem, the theme of the book. Yet he states that, "after reading Carl Van Vechten one has the impression that other writers have merely scratched the surface"—and descants upon its "scientific" accuracy.

Now, it must be obvious that the one statement cancels the other. For if he doesn't know the locality, the type, the setting and the atmosphere which the book portrays, he cannot know whether that portrayal is accurate or not. The implications are disastrous. I cannot imagine Van Wyck Brooks, Ernest Boyd or H. L. Mencken thus sinning against their critical lights and so lightly imperiling their critical reputations. The explanation which suggests itself is that, critically, one measure is used for white men's work dealing with white men and another for any man's work dealing with Negroes; and in such cases some white critics are not above surrendering themselves to "the emotions of a cult" and endorsing something bizarre and "exotic" just because it falls in with the present ephemeral jazz idea of what "the Negro" is. That idea, as I have shown elsewhere, is largely a conventionalized expression of their own inner need for a new evocation and argues, as [Oswald] Spengler somewhere shows, the final exhaustion of the artistic impulse within the white race.

Before we can properly consider the colored critics of the book it is necessary to note Miss [Mary White] Ovington's furtive release on *Nigger Heaven* for which I am indebted to an Ohio editor after trying unsuccessfully for two weeks to find it in New York.

As was to be expected, Miss Ovington sings soprano to the charming tenor and baritone in her cultural corner, concerning whom I will speak further on. She seems to find it a hard job, though, in reality, what she does is to furnish the materials for one of the strongest indictments against the book.

"How good this picture is—I for one, can't say," she tells us—and by "good" it is clear that she means accurate. But that puts her out of court as a validator on the sociologic side.

Her opening paragraph is apologetic. "The colored reader," she begins, "who is not familiar with Van Vechten's other novels may think that in *Nigger Heaven* the colored man is given a rotten deal." Now, since ninety-nine per cent of the probable colored readers of the book are presumptively "not familiar with Van Vechten's other novels" Miss Ovington's words suggest and imply that the book, as read, produces the impression in the Negro readers' minds that "the colored man is given a rotten deal" in its pages. This view is hers—not mine.

But this is not the worst. The concluding words of the sentence quoted above are these: "so largely is the book concerned with the Negro's sensual life." She goes on to cite the very books to which I had directed attention in my review of September 1 and she insists that they are even more devoted to the sensual life than this one is.

Thus, she established for the author a definite addiction to the painting of "sensual life," to dirt and disrepute. Again the indictment is hers, not mine; I had referred to them only for a comparison of literary form. And, as if that were not damnatory enough, she admits my charge of unreality in the characters and atmosphere of the book without seeming to be aware of how much she is admitting.

"This novelist," she says, "loves the tale that seems unreal and impossible, repugnant to common-sense," and she describes the author as "this modernist who likes to draw the impossible." Dear me! It begins to look as if the author's reputation is oozing out between the clenched fingers of his amiable friend. One might well ask Providence to save him from such friends, who essay literary criticism without mental discipline enough to maintain consistency. For Miss Ovington "boosts" the book, and in her closing sentence she advises to "look in on the place," i.e. Nigger Heaven—which reminds me of Mr. James Weldon Johnson's closing sentence in which he also recommends that we read *Nigger Heaven.*

Miss Ovington's critique is "raw" work in a double sense. She writes as if she had been conscripted into a species of defensive warfare for which she has neither aptitude nor inclination.

Mr. James Weldon Johnson in *Opportunity Magazine* for October flies to the defence of his friend's imperiled prestige with a vigor which dispenses with both discretion and the facts. With the disdainful dogmatism of a Brahmin pundit he coolly assures us that "the story comprehends nearly every phase of life in the Negro metropolis." To which one may reply in the words of the sainted [William Cowper] Brann: "Excuse my French, but it's —— not true." If it were true, it would be interesting—and unique. In the very last sentence of his duty-to-a-friend, Mr. Johnson writes: "This reviewer would suggest reading the book before discussing it." It could be wished that he had taken his own advice more seriously. For one who reads the book in any other than the mood of a propagandist or a back-scratcher must see that it doesn't even touch such vital and obtrusive "phases of life" in the Negro metropolis as the churches and their influence, politics, the labor movement, the lodges and fraternalism, economic penetration by whites, the lodger evil, prostitution, organized superstition, or the newspapers. I am not saying that these things should be in such a novel, but their absence proves that the Brahmin's ponderous dogmatism was not dictated by anything remotely related to the truth.

In the same paragraph he says that "Mr. Van Vechten is the only white novelist I can now think of who has not viewed the Negro as a type, who has not treated the race as a unit, either good or bad." This is exasperating — from a professional literateur. Surely, one need not know as much as Macauley's proverbial schoolboy to have read Mark Twain, Joseph Conrad, or, more recently, Mrs. [Sarah G.] Millin, T[homas]. S. Stribling, H[ubert]. A[nthony]. Shands, Gertrude Sanborn and Paul Kester, to mention only a few. But perhaps Mr. Johnson doesn't read much along these lines.

Shands' *White and Black*, Miss Sanborn's *Veiled Aristocrats*, Stribling's *Birthright* and Mrs. Millin's *God's Stepchilden* have all appeared within the last four years. Three of these stand artistically miles above *Nigger Heaven*, and in none of them is the Negro "viewed as a type" or "treated as a unit, either good or bad." Thus, partisanship and literary criticism are seen again to be bad yoke-mates.

And before passing on to other expressions of opinion on the book it may be worthwhile to draw attention to the fact that most of the dubious commendation of *Nigger Heaven* comes from a certain group of "guardians of the gate," which may explain some things. And, as to the critical equality of this flood of raucous rhetoric, inept opinion and juvenile sentimentalities, let it be borne in mind that not one of these "guardians of the gate" has ever known enough of either literary art or criticism to recognize unaided any product of genius from their own race, or any other, when they first met it face to face.

From Dunbar to Countee Cullen, from James Edwin Campbell to Claude McKay, [Langston] Hughes and [Jean] Toomer — good, bad or indifferent — every Negro of real or alleged merit in literature or any other art has had to be first pointed out by white critical opinion before these hounds of spring could bay upon the trail. This is a shameful fact (and I challenge them to maintain any denial of it) which is symptomatic of the critical worthlessness of these "guardians of the gate" who are, indeed, so conscious of their own utter incompetence in this respect that they gladly resign the risks of opinionizing on Negro literature every week into the hands of a white spinster who godmothers their group.

To return to Mr. Johnson for a moment. After Miss Ovington's characterization of *Nigger Heaven* as "so largely concerned with the Negro's sensual life" and of its author as largely addicted to dirt characterizations exactly coinciding with those made by writers in the *New York Age, New York News, Chicago Defender, Pittsburgh Courier* and *Heebie Jeebies* it is with a sense of shock that one reads Mr. Johnson's description of the same book as a "scheme for the interpretation of Negro life in America that opens up a new world for colored writers."

And, curiously enough, he is the only one writing on the book who offers an explicit defence of its title. On this matter it must be remembered that Van Vechten went out of his way to introduce one single footnote in which he expressly tells his readers that, while the word "nigger" is often used among Negroes, it is by them considered the deadliest insult when used by a white man. Consequently, Van Vechten knew just what he was doing when he used the title — and he took pains to serve notice on the Negro boobs that he knew. So that Mr. Johnson's labored defence of the title is "sort of queer."

I was given to understand that Mr. Walter White intended to enter the lists in defence of his friend's book with a critical rejoinder to my review of September 1, but his appearance on the stand has been so long delayed that I am compelled to forego the pleasure of dealing with it — in the present summary.

In the *New York Age* of September 4, under the caption "A Novel With a Moral," there appeared an anonymous review of Van Vechten's book in the form of an editorial. Now, it is not customary to present book reviews as editorials; and *The Age*, being a well-edited weekly, was, doubtless, aware of this. We are, therefore, driven to conclude that the authority behind the opinions expressed wished, for some unknown reason, to claim the protection of anonymity — to which, of course, he is entitled. But "it gives one furiously to think," as the French phrase it.

Oddly enough, this "Mysterious Mister X" opens his commendatory comments with the same admission and defence with which Miss Ovington opens. "The average reader of *Nigger Heaven* . . . is apt to murmur disgustedly 'rotten!' as he reaches the final chapter . . . " he tells us; and, like Miss Ovington, he admits that "it is largely devoted to the delineation of the vicious and degenerate phases of night life in Harlem. (Page Mr. Johnson!) Most of the leading characters are frankly immoral in their sexual relations," which is but the plain and simple truth. But what a lurid light it casts on the mental processes of those who pretend to admire the book as comprehending "nearly every phase of life in Negro metropolis" and as furnishing "a scheme for the interpretation of Negro life in America that opens up a new world for colored writers."

The anonymous writer tells us further that Van Vechten "has painted with deft touch the pursuit of sensuality as the chief end of life of the queer characters whom he puts in his books." It was natural that, in seeking to depict a "Nigger Heaven" he should people it with the same sort of abnormal characters.

"Most of his characters are extravagant types, with their perverse characteristics emphasized by painting in high colors."

But the book, in this writer's opinion, is valuable because of its moral—an opinion for which I can have some sympathy, although I cannot share it. This review was, on the whole, well written: certainly, it was much better written than the half-column in the *New York News* of the same date, which condemned the book mainly on the core of its title, with a passing reference to outraged hospitality.

This "comic strip" was furnished by *The* [New York Inter-State] Tattler, which printed Miss Ovington's review with a host of typographic absurdities. We were treated to "the working of rare prejudice," introduced to "Mary Love, a literarian," and to "sycophants who drink and shout" and were finally informed that "His hero is no puppet, but a young man suffering from bitter disappointment."

The *Boston Guardian* outdid itself in demonstrating the English language is an Eleusinian mystery to some Negroes who speak it more or less. I have room for only a few samples from its "review" of October 2.

> "The characters are caricatured in lifelike simplicity, demonstrating the author's intimate association and inescapable observation of Harlem's Negro, keeping the treatise within the bounds of propriety."

> "The delineation of the noxious cabaret with jazz accoutrements revealed an amazing finesse never attempted before by any author of fiction."

> "At the close of a few chapters, when Rudolph (sic.) was being depicted, a harrowing episode would happen and, with sudden abandon, the author obscured Rudolph into a realm of deliberate doubt."

> "Books, furnishing and decorations were descriptively narrated with a conception of ability and judgment clearly demonstrating the author's intimacy of his surroundings."!!!

The scheme of rhetoric, grammar and punctuation belongs to Mr. [William Monroe] Trotter, the *Guardian's* editor, a learned graduate of Harvard. What he meant to say I have not yet been able to ascertain, except that in his closing sentence he, too, advises us to read *Nigger Heaven.*

The Whip, The Defender and *Heebie Jeebies* of Chicago and the *Pittsburgh Courier* all carried critical comments of a quality higher than the average quality of the New York newspapers. Unfortunately, I haven't a copy of *The Defender's* review, but I can recall its pungency and thoroughness.

On October 2 *Heebie Jeebies,* under the caption "*Nigger Heaven* Displeases Critics," declared that "no colored reviewer, so far, has been able to swallow the work as a whole." That was before Mr. James Weldon Johnson had written for *Opportunity.* Mr. J's article was an earlier summary of critical opinions—without assessing their value. To it I am indebted for valuable information concerning reviews from the *Washington Tribune*, from [Joseph D.] Bibb of *The [Chicago] Whip*, and a letter from Charles S. Johnson, editor of *Opportunity*, to Van Vechten, which last, being originally a private communication, I shall pass over—at present.

Mr. [Harry B.] Webber, in *The [Pittsburgh] Courier*, drew attention to the fact that I had for many years been prophesying exactly what happened, viz.: that if Negro writers continued to ignore the masses of human material available in Harlem and elsewhere, some white writer would come along and utilize them in ways of which Negroes might not approve.

Mr. [Phil A.] Jones of *The Defender* remarked that "*Nigger Heaven* easily takes its place at the bottom of the list. It is drivel, pure and simple . . . 286 pages of lurid detail about women's undergarments . . . slushy scenes in Harlem cabarets . . . grotesque character names . . . impossible dialect . . . and general confusion."

Mr. Bibb improved the opportunity to hurl some caustic contempt at Harlem's beribboned "intellectuals" in words which were well-deserved. The paragraphs devoted to this castigation were classic and ought to be preserved.

The comments of *The Courier*, in sheer quantity and persistence, surpassed those of every other newspaper. On September 4 appeared the letter of Charles S. Johnson, already referred to. On September 11 Harry B. Webber's formal review was presented, taking much the same ground that I had taken in *The Amsterdam News*. Along with it appeared a critique by Merle Spandan, a young Jew. The young Negro's review soared far above the critical level of the Jew's, which was seemingly inserted by way of redressing the balance.

On November 6 Mr. Floyd Calvin took his fling at Van Vechten and made the same score as to Mr. V's inclinations to filth that Miss Ovington did. His closing sentence was worth remembering: "recall who in high places commended the book and you will recall who is responsible for your world's greatest Negro city being known as *Nigger Heaven*." Mr. George S. Schuyler in the same issue found the book to be "good reporting about a certain side of Harlem life. . . . devoted largely to reporting the activities of (Negroes) in the higher and lower strata of the underworld of the black city, as well as the antics and aspirations of the 'social strivers.'"

Taken altogether, the collective reactions to Van Vechten's book were indicative of a keen appreciation of the relation which literature bears to life: for even those who took the wrong turning on the road to knowledge were found resting their commendations and condemnations upon this relationship. This outburst of critical activity may conceivably induce both Negro editors and white writers to recognize the existence of a critical leaven at the core of the unbaked cake of "The Negro Renaissance."

I doubt that such followers as Van Vechten ever supposed the existence of anything more in it than the monkeyfied reflection of themselves—which is what the berriboned boys of "The Harlem School" mostly amount to at present. Within the next ten years, to change the figure, the froth will be blown off the tankard and we will lift to our lips the real beer of literature with life in it, with snap and tang and color, brewed by Negro writers freed from the leading-strings of Greenwich Village neurotics, who, like Van Vechten, mistake near-beer for the genuine lager.

The "Harlem Renaissance"

The "Harlem Renaissance" is a much-debated concept — its very existence and name are challenged by some. In general, "the Harlem Renaissance" refers to the literary outpourings, mostly by Black writers working on Black subject matter with a new sense of confidence and achievement, that reached much wider audiences in the period of the 1920s, particularly the second half of the decade. (Some would date the "Renaissance" from 1917 through about 1935.) The location of the "Renaissance" is also contested — some emphasize its national or international character, while most locate it in New York City, particularly Harlem. Much-discussed aspects of the "Renaissance" concern the authors, their audiences, their themes and subject matter, the quality of their work, and the disproportionate role played by white publishers and white patrons in shaping their artistic works. In his writings, Harrison candidly discusses such issues.[30]

119. "'No Negro Literary Renaissance,' Says Well Known Writer," *Pittsburgh Courier*, March 12, 1927, 2:1, HHHP Wr.

The *Pittsburgh Courier* of March 12, 1927, contained Harrison's provocative "No Negro Literary Renaissance," which, the editor quickly pointed out, did not necessarily reflect the paper's views. The *Courier* claimed that it was "simply trying to arouse helpful and constructive discussion, out of which may grow a practical and sound program for our younger writers." It also gave assurance that "equal space" would be given "to any literary critic qualified to reply." Harrison's argument — that the idea of a "Negro Literary Renaissance" overlooked "the stream of literary and artistic products which have flowed uninterruptedly from Negro writers from 1850 to the present" — somewhat anticipated a similar point by Chidi Ikonné that "the Literary Awakening was only a moment in a long but continued development of racial pride and self-confidence in literature." Harrison's corollary — that a sector of the white race, sensing impending doom, sought salvation among "primitives," disproportionately influenced many Black writers, and invented the "renaissance" — has also, in varying forms, been part of the historic debate on the renaissance. In this article Harrison makes the point that African Americans have much to give toward "a genuine literary renaissance," suggests what such a renaissance would look like, and reiterates his previously articulated point about the "guardians of the gate" waiting for white recognition of a new talent before acknowledging that person.[31]

NEW YORK, March 10.—Doubtless you who now read these lines are "genuinely interested" in the Negro as he has been exhibited in recent or contemporary literature by white and Negro writers. Perhaps you are even one of the intelligentsia (the "g" is hard as in "get"), or one of the "new" Negroes. Of course, you know who wrote *The American Cavalryman, The Leopard's Claw, Veiled Aristocrats* or *The Vengeance of the Gods.* No? Really? Dear me! But we will let that pass. These things are fiction and are not perhaps important. Though I did think that since you have bought and read *Nigger Heaven* you might have also read Miss [Gertrude] Sanborn's book wherein a white author does try to hold your race up.

Well then—But, surely, you know who is Alrutheus Ambush Taylor, and are acquainted with that fine sonnet on *The Mulatto*; have read [William] Ferris' book, or at least know it by name? What! *Sidelights on Negro Soldiers*, then? Or, *Two Colored Women With the A. E. F.*, or that immortal poem by the Baltimore poet entitled "Lenox Avenue"? No? Then exactly what do you mean when you talk about a Negro literary renaissance?

Seriously, the matter of a Negro literary renaissance is like that of the snakes of Ireland—there isn't any. Those who think that there is are usually people who are blissfully ignorant of the stream of literary and artistic products which have flowed uninterruptedly from Negro writers from 1850 to the present. If you ask them about the historical works of Major [Joseph T.] Wilson, George Williams, William C. Neill, William Wells Brown, Rufus L. Perry, Atticus G. Haygood; the essays of T. Thomas Fortune, the fictional writings of Negroes from Francis E. Watkins to Pauline Hopkins, [Paul Laurence] Dunbar and [Charles W.] Chesnutt, they stammer and evade to cover up their confusion. And if anyone who thinks that this is true only of casual colored people, I beg him to consider the following case:

In the year 1905 Professor W. E. B. Du Bois of Atlanta University was hailed by black and white people as pre-eminently the "scholar" of the race. If anyone was an authority on the Negro American he was assuredly "it." In that same year the learned literateur brought forth under the auspices of Atlanta University a work which was meant to be authoritative. It was entitled *A Select Bibliography of the Negro American.* Now, when this family album was assembled Charles W. Chesnutt, the greatest Negro-American novelist, had already published *The Conjure Woman, The Wife of His Youth, The House Behind the Cedars* and *The Marrow of Tradition.* Yet you will search Dr. Du Bois' bibliography of 1905 in vain for any mention of Chesnutt.

But that is nothing unusual for Mr. Du Bois. In his family magazine [the *Crisis*] for February, 1927, he lists under "The Looking Glass" an unusual article by a black West Indian author [Harrison] in a white magazine called *The Modern Quarterly*—but he studiously refrain's from mentioning the writer's name, although it was and is perfectly well known to him. He did something similar to Mr. George Schuyler recently. The significant thing is that this is not peculiar to Mr. Du Bois, but is a common trait of all our "guardians of the gate." They blissfully wait until some white person stumbles on him (as was the case with Dunbar, William Lonsdale Brown, Charles Gilpin and Countee Cullen) before they venture to acknowledge him; with the result that each such casual discoverer thinks that the stream of Negro literary production bubbled up at the precise point that he discovered it. And, so long as through the niggardly narrowness or the critical defect of such people the white man (who doesn't know our literary history) remains our only vendor of values in Negro writings, so long will we be cursed with Jejune Jazz artists who must have managed to hop over both [Robert] Burns and Dunbar in their wild gyrations.

For, let it be said once for all, that if the hysteria of the uneducated kiddies with which we are being deluged at this time is poetry, then the writings of [John] Milton, [John] Keats, [James Russell] Lowell, [Paul Laurence] Dunbar, [Walter Everette] Hawkins and Claude McKay must be something else. At the moment of writing this I learn that one of these kiddies who has perpetrated two books of alleged "poems" is engaged in studying at school, for the first time, Milton's *Paradise Lost*. One does insist that a violinist should have studied the violin and what has been done on it before venturing to ask people to pay for his performances. The same applies to a washerwoman with clothes—and to the entire range of art that links the two. One doesn't object to youth: [George Gordon, Lord] Byron, [Percy Bysshe] Shelley, Keats and [Alfred, Lord] Tennyson were all youths when they mastered the technique of the verse. But they mastered it first. And, after all, literature is the expression of life-values in terms of word-values. How, then can we get literature from those who haven't lived, who haven't even read?

Over the Van Vechten matter Chicago, Pittsburgh and even Charleston have begun to sneer at this mushroom mentality, product of that enfeeblement which follows whenever the more sturdy types of mankind ape the more sophisticated and neurotic without understanding what they ape. The Negro has something to give to American literature; but that something will follow the line of *The Chipwoman's Fortune* rather than those of *Salome* or *Lulu Belle*. [HH crossed out "It will meet itself in the able work of Walter White (his first novel)."] In scholarship it will build on [Benjamin] Brawley, [Alrutheus Ambush] Taylor, [William A.] Sinclair, [John Wesley] Cromwell and [Carter G.] Woodson—that is, something more solid than the mere knowledge of their names! It will see in [Claude] McKay and [Lucian B.] Watkins the only capable poets of our race today—as Dunbar was two decades ago—and will recognize in Countee Cullen (who is NOT a minister's son!) the one youngster marked out by Nature for a poet, with a fine development ahead of him rather than adequate achievement behind him. It will discover the virile short stories of William Pickens and the reason why no white critic praises them. It will pounce on the early work of Kelly Miller and Du Bois (before the one began to talk twaddle in print and the other to imitate himself, like an ancient but animated dowager). But in that day the Negro writer will be going for his authority on race-values, Not to Mr. [Edward Byron] Reuter (who lists Kelly Miller as a mulatto!) nor to Mr. [Melville J.] Herskovits (who in a review of [Percy Amaury] Talbot's recent work on Nigeria shows a woeful ignorance of that author's earlier studies), but to the place where he should go — to the broad bosom of his own people.

This "Negro literary renaissance" has its existence at present only in the noxious night life of Greenwich Village neurotics who invented it, not for the black brothers' profit but for their own. Nor do their darker dupes stand on any safer ground. If any-one, in public, should care to pick any decade between 1850 and 1910 I will undertake to present from among the Negroes of that decade as many writers and (with [Arthur] Schomburg to back me) as many lines of literary and artistic endeavor as he can show for this decade. And I go further! I will also undertake to show (with perhaps three ex-ceptions) more able Negro writers for any decade in that period than can be found today. The challenge is open to anyone — but I do suggest that they read some of the things referred to before they take up the gage.

And now a word in closing about this Negro Harlem which the neurotics of the New Jerusalem have discovered. It has brains: I say this because I know, having lived in it for twenty years. I can walk a mile from the place where this is written and converse with the ablest economist of our race [HH crossed out "I used to teach economics to whites"]. A few blocks north I can shake hands with our best biologist (barring Ernest Just). I am acquainted with a journalist who slings niftier prose than anyone else whom I know, and a scholar whose book reveals a wider historic knowledge of racial contacts than any other scholar, white or black. Their names? Well, you would not recognize them if I gave them here. For Harlem doesn't "boost" Harlem.

Some time soon there will be a genuine literary renaissance, a release of creative en-ergy which will face the task of expressing the life values of our people in prose-forms redolent with the tang of great literature, with poetry that bubbles up honestly and spontaneously out of the wide experience and understanding of the Head: out of the warm intuitions of the Heart. But, depend upon it, there will be nothing in that Real Renaissance for neurotics to exploit. The men and women who create it will have to stand crucifixion upon the publishers' calvarys; they will not care to publish their writ-ings. (For so long as the Negro plays the mountebank or the coward so long will his Boys' Brigades be worth playing with.) None of the white experts on "Negro" literature today seem to have heard of [probably R. Frank] Taylor, [probably William Wells] Browne [Brown] or [J. A.] Rogers, while they are tying ribbons on the little tabby-kittens whose reputations will be as dead as David's sow a short ten years from now. Even so, in that day to come, will they ignore all those who will be doing the good work in which neurotics find no bait for their perverted self-esteem.

120. "Cabaret School of Negro Literature and Art," c. May 1927, HHHP Wr; published as "Cabaret School of Negro Writers Does Not Represent One-Tenth of Race: Dr. Hubert H. Harrison Takes Shot at 'Midnight Maniacs from Greenwich Village' in Article; 'Opportunity Still Open for True Creative Art from Younger Generation' Says Noted Race Critic," *Pittsburgh Courier*, May 28, 1927, 1:3.

In the following article on the "Cabaret School of Negro Literature and Art," Harrison maintains that "Negro society, especially in its upper reaches, takes its standards of value ready-made from white society." He then reviews how whites "discovered" Harlem "with certain 'fixations' about the Negro in their minds" and how, as their conceptions sold, they enticed younger Black artists with whom they would mix in cabarets to write similarly. The result, wrote Harrison, was that "nine-tenths of Negro life is still unrepresented by the artists of the Cabaret School" and the opportunity to write about it was "still open for true creative artists from the younger generation of Negroes."[32]

NEW YORK, May 26. — As late as ten years ago the word cabaret was regarded among us as merely a Frenchified term for a "dive" and the thing itself was treated accordingly. No respectable young woman would let herself be found in one — even with an escort. But things have changed since then, and now our most respectable "advancement" organizations hold their "benefits" and other entertainments in these places. Since no change has come over the character of the cabaret during the past decade we are forced to look for the explanation in some change in the attitude of society — colored and white — toward the cabaret itself and what goes on there. And at the very outset we are faced with the significant fact that Negro society, especially in its upper reaches, takes its standards of value ready-made from white society whose changes of taste, amusements and ideals will be found reflected more or less faithfully in the practices of Negro people. When we consider the historical circumstances under which Negroes developed in America such a relationship seems perfectly natural in itself. But some of its by-products are rather bizarre. Take this matter of the cabaret, for instance.

The great city, whether it be New York, Chicago or St. Louis, sucks into its huge maw most of the country areas, dominates the life of the nation and fixes, sometimes arbitrarily, the cultural standards for all the people. The products of "Tin-Pan Alley" are rapidly diffused over the hamlets of the far South and the ranches of the "wild" West — thanks to the modern means of rapid communication. To the printed copies of song hits, the travelling vaudevillian and the phonograph records, we have recently added radio broadcasting; so that the "sweet magnolias," "ole black mammy," "brown-skin baby" and "red hot mama" of a score of Jew boys in "the roaring forties" of Broadway can more readily and rapidly ruin the spontaneous artistic impulses of millions of people, and enthrone in their simple souls art-forms that bear no necessary relation to their own lives — or to any other.

Art as related to life is dying down among the white race, as [Oswald] Spengler and other competent authorities insist. Pictorially, they have been seeking salvation among "primitives," from the South seas to the Congo forests, as witness [Pablo] Picasso, [Henri] Matisse, [Paul] Gauguin, [Vincent] van Gogh and even Winold Reiss. They go to China for card games, to Old Egypt for dress designs, to the orient for their "new" religions and to the Negro "down South" or in Harlem cabarets for the zip, pep and verve needed to make their literature and art stand up. The really funny feature in all this is that the black brother remains unconscious of the fact that he is giving creative inspiration to the whites when he starts in to imitate from them their imitation of him.

When these whites seeking local (and other) color, first "discovered" the Negro they came to Harlem (which is within nickel distance of Broadway and Greenwich Village) with certain "fixations" about the Negro in their minds, the most basic of which was the characteristic American one that he existed to furnish entertainment to others. Whatever about him was quaint, queer, odd, bizarre and different was seized upon as the essential he, the "real" Negro, the thing for which white editors, publishers and readers had been waiting all these years. The cabaret, of course, was the earliest and easiest point of contact for these discoverers of "The New Negro." There they could find not only a great variety of "types" as conceived by them; but, under the influence of post-war gin and Volstead whisky they could revel in an "atmosphere" which was to them "realistic" and redolent of the "genuine" Negro.

As soon as the resultant "stuff" began to sell, the colored cognoscenti, Harlem's high intelligentsia, flocked to the new centers of cultural exposition like a swarm of bees, and, in order that they might "get in on the graft" and sell their "stuff" downtown, they laid themselves out to attain the imitation which is the most fruitful form of flattery. Their doors were opened to the official expositors, they competed for the honor of entertaining them and shepherded their guests about Harlem with the air of exclusive proprietors. But having attached themselves to the new cultural apostles in the capacity of kite-tails, they had to follow where these led. Cabaret parties became the order of the night, and at the cabarets the colored cognoscenti soon learned to see with the eyes of the angels whom they were entertaining—not entirely unawares. The grotesque antics of bibulous baloons furnished the esthetic principles upon which a "new" art for the New Negro was predicated. The range of their application reached from portrait painting and magazine illustrations to fiction and poetry.

Oddly enough, this didn't "catch on" in the Negro newspapers, but the larger "race" magazines, deriving their prestige wholly or in part from the white world, cheerfully transformed themselves into official vehicles for the exposition of these new principles. Grotesque caricatures of the Negro appeared monthly on the covers and in the pages. Young "poets"—extremely young—were seduced by the opportunity for self-advertising into contributing alleged poems in which many lines consisted of one word each, and rhythm, cadence and idea were conspicuous by their absence. The riot was on. In prose, genuine masters like John Matheus and the real critics like Frank Horne were swamped by the turgid tide of trumpery pish-posh and could hardly be heard for the babel of callow cackling. Many who began with sound artistic impulse but weak wills, like Zora Neale Hurston and Helene Johnson were soon swimming with the tide of tenth-rate marketeers, nibbling at the fleshpots of Egypt, and headed for oblivion. Meanwhile the blowers of the ebony flutes and tawny tin-trumpets are happy in the moment in their own fools' paradise constructed of such literary materials as have floated up out of the cabaret into the cloudy culture in which they have their being.

The Cabaret School of Negro Literature is apt to be a bit brash in its handling of language, and already it has acquired some reputation for coarse vulgarity and indelicate expression. This, too, is a trait imitated from its Greenwich Village godfathers. Both sets, like Billy Sunday, often mistake the language of the gutter for the language of the common people and, since, "spice" rhymes with "nice," they sometimes think that they are nifty when they are only being nasty. This would be only a venial error if it were not for the fact that already a raft of vulgar and suggestive songs and indecent vaudeville acts are tending to identify Negro-ness with nastiness and giving the whole race a bad name. It is a poor defense to hide behind the claim of representing the humbler elements of society. For, in the first place, the real representation of these elements among us is still left to white writers who attempt it with artistic seriousness — like [Thomas] Stribling, [Eugene] O'Neill, Paul Green, Mrs. [Julia] Peterkin and DuBose Hayward, or humorously — like Octavus Roy Cohen. And in the next place, the outstanding literary figures that have come up from these elements — like [John] Bunyan, [Robert] Burns, Gerald Massey, Dunbar and McKay — have not been notorious for vulgarity of that, or any other sort. But it well illustrates the ancient adage that "evil communications corrupt good manners."

On the whole, then, the influence of the cabaret, whether direct or indirect, has not been quite wholesome for Negro "literature." Nine-tenths of Negro life is still unrepresented by the artists of the Cabaret School, still waiting for those who have gumption and courage enough to eschew the namby-pamby colored Brahmins and the seductions of the midnight maniacs from downtown. The opportunity, thank goodness, is still open for true creative artists from the younger generation of Negroes.

121. "Harlem's Neglected Opportunities: Twin Source of Gin and Genius, Poetry and Pajama Parties," *Amsterdam News* (November 30, 1927).

In "Harlem's Neglected Opportunities," Harrison treats Harlem as "a modern community facing modern problems." He concentrates on those not-so-good features of the community in the hope "that we may bend our moral muscle to the task of collective self-improvement." In the course of his analysis he focuses on the lack of business develop-ment, calls for more civic consciousness, and hypothesizes that "any population as marked as the Negro obeys the law of social pressure in its formative stage"—and this explains the tendencies to stick together under pressure and "fly apart" when the pressure is removed.

In the face of the "panning" which Negro Harlem has been getting from Chicago and elsewhere, one hesitates to add fire to fury and admit that Harlem is not quite up to Durham, N.C., Nashville, Tenn., or the Windy City in seizing the opportunities pre-sented to it. Unpleasant truths are always distasteful, even though, like purgatives, they may leave the system better.

One recalls what a hornet's nest the late Dr. [Booker T.] Washington raised when, in an effort to lift the level of ministerial efficiency, he castigated "those who had more perspiration than inspiration, and more lung power than brain power." Of course he meant to do good, but his critics didn't consider that. Yet, in spite of them and because of his brave words, good has come, and today there is in the Negro ministry a larger percentage of men like William Lloyd Imes of New York and Everett Daniels of Detroit. So the journalist, like every other commentator on contemporary life, must risk telling the truth sometime, even in New York—in the none too certain hope that good will come thereof.

Harlem in the Spotlight

Ever since the literary gents from Greenwich Village "discovered" Harlem as the twin-source of gin and genius, poetry and pajama parties, the spotlight of publicity has been playing on it. But, as we see in the theatre, a spotlight often shows an object in false colors. And so it is with Negro Harlem, which is something of a cross between Hells Half Acre and a Fool's Paradise. It is a modern community facing modern problems, and in it the germs of a modern social intelligence are afloat on the abyss—as else-where.

Some of its aspects are promising, while others are frankly depressing. In a later arti-cle I shall have much to tell of Harlem's splendid promise; in the present article I confine myself to those features that are "not so good" in the hope that we may bend our moral muscle to the task of collective self-improvement.

The Bug in the Queen's Bed

The modern Harlemite lives in one of the most beautiful sections of New York, with spacious avenues, splendid apartments, wonderful theatres and all the social accessories that minister to comfort, self-respect and luxury. Yet he often reminds the critical out-sider of the bug in the queen's bed who looks around at the manifold glories of period upholstery, snowy linen and gorgeous curtains and purrs contentedly: "See how ele-gantly I'm situated." But the poor bug had nothing to do with the grandeurs of which he boasts, and has to make himself very scarce when the chambermaid comes around. Despite our boasted advantages, it was left to Negro Harlem in the days immediately preceding the Elks' Convention to show the rest of Negro America that we have been lying down contentedly under a legal prohibition which, even in Richmond, Va., did not exist for Negro Elks. And it is generally known that the lack of hotels among us was primarily responsible for the fact that hundreds of Negro Elks were accommodated in certain large hotels downtown which will not ordinarily receive Negroes.

But the white man knows full well when and where the dollars drop. In fact, it is quite certain that white people made more money off the Elks' Convention than colored people did. And this was by no means the fault of the Elks' entertainment committee, but was due to general conditions in Harlem which indict us all equally.

Another curious feature of Harlem life is revealed when one observes the managers of such large-scale enterprises as exist in Harlem, the heads of the big social service institutions and most of the prominent leaders, have come from other cities — many of them quite recently.

Doubtless this is due in part to the fact that Harlem, like the rest of New York, is largely populated by people who were born elsewhere. But when one notes the manifest mutual envy, jealousy and hatred existing among Negroes and Negro groups in Harlem, one is tempted to attribute the phenomenon partly to that cause. I have heard it said, in places as far apart as Chicago and Lynchburg, that "Harlem Negroes hate each other harder than any other Negroes in the country."

Can We Pull Together?

The first duty which any community owes to itself is that of social cohesion, of collective sticking together, and it seems that in this respect Harlem is still neglecting one of its greatest opportunities. A public opinion is not always susceptible of statistical proof, or even of statistical preservation, but ten minutes casual conversation with any Negro in Harlem will acquaint one with the general belief that we are backward in this respect. Some lay it to the inevitable social consequences of metropolitan life. "For safety's sake," they say, "you can't afford to be as friendly with people in a big city as in Chittling Switch, Miss." There is some truth to that. And yet — Chicago is a very big city.

Some have laid it to the diversity of origins of the Harlem population, which makes it hard for the West Indian to "understand" the American, for the Bostonian to sympathize with the Virginian or for the New Yorker to properly appreciate the chap from Charleston. I have my own idea of the matter, and I give it here for what it may be worth.

As I see it, any population as marked as is the Negro obeys the law of social pressure in its formative stage. The convergent pressure from outside tends to make its units stick together, while the removal of that pressure makes them fly apart. The Jews in Europe and the Negroes in the South are cases in point.

Now, despite all our talk, the cities of New York and Boston are those in which the least pressure of prejudice is put upon the Negro masses. And those cities are precisely the ones in which the Negro, by himself, has accomplished least. The complete deduction is one which I would rather not draw. But many Harlemites have drawn it themselves.

Educational Opportunities Going to Waste

Whatever hatred we may nourish against the white man of the South for hindering us educationally, none of it will lie against the white man of New York. In South Carolina $10.34 is spent annually for the education of each white child and $1.70 for the education of each colored child. In six counties of Georgia the annual cost of a Negro's education was, in 1915, 39 cents.

If the Negro from South Carolina or Georgia doesn't know his place in the world, he has a very good excuse. But the white man of New York offers to the Negro child as good an education as that offered the white child—and it is a free gift. Grammar school, high school and college are absolutely free. Evening schools and evening colleges are the same.

When the Negro's free college course is completed, he can start teaching in any school in the city. Six of my friends are teaching in high schools that I would call "white," but there are neither white nor black schools in New York—only public schools.

And what does the young Harlem Negro do with this wealth of opportunity? You can see him on any summer's night out on the sidewalk gyrating and contorting himself like a pet monkey, doing the "Charleston" or the "black bottom." The Jew overflows City College, while the Harlem Negro in whose very mouth the building is situated, musters about twenty-five or thirty. Recently the Board of Education started enrolling students for an evening high school at P.S. 139 (in West 140th street). The minimum required was 500. They enrolled 197. Naturally, they had to close down the school.

The Public Library recently acquired the Schomburg collection, a large number of books on every phase of Negro life, history, art and culture. Harlem's interest in it is so great that when a white man from Hungary wanted to talk with me, I took him up there, because we would not be disturbed by anyone!

In order to draw people there, the librarian had transferred to that department the newspapers, which many go up to read. At this point I must pay a tribute to the young Negro women of Harlem. They use the library (downstairs); they read and study, they go to high school in far greater numbers than the young men. What that promises for the future it isn't pleasant to contemplate.

In respect to music, I have space for just one remark: the College of the City of New York, through Professor Baldwin, furnishes every Sunday afternoon, from November to May, an organ recital which is attended by thousands of music lovers from all over the city. It is entirely free; it is within easy walking distance, just over the hill. Yet one never finds ten Negroes at any time.

Negro Harlem an Economic Washout

In a business sense, Negro Harlem is peculiar. For all our bluff and bluster we have no Negro bank. Chicago has three. Negro business, for the most part, still goes on crutches — except for the undertaker, the barber, and perhaps the realtor, who is generally the economic jackal for the white real estate lion. Chicago has many streets full of Negro businesses. We have had no life insurance companies. Chicago's Negro not only organized and perfected several, but one of them has reached out and annexed New York as a business colony of Chicago. This annexation was celebrated by a big dinner in March at the Renaissance Casino. What Harlem needed was a day of mourning — but no one seemed to see that.

The banking situation is symbolic of the general economic situation. Some millions of Negro dollars are lent out by the white bank to white business men to perfect the strangle-hold of white business on the pockets of the community. So that, until a Negro bank arises in Harlem, the thrift of Harlemites becomes a means of harnessing them more hopelessly to the chariot wheels of white business.

In the meanwhile, our local attempts to organize large-scale businesses generally end in failure. From shoe store to department store they go down in disaster, while a half-hostile public looks on, grinning at the failure which its support might have changed to success.

In the long list of Harlem's neglected opportunities there is not one as tragic as this one of Negro business. Of course, it can be "explained." But one wonders whether, in this case, "explaining" helps us any.

While productive business struggles under such handicaps the business that panders to ephemeral pleasure flourishes in our faces. They are the poolrooms, the night clubs and cabarets, the dance halls, the numbers, the Italian rum shops — all these make money for their proprietors.

Have We a Civic Sense?

The total picture is not, of course, all black. I am merely giving here the darker side of a civic reality. But these things are true. And, being true, it behooves us to give over bragging about things that were not contributed by us and get down to brass tacks. The small army (or shall I say company?) of homeowners constitute our best civic asset. But Brooklyn beats us hollow in that respect. And, after all, the development of a civic sense is a duty which devolves upon the entire community.

An illustration may help to make this clear: The beauty of Harlem's two main avenues, Seventh and Lenox, is largely the product of the trees, which serve to set them off during the summer months. Four years ago certain official Dogberries began to chop these trees down, first lopping off branches here and there and later laying the trees themselves low in spots. And in all that time not a word of protest has come from our local organizations, whether of rent-payers or home-owners. If there existed in Harlem even an embryonic civic consciousness such a thing would have been challenged long ago.

And yet it is out of the development of a civic consciousness, of each citizen's organic relationship to the community and the community's responsibility for each citizen, that the Greater Harlem will arise. The newer Harlem will not neglect the opportunities which now lie around us on every hand, challenging the manhood within us to rise to the level of our social needs.

Miscellaneous Reviews

122. "Review of *The Story of Mankind* by Hendrik Van Loon," *Negro World* 12 (February 18, 1922): 5.

Hendrik Willem Van Loon (1882–1944), a popular writer, journalist, lecturer, and historian, was born in Rotterdam, Netherlands, arrived in the United States in 1902, and became a naturalized U.S. citizen in 1919. He wrote and illustrated the best-selling *The Story of Mankind* (1921), which was praised by Harrison for its storytelling and for the attention it gave to early Egyptian civilization. Van Loon's book won the Newbery medal for the most distinguished book for juveniles.[33]

The Story of Mankind, by Hendrik Van Loon, 186 pages. Published by Boni and Liveright, 105 West Fortieth street, New York.

Dr. Van Loon is Dutch: so was the great [Desiderius] Erasmus, and this book reminds me that Holland has always been in the lead in that noble march of souls facing toward the light which, for want of a better name, we call Humanism. The points of resemblance between Erasmus and his later countryman are many, but since our present object is not an academic one we must omit them. It may suffice to say that Erasmus also wrote for young people (although the scholars have forgotten it) as Mr. Van Loon does in this book; that he passed the human possession through the alembic of his mild and gentle humor and remained always the champion of the wider world, as against the narrowing claims of countries, creeds and dogmas. In these aspects Van Loon is a worthy spiritual descendant of the great humanist of the sixteenth century.

The Story of Mankind was written for young people — but you would hardly ever suspect it, except when you look at the pictures. Perhaps, too, the style gives away the secret of its purpose. Isn't it passing strange then, whereas history is, in its ultimate terms, a story told, the usual historian is so heavy that no one thinks of going to his pages for a story. Yet in the end the story-teller wins as against the archaeologist, statistician and battle expert. The *Child's History of England*, Plutarch, [Thomas Babington] Macaulay and [William H.] Prescott will always find readers because they know "how to tell a story." And it is because Dr. Van Loon makes a story of man's history that his work holds the interest of all readers.

The average outline of universal history intended for white people's children generally begins with Greece; because there was no white group anywhere which played any commendable part on the stage of civilization prior to twenty-four hundred years ago. Therefore, since education follows social theory, and white men are on top today, white children must be taught that white men were always on top; that prior to then there was nothing known of civilization or culture, and hence their notion of civilization's history requires a Greek beginning. From this vicious view of history Mr. Van Loon's book is entirely free.

He begins where Mr. [H. G.] Wells begins, but he tells the same story to that more exacting audience which stretches from the nursery to the orchestra seats. He sketches the life of prehistoric man as he dodged tigers and hunted wild horses, hid from the thunder and sharpened his stone axe. And as he traces their course on the upward trail, he comes to the first encampment and stops to tell us of Egypt — the first land of culture and civilization. I venture to quote some of what he says as an indication of the matter and manner:

> The valley of the Nile had developed a high stage of civilization thousands of years before the people of the West had dreamed of the possibilities of a fork, or a wheel or a horse. And we shall, therefore, leave our great-great-grandfathers in their caves while we visit the southern and eastern shores of the Mediterranean, where stood the earliest school of the human race.
>
> The Egyptians have taught us many things. They were excellent farmers. They knew all about irrigation. They built temples which were afterwards copied by the Greeks, and which served as the earliest models for the churches in which we worship nowadays. They had invented a calendar which proved such a useful instrument for the purpose of measuring time that it has survived with a few changes until today.

Then he goes on to tell how our letters, which lie at the roots of civilization, have been developed out of the ancient Egyptian hieroglyphs. He explains the rise and fall of Egypt, and the passing of the sceptre to other hands.

In the same spirit he sweeps over Asia Minor, bringing before the reader the spectral sciences figures of Sumerians, Akkadians and the other elements of the great Semitic melting. He even finds space for Moses and the little people who have played such a striking part in the development of the western world.

Then the Greeks enter the tale and from that point the story follows the usual course. But it never sinks to the usual level. It glows and gleams and grips you so that you feel the thrill of one who stands on the sidewalk and sees the moving multitude go by in a gorgeous procession whose beginning and end are beyond the reach of the eyes; but whose passing is a vivid reality.

123. "*Satyricon* of Petronius," letter to the editor, *New York Times*, October 22, 1922.

In the fall of 1922 Harrison became involved in the issue of access to books in libraries and the struggle against censorship. Earlier in the year John S. Sumner, secretary for the Society for the Prevention of Vice (founded by Anthony Comstock), led a campaign of censorship against the *Satyricon* of Petronious, the first novel in Latin, by Gaius Petronious (probably Titus Petronious Niger Arbiter, d. 66 A.D.). The satirical masterpiece was available in France, England, and Germany, but access was delayed in New York. On September 14, Ernestine Rose, librarian at the 135th Street Public Library, wrote to Harrison, in response to his request that the library purchase the *Satyricon* and other books. She advised him that there was "a delay about entering this book officially in our catalogue because of the possibility of censorship." On October 16, Harrison, as president of the Liberty League, wrote the following letter to the editor of the *New York Times*.[34]

To the Editor of *The New York Times*:

Isn't the contention of the New York Vice Society in the matter of Petronious getting to be more than a little absurd? There isn't the slightest danger of any intelligent person confounding the *Satyricon* of Petronious with the work of John Barclay, unless that person is entirely ignorant of Latin literature in general and Petronious in particular.

My own copy of the *Satyricon* as published by [Robert] Garnier contains the Latin text and a French translation by Heguin de Guerle, with critical commentaries by J. N. M. de Guerle. I have had it for more than fourteen years, yet it has never occurred to me that it was a nasty book. I have been able to glean from its pages a much better understand of how people actually lived in Imperial Rome than could be had from the pages of [Theodor] Mommsen, [William] Ihne or even [Victor] Duruy. Of course the *Satyricon* is a classic in both senses of the word; and as a classic it should be better known.

Some years ago Professor Harry Thurston Peck of Columbia University published a translation of a portion of it under the title of *Trimalchio's Feats*. (*Coena Trimalchionis*). This translation was remarkable for the fidelity with which the linguistic flavor of the Latin original was reproduced in English. Every bit of Latin slang was represented by an equivalent piece of English argot. In short, it was one of the finest bits of American classical scholarship that had appeared in our period. Yet the New York Public Library people have put it on their disingenuous Index Expurgatorious.

After all, are the people of the United States less worthy to exercise freedom than the people of Spain, Brazil or France? Public library officials as well as the self-constituted censors of literary and artistic morals seem to assume that the only proper answer is a violent affirmative. Of course we don't want to poison the morals of youth: the sensational newspapers and the so-called comic supplements will attend to that, unhampered by the censorious meddling of professional sewage seekers. But, after all, grownups also have some rights in this matter, since they are the ones who actually pay for all the literature that is bought. Besides, [William] Shakespeare, [Honoré de] Balzac, [François] Rabelais, Vergil [Publius Vergilius Maro] and [Decimus Junius] Juvenal were grown-ups, writing for grown-ups. Mr. [John S.] Sumner and others like him seem to take it for granted that *St. Elmo, Eric*, and *Jasper's Old Shad* should set the standards for all literature. In the racy language of our local Montmartre we ask them: "Where do you get that stuff?"

> HUBERT H. HARRISON
> President of the Liberty League
> New York, Oct. 16, 1922

124. "On Reading Negro Books," *Boston Chronicle* (June 7, 1924), HHHP Wr, reprinted in *The Embryo of The Voice of the Negro* 1 (February 1927): 1, 3.

Harrison's June 7, 1924, *Boston Chronicle* column, "The Trend of the Times," discussed some of the difficulties faced by young Black writers and offered some suggestions on what the reading public could do to support their efforts. Harrison cited difficulties with white publishers and questions about the market, and urged readers to "make it a point of pride" to buy Black books.

The young Negro writer has a hard row to hoe. When he writes a book which tells the truth about Negroes he generally finds that white publishers want something else. And even after he has secured a publisher he finds that our people don't buy enough copies to afford him a living from the royalties. Part of this is due to the old notion which many of us have that Negro books are necessarily of inferior quality. This is not true. Negro writers like Alain Leroy Locke and Charles Johnson of *Opportunity*, J. A. Rogers, William A. Sinclair, W. E. B. Du Bois and Kelly Miller have written and do write quite as well as white people—some of them better. Yet Negroes bought more copies of the *Outline of History* (which attenuates the race's contributions to culture) than of *The Aftermath of Slavery*.

It seems to me that only when

> ". . . . Faith made whole with deed
> Breathes its awakening breath
> Into the lifeless creed"

of Racial Self-Consciousness and Solidarity will the Negro author's really big chance come. The Negro author and the Negro artist must both await the Negro Renaissance when the soul of the race is on fire with the purpose of proving its mettle, achieving for itself the things by which it will be judged in the future, and eager to listen to

> "Bards who from thy roots shall spring
> And proudly tune their lyres to sing
> Of Ethiopia's glory."

In the meanwhile each of us might make it a point of pride to buy a Negro book — and read it. There is much of genuine inspiration in many of them and something of genuine greatness in some.

After all, neither in literature and history nor in the social sciences can we depend on writers of the white race to do justice to ours. I have always urged that we should raise up our own historians, scholars, sociologists, anthropologists — and even Egyptologists. But what is the use of their writing if we will not read? They also acquire appreciation and support; and we should give these to them. For by so doing we will keep alive the sparks of genius and kindle them into a blaze which will light our footsteps up the heights.

What they can give us cannot be given by any other group of writers — to us. To get from them we must give to them and the more we give them the more they can and will give us. Suppose *YOU* begin!

125. "Hayti Finds a Friend: *Black Hayti — A Biography of Africa's Eldest Daughter*," *The West Indian Statesman* (January 1927); copy pasted in Blair Niles, *Black Haiti*, HHHP Bo; reprinted in *The Voice of the Negro* 1, no. 1 (April 1927): 6–7.

The explorer and author Blair Niles (d. 1959) was born in Coles Ferry, Virginia. Some of her early works included *Casual Wanderings in Ecuador* (1923) and *Colombia, Land of Miracles* (1924). In this laudatory review of her 1926 book, *Black Haiti*, Harrison commends her perception and understanding and recommends it highly to *West Indian Statesman* readers.

It is much to be regretted that such a splendid book should be found in such a shoddy fashion, and one hopes that the subsequent editions will fare better in this respect. For this book is of the kind that gets "subsequent editions." Out of the welter of trumpery scribblings, of ephemeral "impressions" and printed "travelogues" by car-window sociologists, *Black Hayti* rises like a majestic lighthouse to set an example and point the proper way. The seeing eye and the understanding mind have combined to produce a work of conspicuous merit whose kind and quality evade off-hand classification of the conventional sort.

Its fifteen chapters include sketches, impressions, description, history, biography and travel — which, being compounded in the alembic of genius, gives us literature. How to distill the essence of this composite which is itself the distillation of the flavour and fragrance of an exotic culture compounded of the African bush, and boulevards of Paris and the intellect of Europe — how to capture the inimitable magic of it and fix the result in a few hundred words is a problem before which an honest reviewer might well give up in despair.

The table of contents offers us no assistance. Running one's eye down this menu, one stumbles on such titles as "A Monkey on a Post Card," "The Black One is Your Cock," "The Flowered Shirt," "Four Lieutenants and The Prisoner Who Drummed" — and not one of these (not even the last) suggests what it contains. The opening chapter entitled "The Mariner's Hayti" indicates with dry ironic unction the ways in which Haytians "spoof" white visitors who come to their island with the fixed notion that the people are cannibals and savages. The Haytian *blaguer* who told the sea-captain, "If I could get you alone I'd cut your heart out and eat it" was only "kidding" him, as Hannibal Price protests that his countrymen so often do. And out of such "kidding" the humorless white compiles his distorted tales of cannibalism and other horrors.

Not that Hayti is free from Voodoo and Obeah superstitions. In those respects it fairly equals our own country with its new Messiahs, its spiritualist seances, its "live-and-never-die" cults or its fear of 13. But in Hayti these things are restricted to the peasantry of the interior. In Port au Prince, Gonaives, and the other large cities there flourishes an educated, refined and well-bred Hayti, conversant with a culture, social and intellectual, far in advance of that of Negro America, with its outstanding poets like Oswald Durand, its historians and scholars like [Thomas] Madiou [fils], and the Baron [Pompée Valentin] de Varstey of the past, and [Jacques Nicolas] Léger and [Dr. J. C.] Dorsainvil of the present. Mrs. Niles portrays both these Haytis with a sympathetic understanding marvelous in an outsider: etches them in with a deftness that is all the more amazing because it seems so casual. And that other Hayti which is the land, she makes you feel the charm of its sun-bathed squares, the glamour of its land-scapes, the wonder of its everlasting hills, the time-defying grandeur of its magnificent ruins. And while she takes you on a personally conducted tour from point to point, she unfolds in a seeming incidental way the long panorama of its history through which stalks the majestic figures of Toussaint [Louverture], [Henri] Christophe, [Jean-Jacques] Dessalines and many another worthy of whose memory all Haytians are proud.

"For to the Haytians," she tells us, "their heroes are not lay figures stuffed with noble sawdust, but men — Africans of extraordinary personality." Our author treats them accordingly, and when she deals with history she commands the Carlylean gift of making it live again.

Of the American Occupation she is neither partisan nor opponent. She tells us in her chapter on "The Four Lieutenants and the Prisoner Who Drummed," "But then I was happily not in Hayti to conduct an investigation. I was under no obligations to conclude this or that. I was merely indulging an incurable passion for life; for following the lure of the road, and for letting impressions happen, rather than going after them." She takes sides in no quarrels, literary or political; she describes. And reading her descriptions, one looks, as it were, through her eyes — or sees Hayti as she was and is, and one dreams, perchance, of what she may become. She writes objectively — I would have said impersonally; but I recall her enthusiastic sketches of the Haytian peasant women in their regal independence, the pathos and poignancy with which she described the last phases of L'Ouverture's life and the genial humanism with which she treats Durand: And every now and then a gleam of warm wisdom flashes out to thrill and illuminate, as when she compares white France with black Hayti and says that, "In the bringing together of these two elements each has intensified the racial quality of the other. In the United States the Anglo-Saxon influence to some extent denatured the African. In the Spanish-American countries, a certain austerity in the conquerors subdues the Negro; but in Hayti the mingling of France with Africa was like giving to Africa a drink of champagne; with the result that the personality of Hayti is singularly vital." And there you are!

Altogether, it is a glorious book — and I feel sure that it will live to become a classic. Here is Hayti's friend at court in the kingdom of letters, doing for the black republic what, on a grander scale Miss Mary Kingsley of sainted memory did for black West Africa.

11 Theater Reviews

I n the first week of January 1917, Harrison delivered a probing talk on "The Art of the Theater and How to Understand It" at Lafayette Hall on 131st Street in Harlem which he and his listeners had renamed The Temple of Truth. In that talk Harrison explained that "criticism" didn't mean what most people thought and that the critic's job was not to find fault, but to interpret and explain so that listeners are able "to perceive for themselves wherein the thing of which he tells is either good or bad — and why." The critic's duty was to help the observer see and understand what the art in general and the production in particular aimed to do, and whether or not the goal was accomplished. Good criticism would help theatergoers "to form reasoned judgments of their own" and gain "an intelligent understanding" of what they saw and heard.

After discussing the function of the critic, Harrison examined the part which the people play in shaping the contemporary stage. He emphasized that drama was a social product, "a presented picture of human beings in their social relations," and its "social character" could be expressed either through the point of view of the audience, or through the point of view of the author.[1]

These themes marked his work as a drama critic.

Focusing on Harlem: Early Theater Reviews

A flow of southern and Caribbean immigrants increased Harlem's Black population to more than fifty thousand by the summer of 1915. The community was poised to play a more important role in local and national politics. As Harrison considered concentrating his work in the Black community he decided to analyze African American society and determine what was truly distinctive in it. He had previously analyzed economic, political, social, and educational aspects of "Negro" existence, read the history, and frequented community haunts. He now attempted to analyze the psychology of the "Negro" and his entrance to this subject was through the frontier of art. He applied his finely honed critical tools to the stage in order to gain a perspective on the psychology of race relations in the United States.[2]

In July 1915 Harrison began writing a book on "Negro Society and the Negro Stage." He intended "to create the impression that it had been written by a white man," for which he felt he didn't "owe any one an apology." His reasons were ones that he would cite over the years. First, he believed that his subject matter—within-race color discrimination— coming from a Black man, would be too controversial for many race leaders, most of whom were of lighter complexion, and most of whom, he felt, practiced such discrimination. A probable second reason was that he believed many Black leaders were so dependent on white leadership that they would not accept contributions from undiscovered Blacks, but only from whites or white-discovered Blacks. This belief would later lead him to advise J. A. Rogers to pretend that he was "white" in order to get his (Rogers's) first book published.[3]

When Harrison began, his study was to be "of the Negro vaudevillian and the social conditions lying back of his art." He "knew practically nothing of Negro actors in the legitimate drama." This was understandable because Black actors had previously been forced from the "white stage," and, as historian Nathan Huggins points out, there had been "no truly Negro ethnic theater."[4] At the time of his initial writings comedy and vaudeville dominated the Black theater, and the future big three of New York's Black stage—the Anita Bush Stock Company, the Lafayette Stock Company, and Ridgely Torrence's Negro Players—were still in embryo.[5]

126. "Negro Society and the Negro Stage, Preamble [Part 1]," written c. July 1915, *The Voice* (September 19, 1917), HHHP Wr.

In the two-part article "Negro Society and the Negro Stage" Harrison describes how "the drama as art becomes at once a record of individual expression and of social expression" and "the author and the age are equally on view." In the process he highlights the "distinctness" of "Negro" drama and the importance of the African American audience. Of particular interest in part 2 (see selection 127) is the attention he pays to the repetitive phrase "the . . . is brown-skin" used by the comedian "String Beans" [Butler May]. Harrison argues "that the dramatic and comic value of the refrain lies solely in the fact that color is the great social obsession among our Negroes." In this focus on repetition he anticipates the point made by Houston Baker Jr. in *Modernism and the Harlem Renaissance*, that the "modern" African American narrator can develop a "liberating" "mastery of form" by using "strategies such as repetition" in "order to ensure attention" and "find a voice."[6]

> *PREAMBLE*
>
> This series of articles was intended to form a book which was begun in July 1915. At that time I knew practically nothing of Negro actors in the legitimate drama. The Anita Bush Stock Company, the Lafayette Stock Company, and Mr. [Ridgely] Torrence's Negro Players were still in the future. But we did have vaudeville—good, bad and in-

different—and the proposed book was intended as a study of the Negro vaudevillian and the social conditions lying back of his art. In fact, in one sense, it may be considered as a study of its amusements—serious as well as frivolous.

As I worked at it many new ideas came to me and I had begun to see the wood through the trees when certain happenings of a personal nature forced me to stop. I have never been able to take up the thread again. Perhaps I never shall—unless *The Voice* grows rich rapidly enough to free my hands from the details of management and liberates me for this and other work of a "higher" sort.

But, as it is, I am reprinting certain portions of the unfinished book here because I believe that they may be of some value to my race as a partial explanation of its own social mind.

I hope that the readers of *The Voice*, who find my editorials easy reading, will forgive a few big words here and there and pardon the flavor of literature which hangs about these articles; remembering that they were planned as portions of a book. The book would have been published in such a way as to create the impression that it had been written by a white man—for which I don't owe any one an apology. So, here goes!

"The Play's the Thing"—*HAMLET*

One of the most competent critics of the last century defined literature as a criticism of life. As a definition this is almost valueless; but as a description of the real function of literature it is matchless. And it may be worthwhile to insist that this is true not only of the art of letters but of every other art. This is the only fruitful view which lifts all out of the domain of the dilettante and disposes once for all time the senseless twaddle about "Art for art's sake." Broadly speaking, an art is one kind of human activity, the end of which is pleasure. But, since what is pleasure depends upon the kind of mind to which it is presented, and the kind of mind is determined by social inheritance and surrounding social conditions, it is inevitable that, in drawing its available materials from these, every art must reflect that in some way. Furthermore, every artist *selects* his materials from the mass available and, in so doing, registers his individual preferences, the sum of which constitutes the taste or culture of his time; and by means of this the mind of a period or a people is revealed. Thus, whether we are noting the things selected or those rejected, every art erects a mirror of the social soul, and whatever allowances must be made for the known laws of its refraction, that mirror will reflect only what it receives. That is why it is possible to reconstruct and interpret the life of any period from its literary and artistic remains as [Heinrich] Schliemann, [Salome] Reinach and the Egyptologists and Assyriologists have done.

In the light of the foregoing it will be seen that the drama as one of the arts of life deserves the earnest attention of the social historian and the sociologists quite as much as the attention of those whom Jeremiah Curtin described in his caustic phraseology as "damned literary fellows." I speak of the drama as acted on the public stage and omit all reference to such closet-dramas as [Percy Bysshe] Shelley's *Prometheus Unbound* and [Alfred, Lord] Tennyson's *Harold*. For it is the former which presents the mental and spiritual traits of a people and reflects in different ages and levels of society those special modifications which changing times and special circumstances produce. Of the human vehicles of society's entertainment Shakespeare (himself an actor) tells us that "they are the abstract and brief *chronicles* of the times," and of their art, that its end, "both at the first and now, was and is, to hold, as 'twere, the mirror up to nature; to show virtue her own feature, scorn her own image, *and the very age and body of the time his form and pressure.*"

So the drama as art becomes at once a record of individual expression and of social expression; the author and the age are equally on view. Besides, if we consider merely the mechanism by which it is presented, we are compelled to consider the actor's as well as the author's share therein and must avoid the danger of confounding the two. In this brief essay I shall endeavor to present from the viewpoint of the privileged outsider the art of the Negro actor; the social background of the art and the connections between them; and if by so doing a glimpse of the Negro's soul as modified by his social environment may be obtained, the gain will be the reader's.

To round out the social picture I also propose to consider the special characteristics of the Negro play-goer. His response to the actor's stimulus reacts upon the actor's art and that of the playwright — determines to a measurable extent the form and substance of the Negro drama and its mode of presentation. I am well aware that most white and black people will be inclined to deny at the outset that there is or can be such a thing as a Negro drama as distinct from the American drama. I can but bespeak their patience for the present, merely promising that if Negro society be in any sense distinct from American society, and the drama a mirror of social situations, the presumption at the outset is against their view. I would also suggest that they ask themselves why it is that a manager of a theater like the Lafayette in New York, catering as we say, to a Negro public, finds it necessary to provide dramatic entertainment with that special fact in view.

THE NEGRO COMEDIAN TODAY

When we speak of the Negro actor in America today we exclude from our consideration the Negro tragedian and the actor in the "legitimate" drama. Under the stress of the social situation this type has disappeared. There were a time when Ira Aldridge, "the Black Roscius," was playing Othello to Edwin Booth's Iago before large audiences. Today no Negro actor can be found doing such a thing. It is not because there are no living Negroes of sufficient histrionic ability. Neither is it true that the Negro's talent does not run in that direction. Anyone who has seen Mr. Charles Burroughs sustained impersonations of the different characters in "Macbeth" will be disinclined to accept any such simple explanation. The real explanation is to be found in the [fact that weal] or woe, we [see that] in America there is a body of opinion which insists that the Negro must be kept "in his place." That place is one collectively lower than that of the rest of the American people. We insist on this in church, in school, in government, and public places and the conditions prevailing before the floodlights reflect themselves behind them.

It is hardly reasonable to expect, when we take a people as inferiors, as the butt of our jokes, that we should allow representatives of the same people to stand where they can be the recipients of our serious admiration and applause unmodified by a due consciousness of our superiority. The fact that Negroes are barred from our best hotels will naturally operate to bar them from the best places on the stage also. The comedian, as the term is understood in America, ministers to our enjoyment in an inferior capacity —as mountebank—wherefore we will accept Negro comedians but not Negro actors in the legitimate drama.

127. "Negro Society and the Negro Stage, Part 2," written c. July 1915, *The Voice* (October 3, 1917): 5, 8, HHHP Wr.

In part 2 of this series Harrison offers insightful comments on the role of Black playwrights, actors, and theatergoers in the Black theater and on the "craze for color [that] runs all through Negro society in the United States."

I can well remember what a sensation it caused when [Bob] Cole and [J. Rosamond] Johnson in the Fall of 1910, after an absence of more than four years, returned to vaudeville at the Fifth Avenue Theatre, New York City. Cole had made his initial hit in New York several years before by his humorous song in the character of a tramp who had gone into a small chicken coop and got covered with vermin. The comedy was entitled "A Trip to Coontown." It was what we were prepared to accept as a proper, conventional picture of Negro life, and it scored a tremendous success. But in the next few years Cole had drifted farther and farther away from this "coon" ideal, until in "The Shoo-Fly Regiment" and "The Red Moon," he and J. Rosamond Johnson were producing not "coon" comedy, but artistic comedy. It was under the influence of this higher ideal that they began to appear before white audiences in correct and unobtrusive evening dress for their act of "high class" singing, piano playing and clever dialogue. It didn't pay. The *New York Age*, at that time the foremost Negro weekly in America, observed that:

The most marked change—the change of changes—that was quickly noted by Cole and Johnson was the attitude of the audience toward the colored acts. They soon discovered that the average white thatregoer of today is not disposed to enthuse to any extent over the work of a performer of ebony hue unless he resorts to low comedy and comes up (down?) to the playgoers idea of how a colored performer should dress, talk, and act. In short, their observations caused them to conclude, without much deliberation, that the majority of white patrons do not highly appreciate a refined colored act. . . . They found nine out of every ten colored actors resorting to low comedy and wearing grotesque costumes. . . . Cole and Johnson were wise enough to make a number of changes post haste which they found to prove exceedingly advantageous. . . . The white public in particular seems inclined to view the race on and off the stage in a humorous vein. To depict the intelligent and cultured Negro on the stage as he exists today fails to evoke generous applause. Such a picture seems to be repulsive to three-fourths of the whites who patronize vaudeville houses.

The unparalleled and long-continued success of [Bert] Williams and [George] Walker, America's peerless comedians, was due largely to the fact that they have never disputed the claims of that social convention which has decided how Negroes shall appear upon the stage. The status of the Negro actor is determined by the status of his own social group and, in turn, determines the relation which he shall maintain to his public, be that public black or white. It decrees that in playing before white audiences he must appear only in Negro roles, and must strive at his peril to present their conception of what a Negro is or should be.

So only can he be sure of securing their support and that measure of success upon which his economic welfare depends.

But this basic fact has another consequence which serves to determine the whole scope of the Negro drama. The Negro playgoer is also a creature of his times and conditions. His general ideas and preferences, his very notion of himself and his group, are to a large extent built upon such models as he gets from the larger world which touches him at so many points. The Negro actor, and the Negro playwright are trying to present a picture of life and manners; but they must make it pay and must, therefore, select for presentation those aspects of both which their audiences will accept. When the Negro actor appears before a Negro audience to present a picture of Negro life, he may play to that conception of life and its stage-presentation which they have derived from white people, which, as I said before, is neither a high nor a serious one. Or, he may play to their higher ideals and the real lives they live. But, I think, that if he chooses the latter, the support which he will get will not be very much larger than that which would be given him by white theatregoers for doing the same thing. At any rate, not just at present.

However this may be, the Negro actor on a vaudeville circuit has to play before both white and colored audiences and whether he plays to the one view or the other he cannot avoid making his art the vehicle of a certain quantity and quality of social criticism. To anyone who has reflected at all on the matter, the mere scope of this criticism is of tremendous significance. Most of us who call ourselves educated are so prone to cut life into sections, according to the patterns in the book that we often miss the meaning of the actual flow of the common life about us. In studying the stage, as well as other things, we often mistake the map for the country, and thereby lose the touch "of splendor in the grass, of glory in the flowers." These passing quips and seemingly idle jests, these light pre-occupations of the comic spirit are the certain index of social situations, which it should profit us to understand. And it is here especially that the artistic value of the Negro playwright and the Negro comedian manifests itself. Consciously and unconsciously, they present phases of Negro life in its social and moral aspects which the writer of Negro books dares not touch. For instance, when "String Beans" sings that funny little song in which he tells us that "the . . . is brown-skin," and forces the phrase on our attention at the end of every second line: we learn that the dramatic and comic value of the refrain lies solely in the fact that color is the great social obsession among our Negroes. Other things being equal, one's social value in this group is in direct ratio to one's lightness — a fact with many implications as to the Negro character and the forces which moulded it. And, when in the last verse of the song as originally rendered the comedian informs us that:

> "We got a horse in our stable
> And he's brown-skin."

he registers his own caustic condemnation of social valuation by reducing it to an absurdity.

Perhaps we might profitably pause to consider the matter of color and its value in Negro society at the outset. It may serve to suggest the real essence of my point of view. How often have I heard Negro speakers dilating before white audiences on the evil effects of "color prejudice," ignoring the fact that there is no such thing as color prejudice in America — except among "colored" people. In Negro society alone does one hear references made to "good" color and "good" hair — "good" in this sense standing for similarity to white people's. These phrases run the whole gamut from "tantalizin browns," to "high yallers." On several occasions I have heard people of "high" color, referring disparagingly to others as "black niggers," and "loads of coal." Indeed, the slang term "nigger" is heard more frequently among Negroes themselves than among white people; and in love, courtship, marriage and their social life generally, lightness of color is perhaps the greatest desideratum. The craze for color runs all through Negro society in the United States (and in the West Indies, except, perhaps, in Hayti). In fact, in so far as there is any society at all in the Fifth avenue meaning of the term — it is a mulatto society. Anyone who cares to take the trouble to observe our Negroes closely, can satisfy himself of the truth of this statement. The darker men and women are always made to feel in ever so many ways that they, as inferiors, are not a welcome part of the upper crust. There can be no doubt that the mulatto, as such, no matter how ignorant or uncouth he may be, thinks himself superior to the black or brown person.

This results in a sort of silent ostracism of the blacks, which can be made very galling. Of course this feeling finds no frank expression in words, and is hidden with especial care from the white outsider. The same shuffling, shamefaced attitude is maintained by them on this matter as is maintained by Northern white people, who may be thrown into casual contact with Negroes at any social gathering of white people. A Negro physician, who attended a recent Negro medical congress in Chicago, tells me that at their dances which were given in their honor, although there was a fair sprinkling of dark men, there were but three dark women present, and these were ceremoniously shunned by men and women alike.

This social separatism finds its most striking organized form in the churches. For instance, in Washington, D.C., the great Presbyterian Church presided over by Dr. H. K. [Francis James] Grimké, one of their greatest and most highly cultured preachers, is a mulatto church. If a dark person happens to stray within its sacred precincts the impalpable forces of social ostracism are set in motion until he learns that he is "in the wrong church." St. Philip's Church, the largest and richest Episcopalian church among New York Negroes, was run on a similar basis, up to a few years ago.

Such slight mitigation of this ban as has been effected was caused by the influx of a darker West Indian element. The rector of this church is practically indistinguishable from a white man, and his curate is almost so. I was informed by a young man who mingles in this church's social life that he overheard the mulatto daughters of one of its highest dignitaries discussing the matrimonial merits of a certain young doctor. Said one fair damsel, "Of course, he is too dark for our set; but then, he has made his way and bought his own home, you know." From which we may conclude that the dark complexion in Negro society in America is a stain, which, like many others in other societies, may be washed away by wealth. Yet many of these mulattoes are the foremost in writing and speaking against the caste-proscriptions from which their race suffers at the hands of white people.

One of the curious social products of this attitude, is the large number of advertisements appearing in Negro newspapers all over the country, of "anti-kinks," skin-bleaches, blond face-powders and other devices for straightening the hair and lightening the complexion of Negroes who, it seems, are no longer pleased with the visible marks of their racial ancestry. When the *Evening Mail*, a white paper, remonstrated with *The New York Age*, a Negro paper, against the unseemly number of such advertisements in its columns, Mr. Fred R. Moore, the editor of *The New York Age*, replied, that black people used such things to make themselves lighter in order that they might get work, since white people in New York preferred to employ light Negroes. This, of course, is not true.

Reviews from the 1920s

128. "Canary Cottage: A Dramatic Opinion," c. 1920, HHHP Wr., reprinted in *Negro World* (October 30, 1920), HHHP Scr B.

Toward the end of 1920 Harrison wrote several theater reviews for the *Negro World* including an extremely laudatory October 30th one of "Canary Cottage," the previous week's musical comedy at the Lafayette Theatre. The show was a bit defective in some of the speaking parts, but his was more than overcome by its stagecraft, its clever plot, the chorus and orchestra, and the good acting throughout. Harrison was also pleased that it was not marred by "the usual contemptible 'niggerisms' which so many of our actors insistently obtrude" into shows.

It is more than two years since I turned my back on the business of dramatic criticism, and, besides, when a person saunters into a theatre and puts down his money for a seat he is entitled to the luxury of enjoying himself — if he can — and of making cynical remarks if he can't. It is not to be expected that he will resurrect the buried tools of an old trade and throw in gratis a half column of kindly appreciation. But the musical comedy billed at the Lafayette last week under the somewhat meaningless title of *Canary Cottage* was a piece of such commanding excellence that it sheerly lifted me out of my seat. Honor to whom honor is due; and I take off my hat to this marvel of melody and stagecraft in which the Quality Amusement people present Shelton Brooks and his associate players.

I have been watching musical comedy at the Lafayette Theatre since it was first built. I have seen and enjoyed in varying degrees the *Darktown Follies*, *The Smart Set* and *The Smarter Set*, *Darkydom*, *Broadway Rastus* from 1915 to date, and the other Negro "musical comedies." I have also critically observed their presentations of Broadway musical comedies from the days of *Madame Sherry*.

But not one of these "shows" has ever come within hailing distance of *Canary Cottage*. It outshines them all in cleverness with which it fairly ripples. It has something to which none of them except the recent *Bamboula* ever made any pretense, namely, melodic consistency. Its chorus is in a class by itself for form, dancing dress and efficient team-work. And over and above all, it really presents a plot. The essence of this plot (narrow as it is in range of ideas), is cleverness. Perhaps it is, in that respect, too highly sophisticated. Yet the steps of its development were quite clear to the audience which was convulsed by the increasing humor of its situations and dialogue.

Broadway Rastus rose to the level of theatrical dignity only in the able acting of one person, Emmett Anthony; *Bamboula* lacked able actors. But *Canary Cottage* was built by Mr. [Oliver] Morosco as firmly and consistently as a drama. It therefore makes considerable demands on the dramatic abilities of the cast, and, as a result, every part was acted as it should be. Perhaps there were but few gleams of great genius, but there was good acting everywhere — and this is unusual in a musical comedy in Harlem. The only observable defect seems to be in the enunciation of most of those who have speaking parts. Their words were often unintelligible in the first balcony. But this could have been due to the defective acoustics of the Lafayette Theatre. [It wasn't though — H. H.]

The musical numbers were excellently rendered by the chorus and orchestra, and Mr. Shelton Brooks' turn at the piano in the second act was highly diverting on account of his harmonic "stunts." [handwritten insert — "The numbers sung by Mrs. Powers and Brooks were exceptionally good, while Miss Edith Purnell as 'Pauline Hugg' attained the happy distinction of being the most beautiful young woman seen on the Lafayette's stage in many a day. (Miss Purnell, by the way, is brown instead of 'white.')"] [The printer left this out — H. H.]

The chorus deserves a paragraph by itself. So many of the choruses recently seen at the Lafayette seem to have had their clothes thrown at them; this chorus is clothed and costumed as if someone had paid real money to a costumer for the things that they wore. They were perfect in every detail. And as to dancing! The girls of *Canary Cottage* know what dancing is. They danced, not as if the stage manager was holding a whip over them. They danced as if they enjoyed it. There was music in the simplest movement of their legs. (And those extremities were very well selected for their work.) They were good to look at — exceedingly good — and they worked for the honor of their company.

Altogether, this musical comedy is the best yet. It pleases without dirt and tickles without the usual contemptible "niggerisms" which so many of our actors insistently obtrude even into a Broadway show. If the name of the piece could be changed to one with more meaning it should have a long and pleasant run at the various theatres on the Q[uality]. A[musement]. C[ompany]. circuit.

129. "The Emperor Jones," *Negro World* (June 4, 1921): 6, copy in Eugene O'Neill, *The Emperor Jones*, HHHP Bo.

During 1921 Harrison began a correspondence with America's leading playwright, Eugene O'Neill, based on his review of O'Neill's play, *The Emperor Jones*. The play opened on November 1, 1920, at the Provincetown Theater on MacDougal Street in Greenwich Village. After its debut on January 29, 1921, at the Princess Theater on Broadway, its scheduled two weeks' run was extended to six months and 204 performances. The Broadway show starred the former Lafayette player Charles Gilpin in the title role and was a tremendous success. Subsequently "The Emperor" went on a two-year road tour in the United States, after which it played in Paris (1923) and then opened in London at the Ambassador's Theatre in the West End (September 1925). It closed in five weeks, after receiving mixed reviews. In London the work of Paul Robeson as Jones drew raves, though O'Neill was criticized for mounting "a brutal attack on the nerves." It was said that he "shocks and surprises but he does not charm, he does not amuse."[7]

Harrison reviewed the Broadway/Gilpin show in the *Negro World* of June 4 and described it as "a work of genius." The paper had previously published, on March 26, 1921, a letter from William Bridges, which argued that *The Emperor Jones* slandered Negroes.[8] O'Neill viewed matters differently and subsequently explained that he had written the play to provide a precedent to facilitate playwrights creating plays "for the Negro as a serious actor." This, he added, was to counter the existing practice whereby Black roles were played by white actors in black face in all but musical comedy and vaudeville. While many Black newspapers agreed with Bridges's criticism, Harrison saw things differently and judged "*The Emperor Jones*, as written by O'Neill and acted by Gilpin," as "a great play acted by a great actor and in a noble manner."

On June 9, O'Neill wrote to Harrison and said that he was "indeed grateful" to Harrison for sending his review. He said: "I have read it with the greatest interest and consider it one of the very few intelligent criticisms of the piece that have come to my notice. You know what you are writing about. I wish I could say the same for many others who have praised it unwisely for what it is not." O'Neill added that he would be "only too glad to give all the publicity I can to your article." He also hoped "to write another Negro play" which he had in mind — in which case his association "with Mr. Gilpin, always a pleasant one from the very start, may be continued and his [Gilpin's] 'Where do I go from here?' may find a solution to his liking." O'Neill considered Gilpin "a wonderful actor" who "should not go playless" and he asked Harrison: "Don't you think the writers among your race should be encouraged — and urged — to try and write plays for him? Something very fine for the Negro in general might evolve from such an attempt." O'Neill then commented further:

> I am glad to see you remonstrate with those of your people who find fault with the play because it does not "elevate." Such folk do not realize that the only propaganda that ever strikes home is the truth about the human soul, black or white. Intentional uplift plays never amount to a damn — especially as uplift. To portray a human being, that is all that counts.
>
> And, by the way, the same criticism of "Jones" which you protest against is a very common one made by a similar class of white people about my other plays — they don't "elevate" them. So you see!

Finally, O'Neill assured Harrison "that in any theatre with which I have connection, all the usual courtesies to a dramatic critic will be extended to you."[9]

As he later indicated, Harrison understood *The Emperor Jones* story as an inversion of the career of Marcus Garvey. In "Marcus Garvey at the Bar of United States Justice" (selection 64), which was written around July 1, 1923, Harrison described the play as "a fine picture of the psychology of the whole Garvey movement." Similar interpretations were subsequently offered by Robert Morss Lovett on July 11, 1923, by Charles S. Johnson in August 1923, and by James Weldon Johnson in 1930. Garvey came from a West Indian island to a modern, large country; Brutus Jones left from a modern, large country for a West Indian island. Each, with considerable pomp, attracted a large, passionate, and generous-giving following and each leader's life followed a tragic course. To Harrison, the parallels and similarities were evident from the beginning. In his review, although he knew it not to be the case, he wrote that "the play was written about eight or ten years ago." Later, when O'Neill informed him that "I wrote the play last summer, not eight or ten years ago" Harrison wrote on his copy of the letter, "as I knew very well." Harrison's misrepresentation suggests that, seeing the parallels with Garvey, he put the incorrect date in the article so that he could make his carefully worded points while writing for Garvey's *Negro World*. This was similar to the careful method he used to critize Woodrow Wilson during the war.[10]

It was on the last day of its long run at the Princess Theatre that I went to see *The Emperor Jones*, joint product of the genius of Eugene O'Neill and Charles Gilpin. Not that I had undervalued the rumors of its excellence that had reached my ears in Harlem, but having plotted Mr. Gilpin's curve as early as 1917 in *The Voice* and knowing that his abilities as an actor placed him in Class A, the pull of the white critics' praise was not so strong on me as on many others of the colored fraternity. But now that I have seen the play I would not have missed it for a trip to France.

I am still at a loss to understand how this play could ever become a Broadway success. For its character, quality and excellence are far above the Broadway level. It is a work of genius, too delicate in its technique to be lightly classed in any of the usual groups, and, like a work of genius, it stands on its own feet and justifies itself. I am speaking, of course, of the play as acted [HH crossed out *acted* and wrote *written*]. Of Mr. Gilpin's part I shall speak farther on. In the book by Boni and Liveright, which contains the text of this and two other plays by Eugene O'Neill, it is described as "a study of the psychology of fear and race superstition." A censorious critic might cavil at the propriety of the last four words, but the rest of the statement is quite correct. It is pre-eminently a psychological study. (The word "psychology" and its derivatives are so much misused nowadays that I must apologize for using it — especially in *The Negro World*.)

The play was written about eight or ten years ago. It presents the spiritual changes that take place in the soul of Brutus Jones when fear strips from him one by one his success, bravado, self-sufficiency, grit and the accumulated stock of restraints and supports with which "civilization" had supplied him. It is necessary to resort to a figure to help the reader to see how this is done. Take the old-fashioned spy-glass; when it is shut [HH changed this to *open*] that is, as short [HH changed this to *long*] as it can be made, you can "telescope" it back. Just imagine that you could "telescope" back the most advanced section, thus sliding the one into the other, until you have reduced its total length to the length of the "original" section — the one nearest the eye — and you will have the method used by the dramatist in stripping the soul of "the emperor" down to its bare essentials. And that is why the play does not follow the conventional European order of acts and scenes. Besides, it is a one-man play, mostly monolog.

It will thus be seen that the external setting of the drama is really of no importance whatsoever. Instead of being set in "an island in the West Indies as yet not self-determined by white marines" it could just as readily be set in Africa or South Carolina. The "action" is within the man, not without. It doesn't purport to give history, and therefore the question of historic accuracy or even probability is quite beside the point.

The play is presented in eight scenes. In the first of these we see Brutus Jones as a successful faker lording it over a group of his people in the style of emperor. From an Alabama field hand who had done time as a convict and killed his man more than once, he had landed among a mass of Negroes in a primitive state of intellect, and by the superior cunning, chicanery and cool nerve supplied by civilization had managed to rise "from stowaway to emperor in two years." Whence it is obvious that Brutus Jones is a man of considerable ability. By appeals to the supernatural and the far away he manages to fool and cow the people while he sucks up every dollar in sight. And this is how he justifies his methods to the cringing cockney who serves as foil to "his majesty."

[Jones —] "Dere's little stealin' like you does and dere's big stealin' like I does. For de little stealin' dey gets you in jail soon or late. For de big stealin' dey makes you emperor and puts you in de hall of fame when you croaks. . . ."

Smithers — "And I bet you got yer pile o' money 'id some safe place.

Jones — I sho' has! And it's in a foreign bank, where no pusson don't ever git it out but me, no matter what come. You didn't s'pose I was holdin' down dis Emperor job for de glory in it, did you? Sho'! De fuss and glory part of it, dat's only to turn de heads o' de low-flung bush niggers dat's here. Dey wants de big circus show for deir money. I gives it to 'em, an' I gits de money. De long green; dat's me every time!"

But the people "get wise" in time to their Emperor's graft, and under the leadership of Lem set out to "get" him. First, they desert the "palace" and take to the woods, whence the coughing boom of the tom-tom warns Jones of the beginning of the end of his imperial job; then they begin to make powerful "medicine" to offset the might of the Emperor's charm — a silver bullet. Jones in the meanwhile has made the necessary preparations for absconding (i.e. his "get away") and sets out for the edge of the forest through which he must pass. He reaches it tired and hungry, only to find that the food which he had hidden there against just such an emergency has been removed and he must face the awful ordeal of crossing the dark forest at night worn, weary and hungry. With splendid courage and grim determination he sets out to do this. But fate is against him. The forest is full of specters which haunt him, and as the visions of his past life appear, he fires the shots from his pistol, including the silver bullet, which was his "charm," reserved for himself.

It is in the selection of these six episodes (scenes 2 to 7) that the skill of the playwright is put in evidence. The first shot drives off "the little formless fears," which indicate the origin of the other specters. The second shuts out the spectre of Jeff, the man whom he had killed in a game of craps, while the third dissipates the horrors of the convict-camp of his earlier days in which he had killed a prison guard who haunts him. So far it is his own personal existence which "telescopes" back. But the soul of the individual is a bud on the stem of ancestry; the base of the individual's mind is bedded in the roots of his race, which is moulded of that race's experience. And in the succeeding scenes the specters are the past horrors of racial experience, which rise from the roots of Jones's subconscious mind. Dogged by these "haunts" he finds himself put up for sale as a slave on a special auction block, then on a ghostly slaveship in the dreaded "middle passage," and, finally, he is about to be offered by a Congo-witch-doctor as a human sacrifice to a phantom crocodile-god on the banks of the Congo. From each agony he frees himself by a shot from his pistol, until, in the seventh scene his last shot is spent.

In the meanwhile the beat of the tom-tom grows at each shot louder, nearer, more rapid and menacing, and the man's soul is stripped by his increasing terror down to its primitive essentials. In the grip of this terror, instead of getting through the forest, he loses his way, turns in a circle and comes back to the point at which he first entered it. There, led by Lem, a chief whom he had injured and who waits there with a sublime confidence that the power of his "charm" will bring the Emperor back, he is shot by the soldiers of his own Negro army. And that is the end of *The Emperor Jones*. If the tale has any moral, it might be this: That the good Lord watches over the poor and ignorant to protect them even from clever sharpies of their own tribe.

Such is the play as written. The play as produced was a marvel of stage-setting and stage-effects. In fact its great success depends as much on the effective handling of the stage director's part as on anything else. The play was originally billed for a run of two weeks at the Princess Theatre, but the genius of Charles Gilpin in the title-role made it a six months' sensation. Mr. Gilpin's acting is creative acting. It shows comprehension, power, mastery. In the character of an inflated mountebank with a ballast of a shrewd common sense and a cargo of cool confidence, he plays up to, but never overplays, the part. And when the naked soul is stripped by terror of all its trappings, we see the terror, yet cannot blink the courage which carries Brutus Jones through to the awful end of his ordeal. Gilpin acts with taste and discrimination. He holds his reserves of dramatic vigor well in hand, and doesn't use them until he has need of them. Then, in the third, fourth, fifth and six scenes, he "turns them loose" and rises to crescendoes of effective intensity. And in this, as in other things, it can be truly said that no white actor on Broadway during recent years has surpassed this Negro actor. And it may be fairly questioned whether any has equalled him. His genius in his line is a credit to the dramatic powers of the race to which the great Ira Aldridge belonged.

Among our own writers a previous study of the technique of the drama is not considered a necessary prerequisite to the uttering of opinions on things dramatic; and we find that while some of them, unable to form any qualified judgements of their own, simply re-echo the encomiums of the white writers without understanding the whys and wherefores; a few others with commendable racial pride, but unfortunate misunderstanding, object that the play "does not elevate the Negro." It is necessary to explain, therefore, that the drama is intended to mirror life, either in realistic outward terms, or, as in this case, in the imaginative terms of inner experience. Mr. O'Neill, in portraying the soul of an ignorant and superstitious person of any race could not be so silly as to put in that person's mouth the language of a different sort of person. He did the best he could — and he did it very well. And Mr. Gilpin, in acting the play, had to act what was in the play. He couldn't act anything else. When the forms of expression now current among our illiterates should have died out, then, and not till then, will [it] be unseemly in a play of contemporary character to reproduce these terms.

> "The fault, dear Brutus, is not in our stars,
> But in ourselves."

To those who have an understanding of the drama and its laws, *The Emperor Jones*, as written by O'Neill and acted by Gilpin, will be known for what it is: a great play acted by a great actor and in a noble manner.

130. "The Negro Actor on Broadway: A Critical Interpretation by a Negro Critic" ["Written after a Dinner Table Discussion on Negro Actors with Theodore Dreiser, Ludwig Lewisohn, H. L. Mencken and Others at Hotel Brevoort, Reported in the *[New York] Tribune* by Burton Rascoe June 4th 1923"], (c. June 4, 1923), HHHP Wr.

On June 4, 1923, in a memorable literary and social evening, Harrison attended a testimonial dinner at the Hotel Brevoort honoring book publisher Horace B. Liveright for his role in the successful fight against the so-called Clean Books bill, which Harrison correctly pointed out was "a piece of legislation designed to terrorize publishers and writers of books." Harrison sat at the guest table along with toastmaster and park commissioner Franklin D. Gallatin, state senator and future mayor of New York James J. Walker, writers Fannie Hurst and Anita Loos, journalist Elmer Davis, and a host of literary personages including Heywood Broun, critic and columnist of the *New York World*; Burton Rascoe, literary editor of the *New York Tribune*; Mr. and Mrs. Liveright; Mr. and Mrs. Ludwig Lewisohn; Mr. and Mrs. Carl Van Vechten; the novelist Theodore Dreiser; journalist and critic Henry L. Mencken; publisher B. W. Huebsch; author and editor Charles Hanson Towne; and author Konrad Bercovici. The night's speakers included Gallatin, Walker, Broun, Rascoe, and Harrison.[11]

Rascoe, in his column in the *Tribune*, described how Mencken asked him for an introduction to Harrison, and within a short while "Dr. Harrison was the center of the most serious discussion of the evening" as "Dreiser, Broun, Towne and Fleisher came and talked with him." Later on that night Harrison elaborated on his earlier comments in eight hand-written pages on "The Negro Actor on Broadway." His discussion centered on two plays at the Ethiopian Art Theatre, Willis Richardson's *The Chip Woman's Fortune* and Oscar Wilde's *Salome*, and he judged that the Richardson play provided "the basis and justification for a real Negro theater."[12]

The Ethiopian Art Theatre — which is a company of actors and not a play-house — has come and gone, having furnished in the interim a seven day sensation for sophisticated Broadway. The two plays which they presented (I speak only of those which I saw) were *The Chip Woman's Fortune* and Oscar Wilde's *Salome*, and critical opinion was divided only on the merits of the latter. Concerning the former, it is agreed that the Negro actors achieved as notable a success this season as Charles Gilpin did in *The Emperor Jones*. A brief estimate of the relative merits of both plays by a writer of the race to which the players belong may therefore be in order at this time.

On general human and artistic grounds, a company of Negro actors on Broadway is simply a company of actors, and the racial identity of the performers would seem to have no value in the esthetic estimate of their work, provided that they were at home in the English language and the conventions of the American stage. And yet this is but reasoning *in vacuo*. The fact remains that a company of Negro actors on Broadway is an unusual phenomenon; a special fact which has to be explained on special grounds that must take into consideration the expectations of the world of white critics, playgoers and the public at large in the light of their previous contact, with Negro actors in the legitimate drama. Not only is the play a projection of life and life's forces onto the stage, but so also are the opinions, judgments and the other reactions of human minds in regard to the play and the players. In short, then, these Negro actors and their acting are new things which must *justify* themselves. From that point of view we must face this first question: What was the contribution, the new and unique thing, which these players contributed to *Broadway*?

On the face of it, it should seem that this must consist in something which Broadway as such did not have. And that is precisely the reason why we are justified in ranking their production of *The Chip-Woman's Fortune* higher than that of *Salome*. For the former is a Negro play, conceived by a Negro playwright, presenting a characteristic Negro situation, with a distinct racial atmosphere and background. All the elements from which it draws its significance and value are Negro elements. *Salome*, however one may like it as dramatic form, is distinctively a hot-house product. It deals with hot-house passions, situations and characters. It is a highly sophisticated product of a spiritual boulevardier. Its atmosphere is strongly painted with the heavy odors of that spiritual and artistic miasma which the French, who first experimented along that line, describe as "decadent." It is not necessary to argue that Negro actors are either temperamental or artistically unable to present such an exotic as capably as white actors. One needs merely insist that even if they had done it better their achievement would still not be as valuable a contribution to Broadway as *The Chip-Woman's Fortune* for the reasons already given. It must be obvious that any group of workers can do more and better work on their own ground with materials native to their experience than they can on alien ground with alien materials.

So much for the argument on general critical grounds. Let us see whether reference to the matters of detail will furnish confirmations. As dramatic material *The Chip Woman's Fortune* was surprisingly thin—barely an incident in the daily life of a Negro worker's family which was living beyond its means. The graphophone hadn't been paid for and the men were coming to cart it back to the store. (The rest of the story is omitted because it must be already well known to those for whom alone this critique can have any value or importance.)

It was the acting, and the acting only, that gave this thin and feeble theme life, depth and poignancy. It was here that Miss Evelyn Preer reveled herself as an actress of power, originality and imagination. It is true that the art of acting doesn't merely, or even mainly, consist in the *reading* of one's lines, as so many Philistines suppose. Yet the mere reading of her lines was a revelation of the range and reach of that particular element of Miss Preer's art such as we haven't had since the palmy days of [Helena] Modjeska and Eleanor Duse. It was a study in tonality and nuances that made it one of the memorable achievements of the American stage. But it was at that point of presentation that lies midway between what we call "business" and body-control that this Negro girl lifted Broadway's art of two-dimensional acting into the body, breadth and depth of three dimensions. Without moving from the chair to which she was (*en caractère*) tied by sickness, she embodied all that there was of the whimsical, the humorous, the sordid, pathetic and tragic in the character and its surroundings and circumstances. What she did, as art, will never escape from the memory of those who have seen it.

The acting of Sidney Kirkpatrick as the impecunious husband was all that was set down in the written play. It was adequate—but no more. On the other hand the excellence of Miss Laura Bowman's rendition of the old Chip-woman is apt to be overlooked by many who saw it. I have known Miss Bowman for years, am quite familiar with her voice and movements; yet (because I had neglected to look at the program) it was not until after the play that I realized that it was she who had played the title-role. And that only after I had been told so. I give "the undoctored incident" as an indication of the power of illusion which she put into her acting. During all my years as a theater-goer this has happened to me only twice. And it is somewhat significant that the only other case was that of another Negro actress—Miss Cleo Desmond.

Altogether, *The Chip-Woman's Fortune* was great as art and high in interpretive quality. It made Broadway realize the novel possibilities that lie in Negro life apart from its mountebank moments. And it suggested that no white actors anywhere can equal Negro actors in the interpration of Negro life. If Broadway can take these two lessons to heart it will have been splendidly benefitted.

In their rendition of *Salome* the Negro players had a difficult piece of interpretation to do, and it is very much to their credit that they did it in such a way as to achieve a marked measure of commendation. But when I saw the play it suffered from poor and imperfect lighting, and because of this the work of Kirkpatrick as Herod was robbed of its maximum histrionic effect. But apart from this interpretation of the part was markedly uneven. In the purely emotional passages his resonant voice and compelling personality stood him in good stead. But he failed to intellectualize it when Herod, faced with the sadistic determination of Salome, realized that he had been trapped by his promise and endeavored to secure from her a cancellation of his kingly word. The words of the Judean tetrarch implied cajolery, bribery and persuasion. But the actor poured them forth in a torrential stream of turgid and passionate appeal that was inconsistent with the requirements of the situation. According to the text, Herod was delicately jingled, but not so drunk that he couldn't rise to the intellectual needs of that crisis, since he could consistently disguise his motive for keeping John the Baptist alive against the justified demands of Herodias. The error in interpretation at this point was, therefore, a cardinal error in Mr. Kirkpatrick's understanding of the requirements of the case.

Miss Bowman's Herodias was a very effective rendering of that character. She kept her dynamus well in hand when it would have been very easy "to tear a passion to tatters"; and, with a skillful economy of means, she gave a well-rounded presentation of the dissolute and ambitious queen at that moment in her life when her sordid successes in profligacy had turned to Dead Sea fruit on her lips. Miss Preer's Salome was decidedly not as good as her rendering of the Negro wife in *The Chip Woman's Fortune*. Anyone who essays to play the part of the daughter of Herodias must be able to dance convincingly; and the most kindly critic cannot concede that Miss Preer could. For the rest, she threw off flashes of genius here and there that only served to illumine the fact that the part was not a perfect fit. Yet, it must be said that the marvel of her voice — especially when seducing the soldier from his duty — made amends for much. And when she let herself go in the perverted passion for John the Baptist she lifted Wilde's conception to the heights of tense reality.

Neither in the character of John nor in the other minor characters was there any particular scope for acting; but that was due to the author's dramatic form rather than to any defect on the part of the actors who were cast for those parts.

On the whole, then, their presentation of *Salome* was good rather than great. And I still insist, as I said to Theodore Dreiser, that there are at least ten white companies on Broadway that could do it as well. But not one of them, in my opinion, could even come near to the flawless perfection of *The Chip-Woman's Fortune*. In this dramatic gem, rather than in the more ambitious *piéce de resistance*, the Negro actors of the Ethiopian Art Theatre justified to the full their temporary presence on Broadway. And if white producers want to be fair to the histrionic gifts of the American Negro; if they wish to give Broadway a genuine opportunity to judge of the dramatic richness of Negro life and the possibilities of the enrichment of the resources of the American stage from that source they will turn to pieces like *The Chip Woman's Fortune* and Ridgely Torrence's *Granny Maumee* and *The Rider of Dreams*. It is here that they will find the basis and justification for a real Negro theater.

12   Poets and Poetry

On April 19, 1905, in one of his first public lectures, a talk on Paul Laurence Dunbar, Harrison contended that "poetry as an art ranks second only to music" and that people "are decidedly deficient in culture if unable to appreciate either." He believed that Black people had a "vivid imagination" and a gift for poetry, and in all his publications, beginning with *The Voice* in 1917, he included a "Poetry for the People" section. One of his major contributions to the *Negro World* (as identified in his diary) was "herding 'poetry' to 1 section" and the establishment of "Poetry for the People" on the "Magazine Page." Harrison not only published poems and encouraged poets: he also occasionally wrote poems and he included among his closest friends the poets Andy Razaf[keriefo] and Claude McKay.[1]

131. Gunga Din (pseudonym), "The Black Man's Burden (A Reply to Rudyard Kipling)," *Colored American Review* 1, no. 4 (December 1915): 3; reprinted as Unity League Leaflet no. 1, c. January 21, 1917, HHHP Wr; reprinted as "The Black Man's Burden (A Reply to Rudyard Kipling)," in *New Negro* 4 (October 1919): 13; and reprinted as "The Black Man's Burden," in *When Africa Awakes*, 145–46.

In 1915 Harrison, under the pseudonym "Gunga Din," wrote a poetic response to Rudyard Kipling's "The White Man's Burden." ["Gunga Din" was the name of the "black-faced" Indian water carrier for British troops in Rudyard Kipling's poem of the same name.] Kipling's poem, addressed to the United States and subtitled "The United States and the Philippine Islands," was published in the February 1899 issue of *McClure's Magazine*, and, according to a commentator quoted by journalist Mark Sullivan, "In winged words it circled the earth in a day, and by repetition became hackneyed in a week." The poem's imperialism-reinforcing title, rather than its more subdued and ironic message, was seized on by many and led Winslow Warren, an original officer of the Anti-imperialistic League, to comment in the *Boston Evening Transcript* that "never was there such a case of a nation's blindly assuming as a right and duty something which had no foundation but in our lust for domain and power." He added that people's memories were apparently quite short; they didn't seem to run back "to times before the Civil War when the slave masters of the South talked of manifest destiny, of the white man's burden, and of the benefits of the white man's rule in promoting the happiness and civilization of the Negroes in slavery."[2]

In the wake of Kipling's poem, Henry Labouchère, on February 12, 1899, cabled "The Brown Man's Burden" to the *New York World* and *Chicago Tribune*, and it was subsequently picked up by many anti-imperialist publications. In addition, a parody of Kipling's poem, Ernest H. Crosby's "White Man's Burden," appeared in the *New York Times* on February 15, 1899.[3] Sixteen years later came Harrison's poem:

> Take up the Black Man's burden —
>   Send forth the worst ye breed,
> And bind our sons in shackles
>   To serve your selfish greed.
> To wait in heavy harness,
>   Be-deviled and beguiled
> Until the Fates Remove you
>   From a world you have defiled.
>
> Take up the Black Man's burden —
>   Your lies may still abide
> To veil the threat of terror,
>   And check our racial pride;
> Your cannon, church and courthouse
>   May still our sons constrain
> To seek the white man's profit
>   And work the white man's gain.
>
> Take up the Black Man's burden —
>   Reach out and hog the earth,
> And leave your workers hungry
>   In the country of their birth.
> Then, when your goal is nearest,
>   The end for which you fought,
> Watch Teuton trained efficiency
>   Bring all your hope for nought.
>
> Take up the Black Man's burden —
>   Reduce their chiefs and kings
> To toil of serf and sweeper,
>   The lot of common things.

Sodden their soil with slaughter
    Ravish their lands with lead;
Go, sign them with your living
    And seal them with your dead.

Take up the Black Man's burden —
    And keep your old reward;
The curse of those ye cozen,
    The hate of those ye barred
From your Canadian cities
    And your Australian ports;
And when they ask for meat and drink,
    Go, girdle them with forts.

Take up the Black Man's burden —
    Ye cannot stoop to less.
Will not your fraud of freedom
    Still cloak your greediness?
But, by the gods ye worship,
    And by the deeds ye do,
These silent, sullen peoples
    Shall weigh your gods and you.

Take up the Black Man's burden —
    Until the tale is told,
Until the balances of hate
    Bear down the beam of gold.
And while ye wait, remember
    That Justice, though delayed,
Will hold you as her debtor, till
    The Black Man's debt is paid.

        "Gunga Din"

 132. "Another Negro Poet," *Negro World* (March 12, 1921): 8, HHHP Scr B.

In the March 12, 1921, *Negro World* Harrison discussed the passing of Lucian B. Watkins (1879–1921), who was born in Virginia and known as the "soldier-poet." Harrison observed that Watkins's death (from war wounds) "served to remind us that our Negro poets never get properly noticed by us until they have been taken up either by death or by the white people." He then used these comments to introduce the poetry of the brilliant and radical

Jamaican Claude McKay (1890-1948) who had "recently returned" to the United States after a year in London, where the British people had acknowledged "his poetic gifts."

> The passing of Lucian B. Watkins, whose loss to the race was so ably set forth in an editorial by Mr. [William H.] Ferris in the issue of last week, has served to remind us that our Negro poets never get properly noticed by us until they have been taken up either by death or by the white people. This is most unfortunate and it is to be hoped that we may soon pass from under this shadow. At present we have with us, in the flesh, another great black poet who has recently returned to us after a year in London where his poetic gifts have received fitting acknowledgements from the British people. We refer to Claude McKay who brought out while in England a small volume of high grade verse entitled *Spring in New Hampshire and Other Poems.* The tide of commendation which it called forth reached its highest mark in the *Cambridge Magazine,* a periodical which sells for a dollar and a quarter a copy.
>
> And yet, which of our Negro literatii knows anything about McKay? Nevertheless, his talents are so well known among the whites that upon his return from England he was promptly offered a position as associate editor of the *Liberator,* one of the most prominent of America's magazines. This offer has been accepted — and none of the subscribers has left the magazine. This is the first time that a Negro has held such a position in America; although the writer of this has himself been on the staff of the same magazine during 1911 when it was under the editorship of Piet Vlag and was known as *The Masses.*
>
> If McKay had waited until one of our "race" publications had given such recognition to his genius he would have starved to death first. Yet his famous poem of New Negro manhood, entitled "If We Must Die," has been quoted in Congress and been recited by many of our readers and elocutionists. The volume, *Spring in New Hampshire,* is published by Grant Richards, Ltd., of St. Martin's Street, London. The book may, however, be obtained direct from Mr. McKay whose present address is care of *The Liberator,* 138 West 13th Street, New York. A review of the book and formal estimate of its writer's genius will appear in these columns later.

133. "Poetry of Claude McKay," review of *Spring in New Hampshire and Other Poems* by Claude McKay, *Negro World* (May 21, 1921), in HHHP Bo and in HHHP Scr B.

On February 18, 1921, Harrison received a copy of Claude McKay's *Spring in New Hampshire and Other Poems,* inscribed by the author. His review appeared in the May 21 *Negro World.* On the same date, a second review by Harrison — of McKay's *Harlem Shadows* — appeared in the *New York World* and described McKay as "the greatest living poet of Negro blood in America today."[4]

The island of Jamaica has given us three Negroes who, along different lines, have risen into permanent prominence: Marcus Garvey, president of the Black Star Line and head of the most widely discussed movement in modern Negrodom; Joel A. Rogers, author of two books which stand without a peer in the output of Negro writing (*From Superman to Man* and *As Nature Leads*); and Claude McKay, whose proud title to distinction consists of two simple words: The Poet. Mr. McKay began to write poetry before he left Jamaica, where he published three volumes of verse. Unfortunately (for us) his interest in his own fame is so slim that he did not take the trouble to preserve any copies of these earlier volumes, and we are left to speculate as to their quality.

Since he came to America Mr. McKay has worked at various jobs, depending firstly on his hands to earn a living for himself. While on one of these jobs he was "discovered" by *Pearson's Magazine* and Max Eastman's *Liberator* of which he is at present associate editor. He has come to the fore by sheer virtue of the spiritual quality of poetic ability which no hardships could suppress. Without any aid from Negro editors or publications he made his way because white people who noted his gifts were eager to give him a chance while Negro editors, as usual, were either too blind to see or too mean-spirited to proclaim them to the world. His manly, stirring poem, "If We Must Die," first appeared in a white publication from which it was elevated to the dignity of a place in the *Congressional Record*. It was then that the Negro reading public discovered him for themselves without any aid from their top-lofty mentors who are always "ready to bring forward young writers" — after they have been proclaimed by white critics.

Mr. McKay's slim little volume, *Spring in New Hampshire and Other Poems*, which was published last year in London, is now before us. It reveals the author as a poet with a fine and delicate technique and a curiously cultivated restraint. It is equally free from jingling and splurging and from the flaring fan-tolds of the free-verse comedians who now hold the centre of the stage in that garish masquerade entitled "The New Poetry." The genuine breath of the tropics is felt in most of these poems, yet it seldom blows tornado blasts. The fine artistic feeling of the poet controls and tempers it to fine effects. Take, for instance, the last ten lines of "North and South":

> A breadth of idleness is in the air
> > That casts a subtle spell upon all things,
> And love and mating-time are every-where,
> > And wonder to life's commonplaces clings.
> The fluttering humming-bird darts through the trees
> > And dips his long beak in the big bell-flowers,
> The leisured buzzard floats upon the breeze
> > Riding a crescent cloud for endless hours;
> The sea beats softly on the emerald strands —
> > O sweet for dainty dreams are tropic lands!

It would have been very easy to vulgarize such a theme, to indulge in what Amy Lowell calls "lazy writing," and to tread the common ground of commonplace figures. Instead, we find that the words and the measure create and appropriate tone-color (or "atmosphere") in which the scene is set, and the nuances make a something that is finer than melody. The fourth line of the quoted portion is the golden touch of genius.

Sometimes the hidden melody of his verse is so fine that those who think that poetry is compounded of jingles and junk will fail to find it. But there it is just the same, like a theme of [Edward Alexander] McDowell's, waiting for the ear of beauty to find it, as in this half-stanza of his "Exhortation" (to Ethiopia):

> In the East the clouds grow crimson with the new dawn that is breaking,
> > And its golden glory fills the western skies: —
> > Oh my brothers and my sisters, wake! Arise!
> For the new birth rends the old earth, and the very dead are waking.
> > Ghosts are turned flesh, throwing off the grave's disguise,
> > And the foolish — even children — are made wise;
> For the big earth groans in travail for the strong, new world in making —
> > Oh my brothers, dreaming for long centuries,
> > Wake from sleeping: to the East turn, turn your eyes!

This will stand the test of thinking and that quality of thought stands out in most of Mr. McKay's work. He means something. He doesn't let the rhyme rule the thought nor the ink guide the pen.

Perhaps the most arresting poem in this volume is the one entitled "A Memory of June." Its theme is too intimate for reproduction here; but it is the one in which our poet comes nearest to letting himself go. "The Lynching," "On Broadway," "Harlem Shadows" and "The Harlem Dancer" are noteworthy presentations of familiar themes.

We feel that the work of this poet should be better known. It is high in aim, in thought, in technique. And we gladly bespeak for this volume of genuine poetry a place in the affections of our folk.

---

134. "Black Bards of Yesterday and Today," review of *The Book of American Negro Poetry*, selected and edited by James Weldon Johnson, *National Star* (December 16, 1923), HHHP Wr.

In the December 16, 1923, *National Star* Harrison offered a particularly harsh criticism of *The Book of American Negro Poetry* (1922) by James Weldon Johnson, the secretary of the NAACP. Johnson's anthology, the first of its kind, contained work from thirty-one poets. Eight years earlier, in a May 6, 1915, *New York Age* editorial, Johnson had offered lavish praise for Harrison, calling for an outdoor lecture series by him in Harlem that would serve as a "university extension" for the man and woman in the street and "would be more than equivalent to a year of college, and of incalculable benefit to the community." Harrison's 1923 book review, however, was extremely critical and suggested crass, selfish motives in Johnson's selection and presentation of materials. Though many of Harrison's comments were justified, the review undoubtedly strained relations between the two activist writers.[5]

Very few Americans are acquainted with the quantity and quality of poetry which has been produced by their colored compatriots; and it is much to be regretted that Mr. Johnson's volume will not tend to increase either their understanding or appreciation. For the bulk of the poems here presented are even below the standards of mediocrity. The best Negro poems have been omitted and we are asked to form our opinion on the total body of Negro poetry from what is very near to the worst.

Take the [Paul Laurence] Dunbar selections for example. In his introductory essay Mr. Johnson tells us that he was a friend of the poet. But if he had entered into a conspiracy to suppress the record of which Dunbar's claims to consideration rest, he could hardly have done worse by him. What would be thought of an anthologist who had to select eight pieces from [Alfred, Lord] Tennyson for the perusal of people who were dimly aware of Tennyson's fame but unacquainted with his works — if he should fail to select anything from "In Memoriam," the songs in "The Princess," "St. Agnes' Eve," "Ulysses," "The Lotus Eaters," "The Two Voices," "The Dream of Fair Women," or "The Idylls of the King"? We should expect the omission of some of these and the substitution of others; but to omit *all* of them from any list of eight would savor of incompetence — or something worse.

Lovers of poetry will fail to understand the unknown principle of selection by which Mr. Johnson omits Dunbar's magnificent "Ode to Ethiopia," "When Malindy Sings," "Love's Apotheosis," or "When Sleep Comes Down," and substitutes poems that are uniformly below Dunbar's highest standards of excellence — as anyone may satisfy himself by picking either the "Lyrics of Lowly Life" or "Lyrics of the Hearth-side."

This same literary dishonesty is seen all through Mr. Johnson's book. Every person who is half-way well-read in recent literature knows that Theodore Henry Shackleford wrote, like [Ernst] Lissauer, a "Hymn of Hate" — sublime, awful, a perfect expression of perfect hate. It is, out and out, the ablest of Mr. Shackleford's poems. But Johnson, in emasculating Shackleford dodged this one and represented this young master by one of the silliest pieces of his earliest days that could be found. Lucian B. Watkins, who wrote some things as beautiful as McKay at his best, is treated in the same dishonest fashion. Someone should protest emphatically against this contemptible attempt of Mr. Johnson to glorify his own mediocre verses by stripping off the gold from the genius of others that they may not outshine his own drab productions.

I have not referred to the preface in which Mr. Johnson puts his best foot forward; because I cannot see how one who has spoiled a dinner by incompetent cooking can plead in extenuation that he has laid the table with every fork in its place. We are concerned with the meal because that is what we have been asked to eat.

As a proof of his powers of critical and poetic discernment, Dr. [HH changed this to *Mr.*] Johnson's book is a hopeless fizzle. And it serves to enforce what I said [HH crossed out *in the* Negro World,] some months ago, that Negro writers like Mr. Johnson lack the power of critical judgement. No person with a modicum of that power could imagine that there was any poetry in the "Litany of Atlanta," by Dr. Du Bois; in D. Webster Davis' "Weh Down Souf"; Mr. Johnson's "Sence You Went Away" and "O Southland"; the first two poems by John Wesley Holloway, or the absolute trash of William Stanley Braithwaite. To call these things poetry is to drive young and aspiring bards like Walter Everette Hawkins and [Andrea] Razafkeriefo to write simple trash in sheer despair. Every time we dishonestly praise trash we, as a race, keep back our artists from doing as good work as white artists are doing. And for this contemptible trick of Mr. Johnson's there is very little excuse.

Of the verses (for we cannot call them poetry) of W[illiam]. S[tanley]. Braithwaite, Mr. Johnson prints 12. In 11 of these there is not a single gleam of either genius or efficiency in versifying, and only one is above the capacity of a 12-year-old school-boy. It is obvious that the anthologist is paying his debt to a mutual admiration society and not doing honest work as a guide to public taste. Braithwaite's "Song of a Syrian Lace Seller," which is better than all these — is omitted.

Then too, the volume lacks proportion. Dunbar gets eight pages while the selector allocates 20 for himself, of which only two poems are worth while. Mr. Johnson's idea of poetry is so bizarre that he prints five pages of Asiatic prose ("The Litany of Atlanta") by his associate, Dr. Du Bois, in this queer hodge-podge as poetry. Three of the ablest young poets of today — Theodore Henry Shackleford, Lucian B. Watkins and George Reginald Margetson, have been emasculated in this selection. Their early endeavors, full of imperfections, from which their latter work is free, are served up as representative of these men only in that the shortcomings . . . . [The rest of the piece is missing.]

13

The International Colored Unity League and the Way Forward

On Sunday March 23, 1924, Harrison took a long walk in Harlem with Edgar Grey and articulated the core program for the International Colored Unity League, his final organizational effort. The ICUL program was the most comprehensive and most unitary developed by Harrison. It included political, economic, and social goals and centered on a plan to enfranchise Southern Blacks and consolidate the Black vote regardless of political affiliation. It also called for self-help initiatives, a halt to condemnation of other Black organizations, and a conciliatory attitude toward the Black church. In addition, the ICUL program had an innovative call for a "Negro nation" in the United States. This preceded a similar call from the Communist Party by four years and came one week after Marcus Garvey addressed 6,000 people in Madison Square Garden, demanding "Africa for the Africans."[1]

In June 1924 Harrison discussed the ICUL plan publicly. Politically, the ICUL sought to unite "the power of the Negro" to demand proper representation in federal, state, and local government. It planned to filibuster and tie up legislative processes until Congress enforced the Fourteenth and Fifteenth Amendments. Economically, the ICUL aimed to develop self-sustaining efforts including cooperative farms, stores, and housing. Socially, the League would develop scholarship programs for youth, oppose restrictive laws, and address problems "in terms of the American culture and consciousness." The ICUL wanted a Black homeland in America so that African Americans could demonstrate their equal competence "under the protection of Old Glory and under modern civilized conditions." Idaho, Wyoming, and Montana were considered possible homeland sites, and though no one would be forced to live in the homeland state, the ICUL would try to convince people the plan was sound and advantageous. The idea of African Americans trying to establish "a Negro state in Africa" was deplored.[2]

Harrison believed that with this program it would be possible "to unite the Race without the sorry spectacle of Race leaders wasting their energies in internal squabbles." The

Hubert Harrison delivering the last lecture in a class on "World Problems of Race" at 200 W. 135th Street, New York, September 9, 1926, from the Hubert Harrison Papers. As Harrison sought to build the International Colored Unity League he lectured for the Institute for Social Studies (ISS), an independent educational institute that studied the vital social problems affecting the lives "of the great masses of the people" as a step toward "complete social emancipation." In these classes Harrison taught many current and future Black activists.

League emphasized cooperation and deplored the "envy, malice and uncharitableness" which "kept Negro 'leaders' eternally bickering and fighting with each other." Harrison urged "less fighting among ourselves and more fighting against the common enemy," and he emphasized that "the sort of unity which helps us most will not come from the 'intellectuals' for the Race, many of whom keep too far away from the masses. It must come from the masses themselves in a rush of racial enthusiasms and good-will, in a common purpose and a common aim." To set a good example the ICUL would refrain from criticism of any Black organizations or movements and would seek to present the better side of Black strivings and achievements. Black churches, ministers, teachers, and journalists were viewed as "a mighty instrument for racial betterment" whose support must be enlisted; "leading, rather than leaders" was needed, and they were already providing it. If their work could be linked and made conscious of itself, a true patriotic service to the nation and the race would be rendered. The ICUL's position was that "America needs the Negro, and the Negro needs America."[3]

By early June the ICUL was organized in Harlem and in Orange and Montclair, New Jersey. Harrison and J. A. Rogers went on a speaking tour for "the political awakening and enlightening of the masses" and to spread ICUL principles. They both traveled to Boston, and Harrison was scheduled to go to Philadelphia, Virginia, Ohio, Indiana, Michigan, Illinois, Wisconsin, Missouri, Kansas, and Washington, D.C. While traveling in the Midwest, Harrison was forced to finance his trip by talks for other organizations, and financial difficulties concerning his travel and his near-destitute family were a constant pressure.[4]

A 1926 list of ICUL officers in addition to president Harrison included Hodge Kirnon, vice-president; John I. Lewis, secretary; J. Dominick Simmons, treasurer; and Reuben Berry, Casper Holstein, Rabbi Arnold Josiah Ford, William H. Price, William J. Gordon, and Mme. Marie Barrier Houston, executive committee members. Harrison lectured for the ICUL in 1926 and 1927 and put out one issue of the *Embryo of The Voice of the Negro* and two issues of *The Voice of the Negro* in 1927. His health problems worsened, however, and within seven months of the last issue of *The Voice of the Negro*, Harrison died from complications related to acute appendicitis.[5]

 135. "Program and Principles of the International Colored Unity League," *The Voice of the Negro* 1, no. 1 (April 1927): 4–6, reprinted in *The Voice of the Negro* 1, no. 2 (May 1927): 12–13.

In the February 1927 *Embryo of The Voice of the Negro* Harrison, explained that a race problem was the sum of the differences between two or more races in friction, and its solution had to be worked out or fought out by forces more complex than those of mere logic and argument. The "Negro problem in America" was not insoluble but the task was daunting. Although the problem was "primarily of the white man's making," it was "the colored man [who] must do most of that work."[6]

The way to proceed was by organizing and that required a solidarity whose great binding force was "LOVE: love of race, love for one another, a blood-is-thicker-than-water policy, racial support and self-support, racial respect and self respect." Every lynching bee and Jim Crow car taught the need to "stand by each other; one for all and all for one, in matters of money, mind, politics and religion," in order to survive and succeed. The organizing that was needed had to be done where people were — in Boston or Bridgetown, Jamaica or Georgia, and Harrison explained that "the old advice is still valuable: 'Cast down your buckets where you are!'"[7]

The centerpiece of the first issue of the April 1927 *The Voice of the Negro* was the official "Program and Principles of the International Colored Unity League" drafted by Harrison. The introduction called the program "the most startling solution of America's race problem" and explained that with this program "The New Negro has come forward" to "take his future in his own hands and mold his own destiny."

The New Negro has come forward, neither to whine, to wheedle, nor to make petitions or vain demands; but to take his future in his own hands and mold his own destiny by mobilizing his manhood and his money, his resources of head, hand and heart. Realizing that whatever is given by goodwill today may be taken away by ill-will tomorrow, he is seeking his own salvation by consolidating in his own hands and under his own control those forces for racial uplift and security, which are already his, to the end that he may thereby win the things he wants: political equality, social justice, civic opportunity and economic power.

General Objects

The International Colored Unity League was organized as the instrument by which these objects might be carried out. The League exists to serve the interests of the great masses of our people, and anyone who sincerely desires, to devote his abilities to them will find his opportunity within its ranks. It holds out the hand of fellowship and brotherhood to all those of Negro blood, however diverse their purposes, provided those purposes be good. It reserves all its energies and fighting-power for those evil conditions created by race-prejudice, and has none to spare for the criticism of other Negroes who are fighting in their own way for the uplift of the race. It aims to bring Negroes together in social and spiritual concord, and to secure ultimately by their co-operation a homeland in America where Negroes can remove the stigma of alleged inferiority by demonstrating to the rest of the nation that they are as capable of democratic self-government under American institutions as any other racial element in this country of ours.

Political

In the meanwhile the Negro in America will achieve neither political self-respect nor political power until he undertakes his own political thinking and uses the votes which he has in the North to secure the vote for his brother in the South. The doctrine of "RACE FIRST!" is the only one which promises political action by organized Negro voters along the lines of their sadly-neglected group interests. The political program of the Unity League aims to unite the political power of the Negro around these three points: (1) Representation in Congress and in State and Municipal legislatures, (2) Utilizing the balance of power in doubtful states, irrespective of previous party affiliations, (3) Enforcement of the 14th and 15th amendments to the Constitution. By these means the Northern Negro will use his political power to get the ballot into the hands of the Southern Negro, and thus put the political power of the Negro all over the nation on a footing of permanent security and beyond the freaks of friendship or the reach of enmity. The immediate program must include an attack upon "Lily White-ism" by demanding the reduction of representation in the national conventions of political parties to the basis of votes actually cast in national elections.

Economic

We Negroes must finance the foundations of our own future and use our available wealth:

To tighten our grip on the land by buying agricultural land in the neighborhood of those cities where we live in large numbers,

To feed ourselves by raising meat, poultry, eggs, milk, vegetables and other farm-products co-operatively for sale to ourselves at rock-bottom prices, thus eliminating the hordes of white middlemen that swarm in Negro neighborhoods and suck our economic life blood, keeping the cost of living unusually high by charging us prices higher than those paid by white workers who get higher wages than we do,

To maintain our own co-operative groceries and butcher-shops in those sections of cities where we live, and to serve them from our own farms by means of our own trucks.

To encourage property-owning in the suburbs of large cities that we may not always be paying our earnings away in high priced city apartments.

To erect our own apartment houses, halls and casinos in our own neighborhoods, so that our rents shall return into the race's pockets in the form of profits which may give employment to our architects, engineers, artists, business men and workers.

And ultimately, to link up the Negro farmer on the land, North and South, with the selling centers in the cities, ensuring them the highest market prices for their cotton, corn, potatoes, oranges and other farm products, thus keeping the cycle of Negro industry and commerce as far as possible within the Negro's control.

Social

It is one of the social aims of the League to foster the elements of racial strength and co-operation already existing in the Negro Church, which has done more for the education and spiritual uplift of the masses than any other agency in the race. The great secret and fraternal organizations have shown us in their benevolent work how great and practical a thing is self-help; while, the Negro newspapers, both national and local, together with the Negro school teachers, have faithfully contributed both light and leading. The League will strive to work in friendly and active co-operation with all these institutions and will always render to them such assistance as opportunity may bring within its power.

Scholarships

The spirit of Youth is struggling to express itself in national and international concerns, to bring hope, ambition and human aspiration into the orbit of public affairs. The League champions this spirit in a practical form and at its first National Congress will arrange to maintain scholarships in the best Northern schools for deserving Negro boys and girls from Southern states.

It will strive to unite the Negro, North and South, in an effective attack on all "Jim Crow" laws, and force the repeal of them by political, economic and educational pressure; to put an end, once and for all, to lynch-law and mob-violence, not by vain petitions but by effective means; to secure justice and absolute equality before the law and at the polls in every state, and to demonstrate to their enemies the power and importance of Negroes when they stand together.

A Negro Homeland in America

America is ours and we are hers. This is the foundation principle of all our racial strivings. Without it there could be no moral or patriotic foundation to our case. It is on that principle that we urge as a final solution of the graver aspects of the American race-problem the setting up of a state, or states, in the Union as a homeland for the American Negro, where we can work out the ultimate economic and racial salvation as a part of the American people. Any Negroes, so desiring, could continue to dwell in any state in the Union as at present, under such conditions as such states may see fit to maintain; while the Negro state would serve as a conduit to drain off Negroes from those states where they are denied a square deal. There the Negro's aspiration to be as great as other men can flower and bear fruit; there Negroes can become governors, generals, judges, United States senators and Congressmen, without being hampered by political tricksters and fair-weather promisers.

The Campaign of Enlightenment

The League maintains that its program contains ill will to no one and carries to the Negro the gospel of salvation by his own works by faith in himself and his future. To spread this gospel the League engages in a campaign of enlightenment and sends out speakers to tour the country North and South, establishing branches securing members, raising funds and making friends.

The League's Magazine

The League is also engaged in launching a monthly magazine to be known as *The Voice of the Negro* and to serve as the organ of the Unity Movement. This Magazine shall be always free from condemnation of other Negro movements; full of the spirit of helpful uplift and co-operation and replete with information about what is taking place in every quarter of the colored world. It shall strive to educate racial sentiment and guide it in channels of usefulness and co-operation, give publicity to all those who are achieving the things that will bring inspiration to others, and bring forward some of those struggling geniuses of our race who languish for lack of opportunity.

136. "The Right Way to Unity," *Boston Chronicle* (May 10, 1924), HHHP Wr.

During the first half of 1924 (around the time he was develping the ICUL program), Harrison wrote a weekly "Trend of the Times" column for the *Boston Chronicle*. The *Chronicle* championed support for racial equality, anti-discrimination and federal antilynching legislation, voting rights, Black representation on the Boston city council and Massachusetts General Court, and the removal of Jim Crow segregation from the military. Harrison's *Chronicle* columns provide samples of some of his pithiest writing. The following three articles were written after he completed a speaking tour in Massachusetts for the ICUL and they reflect the direction of that organization's work. In the first piece, Harrison emphasizes that efforts at "race unity" should emphasize a bottom-up approach and focus on unity of purpose; in the second, he lauds the "common people" as the "dependable back-bone of every good cause"; and in the third, he calls for cooperative efforts in economics.[8]

During the last decade there has been a commendable striving on the part of prominent Negroes to attain unity for the masses. Unfortunately, many of them have not been quite clear as to just what they meant by that much mis-used word. Some seemed to mean unity of thought and ideas; others unity of purpose; and yet others meant unity of action. It should be self-evident that not all of these are humanly possible, or even quite desirable. For, manifestly, there is but one place in which one may reasonably expect unanimity of thought and ideas—and that is in the grave-yard. Besides, unity of organization, while not perhaps impossible, is rather a difficult thing to achieve. The largest organization among Negroes anywhere in the world today is the Baptist Church which numbers over four million. Yet even with the spiritual forces on its side it has not been able to get all the Negroes of America with-in one fold after more than a hundred years.

But it should seem that unity of purpose and aim is well within our possibilities, and this has received recently the attention of some of our best minds. Why, then, have we got no nearer to the goal? With all due deference to these same best minds, I believe that the fault lies entirely with the uniters. They have generally gone at the problem from the wrong end. They have begun at the top when they should have begun at the bottom. To attempt to unite the "intellectuals" at the top is not the same thing as uniting the Negro masses. For, very often the "intellectuals" assume the air of superior beings who are made of finer clay and expect that the others will run to seek them out. When you consider [that the intellectuals in] thirty years were unable to reduce the number of lynchings, and that the ordinary uneducated Negroes did this just by picking up their feet and coming away from the South in large numbers, it becomes apparent that these Negro masses sometimes have more effective brains in their feet than the "intellectuals" have in their heads.

The way to unity lies through the hearts of the multitude. First set those hearts on fire with a common zeal for a common object, equally desired and equally attained by all in common, and the fire of that common feeling will flame in every lodge, every church, every city and state in the nation. From the nature of the case unselfishness, humility, courage, and helpfulness must be the fuel that will go to the kindling of such a flame. But light the fire at the bottom of the pile. . . . Then "your young men shall see visions" — and your young women too. And, in the meanwhile, "where there is no vision the people perish."

137. "The Common People," *Boston Chronicle* (May 17, 1924), HHHP Wr.

A constant theme throughout Harrison's life was "the common people." Whether it was learning to have his "heart open to the call of those who are down" while on St. Croix; writing about the poetry of Paul Laurence Dunbar, Robert Burns, or Claude McKay; teaching at a home for colored women; urging the rank and file of the Socialist Party to vote; posing an alternative to the leadership strategies of Booker T. Washington and W. E. B. Du Bois; imploring the Talented Tenth to come down from their Sinais; reviewing the early life of James D. Corrothers or Booker T. Washington; lecturing on the novels of Charles Dickens; or agitating for better hospital services in Harlem, a concern for the common people was always there. Harrison considered the common people to be the "sources of our literature and art" and the "dependable backbone of every good cause." His entire life he lived among the common people, and he focused his educational, oratorical, journalistic, and political skills on them.[9]

In the following "Trend of the Times" column from the 1924 *Boston Chronicle*, Harrison defends those whom he views as "the real test of our theories of brotherhood and racial solidarity" and the key to future progress.

In one of his characteristic moods Lincoln expressed a happy thought when he said that "God must have loved the common people because he made so many of them." The idea implied is that since they make up the great majority of human kind they deserve more devotion than the aristocrats. And this is as true of our race as of others. According to the Christian doctrine, nobody came from heaven to save the righteous — it was to save sinners that the trip was taken. And, all along, the Carpenter of Nazareth stuck to the "publicans and sinners" and people who were not respectable or in "good society", avoiding the Pharisees and Sadducees, the Scribes, the Sanhedrin and the high priests.

I often think of this when I hear great masses of my fellow-men referred to as "rats"; and I recall how in the great Washington and Chicago race-riots it was the "rats" who upheld the honor of the race and fought to maintain its safety from murderous assaults. I feel that we owe them a vast debt of gratitude, even though they belong to the lowest levels of those whom we call the Common People. Much golden eloquence has been squandered upon the successful and the good; much stern condemnation has been vented upon the wicked and the unclad. I venture now to plead for those of our poor brothers and sisters who are despised and rejected of men. For after all they are the real tests of our theories of brotherhood and racial solidarity.

By and large, the Common People are the real race. They may not have much to give, but, such as it is, they give it without stint: loyalty, respect, friendliness and help in the hour of need. Sometimes their ignorance is played upon and their loyalty and devotion outraged; but when you do the right thing by them they always do the right thing by you. They are a perpetual reservoir of healthy enthusiasm and their rough but genuine appreciation is like a tonic to the soul that is sick of the shams and insincerities of those who call themselves "cultured." They are the dependable back-bone of every good cause and making of many. Out of the bosom of the Common people rise the sources of our literature and art, and the real, living virile society is the genuine life they live. Divorced from that, art is finical and literature flabby and what is called "society" becomes only the drumming of drones. It is better to have their good opinion when you are dead than the blessing of the Brahmins while you live. For while the one is real and abiding, the other is like "a tale told by an idiot, full of sound and fury and signifying — nothing."

138. "The Roots of Power," *Boston Chronicle* (June 21, 1924): 1, HHHP Wr.

In this final editorial from the *Boston Chronicle*, Harrison called for cooperative economic work. He had been inspired by cooperative efforts throughout his life. He witnessed the value of "communal extensions" on St. Croix. He was attracted by the Socialists' efforts toward a "cooperative commonwealth." He was stimulated by the cooperative approach to education at the Modern School. The potential of Black businesses and banks serving the community inspired him. His boyhood friend and sharer of political programs, D. Hamilton Jackson, was the driving force of the cooperative labor movement in St. Croix. Grace Campbell and Richard B. Moore, his friends and co-workers, played prominent roles in cooperative movements in Harlem.[10]

To Harrison, cooperative programs were a necessary positive step. He was an unrelenting foe of white supremacy, but he was also convinced that not all shortcomings should be blamed on it. He believed it was important to be proactive, to build alternate structures and organizations. He believed that cooperative producing, consuming, saving, and investing efforts could stem the flow of money from the community. Steps could then be taken to build political and economic structures that could help organize political power and spur the ambition of youth. To Harrison such positive cooperative efforts were the "Roots of Power." They indicated, as the words of *The Voice* masthead said, "The future in the distance."

It is easy to win applause and approval among our people by charging every one of our shortcomings up to the white people. But, just the same, it isn't true. For instance: the white people instead of being responsible for color prejudice among us, have done their best to discourage it by calling us all by the same contemptuous epithets and by lynching and jim crowing us impartially. So that's one thing we can't blame them for.

Again, while we are tying to unkink our hair most white people have been trying to get a kink into theirs. And it certainly is not the white people's fault that we city-Negroes spend so much of our money on high-rent apartments that we can't own homes, or wear so much "millionaires clothes" that we can't own land. Our morning luncheons, afternoon-teas, moonlight dances, card parties and other apings of moneyed aristocracy are not forced on us by white people. We deliberately choose to begin initiating them at the wrong end, and not at the right end — like the Japanese.

But these things won't last forever. Therefore it is high time to undertake the removal of some of the things that stand in the way of our progress. Consider, for instance, our spendings. In the city districts where so many of us live in the North we find a streak of daily emigration pouring out every morning to the four points of the compass, and a thin stream of daily white immigration flowing in. On Saturday nights the returning colored flood sweeps back into its home areas with its wages; but most of it floats out with the thin white tide. None of that cash outgo is available for the building of economic structures in the home district which would spur the ambition of Negro boys and girls or increase the power of its inhabitants over newspapers and public opinion. And in the meanwhile, we grumble when the bank that collects our savings lends them out to white men to fertilize white businesses in our midst and will not lend them to Negroes to fertilize Negro business. We complain when white politicians and their colored lackeys gerrymander our districts so that we can not get the control of Negro district by Negro voters and "sing the blues" over the way in which we are treated by the police, the boards of health and street cleaning, and the wielders of power.

But it all goes back to our own neglect of economic co-operation. The American Negro, like the European Jew in the middle ages, is shut out of a great many things. But he isn't shut out of making money — and hanging on to it. And now, as then, money is power. But power, to be effective, must be concentrated; and that concentration must be in our own hands.

Biographical Sources on Harrison

The two major sources of biographical material on Harrison are the Hubert Henry Harrison Papers (HHHP), a private collection that includes Harrison's diary (HHHDI), writings, correspondence, scrapbooks, books, and miscellany, and Jeffrey B. Perry, *Hubert Henry Harrison, The Father of Harlem Radicalism*, vol. 1 (Baton Rouge: Louisiana State University Press, forthcoming).

Harrison's two books, *The Negro and Nation* (New York: Cosmo-Advocate Publishing Company, 1917), and *When Africa Awakes: The "Inside Story" of the Stirrings and Strivings of the New Negro in the Western World* (New York: Porro Press, 1920), contain editorials, articles, and reviews. Of the publications he edited, there are scattered issues of *The Voice* (1917–19), the *New Negro* (1919), and the *Negro World* (1920), and a complete set of the *Embryo of the Voice of the Negro* (1927) and the *Voice of the Negro* (1927).

The best sketch by a contemporary of Harrison is that of Joel A. Rogers, "Hubert Harrison: Intellectual Giant and Free-Lance Educator (1883–1927)," in J. A. Rogers, *World's Great Men of Color*, 2 vols. (New York: J. A. Rogers, 37 Morningside Ave., 1946 and 1947), 2:611–19, which is also reprinted as "Hubert Harrison: Intellectual Giant and Free-Lance Educator," in Joel A. Rogers, *World's Great Men of Color*, 2 vols., ed. with intro. by John Henrik Clarke (New York: Collier Books, 1972), 2:432–42. Another excellent contemporary sketch is Richard B. Moore, "Hubert Henry Harrison (1883–1927)," in *Dictionary of American Negro Biography*, Rayford W. Logan and Michael R. Winston, ed. (New York: W. W. Norton, 1982), 292–93. Geraldo Guirty, author of "Crucian Becomes Eloquent Harlem Protester of Injustice," *St. Thomas Daily News*, February 10, 1984, and John G. Jackson, who wrote *Hubert Henry Harrison: The Black Socrates* (Austin: American Atheist Press, 1987), are people who knew Harrison in their youth.

An original biographical article on which most later information on Harrison's early years appears to be based is "Dr. Harrison's Rise as Orator Is Like Fiction: Educator, Writer and Speaker Now Ranks with Best in His Line," *Chicago Defender*, January 19, 1924.

Around the time of Harrison's death, biographical sketches appeared in Joseph J. Boris, *Who's Who in Colored America: A Biographical Dictionary of Notable Living Persons of Negro Descent in America* (New York: Who's Who in Colored America Corp., 1927), 86–87; "Hubert Harrison Dies: Harlem Scholar Succumbs after 'Minor' Operation: Came to America in 1900 from St. Croix, Virgin Islands, Where He Was Born — Unusual Ability Forced Recognition Here," *Amsterdam News*, December 21, 1927; Oscar J. Benson, "Literary Genius of Hubert Harrison," *New York News*, December 24, 1927; Hodge Kirnon, "Hubert Harrison: An Appreciation," *Negro World*, December 31, 1927; "Garvey Aid and Author Passes Away: Hubert H. Harrison Dies in New York," *Chicago Defender*, December 24, 1927; "Hubert Harrison Dies Suddenly in Bellevue Hospital: Complications Following Operation Brings Death," *New York Age*, December 24, 1927; "Dr. Harrison Dies after Operation," *Pittsburgh Courier*, December 24, 1927; "Lament Dream of Dr. Hubert Harrison: Eulogized by Several Who Knew His Life and Work," *Amsterdam News*, December 28, 1927; "Dr. H. H. Harrison, Noted Colored Lecturer, Dies," *Survey Graphic*, December 20, 1927; "Celebrated Harlem Mass Leader Dies after Operation," *New York News*, December 24, 1927; "The Death of Hubert Harrison," *New York News*, December 31, 1927; "Hubert H. Harrison!" *Pittsburgh Courier*, December 31, 1927; and "Obituary: Hubert H. Harrison," *New York World*, December 18, 1927.

During the Depression two other biographical sketches were prepared: one by J. A. Rogers for the Federal Writers' Project, which was published only much later as "Hubert Harrison," in *The Negro in New York: An Informal Social History*, ed. Roi Ottley and William J. Weatherby (New York: New York Public Library, 1967), and Louis B. Bryan, "Brief History of the Life and Work of Hubert Harrison," also in *The Negro in New York*.

A third wave of biographical sketches includes Irwin Marcus, "Hubert Harrison: Negro Advocate," *Negro History Bulletin* 34, no. 1 (June 1971): 18–19; Ralph L. Crowder, "Street Scholars: Self-Trained Black Historians," *Black Collegian* 9, no. 3 (January–February 1979): 8–20, 80; Helen C. Camp, "Hubert Henry Harrison, April 27, 1883–December 17, 1927," in *American Reformers,* ed. Alden Whitman (Bronx: H. H. Wilson, 1985), 406–7; and three very similar pieces by Wilfred David Samuels all titled "Hubert H. Harrison and the 'New Negro Manhood Movement.'" These appear in Wilfred D. Samuels, "Five Afro-Caribbean Voices in American Culture, 1917–1929: Hubert H. Harrison, Wilfred A. Domingo, Richard B. Moore, Cyril V. Briggs, and Claude McKay," Ph.D. diss., University of Iowa, 1977, 50–77; Wilfred D. Samuels, *Five Afro-Caribbean Voices in American Culture* (Boulder: Belmont Books, 1977), 27–41; and in *Afro-Americans in New York Life and History* 5, no. 1 (January 1981): 29–41. A 1983 footnote sketch by Robert A. Hill is provided on "Hubert Henry Harrison," in *The Marcus Garvey and Universal Negro Improvement Association Papers*, ed. Robert A. Hill (Berkeley: University of California Press, 1983), 1:210–11.

Very useful for the socialist period is the chapter "Local New York, the Colored Socialist Club, Hubert H. Harrison, and W. E. B. Du Bois," in Philip S. Foner, *American Socialism and Black Americans: From the Age of Jackson to World War II* (Westport, Conn.: Green-wood Press, 1977), 202–19, and Winston James, "Notes on the Ideology and Travails of Afro-America's Socialist Pioneers, 1877–1930," *Souls* 1, no. 4 (fall 1999): 45–63.

The first lengthy treatment of Harrison was Jeffrey B. Perry, "Hubert Henry Harrison 'The Father of Harlem Radicalism': The Early Years—1883 through the Founding of the Liberty League and *The Voice* in 1917," Ph.D. diss., Columbia University, 1985, which includes an extensive bibliography. This was followed by Jeffrey B. Perry, "Hubert Henry Harrison," in *Encyclopedia of African American Culture and History*, ed. Jack Salzman, David Lionel Smith, and Cornell West (New York: Macmillan, 1995), 1230–31; Jeffrey B. Perry, "Hubert Henry Harrison," in *American National Biography*, ed. John A. Garraty and Mark C. Carnes, 24 vols. (New York: Oxford University Press, 1999), 10:212–14; Jeffrey B. Perry, "Hubert Harrison: A Brief Sketch for Black History Month," *Black World Today*, February 18, 1999, <http://www.tbwt.com/views/feat904.asp>; and Jeffrey B. Perry, "An Introduction to Hubert Harrison, 'The Father of Harlem Radicalism,'" *Souls* 2, no. 1 (winter 2000): 38–54.

Shorter pieces subsequent to the lengthy treatment include Portia James, "Hubert H. Harrison and the New Negro Movement," *Western Journal of Black Studies* 13, no. 2 (1989): 82–91; Barbara Bair, "Hubert H. Harrison (1883–1927)," in *Encyclopedia of the American Left*, ed. Mari Jo Buhle, Paul Buhle, and Dan Georgakas (Urbana: University of Illinois Press, 1990), 292; Patrick Innis, "Hubert Henry Harrison: Great African American Free-thinker," *Secular Subjects* (St. Louis, Mo.: Rationalist Society of St. Louis, 1992); Greg Robinson, "Hubert Henry Harrison," in *Encyclopedia of New York*, ed. Kenneth T. Jackson (New Haven: Yale University Press, 1995), 530; the chapter "Hubert Henry Harrison, New Negro Militancy, and the Limits of Racialized Leadership, 1914–1954," in Kevin K. Gaines, *Uplifting the Race: Black Leadership, Politics, and Culture in the Twentieth Century* (Chapel Hill: University of North Carolina Press, 1996), 234–60, 286–88; and the chapter "Dimensions and Main Currents of Caribbean Radicalism in America: Hubert Harrison, the African Blood Brotherhood, and the UNIA," in Winston James, *Holding Aloft the Banner of Ethiopia: Caribbean Radicalism in Early Twentieth-Century America* (New York: Verso, 1998), 122–84.

Notes

Introduction

1. "Hubert Harrison: Intellectual Giant and Free-Lance Educator (1883–1927)," in J. A. Rogers, *World's Great Men of Color*, edited with an introduction, commentary, and new bibliographical notes by John Henrik Clarke, 2 vols. (New York: Collier Books, 1972), 2:432–42, esp. 432–33. The themes in this introduction are treated in greater depth in Jeffrey B. Perry, *Hubert Henry Harrison: The Father of Harlem Radicalism*, vol. 1 (Baton Rouge: Louisiana State University Press, forthcoming). The principal sources on Harrison's life can be found in the preceding section of this work, "Biographical Sources on Harrison."

2. Henry Miller, *Plexus* (New York: Grove Press, 1965), 560–61.

3. William Pickens, "Hubert Harrison: Philosopher of Harlem," *AN*, February 7, 1923. Pickens added that Harrison was a "'walking cyclopedia' of current human facts," especially history and literature, and it made "no difference" whether he spoke about "*Alice in Wonderland* or the most extensive work of H. G. Wells; about the lightest shadows of Edgar Allan Poe or the heaviest depths of Kant; about music, or art, or science, or political history."

4. W. A. Domingo, interview with Theodore Draper, January 18, 1958, New York, Theodore Draper Papers, Robert W. Woodruff Library for Advanced Studies, Emory University, Atlanta, Georgia, preliminary listing as box 20, folder 7, "Negro Question for Vol. 1 (cont.)," notes re W. A. Domingo, 2. Harlem activists Hodge Kirnon and A. Philip Randolph also praised Harrison. Kirnon emphasized that Harrison "lived with and amongst his people" and that he was "the first Negro whose radicalism was comprehensive enough to include racialism, politics, theological criticism, sociology and education in a thorough-going and scientific manner." Randolph explained that "Harrison was far more advanced than we were" and his mind "reached in all areas of human knowledge." See Hodge Kirnon, "Hubert Harrison: An Appreciation," *NW*, December 31, 1927, and "The Reminiscences of A. Philip Randolph," interview with Wendell Wray, July 25, 1972, p. 154, in Oral History Project, Butler Library, Columbia University, New York.

5. The Socialist Party was the nation's largest class-radical movement and the "New Negro"/Garvey movement was the nation's largest race–radical movement. See James Weinstein, "The Fortunes of the Old Left Compared to the Fortunes of the New," in *Failure of a Dream? Essays in the History of American Socialism,* ed. John H. M. Laslett and Seymour Martin Lipset (Garden City, N.Y.: Anchor Press/Doubleday, 1974), 677–712, esp. p. 679, and Tony Martin, *Race First: The Ideological and Organizational Struggles of Marcus Garvey and the Universal Negro Improvement Association* (Westport, Conn.: Greenwood Press, 1976), p. ix.

6. This seeming incongruity was made possible by the political-economic system of the United States in which a system of racial oppression was central to capitalist rule. Theodore W. Allen, "The Most Vulnerable Point," an unpublished manuscript dated October 1972, which is in the possession of the author, elaborates the position that "[t]he principal aspect of United States capitalist society is not merely bourgeois domination, but bourgeois white-supremacist domination." Allen's discussion of the origins of the system of racial oppression and of that system's centrality to class rule in the United States is developed in Theodore William Allen, *The Invention of the White Race,* 2 vols. (New York: Verso, 1994 and 1997), 1:32–35, 1:133–35, 1:143–50 and 2:221–2, 2:239–59.

7. Domingo, interview with Draper, January 18, 1958. Rogers writes simply, "The Garvey Movement and the *Messenger* Group [led by Randolph and Owen], the first racial, the second economic in doctrine, had only radicalism in common and later became enemies. Both, however, represent eras in the progress of the Afro-American, and both were fructified by the spirit and teaching of Harrison." See *WGMC* 2:437.

8. On Harlem see Richard B. Moore, "Africa Conscious Harlem," *Freedomways* 3, no. 3 (summer 1963): 320. Cary D. Wintz, *Black Culture and the Harlem Renaissance* (Houston: Rice University Press, 1988), 1, 22, writes that in "the period between World War I and 1920" the "locus of black leadership shifted from Tuskegee to New York," and "Harlem, in short, was where the action was in black America in the decade following World War I." Claude McKay, *Harlem: Negro Metropolis* (1940; New York: Harcourt Brace Jovanovich, 1968), 16, calls Harlem "the Negro capital of the world." Mark Naison, *Communists in Harlem During the Depression* (Urbana: University of Illinois Press, 1983), p. xvii, points out that Harlem was "the largest black community in the nation and an intellectual and cultural center of international importance."

9. On Harrison as the "Father of Harlem Radicalism" see *The Negro in New York: An Informal Social History,* ed. Roi Ottley and William J. Weatherby (New York: New York Public Library, 1967), 223; Jervis Anderson, *A. Philip Randolph: A Biographical Portrait* (New York: Harcourt Brace Jovanovich, 1973), 80; Warren J. Halliburton with Ernest Kaiser, *Harlem: A History of Broken Dreams* (Garden City, N.Y.: Doubleday, 1974), 45; Helen C. Camp, "Harrison, Hubert Henry (April 27, 1883–December 17, 1917)," in *American Reformers: An H. W. Wilson Biographical Dictionary,* ed. Alden Whitman (Bronx: H. H. Wilson, 1985), 406–7; Jeffrey B. Perry, "Hubert Henry Harrison, 'The Father of Harlem Radicalism': The Early Years — 1883 through the Founding of The Liberty League and *The Voice* in 1917," Ph.D. diss., Columbia University, 1986; Jeffrey B. Perry, "Hubert Henry Harrison," *Encyclopedia of*

African American Culture and History, ed. Jack Salzman, David Lionel Smith, and Cornel West (New York: MacMillan, 1995), 1230–31; Jeffrey B. Perry, "Hubert Henry Harrison," *ANB* 10:212–14; Jeffrey B. Perry, "An Introduction to Hubert Harrison 'The Father of Harlem Radicalism,'" *Souls* 2, no. 1 (winter 2000): 38–54; Robert A. Hill, "On Collectors, Their Contributions to the Documentation of the Black Past," in *Black Bibliophiles and Collectors: Preservers of Black History*, ed. Elinor Des Verney Sinnette, W. Paul Coates, and Thomas C. Battle (Washington, D.C.: Howard University Press, 1990), 47–56; and Winston James, *Holding Aloft the Banner of Ethiopia: Caribbean Radicalism in Early Twentieth-Century America* (New York: Verso, 1998), 1.

10. The quotation is from HH, "Prejudice Growing Less and Co-Operation More," *PC*, January 29, 1927 (selection 83).

11. *WGMC* 2:432; HH, "On a Certain Condescension in White Publishers [Part I]," *NW* 12, no. 4 (March 4, 1922): 7, HHHP Scr B (selection 98); "Lament Dream of Dr. Hubert Harrison: Eulogized by Several Who Knew His Life and Work," *AN*, December 28, 1927; Hubert Harrison Memorial Church Booklet, c. December 22, 1929, Egbert Ethelred Brown Papers, box 1, "Harlem Unitarian Church," SCRBC, NYPL, New York. Tony Martin, *Literary Garveyism: Garvey, Black Arts and the Harlem Renaissance* (Dover, Mass.: Majority Press, 1983), 5, describes Harrison as "Harlem's best known and most respected intellectual."

12. Baptism Record of "Hubert Henry [Harrison]," July 7, 1883, in "Baptisms Solemnized During the Years March 3, 1883–October 21, 1899," St. John's Anglican Church, Christiansted, St. Croix, United States Virgin Islands, 9; "Declaration of Intention [to Naturalize]," no. 114310, June 22, 1915, National Federal Records Center, New York, *Naturalization Records*, vol. 172, docket no. 42659 and, in the same docket, "Petition for Naturalization," filed June 22, 1922 and approved September 26, 1922; HHHDI, cover; *WGMC* 2:433; "Dr. Harrison's Rise as Orator Is Like Fiction: Educator, Writer and Speaker Now Ranks with Best in His Line," *CD*, January 19, 1924.

13. Daniel Bell, "The Background and Development of Marxian Socialism in the United States," in *Socialism and American Life*, ed. Donald Drew Egbert and Stow Persons, 2 vols. (Princeton: Princeton University Press, 1952), 1:213–405, esp. 268; Philip S. Foner, *The Spanish-Cuban-American War and the Birth of American Imperialism 1895–1902*, 2 vols. (New York: Monthly Review Press, 1972), esp. 1:x; and Rayford W. Logan, *The Betrayal of the Negro: From Rutherford B. Hayes to Woodrow Wilson*, new enl. ed., originally published as *The Negro in American Thought and Life: The Nadir, 1877–1901* (New York: Dial Press, 1954; New York: Macmillan, 1970), 11, 62.

14. HHHDI, May 20, 1908.

15. HH to the editor, *NYS*, December 8, 1910 (selection 52), and December 19, 1910; Charles W. Anderson to Booker T. Washington, September 10 and October 30, 1911, *BTWP*, 11:300–301, 351.

16. HH, "The Negro and Socialism: 1 — The Negro Problem Stated," *NYC*, November 28, 1911; HH, "Race Prejudice — II," *NYC*, December 4, 1911; HH, "The Duty of the Socialist Party," *NYC*, December 13, 1911; HH, "How to Do It — And How Not," *NYC*, December 16, 1911; HH, "Summary and Conclusion," *NYC*, December 26, 1911; HH, "The Black Man's

Burden [I]," *ISR* 12, no. 10 (April 1912): 660–63; HH, "The Black Man's Burden [II]," *ISR* 12, no. 11: (May 1912): 762–64; HH, "Socialism and the Negro," *ISR* 13, no. 1 (July 1912): 65–68; and W. E. B. Du Bois, "Socialism and the Negro Problem," *New Review* 1, no. 5 (February 1, 1913): 138–41, quotation 140; HH, "Race First versus Class First," *NW*, March 27, 1920. (See selections 9–15 and 30).

17. HH, "Southern Socialists and the Ku Klux Klan," c. 1914, HHHP Wr; reprinted in *NW*, January 8, 1921; HH, "Race First versus Class First"; and HH, "An Open Letter to the Socialist Party of New York City," *NW*, May 8, 1920. (selections 15, 30, and 33.)

18. HHHDI, September 28, 1914.

19. HH to the editor, "New York Lecture Centers," *TS*, August 22, 1914; HHHDI, September 28, 1914. On Harrison's pioneering role in Harlem soapbox oratory see "Reminiscences of A. Philip Randolph," 152; Lester A. Walton, "Street Speaker Heralds Spring in Harlem: Negro Orators Resume Soap Box Talks on Various Topics," *NYW*, March 23, 1928; Robert A. Hill, "On Collectors," in Sinnette et al., *Black Bibliophiles*, 47, which refers to Harrison as "the major innovator in that band of black street orators" that "took history into the streets in Harlem in 1917"; and Theodore G. Vincent, *Black Power and the Garvey Movement* (San Francisco: Ramparts Press, 1972), 137, which maintains that: "Harrison was the most famous of [Harlem] Renaissance street-corner orators."

20. HH, "Introductory," in HH, *WAA*, 5–8. Harrison is considered the originator (among African Americans) of the "race first" concept which he said derived from "the American doctrine of 'Race First.'" See HH, *N&N*, 3 n.; Robert A. Hill, "Introduction: Racial and Radical: Cyril V. Briggs, *The Crusader* Magazine, and the African Blood Brotherhood, 1918–1922," in *The Crusader*, 6 vols. (New York: Garland Publishing, 1987), 1:lviii n. 122; HH, "Program and Principles of the International Colored Unity League," *The Voice of the Negro* 1, no. 1 (April 1927): 4–6 (selection 135); and Hodge Kirnon, "Hubert Harrison: An Appreciation," *NW*, December 31, 1927.

21. HH, "Negro Society and the Negro Stage, Preamble [parts 1 and 2]," c. July 1915, HHHP Wr (selections 126 and 127). On this subject see Nathan I. Huggins, *Harlem Renaissance* (New York: Oxford University Press, 1974), 9, 139, and 245, which emphasizes that "the theatrical stage itself, more than any other cultural phenomenon, opens a perspective into the pathology of American race relations." Also see the 1924 comment of Alain Locke that "African art . . . [is] perhaps the ultimate key for the interpretation of the African mind." Michael R. Winston, "Alain Leroy Locke," in *DANB*, 398–404, quotation p. 401.

22. In 1916 Harrison began speaking of a "New Negro Manhood Movement." See, for example, "When the Negro Wakes, A Lecture of 'The Manhood Movement' among the Negro People of America by Hubert Henry Harrison at the Temple of Truth Lafayette Hall, 165 W. 131st St., Sunday Dec. 24, 1916 at 8 P.M.," handout, HHHP Scr 34. The subject of manhood has been a major concern in much Black protest and literature at least since Frederick Douglass detailed his forceful rejoinder to his overseer ("you shall see how a slave was made a man") in his 1845 *Narrative of the Life of Frederick Douglass, an American Slave* (New York: Anchor Books, 1989). The struggle for manhood has often been viewed as a striving

for power, self-determination, and autonomy in the face of vicious white supremacy. See *OCAAL*, 475–77, esp. 475–76, and W. A. Domingo, "Gift of the Black Tropics," in *The New Negro*, ed. Alain Leroy Locke (New York: Albert and Charles Boni, 1925), 346–49, esp. 349, which points out that an "assertion" of "manhood" in "an environment that demands too much servility and unprotesting acquiescence from men of African blood" indicates an "unwillingness to conform and be standardized, to accept tamely an inferior status and [to] abdicate" one's "humanity." In recent years "manhood" has come under increased scrutiny in terms of its male-supremacist implications.

23. By 1917 and the founding of the Liberty League Harrison was also speaking of a "New Negro Movement." Over the years he and others would use both phrases, with "New Negro Movement" predominating. See HH, "Launching the Liberty League," *The Voice*, July 4, 1917, which discusses "this 'New Negro Movement." See also HH, "Program and Principles of the International Colored Unity League," *The Voice of the Negro* 1, no. 1 (April 1927): 4–6, and Hodge Kirnon, "Hubert Harrison," *NW*, December 31, 1927. Winston James, *HATB* 123, refers to Harrison's "pioneering role in what became known as the New Negro radicalism," and Robert A. Hill, *MGP* 1:lxx, considers Harrison the chief intellectual spokesman of the 'new Negro' nationalism." Virgin Islander Frank R. Crosswaith, special organizer of the Brotherhood of Sleeping Car Porters and a prominent Socialist, wrote: "The story of the New Negro's fascinating fight for a man's place in our time, is the story of Hubert H. Harrison. . . . [He] will stand for all time as a symbol of inspiration to the men and women of the Negro race." Frank R. Crosswaith to Mrs. [Irene Louise ("Lin")] Harrison, December 20, 1927, HHHP Co.

24. HH, "Launching the Liberty League," *The Voice*, July 4, 1917, explains that the Liberty League and *The Voice* put forth "the new demands and aspirations of the new Negro" and that "this 'New Negro Movement' represented a breaking away of the Negro masses from the grip of old-time leaders." Although Harrison was instrumental in building a "New Negro Movement," the term "New Negro" had been used before. Booker T. Washington wrote on "The New Negro Woman" in *Lend a Hand* in 1895; Bishop Henry McNeal Turner spoke of the "New Negro" in *Constitution*, September 15–October 15, 1895; Sutton Griggs used the phrase in *Imperium in Imperio* in 1899; Washington collaborated on *A New Negro for a New Century* in 1900; and William Pickens wrote a series of essays published as *The New Negro, His Political, Civil, and Mental Status, and Related Essays* in 1916. See Logan, *Betrayal of the Negro*, 289, 341, and 420; August Meier, *Negro Thought in America 1880–1915: Racial Ideologies in the Age of Booker T. Washington* (1963; Ann Arbor: University of Michigan Press, 1966), 258–59; and Gerald Early, *Speech and Power: The African-American Essay and Its Cultural Content from Polemics to Pulpit*, 2 vols. (Hopewell, N.J.: Echo Press, 1992), 1:45.

25. Harrison depicts the new reality of the "New Negro" in "As the Currents Flow," *NN* 3, no. 7 (August 1919): 3–4 (selection 24). See also Huggins, *Harlem Renaissance*, 53–54 and 59, which states that "the New Negro was militant and self-assertive," "would not be content with second-class citizenship," and emphasized "race consciousness and racial coopera-

tion." On Harrison's movement as the basis for the Garvey movement see Anselmo Jackson, "An Analysis of the Black Star Line," *Emancipator*, March 27, 1920, and William H. Ferris, "The Spectacular Career of Garvey," *AN*, February 11, 1925.

26. Alain Leroy Locke served as special editor for the March 1925 *Survey Graphic* (subtitled *Harlem: Mecca of the New Negro*) which included a wide variety of articles, stories, and poems by prominent Black writers. Eight months later he brought out *The New Negro*, an anthology which included, in revised form, many of the pieces from the *Survey Graphic*. Though Locke noted a "new race consciousness" and "internationalism," that the "rank and file" were becoming leaders, and that the "New Negro" was "an augury of a new democracy in American culture," his work also tended to transform the militancy associated with the more political New Negro movement into what Henry Louis Gates Jr. refers to as a more "apolitical movement of the arts." See Henry Louis Gates Jr., "The Trope of a New Negro and the Reconstruction of the Image of the Black, *Representations*, no. 24 (fall 1998): 129–55, esp. 147; *NAAAL*, 960–70, esp. 960, 964–65, and 969; and *OCAAL*, 340–41. Tony Martin correctly emphasizes the major literary importance of the Garvey movement and the *Negro World* (beginning around 1920 when Harrison became editor) to the literary epoch known as the Harlem Renaissance. See Martin, *Race First*, 91–92; Martin, *Literary Garveyism*, pp. ix–x, 2, 5; and Tony Martin, *African Fundamentalism: A Literary and Cultural Anthology of Garvey's Harlem Renaissance* (1983; Dover, Mass.: Majority Press, 1991), pp. xv–xvi. The Harrison papers make clear that the Garvey movement was a component part of the New Negro movement and that Harrison was a principal architect of the *Negro World's* mass literary appeal. His efforts also contributed to the climate which led to the *New York Age* editorial and symposium "New Negro — What is He?" (*New York Age*, January 24, 1920, and February 7 and 28, 1920), as well as to Locke's widely known publication.

27. HH, "Our Professional Friends," *The Voice*, November 7, 1917, HHHP Wr (selection 45), and "Shillady Resigns," *NW*, June 19, 1920, 2 (selection 57).

28. HH, "Shillady Resigns," 2; HH, "The Liberty League of Negro-Americans," *The Voice*, July 4, 1917 and reprinted in *The Voice*, September 19, 1917 (selection 18). In this period, according to the historian Robert L. Zangrando, the NAACP refused, on constitutional grounds, to push openly for federal antilynching legislation. For several years, in response to lynching and mob violence, it had taken the approach of "on site investigations, efforts at prosecution [under state law], fund-raising, protest meetings, news releases, and a campaign to win passage of appropriate civil rights legislation." NAACP failure to wholeheartedly support the antilynching legislation reflected the fact that it "was reaching for southern support and still pulling its punches on the matter of federal statute." For the time being, "Exposé" remained its "chief weapon." Thus, the Liberty's League's call for federal antilynching legislation was, as Harrison claimed, a "startling" initiative. See Robert L. Zangrando, *The NAACP Crusade against Lynching, 1909–1950* (Philadelphia: Temple University Press, 1980), 26–27, 31, 44, 50–72, and HH, "The Liberty League of Negro-Americans."

29. HH, "Marcus Garvey at the Bar of United States Justice," *ANP*, c. July 1923, HHHP Wr (selection 64); HH, "Two Negro Radicalisms," *NN* 4, no. 2 (October 1919): 4–5, HHHP Wr (selection 27). On *The Voice* circulation see HH, "Owing to the High Cost of Manhood

The Voice Has Gone up to 5 Cents," *The Voice*, October 18, 1917 and HH, "Advertising in the Voice," *The Voice*, July 10, 1917. On the use of a multiplier in determining the readership of Black newspapers see Frederick G. Detweiler, *The Negro Press in the United States* (Chicago: University of Chicago Press, 1922), 6, 11–12, 15.

30. Jackson, "An Analysis of the Black Star Line," *Emancipator*, March 27, 1920; Ferris, "The Spectacular Career of Garvey," *AN*, February 11, 1925; Draper interview with Domingo, January 18, 1958; *WGMC* 2:436.

31. The Liberty Congress's wartime demands for equality were clear forerunners of the March on Washington Movement (MOWM) led by A. Philip Randolph during World War II and of the August 28, 1963, March on Washington during the Vietnam War led by Randolph and Martin Luther King Jr. The MOWM led to President Franklin Delano Roosevelt's signing of Executive Order 8802 on June 25, 1941, which stated that it would be the "policy of the United States that there shall be no discrimination in the employment of workers in defense industries or Government because of race, creed, color, or national origin," and which called for the establishment of a Fair Employment Practices Committee. After Order 8802, the African American presence in war industries increased from 3 to 8 percent. The 1963 march led to the 1964 Civil Rights Act, which forbade discrimination in public accommodations and employment. See Herbert Garfinkel, *When Negroes March: The March on Washington Movement in the Organizational Politics for FEPC* (Glencoe, Ill.: Free Press, 1959; New York: Athenaeum, 1969), 56–57, 6–61, 117–21, and 127–31; James Gilbert Cassedy, "African Americans and the American Labor Movement," *Prologue* 29, no. 2 (summer 1997): 113–20, esp. 119; Paula E. Pfeffer, *A. Philip Randolph, Pioneer of the Civil Rights Movement* (Baton Rouge: Louisiana State University Press, 1990), 269–71; and *The Chronological History of the Negro in America*, ed. Peter Bergman, assisted by a staff of compilers under the direction of Mort N. Bergman (New York: Harper and Row, 1969), 493, 583.

32. HH, "The Descent of Dr. Du Bois," *The Voice*, July 25, 1918 (selection 54); HH, "When the Blind Lead," *NW*, c. February 1920 (selection 55); Mark Ellis, "'Closing Ranks' and 'Seeking Honors': W. E. B. Du Bois in World War I," *JAH* 79, no. 1 (June 1992): 96–124; Mark Ellis, "W. E. B. Du Bois and the Formation of Black Opinion in World War I: A Commentary on 'The Damnable Dilemma,'" *JAH* 81, no. 4 (March 1995): 1584–90.

33. HH, "The Descent of Dr. Du Bois." Du Bois apparently never forgot Harrison's criticism — he never once mentioned Harrison by name in the pages of the *Crisis* and seemingly went out of his way to avoid doing so. See Hodge Kirnon, "Kirnon Flays Monthly Magazines," letter to the editor [February 17], *New York News*, February 28, 1928; Irma Watkins-Owens, *Blood Relations: Caribbean Immigrants and the Harlem Community, 1900–1930* (Bloomington: Indiana University Press, 1996), 97; and HH, "No Negro Literary Renaissance: Says Well Known Writer," *PC*, March 12, 1927 (selection 119).

34. HH, "The Voice Is Coming Out to Stay!" leaflet, c. July 4, 1918, HHHP Wr; HH, "The Resurrection of the Voice," *The Voice*, July 11, 1918; HH, "To Our People in Washington, D.C.," *The Voice*, July 11, 1918; HH, "The Need for It" [and The Nature of It]," *New Negro*, September 1919 (selection 26); George Hutchinson, *The Harlem Renaissance in Black and White* (Cambridge, Mass.: Belknap Press of Harvard University Press, 1995), 212–13, explains

that in January 1918, Oswald Garrison Villard took over the editorship of the *Nation* and "returned the magazine to its former crusading self, with the example of William Lloyd Garrison's *Liberator* clearly in mind." He "made the attack on racism a major issue" and *The Nation* became a progressive organ that "tended toward socialism."

35. HHHDI, March 17 and 18 and August 18, 28, and 31, 1920 (selections 60, 62–63).

36. HHHDI, August 18, 1920, c. April 1923 [Notes on Marcus Garvey], and March 23, 1924.

37. On May 31 and June 1, 1921, Tulsa was torn by what the *New York Times* described as "one of the most disastrous race wars ever visited upon an American city." The "Negro quarter" in north Tulsa, comprising more thirty densely populated blocks, was wiped out by fire. Six thousand African Americans were put "under heavy guard in hastily established detention camps" and, on June 1, "500 whites began the invasion of the negro quarter" as private airplanes circled the city and dropped deadly bombs on the Black community in the first-ever air attack on U.S. soil. Overall, some forty city blocks were looted and leveled; twenty-three churches and 1,000 homes and businesses were ruined; Black men were forced to march, en masse, through town with their hands up; and the state militia was activated. Estimates indicate that as many as two to three hundred Black citizens were killed, and many more may have been buried in mass graves and therefore not counted. See "Negroes Meet Today to Seek Tulsa Redress: Hubert Harrison of Colored Liberty League Wires Oklahoma Gov. to Punish Responsible Whites," *NYC*, June 5, 1921; "85 Whites and Negroes Die in Tulsa Riots as 3,000 Armed Men Battle in Streets; 30 Blocks Burned, Military Rule in City," *NYT*, June 2, 1921; Scott Ellsworth, *Death in a Promised Land: The Tulsa Race Riot of 1921* (Baton Rouge: Louisiana State University Press, 1982), esp. 61–67; R. Halliburton, "The Tulsa Race War of 1921," *Journal of Black Studies* 2, no. 3 (March 1972): 333–76; "The Race War in Tulsa, Okla.," *NW*, July 9, 1921; "Home Guards Set Fire to Buildings While Airplanes Dropped Bombs on Homes in Negro District in Tulsa," *NW*, June 18, 1921; "Tulsa Negroes' Homes Fired," *Chicago Daily News*, June 1, 1921; *NYB*, 1921–1922, 79; "The Tulsa Riot," *Crusader* 4, no. 5 (July 1921): 5-6; Sam Howe Verhovek, "75 Years Later, Tulsa Confronts Its Race Riot," *NYT*, May 31, 1996; "Oklahoma Clears Black in Deadly 1921 Race Riot," *NYT*, October 26, 1996; and Brent Staples, "Searching for Graves — and Justice — in Tulsa," *NYT*, March 20, 1999.

38. HH, "Shillady Resigns," 2; "Dr. Harris[on] Candidate for Congress on Socialist (Single Tax) Ticket," *CD*, June 7, 1924; "Wants State for Negroes," *BC*, June 21, 1924; "Negroes Plan New American State," *CSM*, June 7, 1924; "Separate Colored State Urged by Harrison," *NYN*, August 2, 1924; "Separate State for Negroes Urged," Baltimore *Afro-American*, August 8, 1924; "Lecturer Proposes Independent State for Negro Citizens," *PC*, August 30, 1924; Joseph G. Tucker, "Special Report of Radical Activities in the Greater New York District for Period Week Ending July 26, 1924," file 61-23-297, U.S. Department of Justice, Federal Bureau of Investigation, Washington, D.C.; "Wants Exclusive Negro Territory in U.S.," *NYW*, August 3, 1924, HHHP Scr D. Previously, Harrison had articulated two other subsequent Communist International positions — that it was a principle duty of whites to challenge white supremacy; and that "the cause of the Negro" was "revolutionary." A fourth Commu-

nist contribution — that the "Negro" question was sociohistorical rather than biological — was regularly maintained by Harrison, though he also seemed to emphasize biological factors at times.

39. Richard B. Moore, "Afro-Americans and Radical Politics," in *Richard B. Moore, Caribbean Militant in Harlem: Collected Writings 1920–1972*, ed. W. Burghardt and Joyce Moore Turner (Bloomington: Indiana University Press, 1988), 215–21. Wintz, *Black Culture and the Harlem Renaissance*, 3, writes that Harlem "symbolized the central experience of American blacks in the early twentieth century — the urbanization of black America."

40. *WGMC* 2:432; State of New York, Department of Health of the City of New York, Standard Certificate of Death, December 17, 1927, Register No. 28066; "Lament Dream of Dr. Hubert Harrison"; "Harlem Community Church Renamed in Honor of the Late Hubert Harrison," *NYA*, May 12, 1928; "New Exhibition is Opened at 135th St. Public Library," *HHN*, May 13, 1925; and "Hubert Harrison's Portrait in Library," *AN*, September 10, 1930.

41. Winston James, *HATB* 123.

42. On a general historical neglect traced in part to hostility against West Indians and in part against radicalism — both racial and social — see Cyril Briggs to Theodore Draper, March 17, 1958, in Theodore Draper Collection, box 31, envelope — "NEGRO Cyril V. Briggs," Hoover Institution, Stanford, Calif. Tony Martin, *Race First*, points out that "for two decades or so after his death [in 1940] Garvey was all but relegated to the position of an unperson" as "Afro-American, West Indian and African history books, with few exceptions, failed to mention him or glossed over his career in embarrassed and contemptuous haste." It was only with "the Black Power revolution of the 1960s" that the race–activist Garvey received renewed recognition.

43. *WGMC* 2:439.

44. HH, "The Negro a Conservative," *TS* 41, no. 37 (September 12, 1914): 583 (selection 6); *WGMC* 2:439.

45. In 1923 Hodge Kirnon commented on how *The Messenger* had "yet to speak of Hubert Harrison and his notable work in behalf of radicalism and general modern thought among Negroes and white alike . . . [despite the fact that] Harrison was the first Negro to introduce liberal and radical ideas in the various departments of learning among Negroes in New York . . . [and despite] the fact that the editors of the *Messenger* have derived much of educational worth from him" (Hodge Kirnon, "Some Impressions of the *Messenger* Magazine [1923]," reprinted in Martin, *African Fundamentalism*, 95–96). Kirnon, in a 1928 letter to the editor of the Black weekly *New York News*, commented on the "ominous" "concerted silence" from Du Bois and the NAACP's *Crisis*, from Randolph's *Messenger*, and from the Urban League's *Opportunity* after Harrison's death (Hodge Kirnon, "Kirnon Flays Monthly Magazines"). Edgar M. Grey noted how "big Negro newspapers and business houses, schools and other organizations who had positions allowed themselves to be so hateful that they would not hire him [Harrison]" (Edgar M. Grey, "Why Great Negroes Die Young," *NYN*, December 31, 1927). A list of prominent individuals in African American or leftist circles whose work Harrison criticized includes Booker T. Washington, Kelly Miller, Charles W. Anderson, Fred R. Moore, A. Philip Randolph, Chandler Owen, W. E. B.

Du Bois, Marcus Garvey, Robert Russa Moton, James Weldon Johnson, Ernest Untermann, Ida Raymond, Joel Spingarn, Oswald Garrison Villard, Mary White Ovington, and Carl Van Vechten.

46. Harrison's comments on himself as an "inveterate critic" appear in his copy of David Duncan, *Life and Letters of Herbert Spencer*, 2 vols. (New York: D. Appleton, 1908), 2:246, 273. See also HH to Jaime C. Gil, April 19, 1921, HHHP Co; HH, "On Praise: From the Arable of Abulfeda, Prince of Humah (in Syria), 1328. Done Into Modern English by Hubert H. Harrison," *NW*, January 1, 1921, HHHP Scr 35 (selection 88); and HH, "Bridging the Gulf of Color," c. April 22, 1922 (selection 93); HH, "To the Young Men of My Race," *The Voice*, January 1919 (selection 56). Baal, a god of the Canaanites often represented by a calf, was considered a false god by the Israelites. See Hosea 13:1 and Joel Brinkley, "Archaeologists Unearth 'Golden Calf' in Israel," *NYT*, July 25, 1990.

47. Harrison was compared to Socrates by his peers. The journalist Cleveland G. Allen wrote that Harrison "was a great scholar, and his scholarship and attainments were used unselfishly for the good of others. . . . He was the Socrates of his day, and one of the Prophets of his age" (Cleveland G. Allen to Mrs. [Irene] Harrison, 1927, 1927, HHHP Co). See also Oscar Benson, "Literary Genius of Hubert Harrison," *NYN*, December 24, 1927; Claude McKay, *A Long Way from Home: An Autobiography* (New York: Lee Furman, 1927; New York: Harcourt, Brace and World, 1970), 41–42; and John G. Jackson, *Hubert Henry Harrison: The Black Socrates* (Austin: American Atheist Press, 1987).

48. "Aunt Mamie" [Mary C. Francis], "Interview with William Harrison," February 1, 1951, in "William Harrison Notebook," HHHP Mi; HH to the editor, "A St. Croix Creole," *NYEP*, May 15, 1922 (selection 81). D[avid] Hamilton Jackson (1884–1946), known as the "Black Moses of St. Croix," was the son of Wilford (sometimes spelled Wilfred) and Elisa Jackson, both teachers. In 1915 he put out the first issue of the *Herald*, a voice of the laboring and poor people of the island, and he was selected as St. Croix's delegate to go before the King of Denmark and the Danish Parliament. In January 1916 Jackson led a "General Strike" of some 6,000 Crucian workers who demanded higher wages, the right to free association, better working conditions, and a free press. This struggle led to the first labor union in the Virgin Islands. In 1922 Jackson won the first of many elections to the office of island legislator, and in 1931 he was elected Judge of the Police Court of Christiansted (Karen C. Thurland, interview with author, Christiansted, St. Croix, June 15, 1985; Karen C. Thurland, "Black Moses [D. Hamilton Jackson]," *Virgin Islands Education Review* 1, no. 12 (November 1984): 2–3, 21; Government of the U.S. Virgin Islands, Department of Education, *Profiles of Outstanding Virgin Islanders*, 163–64; Lesmore Howard, "David Hamilton Jackson," in *African Studies Club, 1991 Historical Calendar*; C. E. Rappollee, Despatching Secretary, to Henry M. Hough, Governor, St. Thomas, Virgin Islands of the United States, "Report on activities of one D. Hamilton Jackson," February 10, 1923, RG 59, 811S.00/37, R 18, *FSAA*; and Greg LaMotta, "The Virgin Islands Progressive Guide and the Development of Political Parties in the United States Virgin Islands, 1937–1946," *JCH* 28, no. 1 (1994): 63–83, esp. 74.

49. "Aunt Mamie" [Mary C. Francis], "Interview with William Harrison," February 1, 1951; HH to the editor, "A St. Croix Creole"; Lewisohn, *St. Croix under Seven Flags*, 248–72,

esp. 255, and 308–30, esp. 322–24, 328; Isaac Dookhan, *A History of the Virgin Islands of the United States*, introduction by Richard B. Sheridan (Epping, England, and St. Thomas: Caribbean Universities Press in association with the Bowker Publishing Company for the College of the Virgin Islands, 1974), 151, 161–80, 224–32; Winston James, *HATB*, 201–202, 333 n. 26; Theodore de Booy and John T. Faris, *The Virgin Islands, Our New Possessions and the British Islands* (1918; reprint, Westport, Conn.: Negro University Press, 1970), 37–40, 208; Darwin D. Creque, *The U.S. Virgins and the Eastern Caribbean*, (Philadelphia: Witmore Publishing, 1968), 4–6, 44; Arthur A. Schomburg, "History of the Emancipation of the Virgin Islands," *NW*, April 29, 1922; William W. Boyer, *America's Virgin Islands: A History of Human Rights and Wrongs* (Durham, N.C.: Carolina Academic Press, 1983), 55–57, 60, 70; Neville A. T. Hall, *Slave Society in the Danish West Indies: St. Thomas, St. John, and St. Croix*, ed. B. W. Higman (Baltimore: Johns Hopkins University Press, 1992), 208–27, esp. 212, 215, 226; Norwell Harrigan and Pearl I. Varlack, "The U.S. Virgin Islands and the Black Experience," *Journal of Black Studies* 7, no. 4 (June 1977): 387–410, esp. 391–94; Gordon K. Lewis, *The Virgin Islands: A Caribbean Lilliput* (Evanston, Ill.: Northwestern University Press, 1972), 30–35; Charles Edwin Taylor, *Leaflets From the Danish West Indies: Descriptive of the Social, Political, and Commercial Condition of These Islands* (1888; reprint, Westport, Conn.: Negro University Press, 1970), 125–45, 151–66, esp. 157–58, 165; *New York Herald*, November 28, 1878; and Erik J. Lawaetz, *St. Croix: 500 Years Pre-Columbus to 1990* (Herning, Denmark: Poul Kristensen, 1991), 196–204. During the 1878 struggle English sailors put water casks marked with the word "Liberty" on shore for the insurgents. The "long, long thoughts" is drawn from Henry Wadsworth Longfellow's "My Lost Youth" —

> A boy's will is the wind's will,
> And the thoughts of youth are long, long thoughts.

50. See, for example, "Speaker's Medal to Negro Student: The Board of Education Finds A Genius in a West Indian Night Pupil," *NYW*, April 5, 1903; "Evening School Prizes Awarded," New York *Commercial Advertiser*, April 1, 1903.

51. Oscar Benson, "Literary Genius of Hubert Harrison," *NYN*, December 24, 1927; Hodge Kirnon, "Hubert Harrison: An Appreciation," *NW*, December 31, 1927.

52. HHHP Scr passim; Kirnon, "Hubert Harrison: An Appreciation"; and for a lengthy self-appraisal see Harrison's handwritten comments in his personal copy of Duncan, *Life and Letters of Herbert Spencer*, 2:246, 261, 266, HHHP Bo.

53. HHHDI, September 18, 1907.

54. HHHDI, passim.

55. HHHDI, November 25, 1907 (selection 3); Antonio Gramsci, *"The Modern Prince" and Other Writings* (New York: International Publishers, 1957), 118–20; Antonio Gramsci, *Selections from the Prison Notebooks* (New York: International Publishers, 1971; New York: International Publishers, 1978), 5–11; and Manning Marable, *Black Leadership* (New York: Columbia University Press, 1998), 97–101.

56. The break from religion made possible a healthy, critical approach to all matters. The step had a certain logic as had been noted in 1844 by a young Karl Marx who was similarly

developing his own critical talents and worldview. Marx concluded that "criticism of religion is the premise of all criticism." See Karl Marx, "Toward the Critique of Hegel's Philosophy of Right," *Deutsche-Französische Jahrbücher*, reprinted in *Marx and Engels: Basic Writings on Philosophy and Politics* ed. Lewis S. Feuer (Garden City, N.Y.: Doubleday, 1959), 262–66, quotation 262.

57. HHHDI, November 11, 1907.

58. W. E. B. Du Bois, *The Autobiography of W. E. B. Du Bois: A Soliloquy on Viewing My Life from the Last Decade of Its First Century (1960)*, ed. Herbert Aptheker (New York: International Publishers, 1968; New York: International Publishers, 1971), 236–53, esp. 239; Irene Diggs, "The Amenia Conferences: A Neglected Aspect of the Afro-American Struggle," *Freedomways* 13, no. 2 (second quarter 1973): 117–34, esp. 117; Louis R. Harlan, *Booker T. Washington, The Making of a Black Leader, 1856–1901* (New York: Oxford University Press, 1973), and *Booker T. Washington, The Wizard of Tuskegee, 1901–1915* (New York: Oxford University Press, 1982); Raymond W. Smock, ed., *Booker T. Washington in Perspective: Essays of Louis R. Harlan* (Jackson: University of Mississippi Press, 1988); *BTWP*; Emma Lou Thornbrough, "Booker T. Washington," *DANB*, 633–38; William F. Mugleston, "Booker T. Washington," *ANB* 22:751–56; Michael Louis Goldstein; "Race Politics in New York City, 1890–1930: Independent Political Behavior," Ph.D. diss. Columbia University, 1973, 134–35; Marsha Hurst Hiller, "Race Politics in New York City, 1890–1930," Ph.D. diss. Columbia University, 1972, 134; Logan, *Betrayal of the Negro*, 276–312; C. Vann Woodward, *Origins of the New South, 1877–1913* (Baton Rouge: Louisiana State University Press, 1951; Baton Rouge: Louisiana State University Press, 1966), 357–60; August Meier, *Negro Thought in America, 1880–1915: Racial Ideologies in the Age of Booker T. Washington* (Ann Arbor: University of Michigan Press,1963; Ann Arbor: University of Michigan Press, 1987), 103; August Meier and Elliott Rudwick, "Attitudes of Negro Leaders toward the American Labor Movement from the Civil War to World War I," in *The Negro and the American Labor Movement*, ed. Julius Jacobsen (New York: Doubleday, 1968), 40; and Booker T. Washington, "Industrial Education for the Negro," in Booker T. Washington et al., *The Negro Problem*, with a new preface by August Meier (New York: Arno Press and the New York Times, 1969), 7–29.

59. See HHHP Scr 5, "*The Negro American*, vol. VIII, *The Negro Factions: The Negro Factions, The Protestants, The Subservients.*"

60. Harrison later wrote that "during the Civil War it was not the nation that saved the Negro, but the Negro that saved the nation." He also discussed how "the original Thirteenth Amendment . . . was passed in 1860 by both Houses, having as its purpose the making of slavery perpetual in the United States, and forever forbidding the bringing up of the subject in Congress except by a member from a slave-holding State." He called attention to the fact that Lincoln "was in favor of this amendment" and was, therefore, not an abolitionist at heart as was popularly believed. See HH, "'Negro Saved Nation' in 1861," *Embryo of the Voice of the Negro* 1, no. 1 (February 1927): 3–4, and Abraham Lincoln, "Unfinished draft of letter to C[harles] D. Robinson," August 17, 1864, in *Letters and Addresses of Abraham Lincoln*, ed. Mary Maclean (New York: Trow Press, 1903), 303–5. Harrison also cited Lincoln's statement in his first inaugural address of March 1861, that "I have no objection to its [the proposed

13th amendment's] being made express and irrevocable" and his August 22, 1862, letter to Horace Greeley in which he wrote, "If I could save the Union without freeing any slave, I would do it." In November 1924 Harrison (who did not become a citizen until 1922) stated that he "never voted the Republican ticket." See "Colored Orators Close Campaign in the County: New York Orator Charges the G.O.P. Has Greatly Neglected His People," *Leader Tribune*[?], [Marion, Ind.?], November 1, 1924, HHHP Mi and "Hubert Henry Harrison," Certificate of Naturalization, September 26, 1922, no. 1806138, DJ-IN.

61. The shift from the Republican to the Democratic Party by Black voters began well before the New Deal. In Harlem, in particular, Tammany was able to pull votes in local elections—in 1917 John Hylan received about 27 percent of the Black vote for mayor, and in 1921 (when he campaigned at Liberty Hall) he won almost 70 percent. Al Smith reportedly received 60 to 70 percent of the Black vote when he ran for governor. Tammany chief Charles F. Murphy worked closely with Ferdinand Q. Morton, the UCD head (whom Harrison defended and featured in *The Voice*), and Tammany provided Blacks with patronage in the form of city jobs and business contracts. See *MGP* 7:64, n. 4; Edwin R. Lewinson, *Black Politics in New York City* (New York: Twayne Publishers, 1974), 58–64; Nancy J. Weiss, *Farewell to the Party of Lincoln: Black Politics in the Age of FDR* (Princeton: Princeton University Press, 1983), 6; and Edgar M. Grey, "Party Machinery in Harlem: Tammany Hall," *AN*, December 15, 1926. In Frances Dearborn (pseudonym for HH), "The Black Tide Turns in Politics," unpublished manuscript c. December 1921 (selection 42), Harrison discusses the developing independence among Black voters.

62. See HH, "Sabotage Coming in Silk Mills If Boyd Is Jailed," *NYW*, December 1, 1913.

63. "Race relations" is used with caution and note is made of the comments of Winston James in *HATB* 313 n. 1, that the "race relations" paradigm "takes for granted far too much of what needs to be explained . . . including the very notion of 'race' itself." It is, James adds, "predicated upon a reified idea of 'race' located in nature" and it fails to see the phenomenon "as a product of human society, human history, and human invention conditioned by power relations between different groups of people." On this subject also see Robert Miles, *Racism* (London: Routledge, 1989), 72.

64. Ernest Allen Jr., "The New Negro: Explorations in Identity and Social Consciousness, 1910–1922," in *1915, The Cultural Moment: The New Politics, the New Woman, the New Psychology, the New Art and the New Theatre in America,* ed. Adele Heller and Lois Rudnick (New Brunswick: Rutgers University Press, 1991), 58.

65. In 1926 Harrison argued that the King James version of the Bible does not "contain the word 'race' in our modern sense of a breed of people" and "that goes to show that as late as 1611 our modern idea of race had not yet arisen." The view "that white people are superior and darker people inferior," he explained, "arose as the mental reflex of a social fact . . . the military and political dominations exercised by European whites over the darker people." In this setting science "reflect[ed] the concepts and ideas which saturate[d] the scientists," who were "too frequently full of racial 'fixations.'" For this reason he found "the racial pronouncements of American and British anthropologists, sociologists, psychologists and biologists" to be "worth so little, as science, where Negroes are concerned." See HH, "World

Problems of Race," typescript, July 8, 1926, HHHP Wr, reprinted in *PC*, December 31, 1926.

66. Aida Harrison Richardson and William Harrison (daughter and son of Hubert Harrison), interview with author, August 4, 1983, New York City.

67. Monroe N. Work, *NYB*, *1921–1922* 53, explained that "The growth of racial consciousness among Negroes is manifesting itself in race literature, more faith in Negro leadership, the demand for patronage of Negro business, the boycotting of white firms which do not treat Negroes with courtesy, the moving away from communities in which lynchings have taken place, and boycotting of white insurance companies whose agents fail to treat Negroes with courtesy."

68. HH, "As Harrison Sees It," *AN*, October 6, 1926; HH, "The Negro and the Labor Unions," *The Voice*, c. 1917 (selection 16); "Negroes Meet Today to Seek Tulsa Redress," *NYC*, June 5, 1921.

69. In his second copy of Lothrop Stoddard's *Rising Tide of Color*, received in Philadelphia on July 7, 1924, Harrison challenged Stoddard's notion that white solidarity was a constant. Harrison wrote on p 169, "As in the 5th, 11th, 16th, 17th, 18th & 19th centuries? Well that is too funny!" On p. 170 he added that "since the end of the Crusades the white race has never exhibited any of this mythical solidarity. At best, there have been temporary leagues of competing conquerors and 'balances of power.' The near-record among themselves has been illuminating on this point. Spain vs. Holland, England vs. Spain, England vs. France, Germany vs. Austria, Austria vs. Italy, France and England vs. Russia, England vs. America, America vs. Spain, Allies vs. Central Powers. *Some* solidarity!"

70. Huggins, *Harlem Renaissance*, 8–9, 49, 307–8. In contrast to Harrison's view, Amy Ashwood Garvey, first wife of Marcus Garvey, described her husband as "a strange mixture of a man — [a mixture of] racial doubts and racial aspirations." See *MGP* 1: xc.

71. HH, "Race First versus Class First," (selection 30). George W. Stocking Jr., *Victorian Anthropology* (New York: Free Press, 1987), 112, in discussing self-educated scholars, like Harrison, points out that: "Standing outside the normal process by which intellectual traditions are transmitted, the autodidact may embody the spirit of his age in an unusually direct way."

72. *MGP* 1:lix, lxvi–lxviii, 210–11, esp. 211 n. 1, which cites the *NW*, September 10, 1921, 5, and HH, "Marcus Garvey at the Bar of United States Justice." A detailed list of Liberty Leaguers who went on to hold positions in the UNIA is found in Perry, "Hubert Henry Harrison," 578–79.

73. W. E. B. Du Bois, "Close Ranks," *Crisis* 16 (July 1918), 111, reprinted in *W. E. B. Du Bois: The Crisis Writings*, ed. Daniel Walden (Greenwich, Conn.: Fawcett Publications, 1972), 257–58, esp. 257; *Crisis* 14 (June 1917): 59; Ellis, "'Closing Ranks' and 'Seeking Honors,'" 96–124, esp. 96, 98, 122; and Ernest Allen Jr., "'Close Ranks': Major Joel E. Spingarn and the Two Souls of Dr. W. E. B. Du Bois," *CBS*, no. 3 (1979–1980): 25–38. The Du Bois editorial was a significant departure from the position taken by the NAACP as recently as its May 1917 national conference, at which time it proclaimed that "[a]bsolute loyalty in arms and civil duties need not for a moment lead us to abate our just complaints." See Roy Talbert Jr.,

Negative Intelligence: The Army and the American Left, 1917–1941 (Jackson: University Press of Mississippi, 1991), 121. See also William Jordan, "'The Damnable Dilemma': African-American Accommodation and Protest During World War I," *JAH* 81 (March 1995): 1562–83 and Ellis, "W. E. B. Du Bois and the Formation of Black Opinion in World War I," 1584, 1587, and 1590.

74. Du Bois, "Close Ranks," 111; HH, "The Descent of Dr. Du Bois"; HH, "When the Blind Lead." Mark Ellis also concludes that "a day-to-day study of the events leads to the conclusion that 'Close Ranks' was a quid pro quo, and that the editorial and the captaincy were firmly linked." See Ellis, "W. E. B. Du Bois and the Formation of Black Opinion in World War I," 1584, 1587, and 1590.

75. See also W. E. B. Du Bois, "Talented Tenth," in B. T. Washington et al., *Negro Problem*, 33–75, quotations 42, 75. Interestingly, according to David Levering Lewis, Martin Luther King Jr.'s early assessment (in *Stride toward Freedom*) of Du Bois's "Talented Tenth" concept was that it was "a tactic for an aristocratic elite who would themselves be benefited while leaving behind the 'untalented' 90 per cent." See David Levering Lewis, "W. E. B. Du Bois and the Dilemma of Race," *Prologue* 27, no. 1 (spring 1995): 37–44, quotation 43.

76. HH, "The Line-Up on the Color Line," *NW*, December 4, 1920 (selection 72).

77. Du Bois, "Close Ranks," 111; HH, "The Descent of Dr. Du Bois"; HH, "When the Blind Lead"; HH, to Stoddard, August 21, 1920; Allen, "'Close Ranks,'" 26, 31; HH, "The Problems of Leadership," *WAA*, 54–55.

78. Du Bois would reach a similar conclusion in 1940 in his autobiography *Dusk of Dawn*. At that time Du Bois explained that Booker T. Washington had proposed "a flight of class from mass in wealth with the idea of escaping the masses or ruling the masses through power placed by white capitalists." Du Bois added that he, in turn, had opted for "flight of class from mass through the development of a Talented Tenth; but the power of this aristocracy of talent was to lie in its knowledge and talent and not in its wealth." The problem with this, as Du Bois later realized, was that it, too, "left controls to wealth"—a problem which he admitted that he never foresaw. By 1940 Du Bois concluded that "the mass and class must unite for the world's salvation." This was the position—the unity of the leadership class with the mass—that Harrison arrived at as early as 1916. See W. E. B. Du Bois, *Dusk of Dawn: An Essay toward an Autobiography of a Race Concept* (New York: Harcourt, Brace, 1940; New York: Schocken Books, 1971), 216–17, and Huggins, *Harlem Renaissance*, 5.

79. In HH, "Our Larger Duty," *NN* 3 no. 7 (August 1919): 5–6 (selection 25), Harrison stressed that "before the Negroes of the western world can play any effective part they must first acquaint themselves with what is taking place in the larger world where millions are in motion." The historian Robin D. G. Kelley, in "'But a Local Phase of a World Problem': Black History's Global Vision, 1883–1950," *JAH* 86 no. 3 (December 1999): 1045–77, points out on p. 1056, that Harrison's *When Africa Awakes* was "one of the most profound and widely read texts linking black concerns with international politics."

80. HH, "Education and the Race," *WAA*, 126–28 (selection 36); HH, "Opening the Doors," *BC*, April 5, 1924, HHHP Wr; HH, "The Feet of the Young Men," *BC*, March 22, 1924, HHHP Wr. Judith Stein, *WMG* 44–45, writes that "Harrison believed that education

— the attainment of enlightenment and knowledge—was a prerequisite for, not a by-product of, socialism." See also "Reminiscences of A. Philip Randolph," 153.

81. HH, "Education and the Race," 123.

82. See Du Bois, "The Talented Tenth," and Booker T. Washington, "Industrial Education for the Negro," both in Washington et al., *Negro Problem*, 1–29, 33–75, esp. 33; Paul Avrich, *The Modern School Movement: Anarchism and Education in the United States* (Princeton: Princeton University Press, 1980), 7, 15–18; David Levering Lewis, *When Harlem Was in Vogue* (1979; New York: Vintage Books, 1981), 7; HH, "The Voice of the Negro: *The Everlasting Stain*—by Kelly Miller," (unidentified published article, c. 1924), HHHP Wr; HH, "Education and the Race," 126–28, esp. 128.

83. HH, "The New Knowledge for the New Negro," *WAA*, 131–34, esp. 131; HH, "The World We Live In," *BC*, January 19, 1924, HHHP Wr; HH, "Read, Read, Read!" *The Voice*, July 18, 1918, HHHP Wr (selection 39); HH, "Reading for Knowledge," *The Voice*, September 1918, reprinted in *WAA*, 123–26; HH, "A Few Books," *BC*, March 1, 1924, HHHP Wr; HH, "Negro Culture and the Negro College," *NN* 4, no. 1 (September 1919): 4–5 (selection 35); and HH, "The Racial Roots of Culture," *WAA*, 129–31.

84. HH, "Read! Read! Read!" and HH, "Reading for Knowledge." Harrison's "Read! Read! Read!" calls to mind Frederick Douglass's response, only one month before his death, to the question about what strategy he would recommend to African Americans entering the twentieth century. At that time the elderly Douglass, speaking from the depth of his being and richness of his life's experiences, advised "Agitate! Agitate! Agitate!" See Nathan Irvin Huggins, "Plus Ça Change . . . ," in *Revelations: American History, American Myths*, ed. Brenda Smith Huggins (New York: Oxford University Press, 1995), 244.

85. "Infidelity among Our Ministers: A Startling Lecture by Hubert H. Harrison at Lafayette Hall 165 West 131st St, New York on Sunday, Dec. 10th, [1916,] at 8 P.M.," handout, HHHP Scr 34; HH, "Harlem's First and Foremost Forum," *Embyo of the Voice of the Negro* 1 (February 1927): 1; HH, "Reading for Knowledge," *WAA*, 124; and HH, "The New Policies for the New Negro," *The Voice*, September 4, 1917, HHHP Wr, (selection 43).

86. HH, "The Problems of Leadership," 54–55.

87. See also Perry, "Hubert Henry Harrison," 577–90, and Perry, *Hubert Harrison*.

88. See also HHHDI, c. April 1923.

89. HH to the editor, *NYTSRB*, April 13, 1907, and April 27, 1907 (selection 97); HH, "On a Certain Condescension in White Publishers" [Part I], 7 (selection 98); Martin, *Literary Garveyism*, 91–92; HH to Clifford Smyth, February 23, 1923, HHHP Co.

90. HHHDI, March 17, 1920; Martin, *Literary Garveyism*, 5 and the section "Poetry for the People," 43–90.

91. HH, "The Right Way to Unity," *BC*, May 10, 1924, HHHP Wr (selection 136); HH, "The Common People," *BC*, May 17, 1924, HHHP Wr (selection 137); HH, "Program and Principles of the International Colored Unity League," 4–6.

92. HH, "The Right Way to Unity."

Chapter 1. Developing Worldview

1. Logan, *The Betrayal of the Negro*, 244–45; Edmund Wilson, *Patriotic Gore: Studies in the Literature of the American Civil War* (1962; New York: Oxford University Press, 1969), 604–16; Donald Bogle, *Toms, Coons, Mulattoes, Mammies, and Bucks: An Interpretive History of Blacks in American Films* (1973; new exp. ed. New York: Continuum, 1989), 8. Lawrence W. Levine, *Black Culture and Black Consciousness: Afro-American Folk Thought From Slavery to Freedom* (New York: Oxford University Press, 1977), 128, points out that in one popular slave trickster tale a slave steals some chickens and afterwards, when the master questions what is being cooked, says he thought they were possums. Booker T. Washington alluded to "chickens (gathered from miscellaneous sources)" in his famous Atlanta Exposition Address of September 18, 1895. See *BTWP* 3:581, 583, 586.

2. See "'Negro' with a Capital 'N,'" *NYT*, March 7, 1930, 22.

3. HH, *WAA*, 8.

4. On Buckle (1857–61) see Henry Thomas Buckle, *History of Civilization in England* (London: W. J. Parker and Son, 1857–61) condensed by Clement Wood in 1926 (New York: Frederick Ungar Publishing, 1964), pp. v, x, and see the comments of Sir Leslie Stephen in *Encyclopaedia Britannica* (Chicago: Encylopaedia Britannica, 1929), 4:321, that Buckle "popularize[d] the belief in the possibility of applying scientific treatment to historical problems." On the Reconstruction notebooks see HHHDI, November 15, 23, and 25, 1908. See also W. E. B. Du Bois, "Reconstruction and Its Benefits," *AHR* 15 (July 1910): 781–99; "Reconstruction Seventy-Five Years After," *Phylon* 4, no. 3 (third quarter 1943): 205–12, esp. 205; W. E. B. Du Bois, *Black Reconstruction in America: An Essay toward a History of the Part Which Black Folk Played in the Attempt to Reconstruct Democracy in America, 1860–1880* (New York: Harcourt, Brace, 1935); *A Documentary History of the Negro People in the United States*, ed. Herbert Aptheker (New York: Citadel Press, 1951), 2:874, 886; and David Levering Lewis, *W. E. B. Du Bois: Biography of a Race* (New York: Henry Holt, 1993), 154, 383–85, 462.

5. Gordon Stein, *The Encyclopedia of Unbelief* (Buffalo, N.Y.: Prometheus Books, 1985), 247, explains that *free thought* should be distinguished from *freethought*. *Free thought* refers to thought that is free, and usually means free from dogmatic religious assumptions. *Freethought* refers to a movement with a tradition and a philosophical base. Harrison interacted with the freethought movement, its organizations, and its publications. On essentials of freethought see *TS*, September 12, 1914, 586; George Jacob Holyoake, "English Secularism: The First Stage of Freethought," excerpts from his *Origin and Nature of Secularism* (1896), reprinted in *An Anthology of Atheism and Rationalism*, ed. and comp. Gordon Stein (Buffalo: Prometheus Books, 1980), 300–303; and Joseph Jablonski, "Freethought," in *EAL* 243–44.

6. On Black freethinkers and atheists see John G. Jackson, "The Black Atheists of the Harlem Renaissance: (1917–1928)," from a talk at the 1984 American Atheists Convention, <http://www.atheists.org/Atheism/roots/harlem/harlem.html>; John G. Jackson, "Hubert Henry Harrison: The Black Socrates," *American Atheist* (February 1987): 18–20; John Ragland, "No More Ham," *American Atheist* (February 1987): 25–34, esp. 25–28; Walter E. Hawkins, to the editor, *TS* (March 6, 1926), reprinted as "A Tantalizing Letter," in *American Athe-*

ist (February 1987): 21; James, *HATB*, 76–77; R. Murray-O'Hair, "Atheists of a Different Color: A Minority's Minority," *American Atheist* (February 1987): 17; Lewis, "W. E. B. Du Bois and the Dilemma of Race," *Prologue* 27, no. 1 (spring 1995): 43; and Lewis, *W. E. B. Du Bois*, 65–66, 198, and 216. Also of note is that Frederick Douglass, in a famous July 4, 1852, speech, proclaimed "For my part, I would say, welcome infidelity! welcome atheism! welcome anything! in preference to the gospel as preached by the Divines!" This statement takes on additional meaning in light of the fact that the atheist Ottilie Assing, his intimate companion of twenty-eight years, said that Douglass's encounter with Ludwig Feurbach's *The Essence of Christianity*, which holds that man created God, "accomplished a complete revolution of his opinions." See Maria Diedrich, *Love across Color Lines: Ottilie Assing and Frederick Douglass* (New York: Hill and Wang, 1999), 227–30, quotation 229.

7. On Francis Reynolds Keyser see Floris Barnett Cash, "Radicals or Realists," *Afro-Americans in New York Life and History* 15, no. 1 (January 1991): 7–17, esp. 7–10, 13, and 30 n. 16; Charles Flint Kellogg, *NAACP: A History of the National Association for the Advancement of Colored People*, vol. 1, 1909–1920 (Baltimore: Johns Hopkins University Press, 1967; reprint, Baltimore: Johns Hopkins University Press, 1973), 1:47–48, 61, 304, 306; Rackam Holt, *Mary McLeod Bethune: A Biography* (Garden City: Doubleday, Doran, New York, 1964), 102–104; Emma Gelders Sterne, *Mary McLeod Bethune* (New York: Alfred A. Knopf, 1957), 163; and Mary McLeod Bethune, "A Tribute to My Friend and Co-Worker Frances Reynolds Keyser," in Elizabeth Lindsay Davis, *Lifting as They Climb: The National Association of Colored Women* (Washington: National Association of Colored Women, 1933), 213–15.

8. In 1889 Thomas Henry Huxley (1825–1895) explained how he coined the word "agnosticism":

> [Others] were quite sure they had attained a certain "gnosis" — had, more or less successfully, solved the problem of existence; while I was quite sure I had not, and had a pretty strong conviction that the problem was insoluble. . . . So I took thought and invented what I perceived to be the appropriate title of "agnostic." It came into my head as suggestively antithetic to the "gnostic" of Church history, who professed to know so much about the very things of which I was ignorant; and I took the earliest opportunity of parading it at our society to show that I, too, had a tail, like the other foxes. To my great satisfaction, the term took . . . agnostics, they have no creed; and, by the nature of the case, cannot have any. Agnosticism, in fact, is not a creed but a method, the essence of which lies in the vigorous application of a single principle. . . . the fundamental axiom of modern science. Positively the principle may be expressed as in matters of intellect, follow your reason as far as it can carry you without other considerations. And negatively, in matters of the intellect, do not pretend the conclusions are certain that are not demonstrated or demonstrable. That I take to be the agnostic faith, which if a man keep whole and undefiled, he shall not be ashamed to look the universe in the face, whatever the future may have in store for him.

From Thomas Henry Huxley, "Agnosticism," *Nineteenth Century*, February 1889, p. v, reprinted in Stein, *Anthology*, 42–45, quotations 43–44. Pat Shipman, *The Evolution of Racism: Human Differences and the Use and Abuse of Science* (New York: Simon and Schuster, 1994), 40–41, speaks of Huxley's "willingness to test and weigh up any and all beliefs — however sacred — on the scales of intellect."

9. The French naturalist Jean Baptiste Pierre Antoine de Monet de Lamarck (1744–1829) maintained that "All that has been acquired or altered in the organization of individuals during their life is preserved by generation and transmitted to new individuals which proceed from those which have undergone change." This controversial theory had strong proponents at the turn of the century and was subsequently emphatically rejected by those who held that body type was coded in DNA and was unaffected by the body traits acquired by one's parents. Late-nineteenth- and early twentieth-century believers in the heritability of acquired characteristics included August Comte, Lewis Henry Morgan, Herbert Spencer, Lester Frank Ward, George Bernard Shaw, and Henri Bergson. See J. B. Lamarck, *Zoological Philosophy: An Exposition with regard to the Natural History of Animals . . .*, trans. Hugh Elliot (London: Macmillan, 1914), 11, 113; Richard Milner, *The Encyclopedia of Evolution: Humanity's Search for Its Origins*, foreword by Stephen J. Gould (New York: Facts on File, 1990), 262–64, 324–25; Vernon Blackmore and Andrew Page, *Evolution: The Great Debate* (Oxford: Oxford University Press, 1989), 47–51; "Lamarckianism in American Social Science, 1890–1915," in George W. Stocking Jr., *Race, Culture, and Evolution: Essays in The History of Anthropology* (New York: Free Press, 1968), 234–69, esp. 238–40, 242, 253; Stocking, *Victorian Anthropology*, 134–35; and Carl N. Degler, *In Search of Human Nature: The Decline and Revival of Darwinism in American Social Thought* (New York: Oxford University Press, 1991), 21–23, 93.

A succinct critique of the Lamarckian theory has been offered by the paleontologist Stephen J. Gould, *The Mismeasure of Man* (New York: W. W. Norton, 1981), 325, who writes:

> Cultural evolution can proceed so quickly because it operates, as biological evolution does not, in the "Lamarckian" mode — by the inheritance of acquired characteristics. Whatever one generation learns it can pass on to the next by writing, instruction, inculcation, ritual, tradition, and a host of methods that humans have developed to assure continuity in culture. Darwinian evolution, on the other hand, is an indirect process: genetic variation must first be available to construct an advantageous feature, and natural selection must then preserve it. Since genetic variation arises at random, not preferentially directed toward advantageous features, the Darwinian process works slowly. Cultural evolution is not only rapid; it is also readily reversible because its products are not coded in our genes.

10. The issue of a Lamarckian transmission of acquired characteristics is important. In general it raises the question of whether ideas, actions, and capabilities are transmitted socially or biologically. Thomas Dyer, elaborating on the work of George Stocking Jr., explains that "turn-of-the-century racial theory" placed the concept of "adaptation," at "the heart of the question of race formation." Lamarckianism "did not stress the immutability of racial characteristics which many physical anthropologists regarded as essential to an un-

derstanding of the nature of race." Instead, it "emphasized the power of environment as opposed to the importance of heredity." Thus "the racial past of any people was a 'bio-social' past" made up of "elements of biological heredity" and "characteristics acquired through the influence of environment and culture" and "racial heredity" was "ultimately the implicitly Lamarckian product of social and environmental forces." See Thomas G. Dyer, *Theodore Roosevelt and the Idea of Race* (Baton Rouge: Louisiana State University Press, 1980), 37–38; Stocking, "Lamarckianism," 238–40, 244, 265. Historian Ernest Allen Jr. discusses how "the biological aspects of 'race' and their social aspects as manifested in the structuring of social relations" can be "constantly confused with one another." See Ernest Allen Jr., "The New Negro: Explorations in Identity and Social Consciousness, 1910-1922," in *1915, The Cultural Moment*, ed. Heller and Rudnick, 66 n. 35.

11. See Eric Foner, "Thomas Paine," *RCAH*, 814–15; Thomas Paine, *The Age of Reason* (1794), with a biographical introduction on Paine by Philip S. Foner (1948; Secaucus, N.J., 1974), 34–36; 46–47, 50, 190; Stein, *Anthology*, 125; *American Authors: 1600–1900; A Biographical Dictionary of American Literature*, ed. Stanley J. Kunitz and Howard Haycraft (New York: H. W. Wilson, 1938), 589–91; Eric Foner, *Tom Paine and Revolutionary America* (New York: Oxford University Press, 1976); and Philip S. Foner, *The Complete Writings of Thomas Paine*, 2 vols., ed. with notes and intro. by Philip S. Foner (New York: Citadel Press, 1945).

12. HH, "The Attitude of the American Press toward the American Negro," November 1, 1919, 17–18.

13. Walden, *W. E. B. Du Bois: The Crisis Writings*, 53; W. E. B. Du Bois, "My Evolving Program for Negro Freedom," in *What the Negro Wants*, ed. Rayford W. Logan (Chapel Hill: University of North Carolina Press, 1944), 31–70, quotation 49.

Chapter 2. Class Radicalism

1. Philip S. Foner, *American Socialism and Black Americans: From the Age of Jackson to World War II* (Westport, Conn.: Greenwood Press, 1977), 93; Ira Kipnis, *The American Socialist Movement, 1897–1912* (1952; reprint, New York: Monthly Review Press, 1972), 421; Bell, "Background and Development," 1:268–9; David A. Shannon, *The Socialist Party of America* (New York: Macmillan, 1955), 4–5, 17; James Weinstein, *The Decline of Socialism in America, 1912–1925* (New York: Monthly Review Press, 1967), 1; Solon De Leon in collaboration with Irma C. Hayssen and Grace Poole, *The American Labor Who's Who* (New York: Hanford Press, 1925), 97; Charles Leinenweber, "The Class and Ethnic Bases of New York City Socialism, 1904–1915," *Labor History* 22, no. 1 (winter 1981): 31–56, esp. 33; Charles Leinenweber, "The American Socialist Party and 'New' Immigrants," *Science and Society* 32, no. 1 (winter 1968): 1–25, esp. 1; Bruce Dancis, "Socialism and Women in the United States, 1900–1917," *Socialist Revolution*, whole no. 27, vol. 6, no. 1 (January–March 1976): 81–144, esp. 85; and Melvyn Dubofsky, "Success and Failure of Socialism in New York City, 1900–1918: A Case Study," *Labor History* 9, no. 3 (fall 1968): 361–75, esp. 361.

2. Paul M. Buhle, "*The Appeal to Reason*, Girard, Kansas, 1895–1917, 1919–1922; *New Appeal*, Girard, 1917–1919," in *The American Radical Press 1880–1960*, 2 vols., ed. and intro.

Joseph R. Conlin (Westport, Conn.: Greenwood Press, 1974), 1:50–59, esp. 50–51; Bell, "Background and Development," 1:268–9; *National Party Platforms 1840–1968*, comp. Kirk H. Porter and Donald Bruce Johnson (Urbana: University of Illinois Press, 1970), 164–66; John P. Diggins, *The American Left in the Twentieth Century* (New York: Harcourt Brace Jovanovich, 1973), 12–13.

3. Shannon, *Socialist Party*, 11; Bell, "Background and Development," 275; Kipnis, *American Socialist Movement*, 118, 296; Porter and Johnson, *National Party Platforms*, 165; Marc Karson and Ronald Radosh, "The American Federation of Labor and Negro Workers, 1894–1949," in *The Negro and the American Labor Movement*, ed. Julius Jacobsen (New York: Doubleday, 1968), 155–87, esp. 155–57.

4. P. Foner, *American Socialism*, p. xiii.

5. HH, "The Negro and Socialism," 6.

6. Thomas F. Gossett, *Race: The History of an Idea in America* (New York: Shocken Books, 1971), 332–33, and Eugene V. Debs, "The Negro in the Class Struggle," *ISR*, November 1903, reprinted in Eugene V. Debs, *Writings and Speeches of Eugene V. Debs* (New York: Hermitage Press, 1948), 65. Harrison later explained that the "theory" by which the portion of the white race that rules the world and the world's colored majority "justify themselves to themselves is known variously as the Color Line, the White Man's Burden, and Racial Superiority." See HH, "The Theory and Practice of International Relations among Negro-Americans," *NW*, October 22, 1921, HHHP Scr A.

7. On Socialists and the capital "N" see P. Foner, *American Socialism*, 397 nn. 12–13.

8. See Du Bois, "Socialism and the Negro Problem," *NR* 1, no. 5 (February 1, 1913): 140. See also Du Bois, *Black Reconstruction*, 15, where Du Bois describes the Black worker as "the ultimate exploited."

9. On the groupings in the Socialist Party see Shannon, *Socialist Party*, 10–11, and Bell, "Background and Development," 1:275, 277.

10. "The New Review," *NR* 1, no. 1 (January 4, 1913): 1; Theodore Draper, *The Roots of American Communism* (New York: Viking, 1957), 49, 404 n. 35; The New Review Publishing Association to The Central Committee of Local New York, September 1913, LNY, SP, "Letters," R 2636, V: 70; W. E. B. Du Bois, "A Field for Socialists," *NR* 1, no. 1 (January 4, 1913): 54–57, quote p. 54; W. E. B. Du Bois, "Socialism and the Negro Problem," *NR*, 1, no. 2 (February 1, 1913): 138–41, quotation 140; HH, "Socialism and the Negro," *ISR*, 13, no. 1 (July 1912): 66; Mary White Ovington, "The Status of the Negro in the United States," *NR* 1, no. 9 (September 1913): 744–49, quotation 748.

11. Ida M. Raymond to the editor, "A Southern Socialist on the Negro Question," *NR* 1, no. 12 (December 1913): 990–91.

12. Paul Buhle, *Taking Care of Business: Samuel Gompers, George Meany, Lane Kirkland, and the Tragedy of American Labor* (New York: Monthly Review Press, 1999), 13, 15, 46, esp. 46. Herbert Hill, "Race, Ethnicity and Organized Labor: The Opposition to Affirmative Action," *New Politics*, new ser., vol. 1, no. 2 (winter 1987): 31–82, esp. 46; Bernard Mandel, "Samuel Gompers and the Negro Workers, 1886–1914," *Journal of Negro History* 40 (January 1955): 34–60; and Joseph G. Rayback, *A History of American Labor* (New York: Macmillan,

1959; reprint, New York: Macmillan, 1966), 253. Gabriel Kolko, "The Decline of American Radicalism in the Twentieth Century," *Studies on the Left* (September–October 1966): 9–26, points out that the Socialist Party "always maintained its primary contacts with the A. F. of L., which at this time was the most conservative major union in the world."

13. HH, "As Harrison Sees It," 11.

14. Zangrando, *NAACP Crusade*, 36; *MGP* 1:220, n. 1; Florette Henri, *Black Migration: Movement North, 1900–1920* (Garden City, N.Y.: Anchor Press/Doubleday, 1975), 51–53; and Emmett J. Scott, *Negro Migration During the War* (1920; New York: Arno Press and the New York Times, 1969), 14, 52.

15. Edward Robb Ellis, *Echoes of Distant Thunder: Life in the United States 1914–1918* (New York: Coward, McCann and Geoghegan, 1975), 416; "Urges Negroes to Get Arms: Liberty League President Advises His Race to 'Defend Their Lives,'" *NYT*, July 5, 1917; "The East St. Louis Riots," *NYB, 1918–1919*, 8–15, 50; *MGP* 1:220 n. 1; "4 Whites, 3 Blacks Shot as Race Riot Grows in Illinois," *NYW*, May 30, 1917; "Negroes Flee Rioting Mobs," *NYES*, May 29, 1917; "50 Negroes Hurt by White Mob," *NYEM*, May 29, 1917; "Truth about East St. Louis Massacre," *CD*, July 14, 1917, 1, 9; "Sue East St. Louis for Big Riot Damages," *Boston Guardian*, January 19, 1918; Elliot Rudwick, *Race Riot at East St. Louis July 2, 1917* (New York: Atheneum, 1972); and Zangrando, *NAACP Crusade*, 37.

16. Samuel Gompers, "East St. Louis Riots — Their Causes," *American Federationist* 24, no. 8 (August 1917): 621–26, esp. 623, 626; "Urges Negroes to Get Arms"; *NYB, 1918–1919*, 8–15, 50; "Industries Welcomed Negro to East St. Louis; Labor Feared Him and Mob Butchered Him," *New York Tribune*, January 6, 1918, HHHP Scr, 3; "Roosevelt and Gompers Row at Russian Meeting," *NYT*, July 7, 1917; "Labor Denies Riot Blame," *NYT*, July 6, 1917; and "Roosevelt Takes Gompers to Task," *CD*, July 14, 1917; *MGP* 1:220 n. 1.

17. HH, "Purpose of the League," *NYC*, June 5, 1921, reprinted in *NW*, June 25, 1921.

18. William Z. Foster, *The Great Steel Strike and Its Lessons*, (New York: B. W. Huebsch, 1920), 205–206, 208, 210; James R. Barrett, "William Z. Foster," in *Encyclopedia of the American Left*, ed. Mari Jo Buhle, Paul Buhle, and Dan Georgakas (Urbana: University of Illinois Press, 1990), 235–37; Edward P. Johanningsmeier, *Forging American Communism: The Life of William Z. Foster* (Princeton: Princeton University Press, 1994); and Maurice Isserman, "William Z. Foster," *ANB* 8:310–12.

Chapter 3. Race Radicalism

1. HH, "Introductory," 5–8; HH, "Race First versus Class First"; HHHDI, May 24, 1920 (selection 61).

2. HH, "The Need for It," 1 (selection 26); HH, "Race Consciousness," *Voice of the Negro* 1, no. 1 (April 1927): 4 (selection 34).

3. HH, "Introductory," 5–8, quotation 5–6.

4. HH, "Introductory," 6.

5. HH, "Introductory," 7.

6. HH, "Introductory," 5–8; HH, "Stop Lynching and Disfranchisement in the Land

Which We Love and Make the South 'Safe For Democracy,'" handout, c. June 12, 1917, HHHP Mi; "Make a Drive for Liberty on Lincoln's Birthday, July 4th, 1917, with the Liberty League of Negro Americans. The First Mass Meeting," advertisement, c. July 4, 1917, HHHP Scr C; "Negroes Seek Law for Mobs: Want Federal Statute to Cover Lynchings — Young Men and Women in League," *NYC*, June 13, 1917, 4; Zangrando, *NAACP Crusade*, 6; W. James, *HATB*, 1; and Nancy Weiss, *The National Urban League 1910–1940* (New York: Oxford University Press, 1974), 147–48.

7. Joseph R. Gusfield, *Symbolic Crusade: Status Politics and the American Temperance Movement* (Urbana: University of Illinois Press, 1963; Urbana: University of Illinois Press, 1972), 102–3; Zangrando, *NAACP Crusade*, 44. Prohibition of the manufacture, sale, and use of alcohol passed Congress on October 28, 1919, and became the Eighteenth Amendment to the U.S. Constitution on January 16, 1920.

8. See also HH, "How to End Lynching," *BC*, June 25, 1924, HHHP Wr (selection 91), and HH, "Lynching: Its Cause and Cure," *NW*, June 26, 1920, 2 (selection 89).

9. See HH, "Marcus Garvey at the Bar of United States Justice." Harrison describes the "colored races" as "black and brown and yellow" in "The White War and the Colored Races," [1918] *New Negro* 4 (October 1919): 8–10 (selection 67).

10. Zangrando, *NAACP Crusade*, 43–45, esp. 44. A rationale for the NAACP position was articulated earlier in W. R. Harr, assistant attorney general, for the attorney general, to Oswald Garrison Villard, chairman of the NAACP, on December 31, 1911, file 158260-7, RG 60, DNA, *FSAA*, reel 14. Harr wrote, "There is no authority in the United States Government to interfere [with mob violence] because the parties committing such crimes violate the laws of the State where the offense is committed and are punishable in its courts having jurisdiction of the offense. The federal authorities are not authorized to intervene unless it be for the purpose of protecting a citizen in the exercise of rights which he possesses by virtue of the Constitution and laws of the United States." See also Allen, "'Close Ranks,'" 37, and Jane Lang Scheiber and Harry Scheiber, "The Wilson Administration and the Wartime Mobilization of Black-Americans, 1917–1918," *Labor History* 10, no. 3 (summer 1969): 433–58, esp. 456.

11. "Urges Negroes to Get Arms"; "Make a Drive for Liberty"; H. C. Peterson and Gilbert Fite, *Opponents of War: 1917–1918* (Madison: University of Wisconsin Press, 1957), 88.

12. Hill, "Introduction," p. xiii; Baltimore *Afro-American*, June 30, 1917; and "Urges Negroes to Get Arms." For more on the New York Black community's protests in May–July 1917 see Watkins-Owens, *Blood Relations*, 101, which cites *NYT*, May 27 and 31 and June 7, 1917. Judith Stein, *WMG* 42, explains that "In 1917, the advocacy of self–defense was a litmus test of militance, dividing old from aspiring leadership."

13. *MGP* 2:428 nn. 1 and 2; Robert V. Haynes, *A Night of Violence: The Houston Riot of 1917* (Baton Rouge: Louisiana State University Press, 1976), 2, 15–46; Arthur E. Barbeau and Florette Henri, *The Unknown Soldiers: Black American Troops in World War I* (Philadelphia: Temple University Press, 1974), 26–29, 265–66; Aptheker, *Documentary History*, 3:184–85; and Herbert Shapiro, *White Violence and Black Response* (Amherst: University of Massachusetts Press, 1988), 106–109.

14. Barbeau and Henri, *Unknown Soldiers*, 28–31; Aptheker, ed., *Documentary History*, 3:184–85; Jack D. Foner, *Blacks and the Military in American History* (New York: Praeger, 1974), 114–15; Haynes, *Night of Violence*, 90–139; "Houston Race Riot the Result of Series of Mob Executions Says White Editor," *NYA*, August 30, 1917.

15. Barbeau and Henri, *Unknown Soldiers*, 28–31; Aptheker, *Documentary History*, 3:184–85; J. Foner, *Blacks and the Military*, 115; Haynes, *Night of Violence*, 254–323; Richard B. Sherman, *The Republican Party and Black America* (Charlottesville: University of Virginia Press, 1970), 123; Kellogg, *NAACP* 1:260–62; *NYB, 1918–1919*, 67. See also in HHHP Scr 8 the following: "A Military Lynching," *Richmond Planet*, June 5, 1918; "Colored Folks Dazed," *Richmond Planet*, (reprinted from the *Savannah Tribune*), January 12, 1918; "Court Martial is Dangerous Place for a Guilty Man," *Houston Post*, c. November 5, 1917; "2 More 24th Men Turn States' Evidence," *Guardian*, December 1917; "Asks Race to Aid Families of Men of 24th Hanged," *NYN*, December 20, 1917.

16. Kellogg, *NAACP* 1:161–72 and 218; Shapiro, *White Violence and Black Response*, 111–13; Haynes, *Night of Violence*, 65–67; Hill, "Introduction," pp. v–lxvii, esp. p. xii; and James Allen et al., *Without Sanctuary: Lynching Photography in America* (Santa Fe, N.M.: Twin Palms Publishers, 2000), 173–74.

17. Arthur I. Waskow, *From Race Riot to Sit-In, 1919 and the 1960s: A Study in the Connections Between Conflict and Violence* (Garden City, N.Y.: Doubleday, 1966), 21–104, esp. 23, 25, 27, 37–38, 41–42, 47; "Race Riot at Capital [sic]," *NYA*, July 26, 1919; *HR*, 303; "Chicago is in the Grip of Serious Race Riots," *NYA*, August 2, 1919; "Union Labor Leaders Foment Trouble in Chicago," *NYA*, August 16, 1919; Mark Ellis, "J. Edgar Hoover and the 'Red Summer' of 1919," *Journal of American Studies* 28, no. 1 (April 1994): 45; William M. Tuttle, "Labor Conflict and Racial Violence: The Black Worker in Chicago, 1894–1919," *Labor History* 10 no. 3 (summer 1969): 408–32; and *MGP* 1:473 nn. 3–4, which quotes Socialist Charles Edward Russell as saying, "The Negro did not run in Chicago nor in Washington and in my judgment he is not going to run anywhere . . . he will stand and fight."

18. Of interest in relation to Harrison's arguments are the comments of Jared Diamond in his Pulitzer Prize–winning *Guns, Germs, and Steel: The Fates of Human Societies* (New York: W. W. Norton, 1997). Diamond (p. 23) acknowledges "the immediate factors that enabled Europeans to kill or conquer other peoples—especially European guns, infectious diseases, steel tools, and manufactured products." He also emphasizes (p. 25) that "[h]istory followed different courses for different peoples because of differences among peoples' environments, not because of biological differences among peoples themselves."

19. See HHHDI, June 15, 1914. Regarding this sexual double standard, Elinor Des Verney Sinnette, biographer of Arthur Schomburg, writes: "The implicit and explicit social rule of the time was that the women, by and large, remained home attending to household tasks while their mates, gainfully employed during the day, participated at night in the events of their various clubs and lodges." See Elinor Des Verney Sinnette, *Arthur Alfonso Schomburg, Black Bibliophile and Curator: A Biography* (Detroit: New York Public Library and Wayne State University Press, 1989), 36. Carl Degler adds that "the idea that the sexual or

biological function of woman shaped her mind and behavior was socially epitomized in the nineteenth-century idea of 'separate spheres' for men and women. Women's sphere was the home and children; men's was the world of work and power." See Carl N. Degler, *In Search of Human Nature: The Decline and Revival of Darwinism in American Social Thought* (New York: Oxford University Press, 1991), 107.

20. *Emancipator*, April 3, 1920; "Our Reason for Being," *Emancipator*, March 13, 1920; and *MGP* 2:40 n. 2, xlix.

21. "Race First!" *Crusader* 2, no. 7 (March 1920): 8–9, quotation 9. In June 1920 Briggs advised African Blood Brotherhood members and other Blacks to "[a]dopt the policy of race first, without, however, ignoring useful alliances with other groups" and to "[h]elp propagate the 'race first idea.'" He had earlier emphasized his allegiance to the doctrine of "NEGRO FIRST, LAST, AND ALL THE TIME!" Robert A. Hill observes that "Briggs found no difficulty" preaching race first while he simultaneously considered himself a "Bolshevist!!!" (stated in his preceding editorial). See Hill, "Introduction," pp. v–lxvii, esp. p. xxviii; "The African Blood Brotherhood," *Crusader* 2, no. 10 (June 1920): 22; "Negro First!" *Crusader* 2, no. 2 (October 1919): 9; "Race First," *Crusader* 2, no. 7: 8–9; and Andrea Razafkeriefo's critical "Race First," *Crusader* 6, no. 1 (whole no. 42): 26.

22. The unidentified quotation is from the 1912 Socialist Party convention and was signed by Ernest Untermann and J. Stitt Wilson, representing the West, and Joshua Wanhope (editor of the *Call*) and Robert Hunter, representing the East. See Socialist Party, *National Convention of the Socialist Party Held at Indianapolis, IN, May 12 to 18, 1912*, Stenographic Report by Wilson E. McDermut, assisted by Charles W. Phillips, ed. John Spargo (Chicago, 1912), 209–11.

23. HH, [Notes on Marcus Garvey], HHHDI.

24. HH, "The Problems of Leadership," 54–55. In 1923 Garvey wrote, "the negro has become his own greatest enemy. Most of the trouble I have had in advancing the cause of the race has come from negroes. Booker Washington aptly described the race in one of his lectures by stating that we were like crabs in a barrel, that none would allow the other to climb over, but on any such attempt all would continue to pull back into the barrel the one crab that would make the effort to climb out." See MG, "The Negro's Greatest Enemy," *Current History* 18, no. 6 (September 1923): 951–57; reprinted in *The Philosophy and Opinions of Marcus Garvey*, 2 vols., ed. Amy Jacques Garvey (New York: Universal, 1923 and 1925); reprinted in one volume, (New York: Atheneum, 1969), 133. On February 18, 1995, at a Newark, N.J., conference on "Booker T. Washington and Modern Black Leadership Revisited" sponsored by the New Jersey Historical Commission, Professor Louis R. Harlan, biographer of Booker T. Washington, informed the author that he had heard that Washington told "crab stories" and though he couldn't cite a specific instance at the time he thought they might be referred to in the published papers of Claude G. Bowers, who had transcribed Washington speeches in his youth.

25. HH, [Notes on Marcus Garvey], HHHDI; HH, *WAA*, 74–75; "H. H.," "'Just Suppose' a Riddle for 'Scientific Radical' Liars, with Apologies to C. OW.," *NW*, April 10, 1920. Owen

became so disillusioned with socialist radicalism that by 1923 he moved to Chicago, edited the *Chicago Bee*, and became involved with the Republican Party. See *MGP* 5:231, n. 1; Theodore Kornweibel Jr., "Chandler Owen," *DANB*, 476.

26. HH, "One Decade of Harlem's Mental Growth," notes, c. 1925, HHHP Wr; James Weldon Johnson, "An Open Air Lecture Course," editorial, *NYA*, May 6, 1915; HH to James Weldon Johnson, May 12, 1915, James Weldon Johnson Papers, Correspondence, Series 1, Folder 197, Beinecke Rare Book and Manuscript Library, Yale University; HHHDI, June 3, 1915; *Who's Who in Colored America: A Biographical Dictionary of Notable Living Persons of African Descent in America 1938–1939–1940*, 2d ed., ed. Thomas Yenser (Brooklyn: T. Yenser, 1940), 120; Guishard Parris and Lester Brooks, *Blacks in the City* (Boston: Little, Brown, 1971), 45–47.

Chapter 4. Education

1. HH, "The Negro a Conservative" (selection 6).

2. HH, "Education and the Race," 128.

3. HH, "Education and the Race," 128, and HH, "Reading for Knowledge," 124.

4. Harrison worked as an adjunct professor of Comparative Religion at the Ferrer Association's Modern School. See *WGMC* 2:435; Harry Kelly, *The Modern School* (Stelton, N.J.: The Modern School Association of North America, 1920), 2–4; *Socialism and American Life*, ed. Donald Drew Egbert and Stow Persons (Princeton: Princeton University Press, 1952), 1:716 n. 184 and 717; Paul Avrich, *The Modern School Movement: Anarchism and Education in the United States* (Princeton: Princeton University Press, 1980), 3, 7–8; Stein, *Encyclopedia of Unbelief*, 219–21; and Kenneth Teitelbaum, *Schooling for "Good Rebels": Socialist Education for Children in the United States, 1900–1920* (Philadelphia: Temple University Press, 1993), 39.

5. HH, "Education and the Race," 123.

6. HHHDI, March 17, 1920.

7. HH, "Reading for Knowledge," 123.

8. HH, "Our Little Library," *NN*, September 1919, 16.

9. HH, "Our Little Library," *NN*, September and October 1919, p. 16.

Chapter 5. Politics

1. Garvey at first eschewed politics and had what historian Robert A. Hill described as a "static view of political abstinence." See *MGP* 1:lix, lxvi.

2. Much of Harrison's effort aimed to break clear of the "lesser evil" argument that was the basis of Du Bois's decisions in 1912 and 1916. In 1912 Woodrow Wilson had promised "fair justice" to Blacks in a letter to Bishop Alexander Walters, and this led Du Bois to back Wilson and resign from the Socialist Party in order to not violate party discipline. See "Woodrow Wilson's Letter to Bishop Walter in 1912," *NYA*, July 12, 1917. In 1916 Harrison thought that his dissatisfaction with Wilson kept clear of the "temporary aberration" of

"Negro radicals like Randolph and Owen and liberals like Du Bois." He noted that Du Bois praised Wilson and "urged his re–election to the presidency." Du Bois later claimed that he had changed attitudes on Wilson and opted for the Republican, Charles Evans Hughes. But Harrison, unlike Du Bois, did not feel compelled to choose the lesser evil, so he supported neither of the two major parties. Neither did Harrison support Wilson, as did Randolph and Owen. Instead, he favored allowing both parties to work to earn Black support. When Du Bois flopped back to support Wilson and the war effort in his famous wartime "Close Ranks" editorial, Harrison wrote a stinging critique. At that point, in the summer of 1918, Harrison considered Du Bois, like Booker T. Washington before him, a fallen Black leader. See HH [on "Vesey St. Liberals"], n.d., HHHP Wr, where Harrison writes that Du Bois "stumbled and fell from the pinnacle of racial leadership [to] a point to which all the strenuous pulling and handling of his white friends has never been able to lift him since." The NAACP's office was originally at 20 Vesey St. in lower Manhattan. See Logan, *Betrayal of the Negro*, 360–61; Kellogg, *NAACP* 1:161–74; Du Bois, *Dusk of Dawn*, 235–36; "Frances Dearborn" (HH), "The Black Tide Turns in Politics"; HH, "The Real Woodrow Wilson," *NW*, April 9, 1921. In the October 1916 *Crisis*, Du Bois wrote: "under ordinary circumstances the Negro must expect from him [the Republican presidential candidate Charles Evans Hughes], as chief executive, the neglect, indifference, and misunderstanding that he has had from recent Republican presidents. Nevertheless, he is practically the only candidate for whom we can vote." See Sherman, *Republican Party*, 121.

3. See *MGP* 1:xvvi, xciii.

4. Maclean, *Letters and Addresses of Abraham Lincoln*; Du Bois, *Dusk of Dawn*, 258; Kellogg, *NAACP* 1:37, 45 n. 66, 151.

5. HH, "The Grand Old Party," *WAA*, 49–53 (selection 48). On Brownsville see Anne J. Lane, *The Brownsville Affair: National Crisis and Black Reaction* (Port Washington: National University Publications, Kennikat Press, 1971), 6–7, 12–24, 69–130; Henry F. Pringle, *Theodore Roosevelt: A Biography* (1931; New York: Harcourt, Brace and World, 1956), 322–27; Emma Lou Thornbrough, "The Brownsville Episode and the Negro Vote," *Mississippi Valley Historical Review* 44 (December 1957): 469–83; James A. Tinsley, "Roosevelt, Foraker, and the Brownsville Affair," *Journal of Negro History* 4 (1956): 43–45; Logan, *Betrayal of the Negro*, 347–50; "Soldiers Discharged," *NYA*, November 8, 1906; Sherman, *Republican Party*, 57; Seth M. Scheiner, "President Theodore Roosevelt and the Negro, 1901–1908," *Journal of Negro History* (July 1962): 181–82; "Judicial Lynching at Brownsville: November 9, 1906; 167 Black Soldiers Finally Vindicated," *Crisis*, January 1973, 15–17; J. Foner, *Blacks and the Military*, 95–103.

6. Louis R. Harlan, "Booker T. Washington and the Politics of Accommodation," in *Black Leaders of the Twentieth Century*, ed. John Hope Franklin and August Meier (Urbana: University of Illinois Press, 1982), 1–18, esp. 3, 9–11; HH, "The Right Way to Unity"; and Goldstein, "Race Politics in New York City," 187, 391. Nathan Irvin Huggins, *Voices from the Harlem Renaissance* (New York: Oxford University Press, 1974), 5, writes that "the most striking thing about the 'New' as opposed to the 'Old' Negro was that he was urban rather than rural."

7. For background see Hiller, "Race Politics in New York City," 134 and 171, and Goldstein, "Race Politics in New York City," 78–79.

8. See "3,000 Blacks Like Attack upon T. R.: Negro Speaker at Meeting Flouts Colonel's East St. Louis Stand and Recalls His Old Inaction," *NYW*, July 30, 1917.

9. In the reprinted edition Harrison replaced "Africa First" with "Race First." In 1920 he explained that "Africa First" was used "in its racial, rather than geographical sense." See HH, "Introductory," 8.

10. HH, "The Coming Election," *The Voice*, October 18, 1917; Goldstein, "Race Politics in New York City," 216–17; Hiller, "Race Politics in New York City," 230–55; "3,000 Blacks Like Attack upon T. R.," *NYW*, July 30, 1917; Cleveland G. Allen, "Among the Negroes of Harlem," *HHN*, October 17, 1917, 6; and Edwin R. Lewinson, *Black Politics in New York City* (New York: Twayne Publishers, 1974), 56–57.

11. Florette Henri, *Black Migration: Movement North, 1900–1920* (Garden City, N.Y.: Anchor Press, 1975), 88–90; Gilbert Osofsky, *Harlem: The Making of a Ghetto; Negro New York, 1890–1930* (1963; 2d ed.; New York: Harper and Row, 1971), 122–23, 131; Seth Scheiner, *Negro Mecca: A History of the Negro in New York City, 1865–1920* (New York: New York University Press, 1965), 8–9, 221–22; Huggins, *Harlem Renaissance*, 30–31, 35, 39; Charles V. Hamilton, *The Black Experience in American Politics* (New York: G. P. Putnam's Sons, 1973), 3–4.

12. Mark Ellis, "Joel Spingarn's 'Constructive Programme' and the Wartime Antilynching Bill of 1918," *Journal of Policy History* 4, no. 2 (1992): 134–61, esp. 135–36.

13. Du Bois, *Autobiography*, 266. *Black Experience in American Politics*, ed. Charles V. Hamilton (New York: G. P. Putnam's Sons, 1973), p. xii, offers a context for Du Bois's comments. He points out that "the perpetually crisis-oriented environment in which black people have found themselves left little time for the 'luxury' of seemingly abstract philosophical reflections and pursuits." Du Bois "highlighted this problem" during World War I when he stated "'We face a condition not a theory.' There is not the slightest chance for our being admitted to white camps, therefore, it is either a case of a 'jim-crow' officers training camp or no colored officers. Of the two things, no colored officers would be the greatest calamity." For a precursor to Du Bois's "condition not a theory" position see *Proceedings of the National Negro Conference 1909: New York May 31 and June 1* (New York: National Negro Conference Headquarters, 1909), 122, where Judge Wendell Phillips Stafford of the Supreme Court of the District of Columbia said "We are confronted not by a theory but by a fact. That fact is the deliberate and avowed exclusion of a whole race of our fellow citizens from their constitutional rights, accompanied by the announcement that the exclusion must and shall be permanent."

14. HH, "In Case of War . . . What?" *BC*, June 14, 1924. See also Henri, *Black Migration*, 284, and HH, "An Open Letter to the Socialist Party of New York City" (selection 33).

15. Kellogg, *NAACP* 1:250–53, esp. 254 n. 25; Ellis, "'Closing Ranks' and 'Seeking Honors'"; [advertisement] "Harlem People's Forum: Hubert Harrison, Lecturer . . . . This Sunday: Our Professional Friends the 'NAACP' National Association for the Acceptance of Color Proscription," *The Voice*, July 11, 1918; HH, [on "Vesey St. Liberals"]; HH, "In Case of

War — What?" *BC*, June 14, 1924; HH, "Why Is the Red Cross?" *The Voice*, July 18, 1918, HHHP Wr; Scheiber and Scheiber, "The Wilson Administration," 443, 452.

16. HH, "Negroes Form New Party to Combat Republicans," *NW*, August 28, 1920; HH, "Negro Party Brands Bridges as a Faker: Accused of Secretly Working for the Democratic Party — Man Who Attacked Garvey and West Indians Two Years Ago Is Now Threatened with Expulsion" [HH added "Meant for issue of 10/30/20"], *NW*, November 6, 1920, HHHP Scr B; *MGP* 2:431 n. 2.

17. Telephone interview with David Stivers, archivist, the Nabisco Company, Parsippany, N.J., January 9, 1995, and Leonard Brathwaithe to the editor, "A Word of Praise," *NW*, July 31, 1920. J. G. Tucker, Report, July 17, 1920, bureau file OG207369, RG 65, DNA, reel 10, *FSAA*, states that in the *Negro World* "of the 17th instant," the editorial "U Needa Biscuit" appeared "over the initials H. H. (HUBERT HARRISON)."

18. Paul Lewinson, *Race Class and Party: A History of Negro Suffrage and White Politics in the South* (New York: Oxford University Press, 1932), 106, 218–19; W. E. B. Du Bois, "The Gentleman's Agreement and the Negro Vote," *Crisis* 28 (1924): 260–64; and *NYB, 1918–1919*, 44.

19. See Sherman, *Republican Party*, p. iii, and Lawrence W. Levine, "Marcus Garvey and the Politics of Revitalization," in Franklin and Meier, *Black Leaders of the Twentieth Century*, 105–38, esp. 112.

Chapter 6. Leaders and Leadership

1. HH, "Problems of Leadership," 54–55.

2. See Allen, "'Close Ranks,'" 25–38; Mark Ellis, "America's Black Press, 1914–1918," *History Today* 41 (September 1991): 20–23, 25; Ellis, "'Closing Ranks' and 'Seeking Honors,'" 96–124; Ellis, "Joel Spingarn's 'Constructive Programme,'" *Journal of Policy History* 4, no. 2 (1992): 134–61; Jordan, "'The Damnable Dilemma,'" 1562–83; and Ellis, "W. E. B. Du Bois and the Formation of Black Opinion in World War I," 1584–90.

3. See *BTWP*; Thornbrough, "Booker T. Washington," *DANB*, 633–38; *MGP* 1:48, n. 1; *WGMC* 2:383–98; and Mugleston, "Booker T. Washington," *ANB* 22:751–56.

4. "Dr. Washington Abroad: Educator Being Lionized in London," *NYA*, September 8, 1910; "Washington on Race Problem in America: Discusses Problem at Length in the London Morning Post," *NYA*, September 22, 1910; "Negroes Appeal to Europe," *NYS*, December 1, 1910; [Editorial], *NYS*, December 2, 1910; "D," letter to the editor, *NYS*, December 5, 1910.

5. HH to the editor, *NYS*, December 8, 1910; Charles W. Anderson to Booker T. Washington, September 10 and October 30, 1911, *BTWP*, 11:300–01, 351.

6. Allen W. Whaley, "Drive For Liberty," *Boston Guardian*, June 1, 1918; "National Organizer Whaley Issues Appeal to Colored America in Behalf of Great Colored Liberty Congress to Be Held Soon at Nation's Capital," *Boston Guardian*, June 1, 1918; Fred W. Moore, Captain, Q.M.R.C., Intelligence Officer Northeastern Department, to Chief Military Intelligence Branch, Washington, D.C., June 5, 1918, "Subject: Proposed National Convention of

Negroes," MID-10218-153-5; "Negroes Asking for Foretaste of Democracy," *The Voice* 2, no. 1 (July 11, 1918); "Historic Colored Liberty Congress," *Boston Guardian*, July 6, 1918; "Liberty Congress in Interesting Session," *NYA*, July 6, 1918; Allen, "'Close Ranks,'" 25–38; "Address to the Committee on Public Information, 1918," in Aptheker, *Documentary History*, 3:218–22.

7. Aptheker, *Documentary History*, 3:215–18; "Extension of Remarks of F. H. Gillett (R. Mass.)" in *Congressional Record*, [vol. 56 appendix] June 28, 1918, 65th Congress, 2d sess., 502.

8. On the three-pronged offensive see Ellis, "America's Black Press," *History Today* 41 (September 1991): 20–23, 25, and Ellis, "'Closing Ranks' and 'Seeking Honors,'" 96–124.

9. David Levering Lewis, *W. E. B. Du Bois*, vol. 1 of 2 vols. *Biography of a Race* (New York: Henry Holt, 1993); Rayford W. Logan and Michael R. Winston, "William Edward Burghardt Du Bois," *DANB*, 193–99; Thomas C. Holt, "W. E. B. Du Bois," *ANB* 6:944–49; Arnold Rampersad, *The Art and Imagination of W. E. B. Du Bois* (Cambridge, Mass.: Harvard University Press, 1976); *MGP* 1:63 n. 9; Robin D. G. Kelley and Paul Buhle, "W. E. B. Du Bois," *EAL*, 202–205; and J. A. Rogers, "William E. Burghardt Du Bois," *WGMC* 2:593–97.

10. HH, "The Problems of Leadership," 54–55. Allen, "'Close Ranks,'" 26, writes that "Although lacking specific details of the 'drama' which he so unkindly depicted, Hubert H. Harrison's charges proved to be rather incisive in their overall characterization." Allen adds that researchers, working with declassified military documents, have been able to confirm "the essence of the 'script' which Harrison envisioned behind Du Bois' call to 'Close Ranks.'" Allen argues, "Calculated planning on the part of certain persons, there assuredly was; Du Bois' performance, on the other hand, seems to have been propelled by extreme confusion and naivete." See also Ellis, "'Closing Ranks' and 'Seeking Honors,'" 115–17.

11. HH, "The Descent of Dr. Du Bois"; Allen, "'Close Ranks,'" 26; Ellis, "'Closing Ranks' and 'Seeking Honors,'" 96, 122, notes that Elliot Rudwick described "Close Ranks" as a "colossal blunder" and that "Du Bois was scarred by the accusations of treachery from fellow black leaders, and he never forgot them."

12. "Du Bois Appointed: Offered Berth in Intelligence Dept. under Major Spingarn, following *The Crisis* Editorial Asking Race to 'Forget' Its Grievances," *Boston Guardian*, July 20, 1918. The FBI's bureau file, OG 311587, RG 65, DNA, *FSAA*, reel 11, states that "Du Bois, One-Time Radical Leader Deserts and Betrays Cause of His Race" and added that Du Bois "weakened, compromised, disarmed the fight, [and] betrayed the cause of his race." See also *NW*, August 29, 1918.

13. See Paul Laurence Dunbar, *The Complete Poems of Paul Laurence* (1895; New York: Dodd, Mead, 1913), 75.

14. HH, "Shillady Resigns"; *MGP* 5:158–59, n. 5, 442, n. 5; Theodore Kornweibel Jr., *"Seeing Red": Federal Campaigns against Black Militancy, 1919–1925* (Bloomington: Indiana University Press, 1998), 69.

15. HH, "The Problems of Leadership," *WAA*, 54–55; Henri, *Black Migration*, 189, 369 n. 46; and Willard B. Gatewood, *Aristocrats of Color: The Black Elite, 1880–1920* (Bloomington: Indiana University Press, 1990), 343.

16. "White Stool Pigeon Incites Chicago Race Riot," *NW*, July 3, 1920 (dateline "Chicago,

June 23") and "Editorial Notes"; *MGP* 1:337 n. 1, 390, and 402–405, 2:388–89 nn. 1–2, and 531–32; U.S. Department of Justice, Radical Division, Washington, D.C., "Strictly Confidential: General Intelligence Bulletin," no. 48, April 30, 1921, file OG 374217, DNA, reel 12, *FSAA*; Walter H. Loving to Director, Military Intelligence Division, "Subject: Rev. R. D. Jones (Jonas), sometimes known as 'Prophet Jones,'" December 23, 1918, DNA, RG 165, file MID 10218-77-5; and "A Spy Exposed," *Crusader* 2 (July 1920).

17. See *MGP*; Martin, *Race First*; Judith Stein, *The World of Marcus Garvey: Race and Class in Modern Society* (Baton Rouge: Louisiana State University Press, 1986); *WGMC* 2:415–431; E. David Cronon, "Marcus Mosiah Garvey," *DANB*, 254–56; Helen C. Camp, "Marcus Mosiah Garvey, Jr.," in *American Reformers*, ed. Alden Whitman (Bronx: H. H. Wilson, 1985), 338–42; and William F. Mugleston, "Marcus Garvey," *ANB* 8:771–73.

18. See also "Statement of Hubert Harrison. *In re U.S. v. Black Star Line, Inc.*, Post Office Building, New York, Jan. 16, 1922," Marcus Garvey: FBI Investigation File, Microfilm reprint, Scholarly Resources Inc., Wilmington, Delaware. Harrison indicated to Postal Inspector Oliver Williamson that he was editor of the *Negro World* "between January, 1920 and November, 1921 [this date should be 1920], when I gave up the editorship," after which he became "associate editor," "one of the contributing editors." Harrison was listed on the masthead of the *Negro World* as editor from c. March 6, 1920, to c. December 25, 1920 and as contributing editor from c. January 1, 1921 to c. September 9, 1922. Robert A. Hill lists Harrison as contributing editor from January 1, 1921, to c. March 25, 1922. See *MGP* 7:972. On *Negro World* circulation figures see William H. Ferris, "Garvey and the Black Star Line," *Favorite Magazine*, July 1920, reprinted in *MGP* 2:471–73, esp. 472; "Black Star Line Vindicated by White American Jury," *NW*, June 19, 1920, reprinted in *MGP* 2:349–71, esp. 352, 357; Charles Mowbry White interview with Marcus Garvey, August 18, 1920, reprinted in *MGP* 2:602–604; HH, "Marcus Garvey at the Bar of United States Justice," *ANP*, c. July 1923 (selection 64); Raymond Sheldon to Director, Military Intelligence Division, January 21, 1921, DNA, RG 165, MID 10218-412-1; "Report of UNIA Meeting," *NW*, October 25, 1919, reprinted in *MGP* 2:100–105, esp. 100; "Report of UNIA Meeting," *NW*, March 6, 1920, reprinted in *MGP* 2:236; and *MGP* 1:211–12 n. 3, 444 n. 2, 529. On the paper's expansion to ten pages, which occurred as the rival *Emancipator* ceased publication, see the *Negro World* issue of May 1, 1920.

19. Martin, *Literary Garveyism*, 27, adds that he was was "hard put" to identify any similar "primarily political oriented newspaper which devoted so much space, even on its editorial pages, to literary concerns." This combination of politics and literature was primarily effected by Harrison.

20. See Rev. E. Ethelred Brown, "Garvey-istic Devotion," sermon, August 12, 1923, NN-SC, E. Ethelred Brown Papers, reprinted in *MGP* 5:423–31, esp. 425, 430, and Watkins-Owens, *Blood Relations*, 204 n. 63, citing *NYA*, January 21, 1928.

21. "A Walking Encyclopedia," *NW*, September 4, 1920.

22. *Negro World Convention Bulletin*, no. 2, August 3, 1920, cited in *MGP* 1:lxxiv n. 126; HHHDI, August 31, 1920. According to Robert A. Hill, "Garvey repeatedly claimed the worldwide black population to be four hundred million," a figure far above the 261,277,000

found by Monroe N. Work in *NYB, 1918–1919*. See *MGP* 9:161 n. 4, 1:lxxiv and lxxiv n. 126, 1:289 n. 1, 2:478, and 3:560–64 and 585. Arthur Schomburg also criticized Garvey's claim to "control four hundred million followers." See W. James, *HATB*, 213. Hill was able to put together a list of 144 delegates "whose names appeared in accounts of the convention printed in the *Negro World*, the *Negro World Convention Bulletin*, and in the records of the Bureau of Investigation." See *MGP* 2:682–83. A number of these, however, were likely the pseudo-delegates Harrison describes in his August 28 entry.

23. Special Agent P-138 [Herbert S. Boulin], "Report by Special Agent P-138 In Re: Negro Activities (Marcus Garvey)," New York City, August 14, 1920, DNA, RG 65, file OG 329359, reprinted in *MGP* 2:582 and "Declaration of Rights of the Negro Peoples of the World" [August 13, 1920], *NW*, September 11, 1920, reprinted in *MGP* 2:571–78.

24. *MGP* 5:liii, 316–17, 382–83 n. 4; 6:59, 66 n. 4, 357 n. 7; and 7:608 n. 3.

25. Nahum Daniel Brascher to HH, July 3, 1923, HHHP Co. Of interest is the fact that W. E. B. Du Bois concurred with Harrison's assessment of the fairness of the trial and later wrote that "No Negro in America ever had a fairer and more patient trial than Marcus Garvey. He convicted himself by his own admissions, his swaggering monkey-shines in the court room with monocle and long tailed coat and his insults to the judge and the prosecuting attorney." See W. E. B. Du Bois, "A Lunatic or a Traitor," *Crisis* 27, no. 7 (May 1924): 8–9, reprinted in *MGP* 5:583-84. Regarding Harrison's closing paragraph, the historian Judith Stein, *World of Marcus Garvey*, 248, 266, explains that "whether in prison or out on bail, he [Garvey] chanted old formulas" and that "from his deportation in 1927 to his death in 1940, Garvey persistently sought to regain the power and influence that he tasted briefly." She also quotes from George Padmore's description of Garvey in the late 1930s "boasting of former glories."

26. On "African Redemption" in Garvey's program c. 1924 see *MGP* 1:lxix. Garvey wanted "the Negro [to make] of Africa a strong and powerful Republic." See *MGUNIAP* 1:lxvii. On September 25, 1921, he explained that "It is because we have studied history by close scrutiny that we started the Universal Negro Improvement Association as an organization toward the object of empire." See "Speech by Marcus Garvey," *NW*, October 1, 1921, reprinted in *MGP* 4:81–90, quotation 81. See also Marcus Garvey, [editorial letter], *Negro World*, January 26, 1924, reprinted in *MGP* 5:536–47, esp. 539, and "Building Empires," *NW*, October 3, 1925, quoted in *MGP* 1:lii.

Chapter 7. Anti-imperialism and Internationalism

1. On the importance of "global developments" in "determining the fate and destiny of African-Americans" see Gerald Horne, "Race for the Planet: African-Americans and U.S. Foreign Policy Reconsidered," *Diplomatic History* 19, no. 1 (winter 1995): 159–65, esp. 165.

2. *American Labor Year Book 1919–20*, ed. Alexander Trachtenberg (New York: Rand School of Social Science, 1920), 90–92; Ellis, "America's Black Press, 1914–1918," *History Today* 41 (September 1991): 20; Ellis, "'Closing Ranks' and 'Seeking Honors,'" 102 n. 11; HHHDI, April 24, 1917, and March 30, 1918; William Preston Jr., *Aliens and Dissenters: Fed-*

eral Suppression of Radicals, 1903–1933 (New York: Harper and Row, 1963), 87; *MGP* 1:341 n. 2; Sean Dennis Cashman, *America in the Age of the Titans: The Progressive Era and World War I* (New York: New York University Press, 1988), 505; and Patrick S. Washburn, *A Question of Sedition: The Federal Government's Investigation of the Black Press During World War II* (New York: Oxford University Press, 1986), 11–12.

3. "The Negro and the War," c. August 1920, *WAA*, 25; HH, "Introductory," 5–8. On Harrison's use of language that was militant and well understood by the Harlem masses see Directorate of Intelligence, Special Report no. 10: "Unrest among the Negroes," October 7, 1919, reprinted in *Science and Society* 32, no. 1 (winter 1968): 66–79, esp. 77–78.

4. *WAA*, 116.

5. Cashman, *America in the Age of the Titans*, 519; *MGP* 1:304 n. 1.

6. W. James, *HATB*, 129.

7. Hans Schmidt, *The United States Occupation of Haiti, 1915–1934* (New Brunswick: Rutgers University Press, 1971), 3–5; *RCAH*, 364–69, 724, 844; William Foster, *History of the Communist Party of the United States* (New York: International Publishers, 1952), 91; and Philip S. Foner, *The Spanish-Cuban-American War and the Birth of American Imperialism 1895–1902*, 2 vols. (New York: Monthly Review Press, 1972), 1:x.

8. HH, ["Response to Jose Clarana, II"], *NW*, April 30, 1921.

9. The quotation is handwritten in Harrison's copy of Stoddard's *Rising Tide of Color*. Sir Sidney A. T. Rowlatt was a lower judge who went from England to India to head a committee established in 1917 "to investigate revolutionary conspiracies." In a July 19, 1918, report, Bengal, Bombay Presidency, and Punjab were identified as centers of conspiracy and emergency powers were recommended. The recommendations, essentially a continuation of wartime measures, included trials of seditious acts by three judges without juries, arrest and imprisonment in nonpenal custody, and demand for securities from suspects. In February 1919 a bill embodying many of these provisions was presented and on March 18, 1919, the Rowlatt Act became the law of the land. The following day, in response, Mahatma Gandhi decided on a general *hartal*, or cessation of economic activity, coupled with "fasting and prayer," and six hundred people signed a *satyagraha* pledge to launch a nationwide campaign of civil disobedience designed to cripple economic life in India's towns and cities. Delhi boycotted on March 30 and the rest of the country on April 6. This was Gandhi's first political act in India against the British government, and it was met with brutal repression on April 13, when the British massacred hundreds of unarmed demonstrators in Amritsar, a Sikh holy city. This campaign, which cut across geographic, caste, and religious barriers, marked Gandhi's emergence as a national leader. See Louis Fischer, *The Life of Mahatma Gandhi* (New York: Harper and Row, 1950), 175–76; Sudarshan Kapur, *Raising Up: The African-American Encounter with Gandhi* (Boston: Beacon Press, 1992), 24–25; Judith M. Brown, *Modern India: The Origins of Asian Democracy* (1985; 2d ed., New York: Oxford University Press, 1994), 203.

10. "P-138," Report "In Re: 'Negro Activities (AFRICAN BLOOD BROTHERHOOD and attempts of Communists to influence same),'" July 13, 1921, for week of July 10, 1921, Bu. Sec. 202600-2031-7 roll 941 and reel 7, *FSAA*; *MGP* 1:525 and 3:681–82 n. 1; Hill, "Introduc-

tion," pp. v–lxvii, esp. p. xl. On the date that Briggs joined the Communist Party, also see *HATB*, 161–63, and Mark Solomon, *The Cry was Unity: Communists and African Americans, 1917–1936* (Jackson: University of Mississippi Press, 1998), 9.

11. "The Program of the American Arm of the Communist International: Program of the United Communist Party" (section entitled "Negro Problem"), reprinted in *Toiler*, no. 158, February 12, 1921.

12. HH, "The New International," *NW*, May 15, 1920, reprinted as "A New International" in *WAA*, 111–13.

13. Thomas H. Buckley, *The United States and the Washington Conference, 1921–1922* (Knoxville: University of Tennessee Press, 1970), pp. vii, 3–19, 63–74, 76, 172, 185–90; William Roger Louis, *British Strategy in the Far East, 1919–1939* (Oxford: Oxford University Press, 1971), 79–108; *MGP* 3:633 n. 2, 4:190 n. 3, 227 n. 2, and 776 n. 4.

14. HH, [Notes on Marcus Garvey]; HH, "West Indian News Notes to Be Resumed," *NW*, February 4, 1922, 6; British Military Intelligence Report, February 10, 1920, DNA, RG 165, file 10218-364-22-190X, reprinted in *MGP* 2:205–10, esp. 209. This letter was "received from the British" and originally enclosed with a letter from Maj. H. A. Strauss, MID, to the director of MID, February 24, 1920.

15. Schmidt, *The United States Occupation of Haiti*, 118; John W. Blassingame, "The Press and American Intervention in Haiti and the Dominican Republic," *Caribbean Studies* 9, no. 2 (July 1969): 27–43; James Weldon Johnson, "Self-Determining Haiti," *Nation* 111, nos. 2878–2880, 2882 (August 28–September 25, 1920) [four parts]; Herbert J. Seligmann, "The Conquest of Haiti," *Nation* 111, no. 2871 (July 10, 1920): 35–36; *MGP* 1:361, n. 2; John Edwin Fagg, *Cuba, Haiti, and the Dominican Republic* (Englewood Cliffs, N.J.: Prentice-Hall, 1965), 15; Brenda Gayle Plummer, "The Afro-American Response to the Occupation of Haiti, 1915–1934," *Phylon* 43, no. 2 (June 1982): 133–38; and Henry Lewis Suggs, "The Response of the African American Press to the United States Occupation of Haiti, 1915–1934," *Journal of Negro History* 73, nos. 1–4 (spring, winter, summer, fall 1988): 33–45.

16. Schmidt, *The United States Occupation of Haiti*, 17, 67, 83, and 100–105.

17. HH, "Declaration of Intention [to Naturalize]," and HH, "Petition for Naturalization." For a brief discussion of the elliptical arguments used by U.S. government officials and the State Department to argue that the 1917 treaty of cession granted "citizenship in the United States" to Virgin Islanders not wishing to remain Danish subjects, but not "citizenship of the United States," and that they were therefore, "entitled to the protection of the government, but have not the civil and political status of the United States" see William W. Boyer, *America's Virgin Islands: A History of Human Rights and Wrongs* (Durham, N.C.: Carolina Academic Press, 1983), 136–38.

18. HHHDI, November 1, 1923; Ernest Gruening to HH, December 6, 1923, and January 19, 1924, HHHP Co; Ashley L. Totten, "The Truth Neglected in the Virgin Islands," *Nation* 8, no. 7 (July 1926) [part one] and 8, no. 8 (August 1926) [part 2], reprinted in *These "Colored" United States: African American Essays from the 1920s*, ed. Tom Lutz and Susanna Ashton (New Brunswick: Rutgers University Press, 1996), 275–88.

19. The president Harrison was referring to was probably Warren G. Harding. See J. A.

Rogers, *The Five Negro Presidents: According to What White People Said They Were* (New York: H. M. Rogers, 1965), 11–13.

20. For Malliet's series see *PC*, July 2 and 9 and August 13, 1927.

21. Malliet, "Malliet Closes Still Crying," *PC*, August 13, 1927.

22. Malliet, "'Why I Cannot Become Americanized,'" *PC*, August 13, 1927.

Chapter 8. Meditations

1. HHHDI, November 11, 1907, and March 7 and May 20, 1908.

2. See *NYT*, May 20, 1918; *MGP* 1:515 n. 5; Walter White, "The Work of A Mob," *Crisis* 16 (September 1918): 221–23, reprinted in Aptheker, *Documentary History*, 3:227–32.

3. In HH, "Lincoln and Douglass," *Embryo of the Voice of the Negro* 1, no. 1 (February 1927): 2, Harrison wrote, "The worship of its great men is one root of self-respect of a group, a nation, a race; it is high time that Negroes should become familiar with the heroic deeds and splendid achievements of their brothers in blood."

4. *WNBD*, 6.

5. Indication that Harrison was the real author of this apparently satiric poke at Garvey is suggested by his article "The Crab Barrel," *NW*, April 3, 1920, where Harrison explains, "As far as I know the poetic literature of the Negro has not been enriched by satire — except by those who wrote in Arabic, a language with which we of the western world are not sufficiently acquainted." Also see the letter from the poet A. P. Razafkeriefo to "Dear Friend Harrison," October 22, 1917, reprinted in *The Voice*, October 31, 1917, in which "Raz" writes that satire was a trait "second nature" to Harrison.

Chapter 9. Lynching, the Klan, Race Relations

1. *The Negro Almanac: A Reference Work on the Afro American*, 3d ed., comp. and ed. Harry A. Ploski and Warren Marr II (New York: Bellwether, 1976), 275–77; *MGP* 1: 212 n. 9.

2. Allen W. Trelease, "Ku Klux Klan," *RCAH*, 625–26, and David M. Chambers, *Hooded Americanism: The History of the Ku Klux Klan* (New York: New Viewpoints, 1976), esp. 1–8.

3. *Tenth Annual Report of the National Association for the Advancement of Colored People, for the Year 1919* (New York: NAACP, 1920), reprinted in part in *Negro Protest Thought in the Twentieth Century*, ed. Francis L. Broderick and August Meier (Indianapolis: Bobbs-Merrill, 1965), 63–64, quote p. 64.

4. Kenneth T. Jackson, *The Ku Klux Klan in the City: 1915–1930* (1967; New York: Oxford University Press, 1977), esp. 11, and *MGP* 4:715 n. 2 and 1089 n. 2.

5. On the matter of errors in the 1840 census see also George M. Frederickson, *The Black Image in the White Mind: The Debate on Afro–American Character and Destiny, 1817–1914* (New York: Harper and Row, 1971), 239–55 and Leon F. Litwack, *North of Slavery: The Negro in the Free States, 1790–1860* (Chicago: University of Chicago Press, 1961), 40–46.

6. Ernest Crandall to HH, April 22, 1922, HHHP Co.

7. Harrison elsewhere described "The fathers have eaten sour grapes and the children's

teeth are set on edge" [Jeremiah 31:29 and Ezekiel 18:2] as "the old Hebrew statement of the doctrine of social consequences." See "Hubert Harrison Addresses Bronx Rotary Club on 'New Americanism,'" *AN*, July 28, 1926.

8. In Robert Littell to HH, April 27, 1923, HHHP Co, Littel asks forgiveness for his "long delay with your manuscripts." Harrison handwrote on his copy of the letter, "After 6 mos. received back manuscripts of 'The Back of the Black Man's Mind' and 'Bridging the Gulf of Color'—both sent only at Littell's request." On the meetings see *MGP* 5:690 n. 1 and 6:196, n. 7; *NYT*, November 5, 1921; and *NYW*, November 5, 1921.

9. Boanerges was the surname given by Jesus to James and John and suggests a vigorous orator. See Mark 3:17. According to Robert A. Hill, the leading Black in the Republican Party, Henry Lincoln Johnson was among those involved in enabling Garvey to return to the United States, and a bribe to a State Department official was likely involved. See *MGP* 1:lxxxix.

10. HH, "Introductory," 5–6.

11. "Hubert Harrison Addresses Bronx Rotary Club on 'New Americanism,'" *AN*, July 28, 1926, 9.

12. "H. H. H.," "Letter to the Editor," *NW*, October 1, 1921.

13. HHHDI, June 21, 1923. "The Negro and the Nation" was the title of the presentation given by Dr. William A. Sinclair and the subject of the pithy comments of Judge Wendell Phillips Stafford of the supreme court of the District of Columbia at the 1909 meeting which led to the founding of the NAACP. See *Proceedings of the National Negro Conference 1909: New York May 31 and June 1*, 113, 121–22, 168, 211–13, 225. The title was also that of a 1906 book—George W. Merriam, *The Negro and the Nation: A History of American Slavery and Enfranchisement* (New York: Henry Holt, 1906)—and of Harrison's 1917 book.

Chapter 10. Literary Criticism, Book Reviews

1. W. E. B. Du Bois, "Negro Art," *Crisis* 22 (1921): 55 and Theodore O. Mason, "African American Theory and Criticism," in *Johns Hopkins Guide to Literary Theory and Criticism*, ed. Michael Groden and Martine Kresiwirth (Baltimore: Johns Hopkins University Press, 1997).

2. *The New Negro*, ed. Alain Locke (New York: Atheneum, 1968), 7.

3. HH to the editor, *NYTSRB*, April 13, 1907, and April 27, 1907; HH, "On a Certain Condescension in White Publishers" [part 1]; Martin, *Literary Garveyism*, 91–92; HH to Clifford Smyth, February 23, 1923, HHHP Co.

4. Anderson, *A. Philip Randolph*, 61, 192, 259; David J. Garrow, "A. Philip Randolph," in *Biographical Dictionary of the American Left*, ed. Bernard K. Johnpoll and Harvey Klehr (Westport, Conn.: Greenwood Press, 1986), 326–29; William H. Harris, *Keeping the Faith: A. Philip Randolph, Milton P. Webster, and the Brotherhood of Sleeping Car Porters, 1925–1937* (Urbana: University of Illinois Press, 1977); Theodore Kornweibel, *No Crystal Stair: Black Life and the Messenger, 1917–1928* (Westport, Conn.: Greenwood Press, 1975); *MGP* 1:220–21

n. 1 and 307–308 n. 1; William H. Harris, "A. Philip Randolph as a Charismatic Leader, 1925–1941," *JNH* 64 no. 4 (fall 1979): 301–315; "The Reminiscences of A. Philip Randolph," interview with Wendell Wray, July 25, 1972, New York, Columbia University Oral History Project, Butler Library, Columbia University, New York, 152; Paula E. Pfeffer, *A. Philip Randolph, Pioneer of the Civil Rights Movement* (Baton Rouge: Louisiana State University Press, 1990); and Theodore Kornweibel Jr., "Chandler Owen," *DANB*, 476–77.

5. HH, Notes on "The Red Record of Radicalism," c. 1927, HHHP Wr; HHHDI, June 15, 1916; HH, "'Just Suppose': A Riddle for 'Scientific Radical' Liars."

6. "The Independent Political Council," *Messenger* 1 no. 11 (November 1917): 33; *Messenger* (January 1918): 11; Marsha Hurst Hiller, "Race Politics in New York City, 1890–1930," Ph. D. dissertation, Columbia University, 1972 , 235; *WMG*, 47; "Reminiscences of Randolph," 168-74, 219-21; Socialist Party, Local New York, Minutes of Executive Committee, October 10 and 21, 1917, in "Minutes of Central Committee," Socialist Party Minutes, 1900–1936, reel 2639, collection VI:5, New York Socialist Party Papers, Tamiment Institute, Elmer Holmes Bobst Library, New York University, New York; Anderson, *A. Philip Randolph*, 92–96; and "The New Negro," *Negro Worker* 1, no. 1 (December 1918): 8.

7. HH, Notes on "The Red Record of Radicalism"; *WGMC* 2:615; Hill, "Introduction," pp. v–lxvi, quotation p. vi; *WMG* 38–39; *MGP* 2:220 n. 2; P. Foner, *American Socialism and Black Americans*, 268, 286–87; Huggins, *Harlem Renaissance*, 29; and Charles Leinenweber, "The Class and Ethnic Bases of New York City Socialism, 1904–1915," *LH* 22, no. 1 (winter 1981): 32–56, esp. 47.

8. *WMG* 38–39; Cleveland G. Allen, "Among the Negroes of Harlem," *HHN*, December 9, 1917; Leinenweber, "The Class and Ethnic Bases of New York City Socialism," 47; P. Foner, *American Socialism and Black Americans*, 286–87; and Huggins, *Harlem Renaissance*, 29.

9. A. Philip Randolph to Elizabeth Gurley Flynn, secretary, The American Fund for Public Service, Inc. [Garland Fund], January 22, 1925, in "Applications Favorably Acted Upon, I: Gifts 1922–1927," "Messenger," vol. 8, bound file no. 67, American Fund for Public Service Papers, New York Public Library, New York.

10. See W. Burghardt Turner, "Joel Augustus Rogers: An Afro-American Historian," *NHB* 35, no. 2 (February 1972): 34–38; W. Burghardt Turner, "Joel Augustus Rogers: Portrait of an Afro-American Historian," *Black Scholar* 6, no. 5 (January–February 1975): 32–39; *MGP* 5:5–6 n. 2; Rayford W. Logan, "J[oel] A[ugustus] Rogers," *DANB*, 531–32; *KI* 4:244–45; *HR*, 309–10; and *WGMC* 2:432–42.

11. Arthur A. Schomburg, "West Indian Composers and Musicians," *OP* 4, no. 47 (November 1926): 353; *Bibliography of the Negro in Africa and America*, comp. Monroe Work (New York: H. W. Wilson, 1928; New York: Argosy–Antiquarian, 1965), 475. According to Moore, "Africa Conscious Harlem," 315–34, esp. 315–16, the *Letters of Ignatius Sancho* was sold in George Young's "Book Exchange" at 135 W. 135th Street.

12. J. A. Rogers to HH, n.d. [1921?], HHHP Mi; J. A. Rogers, *From "Superman" to Man* (Chicago: J. A. Rogers, 1917; reprint, New York: Helga M. Rogers, 1971), dustjacket; Martin, *Literary Garveyism*, 100.

13. HH, "Our International Consciousness," *WAA*, 95.

14. "T[heodore] Lothrop Stoddard," *National Cyclopaedia of American Biography* (New York: James T. White, 1955), 40:371; Idus A. Newby, *Jim Crow's Defense: Anti-Negro Thought in America, 1900–1930* (Baton Rouge: Louisiana State University Press, 1965), 54–55; Gossett, *Race*, 390–97, quotation 391.

15. Lothrop Stoddard to HH, June 17, 1920, HHHP Co, and HH to Lothrop Stoddard, June 24, 1920, HHHP Co.

16. *MGP* 1:289 n. 5; Roy Hoopes, "The Forty-Year Run," *American Heritage*, November 1992, 45–56; and Clifford Krauss, "Remember Yellow Journalism," *NYT*, February 15, 1998, wk 3.

17. T. Lothrop Stoddard to HH, August 1, 1921, and October 27, 1921, HHHP Co.

18. Claude McKay, *The Negroes in America* [1923], trans. Robert J. Weiner from the Russian, ed. Alan L. McLeod (Port Washington, N.Y.: National University Publications, 1979), 71; Rampersad, *The Art and Imagination of W. E. B. Du Bois*, p. ix.

19. Dorothy B. Porter, "Monroe Nathan Work," *DANB*, 667–68; Linda O. McMurray, *Recorder of the Black Experience: A Biography of Monroe Nathan Work* (Baton Rouge: Louisiana State University Press, 1985); *MGP*,3:509 n. 5; *KI* 5:396.

20. Royall Brandis, "Thorstein Bunde Veblen," *ANB* 22:308–12; and Milner, *Encyclopedia of Evolution*, 446.

21. Hodge Kirnon, cited in HH, "As to 'H. H.,'" *NW*, August 21, 1920; Sinclair Wilberforce, "Harrison Delivers Inspiring Lecture at Harlem People's Forum," *The Voice*, August 1, 1918; HH, "Know Thyself," *NW*, April 16, 1921; Clarke, *Marcus Garvey and the Vision of Africa*, 197; HH, "The Negro at the Peace Congress," *WAA*, 30–32; HH, "Africa and the Peace," *The Voice*, December 26, 1918; "New Exhibition Is Opened at 135th St. Public Library," *HHN*, May 13, 1925. "Hubert Harrison's Portrait in Library," *AN*, September 10, 1930; John E. Bruce, "The Negro Society for Historical Research," box 5, Miscellaneous 13, Ms. 55–13, John E. Bruce Papers, SCRBC; Joseph J. Boris, ed., *Who's Who in Colored America: A Biographical Dictionary of Notable Living Persons of Negro Descent in America* (New York: Who's Who in Colored America Corp., 1927), 87; "Hubert Harrison to deliver 15 lectures on African culture in Brooklyn," April 14–May 12 [1921], HHHP Mi.

22. This article is listed as part 1 in Harrison's combined handwritten and typed manuscript for his "With the Contributing Editor" column of the *Negro World*. Harrison also wrote "The Black Man's Burden: Proem to Part Two," 5 pp., handwritten and dated, November 7, 1920, in HHHP Wr.

23. On Morel see *MGP* 4:315 n. 1; Robert C. Reinders, "Racialism on the Left: E. D. Morel and the 'Black Horror on the Rhine,'" part 1, *International Review of Social History* 13 (1968): 1–28; and HH, "Our White Friends," *NW*, July 3, 1920, 2 (selection 59).

24. Chidi Ikonné, *From Du Bois to Van Vechten: The Early New Negro Literature, 1903–1926* (Westport, Conn.: Greenwood Press, 1981), 6, 38 nn. 18–19, which cites Ernest Hemingway in the *Toronto Star*, March 25, 1922. Jessie Fausset, "'Batouala' is translated," *Crisis* 24–25 (1922–1923), 218–19, and Alice J. Smith, "René Maran's *Batouala* and the *Prix-Goncourt*," *Contributions in Black Studies* 4 (1980–81): 17–34, esp. 17–20. See also *MGP* 4:776 n. 2.

25. "Rene Maran Gets Little Money from Sale of Book," *CD*, April 5, 1923.

26. Robert L. Gale, "Octavus Roy Cohen," *ANB* 5:165–66 and Kellner, *HR*, 75–76.

27. See Rayford W. Logan, "Carter Godwin Woodson," *DANB*, 665–67; *MGP* 9:662 n. 15; Jacqueline Goggin, *Carter G. Woodson: A Life in Black History* (Baton Rouge: Louisiana State University Press, 1993).

28. *NAAAL*, 929–36 and Kellner, *Harlem Renaissance*, 367–68.

29. Robert F. Worth, "*Nigger Heaven* and the Harlem Renaissance," *African American Review* 29, no. 3 (fall 1995): 461–73, esp. 473; *MGP* 7:244 nn. 5–6; Huggins, *Harlem Renaissance*, 93–118; "Novel about Harlem Folk Called Uplift," *CD*, November 6, 1926; L. M. Hussey, "Homo Africanus," *American Mercury* 4 (1925): 86–87; George Hutchinson, *The Harlem Renaissance in Black and White* (Cambridge: Belknap Press of Harvard University Press, 1995), 331.

30. *NAAAL*, 929–36, esp. 933–34; Wintz, *Black Culture and the Harlem Renaissance*, 154–89; Amritjit Singh, "Harlem Renaissance," in *OCAAL*, 340–42, esp. 340; *HR*, pp. xii–xxvii, esp. p. xxiv; and Ikonné, *From Du Bois to Van Vechten*, p. xi.

31. See Ikonné, *From Du Bois to Van Vechten*, p. xi. For other critics of the Renaissance see the chapter "The Black Intelligentsia: Critics," in Wintz, *Black Culture and the Harlem Renaissance*, 130–53 and 248 n. 3. Harrison was challenged by John P. Davis in a pointed, and at times very personal, reply. Davis contested the notion "that there was no Negro Renaissance at the present time" and argued that "the publication of novels, books of poetry, plays, historical treatises and books on Negro folk songs — written by Negroes is unparalleled by any previous decade in American Life." See John P. Davis, "An Answer to Dr. Hubert Harrison's Article," *PC*, April 2, 1927.

32. Twenty months later Alain Locke observed, "The Harlem Renaissance movement of the artistic '20s was really inspired and kept alive by the interest of whites. It faded out when they became tired of the new plaything.'" Alain Locke, "1928: A Retrospective Review," *OP*, January 1929, reprinted in *Voices of a Black Nation: Political Journalism in the Harlem Renaissance*, ed. Theodore G. Vincent (San Francisco: Ramparts Press, 1973), 353–56, esp. 353.

33. Gerard Willem Van Loon, *Hendrik Willem Van Loon* (Philadelphia: J. B. Lippincott, 1972), 127–29, and *WNBD* 1017.

34. J. Krassny, to the editor, "Satyricon of Petronius," *NYT*, October 2, 1922; Ernestine Rose to HH, September 14, 1922, HHHP Co; and Petronius, *The Satyricon*, trans. William Arrowsmith (New York: New American Library, 1959), esp. pp. v–xviii. Anthony Comstock (1844–1915) formed the New York Society for the Suppression of Vice — a private agency that the police granted certain powers to regulate and monitor sexual behavior. In January 1873 he presented to Congress a display on "obscene" material and a proposed bill and a federal anti-obscenity statute (the "Comstock Law") was passed. President Ulysses S. Grant appointed Comstock as a special agent with the U.S. Post Office (the title changed to postal inspector in 1880) and from 1873 until 1913 Comstock oversaw the arrest of more than 3,600 persons for selling obscene pictures, gambling materials, and articles on contraception and abortion. Of the 2,713 cases brought to trial, he had a conviction rate of 98.5 percent. George Bernard Shaw used the word "comstockery" to describe "the American obsession

with regulating morality and suppressing sexuality." See Heywood Broun and Margaret Leech, *Anthony Comstock: Roundsman of the Lord* (New York: A. and C. Boni, 1927); Kenneth T. Jackson, ed., *The Encyclopedia of New York City* (New Haven: Yale University Press and New York Historical Society, 1965), 271; Robert D. Cross, "Anthony Comstock," *ANB* 5:306–308; Beverly A. Brown, "American Smut: A Historical Perspective on Obscenity Laws," *U.S. Postal Inspection Service Bulletin*, September 1994, 33–36, esp. 34; Bruce Shapiro, "From Comstockery to Helmsmanship," *Nation*, October 1, 1990, 335–37.

Chapter 11. Theater Reviews

1. Osofsky, *Harlem*, 122; Henri, *Black Migration*, 88; and Huggins, *Harlem Renaissance*, 139 and 245.

2. HH, "White People versus Negroes, Being the Story of a Great Book," *NW*, January 7, 1922 (selection 102). In "At the Back of the Black Man's Mind," c. November 1922 (selection 94), Harrison wrote that he was "too dark" to get employment on all but one of the four major Black papers in New York.

3. Huggins, *Harlem Renaissance*, 246–49, quotation 246.

4. Kellner, *Harlem Renaissance*, 63, 75, 213–14, 285, 322; Sister Francesca Thompson, "Anita Bush," in *BWA*, 1:205–206; Sister M. Francesca Thompson, "The Lafayette Players, 1915–1932," in *The Theatre of Black Americans*, ed. Errol Hill, 2 vols. (Englewood Cliffs, N.J., 1980), 2:27; *KI* 1:394, 5:111; Kathy A. Perkins, "Theater," *BWA* 2:1161–65, esp. 1162, and 1319.

5. HH, "The Art of the Theater and How To Understand It," c. January 7, 1917, HHHP Wr.

6. Houston Baker Jr., *Modernism and the Harlem Renaissance* (Chicago: University of Chicago Press, 1987), 25–27, 33, 37.

7. *DANB*, 261; *MGP* 7:243–44 n. 4.

8. William Bridges to the editor, *NW*, March 26, 1921; *MGP* 7:243–44 n. 4, which cites Eugene O'Neill to Abdias do Nascimento, founder, Negro Experimental Theater, Rio de Janeiro, January 6, 1944, quoted in Carl N. Degler, *Neither Black nor White: Slavery and Race Relations in Brazil and the United States* (New York: MacMillan, 1971), 181.

9. Eugene O'Neill to HH, June 9, 1921, original pasted in *The Emperor Jones*, copy in HHHP Bo, reprinted as "The Emperor Jones: Famous Author of Famous Play Calls For Negro Dramatists," *NW*, June 25, 1921. On the Black theater and the issue of idealized types see Kornweibel, *No Crystal Stair*, and Theodore Kornweibel, "Theophilius Lewis and the Theater of the Harlem Renaissance," in *The Harlem Renaissance Remembered*, ed. Arna Bontemps (New York: Dodd, Mead, 1972), 171–89.

10. HH, "Marcus Garvey at the Bar of United States Justice" (selection 64); Robert Morse Lovett, "An Emperor Jones of Finance," *New Republic*, July 11, 1923; Charles S. Johnson, "After Garvey — What?" *Opportunity* 1, no. 8 (August 1923): 231–33, esp. 231, which refers to Garvey as "the 'Emperor Jones of Finance'"; and James Weldon Johnson, *Black Manhattan* (New York: A. A. Knopf, 1930; New York: Athenaeum, 1968), 256. For the view that Emperor

Jones also was also drawn from W. H. Ellis, an African American from Texas whom O'Neill met in Mexico, see *Negro History Bulletin* 24 (May 1961): 183–84.

11. Menu and Seating Arrangements for "A Testimonial Dinner to Horace B. Liveright," Hotel Brevoort, Thursday, June 14, 1923, HHHP Mi; HHHDI, June 21, 1923.

12. Burton Rascoe, "A Bookman's Day Book—Thurs. 6/14/23," *New York Tribune*, Magazine and Book Review Section, June 24, 1923, HHHP Scr D.

Chapter 12. Poets and Poetry

1. *Catholic News*, April 22, 1905; [Announcement re HHH Lecture on Paul Laurence Dunbar], June 12, 1905, HHHP Scr, 35; HH, "At The Back of the Black Man's Mind"; HH, [Notes on Marcus Garvey]; HHHDI, March 17, 1920 (selection 60).

2. HHHDI, March 17, 1920; Martin, *Literary Garveyism*, 5, 43–90.

3. Mark Sullivan, *Our Times: The United States, 1900–1925*, vol. 1 of 6 vols.: *The Turn of the Century, 1900–1904* (New York: Charles Scribner's Sons, 1926), 6, and E. Berkeley Tomkins, *Anti-Imperialism in the United States: The Great Debate, 1890–1920* (Philadelphia: University of Pennsylvania Press, 1970), 236–42, esp. 239, which cites Winslow Warren, letter, *Boston Evening Transcript*, February 18, 1899.

4. Tomkins, *Anti-Imperialism in the United States*, 239–40, which cites Ernest H. Crosby, "The White Man's Burden," *New York Times*, February 15, 1899.

5. Claude McKay, *Spring in New Hampshire and Other Poems* (London: Grant Richards, 1920), signed by author February 18, 1921, HHHP Bo; "*Harlem Shadows*: Comments by a Writer of His Race on the Poems of Claude McKay," *NYW*, May 21, 1922.

6. Roger M. Valade III, *The Essential Black Literature Guide* (Detroit: Visible Ink Press, 1996), 199, and James Weldon Johnson, "An Open Air Lecture Course," *NYA*, May 6, 1915.

Chapter 13. The International Colored Unity League

1. HHHDI, March 23, 1924; "Dr. Harris[on] Candidate for Congress on Socialist (Single Tax) Ticket"; "Garvey Proclaims Negroes Right to Self-Government," *NYW*, March 17, 1925, reprinted in *MGP* 5:572–73; "Resolution of the Communist International," October 26, 1928, in Communist Party U.S.A., *The Communist Position on the Negro Question* (New York: Workers Library Publishers, 1934); and Solomon, *The Cry Was Unity*, 68–85.

2. "Dr. Harris[on] Candidate for Congress on Socialist (Single Tax) Ticket"; "Wants State for Negroes: Unity League Launches a National Movement for Political, Economic and Spiritual Co-operation; Dr. Hubert Harrison Touring U.S. In Its Interest," *BC*, June 21, 1924; "Negroes Plan New American State: International Colored Unity League Organizing Branches to Further Project", *CSM*, June 7, 1924; "Separate Colored State Urged by Harrison," *NYN*, August 2, 1924; "Separate State for Negroes Urged," *Baltimore Afro-American*, August 8, 1924; "Lecturer Proposes Independent State for Negro Citizens," *PC*, August 30, 1924; Joseph G. Tucker, "Special Report of Radical Activities in the Greater New York Dis-

trict for Period Week Ending July 26, 1924," file 61-23-297, U.S. Department of Justice, Federal Bureau of Investigation, Washington, D.C.; "Wants Exclusive Negro Territory in U.S.," *NYW*, August 3, 1924, HHHP Scr D.

3. "Dr. Harris[on] Candidate for Congress on Socialist (Single Tax) Ticket"; "Wants State for Negroes"; "Negroes Plan New American State."

4. "Dr. Harris[on] Candidate for Congress on Socialist (Single Tax) Ticket"; "Negroes Plan New American State"; HHHDI, March 23, August 27, September 24, 1924; "League of Women for Community Service: 558 Massachusetts Ave.," *BC*, June 21, 1924.

5. Stationery of the International Colored Unity League, c. 1926, HHHP Mi.

6. HH, "The I.C.U. [International Colored Unity League]," *Embryo of The Voice of the Negro* 1, no. 1 (February 1927): 2. *Voice of the Negro* was also the name of an influential monthly edited by Jesse Max Barber from January 1904 through October 1907. Interestingly, that publication changed its name in November 1906 to *The Voice*. See *DANB*, 27.

7. HH, "The I.C.U. [International Colored Unity League]." The "cast down your buckets" quote was from Booker T. Washington's Atlanta Compromise address of September 18, 1895. See *DANB*, 635–37.

8. "25th Anniversary Edition," *BC*, December 21, 1940.

9. "Dr. Harrison's Rise as Orator Is Like Fiction"; HHHDI, October 27, 1907 and January 27, 1909; HH, "Cabaret School of Negro Literature and Art"; HH, "Election Results," *The Voice*, November 14, 1917; HH, "Education and the Race," 128; HH, "The Harlem Hospital," *NW*, May 7, 1921, 5; HH, "*In Spite of the Handicap* by James D. Corrothers, D.D.: Our Book Review," *NW*, July 10, 1920; and announcement of Hubert Harrison lecture on "Charles Dickens the Novelist of the Common People," *Sabotage*, July 20, 1914.

10. HH, "The Virgin Islands," 7–8 (selection 82); Bell, "The Background and Development of Marxian Socialism in the United States," in Egbert and Persons, *Socialism and American Life*, 1:268–69; "Socialist Platform of 1912," in Porter and Johnson, *National Party Platforms*, 188–91, esp. 189; Harry Kelly, *The Modern School* (Stelton, N.J.: The Modern School Association of North America, 1920), 3–4; HHHDI, March 17, 1920; Stationery of Pioneer Development Corporation, (Promoting a Colored Bank in New York), c. 1919, HHHP Mi; Joyce Moore Turner, "Richard B. Moore and His Works," in Turner and Turner, *Richard B. Moore*, 19–122, esp. 29; HH, "A St. Croix Creole" (selection 81); and *HATB*, 173.

Index of Titles

General Index